Ordnance Survey

STREET ~~ATLAS~~ S

Derbyshire

D1150115

Contents

III Key to map symbols

IV Key to map pages

VI Administrative and post code boundaries

1 Street maps

266 Extra-large-scale maps of town centres
  266 Chesterfield
  267 Derby

268 Town maps
  268 Mansfield
  268 Nottingham
  269 Stafford
  269 Stoke-on-Trent

270 Index of hospitals, railway stations, schools, shopping centres, street names and universities

PHILIP'S

First edition published 1995
First colour edition published 1998
Reprinted in 1999 by

Ordnance Survey®   and   George Philip Ltd, a division of
Romsey Road   Octopus Publishing Group Ltd
Maybush   2-4 Heron Quays
Southampton   London
SO16 4GU   E14 4JP

ISBN 0-540-07533-7 (pocket)

To the best of the Publishers' knowledge, the information in this
atlas was correct at the time of going to press. No responsibility
can be accepted for any errors or their consequences.

The representation in this atlas of a road, track or path is no
evidence of the existence of a right of way.

**The mapping between pages 1 and 269 (inclusive) in this
atlas is derived from Ordnance Survey® Large Scale and
Landranger® mapping, and using revised Land-Line® data.**

Ordnance Survey, Land-line and Landranger are
registered trade marks of Ordnance Survey, the national
mapping agency of Great Britain.

Printed and bound in Spain by Cayfosa

Digital Data

The exceptionally high-quality
mapping found in this book is
available as digital data in TIFF
format, which is easily convertible
to other bit-mapped (raster) image
formats.

The index is also available in digital
form as a standard database table.
It contains all the details found in
the printed index together with the
National Grid reference for the map
square in which each entry is
named and feature codes for places
of interest in eight categories such
as education and health.

For further information and to
discuss your requirements, please
contact Philip's on 0171 531 8440 or
george.philip@philips-maps.co.uk

(22a)	**Motorway** (with junction number)
	Primary route (dual carriageway and single)
	A road (dual carriageway and single)
	B road (dual carriageway and single)
	Minor road (dual carriageway and single)
	Other minor road
	Road under construction
	Pedestrianised area
	County and Unitary Authority boundaries
	Railway
	Tramway, miniature railway
	Rural track, private road or narrow road in urban area
	Gate or obstruction to traffic (restrictions may not apply at all times or to all vehicles)
	Path, bridleway, byway open to all traffic, road used as a public path
	The representation in this atlas of a road, track or path is no evidence of the existence of a right of way
170 / 52 / 267	**Adjoining page indicators**
	The map area within the pink band is shown at a larger scale on the page indicated by the red block and arrow

Acad	**Academy**	Mon	**Monument**
Cemy	**Cemetery**	Mus	**Museum**
C Ctr	**Civic Centre**	Obsy	**Observatory**
CH	**Club House**	Pal	**Royal Palace**
Coll	**College**	PH	**Public House**
Ent	**Enterprise**	Recn Gd	**Recreation Ground**
Ex H	**Exhibition Hall**	Resr	**Reservoir**
Ind Est	**Industrial Estate**	Ret Pk	**Retail Park**
Inst	**Institute**	Sch	**School**
Ct	**Law Court**	Sh Ctr	**Shopping Centre**
L Ctr	**Leisure Centre**	Sta	**Station**
LC	**Level Crossing**	TH	**Town Hall/House**
Liby	**Library**	Trad Est	**Trading Estate**
Mkt	**Market**	Univ	**University**
Meml	**Memorial**	YH	**Youth Hostel**

⇌	**British Rail station**
Ⓜ	**Metrolink station**
⊖	**Underground station**
D	**Docklands Light Railway station**
M	**Tyne and Wear Metro**
⊕	**Private railway station**
⬤	**Bus, coach station**
◆	**Ambulance station**
◆	**Coastguard station**
◆	**Fire station**
◆	**Police station**
✚	**Accident and Emergency entrance to hospital**
H	**Hospital**
+	**Church, place of worship**
i	**Information centre** (open all year)
P P&R	**Parking, Park and Ride**
PO	**Post Office**
Prim Sch	**Important buildings, schools, colleges, universities and hospitals**
River Medway	**Water name**
	Stream
	River or canal (minor and major)
	Water
	Tidal water
	Woods
	Houses
House	**Non-Roman antiquity**
VILLA	**Roman antiquity**

■ The dark grey border on the inside edge of some pages indicates that the mapping does not continue onto the adjacent page

■ The small numbers around the edges of the maps identify the 1 kilometre National Grid lines

The scale of the maps is 3.92 cm to 1 km (2½ inches to 1 mile)	0 — ¼ — ½ — ¾ — 1 mile 0 — 250m — 500m — 750m — 1 kilometre
The scale of the map on pages numbered in red is 7.84 cm to 1 km (5 inches to 1 mile)	0 — 220 yards — 440 yards — 660 yards — ½ mile 0 — 125m — 250m — 375m — ½ kilometre

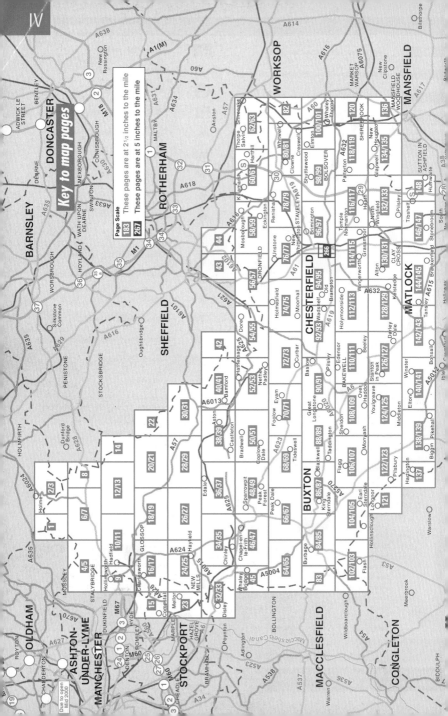

IV

Key to map pages

Page Scale
183	These pages are at 2½ inches to the mile
257	These pages are at 5 inches to the mile

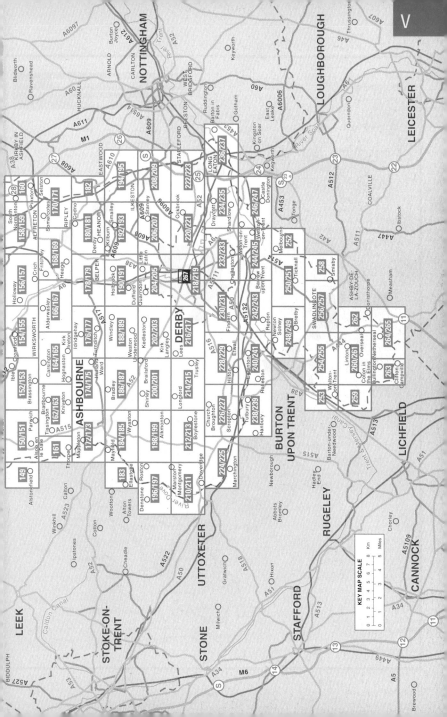

Major administrative and post code boundaries

County and Unitary Boundaries

District Boundaries

Post Code Boundaries

Area covered by this atlas

0   5   10
Kilometres

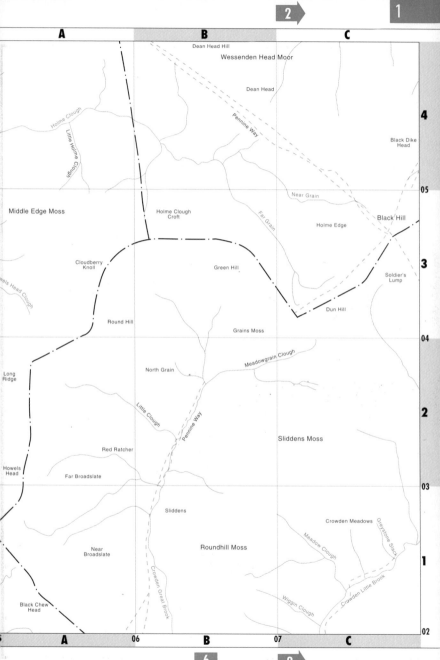

Dean Head Hill

Wessenden Head Moor

Dean Head

Pennine Way

Holme Clough

Little Holme Clough

Black Dike Head

05

Middle Edge Moss

Holme Clough Croft

Near Grain

Far Grain

Holme Edge

Black Hill

4

Wells Head Clough

Cloudberry Knoll

Green Hill

Soldier's Lump

3

Round Hill

Grains Moss

Dun Hill

04

Long Ridge

North Grain

Meadowgrain Clough

Little Clough

Pennine Way

Sliddens Moss

2

Howels Head

Red Ratcher

Far Broadslate

03

Sliddens

Crowden Meadows

Greystone Slack

Meadow Clough

Near Broadslate

Roundhill Moss

1

Crowden Great Brook

Crowden Little Brook

Black Chew Head

Wiggin Clough

02

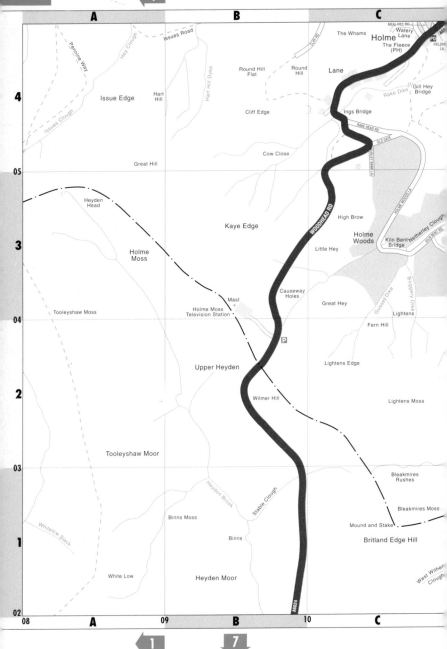

| A | B | C |

4

Pennine Way

Hey Clough

Issues Road

Issue Edge

Hart Hill

Hart Hill Dyke

Issues Clough

Round Hill Flat

Round Hill

Cliff Edge

The Whams

Holme

The Fleece (PH)

Lane

Watery Lane

PO

FIELDHE LA

Rake Dike

Gill Hey Bridge

Ings Bridge

RAKE HEAD RD

OLD GATE

RAKE HEY BANK LA

05

Great Hill

Cow Close

WOODHEAD RD

High Brow

HOLME WOODS LA

3

Heyden Head

Kaye Edge

Holme Moss

Little Hey

Holme Woods

Kiln Bent Bridge

Netherley Clough

Boggery Dikes

04

Tooleyshaw Moss

Mast

Holme Moss Television Station

Causeway Holes

Great Hey

Gussel Dike

Lightens

Fern Hill

Lightens Edge

P

2

Upper Heyden

Wilmer Hill

Lightens Moss

03

Tooleyshaw Moor

Bleakmires Rushes

Heyden Brook

Stable Clough

Bleakmires Moss

Binns Moss

Mound and Stake

1

Whitelow Slack

Binns

Britland Edge Hill

West Wither Clough

White Low

Heyden Moor

A6024

02

| 08 | A | 09 | B | 10 | C |

D   E   F

Brownhill Reservoir

Moss Edge

MOSS LANE RD

White Gate

Crow Hill

Dobb Dike

WEATHER HILL LA

WEST GATE

Hollin Hill

4

Netherley

Ramsden Reservoir

BROWNHILL LA

RAMSDEN LA

Green House Lane

Kirklees Way

RAMSDEN RD

CARTWORTH MOOR RD

COPTHURST RD

WHITE GATE RD

Upper White Gate

Elysium

Kirklees Way

Netherley Brow

Riding Wood Reservoir

Crossley's Plantation

Copthurst Moor

Reynard Clough

Hades

05

EAST VIEW RD

The dge

Yateholme Cote

Ramsden Edge

Peat Pit Moss

Hades Green

Holme Valley Circular Walk

Yateholme Reservoir

Green House Hey Wood

Hades Peat Pits

3

Lower Flat

Cook's Study Hill

LINDHURST RD

Linshaws Scar

The Rakes

Ruddle Clough Moss

Cook's Study Moss

Snailsden Reservoir

04

Great Twizle Clough

Little Twizle Clough

Herbage Flat

Herbage Edge

Elbow End

Great Twizle Hole

Herbage Hill

Ramsden Rocks

Ruddle Clough

Upper Snailsden Moss

Great Twizle Head

Ramsden Clough

Ruddle Clough Knoll

2

Herbage Moss

Lad Clough Knoll

Reaps Dike

Reaps Moss

Snailsden Pike End

Twizle Head Moss

Lad Clough

Snailsden Edge

Laund Moss

Bailie Causeway Moss

Swiner Clough Top

Swiner Dike

03

Swiner Clough

Swiner Clough Moss

Great Grains

Grains Edge

Don Well

River Don

Grains End

Ford

West Withens Clough

Great Grains Clough

Dunford Bridge

1

Grains Moss

Black Grough

Little Grain Clough

Dead Edge Flat

Withens Edge

02

D   12   E   13   F

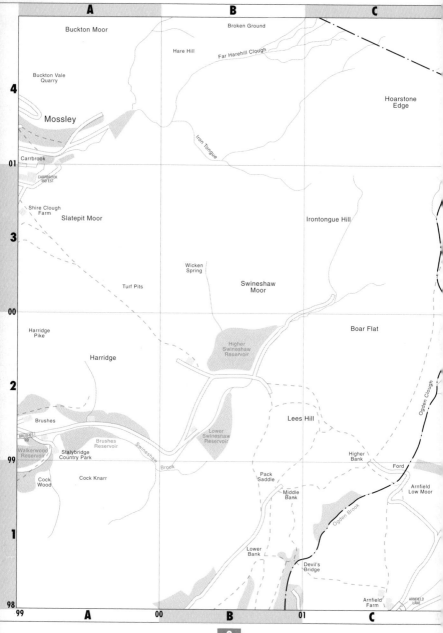

A   B   C

Buckton Moor

Broken Ground

Hare Hill

Far Harehill Clough

Buckton Vale
Quarry

4

Hoarstone
Edge

Mossley

Iron Tongue

Carrbrook

01

CARRBROOK
IND EST

Shire Clough
Farm

Slatepit Moor

Irontongue Hill

3

Wicken
Spring

Turf Pits

Swineshaw
Moor

00

Harridge
Pike

Boar Flat

Harridge

Higher
Swineshaw
Reservoir

2

Ogden Clough

Brushes

Lees Hill

BRUSHES
RD

Brushes
Reservoir

Lower
Swineshaw
Reservoir

Walkerwood
Reservoir

Stalybridge
Country Park

Swineshaw

Higher
Bank

99

Brook

Ford

Cock
Wood

Cock Knarr

Pack
Saddle

Arnfield
Low Moor

Middle
Bank

Ogden Brook

1

Lower
Bank

Devil's
Bridge

Arnfield
Farm

ARNFIELD
LANE

98

99   A   00   B   01   C

Dish Stone
Rocks

Chew Reservoir

Chew
Green

Chew Brook

CHEW RD

Chew
Hurdles

South Clough

Green Grain

Greenfield

Dry Clough

4

Bowerclough Head

Blindstones Moss

Blindstones

Wilderness

01

Ormes Moor

Featherbed Moss

Windgate
Edge

3

Mount
Skip

Arnfield Flats

00

Arnfield Clough

Robinson's
Moss

Arnfield Gutter

Black Gutter

2

Tintwistle
Knarr

Arnfield Brook

Rawkins Brook

Arnfield
Moor

99

Ogden

Didsbury Intake

A628

1

Arnfield
Covert

Rhodeswood
Reservoir

Longdendale
Trail

Tintwistle Low Moor

98

A628

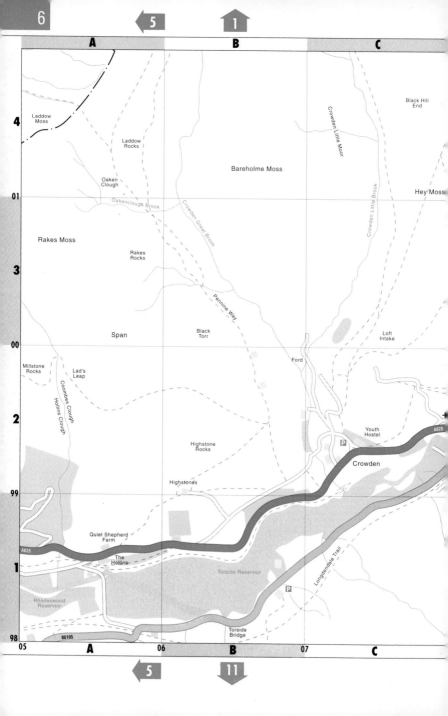

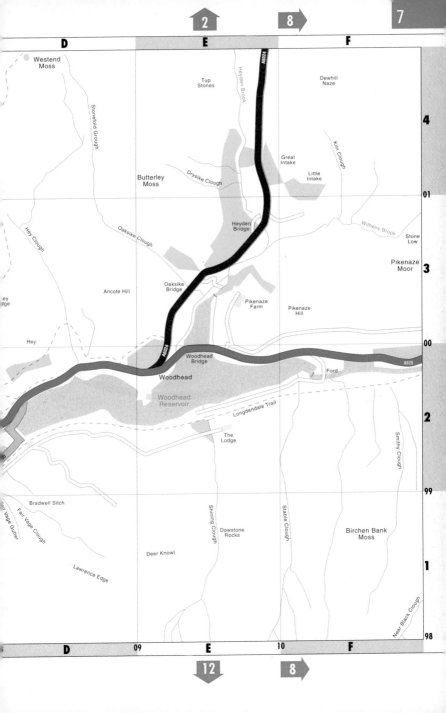

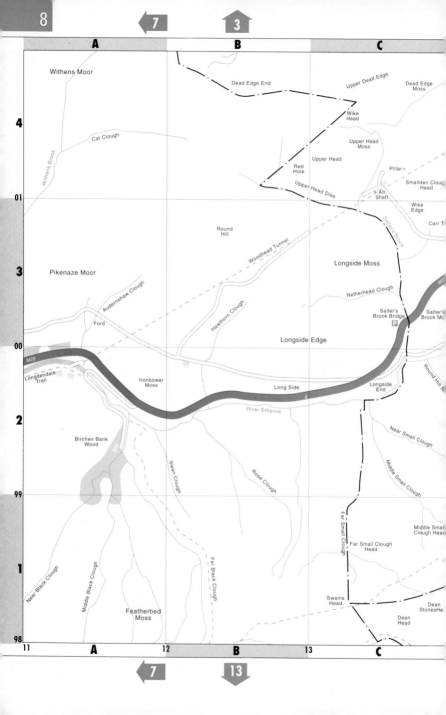

A   **B**   **C**

Withens Moor

Dead Edge End

Upper Dead Edge

Dead Edge Moss

Wike Head

4

Cat Clough

Upper Head Moss

Withens Brook

Red Hole

Upper Head

Pillar

Smallden Clough Head

01

Air Shaft

Wike Edge

Upper Head Dike

Carr T

Round Hill

Salter's Brook

Woodhead Tunnel

Longside Moss

3

Pikenaze Moor

Netherhead Clough

Audenshaw Clough

Hawthorn Clough

Salter's Brook Bridge

Salter's Brook M

Ford

Longside Edge

00

Longdendale Trail

A628

Ironbower Moss

Long Side

Longside End

Round Hill R

River Etherow

Near Small Clough

2

Birchen Bank Wood

Swan Clough

Rose Clough

Middle Small Clough

99

Far Small Clough

Middle Sma Clough Hea

Near Black Clough

Middle Black Clough

Far Black Clough

Far Small Clough Head

Middle Sma Clough Hea

1

Swains Head

Dean StonesHe

Featherbed Moss

Dean Head

98

11   **A**   12   **B**   13   **C**

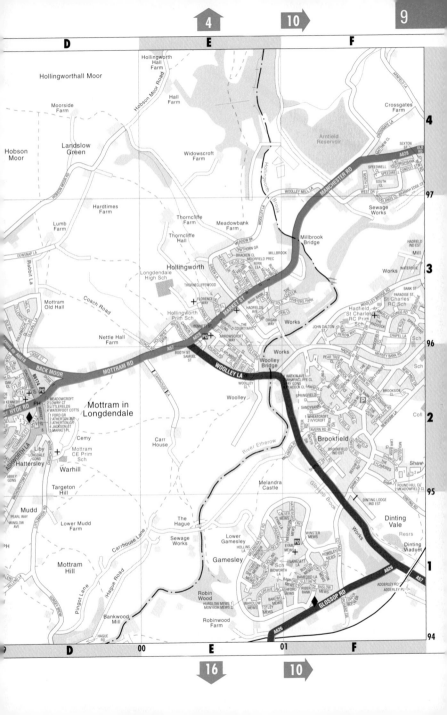

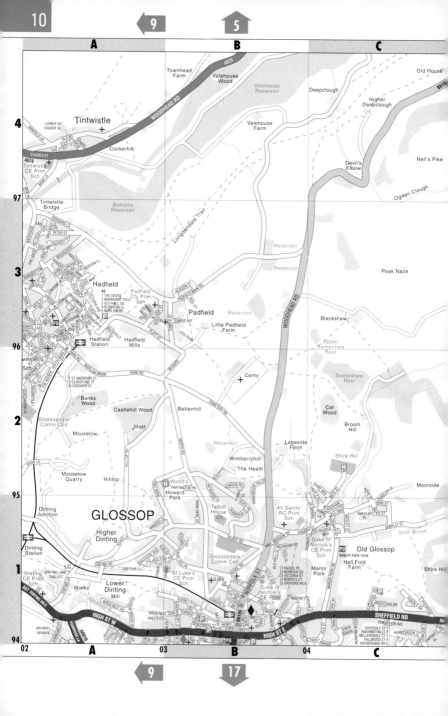

D

E

F

4

97

3

96

2

95

1

94

B6105

Reaps

Long Gutter Edge

White Mare

Torside Naze

Bramah Edge

Peaknaze Moor

Clough Edge

Toreside Clough

Pennine Way

Blackshaw Clough

Glossop Low

Torside Castle

Blake Moor

Cock Hill

Small Clough

Harrop Moss

Dog Rock

Dowstone Clough

Blackemoor Plantation

Yellow Slacks

The Pike

Edge Plantation

Shittern Clough

Lightside

Yellowslacks Brook

Ferny Hole

Wigan Clough

Shelf Benches

Shire Hill

Mossy Lea Farm

Reservoir

Lower Shelf

Little Clough

Wash Brow

Shelf Brook

Doctor's Gate

WOODCOCK RD

A57 SNAKE PASS

Woodcock Farm

HURST RD

Golf Course

05

D

06

E

07

F

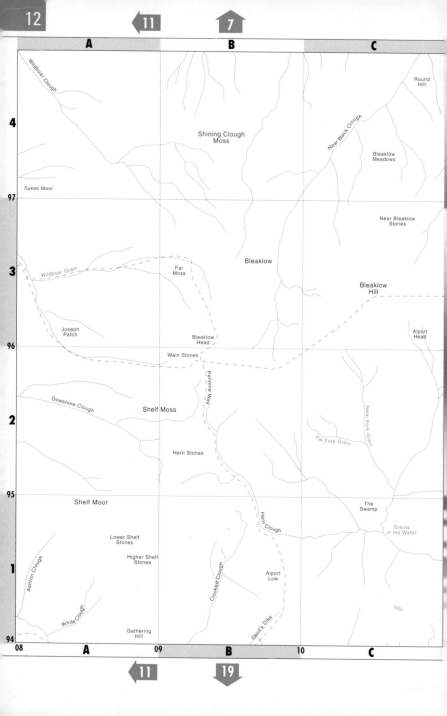

D   E   F

Black
Moss

Middle Black Clough

Featherbed
Moss

White
Stones

Swains Greave

Barrow
Stones

Barrow Clough

4

97

Bleaklow
Stones

Grinah
Stones

Round
Hill

3

96

Westend
Head

Grinah Grain

Deep Grain

2

The Ridge

Ridgewalk Moor

95

River Westend

1

Ravens Clough

Over Wood
Moss

94

11   D   12   E   13   F

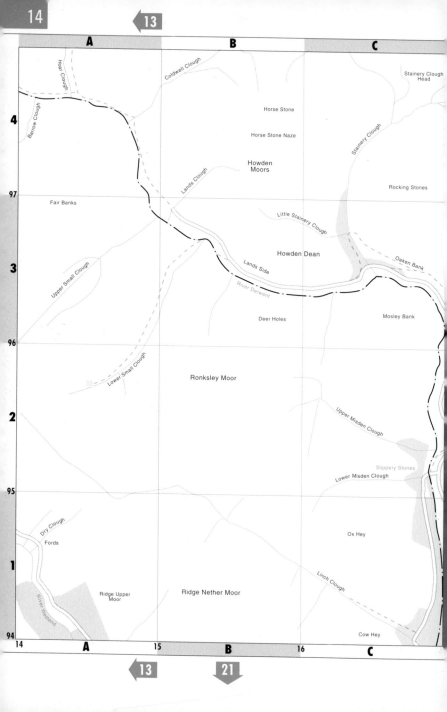

A   **B**   **C**

Hoar Clough

Coldwell Clough

Stainery Clough Head

Barrow Clough

Horse Stone

4

Horse Stone Naze

Stainery Clough

Howden
Moors

97

Fair Banks

Lands Clough

Rocking Stones

Little Stainery Clough

Oaken Bank

Upper Small Clough

3

Howden Dean

Lands Side

River Derwent

Mosley Bank

Deer Holes

96

Lower Small Clough

Ronksley Moor

2

Upper Misden Clough

Slippery Stones

95

Lower Misden Clough

Dry Clough

Fords

Ox Hey

1

River Westend

Ridge Upper
Moor

Ridge Nether Moor

Linch Clough

Cow Hey

94

14   **A**   15   **B**   16   **C**

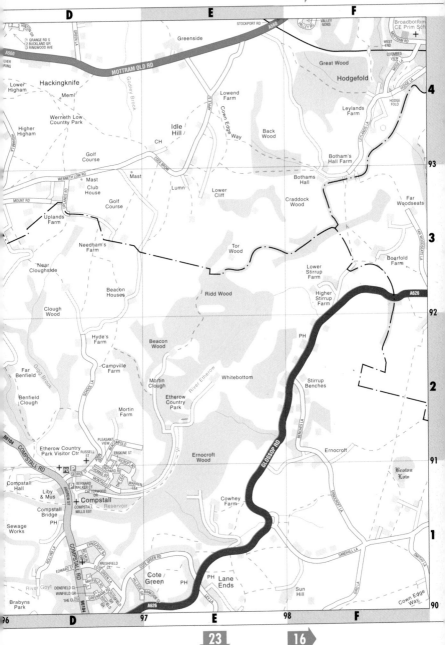

A   B   C

SPRING ST
Broadbottom
Sta
GORSEY INTAKES ST
BANKGATE
KING ST
7 GARDEN ST
8 CROSS ST
MOTTRAM RD

Broadbottom

Warhurst
Fold Farm

SUMMERBOTTOM
LEE BANGS
RD

P
LYMEFIELD
TERR
Visitor
Ctr
1 OLIVE TERR
2 MILL BROW
3 NEW ST
4 ST ANNES ST
5 TEMPERANCE ST
6 ETHEROW BROW

River Etherow

Higher Gamesley

St Margaret's
RC Prim
Sch

Gamesley Fold
Farm

Bankwood Gate

Hargate Hill
Farm

Hargate
Hill

GLOSSOP RD

A626

STORTH MEADOW
MEADOW BANK
STORTH
MEADOW
RISE

Simmondley

Cloud
Farm

HIGH LA

93

Tom Wood

Fields Farm

SPRINGMEADOW

Charlesworth
CE Prim Sch

TOWN LA

Charlesworth

Charlesworth
CE Prim Sch

CHAPEL BROW

Slack
Edge

Woodseats

Woodseats
Farm

Lea
Farm

Lee Head

PO

LEE HEAD

SPRINGFIELD

BOGGARD LA

Back Lane

The Banks

BACK LA

MONKS RD

Coombes Edge

3

FAR
WOODSEATS
LA

Rarewood
House

Mill

Mill

Cown Edge Way

COOMBES LA

Holehouse

Works

Close
Wood

Mares
Back

Chew

A626   MARPLE RD

Hunter's
Inn
(PH)

Chisworth

Bot
Wood

Coombes

92

SANDY LA

**Higher
Chisworth**

NEW MILLS RD

Hilltop
Farm

Far Coombes

Coombes
Tor

Coombes Rocks

Rocks
Farm

2

Intakes Farm

Intakes

Moorside

Cown Edge Rocks

91

SANDHILLS LA

Cown Edge Way

Robin Hoods
Picking Rods

Far Slack

Cown Edge
Rocks

Far Cown Edge
Farm

1

Cloughend Farm

Ludworth Moor

SUN RD

Gun Farm

Near Slack

Cloughead Farm

Smithylane

Brook Bottom
Farm

Far Bradshaw
Farm

Pistol Farm

90

99   A   00   B   01   C

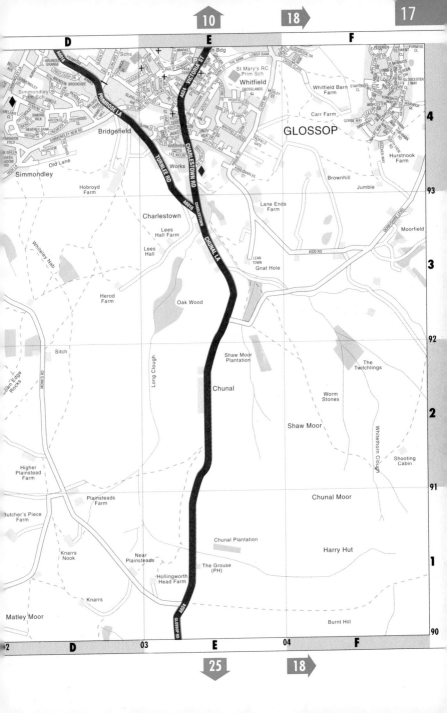

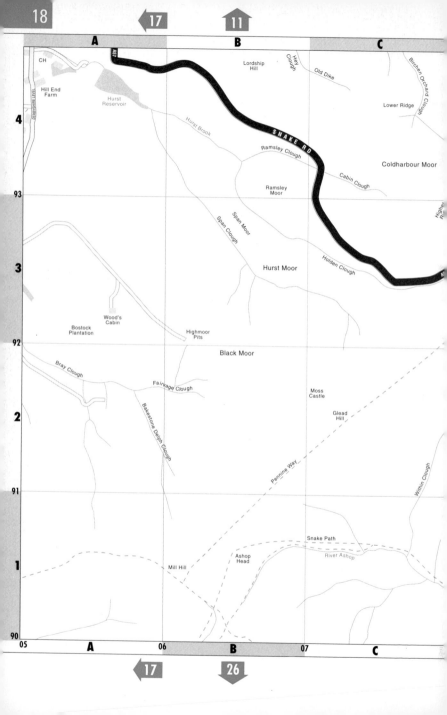

A
B
C

CH

Lordship
Hill

Hey
Clough

Old Dike

Binchen Orchard Clough

Hill End
Farm

Hurst
Reservoir

Lower Ridge

Derwent Level

4

Hurst Brook

SNAKE RD

Coldharbour Moor

Ramsley Clough

Cabin Clough

93

Ramsley
Moor

Span Moor

Higher
R

Span Clough

3

Hurst Moor

Holden Clough

A

Wood's
Cabin

Bostock
Plantation

Highmoor
Pits

92

Black Moor

Bray Clough

Fairvage Clough

Moss
Castle

2

Bakestone Delph Clough

Glead
Hill

Pennine Way

91

Within Clough

Snake Path

River Ashop

1

Mill Hill

Ashop
Head

90

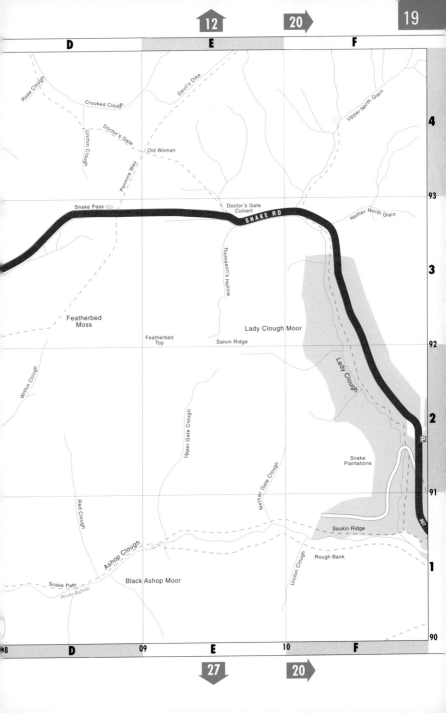

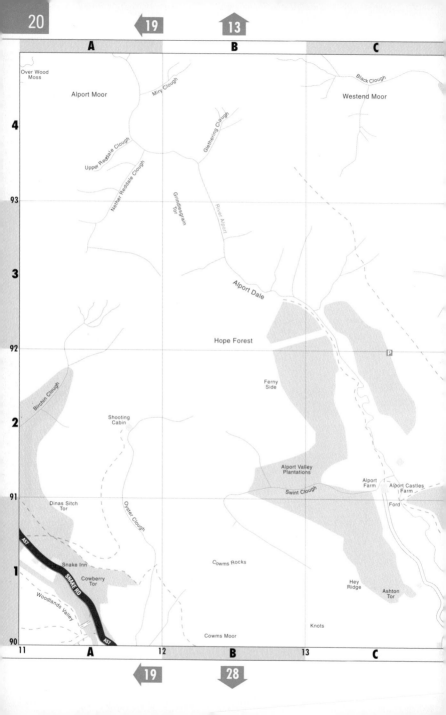

D
E
F

4

93

3

92

2

91

1

90

Upper Wood

Ridge Nether Moor

Banktop Hey

Ford

Ronksley South Plantation

Ridge Clough

Nether Wood Plantation

Ridge Wood

River Westend

Banktop Plantation

Howden Reservoir

Fagney Plantation

Hern Side

West Cable Tip Plantation

Ditch Clough Plantation

Fox's Piece

Fagney Clough

Beaver's Croft

Ditch Clough

Green Clough

Chapel Plantation

Bank Clough

Birchin Hat

Birchinlee East Plantation

Derwent Reservoir

Upper Derwent Valley

Birchinlee Pasture

Birchinlee

Calfhey Wood

Alport Castles

Little Moor

Cote Clough

Castles Wood

Hucklow Lees Barn

Ouzelden Clough

Birchinlee New Piece

Gores Farm

Gores Plantation

Whitefield Pits

Rowlee Pasture

Alport Grain

Gores Heights

Nabs Wood

D
15
E
16
F

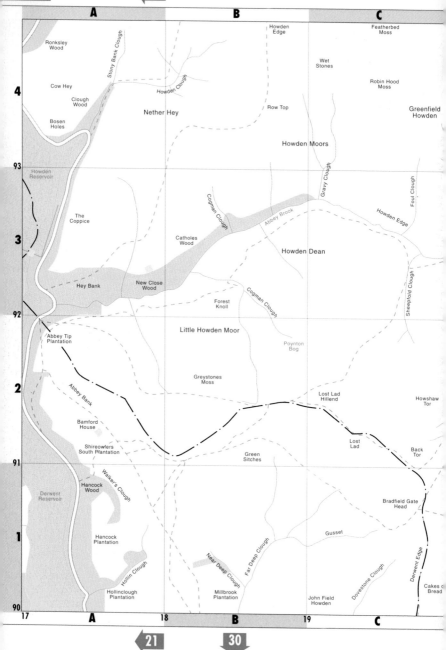

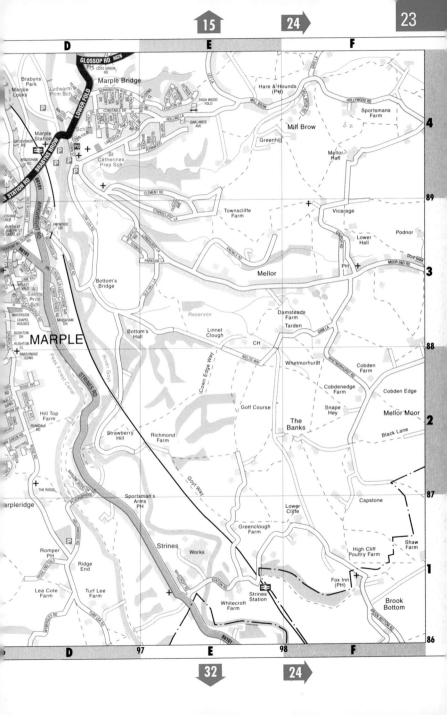

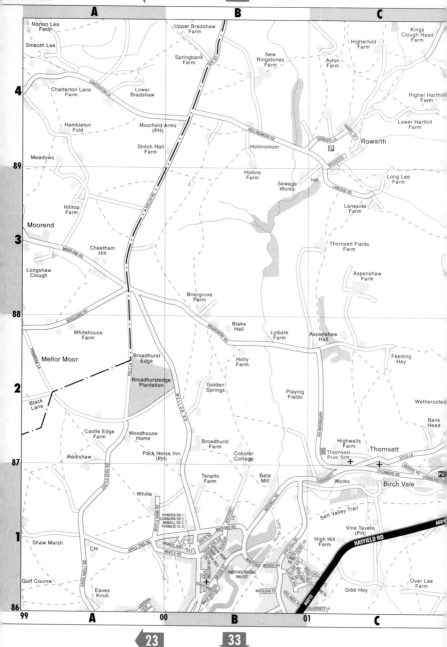

A   B   C

Norton Lea Farm
Smooth Lee
Upper Bradshaw Farm
Kings Clough Head Farm
Higherfold Farm
Springbank Farm
New Ringstones Farm
Ayton Farm
4
Chatterton Lane Farm
Lower Bradshaw
CHATTERTON LA
Higher Harthill Farm
Hambleton Fold
Moorfield Arms (PH)
HOLLINSMOOR RD
Lower Harthill Farm
CHAPEL ST
GOODFARD LA
Rowarth
Meadows
Shiloh Hall Farm
Hollinsmoor
89
Hilltop Farm
Hollins Farm
Inn
BROOKBOTTOM
Long Lee Farm
Moorend
Sewage Works
LANESIDE RD
MOOREND RD
Cheetham Hill
Laneside Farm
3
Thornsett Fields Farm
Longshaw Clough
Aspenshaw Farm
BOGGARD RD
88
Briergrove Farm
Blake Hall
Lydiate Farm
Aspenshaw Hall
Whitehouse Farm
BROADHURST RD
Feeding Hey
PRIMROSE LA
Mellor Moor
Broadhurst Edge
Holly Farm
Wethercotes
2
Broadhurstedge Plantation
Golden Springs
ASPENSHAW RD
Playing Fields
Bank Head
Black Lane
Castle Edge Farm
Woodhouse Home
MELLOR RD
Broadhurst Farm
Highwalls Farm
Thornsett
Redishaw
Pack Horse Inn (RH)
Cobster Cottage
Thornsett Prim Sch
SYCAMORE RD
SHIRT LA
QUARRY RD
87
CASTLE EDGE RD
Tanpits Farm
Bate Mill
THORNSETT
Works
Birch Vale
SPINNERBOTTOM
Whitle
PD
Sett Valley Trail
WHITLE BANK RD
HOWDEN RD 1
COWBURN DR 2
WINHILL RD 3
FERNILEE CL 4
WATFORD RD
Vine Tavern (PH)
High Hill Farm
HAYFIELD RD
A6015
1
Shaw Marsh
CH
APPLE TREE RD
PEVERIL AVE
WHITLE RD
River Sett
Over Lee Farm
Golf Course
WATFORD BRIDGE IND EST
WATBURN RD
Gibb Hey
Eaves Knoll
LATERTON
PACK HORSE RD
A6015
OLLERSETT LA

A   B   C

4

Leygatehead
Moor

William Clough

Pennine Way

Sandy
Heys

89

Mermaid's
Pool

3

Nab
Brow

Hollin
Head

White Brow

River Kinder

Kinder
Reservoir

Blackshaws

Red Brook

Kinder
Head

88

Upper Moor

Marepiece
Wood

Upper
House

Farlands

Booth

Cluther
Rocks

2

The
Cote

Broad
Clough

Kinder
Low

Hill
House
Farm

87

The Three
Knolls

Pennine Way

Tunstead Clough
Farm

Tunstead
House

Stones
House

Kinderlow
End

Oaken Clough

1

The
Ashes

Swine's
Back

Harry Moor

Edale
Cross

86

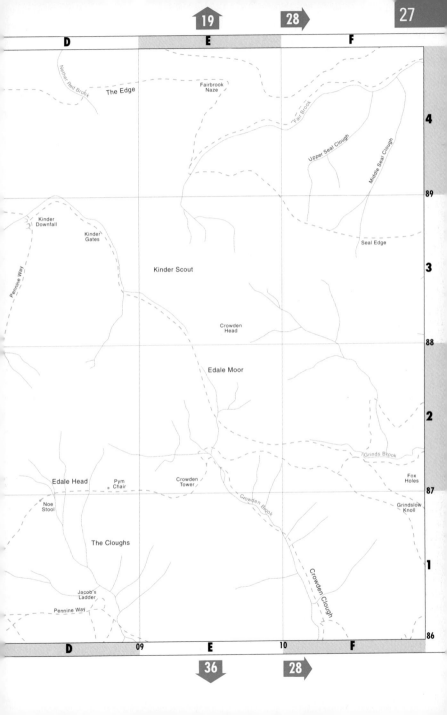

The Edge

Nether Red Brook

Fairbrook
Naze

Fair Brook

Upper Seal Clough

Middle Seal Clough

4

89

Kinder
Downfall

Kinder
Gates

Seal Edge

Pennine Way

Kinder Scout

3

Crowden
Head

88

Edale Moor

2

Grinds Brook

Edale Head

Pym
Chair

Crowden
Tower

Crowden Brook

Fox
Holes

87

Noe
Stool

Grindslow
Knoll

The Cloughs

1

Crowden Clough

Jacob's
Ladder

Pennine Way

86

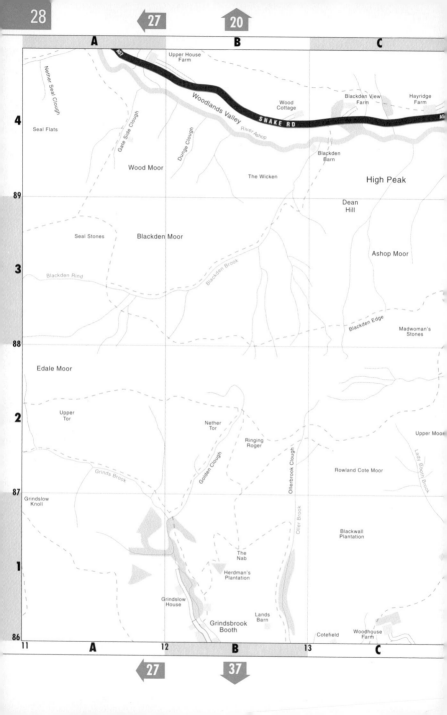

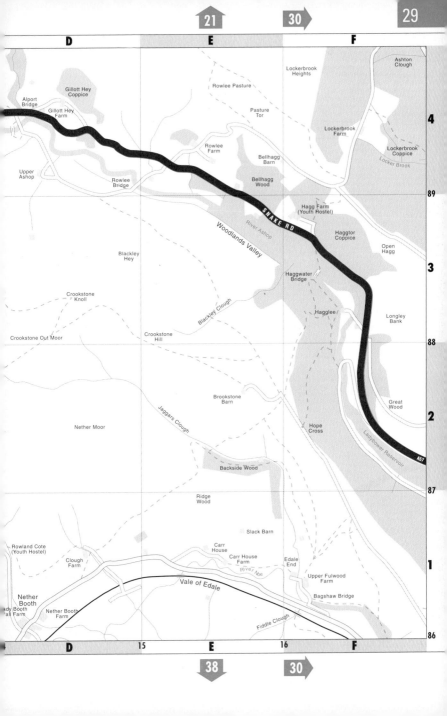

D
E
F

Ashton
Clough

Lockerbrook
Heights

Rowlee Pasture

Gillott Hey
Coppice

Pasture
Tor

Alport
Bridge
Gillott Hey
Farm

Lockerbrook
Farm

4

Upper
Ashop

Rowlee
Farm

Bellhagg
Barn

Lockerbrook
Coppice

Locker Brook

Rowlee
Bridge

Bellhagg
Wood

89

SNAKE RD

River Ashop

Hagg Farm
(Youth Hostel)

Woodlands Valley

Haggtor
Coppice

Open
Hagg

Blackley
Hey

3

Haggwater
Bridge

Crookstone
Knoll

Hagglee

Longley
Bank

Blackley Clough

Crookstone Out Moor

Crookstone
Hill

88

Brookstone
Barn

Great
Wood

Jaggars Clough

Nether Moor

Hope
Cross

2

Ladybower Reservoir

A57

Backside Wood

87

Ridge
Wood

Slack Barn

Rowland Cote
(Youth Hostel)

Carr
House

Clough
Farm

Carr House
Farm

Edale
End

River Noe

1

Upper Fulwood
Farm

Vale of Edale

Bagshaw Bridge

Nether
Booth

dy Booth
all Farm

Nether Booth
Farm

Fiddle Clough

86

D
15
E
16
F

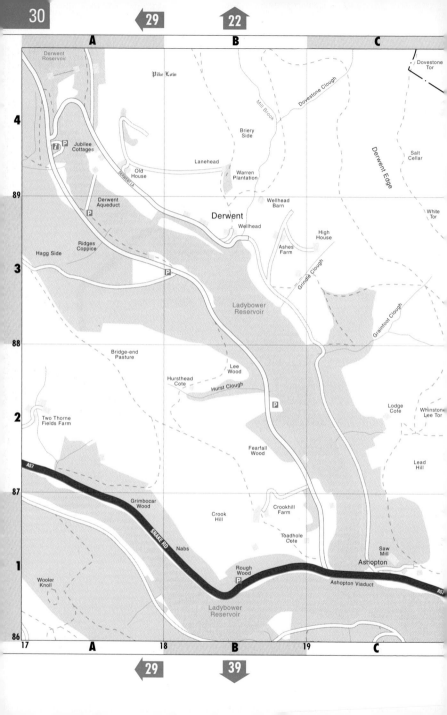

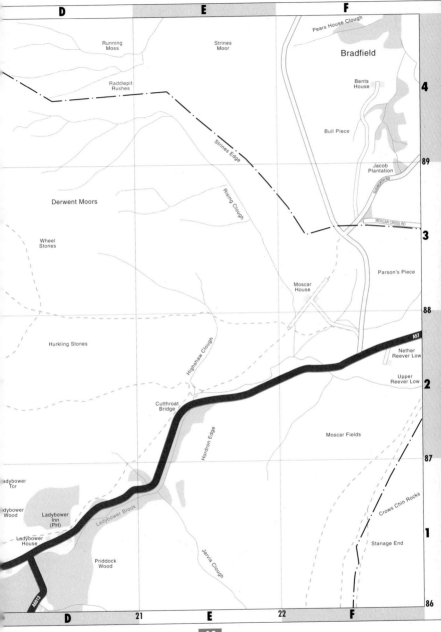

D   E   F

Pears House Clough

Running
Moss

Strines
Moor

Bradfield

Raddlepit
Rushes

Bents
House

4

Strines Edge

Bull Piece

89

Jacob
Plantation

Derwent Moors

Rising Clough

MOSCAR CROSS RD

3

Wheel
Stones

Parson's Piece

Moscar
House

88

Hurkling Stones

Highshaw Clough

A57

Nether
Reever Low

Upper
Reever Low

2

Cutthroat
Bridge

Moscar Fields

Hordron Edge

87

adybower
Tor

Crows Chin Rocks

dybower
Wood

Ladybower
Inn
(PH)

Ladybower Brook

1

Ladybower
House

Stanage End

Priddock
Wood

Jarvis Clough

86

A6013

D   21   E   22   F

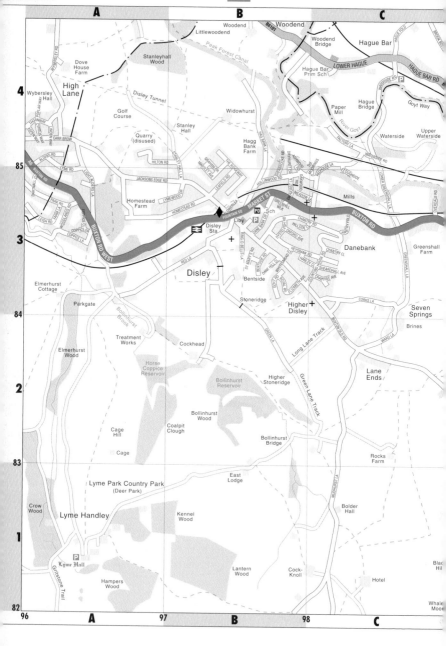

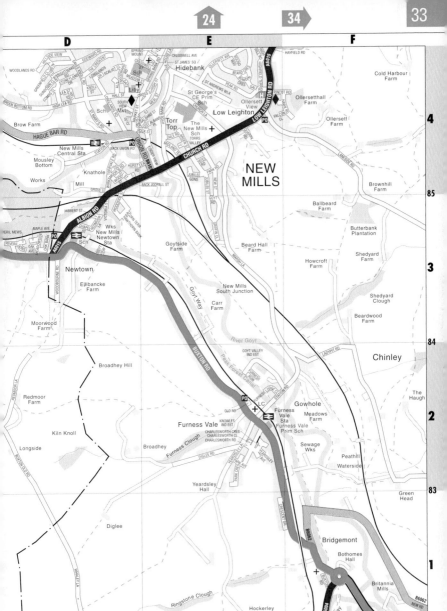

A

B

C

4

Brown
Knoll

Pennine Way

Lee
Farm

River Noe

Grain Clough

Crowden Brook

Upper
Booth

Highfield

85

Tagsnaze
Farm

P

3

Horsehill
Tor

The
Orchard

Door
Clough

Upper
Clough

Roych Clough

Dalehead

Whitemoor Slitch

Whitemoor Clough

84

Roych
Tor

Cowburn Tunnel

Colborne

Chapel Gate

Shaft

Toot
Hill

2

Green
Low

83

Rushup Edge

A625

Bolehill Clough

Tom Moor
Plantation

Hillside
Farm

Rushup Edge
Farm

1

Bettfield
Farm

Coldwall
Farm

A625

RUSHUP LA

Breck Edge

Rushop
Hall

82

08

A

09

B

10

C

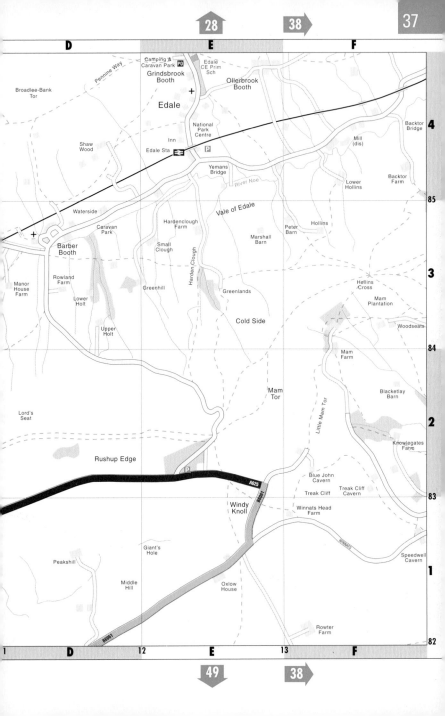

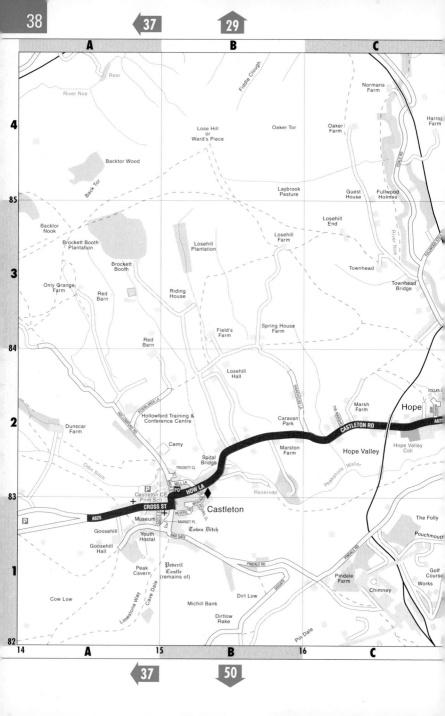

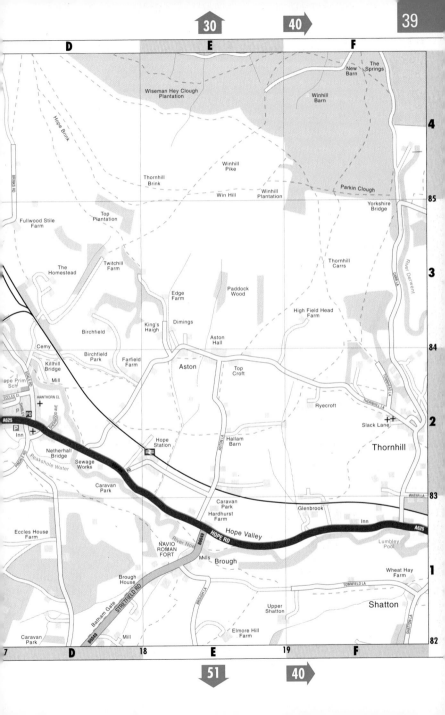

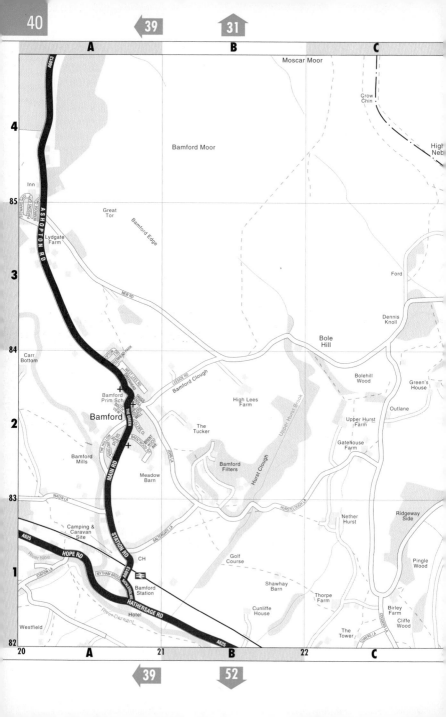

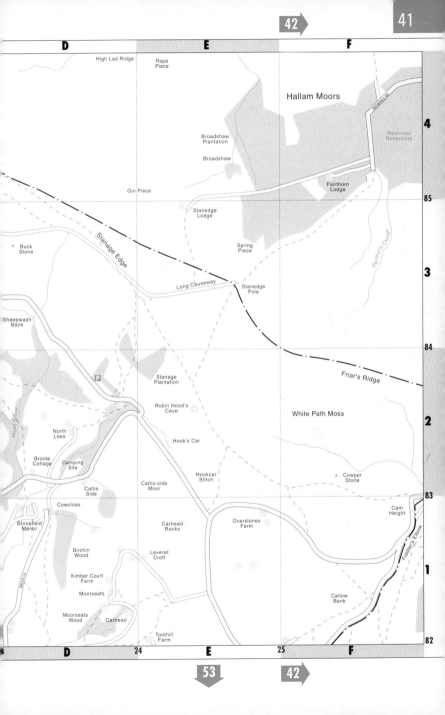

A   **B**   **C**

Lodge Moor

Reservoir Cottages

Wyming Brook Farm

Redmires Plantaion

Works

Wyming Brook Farm

Soughley

REDMIRES RD

WYMING BROOK DR

SOUGHLEY LA

LODGE MOOR RD

Redmires Conduit

BROWN HILLS LA

Peat Farm

Fulwood Grange Farm

Brownhills Farm

Birk's Green Farm

4

Redmires Reservoirs

ROPER L.

FULWOOD HEAD RD

Fulwood Booth

Knoll Top Farm

Douse Croft Farm

DOUSE CROFT LA

M... L... F...

85

Fulwood Head

Wagg Lane

Yarncliffe House Farm

FOXHALL L.

3

White Stones

BASSETT LA

BROWNELL LA

Green House Farm

GREENHOUSE LA

FULWOOD LA

OLD...

Bassett

Rud Hill

Brown Edge Farm

Clough Hollow

Porter Clough

84

Hallam Moors

Moorfield Farm

Brown Edge

Ringinglow

RINGINGLOW RD

2

Lady Canning's Plantation

Upper Burbage Bridge

Ox Stones

83

HOUNDKIRK RD

JANKIN RD

1

Burbage Moor

SHEFFIELD RD

Ford

Houndkirk Moor

82

26   **A**   27   **B**   28   **C**

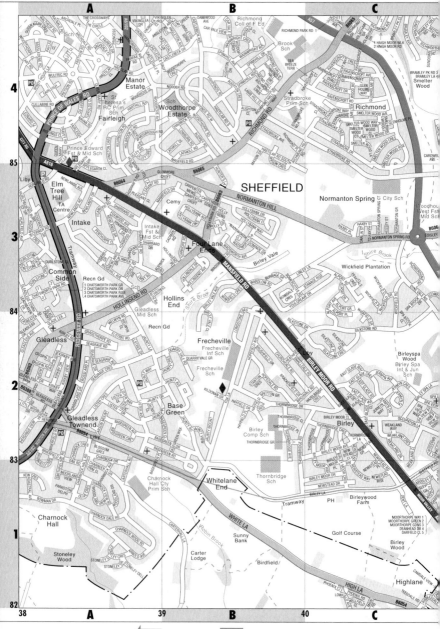

SHEFFIELD

Normanton Spring

Richmond

Manor Estate
Fairleigh
Woodthorpe Estate

Elm Tree Hill
Intake
Common Side
Gleadless

Four Lane Ends
Birley Vale

Wickfield Plantation

Hollins End

Frecheville
Frecheville Inf Sch
Quarry Vale Gr
Frecheville Sch

Birleyspa Wood
Birley Spa

Base Green

Gleadless Townend

Birley

Birley Comp Sch

Whitelane End

Tramway

Thornbridge Sch

Birleywood Farm

Charnock Hall Cty Prim Sch

Charnock Hall

Stoneley Wood

Sunny Bank

Carter Lodge

Robin Brook

WHITE LA

Golf Course

Birdfield

Birley Wood

Highlane

HIGH LA

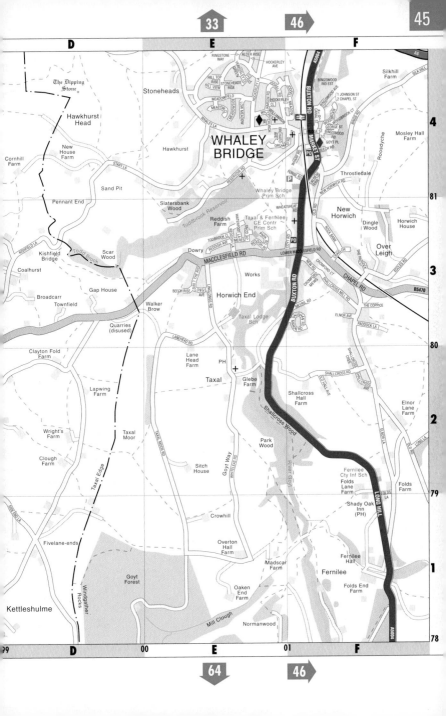

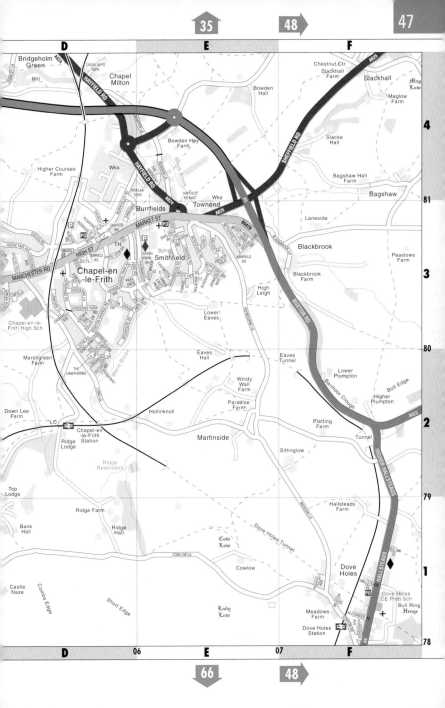

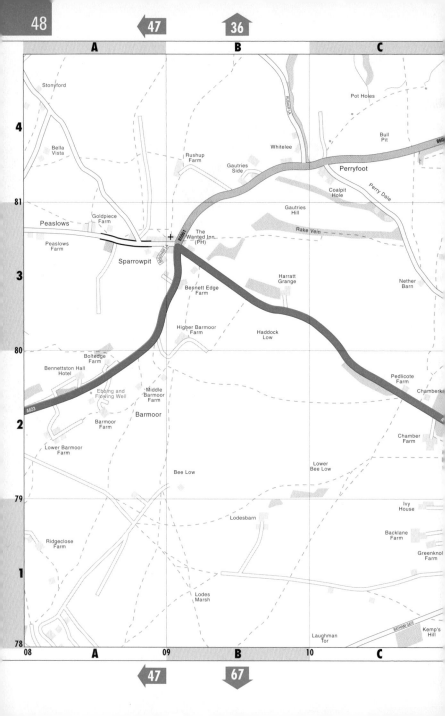

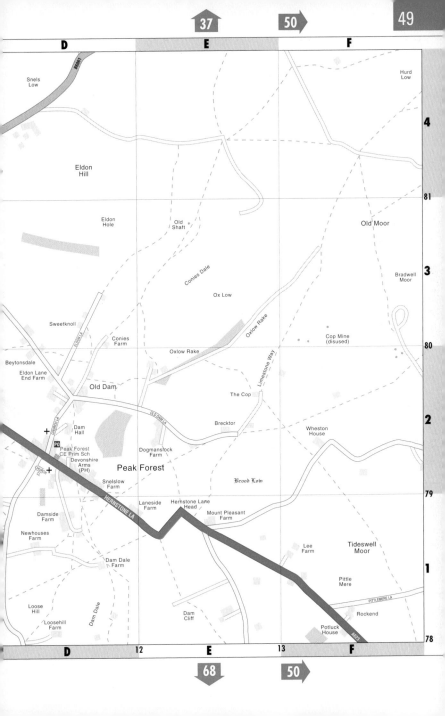

D E F

4

81

3

80

2

79

1

78

Snels
Low

Hurd
Low

Eldon
Hill

Eldon
Hole

Old
Shaft

Old Moor

Conies Dale

Bradwell
Moor

Ox Low

Sweetknoll

Oxlow Rake

Cop Mine
(disused)

Conies
Farm

Oxlow Rake

Beytonsdale

Limestone Way

Eldon Lane
End Farm

Old Dam

The Cop

Dam
Hall

Brecktor

Wheston
House

PO

Peak Forest
CE Prim Sch
Devonshire
Arms (PH)

Peak Forest

Dogmanslock
Farm

Brood Low

Snelslow
Farm

Laneside
Farm

Hernstone Lane
Head

HERNSTONE LA

Mount Pleasant
Farm

Damside
Farm

Lee
Farm

Tideswell
Moor

Newhouses
Farm

Dam Dale
Farm

Pittle
Mere

Loose
Hill

PITTLEMERE LA

Rockend

Loosehill
Farm

Dam Dale

Dam
Cliff

Potluck
House

A623

D E F

12 13

68 50

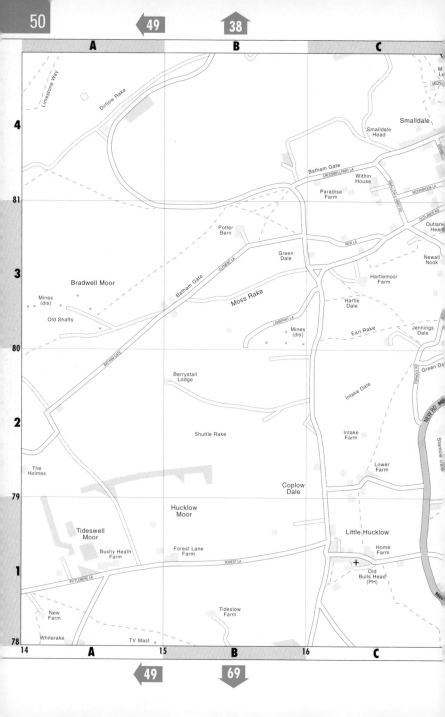

D   **E**   **F**

Caravan Park
Lee House
Brough Lee
Batham Gate
Batham's Farm
B6049
MICHLOW LA
HALL LA
Greet Ditch
Hall Gate View
Bradwell Head
Springfield Rd
Wks
SPRING
Smithy-Hill
NETHERSIDE
MAIN RD
CHURCH ST
FERNBANK
CHARLOTTE LA
HILL
YELLOW HAM LA
TOWN BOTTOM
TOWN GATE
OUTLANDS RD
Bradwell
Bradwell Jun Sch
Bradwell CE Inf Sch
Rebellion Knoll
Shatton Moor
TV Mast *
Shatton Edge

4

81

Bagshawe Cavern
Dale End
JEFFERY LA
BESSIE LA
Bradwell Hills
Bradwell Dale
Over Dale
Overdale Brook
Bradstoll La
Shatton La
Burton Bole End
Burton Bole
Wolf's Pit
Siney Sitch

3

NEW RD
Hill Rake
Hazlebadge Hall
Bradwell Edge
Robin Hood's Cross
DUPER LA
Fold Farm

80

Deadmans Clough
Bleak Knoll
Abney Moor
Abney
Ash House Farm

2

Quarters Farm
Durham Edge
Cockey Farm

79

Nether Water Farm
Camphill (Gliding Field)
Abney Grange

Broad Low
Burrs Mount
Great Hucklow Prim Sch
Gliding Club
Hucklow Edge
Grange Farm
Bretton Brook
Youth Hostel

1

78

7   **D**   18   **E**   19   **F**

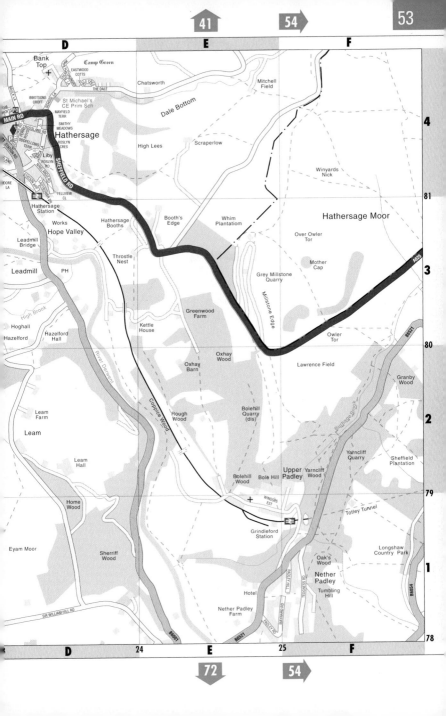

D **E** **F**

Bank Top
Camp Green
EASTWOOD COTTS
IBBOTSONS CROFT
St Michael's CE Prim Sch
Chatsworth
Mitchell Field
THE DALE
MAYFIELD TERR
Dale Bottom

4

MAIN RD
Hathersage
SMITHY MEADOWS
ROSLYN CRES
ODDFELLOWS TERR
Liby
ROSLYN RD
High Lees
Scraperlow
Winyards Nick

81

SHEFFIELD RD
FELLVIEW CL
Hathersage Station
Works
Hope Valley
Hathersage Booths
Booth's Edge
Whim Plantatiom
Hathersage Moor
Over Owler Tor

Leadmill Bridge
Throstle Nest
Grey Millstone Quarry
Mother Cap

3

Leadmill
PH
A625

High Brook
Hoghall
Hazelford
Hazelford Hall
Kettle House
Greenwood Farm
Millstone Edge
Owler Tor

80

River Derwent
Oxhay Wood
Lawrence Field
Granby Wood

Oxhay Barn
B6521

Leam Farm
Coppice Wood
Rough Wood
Bolehill Quarry (dis)
Burbage Brook
Yarncliff Quarry
Sheffield Plantation

2

Leam
Leam Hall
Bolehill Wood
Bole Hill
Upper Padley
Yarncliff Wood

Home Wood
WINDSES EST
Grindleford Station
Totley Tunnel

79

Eyam Moor
Sherriff Wood
Oak's Wood
Nether Padley
Longshaw Country Park

1

Hotel
Tumbling Hill
B6054

SIR WILLIAM HILL RD
Nether Padley Farm
PARKEY HILL
PADLEY RD

B6001
B6521

78

D 24 **E** 25 **F**

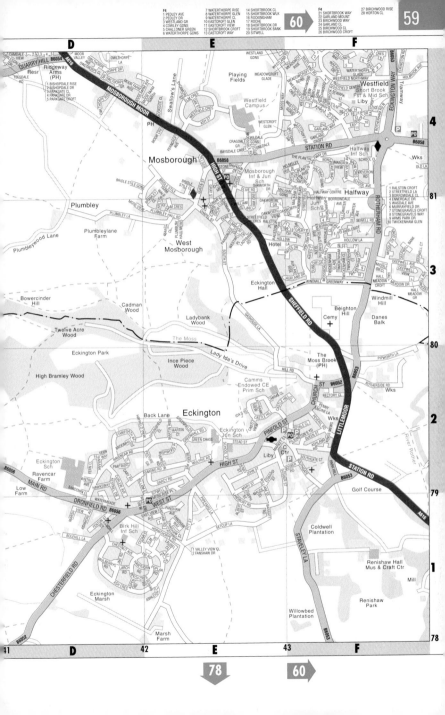

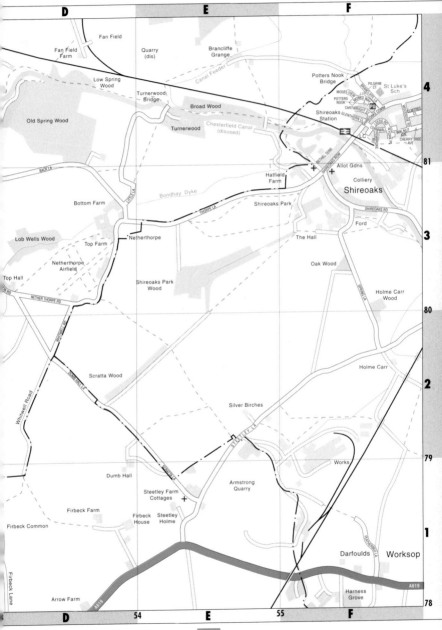

D　　　　　E　　　　　F

Fan Field
Fan Field Farm
Quarry (dis)
Brancliffe Grange
Low Spring Wood
Canal Feeder
Potters Nook Bridge
PILGRIM CT
MOSES VIEW WAY
PITNMS WAY
POTTERS NOOK
CARTWRIGHT CL
St Luke's Sch
ELMTREE

4

Turnerwood Bridge
Broad Wood
Shireoaks Station
GLENTWORN CL
WALNUT AVE
CHERRY TREE AVE
CORNWALL RD

Old Spring Wood
Turnerwood
Chesterfield Canal (disused)

RETHAL TERR
SHIREOAKS ROW
Allot Gdns

81

BACK LA
LITTLE LA

Hatfield Farm
Colliery
Shireoaks

Bottom Farm
Bondhay Dyke
THORPE LA
Shireoaks Park
SHIREOAKS RD

Lob Wells Wood
Netherthorpe
Top Farm
The Hall
Ford

3

Netherthorpe Airfield
Oak Wood
SPRING LA
Holme Carr Wood

Top Hall
TOP RD
NETHER THORPE RD
Shireoaks Park Wood

80

TOP MELDRUM

Scratta Wood
Holme Carr

2

Whitwell Road
STEETLEY LA
Silver Birches

Works

79

Dumb Hall
STEETLEY LA
Armstrong Quarry

Steetley Farm Cottages

Firbeck Farm
Firbeck House
Steetley Holme
FLOUR MILL LA

Firbeck Common

1

Darfoulds
Worksop

Firbeck Lane

A619
Harness Grove

78

Arrow Farm
A619

D　　　54　　　E　　　55　　　F

A **B** **C**

Browtop
Farm

Oldfield

Wks

River Goyt

A5004

LONG HILL

Hadgel Brook

4

Ladbitch
Wood

Hoo Moor

77

Goyt Forest

Goyt Valley

Fernilee Reservoir

Pymchair
Farm

P

Pym Chair

Calfhay
Wood

3

Oldgate
Nick

ERRIDGE CWT

THE STREET

Jep Clough

76

Cats Tor

Withinleach
Moor

Picnic
Area

Bunsal
Cob

2

Foxlow Edge

Sailing
Club

Errwood Reservoir

Thursbitch

75

Errwood
Hall

Picnic
Area

Forest
Trail

A5004 LN

The Tors

Shooter's Clough

River Goyt

1

Wild /Mc

74

99 **A** **00** **B** **01** **C**

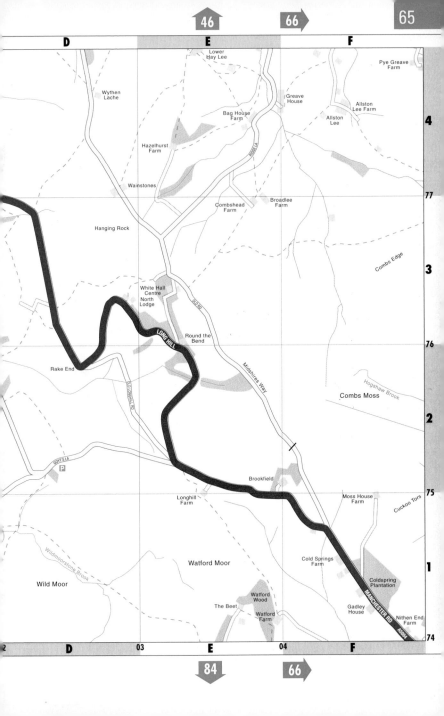

4

Pye Greave
Farm

Lower
Hay Lee

Wythen
Lache

Greave
House

Allston
Lee Farm

Bag House
Farm

Allston
Lee

Hazelhurst
Farm

Wainstones

77

Combshead
Farm

Broadlee
Farm

Hanging Rock

Combs Edge

3

White Hall
Centre
North
Lodge

76

LONG HILL

Round the
Bend

Midshires Way

Rake End

Hogshaw Brook

Combs Moss

2

OLD LONGHILL RD

BOYT'S LA

P

Brookfield

75

Longhill
Farm

Moss House
Farm

Cuckoo Tors

Wildmoorstone Brook

Watford Moor

Cold Springs
Farm

1

Wild Moor

Coldspring
Plantation

Watford
Wood

The Beet

MANCHESTER RD

Watford
Farm

Gadley
House

Nithen End
Farm

74

A **B** **C**

Pyegreave Brook

Hob Tor

Reservoirs

STATION RD
PH
HALLSTEADS
PH
Ashpiece Farm
BUXTON RD

4

P
Bibbington

77

Blackedge Reservoir

3 Combs Moss

Black Edge

Field Farm

Blackedge Farm

Tom Thorn Farm

76

Thorn Head Farm

Batham Gate

BATHAM LANE

Tomthorn

Hogshaw Brook

2

Television Station

Brownedge Plantation

Reservoirs

Turner Lodge

Brookhouse Farm

High Peak Nurseries

Brook House

Breezemount Farm

Waterswallows Green

WATERSWALLOWS LA

Light Wood

Lightwood Reservoirs

Frome Lodge

The Barms Farm

75

Works

Golf Course

DAISYMERE LA

WATERSWALLOWS RD

Hogshaw Brook

1

Fairfield Common

Corbar Hill

NUNSFIELD RD

BROWNEDGE RD

Nunsfield Farm

WATERSWALLOWS
MEWS
DAKIN CT.

TOWN END

Townend Farm

Corbar Woods

John Duncan Sch

CHESTNUT

St Anne's RC Prim Sch

LASCELLES RD

CH

FISSET LA

74

05 **A** **06** **B** **07** **C**

A B C

4

77

3

76

2

75

1

74

11 A 12 B 13 C

Kempshill Farm
Lower Kempshill Farm
Stone Lea Farm

Dam Dale

Hay Dale

Dale Head Farm
Dale Head

Bottom Farm

WATER LA

Sitch House

Wheston

Hall

The Top Farm

Peter Dale

Limestone Way

Cherryslack

Hayward Farm
Hargatewall

Monksdale House

Wind Low
Hargate Hall

Tunstead

MONKSDALE LA

Hill Top Farm

Wormhill Hill

Monk's Dale

Old Hall Farm
Wormhill

Nature Reserve

+
Wormhill Hall

A623

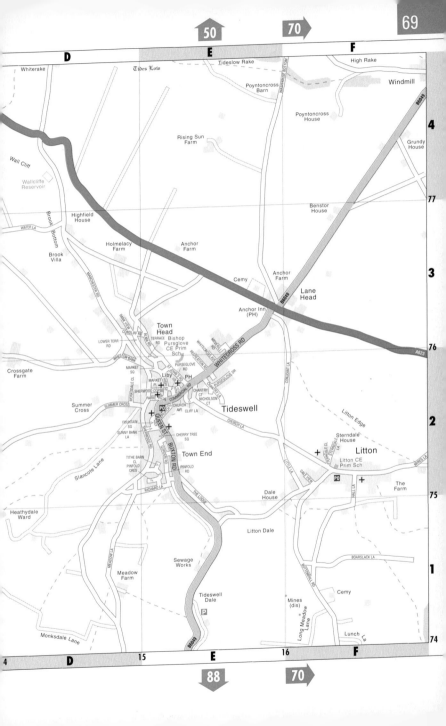

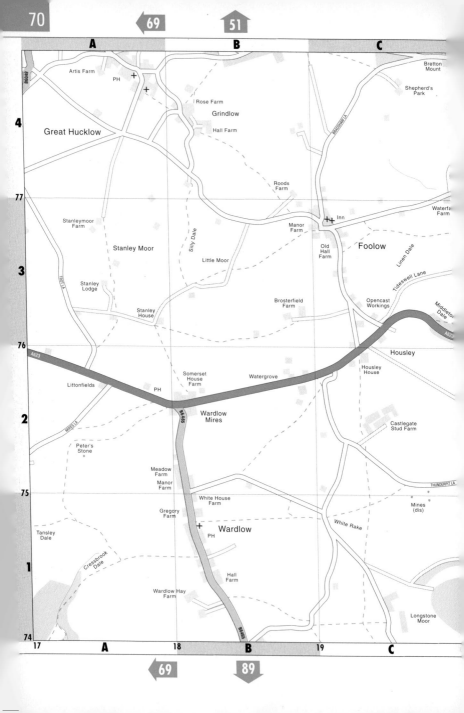

A   B   C

Bretton
Mount

Artis Farm

PH

Shepherd's
Park

Rose Farm

Grindlow

4

Great Hucklow

Hall Farm

BRADSHAW LA

Waterfall
Farm

Roods
Farm

77

Inn

Stanleymoor
Farm

Manor
Farm

Foolow

Old Hall
Farm

Linen Dale

Stanley Moor

Little Moor

Tideswell Lane

3

ROU LA

Silly Dale

Opencast
Workings

Middleton
Dale

Stanley
Lodge

Brosterfield
Farm

A623

Stanley
House

76

Housley

A623

Housley
House

Littonfields

Somerset
House
Farm

Watergrove

MIRES LA

PH

B6465

Castlegate
Stud Farm

2

Wardlow
Mires

Peter's
Stone

THUNDERPIT LA.

Meadow
Farm

Manor
Farm

White House
Farm

75

Mines
(dis)

Gregory
Farm

White Rake

Tansley
Dale

Wardlow

PH

Cressbrook Dale

1

Hall
Farm

Wardlow Hay
Farm

Longstone
Moor

B6465

74

17   A   18   B   19   C

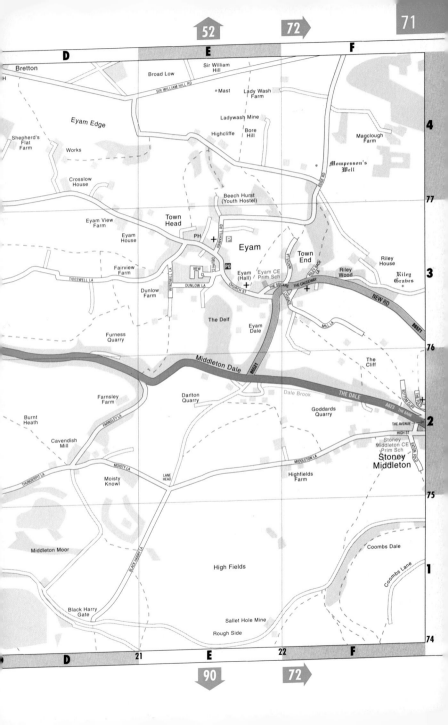

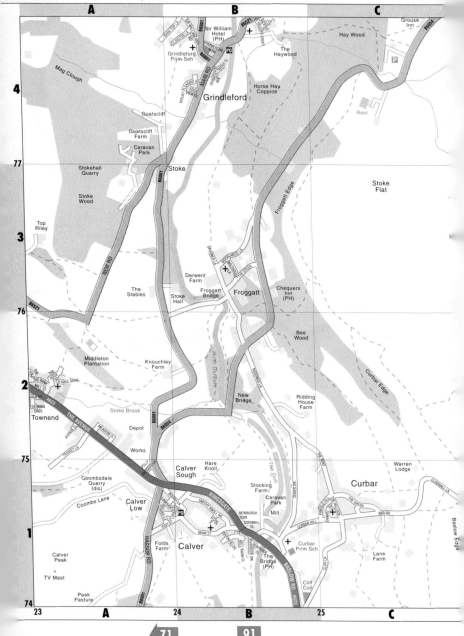

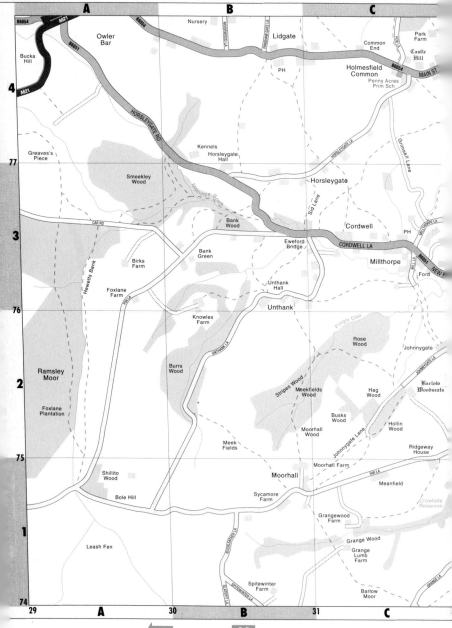

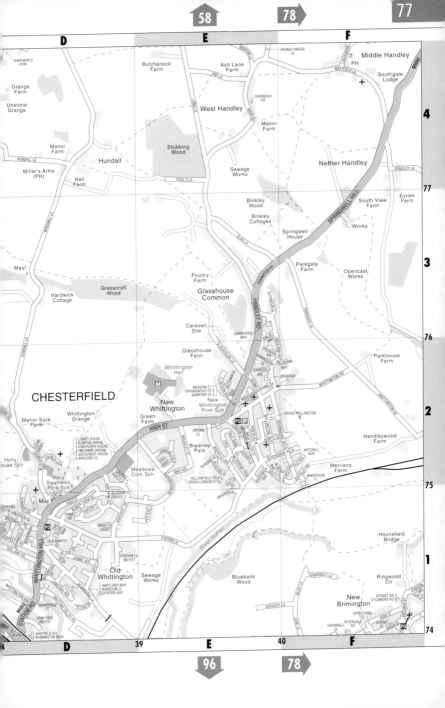

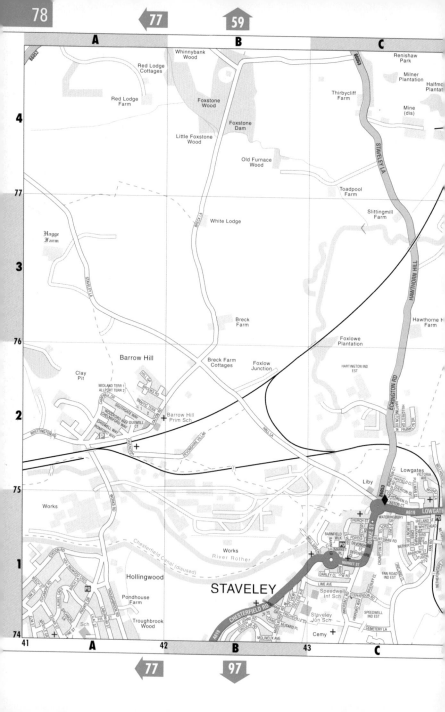

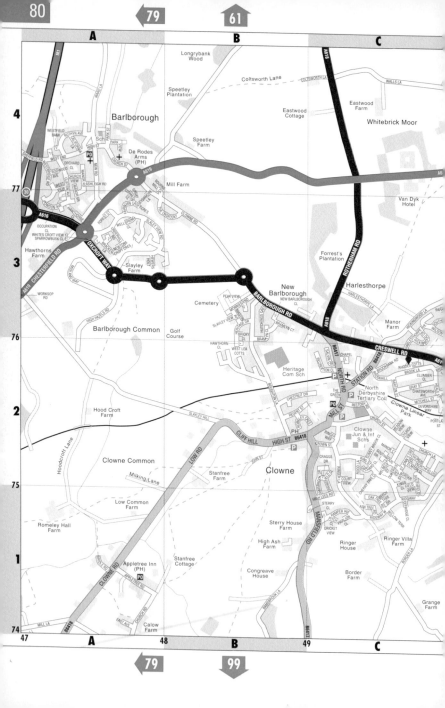

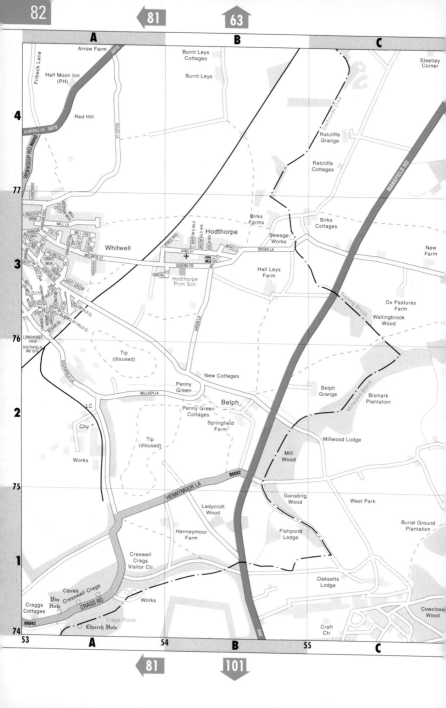

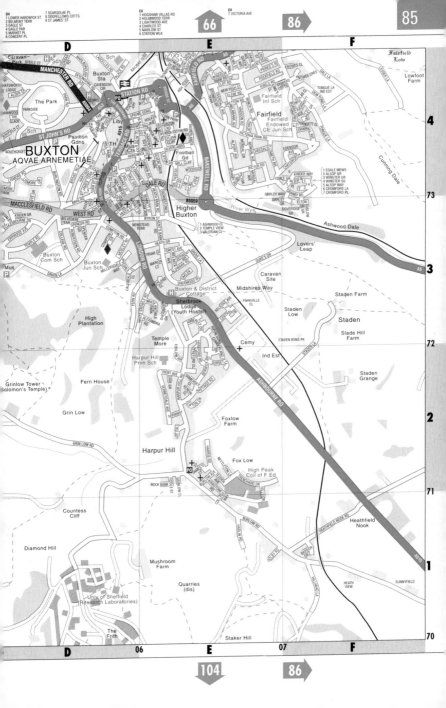

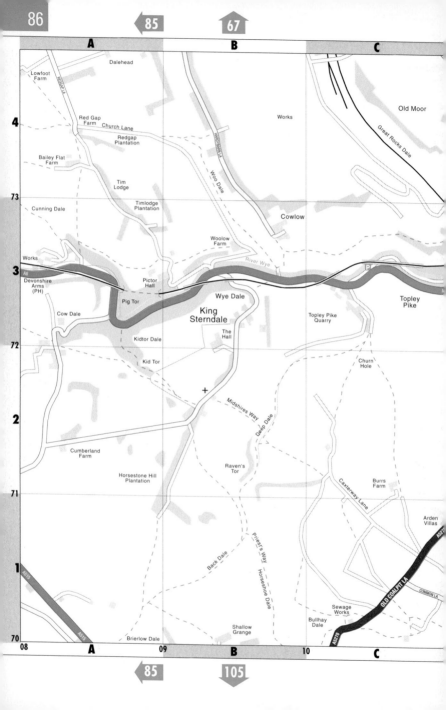

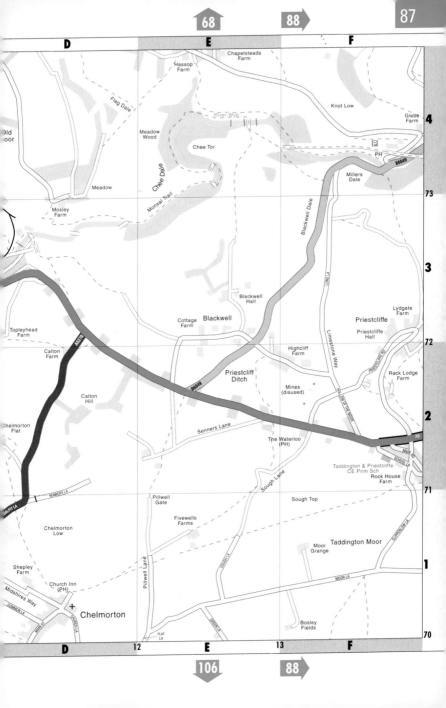

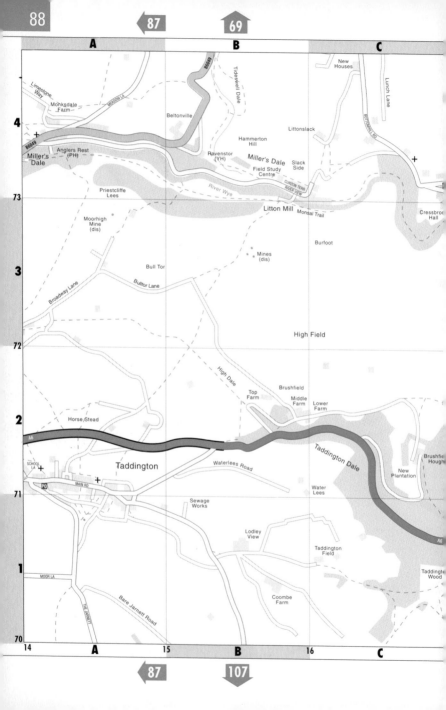

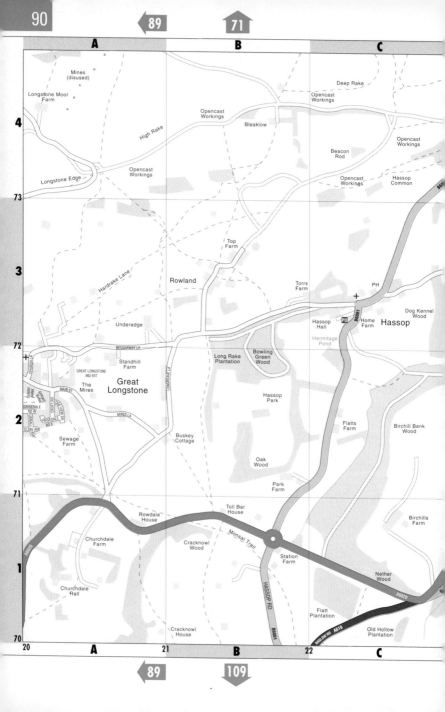

North Cliff
Plantation

Peak
Pasture

HASSOP RD

B6001

Cliff Coll

Grislow
Field

St Mary's
Wood

Bramley
Wood

Stanton
Ford

Gorse Bank
Farm

Bramley
Farm

Back Dale
Mine

BRAMLEY LA

Overlane
House

Back Dale
Wood

Bank
Wood

Shaw Top
P

Bramley
Plantation

Townend
Wood

Baslow
Hall

Bubnell
Farm

Bramley
Dale

Bank
Wood

Bubnell

CALVER RD

Bridge
End

Over
End

Oxpasture

CHURCH LA

Bubnell
Hall

Nether
End

St Anne's CE
Prim Sch

GOOSE
GREEN
VIEW

West
End

Baslow

A623

Park
Side

CHURCH LA   COCK HILL

Hotel
P

Toost Wood

WHEATLANDS LA

Bubnell
Cliff

St Anne's
CL

River Derwent

Toost Bank
Wood

Sewage
Farm

Home
Farm

chill
ank
ood

B6012

BAKEWELL RD

Rymas Brook

Hare Park

Farlow
Paddocks

Nursery

Oldfield
Plantation

PH

HIGH ST

BUS ALLEY

Pilsley

Dukesbank
Plantation

Pilsley CE
Prim Sch

Stud
Farm

Buston
Wood

Chatsworth Park

Oldfield
Plantation

B6048

Redway Wood

Broomhill
Plantation

Park
Wood

Redway Farm

Dunsa
Farm

Queen Mary's
Bower

Handley Bottom
Farm

HANDLEY LA

DUNSA LA

Dunsa

Bridge

Handley
Bottom

Paddocks
Plantation

B6012

4

73

3

72

2

71

1

70

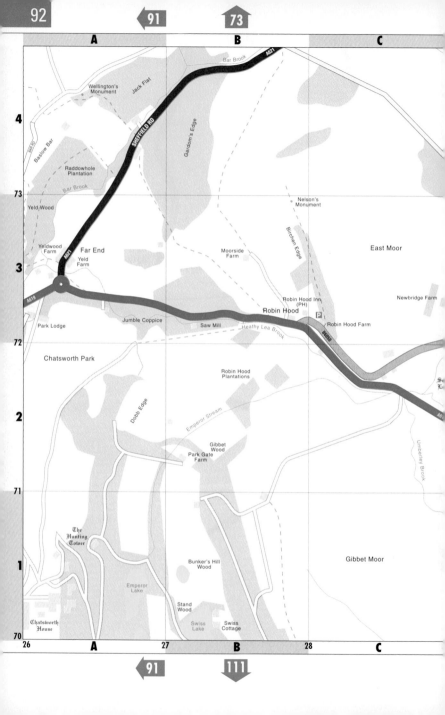

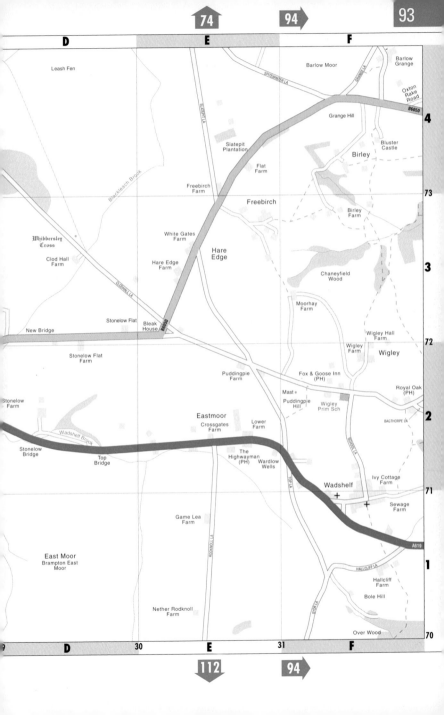

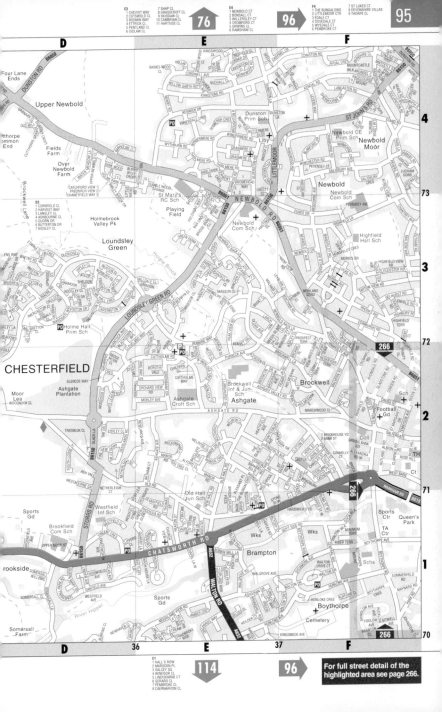

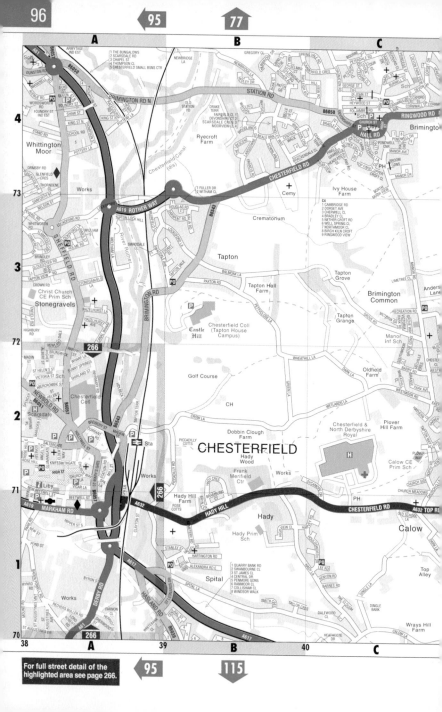

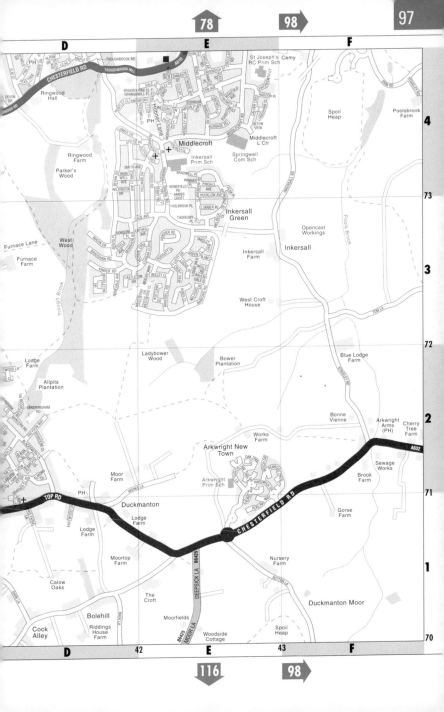

D E F

ALPINE
MAPLE ST
TROUGHBROOK RD
CHESTERFIELD RD
TROUGHBROOK HILL
DIVISION ST
PH
St Joseph's Cemy
RC Prim Sch
DEVON
DR
WOODHOUSE RD
Ringwood
Hall
ST EDWARD'S
CAVENDISH PL
Spoil
Heap
Poolsbrook
Farm

4

Ringwood
Farm
BRADBOURNE CL
GRANGEMILL PL 2
CROMFORD DR
HADDON PL
PH
ELTON
VIEW
Middlecroft
L Ctr

Parker's
Wood
ATTLEE RD
Middlecroft
Inkersall
Prim Sch
Springwell
Com Sch

SMITH AVE
SHIN
WELL
AVE
BRADWELL
WINNAT
PL
PINDALE
HUCKLOW AVE
West
Wood
WILKINSON
DR
BONDFIELD
RD
AMBER
CROFT
HOLBROOK PL
CLUMBER PL

73

Furnace Lane
Furnace
Farm
DOBSON
LA
LATHKILL
AVE
THORESBY
Inkersall
Green
Opencast
Workings
Pools Brook

West
Wood
BRADSHAW LA
KINDER RD
CASTLETON
BEELEY CL
DALE CL
TANSLEY
ALAM
HAVENS
DALE CL
Inkersall
Farm
Inkersall

TOM LA

3

West Croft
House

72

Trough Brook
Ladybower
Wood
Bower
Plantation
Blue Lodge
Farm

Lodge
Farm
TWOOD CL
GE CL
Allpits
Plantation
Bonne
Vienne
Arkwright
Arms
(PH)
Cherry
Tree
Farm

2

SANDRINGHAM
RD
Works
Farm
Sewage
Works
A632
Arkwright New
Town
Moor
Farm
WORKS LA
OAK TREE
HARDWI
PENFOLD
Brook
Farm

FASTWOOD DR
PH
TOP RD
Duckmanton
Arkwright
Prim Sch
ROSS RD
CHESTERFIELD RD
Gorse
Farm

71

Lodge
Farm
Lodge
Farm
Moortop
Farm
Nursery
Farm

DEEPSICK LA
B6425
MOOR LA
BUTTON LA
Duckmanton Moor

1

Calow
Oaks
The
Croft
Moorfields

Bolehill
Riddings
House
Farm
Woodside
Cottage
Spoil
Heap

Cock
Alley
B6425
MOOR LA

70

D 42 E 43 F

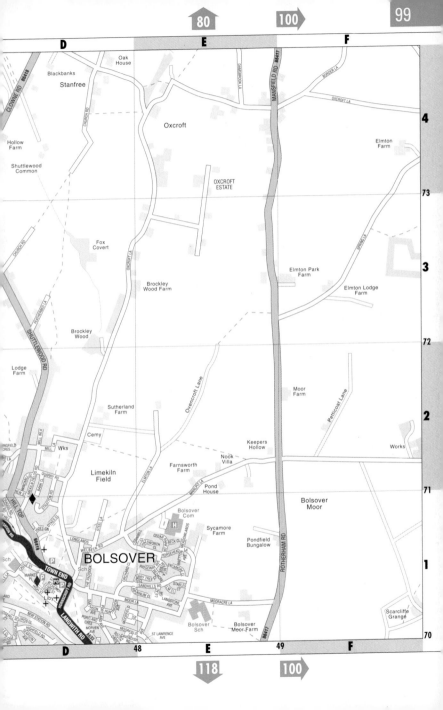

D E F

Blackbanks
Stanfree
Oak House

CLOWNE RD B6418
CHURCH RD
DAMBROOK LA
MANSFIELD RD B6417
BORDER LA
OXCROFT LA

Oxcroft

Hollow Farm

Elmton Farm

Shuttlewood Common

OXCROFT ESTATE

4

73

Fox Covert

OXCROFT LA

CHURCH RD

Elmton Park Farm

SPRING LA

3

Brockley Wood Farm

Elmton Lodge Farm

SHUTTLEWOOD RD

LEVERS DELL LA

Brockley Wood

72

Lodge Farm

Oxencroft Lane

Moor Farm

Petticoat Lane

2

Sutherland Farm

Works

Cemy

MILL WALK
MILL LA

Wks

Keepers Hollow

Farnsworth Farm

Nook Villa

Limekiln Field

ELM TREE LA

Pond House

71

BOLSOVER MOOR

HILL TOP

B6419

MILL WALK
QUARRY LA
BANK CL
STEEL LANE
SHEEP LANE

Bolsover Com

H

Sycamore Farm

ROTHERHAM RD B6417

TOWN END
MARKET PL

BOLSOVER

Sch

Liby

Sch

CEDAR PK CL
BECK CL
MOORLANDS
SYCAMORE
STATION RD
WELBECK RD
LONGLANDS
RIDGEWAY
SANDHILLS RD
LANGSTONE AVE
STABLES CT

Pondfield Bungalow

1

NEW STATION RD
LANGWITH RD A632

ST LAWRENCE AVE

Bolsover Sch

Bolsover Moor Farm

MOORACRE LA

Scarcliffe Grange

70

D 48 E 49 F

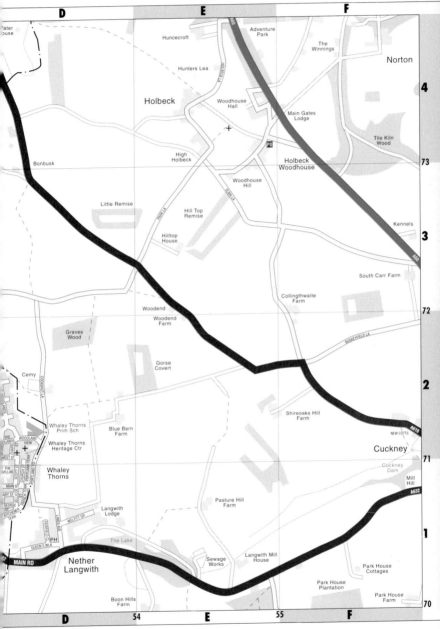

D
E
F

Huncecroft

Adventure Park

The Winnings

Norton

4

Hunters Lea

Holbeck

Woodhouse Hall

Main Gates Lodge

Tile Kiln Wood

PO

Holbeck Woodhouse

73

Bonbusk

High Holbeck

Woodhouse Hill

Little Remise

Hill Top Remise

Kennels

3

Hilltop House

South Carr Farm

Woodend

Collingthwaite Farm

72

Graves Wood

Woodend Farm

Budmeyfield La

Cemy

Gorse Covert

2

Whaley Thorns Prim Sch

Blue Barn Farm

Shireoaks Hill Farm

NEW COTTS

A616

THE ISLANDS

WOODLAND VIEW

Whaley Thorns Heritage Ctr

Cuckney

71

THE VILLAS

Whaley Thorns

Cuckney Dam

Mill Hill

MAIN ST

A632

GEORGE

Langwith Lodge

Pasture Hill Farm

1

PH

QUEEN'S WLK

The Lake

Nether Langwith

Sewage Works

Langwith Mill House

Park House Cottages

Boon Hills Farm

Park House Plantation

Park House Farm

70

D
54
E
55
F

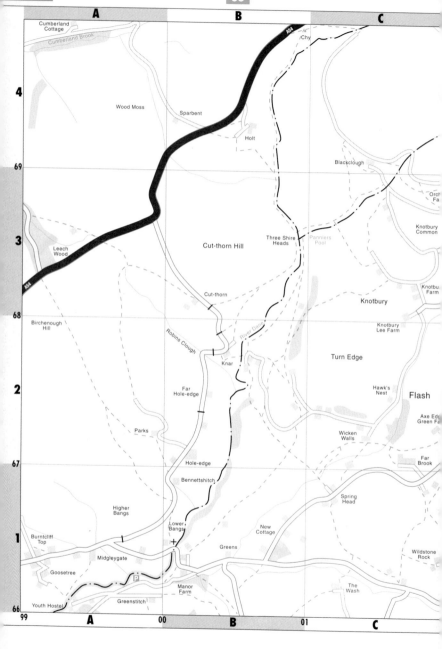

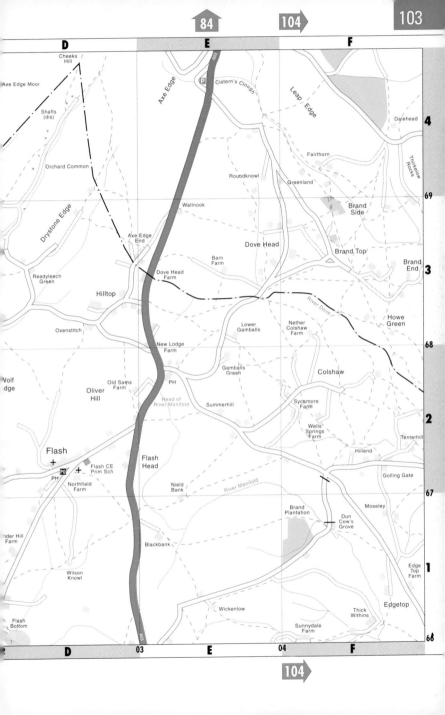

103
85

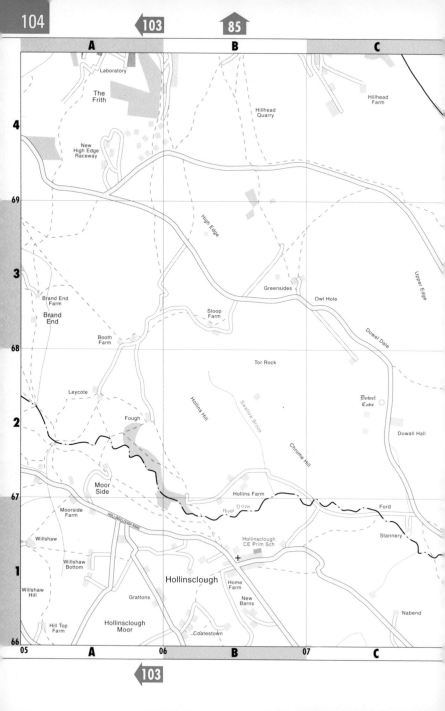

A · B · C

Hillhead Quarry

Hillhead Farm

4

69

High Edge

Upper Edge

3

Brand End Farm

Brand End

Greensides

Owl Hole

Dowel Dale

Stoop Farm

Booth Farm

68

Tor Rock

Dowel Cate

Leycote

Hollins Hill

Swallow Brook

Dowall Hall

2

Fough

Chrome Hill

Moor Side

67

Moorside Farm

HOLLINSCLOUGH RAKE

Hollins Farm

River Dove

Ford

Stannery

Willshaw

Hollinsclough CE Prim Sch

Willshaw Bottom

Hollinsclough

Home Farm

1

Willshaw Hill

Grattons

New Barns

Nabend

Hill Top Farm

Hollinsclough Moor

Coatestown

66

05 · A · 06 · B · 07 · C

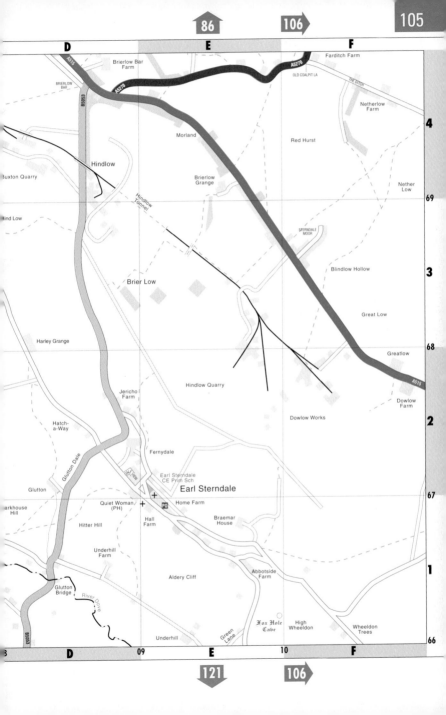

D | E | F

A515
BRIERLOW BAR
Brierlow Bar Farm
Farditch Farm
OLD COALPIT LA
A5270
THE DITCH
B5053
A5270
Netherlow Farm

4

Morland
Red Hurst
Hindlow
Buxton Quarry
Brierlow Grange
Nether Low

69

Hindlow Tunnel
ind Low
SPERNDALE MOOR

Brier Low
Blindlow Hollow

3

Great Low

Harley Grange
Greatlow

68

A515
Jericho Farm
Hindlow Quarry
Dowlow Farm

Hatch-a-Way
Dowlow Works

2

Glutton Dale
Fernydale
Earl Sterndale CE Prim Sch
Glutton
Quiet Woman (PH)
Earl Sterndale
Home Farm
PO

67

arkhouse Hill
Hall Farm
Braemar House
Hitter Hill
Underhill Farm

1

Aldery Cliff
Abbotside Farm
Glutton Bridge
River Dove
Underhill
Green Lane
Fox Hole Cave
High Wheeldon
Wheeldon Trees
B5053

66

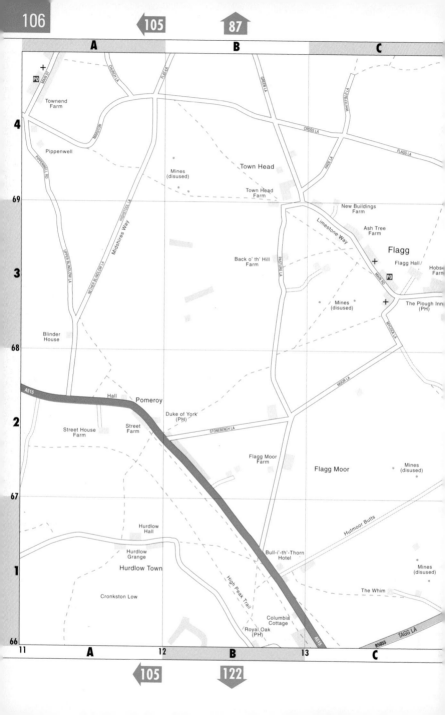

105
87

A B C

105
122

PO
Townend Farm

Pippenwell

CHURCH LA

FLEA LA

GREEN LA

WHITEHILL LA

CROSS LA

FLAGG LA

PICO LA

Town Head

Mines (disused)

Town Head Farm

New Buildings Farm

Ash Tree Farm

Limestone Way

Flagg

Flagg Hall

Hobson Farm

The Plough Inn (PH)

Back o' th' Hill Farm

Mines (disused)

PASTURE LA

MAIN RD

PO

BROOK LA

Blinder House

MIDSHIRES WAY

HORSTON LA

UPPER BLACKLOW LA

WALKER BLACKLOW LA

PIPPENWELL RD

MOOR LA

A515

Hall

Pomeroy

Duke of York (PH)

STONERICH LA

Street House Farm

Street Farm

Flagg Moor Farm

Flagg Moor

Mines (disused)

Hutmoor Butts

Hurdlow Hall

Hurdlow Grange

Hurdlow Town

Cronkston Low

Bull-i'-th'-Thorn Hotel

High Peak Trail

A515

Mines (disused)

The Whim

Columbia Cottage

Royal Oak (PH)

B5055

TAGG LA

4

69

3

68

2

67

1

66

11

12

13

A B C

107
89

A   **B**   **C**

Ashford CE
Prim Sch

River Wye

THE DUKE'S DR

A6 BUXTON

Great Shacklow
Wood

Ashford in
the Water

Little Shacklow
Wood

4

Arrock
Plantation

69

Rose Farm
Opencast Workings

Lower
Farm
Opencast
Workings

Dirtlow
Farm

Top Farm

Kirk Dale

Dirtlow
Plantations

Sheldon

Woodbine
Farm

Cowden
Plantations

3

Magpie Mine
(disused)

Truebell Lane

68

Opencast Workings

Green Cowden
Farm

B5055

Shafts
(dis)

2

Bole Hill

Bole Hill
Farm

Blores Barn
Farm

GREEN LA

Melbourne
Farm

67

Haddon Grove
Farm

B5055

Organ Ground

Opencast Workings

1

Haddon
Grove

Mandale Rake

Haddon Grove
Farms

Mines
(dis)

Twin Dales

66

River Lathkill

17   **A**   **18**   **B**   **19**   **C**

107
124

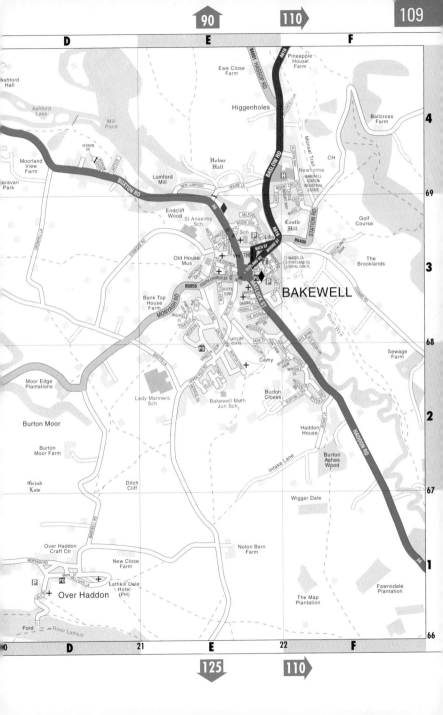

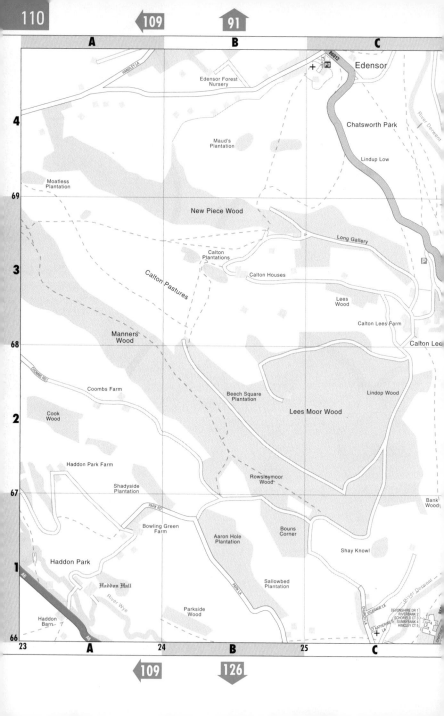

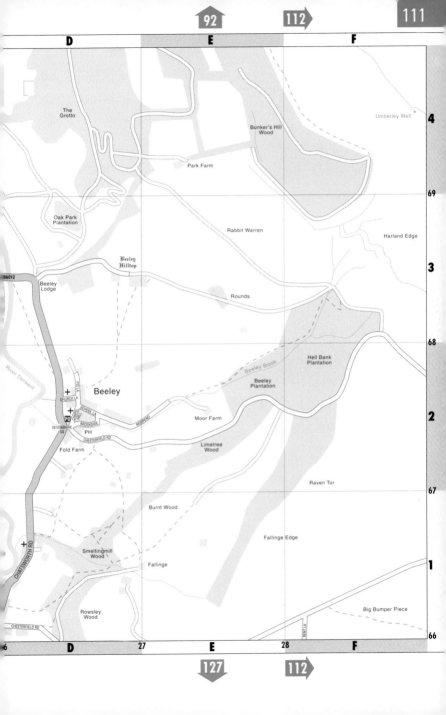

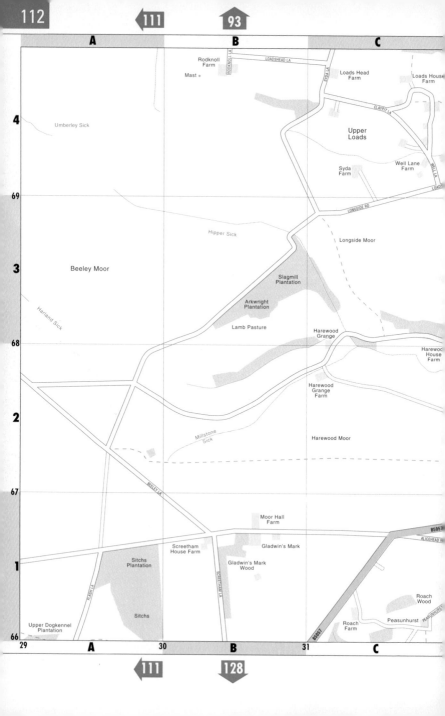

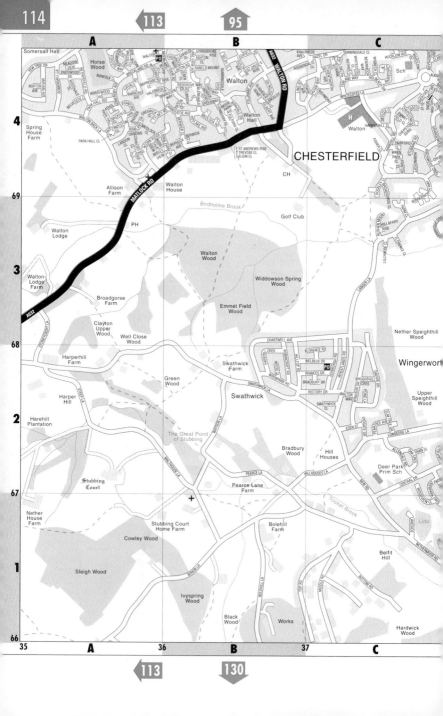

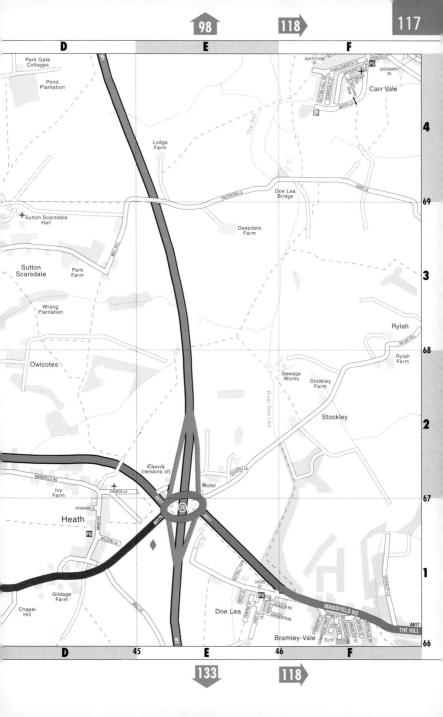

D **E** **F**

Park Gate Cottages

Pond Plantation

NORTH VIEW ST
SPENCER ST
CHARLESWORTH ST
BATHURST ST
GREENWAY DR
Carr Vale
WATER LA

4

Lodge Farm

The Golf

PALTERTON LA
Doe Lea Bridge
CARR LA

69

Sutton Scarsdale Hall

Deepdale Farm

Sutton Scarsdale

Park Farm

MILL HILL

3

Wrang Plantation

Rylah

RYLAH HILL

68

Owlcotes

Rylah Farm

Sewage Works

Stockley Farm

River Doe Lea

Stockley

2

Church (remains of)

CHURCH LA

MANSFIELD RD

Ivy Farm
CHURCH LA

Motel

67

Heath

VICARAGE CL

MAIN RD

PO
WILSON LA.

A617

M617G

29

A617

1

Gildage Farm

MILL LA

NUTHALL TERR
CROSS ST
PO
JACKSON RD
CENTRE ST
OLD ROAD
SCHOOL
GARDEN ROW

MANSFIELD RD

STOCKLEY LA

Chapel Hill

Doe Lea

CAMBRIDGE CRES
STANTON CT
STIRLING CT
BRAMLEY RD
CENTRE ST
BRAMLEY RD
BIRCHMOOR DR
MACBETH ST
HARTINGTON ST
A617
THE HILL

Bramley-Vale

Sch

66

D **45** **E** **46** **F**

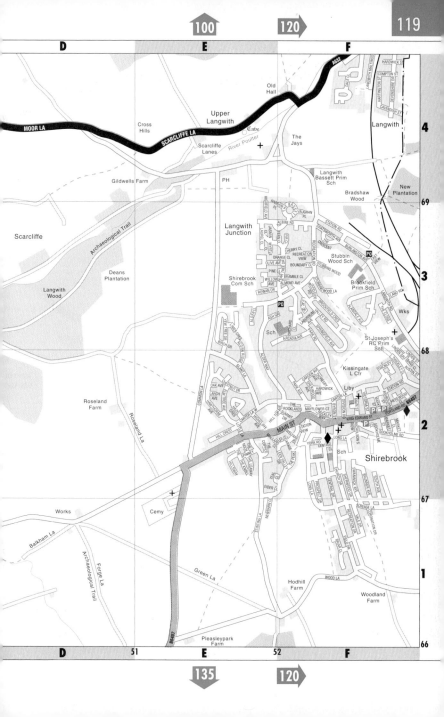

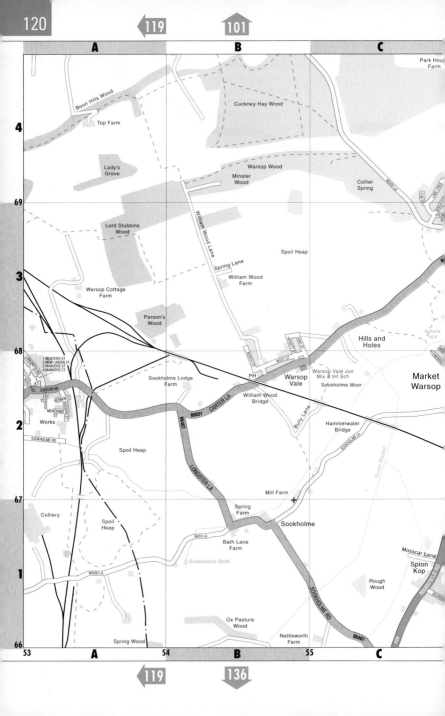

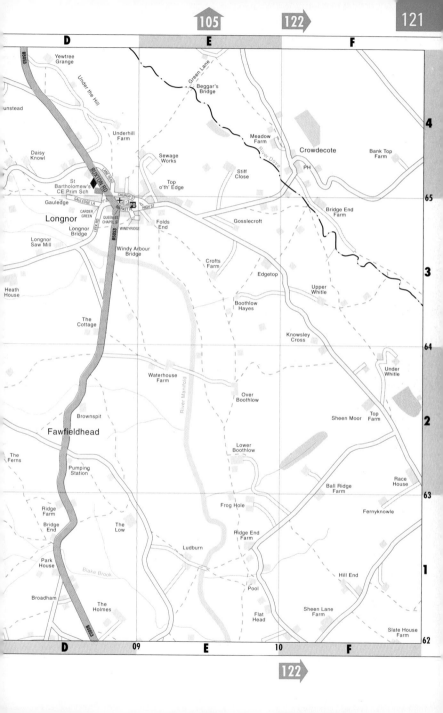

Barrowstones Lane

Milkings Lane

Fern Dale

Summerhill Farm

Limestone Way

4

One Ash Grange Farm

Highlow Farm

DERBY LA

65

Opencast Workings

Mines (dis)

Bruntmoor

THE RAKE

Cales Dale

3

Mines (dis)

Cales Farm

Moscar Farm

Benty Grange

Prospect Mine (dis)

64

LONG RAKE

Darley Farm

Crookdale Plantation

P

Parsley Hay

Upper Oldhams Farm

Arbor Low

New Vincent Farm

Midshires Way

High Peak Trail

Gib Hill

Rookery Plantation

2

Gibhill Plantation

Middleton Common

63

Blake Moor

Tissington Trail

Newhaven Lodge

1

Lean Low

Green Lane

Leanlow Farm

Blakemoor Plantation

A515

62

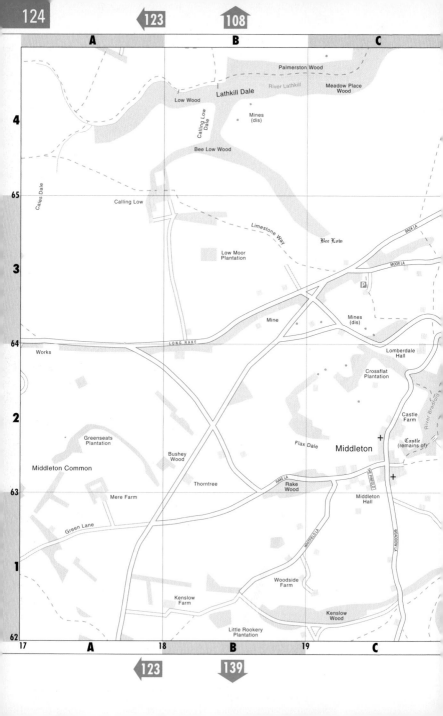

A **B** **C**

Palmerston Wood

River Lathkill

Meadow Place Wood

Lathkill Dale

Low Wood

Calling Low Dale

4

Mines (dis)

Bee Low Wood

Cales Dale

65

Calling Low

Limestone Way

Bee Low

Low Moor Plantation

3

BACK LA

MOOR LA

P

Mine

Mines (dis)

64

LONG RAKE

Works

Lomberdale Hall

Crossflat Plantation

River Bradford

2

Castle Farm

Greenseats Plantation

Flax Dale

Castle (remains of)

Middleton

Bushey Wood

Middleton Common

RAKE LA

Rake Wood

THE PINFOLD

Thorntree

Middleton Hall

63

Mere Farm

WHITFIELD LA

MEADOW LA

Green Lane

1

Woodside Farm

Kenslow Farm

Kenslow Wood

62

Little Rookery Plantation

17 **A** **18** **B** **19** **C**

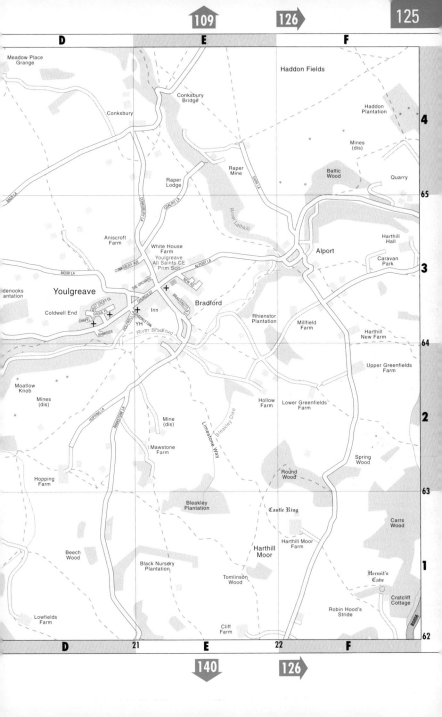

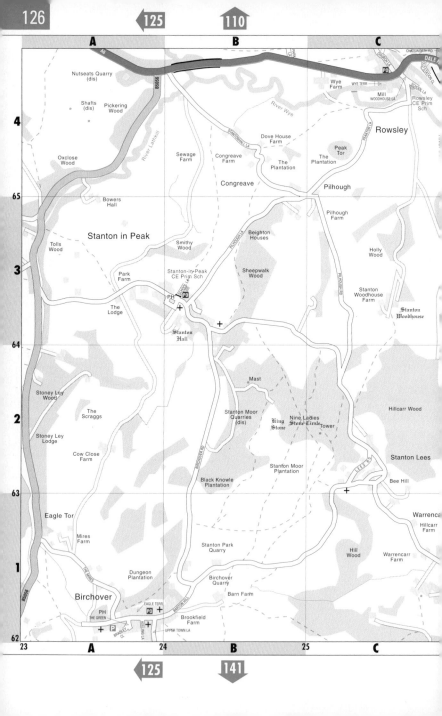

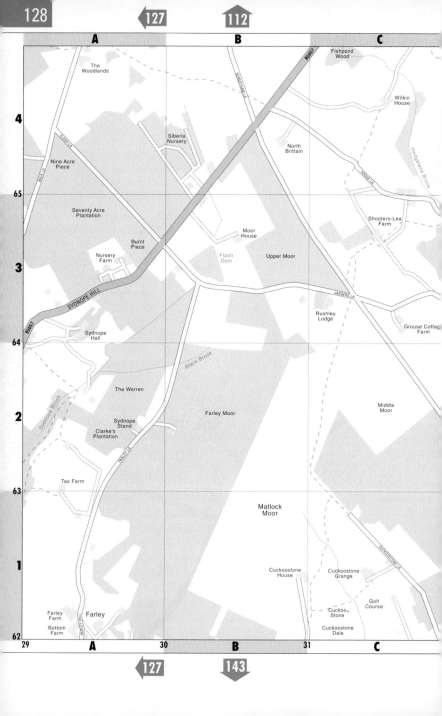

A B C

B9057

Fishpond
Wood

The
Woodlands

Wilkin
House

4

Siberia
Nursery

North
Brittain

FLASH LA

Nine Acre
Piece

BECK LA

Hodgelane Brook

HUDGE LA

65

Seventy Acre
Plantation

Shooters-Lea
Farm

Moor
House

Burnt
Piece

Upper Moor

3

Nursery
Farm

Flash
Dam

SYDNOPE HILL

JAGGERS LA

B9057

Sydnope
Hall

Rushley
Lodge

Grouse Cottage
Farm

64

Black Brook

The Warren

Middle
Moor

2

Farley Moor

Sydnope
Stand

Sydnope Brook

Clarke's
Plantation

FARLEY LA

Tax Farm

63

Matlock
Moor

CUCKOOSTONE LA

1

Cuckoostone
House

Cuckoostone
Grange

Cuckoostone
Cuckoo
Stone

Golf
Course

Farley
Farm

FARLEY HILL

Farley

Bottom
Farm

Cuckoostone
Dale

62

29 **A** 30 **B** 31 **C**

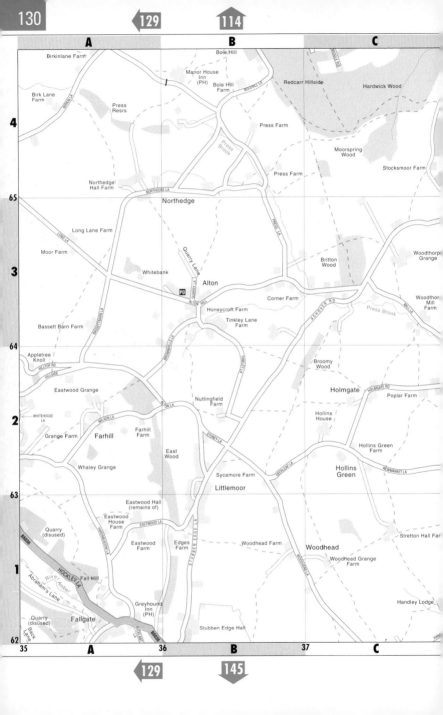

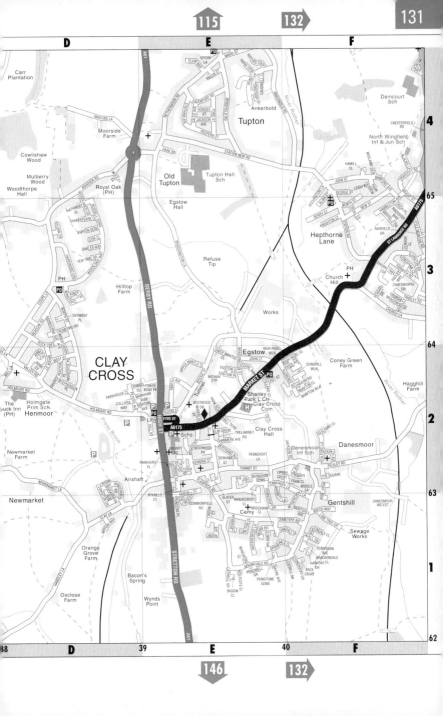

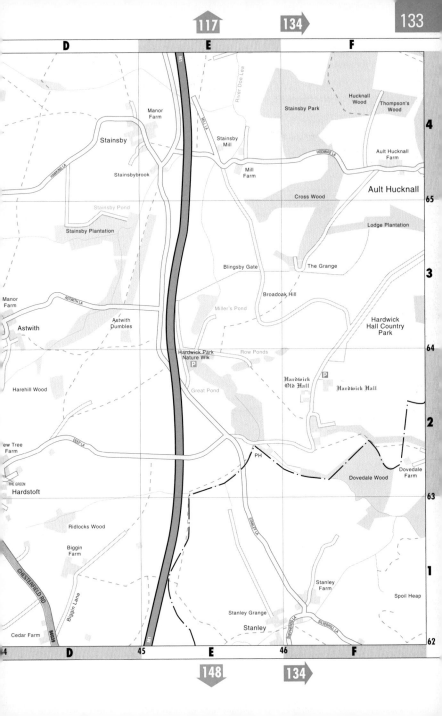

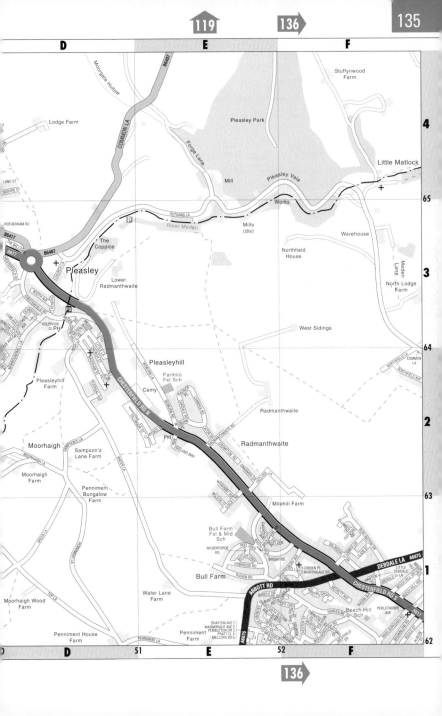

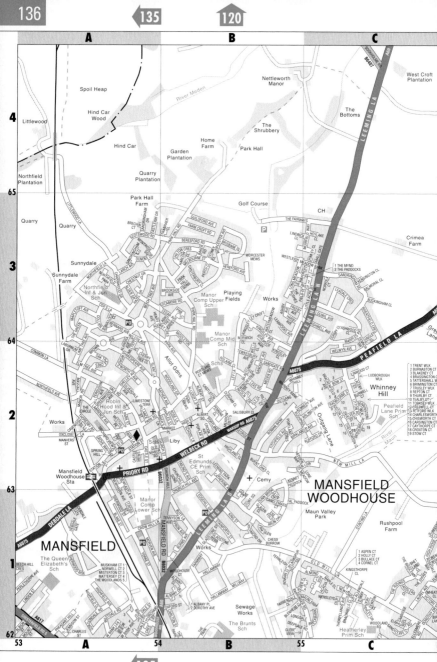

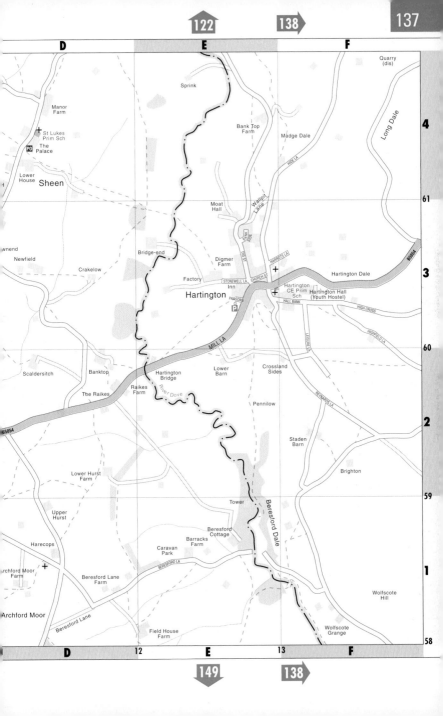

Quarry
(dis)

Long Dale

4

Manor
Farm

St Lukes
Prim Sch
The Palace

Bank Top
Farm

Madge Dale

Lower
House

Sheen

Sprink

Moat
Hall

Walpit Lane

HIDE LA

61

wnend

Newfield

Crakelow

Bridge-end

Digmer
Farm

Factory

HARROTS LA

Hartington Dale

3

Hartington

STONEWELL LA

CHURCH ST

Inn

Hartington
CE Prim
Sch

Hartington Hall
(Youth Hostel)

B5054

HALL BANK

PARSONS

MILL LA

HIGH CROSS

HIGHFIELD LA

LEESIDE LA

60

Scaldersitch

Banktop

Hartington
Bridge

Lower
Barn

Crossland
Sides

The Raikes

Raikes
Farm

River Dove

Pennilow

REYNARDS LA

2

B5054

Staden
Barn

Brighton

Lower Hurst
Farm

59

Upper
Hurst

Tower

Beresford Dale

Harecops

Beresford
Cottage

rchford Moor
Farm

Barracks
Farm

Caravan
Park

Beresford Lane
Farm

BERESFORD LA

1

Wolfscote
Hill

Archford Moor

Beresford Lane

Field House
Farm

Wolfscote
Grange

58

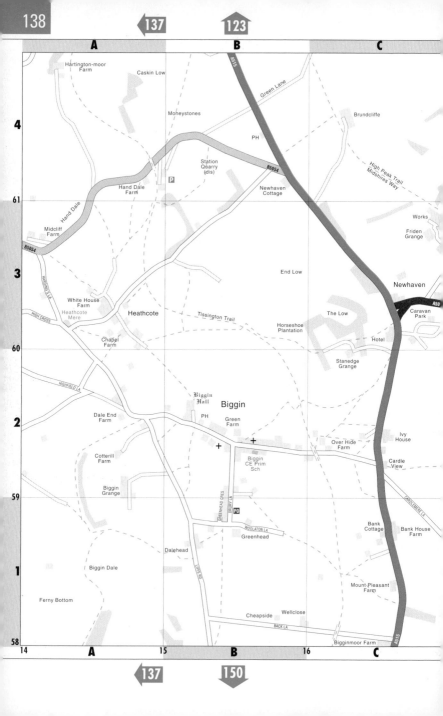

A B C

Hartington-moor Farm

Caskin Low

Green Lane

Moneystones

Brundcliffe

PH

4

Station Quarry (dis)

High Peak Trail
Midshires Way

B5054

P

Hand Dale Farm

Newhaven Cottage

61

Hand Dale

Works

Midcliff Farm

Friden Grange

B5054

End Low

Newhaven

3

HASLING LA

A50

White House Farm

Caravan Park

HIGH CROSS

Heathcote Mere

Heathcote

Tissington Trail

The Low

Horseshoe Plantation

Hotel

Chapel Farm

60

Stanedge Grange

HIGHFIELD LA

Biggin Hall

Biggin

2

Dale End Farm

PH

Green Farm

Ivy House

Over Hide Farm

Cotterill Farm

Biggin CE Prim Sch

Cardle View

Biggin Grange

59

GREENHEAD CRES

DRUBY LA

PO

Bank Cottage

Bank House Farm

BUGOLATON LA

CARDLEMERE LA

Greenhead

Dalehead

1

Biggin Dale

LEES RD

Mount-Pleasant Farm

Ferny Bottom

Cheapside

Wellclose

BACK LA

58

Bigginmoor Farm

A515

14 A 15 B 16 C

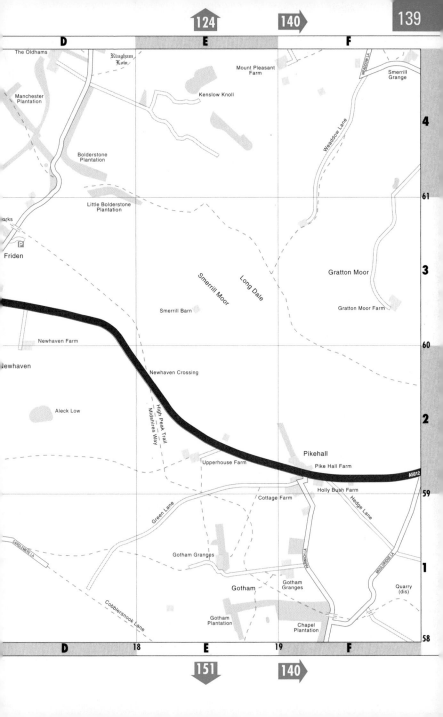

124
140

D
E
F

The Oldhams

Ringham Low

Mount Pleasant Farm

Manchester Plantation

Kenslow Knoll

Smerrill Grange

Weaddow Lane

4

Bolderstone Plantation

Little Bolderstone Plantation

61

orks

Friden

Smerrill Moor

Long Dale

Gratton Moor

3

Smerrill Barn

Gratton Moor Farm

Newhaven Farm

60

Newhaven

Newhaven Crossing

Aleck Low

High Peak Trail
Midshires Way

Pikehall

2

Upperhouse Farm

Pike Hall Farm

A5012

Holly Bush Farm

59

Cottage Farm

Hedge Lane

Green Lane

CARDLEMERE LA

Gotham Granges

Gotham Granges

Ya CHORAGH

MOULDRIDGE LA

1

Quarry (dis)

Gotham

Cobblersnook Lane

Gotham Plantation

Gotham Granges

Chapel Plantation

58

D
18
E
19
F

151
140

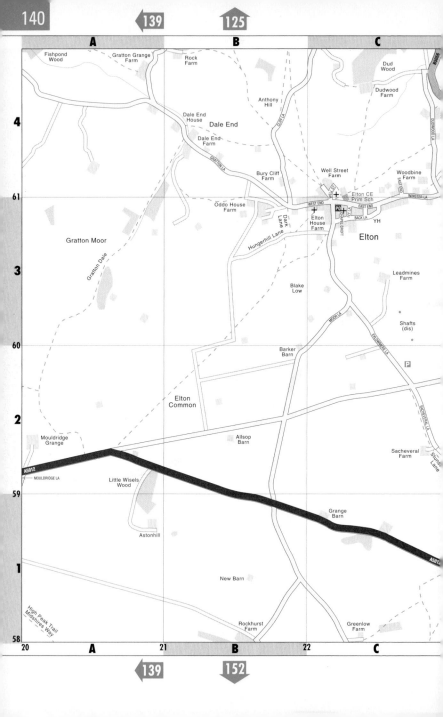

139
125

A　　　B　　　C

Fishpond
Wood

Gratton Grange
Farm

Rock
Farm

Dud
Wood

Dudwood
Farm

Anthony
Hill

Dale End
House

4 Dale End

Dale End
Farm

Woodbine
Farm

Bury Cliff
Farm

Well Street
Farm

Elton CE
Prim Sch

61 Oddo House
Farm

WEST END

EAST END

WINSTER LA

Dark
Lane

Elton
House
Farm

YH

Elton

Hungerhill Lane

BACK LA

Gratton Moor

Leadmines
Farm

3 Gratton Dale

Blake
Low

Shafts
(dis)

MOOR LA

60 Barker
Barn

P

Elton
Common

SACHEVERAL LA

2 Sacheveral
Farm

Mouldridge
Grange

Allsop
Barn

Sitwell
Lane

A5012

MOULDRIDGE LA

Little Wisels
Wood

Grange
Barn

A5012

59

Astonhill

1 New Barn

High Peak Trail
Midshires Way

Rockhurst
Farm

Greenlow
Farm

58

20　　　A　　　21　　　B　　　22　　　C

139
152

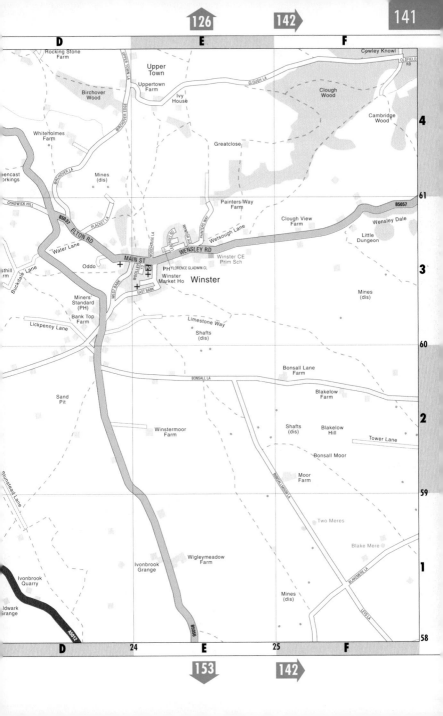

D E F

Rocking Stone Farm
Cowley Knowl
OLDFIELD RD

Upper Town
Uppertown Farm
CLOUGH LA
Clough Wood

Birchover Wood
Ivy House

UPPER TOWN LA
BRIDDLEY EDGE

Cambridge Wood

4

Whiteholmes Farm

Greatclose

BIRCHOVER LA
Mines (dis)

encast orkings

61

CHADWICK HILL
Painters Way Farm

Clough View Farm
Wensley Dale

B5057

B5057 ELTON RD
PLACKET LA

Little Dungeon

Wetsough Lane
WENSLEY RD
PAINTERS WAY

WYNLEA CL

Water Lane

MAIN ST
WOODLEIGH LA

Winster CE Prim Sch

Oddo
Ph
PH FLORENCE GLADWIN CL
WEST BANK

3

Mines (dis)

sthill rm

Buckdale Lane
Winster Market Ho
Winster
EAST BANK

Miners' Standard (PH)
Bank Top Farm
Lickpenny Lane

Limestone Way
Shafts (dis)

60

Bonsall Lane Farm
BONSALL LA

Sand Pit

Blakelow Farm

2

Winstermoor Farm

Shafts (dis)
Blakelow Hill

Tower Lane

Bonsall Moor

Slunsteap Lane

Moor Farm

BONSALL MOOR LA

59

Two Meres

Blake Mere

Ivonbrook Grange

Wigleymeadow Farm

1

Ivonbrook Quarry

BLAKEMERE LA

LEYS LA

ldwark range

Mines (dis)

A5012
B5056

58

D 24 E 25 F

141
127

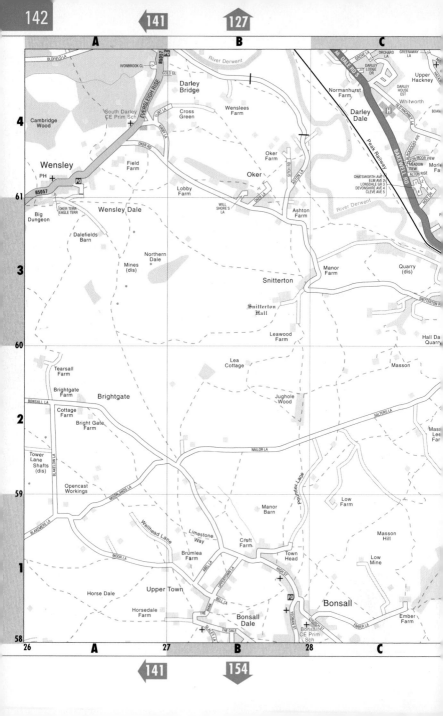

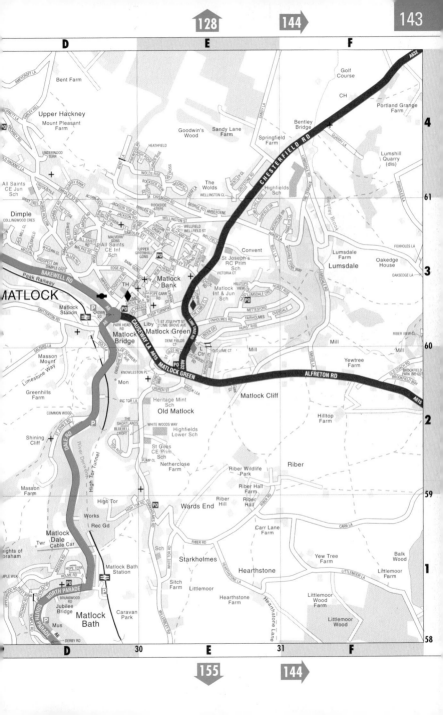

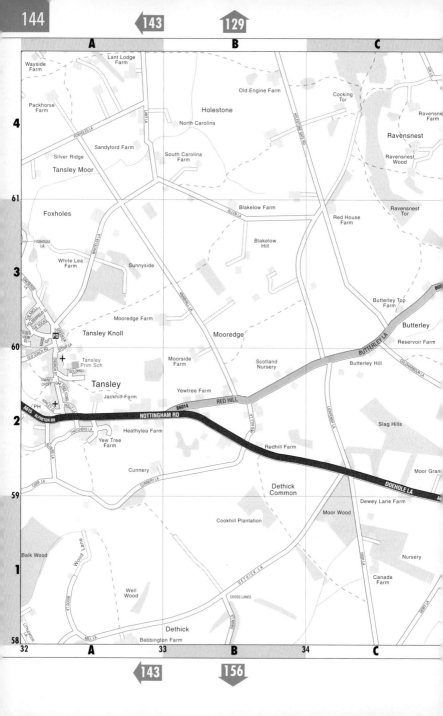

A   B   C

4

Wayside Farm

Lant Lodge Farm

Packhorse Farm

FORKLEE LA

Old Engine Farm

Holestone

North Carolina

Cocking Tor

Ravensnest Farm

Ravensnest

LANT LA

VALLESTONE GATE RD

Silver Ridge

Sandyford Farm

South Carolina Farm

Tansley Moor

61

Foxholes

FOXHOLES LA

WHITE LEA LA

Blakelow Farm

ALLEN LA

Red House Farm

Ravensnest Wood

Ravensnest Tor

3

White Lea Farm

Sunnyside

Blakelow Hill

DARLEY LA

HOLLINGFIELD CL

THE ROCKS

Mooredge Farm

Butterley Top Farm

B6

Butterley

OLD COACH RD

CROSS LA

Tansley Knoll

Mooredge

BUTTERLEY LA

Reservoir Farm

COLDLEY BORDUR LA

60

CHURCH LA

Tansley Prim Sch

GOLDHILL

Moorside Farm

Scotland Nursery

Butterley Hill

OAK TREE COMMON

Tansley

Yewtree Farm

LYDGATE LA

TAWNEY CROFT

Jackhill Farm

RED HILL

2

PH

A615

ALFRETON RD

NOTTINGHAM RD

B6014

Slag Hills

ASKER LA

THATCHERS LA

Heathylea Farm

Redhill Farm

Moor Gran

Yew Tree Farm

DOEHOLE LA

A6

CARR LA

Cunnery

CUNNERY LA

Dethick Common

Dewey Lane Farm

Moor Wood

59

Balk Wood

Wood Lane

DETHICK LA

Cookhill Plantation

Moor Wood

HIGH LA

Nursery

1

WOOD LA

Well Wood

Canada Farm

DEWEY LA

LITTLEMOOR LA

CROSS LANES

MILL LA

ST FRINK

Dethick

Babbington Farm

58

32   A   33   B   34   C

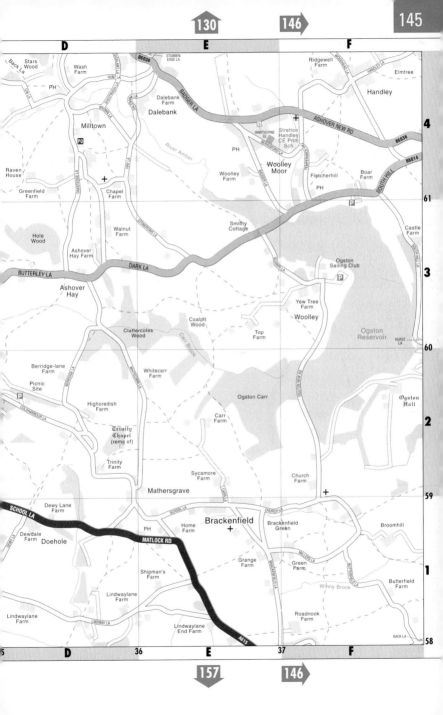

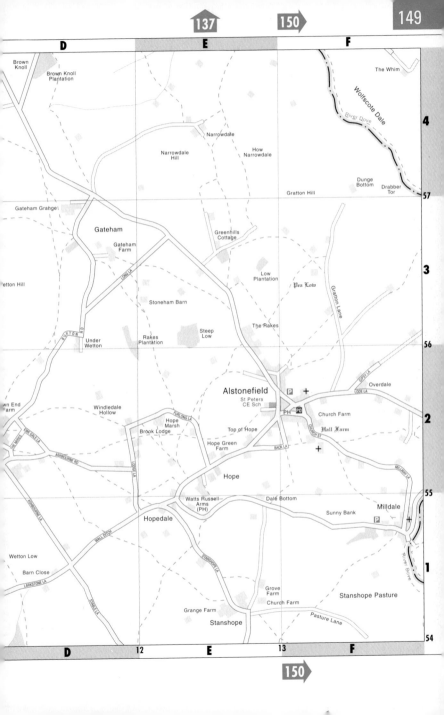

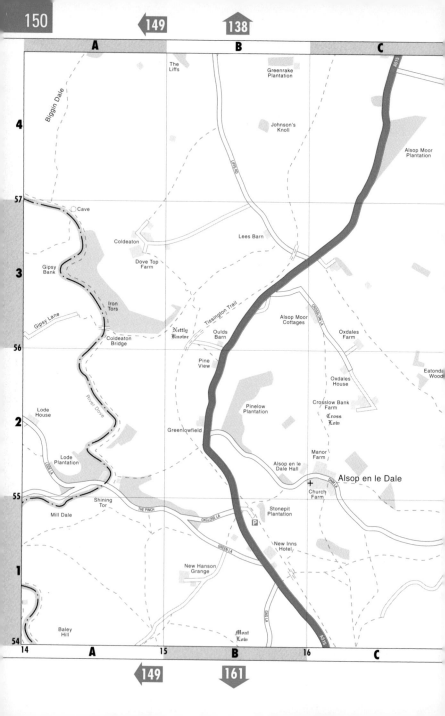

Cobblersnook
Plantation

Uppermoor
Farm

Cobblersnook Lane

The
Nook

Minninglow Lane

White Cliffe
Farm

Mountain
Ash
Farm

Roystone
Cottages

4

The
Bungalow

Middlemoor
Farm

57

Lowmoor
Plantation

Hawks
Low

Lowmoor
Farm

Lowmoor
Cottages

3

Hawkslow
Farm

Twodale
Barn

56

Lombard's
Green

Ballidon
Quarry

2

Dale End
Farm

Hilltop
Farm

Middlehill
Farm

Parwich
Hill

Fields
Farm

Foufinside

55

Peakway

Middlehill
Barn

MONSDALE LA

aton
ale

DAN LA

Close
Farm

ROTHBOURNE
CROFT

Littlewood
Farm

1

Parwich
Lees

Flaxdale
Holding

Parwich
Prim Sch

KILN LA

PO

Parwich

Sycamore
Inn
(PH)

SYCAMORE
COTTS

Pits
Lane

54

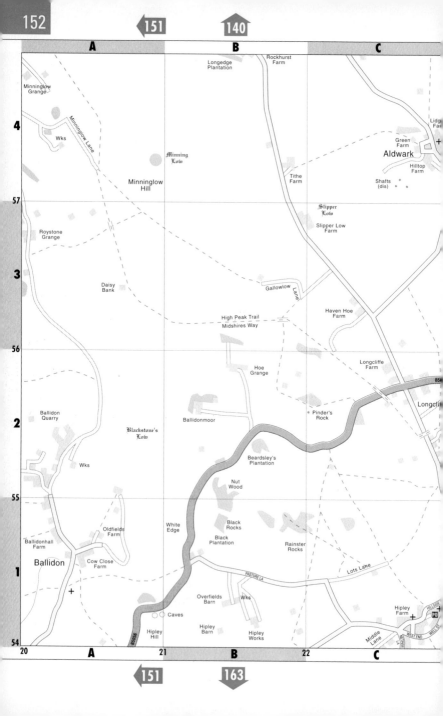

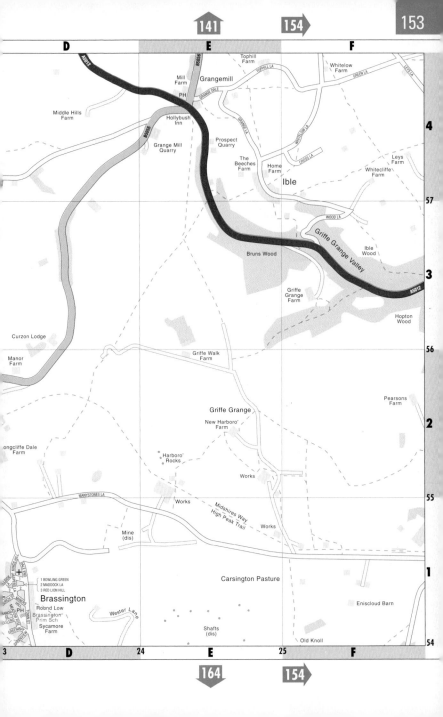

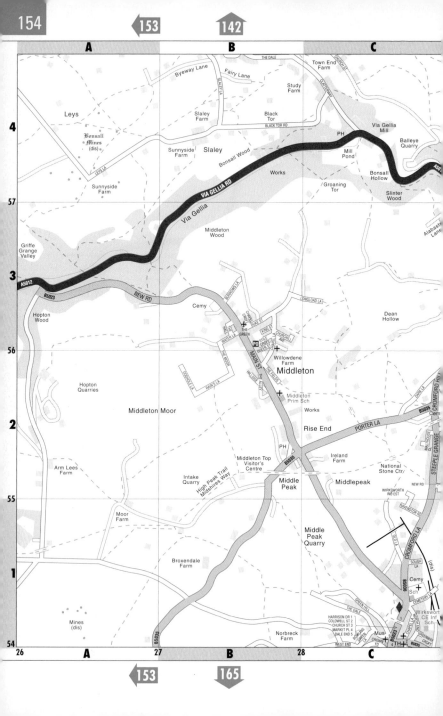

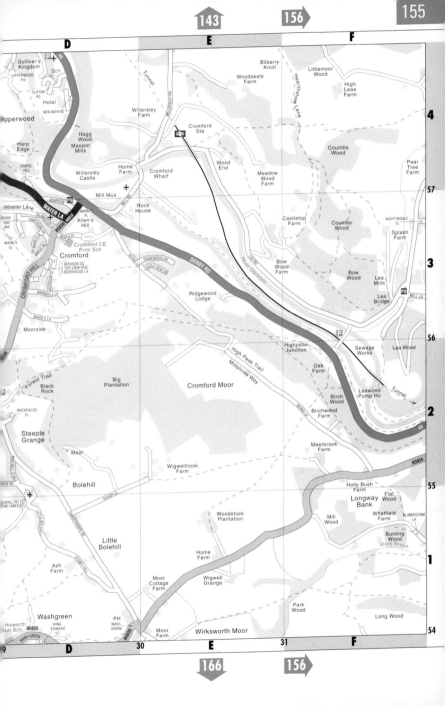

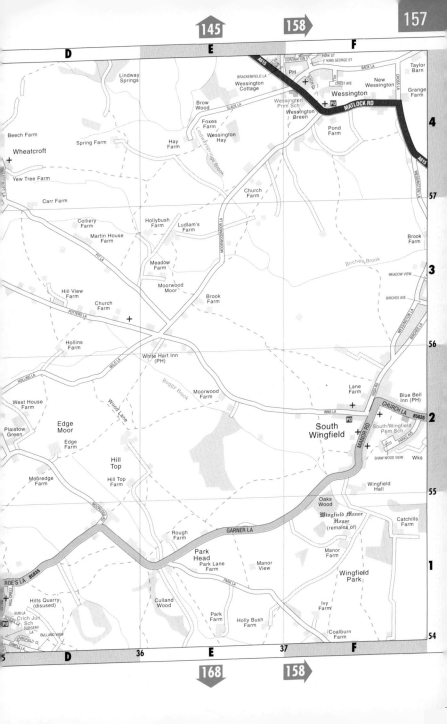

4

57

3

56

2

55

1

54

D
E
F

Taylor Barn
Grange Farm

CORONATION ST
PARK ST
KING GEORGE ST
BACK LA
CREST AVE
New Wessington
Wessington
PH
MATLOCK RD
Wessington Prim Sch
Wessington Green
Pond Farm
Wessington Hay
BRACKENFIELD LA
Wessington Cottage
SLACK LA
Foxes Farm
Brow Wood
Hay Farm
Lindway Springs

Beech Farm
Wheatcroft
Spring Farm
Yew Tree Farm
Carr Farm
Church Farm

Colliery Farm
Hollybush Farm
Ludlam's Farm
Martin House Farm
Meadow Farm
Brook Farm
Hill View Farm
Moorwood Moor
Church Farm
Brook Farm

Birches Brook
MEADOW VIEW
BIRCHES AVE

Hollins Farm
White Hart Inn (PH)

West House Farm
Plaistow Green
Edge Moor
Edge Farm
Wood Lane
Boggy Brook
Moorwood Farm
Lane Farm
Blue Bell Inn (PH)
CHURCH LA
B5035
INNS LA
South Wingfield
South Wingfield Prim Sch
MANOR RD
HIGH RD
PARKS AVE
SHAW WOOD VIEW
Wks

Hill Top
Hill Top Farm
Mooredge Farm
MOORWOOD RD

ROE'S LA
B5035
Hilts Quarry (disused)
SUN LA
Crich Jun Sch
SURGERY
PO
OULLAND VIEW
SPRINGFIELD CL
DIMPLE LA

Rough Farm
Park Head
Park Lane Farm
GARNER LA
PARK LA
Manor View
Culland Wood
Park Farm
Holly Bush Farm
Oaks Wood
Wingfield Manor House (remains of)
Manor Farm
Wingfield Park
Ivy Farm
Coalburn Farm
Wingfield Hall
Catchills Farm

A615
WESSINGTON LA
BECK LA

D
E
F
36
37

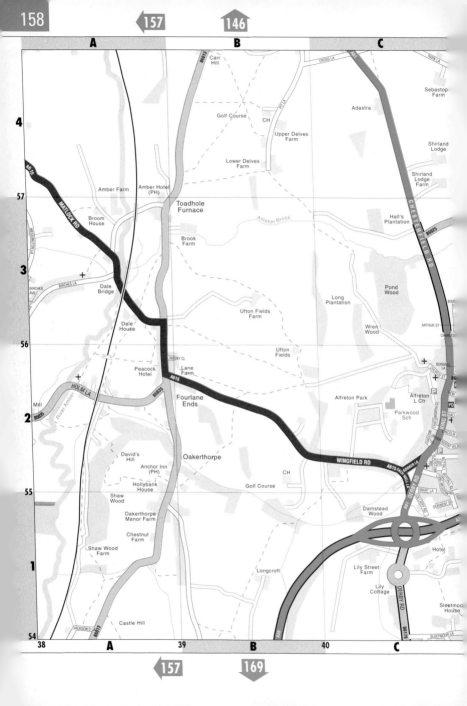

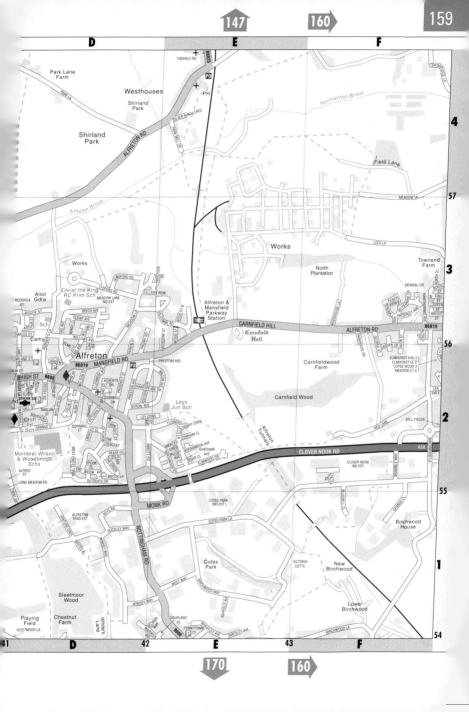

F

D E F

Hanson Grange

Moatlow Farm

Tissington Trail

Hillside

Hall Dale

The Nabs

Stand Low

Newton Grange

4

Dove Holes

Bostern Grange Farm

Upper Taylor's Wood

Standlow

urt's wood

Pickering Cave

Gaglane Barn

53

Ilam Rock

Pickering Tor

Broadclose

Rose Low

Dovedale Wood

Reynard's Cave

Sharplow Farm

3

Air Cottage

Dove Dale

Sharplow Dale

Hollington Barn

52

Jacob's Ladder

Tissington Spires

Moor Barn

Lover's Leap

Twelve Apostles

River Dove

2

Bunster Hill

Dovedale Castle

Thorpe Pasture

Hollington End Farm

WASHBROOK LA

Wash Brook

Cave

Lin Dale

Highfields Farm

Ilam

Thorpe Cloud

Pike House

51

Izaak Walton Hotel

P

Rifle Range

Caravan Park

River Manifold

Hamston Hill

Peveril of the Peak Hotel

The Narrows

1

WINTERCROFT LA

P

Tissington Trail

St Mary's Bridge

Thorpe Mill Farm

Dog and Partridge Hotel (PH)

Station House

ishpond Wood

Thorpe

Broadlowash

The Firs

50

D 15 E 16 F

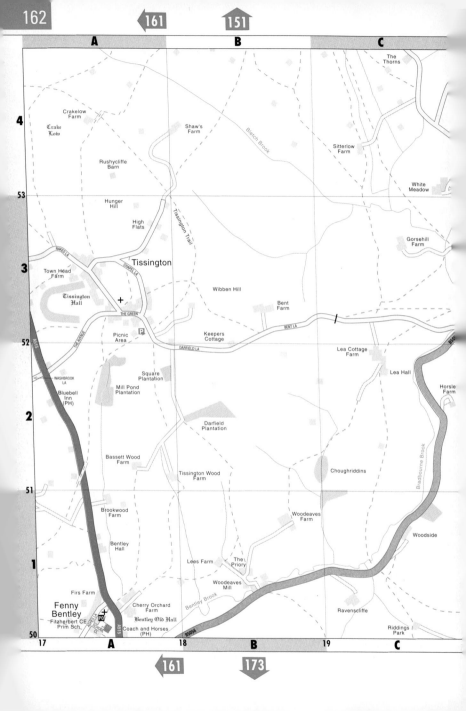

A   B   C

4

Crakelow
Farm

Crake
Low

Shaw's
Farm

Bletch Brook

Sitterlow
Farm

The
Thorns

Rushycliffe
Barn

White
Meadow

53

Hunger
Hill

High
Flats

Tissington Trail

Gorsehill
Farm

Tissington

RAKES LA

Town Head
Farm

CHAPEL LA

Tissington
Hall

Wibben Hill

Bent
Farm

BENT LA

3

THE GREEN

Picnic
Area

Keepers
Cottage

Lea Cottage
Farm

Lea Hall

B5056

52

THE PEAKE

WASHBROOK
LA

DARFIELD LA

Horsle
Farm

Bluebell
Inn
(PH)

Square
Plantation

A515

Mill Pond
Plantation

2

Darfield
Plantation

Bradbourne Brook

Bassett Wood
Farm

Choughriddins

Tissington Wood
Farm

51

Brookwood
Farm

Woodeaves
Farm

Woodside

Bentley
Hall

1

Lees Farm

The
Priory

Firs Farm

Woodeaves
Mill

Ravenscliffe

Fenny
Bentley

Cherry Orchard
Farm

Fitzherbert CE
Prim Sch

PO

Bentley Old Hall

Bentley Brook

Riddings
Park

Coach and Horses
(PH)

A515

B5056

50

17   A   18   B   19   C

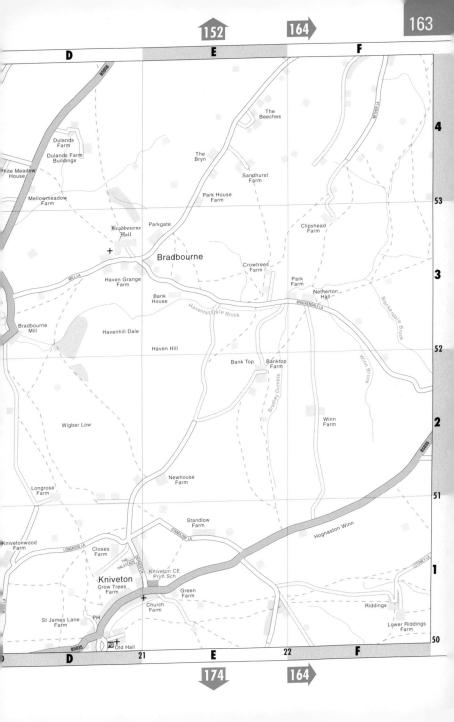

D
E
F

4

The
Beeches

Dulands
Farm

Dulands Farm
Buildings

White Meadow
House

The
Bryn

Sandhurst
Farm

Mellowmeadow
Farm

Park House
Farm

53

Parkgate

Bradbourne
Hall

Clipshead
Farm

Bradbourne

Crowtrees
Farm

Park
Farm

Netherton
Hall

3

MILL LA

Haven Grange
Farm

Bank
House

BRACKENDALE LA

Brackendale Brook

Bradbourne
Mill

Havenhill Dale Brook

Havenhill Dale

Winn Brook

Haven Hill

52

Bank Top

Banktop
Farm

Bradley Dumble

Wigber Low

Winn
Farm

2

B5035

Longrose
Farm

Newhouse
Farm

51

Standlow
Farm

STANDLOW LA

Hognaston Winn

Knivetonwood
Farm

LONGROSE LA

Closes
Farm

LETONEY LA

THE HALSTEADS

BRIDGEGATE

Kniveton CE
Prim Sch

1

WOOD LA

Kniveton

Crow Trees
Farm

Green
Farm

Riddings

St James Lane
Farm

PH

Church
Farm

Lower Riddings
Farm

B5035

Old Hall

50

D
21
E
22
F

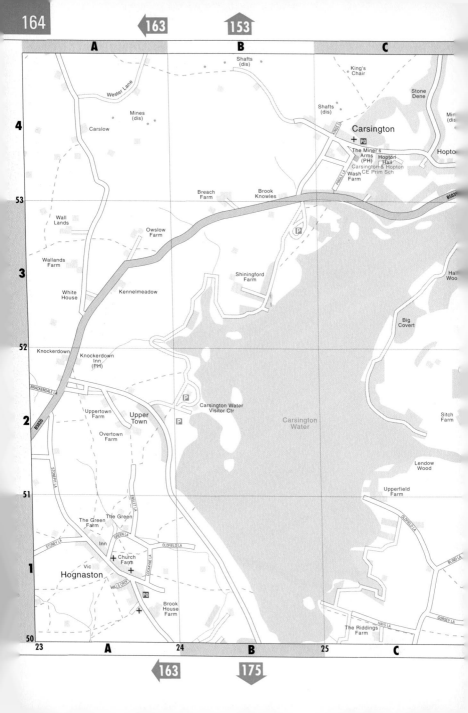

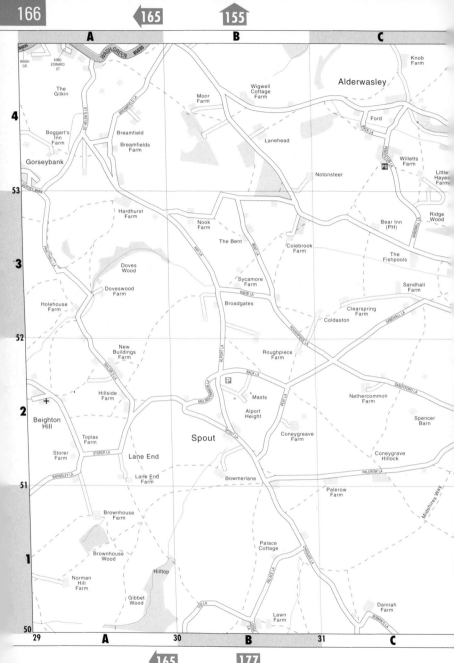

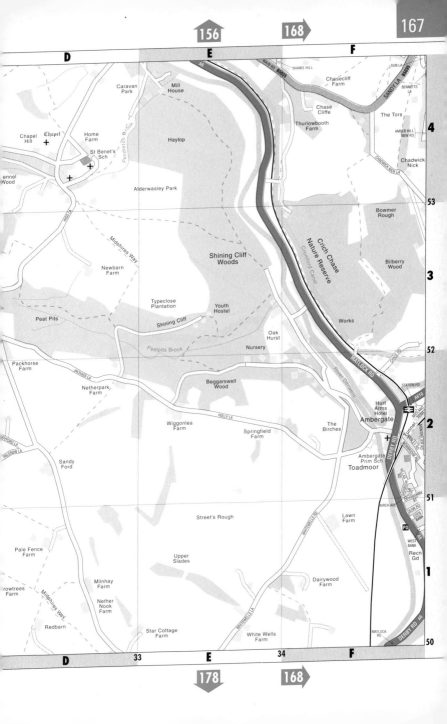

D
E
F

4

53

3

52

2

51

1

50

D
33
E
34
F

Caravan Park
Mill House
SHAWS HILL
Chasecliff Farm
SUN LA
SANDY LA
BENNITTS LA

Chapel Hill
Chapel
Home Farm
St Benet's Sch
Haytop
Chase Cliffe
Thurlowbooth Farm
The Tors
AMBER HILL NEW RD
Chadwick Nick

ennel Wood
Alderwasley Park
CHADWICK NICK LA

Bowmer Rough

Midshires Way
Newbarn Farm
Shining Cliff Woods
Crich Chase Nature Reserve
Cromford Canal
Bilberry Wood

Typeclose Plantation
Youth Hostel

Peat Pits
Shining Cliff
Oak Hurst
Works

Peatpits Brook
Nursery

Packhorse Farm
JACKASS LA
Beggarswell Wood
MATLOCK RD
CHASE RD

Netherpark Farm
Holly La
STATION RD
A610

Wiggonlea Farm
Springfield Farm
The Birches
River Derwent
Hurt Arms Hotel
Ambergate

OXFORD LA
PARROW LA

Sandy Ford
Ambergate Prim Sch
Toadmoor

DERBY RD
Tunnel

BIRCH AVE

Street's Rough
Lawn Farm
WHITEWELLS RD

Pale Fence Farm
Upper Slades
PO
WEST BANK
Recn Gd

rowtrees Farm
Milnhay Farm
Dairywood Farm

Midshires Way
Nether Nook Farm

Redbarn
Star Cottage Farm
White Wells Farm
WHITEWELLS LA
MATLOCK RD
DERBY RD A6

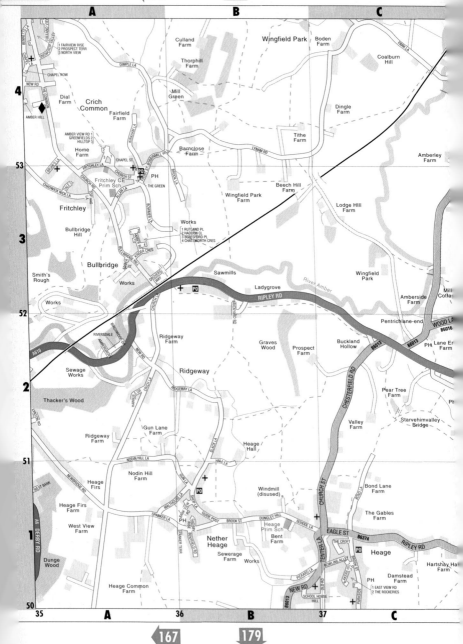

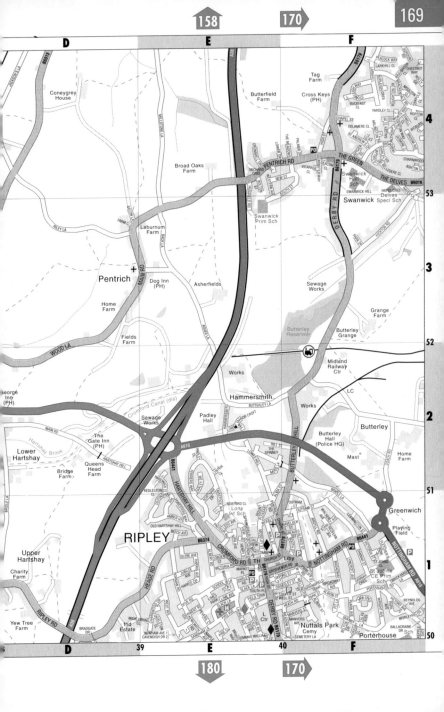

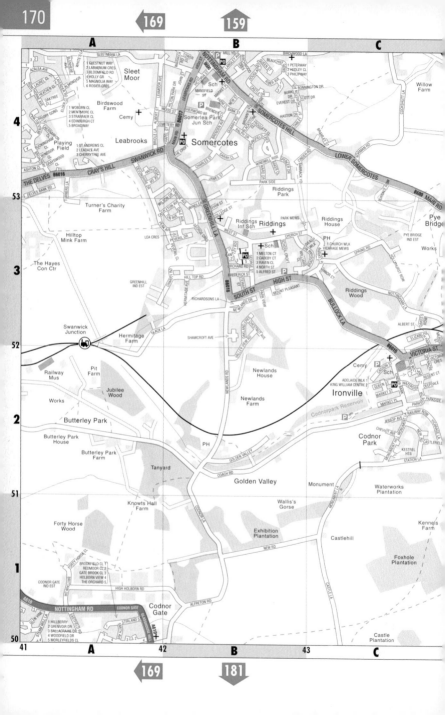

A B C

Sleet
Moor

Birdswood
Farm

1 CHESTNUT WAY
2 LABURNUM CRES
3 BLOOMFIELD RD
4 HOLLY GR
5 MAGNOLIA WAY
6 ROSIER CRES

1 WOBURN CL
2 MENTMORE CL
3 STANMORE CL
4 EDINBURGH CT
5 BROADWAY

Cemy

Leabrooks

1 ST ANDREWS CL
2 LEADALE AVE
3 CHERRYTREE AVE

Somerlea Park Jun Sch

Somercotes

Somercotes Hill

Lower Somercotes

Willow
Farm

Playing
Field

THE DELVES B6016

CRAY'S HILL

SWANWICK RD

Park Side

Riddings
Park

B600 MAIN RD

Pye
Bridge

Turner's Charity
Farm

Riddings
Inf Sch

Riddings

Park Mews

Riddings
House

PYE BRIDGE
IND EST

Works

Hilltop
Mink Farm

LEA CRES

PEVERIL DR

The Hayes
Con Ctr

GREENHILL
IND EST

HILL TOP RD

FREDERICK ST

SOUTH ST

HIGH ST

PH

1 CHURCH WLK
VICARAGE MEWS

Sch

Mount Pleasant

Riddings
Wood

ALBERT ST

RICHARDSONS LA

NEWING DR

BULLOCK LA

Swanwick
Junction

Hermitage
Farm

SLACK LA

SHAWCROFT AVE

Newlands
House

VICTORIA ST

Cemy

Sch

Railway
Mus

Pit
Farm

Jubilee
Wood

Newlands
Farm

ADELAIDE WLK
KING WILLIAM CENTRE

Ironville

Codnorpark Reservoir

Codnor
Park

Works

Butterley Park

Butterley Park
House

Butterley Park
Farm

Tanyard

PH

GOLDEN VALLEY

COACH RD

Golden Valley

Monument

Waterworks
Plantation

Knowts Hall
Farm

Wallis's
Gorse

Kennels
Farm

Forty Horse
Wood

Exhibition
Plantation

Castlehill

NEW RD

Foxhole
Plantation

1 BROOKFIELD CL
2 REDMOOR CL
3 GATE BROOK CL
4 HOLBORN VIEW
5 THE ORCHARD

CODNOR GATE
IND EST

HIGH HOLBORN RD

A610

NOTTINGHAM RD

CODNOR GATE

Codnor
Gate

ALFRETON RD

Castle
Plantation

1 HILLBERRY
2 GRENVOIR DR
3 BALLACRAINE DR
4 WOODFIELD DR
5 MORLEYFIELDS CL

41 A 42 B 43 C

D E F

Sewage Works

Hobsic Farm

PH

Hillbank Farm

Hall Green

Commonside

HOBSIC LA

COMMON SIDE

B6018

4

Crimea Farm

Pye Bridge Junction

River Erewash

Hall Green Farm

HOMECROFT DRI

STONEY L

Rosemaryhill

1 ALBERT AVE
2 CHESTNUT DR
3 CEDAR DRI

MANSFIELD RD

MAIN RD

Selston Green

Selston

Pye Bridge

ALFRETON RD

Pinfold Farm

Liby

Matthew Holland Comp. Sch

NOTTINGHAM RD

B6018

MAIN RD

PYE BRIDGE

Selston CE Inf Sch

HODLEY ST

VICTORIA ST

53

Sleepy Hole

PH

B6018

B600

B600

Golf Course

Langton Hollow

Toadhole

Dove Green

Ashes Farm

Allen's Green

Handstubbing

3

LANGTON HOLLOW

Barrows Green

Barrows Hill

Home Farm

Lea Farm

PH

52

Pye Hill

SELSTON RD

B6016

NEW RD

PYE HILL RD

Liby

BAGSTOCK LA

WEST LA

Jacksdale

P.O

Jacksdale Prim Sch

New Westwood

Westwood Inf Sch

Gate Inn (PH)

Bagthorpe Brook

Manor Farm

Shepherds Rest (PH)

Bagthorpe

Brookside Farm

2

Westwood

Westwood Farm

Yewtree Farm

Wansley Hall

PLAYER LA

LOWER BAGTHORPE

MAIN RD

51

Underwood Green

Plain Spot Farm

Plain Spot

Underwood Hill

Hole in the Wall (PH)

PRIMROSE AVE

Underwood CE Sch

1

FRANCIS ST

BRINSLEY AVE

MAIN RD

PH

Pollington House

MAIN ST

WINDSMOOR RD

New Brinsley

Oaktree Farm

A608

50

D 45 E 46 F

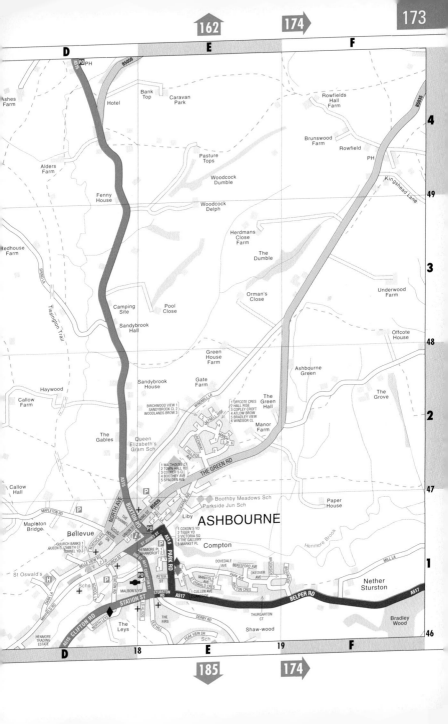

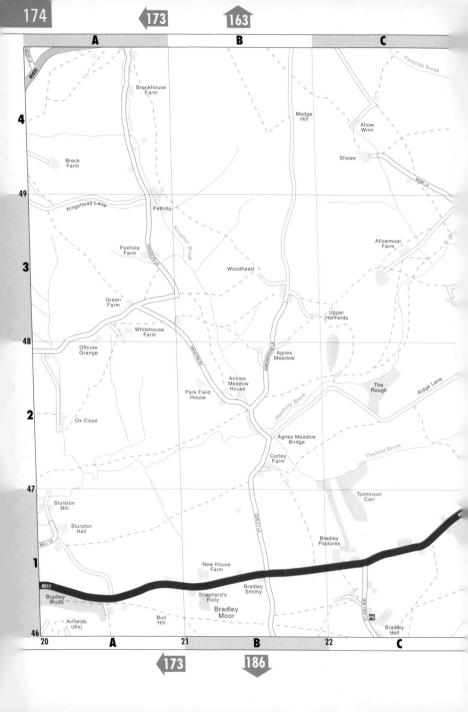

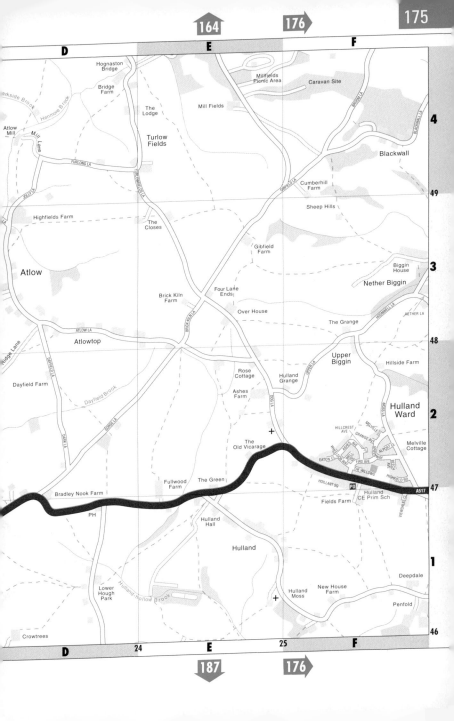

164
176

D
E
F

Hognaston Bridge

Millfields Picnic Area

Caravan Site

arkside Brook

Henmore Brook

Bridge Farm

The Lodge

Mill Fields

BROOK LA

4

Atlow Mill

Mill Lane

Turlow Fields

Blackwall

BLACKWALL LA

FURLONG LA

GREEN LA

Cumberhill Farm

49

JOLLY LA

Highfields Farm

The Closes

Sheep Hills

Gibfield Farm

Biggin House

3

Atlow

Nether Biggin

NETHER LA

Brick Kiln Farm

Four Lane Ends

Over House

The Grange

HOGNHILL LA

dge Lane

ATLOW LA

BRICK KILN LA

48

Atlowtop

Upper Biggin

Hillside Farm

DAYFIELD LA

Rose Cottage

Hulland Grange

UPPER LA

Hulland Ward

2

Dayfield Farm

PARK LA

Dayfield Brook

GREEN LA

Ashes Farm

DOG LA

HILLCREST AVE

MELVILLE

GRANGE AVE

ALPORT CL

Melville Cottage

The Old Vicarage

WHEELDON AVE

CURZON WAY

MOSS AVE

FIRS AVE

BEECH AVE

HIGHFIELD RD

EATON CL

THE WILLOWS

Bradley Nook Farm

Fullwood Farm

The Green

HOLLANT SQ

PO

Fields Farm

Hulland CE Prim Sch

VERNON DALE CL

A517

47

PH

Hulland Hall

Hulland

1

Lower Hough Park

Hulland Hollow Brook

Hulland Moss

New House Farm

Deepdale

Penfold

Crowtrees

46

D
24
E
25
F

187
176

175
165

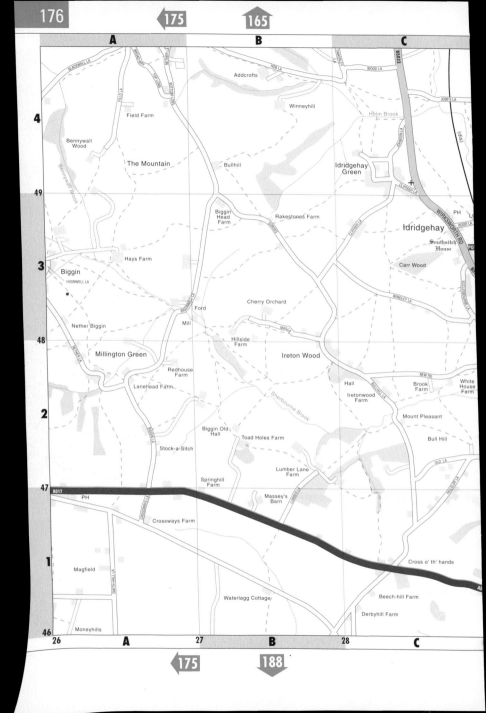

175
188

D
E
F

BOMAN'S LA

Newschool Farm

Shottle
Lodge
Farm

LODGE LANE

HEAVYGATE LA

WILDERBROOK LA

+ The Sycamores

4

Shottle

Manifold Farm

JEBB'S LA

+ Lambhouse

Wallstone Farm

Rookery Farm

Carrbrook Farm

49

Johnson's Carr

White House Farm

Hollyseat

3

Mason's Wood

TOP LA

CALLOWAY LA

Newbuildings Farm

Hollyhouse Farm

LAMBHOUSE LA

Randlepike House

Hole Cottage

Shipley Brook

48

Shipley Lane

Grange Farm

Shottle Hall

2

Franker Brook

WHITE LA

Hill Top Farm

NEW RD

Mill

OLD HALL LA

HIGH CLIFF LA

WIRKSWORTH RD

ASHBOURNE RD

A517

THE DRIVE

Shottlegate

Holme Hurst

Hillclifflane

(dis)

Cowers Lane

47

Hill Cliff Farm

River Ecclesbourne

PH P

Netherhouse Farm

Ridgeway Brook

Round Wood

The Vicarage

PD +

HILL LA

PH

+

PH

Postern House

HAGG LA

1

Wellhole Wood

Turnditch CE Prim Sch

Turnditch

Postern Lodge Farm

B5023

Ash House Farm

WINDLEY LA

B5024

Turnditch Hall

The Lumb

Postern Farm

46

B5023

D
30
E
31
F

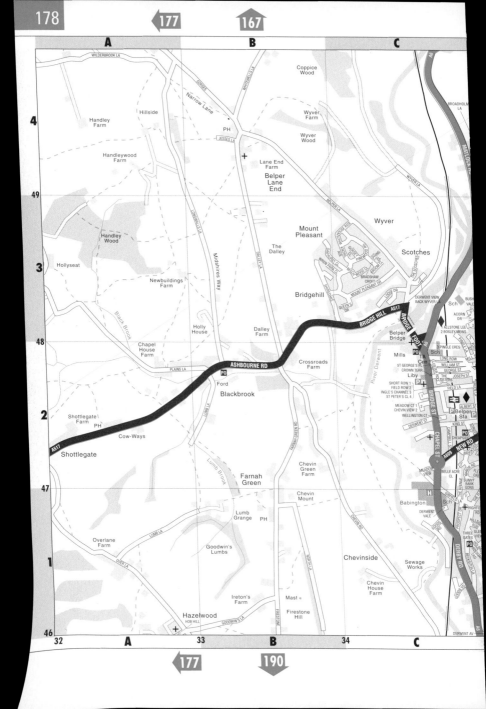

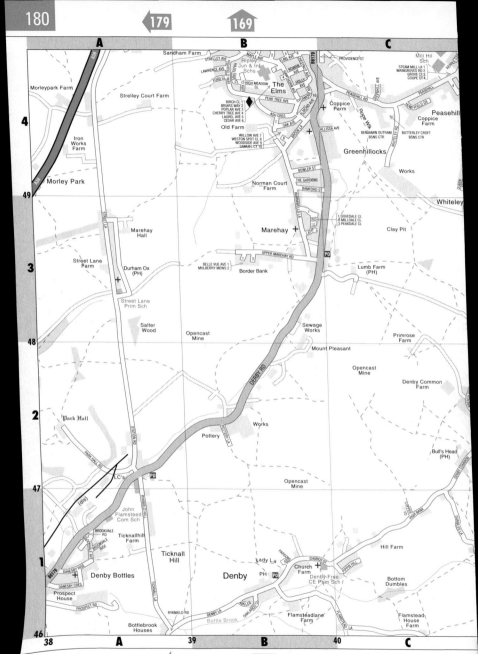

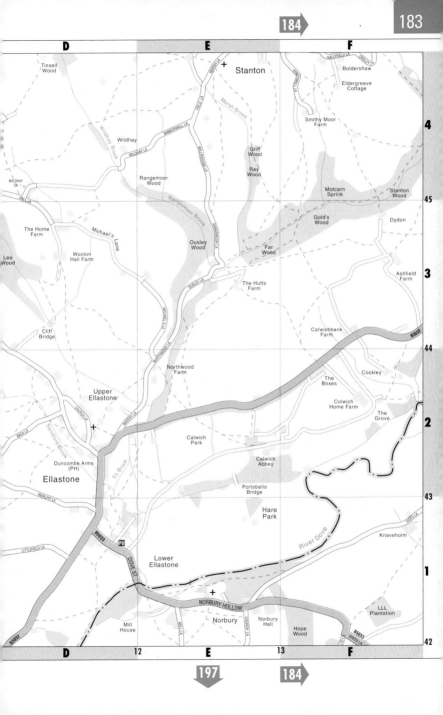

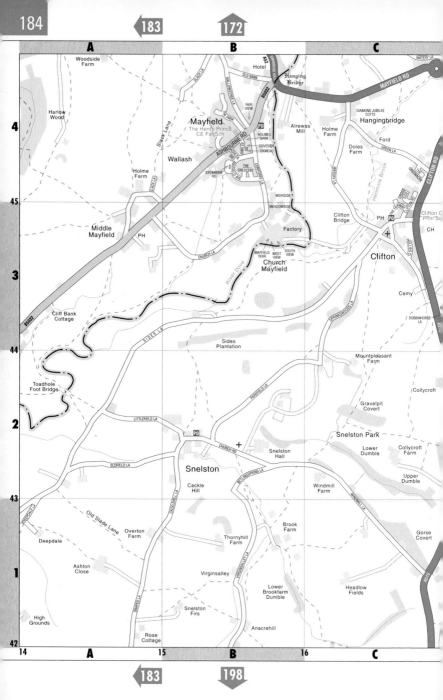

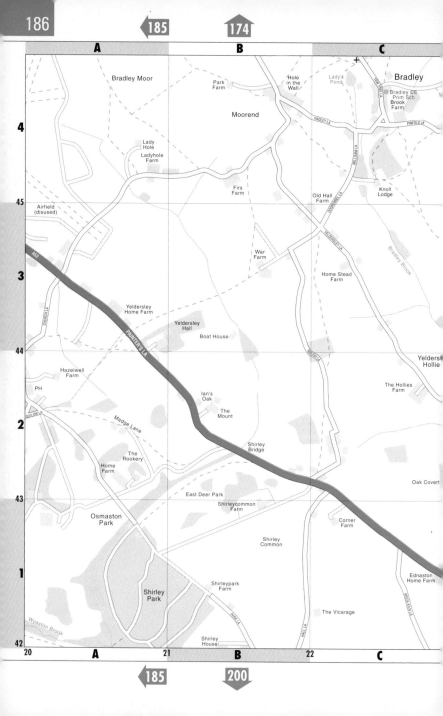

Bradley Moor

Park Farm

Hole in the Wall

Lady's Pond

Bradley

Bradley CE Prim Sch

Brook Farm

HADLEY LA

PINFOLD LA

Moorend

4

Lady Hole

Ladyhole Farm

MILLDAM LA

Firs Farm

Old Hall Farm

Knoll Lodge

45

Airfield (disused)

DOGKENNEL LA

YELDERSLEY LA

Bradley Brook

War Farm

Home Stead Farm

3

CHURCH LA

A52

Yeldersley Home Farm

Yeldersley Hall

Boat House

YELDERSLEY LA

44

PAINTER'S LA

Hazelwell Farm

Yelders Hollie

PH

The Hollies Farm

Ian's Oak

QUILOW LA

The Mount

2

Madge Lane

Shirley Bridge

The Rookery

Oak Covert

Home Farm

East Deer Park

43

Shirleycommon Farm

Osmaston Park

Corner Farm

Shirley Common

1

Ednaston Home Farm

Shirleypark Farm

Shirley Park

PARK LA

PINN LA

BROCK HILL LA

The Vicarage

Wyaston Brook

Shirley House

42

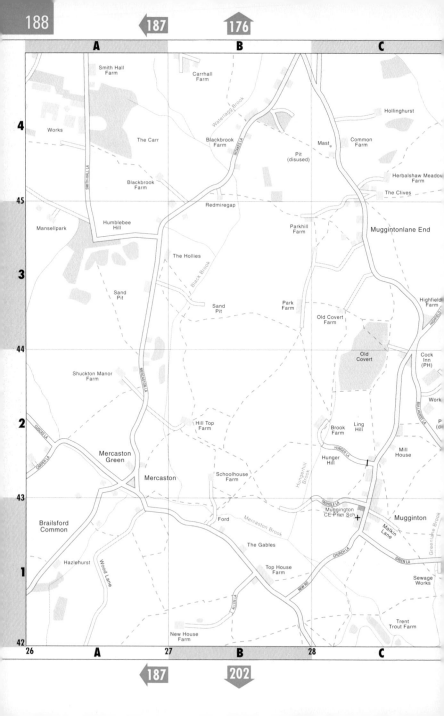

D
E
F

4

B5024

WINDLEY LA

LIME KILN LA

Home
Farm

The
Lilies

Windley

Grove
Farm

River Ecclesbourne

Knowle
Farm

The
Limekilns

Brook
Farm

Hall
Farm

Windley
Hall

WIRKSWORTH RD

WINDLEY LA

B5024

B5023

(dis)

45

Corkley
Farm

Chapel
Farm

Yewtree
Farm

Hole
Farm

NETHER
LA

Puss in Boots
(PH)

B5023

Highfield
Barn

3

Highfield Lane

HIGHFIELD
LA

Brewards
Carr

The
Clouds

Gunhills
Farm

GUNHILLS LA

Windleyhill
Farm

Leasow

Gun Hills

44

Bullhurst
Hill

Mosey-Ley
Farm

Hollybush

BURLAND GREEN LA

Newlands

BROOK LA

Champion
Carr

2

Chilla
Carr

Ivy House
Farm

Draycott
Plantation

Burland-green
Plantation

43

Cocks-hut-Hill

Weston
Underwood

Blind Brook

Marplas
Plantation

Northfield
Plantation

Ireton
Rough

1

Inn
arm

Parkview

Hall Close
Farm

Newkennel
Plantation

42

D
30
E
31
F

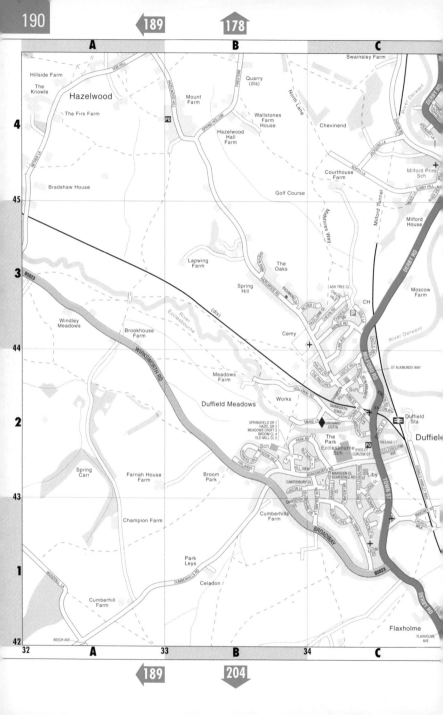

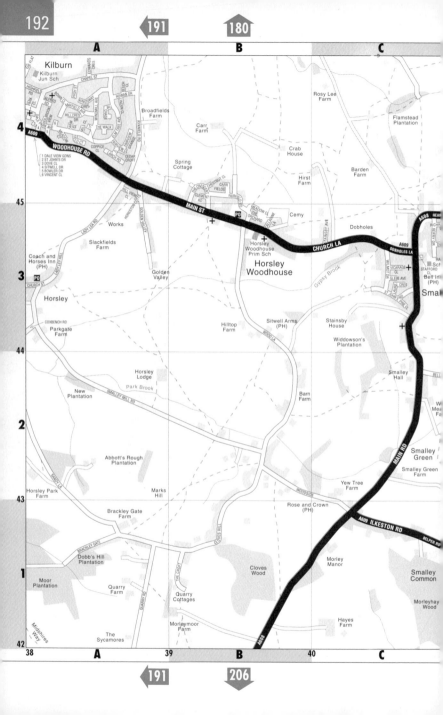

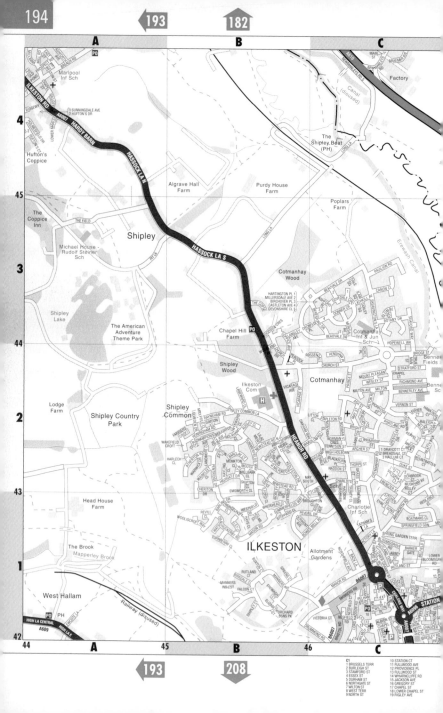

C1
1 BRUSSELS TERR
2 BURLEIGH ST
3 STAMFORD ST
4 ESSEX ST
5 DURHAM ST
6 NORTHGATE ST
7 WILTON ST
8 WEST TERR
9 NORTH ST
10 STATION CT
11 FULLWOOD AVE
12 PROVIDENCE PL
13 FULLWOOD ST
14 WHARNCLIFFE RD
15 JACKSON AVE
16 GREGORY ST
17 CHAPEL ST
18 LOWER CHAPEL CL
19 RIGLEY AVE

A B C

Shepherdswood

Chapel House

Cindershills Wood

B5033

GREEN LA

Queen Adelaide Arms (PH)

Darley Moor

4

Old Queen Farm

Flat Covert

Snelston Common

COCKSHEAD LA

B5033

Common Farm

John Roe's Covert

A515

Quarry (dis)

Grange Cottage

41

Grange Farm

T St

Birchwood Park

Roston Common

Manor House

3

Birchwoodmoor

Cubley Brook

Marstoncommon Farm

Cubley Wood Farm

40

Wood Hay Farm

Accession Wood

The Hollies

HOLLIES LA

Side Gate

Broad Lane

Sammy's Wood

2

Whiterley

Sandhills Farm

Cubley Covert

Holme Lea

Cubley Common

39

Gorse Covert

Cubley Cottage Farm

Common Farm

Mountpleasant Farm

1

Rough Grounds

Birch Field Farm

The Spinney

Brookside Farm

Great Cubley

SHIRE LA

CUBLEY LA

A515

DERBY LA

PO

LONG MEADOW

38

Cubley Fields Farm

Howard Arms (PH)

14 A 15 B 16 C

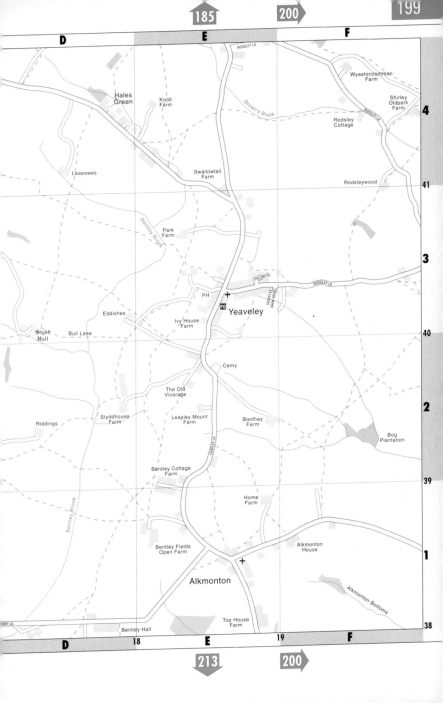

D   E   F

DERBY LA

A52

Brailsford
Mill

BLACK LA

Yew Tree Inn
(PH)

CORNER FARM

THE PLAIN

LIME LA

THE DRIVE

THROSTLE-NEST WAY

4

Ednaston
Hall

Ednaston

Brailsford
Green

Brailsford

Ednaston
House

Hall Farm

PO

CHURCH LA

Brailsford
CE Prim Sch

MAIN RD

PH

Ednaston Hall
Farm

The
Spinney

A52

LA

41

Hollington
Cottage

Churchfields
Farm

Pools
Head

3

Brailsford Brook

Mossnip
Cottage

Peatmoss
Plantation

40

Upper Burrows
Farm

2

Culland
Mount

Slade
Hollow

SLADE HOLLOW LA

Culland
Hall

Culland
Cottage

Cullandmanor
Farm

The
Burrows

39

BURROWS LA

Water
Tower

1

Nunsfield

Longlane

Stoop
Farm

The
Stoop

Glebe
Farm

GLEBE CT

PH

Long Lane
CE Prim Sch

LONG LA

38

D   E   F

24   25

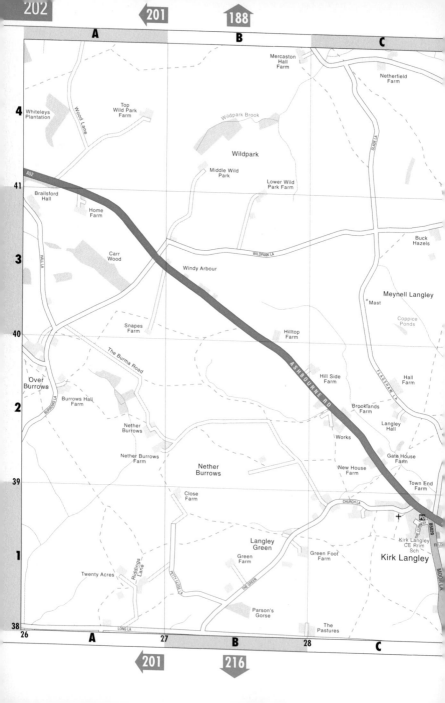

Mercaston Hall Farm

Netherfield Farm

Whiteleys Plantation

Wood Lane

Top Wild Park Farm

Wildpark Brook

Wildpark

Middle Wild Park

Lower Wild Park Farm

SLACK LA

Buck Hazels

Brailsford Hall

A52

Home Farm

HILL LA

Carr Wood

Windy Arbour

WILDPARK LA

Meynell Langley

Mast

Coppice Ponds

Snapes Farm

The Burma Road

Hilltop Farm

Over Burrows

BURROWS LA

Burrows Hall Farm

Nether Burrows

Nether Burrows Farm

Nether Burrows

ASHBOURNE RD

Hill Side Farm

Hall Farm

FLAGSHAW LA

Brooklands Farm

Langley Hall

Works

New House Farm

Gate House Farm

Town End Farm

Close Farm

CHURCH LA

PO

Langley Green

Green Farm

Green Foot Farm

Kirk Langley CE Prim Sch

Kirk Langley

B5020

MOOR LA

Twenty Acres

Riddings Lane

PEVERIL LA

THE GREEN

Parson's Gorse

The Pastures

LONG LA

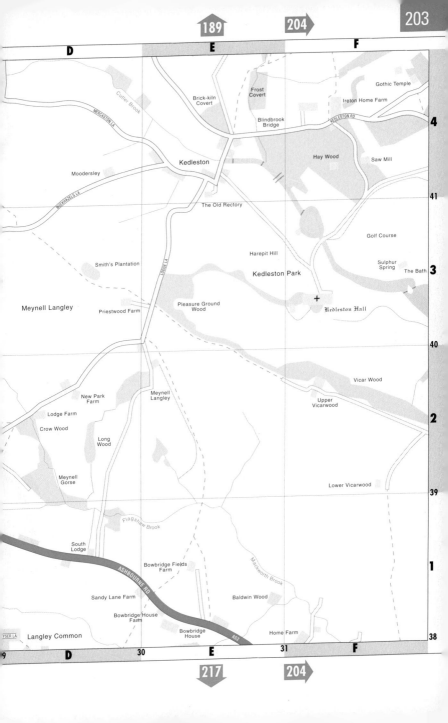

189

204

D · E · F

Cutler Brook

Brick-kiln Covert

Frost Covert

Gothic Temple

Ireton Home Farm

KEDLESTON RD

Blindbrook Bridge

4

MERCASTON LA

Hay Wood

Saw Mill

Kedleston

Moodersley

NUCHAELS LA

41

The Old Rectory

Golf Course

Harepit Hill

Smith's Plantation

Kedleston Park

Sulphur Spring

The Bath

3

LODGE LA

Kedleston Hall

Pleasure Ground Wood

Meynell Langley

Priestwood Farm

40

Vicar Wood

New Park Farm

Meynell Langley

Upper Vicarwood

Lodge Farm

Crow Wood

2

Long Wood

Meynell Gorse

Lower Vicarwood

39

Flagshaw Brook

Markeaton Brook

South Lodge

ASHBOURNE RD

Bowbridge Fields Farm

1

Sandy Lane Farm

Baldwin Wood

Bowbridge House Farm

YSER LA

Langley Common

Bowbridge House

A52

Home Farm

38

9 · D · 30 · E · 31 · F

217

204

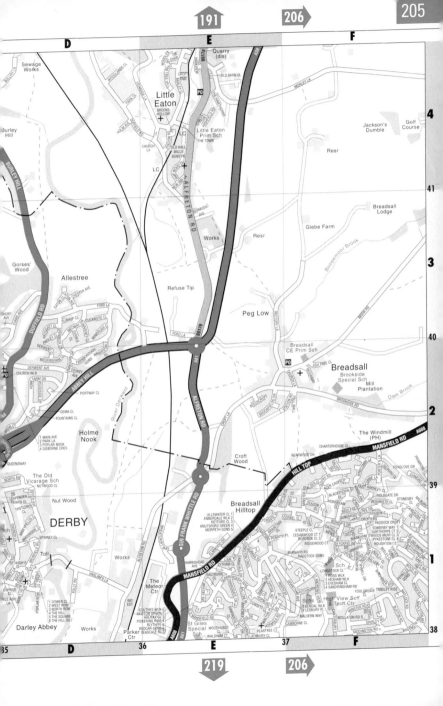

A B C

4

Priory
Cottages

Breadsall
Priory
Hotel

MORLEY LA

QUARRY RD

BRICKYARD LA

PO

PH

Morley
Smithy

Smithy
Farm

Little
Wood

Park
Farm

Hayes
Park
Farm

Almshouses

Golf
Course

Lodge
Farm

Morleymoor

41

Morley House
Farm

Morley
Prim Sch

Morley
Hall

MOOR RD

MORLEY MOOR RD

The Mound

Midshires Way

CHURCH LA

MOSS LA

Spring
Oak
Farm

3

Morley

Top
Farm

Broomfield Coll
(Derbyshire Coll of Ag)

Broomfield
Cottages

Jesse
Farm

40

Broomfield
Farm

Lime
Farm

Ferriby Brook

LIME LA

The
Limes

Kings
Corner

North
Lodge

2

BROOKSIDE
RD

MANSFIELD
RD

A608

1 GLENORCHY CT
2 APPLEGATE CL
3 BRAMBLEBERRY CT
4 TISSINGTON DR
5 CRESSBROOK WAY

Chaddesden
Common

1 HEDGEROW GDNS
2 HEDGEBANK CT

DERBY RD

A608

DERBY

Chaddesden
Wood

PRIMROSE
CL

MEADOW VIEW

HOLMOAK CL

ASHDELL RD

LIME LA

CONSORT
GDNS

SOVEREIGN WAY

39

1 COLUMBINE CL
2 CELANDINE CL
3 DUNKERY CT
4 SELWORTHY CL
5 PORLOCK CT
6 BONNYRIGG DR
7 HAREBELL CL

LARKSPUR

WOODRISINGS

SPRINGWOOD DR

8 ELKSTONE CL
9 CHURCHDOWN CL
10 ARMSCOTE CL
11 BARCHESTON CL
12 CULWORTH CL
13 MOUNTFORD CL
14 LAMPETER CL
15 OXWICH CT
16 BRIDGEND CT
17 SHREWSBURY CL

Birch
Wood

Birchwood
House

1

Oakwood
L Ctr

8 SWANWICK GDNS
9 ANSTEY CT
10 THURLOW CT
11 DELAMERE CL

OAKWOOD
DISTRICT
CTR

1 THORESBY CL
2 BASSINGHAM CL
3 ROSEBERRY CT
4 FIRTREE GR
5 WHYTELEAFE GR
6 BICKLEY MOSS
7 SAMANTHA CT

LOCKO RD

Locko
Park

Locko
Hall

Crow
Wood
Farm

The Lake

38

Hill
Farm

GAINSBOROUGH

LOSCOE RD

A 39 B 40 C

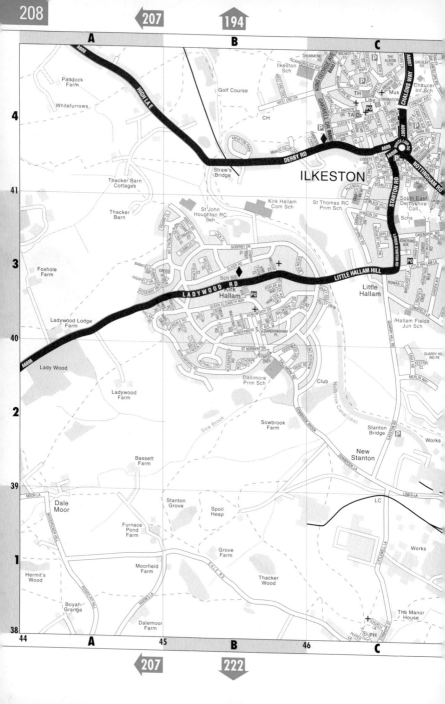

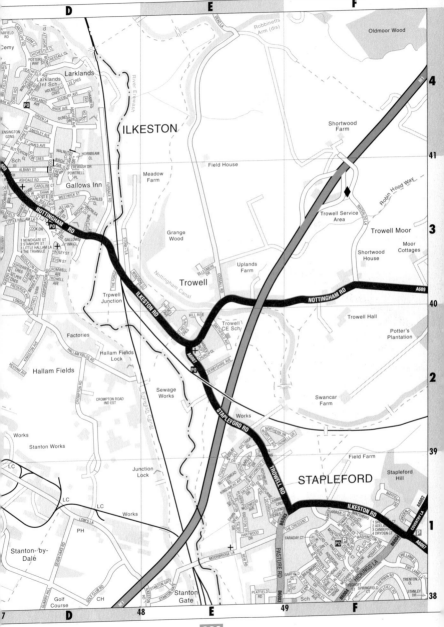

ILKESTON

Larklands

Gallows Inn

Trowell

Trowell Moor

Trowell Service Area

Robin Hood Way

Shortwood Farm

Oldmoor Wood

Field House

Meadow Farm

Grange Wood

Uplands Farm

Shortwood House

Moor Cottages

Trowell Hall

Potter's Plantation

NOTTINGHAM RD   A609

Nottingham Canal

Trowell Junction

ILKESTON RD

Hallam Fields Lock

Hallam Fields

Trowell CE Sch

Hill Rise

Factories

Sewage Works

Swancar Farm

Works

CROMPTON ROAD IND EST

STAPLEFORD RD

STAPLEFORD

Stapleford Hill

Field Farm

Works

Stanton Works

Junction Lock

ILKESTON RD

PASTURE RD

TROWELL RD

Stanton-by-Dale

The Crescent

Faraday Ct

Moorbridge La

New Rd

Stanton Gate

Golf Course

Stanton Gate

1 NEWDIGATE ST
2 STANHOPE ST
3 LITTLE HALLAM LA
4 THE TRIANGLE

Robinnetts Arm (dis)

River Erewash

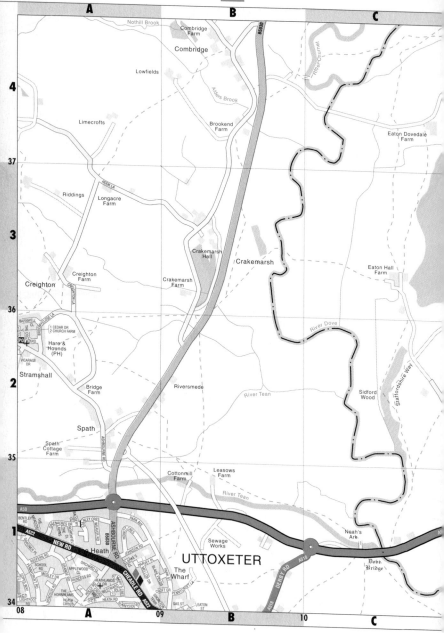

196

4

Nothill Brook

Combridge Farm

Combridge

Lowfields

Limecrofts

Alders Brook

Brookend Farm

Eaton Dovedale Farm

River Churnet

37

HOOK LA

Riddings

Longacre Farm

CREIGHTON LA

3

Crakemarsh Hall

Crakemarsh

Eaton Hall Farm

Creighton Farm

Creighton

Crakemarsh Farm

River Dove

36

BARNWELL

THE ORCHARD

PO

1 CEDAR DR
2 CHURCH FARM

Hare & Hounds (PH)

VICARAGE DR

2

Stramshall

Bridge Farm

ASHBOURNE RD

Riversmede

River Tean

Sidford Wood

Staffordshire Way

Spath

35

Spath Cottage Farm

Cottonmill Farm

Leasows Farm

River Tean

A50

BENTLEY RD

A522

NEW RD

The Heath

ASHBOURNE RD

B5030

PARK AVE

Sewage Works

Noah's Ark

1

UTTOXETER

The Wharf

DERBY RD

A518

Dove Bridge

A522

CHEADLE RD

Sch

LIGHTFOOT RD

THE HOMBRLANS

HEATH CROSS

Heath Rd

GAS ST

EATON ST

A515

34

08   **A**   09   **B**   10   **C**

D
E
F

Morry House Farm

Sch
PO
1 WESTON BANK
2 THURVASTON RD
EAST BANK

Manor House

Marston Montgomery

PH

Sedsall Farm

Eaton Barn

4

Havenhouse Farm

Beggarsbutts

Banktop

The Beeches

37

Waldley

Waldley Farm

Marston Woodhouse

Eaton Wood

Marston Brook

3

Old Woodhouse Farm

Upper Eaton Farm

36

Upwoods Farm

Lady Coppice

Hill Farm

2

Somersal Herbert

Somersal Farm

Holmlea Farm

PO

Victory Farm

Woodhouse Farm

The Hall

Mount Pleasant

35

North Lodge

Brookston Brook

Grove Cottages

Eaton Lodge

Field Farm

1

Mill Cottage

Oaklea

DROVE LA

Doveridge

PH

Mill Farm

A50

34

D
E
12
13
F

River Dove

Sch
PO

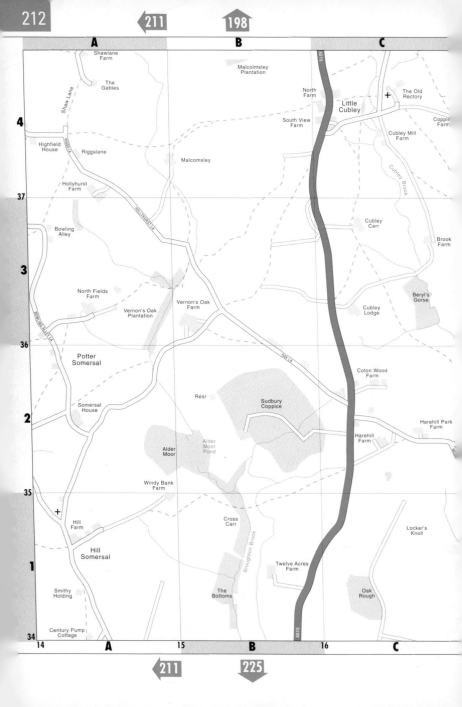

211
198

A

B

C

Shawlane
Farm

Malcolmsley
Plantation

The Gables

North
Farm

The Old
Rectory

Little
Cubley

Coppice
Farm

4

South View
Farm

Cubley Mill
Farm

Shaw Lane

Highfield
House

Riggslane

Malcomsley

RIGGS LANE

Hollyhurst
Farm

37

Cubley Brook

Cubley
Carr

Brook
Farm

Bowling
Alley

HOLLYHURST LA

3

North Fields
Farm

Vernon's Oak
Farm

Beryl's
Gorse

Vernon's Oak
Plantation

Cubley
Lodge

BOWLING ALLEY LA

36

Potter
Somersal

OAK LA

Coton Wood
Farm

Somersal
House

Resr

Sudbury
Coppice

2

Harehill Park
Farm

Alder
Moor

Alder
Moor
Pond

Harehill
Farm

Windy Bank
Farm

35

Locker's
Knoll

Hill
Farm

Cross
Carr

Hill
Somersal

Broughton Brook

Twelve Acres
Farm

1

Smithy
Holding

Oak
Rough

The
Bottoms

Century Pump
Cottage

34

A515

14

A

15

B

16

C

A515

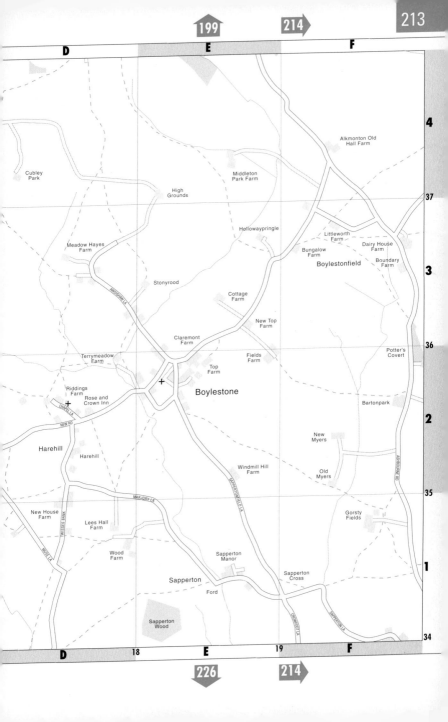

D E F

4

37

3

36

2

35

1

34

Cubley
Park

Alkmonton Old
Hall Farm

Middleton
Park Farm

High
Grounds

Hollowaypringle

Littleworth
Farm

Dairy House
Farm

Meadow Hayes
Farm

Bungalow
Farm

Boundary
Farm

Boylestonfield

Stonyrood

Cottage
Farm

New Top
Farm

Potter's
Covert

Claremont
Farm

Fields
Farm

Terrymeadow
Farm

Top
Farm

Boylestone

Riddings
Farm

Rose and
Crown Inn

Bartonpark

New
Myers

Harehill

Harehill

Windmill Hill
Farm

Old
Myers

MARJORY LA

Gorsty
Fields

New House
Farm

Lees Hall
Farm

Wood
Farm

Sapperton
Manor

Sapperton
Cross

Sapperton

Ford

Sapperton
Wood

NEW RD

CHAPEL LA

WISSIS LANE

ROSE LA

MIDOSHAW LA

SAPPERTONFIELD LA

ASHBOURNE RD

SAPPER LA

DRANFOT LA

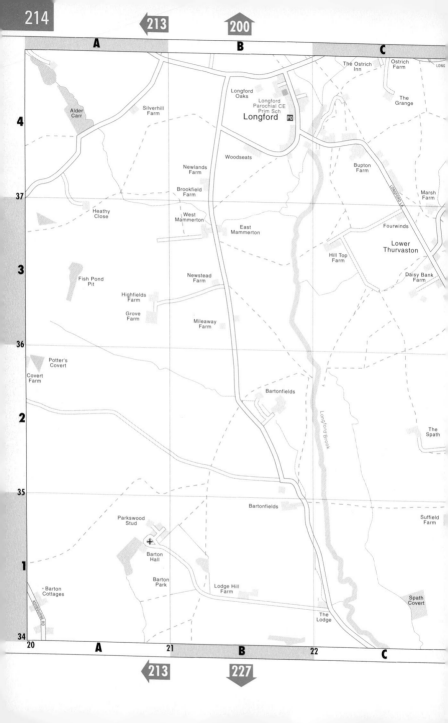

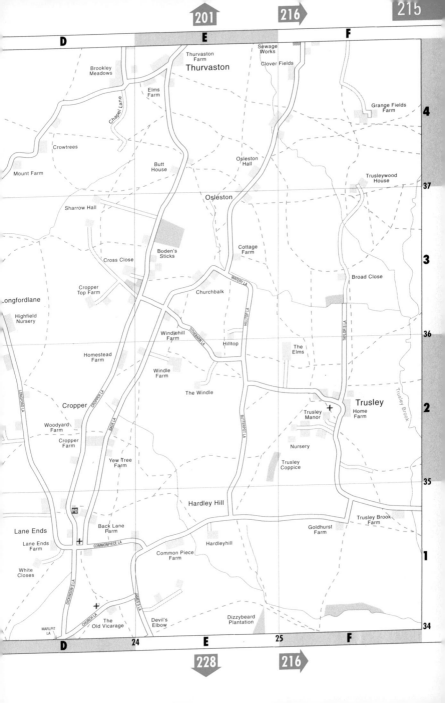

D E F

4

37

3

36

2

35

1

34

Thurvaston Farm
Thurvaston

Sewage Works
Clover Fields

Brookley Meadows

Elms Farm

Chapel Lane

Grange Fields Farm

Crowtrees

Butt House

Osleston Hall

Trusleywood House

Mount Farm

Osleston

Sharrow Hall

Boden's Sticks

Cottage Farm

Cross Close

Broad Close

Longfordlane

Cropper Top Farm

Churchbalk

WATERS LA

ST. GILES HILL

Highfield Nursery

Windlehill Farm

TUNNELPIT LA

Hilltop

The Elms

TAYLOR'S LA

Trusley Brook

Homestead Farm

Windle Farm

The Windle

Cropper

CROPPER LA

BUTTERPOT LA

Trusley
Trusley Manor
Home Farm

LONGFORD LA

Woodyard Farm

BLACK LA

Cropper Farm

Nursery

Yew Tree Farm

Trusley Coppice

Hardley Hill

PO

Back Lane Farm

Goldhurst Farm

Trusley Brook Farm

Lane Ends
Lane Ends Farm

COMMONPIECE LA

Hardleyhill

White Closes

DUCKPADDLE LA

CHURCH LA

Common Piece Farm

WAKES LA

The Old Vicarage

Devil's Elbow

Dizzybeard Plantation

MARLPIT LA

LONG LA

Cherry Tree
Farm

Poplar Grove
Farm

Lees
Hall

Lees

4

Nunclough Brook

Lees Brook

PH

Sewage
Works

37

Hillside
Farm

Black Fir Tree
Farm

Rock House
Farm

Foxfields
Farm

Corner
Farm

3

Woodhouse Lane

Foxfield
Plantation

Hinckley
Farm

Thatched
Farm

Radbourne

Woodhouse
Farm

Old Park
Farm

Ravensdale
Lodge

36

Cunnery
Pond

Ravensdale

+

Birch
Wood

Daysclose
Plantation

Dog Kennel
Pond

Radbourne
Hall

2

Radbourne Brook

The
Rough

The
Rookery

Seedpiece
Plantation

Rookhills
Farm

35

Terrel Hays

Sandpit
Wood

White House
Farm

Smerrills
Farm

Dalbury
Hollow

Bearwardcote
Hall

HAZEL LA

1

Manor
Farm

Top
Farm

+ Dalbury

The
Cottage

34

Bannell's
Lane

217 204

A B C

Mackworth Brook

Markeaton

Old School House

Crem

Markeaton Park

Markeaton Hill

Univ

Broadway

Broadway Park Cl

KEDLESTON OLD RD

Royal Sch for the Deaf

TA Centre

Markeaton Prim Sch

ASHBOURNE RD

Roxhampton

Mackworth

Downing Cl

Sloane Rd

Marylebone Cres

Mackworth Tertiary Coll

New Zealand

Works

Findern St

Kingsway Ret Pk

Bramble Brook

Kingsway

Bemrose Mews

Rough Heanor Farm

Amb HQ

UTTOXETER NEW RD

Bemrose Com Sch

California

St Luke's

Bishop Lonsdale CE Prim Sch

Buntings Cl

Heron Way

Swallow Cl

UTTOXETER RD

Derby City

Wren Park Prim Sch

Mount Carmel St

BURTON RD

Dale Prim Sch

CHAIN LA

Keats Ave

Golf Course

Derby High Sch for Girls

Hotel

PASTURES HILL

St Peter's CE Jun Sch

Lib'y

Old Vicarage Cl

Normanton Park

WARWICK AVE

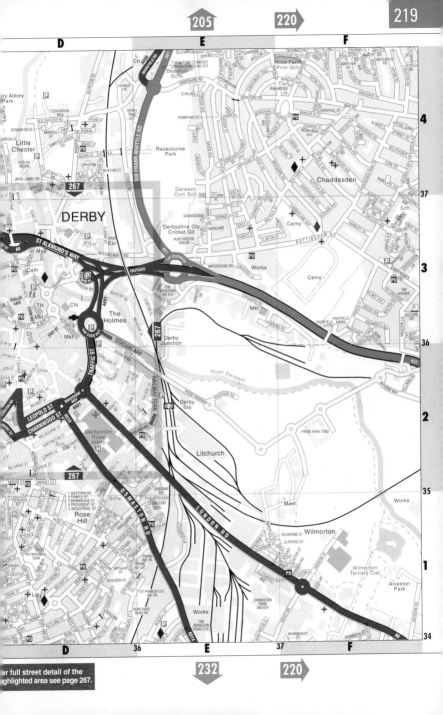

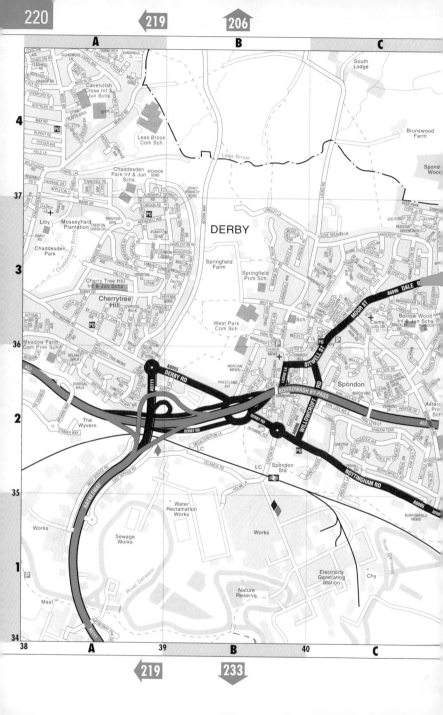

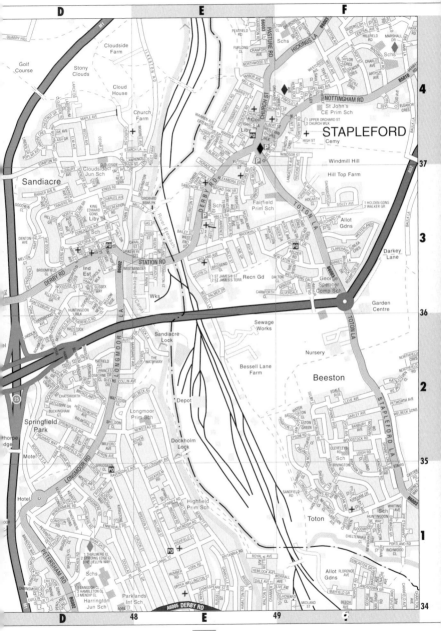

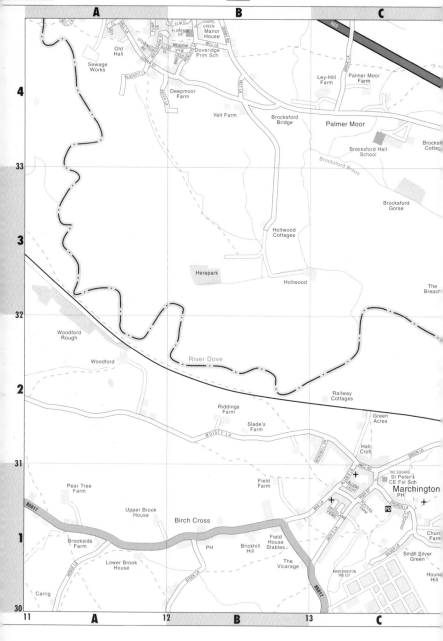

D **E** **F**

Cave
Cottage

Heath House
Farm

Merefield
Gorse

Parkside

Sudbury Park

Somersal
Heath

Brickyard
Farm

Oaks
Green

Sudbury Park
Farm

Gorse
Covert

4

fway
use

Flacketts Lane
Farm

Grove
Plantation

HM
Prison

The Grove

33

West
Broughton

Forest
View

Portway
Head

Sewage
Works

Deercote

Home
Farm

Fiddlers
Farm

Oak
Cottage

Square
Pond

3

West Broughton
Farm

The
Decoy

PH

Aston

32

+
The
Hall

Mus

PO

MAIN RD A50

Sudbury

Sudbury
Prim Sch

Rectory
Farm

Aston
House
Farm

Sewage
Works

Dovebank

Weir
Plantation

River Dove

2

Dovefields
Crossing

Dove
Fields

Aston
Bridge

31

LC

GREEN LA

Sudbury
Dairy

Hotel

LC

Houndhill
Farm

Gliding
Club

Moat
Farm

1

Draycott
in the
Clay

Draycott
Mill

Densey
Lodge

30

D 15 **E** 16 **F**

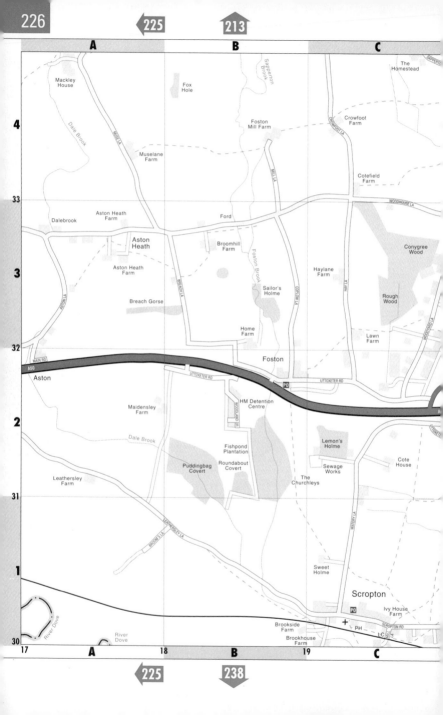

D **E** **F**

Highfield

Highwall
Lodge

Bannell's Farm

MEASE LA

BANNELL'S LA

Bearwardcote
Farm

Bannell's Lane Farm

4

Highfields Farm

A516

Marsh Farm

Hepnalls

33

Oakdene

ETWALL LA

The
Lawns

TINDERBOX LA

MANOR FARM MEWS

SEALWAY CL

BARHILL

3

Ashe Hall

The Marsh

Marsh
Cottage
Farm

BURNASTON LA

Greenacres

ETWALL LA

Burnaston

A516 LA

SUTTON LA

CHURCH LA

PORTLAND ST

BLENHEIM DR

SLADE CL

SANDYPITS LA

32

Etwall Brook

L Ctr

PO

WILLOW PARK

KINGS CL

JOHN PORT

LODGE

Sandypits Farm

RIBER CROFT CL

John Port
Sch

DERBY RD

HILTON RD

Liby

Etwall
Prim
Sch

SYCAMORE CL

GERARD DR

2

Friary Farm

MILL FIELDS

HOLLIES DR

BLAKELOW DR

CHELT

WAM

BECK CR

MAY FIELD

ABURN LA

Etwall

WILLINGTON RD

Lodge Farm

New Close Farm

New Gorse
Fox Covert

Sewage
Works

SPRING

ELMS CR

HENLY

GROVE

Maripit
Plantation

31

JACKSONS LA

Broomhill
Cottages

TYNEFIELD
MEWS

BLAKELEY LA

Etwall Common

Works

1

TYNEFIELD CT

Blakeley Lodge

OLDFIELD LA

Egginton
Common

A50

30

D 27 **E** 28 **F**

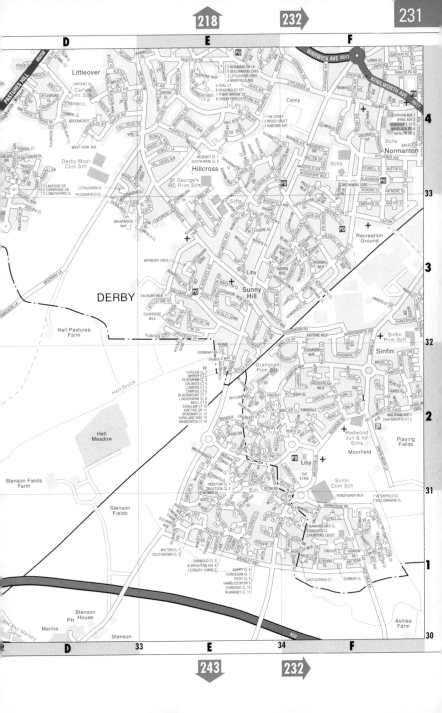

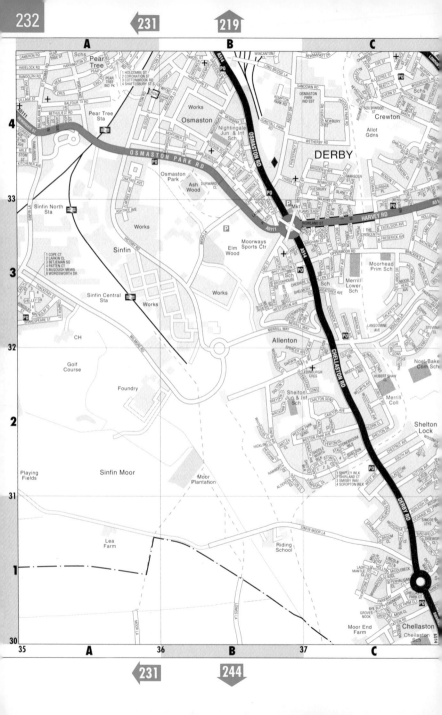

A   B   C

4

33

3

32

2

31

1

30

Draycott
Fields

A6005

DIGBY LA

Derby Rd

MAPLETON

Draycott
Fields

Works

Melbourne
House

WEST AVE

LIME GR

Bankfields
Farm

Draycott

CLEVELAND
AVE

The Park

Caravan
Site

Bedford Drive

Elvaston Castle
Country Park

River Derwent

Drive
Lodge

MAIN RD

Elvaston

CASTLE CT

SILVER
LA

BALL LA

AMBASTON LA

Meadow
Farm

Ambaston

MAIN ST

Ambaston Lane Farm
House

Grange
Farm

OAK RD

Thulston

Thurleston
Grange

Bellington
Wood

Bellington
Hill

Bellington
Farm

Sand &
Gravel Pit

Ambaston
Grange

AMBASTON LA

DERBY RD

A50

Fox Covert
Farm

Glebe
Farm

Elms
Farm

Manor
Farm

Shardlow
Moor

Moor
Farm

PO

Shardlow
Prim Sch

Shardlow

Shardlow
Hall

Brickyard
Plantation

Bird's Nest
Farm

The
Grove

H

INN WAY

ALTS WICK WAY

WEST END

LONDON RD

COLLIERY CL

ASTORIA

NORWAY CL

Alderslade
Farm

ALDERSLADE CL

Aston
Moor

A6

Trent & Mersey Canal

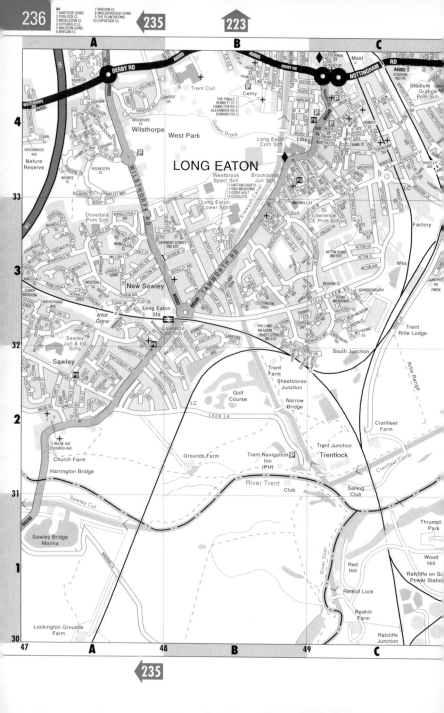

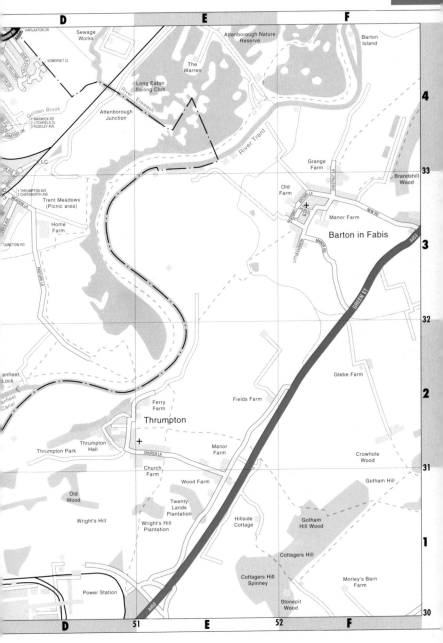

D

E

F

HARLAXTON DR

Sewage
Works

SOMERSET CL

Attenborough Nature
Reserve

Barton
Island

The
Warren

Long Eaton
Sailing Club

River Erewash

Golden Brook

1 WARWICK RD
2 LITCHFIELD CL
3 RUGELEY AVE

ARMITAGE DR

Attenborough
Junction

4

River Trent

LC

Grange
Farm

CHESTNUT LA

Brandshill
Wood

33

NEW RD

1 THRUMPTON AVE
2 CHATSWORTH AVE

MEADOW LA

Trent Meadows
(Picnic area)

Old
Farm

BYRON LA

CHURCH LA

Manor Farm

Barton in Fabis

A453

Home
Farm

LITTLE LA

MARKET RD

3

JUNCTION RD

PASTURE LA

GREEN ST

32

Canfleet
Lock

Glebe Farm

Canfleet
Canal

Ferry
Farm

Fields Farm

2

Thrumpton

Thrumpton
Hall

Crowhole
Wood

Thrumpton Park

CHURCH LA

Manor
Farm

Church
Farm

Gotham Hill

31

Old
Wood

Wood Farm

Twenty
Lands
Plantation

Hillside
Cottage

Gotham
Hill Wood

Wright's Hill

Wright's Hill
Plantation

1

Cottagers Hill

Power Station

Cottagers Hill
Spinney

Morley's Barn
Farm

A453

Stonepit
Wood

30

D

51

E

52

F

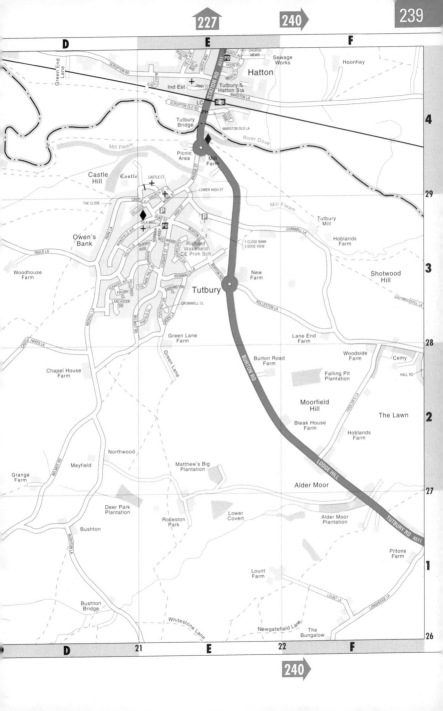

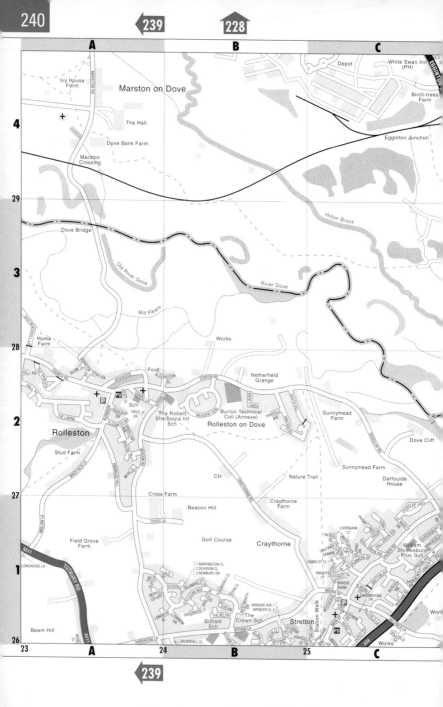

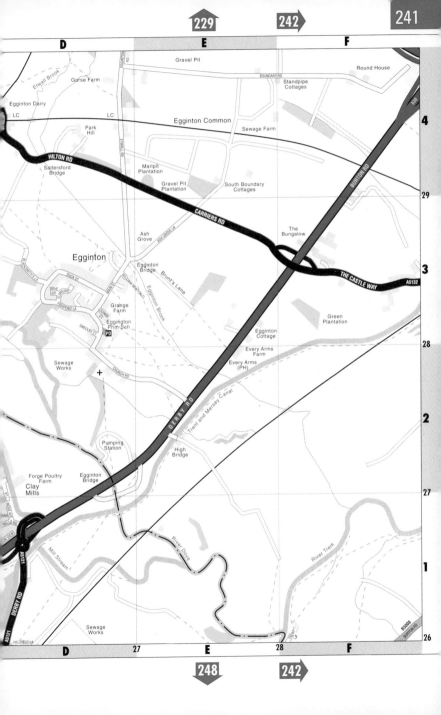

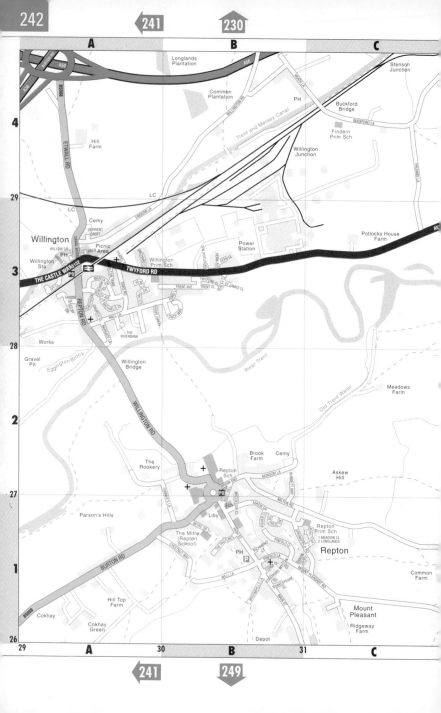

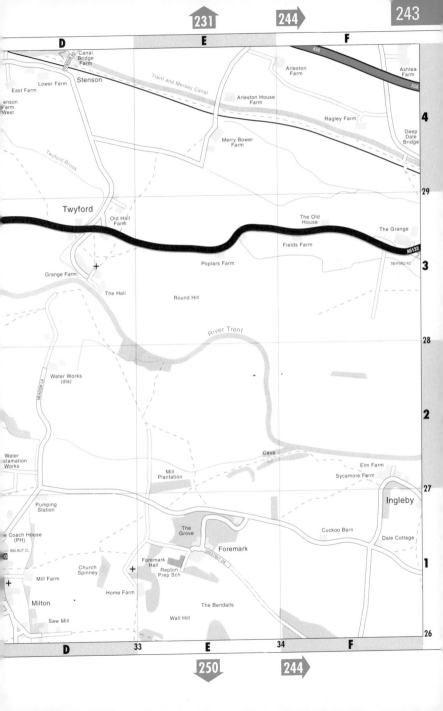

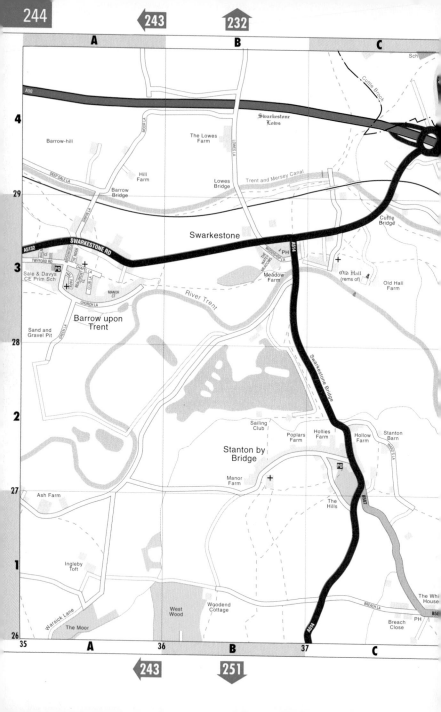

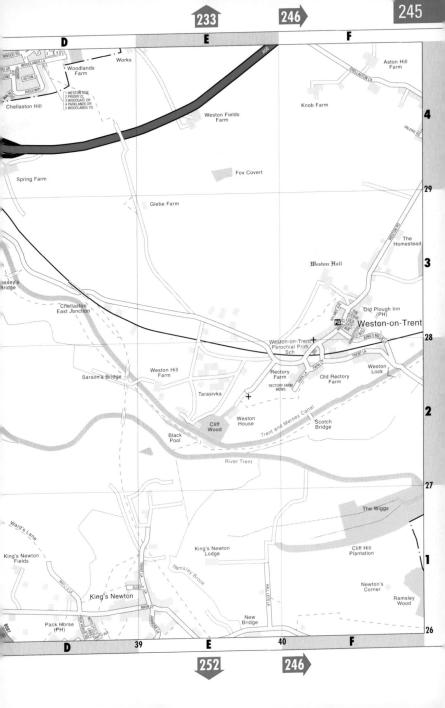

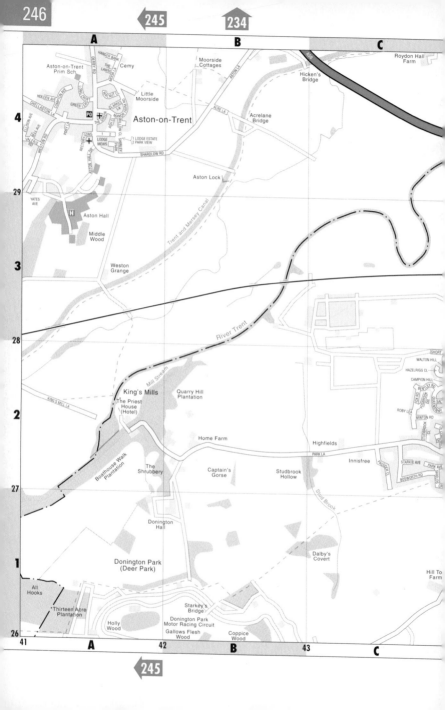

D **E** **F**

River Trent

Cavendish Bridge

The Cavendish Arms (PH)

LONDON RD

DONINGTON LA

TAMWORTH RD

B6540

B6540

Sand and Gravel Pit

WEATHERFIELD LA

M1

4

29

A50

BACK LA

Willow Farm

LC

Trent Farm

Hanover Estate

SYCAMORE RD

GARDE AVE

NEWBOLD DR

TRENT LA

WILLOW DR

VICTORIA ST

HAWTHORNE

STATION RD

RISDYKE RD

New Delight Cottages

MAIN ST

Hemington

HEMINGTON LA

Lockington

Lockington Park

MAIN ST

Lockington Hall

3

Sewage Works

LOCKINGTON RD

Hemington Cty Sch

PO

Daleacre Hill

DALEACRE

KINGS GATE

PO

CHURCH RD

28

THE HORSE SHOES

War Meml

HEMINGTON ST

CHURCH LA

The Dumps

2

CAMPION HILL

RAWDON CL QUEENSWAY

SPITAL

HAULTON DR

HARCOURT PL

MILLERS

P

P PO

THE BARROON

Orchard Cty Prim Sch

MARKET

CHARNWOOD AVE

Cemy

King Street Plantation

ORCHARD AVE

PARK LA

EDEN CL

Sch

DELVEN LA

MOOR RD

MOUNT PLEASANT

EASTWAY

Castle Donington Com Coll

Castle Donington

27

Liby

HALL FARM CL

COOKS AVE

PASTURES

TOWLES

CRABTREE

DONINGTON RD

Field Farm

1

East Midlands Airport

Mast

26

D 45 **E** 46 **F**

241

A   B   C

4

Bendalls Clump

Heath Wood

Warsick

Seven Spouts Farm

ROBIN'S CROSS LA

Orangehill Bridge

25

The Bendalls Farm

Knowle Hill Farm

Brookdale Farm

Orange Hill

Spur's Bottom

Dove Cote Hill

3

Repton Common

Tower

P

The Grange

24

Foremark Reservoir

P

BURTON RD A514

HARROW

2

Fairview Farm

SCADDOWS LA

The Scaddows

Repton Shrubs

Repton Bog

Bondwood Farm

Foremark Park Farm

Basfords Hill Farm

23

Hartshorn Bog

Carver's Rocks

The Scaddows

Pottery House

ASHBY RD

P

1

Top Farm

DERBY RD B5006

BURTON LA

Gravelpit Hill

The Buildings Farm

Smith's Gorse

22

32   A   33   B   34   C

A514 COAL

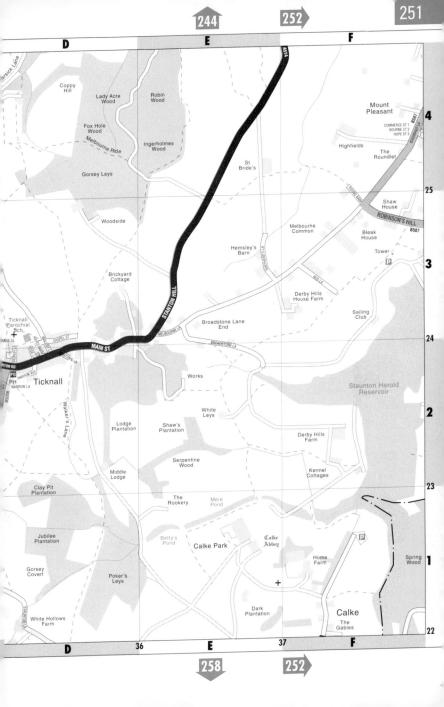

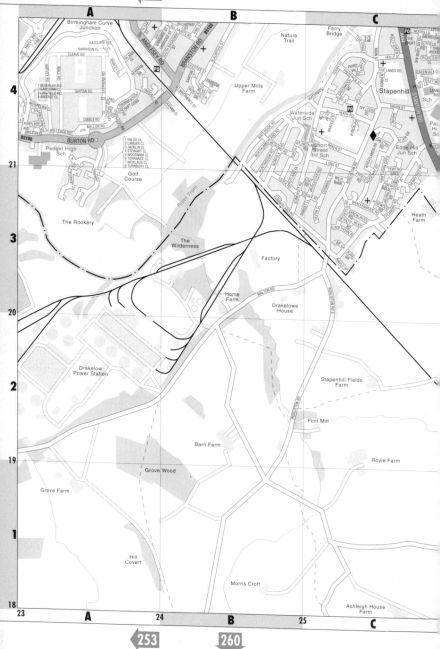

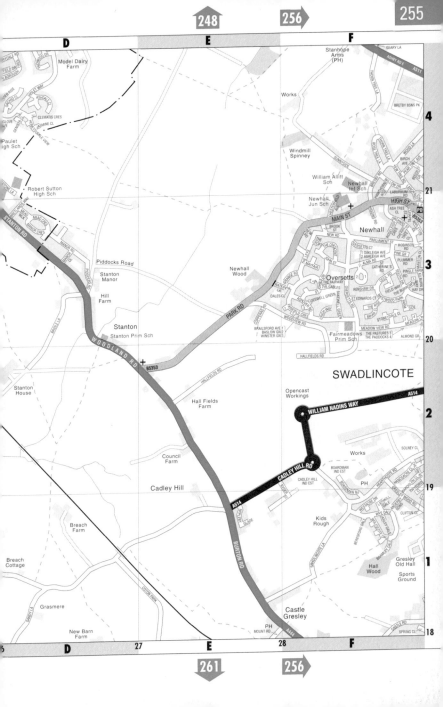

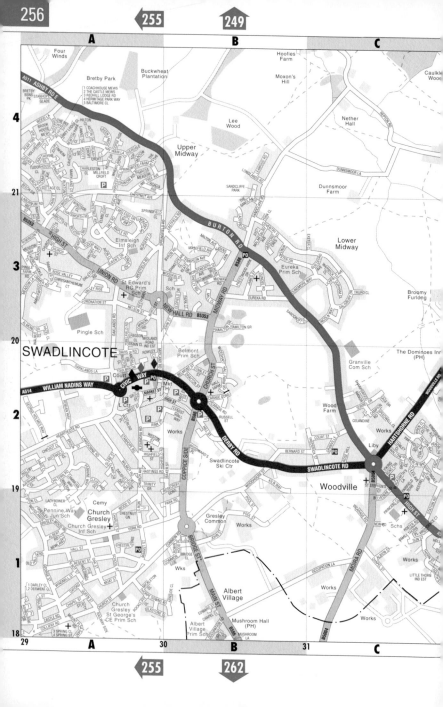

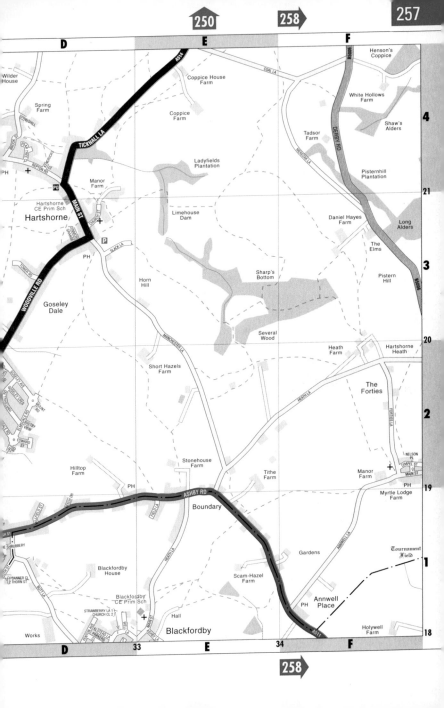

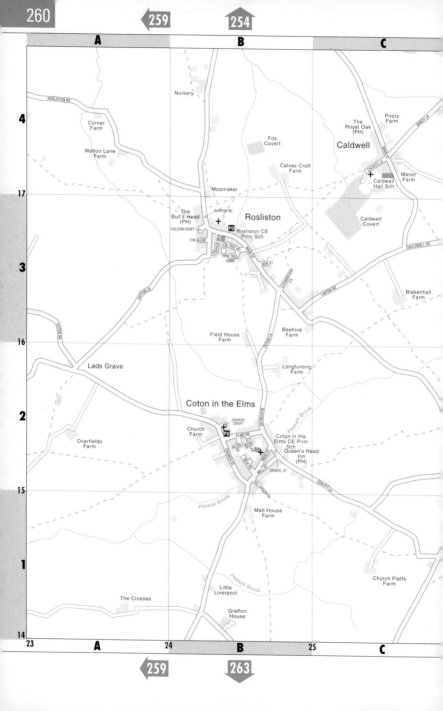

259
254

A   **B**   **C**

4

ROSLISTON RD

Nursery

Corner
Farm

Walton Lane
Farm

Fox
Covert

The
Royal Oak
(PH)

Priory
Farm

Caldwell

Calves Croft
Farm

Manor
Farm

Moonraker

Caldwell
Hall Sch

17

BURTON RD

The
Bull's Head
(PH)

Rosliston

PO

Rosliston CE
Prim Sch

HOLDON CROFT

THE GLEBE

YR TREE RD

YEW TREE
GDNS

NEW ST

STRAWBERRY LA

LINTON RD

Caldwell
Covert

CAULDWELL RD

3

COTON LA

COTON RD

Blakenhall
Farm

Field House
Farm

Beehive
Farm

COTON LA

16

Lads Grave

Longfurlong
Farm

2

Coton in the Elms

Overfields
Farm

Church
Farm

CHURCH
CROFT

PO

BURTON RD

Pessall Brook

Coton in the
Elms CE Prim
Sch

Queen's Head
Inn
(PH)

ELMS RD

GLEBE
CRES

CHURCH END

MAIN ST

CHAPEL ST

COALPIT LA

15

Pessall Brook

Malt House
Farm

1

Church Flatts
Farm

Pessall Brook

The Crosses

Little
Liverpool

Grafton
House

23   **A**   **24**   **B**   **25**   **C**

D
E
F

Princess St
Station St

Knob Fields
A444 Burton Rd

Hill Crest Farm

Coton Park

Sewage Works

High Cross Bank

Castle Gresley Inf Sch

Mount Pleasant Rd

4

Mount Pleasant

Belmot Rd

Grange Farm

17

Manor Farm

Cauldwell Rd

PH

Peartree Cl

Linton

Greenfields

Waterfallows Farm

Linton Heath

Linton Heath

Burton Rd A444

3

Longlands

Princess Ave

Chapel Cl

Linton Prim Sch

Weathern Field

16

Sealwood La

Green La

Middle Hayes Farm

Woodside Farm

Sealwood La

2

Botany Bay Farm

Park Farm

Sealwood Farm

Green Lane

Lullington Rd

15

Potter's Wood

Grange Wood

Gunby Lea

Gunby Rd

1

Craft Ctr

Grangewood Hall

Grangewood Farm

Gunby Farm

Woodfields Farm

Grangewood Lodge

Woodside Farm

Lodge Rd

Grenvue

14

6
D
27
E
28
F

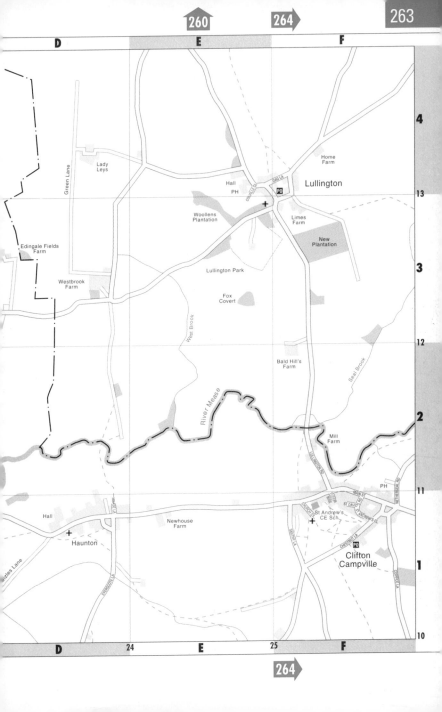

260
264

D   E   F

4

Home Farm

Green Lane

Lady Leys

Hall

PH

ORG LA

PO

Lullington

13

Woollens Plantation

Limes Farm

Edingale Fields Farm

New Plantation

3

Westbrook Farm

Lullington Park

Fox Covert

West Brook

12

Bald Hill's Farm

Seal Brook

River Mease

2

Mill Farm

LULLINGTON RD

Hall

11

Newhouse Farm

St Andrew's CE Sch

MAIN ST

ST DAVID'S

PH

NETHERSEAL RD

ST ANDREW'S CL

BRIDGE LA

Haunton

DARK LA

SPRINGDALE LA

Clifton Campville

CHURCH LA

CHESTNUT LA

PO

COMMON LA

1

Swizzles Lane

10

D   24   E   25   F

264

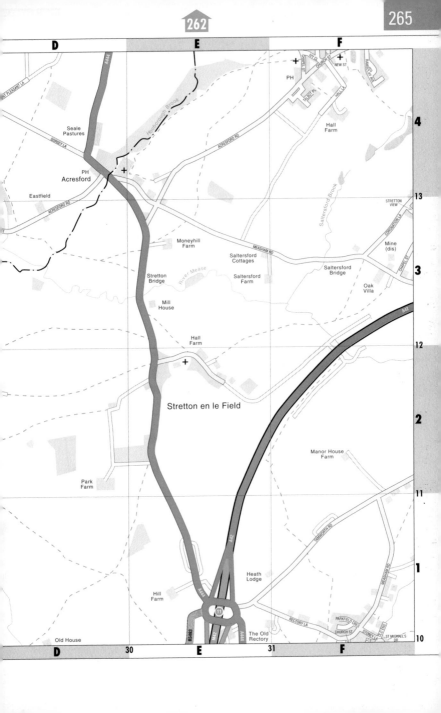

D   E   F

4

Seale
Pastures

DORSEY LA

PH
Acresford

Eastfield

ACRESFORD RD

ACRESFORD RD

Hoddemoor Brook

13

Saltersford Brook

STRETTON
VIEW

CORPORATION LA

MEASHAM RD

Moneyhill
Farm

Saltersford
Cottages

Mine
(dis)

CHAPEL ST

Saltersford
Farm

Saltersford
Bridge

3

River Mease

Stretton
Bridge

Oak
Villa

Mill
House

Hall
Farm

12

Stretton en le Field

2

Manor House
Farm

Park
Farm

11

Hall
Farm
New St

PH

Hall
Farm

TAMWORTH RD

1

Heath
Lodge

Hill
Farm

RECTORY LA

PARKFIELD CRES

STONEY CL

MEASHAM RD

ST MICHAEL'S
DR

Old House

The Old
Rectory

CHURCH ST

B5493

A444

10

D   30   E   31   F

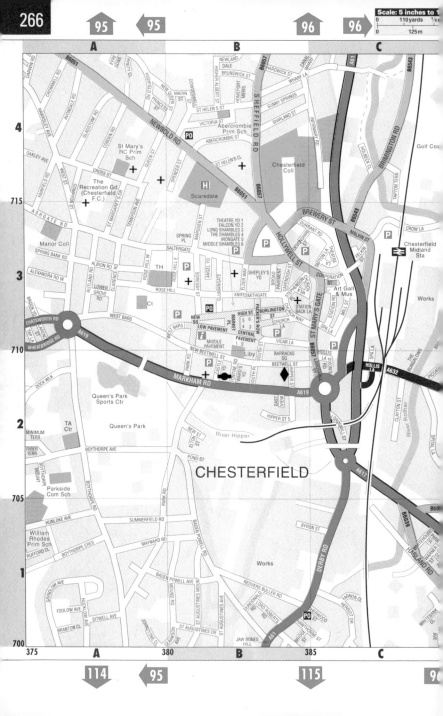

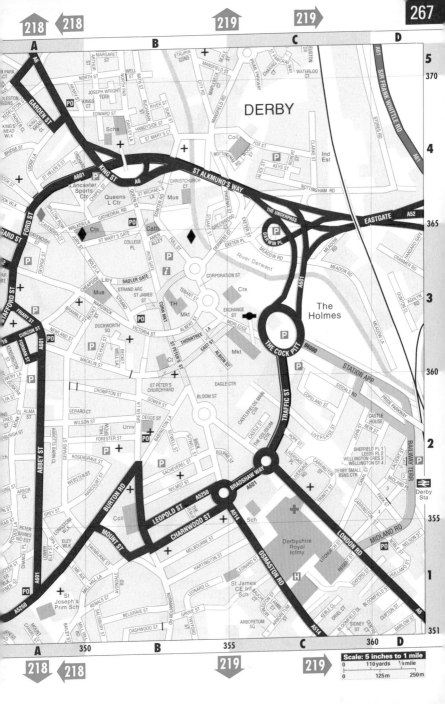

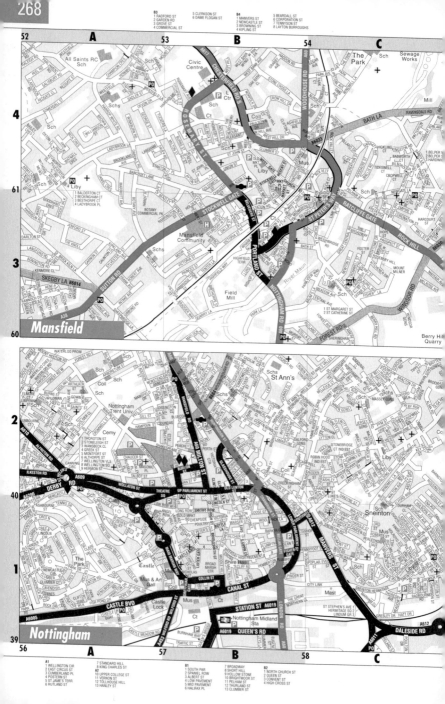

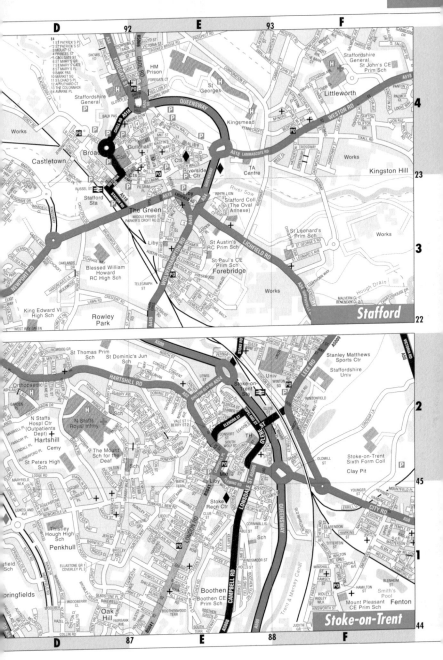

Stafford

Stoke-on-Trent

Index

Street names are listed alphabetically and show the locality, the Postcode District, the page number and a reference to the square in which the name falls on the map

Cambridge Rd **1** Brimington S43 .. **96 C4**

Full street name
This may have been abbreviated on the map

Location Number
If present, this indicates the street's position on a congested area of the map instead of the name

Town, village or locality in which the street falls.

Postcode District for the street name

Page number of the map on which the street name appears

Grid square in which centre of the street falls

Schools, hospitals, sports centres, railway stations, shopping centres, industrial estates, public amenities and other places of interest are also listed.

Abbreviations used in the index

App Approach	La Lane
Arc Arcade	N North
Ave Avenue	Orch Orchard
Bvd Boulevard	Par Parade
Bldgs Buildings	Pk Park
Bsns Pk Business Park	Pas Passage
Bsns Ctr Business Centre	Pl Place
Bglws Bungalows	Prec Precinct
Cswy Causeway	Prom Promenade
Ctr Centre	Ret Pk Retail Park
Cir Circus	Rd Road
Cl Close	Rdbt Roundabout
Comm Common	S South
Cnr Corner	Sq Square
Cotts Cottages	Strs Stairs
Ct Court	Stps Steps
Ctyd Courtyard	St Street, Saint
Cres Crescent	Terr Terrace
Dr Drive	Trad Est Trading Estate
Dro Drove	Wlk Walk
E East	W West
Emb Embankment	Yd Yard
Ent Enterprise	
Espl Esplanade	
Est Estate	
Gdns Gardens	
Gn Green	
Gr Grove	
Hts Heights	
Ho House	
Ind Est Industrial Estate	
Intc Interchange	
Junc Junction	

Town and village index

Abney ... 51 F2
Aldercar ... 182 A2
Alderwasley ... 166 C4
Alfreton ... 159 D2
Alkmonton ... 199 E1
Alsop en le Dale ... 150 C2
Alstonefield ... 149 E2
Alton ... 130 B3
Ambergate ... 167 F2
Apperknowle ... 58 A1
Ashbourne ... 173 E1
Ashby-de-la-Zouch ... 258 B1
Ashford in the Water ... 108 C4
Ashover ... 129 F2
Aston-on-Trent ... 246 A4
Atlow ... 175 D3
Ault Hucknall ... 133 F4
Awsworth ... 195 E4
Bakewell ... 109 F3
Ballidon ... 152 A1
Bamford ... 40 A2
Barlborough ... 80 A4
Barlow ... 75 F1
Barrow Hill ... 78 A2
Barrow upon Trent ... 244 A3
Barton in Fabis ... 237 F3
Barton Turn ... 253 D1
Baslow ... 91 F3
Beeley ... 111 D2
Beeston ... 223 F2
Belper ... 179 D2
Biggin ... 138 B2
Birch Vale ... 25 D1
Birchover ... 126 A1
Blackfordby ... 257 E1
Blackwell ... 147 F1
Bolsover ... 99 D1
Bonsall ... 142 C1
Borrowash ... 221 E1
Boylestone ... 213 E2
Brackenfield ... 145 E1
Bradbourne ... 163 E3
Bradley ... 186 C4
Bradwell ... 51 D4
Brailsford ... 201 F4
Bramley-Vale ... 117 F1
Branston ... 253 F4
Brassington ... 153 D1
Breadsall ... 205 F2
Breaston ... 235 E4
Breedon on the Hill ... 252 C1
Bretby ... 249 D2
Brimington ... 96 C4
Brinsley ... 182 C3
Broadbottom ... 16 A4
Bullbridge ... 168 A3
Burnaston ... 229 F3
Burton upon Trent ... 248 A2
Buxton ... 85 D4
Caldwell ... 260 C4
Callow ... 165 D2
Calow ... 96 C1
Calver ... 72 B1
Carsington ... 164 C4

Castle Donington ... 247 E2
Castleton ... 38 B1
Chapel-en-le-Frith ... 47 D3
Charlesworth ... 16 B3
Chellaston ... 230 B3
Chelmorton ... 87 D1
Chesterfield ... 96 B2
Chinley ... 34 C1
Church Broughton ... 227 D4
Clay Cross ... 131 D2
Clifton ... 184 C3
Clifton Campville ... 263 F1
Clowne ... 80 B2
Codnor ... 181 E4
Common Side ... 75 E2
Compstall ... 15 D1
Cossall ... 195 E1
Coton in the Elms ... 260 B2
Creswell ... 81 F1
Crich ... 156 C1
Cromford ... 155 D3
Curbar ... 72 C1
Dale ... 207 F1
Darley Dale ... 127 E1
Denby ... 180 B1
Denstone ... 196 B3
Derby ... 219 D3
Disley ... 32 B3
Donisthorpe ... 262 C1
Dore ... 55 F4
Dove Holes ... 47 F1
Doveridge ... 211 D1
Draycott ... 234 C4
Dronfield ... 56 C1
Duffield ... 190 C2
Earl Sterndale ... 105 E2
Eastwood ... 182 C2
Eckington ... 59 E2
Edale ... 37 E4
Eggington ... 241 D3
Ellastone ... 183 D2
Elton ... 140 C3
Elvaston ... 234 A3
Etwall ... 229 E2
Eyam ... 71 E3
Fenton ... 269 E1
Findern ... 230 B1
Flagg ... 106 C3
Fritchley ... 168 A2
Gamesley ... 9 E1
Glapwell ... 134 B4
Glossop ... 10 A1
Grassmoor ... 115 F2
Great Cubley ... 198 C1
Great Longstone ... 90 A2
Grindleford ... 72 B4
Hadfield ... 10 A3
Hallam Moors ... 41 F4
Hanbury ... 238 A3
Harthill ... 61 F3
Hartington ... 137 E3
Hartshorne ... 257 D3
Hassop ... 90 C3
Hathersage ... 53 D4
Hatton ... 239 E4

Hayfield ... 25 E1
Hazelwood ... 190 A4
Heage ... 168 C3
Heanor ... 181 E1
Heath ... 117 D1
High Lane ... 32 A4
Hilcote ... 148 B1
Hilton ... 228 B1
Holbrook ... 191 E3
Hodthorpe ... 82 B3
Hognaston ... 164 A1
Hollingworth ... 9 E3
Hollinsclough ... 104 B1
Holloway ... 156 A3
Holme ... 2 C4
Holmesfield ... 75 D4
Holmewood ... 116 C1
Holymoorside ... 113 E4
Hope ... 38 C2
Horsley ... 191 F3
Hulland Ward ... 175 F2
Ible ... 153 F4
Idridgehay ... 176 C3
Ilkeston ... 208 C4
Ironville ... 170 C2
Kilburn ... 192 A4
Killamarsh ... 60 B3
Kimberley ... 195 F4
Kirby-in-Ashfield ... 160 C2
Kirk Ireton ... 165 E1
Kirk Langley ... 202 C1
Kniveton ... 163 D1
Langley Mill ... 182 A2
Langwith ... 119 F3
Linton ... 261 E3
Little Eaton ... 205 E4
Litton ... 69 F2
Lockington ... 247 F3
Lodge Moor ... 42 C4
Long Duckmanton ... 98 A2
Long Eaton ... 236 B4
Longford ... 214 B4
Longnor ... 121 D3
Lount ... 258 C3
Lullington ... 263 F4
Mackworth ... 217 F4
Mansfield ... 136 A1
Mansfield ... 268
Mansfield Woodhouse ... 136 C2
Mapperley ... 193 F2
Marchington ... 224 C1
Market Warsop ... 120 C2
Marple ... 23 D4
Marsh Lane ... 58 C2
Marston Montgomery ... 211 F4
Mastin Moor ... 79 E2
Matlock ... 143 D3
Matlock Bath ... 143 D1
Mayfield ... 184 B4
Melbourne ... 252 A4
Middleton ... 124 C2
Middleton
  (Nr Wirksworth) ... 154 B2

Moira ... 262 C2
Monyash ... 107 E1
Morley ... 206 B3
Morton ... 146 C3
Mosborough ... 59 E4
Mottram in Longdendale ... 9 D2
Nether Heage ... 168 B1
Nether Langwith ... 101 D1
Netherseal ... 264 C4
Neverthorpe ... 79 D1
New Houghton ... 134 F4
New Mills ... 33 E4
Newton ... 148 A2
Newton Solney ... 248 C4
North Wingfield ... 132 A4
Northwood ... 127 D3
Nottingham ... 268
Ockbrook ... 221 E3
Old Brampton ... 94 B2
Osmaston ... 185 F2
Over Haddon ... 109 D1
Overseal ... 262 A2
Palterton ... 118 A3
Parwich ... 151 F1
Peak Dale ... 67 D3
Peak Forest ... 49 D2
Pentrich ... 169 D3
Pilsley ... 132 B1
Pinxton ... 160 B4
Pleasley ... 135 D3
Poolsbrook ... 98 A4
Quarndon ... 204 B3
Radmanthwaite ... 135 E2
Renishaw ... 79 D4
Repton ... 242 C1
Ridgeway ... 168 B2
Ripley ... 169 E1
Risley ... 222 C2
Rocester ... 197 D2
Rodsley ... 200 A3
Rolleston ... 240 A2
Rosliston ... 260 B3
Rowland ... 197 F4
Rowsley ... 126 C4
Sandiacre ... 223 D3
Scarcliffe ... 118 C3
Scropton ... 226 C1
Selston ... 171 F4
Shardlow ... 234 C1
Sheffield ... 43 D4
Shipley ... 194 A3
Shirebrook ... 119 F2
Shireoaks ... 63 F3
Shirland ... 146 B1
Shirley ... 200 C4
Shottle ... 177 F4
Smalley ... 192 C3
Smisby ... 258 A2
Snelston ... 184 B2
Somercotes ... 170 B4
Somersal Herbert ... 211 F2
South Normanton ... 160 A4
South Wingfield ... 157 F2
Spinkhill ... 60 B1

Spout ... 166
Stafford ... 269
Stanley ... 207
Stanton ... 183
Stanton in Peak ... 126
Stanton-by-Dale ... 222
Stapleford ... 223
Staveley ... 78
Stoke-on-Trent ... 269
Stonebroom ... 146
Stoney Middleton ... 71
Stramshall ... 210
Stretton ... 146
Stretton en le Field ... 265
Sudbury ... 225
Sutton in Ashfield ... 148
Sutton on the Hill ... 228
Swadlincote ... 256
Swanwick ... 169
Swarkestone ... 244
Taddington ... 88
Tansley ... 144
Temple ... 116
Thornhill ... 39
Thorpe ... 161
Thorpe Salvin ... 62
Thrumpton ... 237
Thurvaston ... 215
Tibshelf ... 148
Ticknall ... 251
Tideswell ... 69
Tintwistle ... 10
Tissington ... 162
Toadmoor ... 167
Totley ... 55
Trowell ... 209
Trusley ... 215
Tupton ... 131
Turnditch ... 177
Tutbury ... 239
Underwood Green ... 171
Unstone ... 76
Uttoxeter ... 210
Walton-on-Trent ... 253
Wensley ... 142
Wessington ... 157
West Hallam ... 207
Weston Underwood ... 189
Weston-on-Trent ... 245
Westwood ... 171
Whaley Bridge ... 45
Whaley Thorns ... 101
Whitwell ... 81
Willington ... 242
Windley ... 189
Wingerworth ... 114
Winster ... 141
Wirksworth ... 165
Woodthorpe ... 95
Woodville ... 256
Yeaveley ... 199
Youlgreave ... 125

1st Ave DE7 .... 208 C4
2nd Ave DE7 .... 208 C4
3rd Ave DE7 .... 208 C4
Abba Cl NG16 .... 195 F4
Abbey Brook Dr S8 .... 56 C4
Abbey Croft S40 .... 95 D4
Abbey Gdns SK14 .... 9 D2
Abbey Hill
  Breadsall DE21, DE22 .... 205 D2
  Derby DE21, DE22 .... 205 D2
Abbey Hill Rd DE22 .... 204 B1
Abbey La DE22 .... 205 D1
Abbey Lodge Cl DE11 .... 256 A4
Abbey St Derby DE1 .... 267 A2
  Ilkeston DE7 .... 194 C1
Abbey View Dr S8 .... 43 D2
Abbey View Rd S8 .... 43 D2
Abbey Yd DE22 .... 205 D1
Abbeydale Park Cres S17 ... 55 F3
Abbeydale Park Rise S17 ... 55 F3
Abbeydale Rd S8 .... 43 D4
Abbeydale Rd S Dore S8 ...... 56 A4
  Sheffield S17 .... 56 A4
Abbeyfields Cl DE22 .... 205 D1
Abbeyhill Cl S40 .... 95 D2
Abbot Beyne Sch The
  DE15 .... 248 A2
Abbot Cl DE21 .... 205 F1
Abbot Rd DE7 .... 208 B3
Abbots Cl DE11 .... 195 E2
Abbots Gr DE56 .... 179 D3
Abbotsford Dr NG3 .... 268 B2
Abbotsford Mews DE7 ...... 194 B2
Abbotsholme Sch ST14 ...... 197 D1
Abbott Rd DE55 .... 159 D2
Abbott St Heanor DE75 ...... 181 F1
  Long Eaton NG10 .... 236 B3
Abbotts Barn Cl DE1 .... 267 A2
Abbotts Cl DE11 .... 256 A3
Abbotts Croft NG19 .... 135 F1
Abbotts Rd DE11 .... 256 A4
Abell St DE24 .... 142 B1
Abells DE5 .... 180 B1
Abercrombie Prim Sch
  S41 .... 266 B4
Abercrombie St S41 .... 266 B4
Aberdare Cl DE21 .... 206 A1
Aberdeen St NG3 .... 268 C2
Abingdon Bsns Ctr The
  DE24 .... 219 E1
Abingdon St DE24 .... 232 B4
Acacia Cl Chesterfield S40 ... 95 E3
  Derby DE3 .... 217 F1
  Sheffield S14 .... 43 E3
Abney Dr S14 .... 43 E3
Abney Rd S14 .... 43 E3
Acacia Ave Brimington S43 ... 97 D4
  Derby DE3 .... 217 F1
  Swadlincote DE11 .... 256 A4
Acacia Cres S21 .... 60 A3
Acacia Ct NG10 .... 136 C1
Acacia Dr
  Lower Pilsley S45 .... 132 A2
  Melbourne DE73 .... 252 A4
Acacia Gdns NG16 .... 195 F4
Acer Cl Killamarsh S21 ...... 60 B3
  Pinxton NG16 .... 160 B2
Acer Croft DE21 .... 205 F2
Acorn Ave NG16 .... 195 E4
Acorn Bsns Pk NG18 .... 268 B3
Acorn Cl DE24 .... 232 C2
Acorn Dr DE56 .... 179 D3
Acorn Ridge
  Chesterfield S40 .... 114 A4
  Matlock DE4 .... 143 D3
  Shirebrook NG20 .... 119 E3
Acorn Terr SK22 .... 33 D3
Acorn Way Belper DE56 ...... 179 D3
  Derby DE21 .... 220 B3
  Morley DE21 .... 220 B3
Acre La NG20 .... 246 B4
Acre St SK13 .... 17 E4
Acreage La NG20 .... 119 F1
Acrefield Way DE73 .... 233 D1
Acres Rd S45 .... 132 A2
Acres The S45 .... 132 A2
Acres View Cl S41 .... 95 F4
Acresford Rd
  Donisthorpe DE12 .... 265 E4
  Netherseal DE12 .... 265 D3
  Overseal DE12 .... 262 A1
Acton Ave NG10 .... 236 C3
Acton Cl NG10 .... 236 C3
Acton Gr NG10 .... 236 C3
Acton Rd Derby DE22 .... 217 F3
  Long Eaton NG10 .... 236 C3
Acton Road Ind Est NG10 ... 236 C3
Acton St NG10 .... 236 C3
Adale Rd DE7 .... 193 D4
Adam Bede Cres DE4 ...... 165 F3
Adam St DE7 .... 209 D3
Adam's Rd DE6 .... 217 D4
Adams Cl DE75 .... 193 E4
Adams Ct DE7 .... 194 C2
Adastral Ave S12 .... 44 A1
Adderley Pl SK13 .... 9 F1
Adderley Rd SK13 .... 9 F1
Addison Dr DE55 .... 159 D2
Addison Rd Derby DE24 ...... 232 B4
  Stonebroom DE55 .... 146 C2
Addison Sq DE4 .... 155 D3
Addison St
  Nottingham NG1 .... 268 A2
  Tibshelf DE55 .... 148 A4
Addison Villas NG16 .... 182 C1
Adelaide Cl Derby DE3 ...... 217 F2
  Stapleford NG9 .... 209 F1
Adelaide Cres DE15 .... 248 B1
Adelaide Wlk NG16 .... 170 C2
Adelphi Cl DE23 .... 231 D3
Adin Ave S44 .... 98 C3
Adlington Ave S42 .... 115 E1
Adlington La S32 .... 72 B4
Admiral Cl DE79 .... 181 E1
Adrian Cl NG9 .... 223 F1
Adrian St DE24 .... 232 B3
Adwick Cl DE3 .... 217 E1
Agard St DE1 .... 218 C3
Agnesmeadow La DE6 ...... 174 B2
Ainley Cl DE23 .... 232 C4
Ainsworth Dr DE23 .... 231 F4
Ainsworth St S14 .... 231 F4
Aintree Ave S21 .... 59 F1
Aintree Cl Branston DE14 ... 254 A4
  Kimberley NG16 .... 195 F4
Airedale Cl NG10 .... 236 A3
Airedale Wlk DE24 .... 233 E3
Akley Bank Cl S17 .... 55 F3
Alabaster La DE4 .... 155 D3
Alandale Ave NG20 .... 119 F3
Albany Cl NG19 .... 136 B1
Albany Cl NG9 .... 209 F1
Albany Dr NG19 .... 136 B1
Albany Inf Sch NG9 .... 209 F1
Albany Jun & Inf Schs
  NG9 .... 209 F1
Albany Pl NG19 .... 136 B1
Albany Rd DE22 .... 218 B2
Albany St DE7 .... 209 D3
Albemarle Rd DE21 .... 220 A4
Albert Ave Chesterfield S43 ... 77 F2
  Stapleford NG9 .... 209 F4
  Westwood NG16 .... 171 D2
Albert Cres DE21 .... 220 A2
Albert Rd Breaston DE72 ...... 235 D4
  Chesterfield S43 .... 77 E2
  Derby DE21 .... 220 A2
  Long Eaton NG10 .... 236 B4
  Ripley DE5 .... 169 E1
  Sandiacre NG10 .... 223 D3
  Sheffield S8 .... 43 D3
  Swadlincote DE11 .... 256 A1
Albert St Belper DE56 .... 178 C2
  Derby DE1 .... 267 B3
  Eastwood NG16 .... 182 C2
  Eckington S21 .... 59 E1
  Hadfield SK13 .... 10 C4
  Ilkeston DE7 .... 194 C1
  Ironville NG16 .... 170 C3
  Mansfield NG18 .... 268 B3
  Mansfield Woodhouse
    NG19 .... 136 B2
  [⑧] Nottingham NG1 .... 268 B1
  Ripley DE5 .... 169 F1
  Somercotes DE55 .... 170 A4
  South Normanton DE55 ...... 160 A3
  Stapleford NG9 .... 223 E4
Albert St N S41 .... 76 C1
Albert Village Prim Sch
  DE11 .... 256 B1
Alberta Ave NG16 .... 171 F4
Albine Rd NG20 .... 119 F3
Albion Ctr The DE7 .... 208 C4
Albion Rd Chesterfield S40 ... 266 A3
  Long Eaton NG10 .... 236 C4
  New Mills SK22 .... 33 D3
Albion St Derby DE1 .... 267 B3
  Ilkeston DE7 .... 194 C1
  Mansfield NG19 .... 135 F1
  Ripley DE5 .... 169 F1
  Woodville DE11 .... 256 C1
Albrighton Ave DE24 .... 231 E1
Alcock Ave NG18 .... 268 C1
Aldam Cl S17 .... 55 F2
Aldam Croft S17 .... 55 F2
Aldam Rd S17 .... 55 F2
Aldam Way S17 .... 55 F2
Alder Brook SK23 .... 205 F2
Alder Cl Derby DE21 .... 136 C1
  Mansfield NG19 .... 119 E3
  Shirebrook NG20 .... 119 E3
Alder Cl DE21 .... 219 D4
Alder Gr Burton u T DE15 ... 254 C4
  Buxton SK17 .... 85 D4
  Mansfield Woodhouse
    NG19 .... 136 A3
Alder Rd NG19 .... 179 D2
Alder Rise SK23 .... 45 E3
Alder Way NG19 .... 119 E2
Alderbrook Cl DE13 .... 240 A2
Aldercar Inf Sch NG16 ...... 182 A2
Aldercar La NG16 .... 182 A3
Aldercar Sch NG16 .... 182 A2
Alderd Cl S21 .... 60 C4
Alderfen Cl DE24 .... 232 B2
Alderley Cl DE21 .... 206 A1
Aldern Way DE45 .... 109 F4
Alderney Rd S2 .... 43 D4
Alders Ave SK23 .... 45 E3
Alders Brook S45 .... 228 B1
Alders La Chinley SK23 ...... 34 C1
  Tansley DE4 .... 144 A2
Alders Rd SK6 .... 32 A4
Alders The S42 .... 113 E4
Aldersgate Derby DE22 ...... 217 F4
  New Mills SK22 .... 33 D4
Alderside Cl DE24 .... 234 A1
Aldersley Cl DE65 .... 230 B1
Alderson Pl S2 .... 43 D4
Alderson Rd S2 .... 43 D4
Alderson Rd N S2 .... 43 D4
Aldred's La DE75, NG16 ...... 182 A1
Aldridge Cl NG9 .... 223 F1
Aldwark Rd SK17 .... 85 E3
Aldwych DE22 .... 218 A3
Alexander Ave NG16 .... 171 E4
Alexander Rd
  Dove Holes SK17 .... 47 F1
  Nottingham NG7 .... 268 A1
Alexander St NG16 .... 182 C1
Alexander Terr NG16 .... 160 B1
Alexandra Ave NG19 .... 136 A3
Alexandra Cl DE15 .... 248 A2
Alexandra Gdns DE23 ...... 219 E1
Alexandra Rd
  Burton u T DE15 .... 248 A2
  Buxton SK17 .... 85 D4
  Dronfield S18 .... 57 D1
  Long Eaton NG10 .... 236 B4
  Overseal DE12 .... 262 A2
  Sheffield S2 .... 43 D4
  Stafford ST17 .... 269 E3
  Swadlincote DE11 .... 256 A2
Alexandra Rd E S41 .... 96 B1
Alexandra Rd W S40 .... 266 A3
Alexandra St NG9 .... 223 E3
Alexandre Cl DE23 .... 231 E3
Alford Cl S40 .... 95 E2
Alfred Cl NG3 .... 268 B2
Alfred Cl NG18 .... 268 B4
Alfred Rd DE56 .... 192 A4
Alfred St Alfreton DE55 ...... 158 C2
  Pinxton NG16 .... 160 B2
  Ripley DE5 .... 169 F1
  Somercotes DE55 .... 170 B3
  South Normanton DE55 ...... 159 F3
Alfred St Central NG3 ...... 268 B2
Alfred St N NG3 .... 268 B2
Alfreton Cl DE55 .... 158 C2
**Alfreton & Mansfield
  Parkway Sta** NG16 ...... 159 E3
Alfreton Rd Blackwell DE55 ... 147 F1
  Breadsall DE21 .... 205 E3
  Derby DE21 .... 205 E3
  Derby DE21 .... 205 E3
  Holbrook DE7 .... 191 E1
  Little Eaton DE21 .... 205 E3
  Matlock DE4 .... 143 D3
  Nottingham NG7 .... 268 A2
  Pinxton NG16 .... 160 B2
  Selston DE55, NG16 .... 171 E3
  Tansley DE4 .... 143 F2
  Tibshelf DE55 .... 147 F2
Alfreton Trad Est DE55 ...... 159 D1
Algar Cl S2 .... 43 F4
Algar Cres S2 .... 43 F4
Algar Dr S2 .... 43 F4
Algar Pl S2 .... 43 F4
Algar Rd Sheffield S2 ...... 43 F4
  Stoke-on-T S14 .... 269 D1
Alice St DE7 .... 267 C4
Alice Way S18 .... 76 C3
Alicehead Rd S45 .... 113 D1
Alison Cl DE21 .... 219 F4
All Saints CE Fst Sch
  ST14 .... 196 C3
All Saints CE Inf Sch DE4 ... 143 D4
All Saints CE Jun Sch
  DE4 .... 143 D4
All Saints Cl DE3 .... 217 E1
All Saints Prim Sch SK6 ... 23 D3
All Saints RC Comp Sch
  NG19 .... 268 A4
All Saints Rd
  Burton u T DE14 .... 254 B4
  Stoke-on-T S14 .... 269 E1
All Saints' RC Prim Sch
  SK13 .... 10 B1
All Saints' Rd DE4 .... 143 D3
All Saints' St NG7 .... 268 A2
Allan Ave DE23 .... 230 C4
Allan La DE55 .... 168 A3
Allandale Rd DE75 .... 181 D2
Allcroft St NG19 .... 136 B2
Allen Hill DE4 .... 143 D3
Allen La Ashover DE4 .... 144 B3
  Weston Underwood DE6 ... 188 B1
  Stoke-on-T S14 .... 269 D2
Allen's Green Ave NG16 ... 171 F3
Allen's La S14 .... 224 C1
Allenby Cl S8 .... 56 C4
Allenby Dr S8 .... 56 C4
Allendale DE7 .... 194 C3
Allendale Rd S42 .... 114 C2
Allendale Way NG19 .... 136 C1
Allenpark Inf Sch DE24 ...... 232 B3
Allens Croft ST14 .... 224 C1
Allenton Com Prim Sch
  DE24 .... 232 B3
Allestree Cl DE24 .... 232 C4
Allestree Dr S18 .... 56 B1
Allestree La DE22 .... 204 B2
Allestree St DE24 .... 232 B4
Alley The DE4 .... 154 B2
Alleyne St S41 .... 201 F4
Allison Ave DE7 .... 256 A2
Allissa Ave DE5 .... 180 C4
Allpits Rd S44 .... 96 C2
Allport Terr Barrow Hill S43 ... 78 A2
  Blackwell DE55 .... 147 E1
Allsops Pl S41 .... 95 F4
Allstone Lee DE56 .... 178 C3
Alma Cl NG3 .... 268 A2
Alma Cres S18 .... 57 E2
Alma Hill NG16 .... 195 F4
Alma Hts DE3 .... 217 F1
Alma Rd
  North Wingfield S42 .... 132 A4
  Nottingham NG3 .... 268 C2
  Selston NG16 .... 171 F3
  Swadlincote DE11 .... 255 F3
  Tideswell SK17 .... 69 E2
Alma St Alfreton DE55 .... 159 D2
  Buxton SK17 .... 85 E4
Derby DE22 .... 267 A2
Fenton ST4 .... 269 E3
Melbourne DE73 .... 252 A4
North Wingfield S42 .... 131 F3
Ripley DE5 .... 169 E2
Alma St W S40 .... 95 F1
Almond Ave Ripley DE5 ...... 180 B4
  Shirebrook NG20 .... 119 F3
Almond Cl Calow S44 .... 97 D2
  Kimberley NG16 .... 195 F4
Almond Cres S43 .... 79 E2
Almond Cl DE13 .... 240 C1
Almond Dr S21 .... 60 B3
Almond Gr
  Swadlincote DE11 .... 256 A3
  Swanwick DE55 .... 170 A4
Almond Rise NG19 .... 136 C1
Alms Rd DE6 .... 211 E1
Alnwick Dr S12 .... 44 A3
Alnwick Rd S12 .... 44 A3
Alpha Rd SK23 .... 34 C1
Alpha Terr NG1 .... 268 A2
Alpine Gr S43 .... 80 A4
Alport Ave Buxton SK17 ...... 85 E4
  Sheffield S12 .... 44 C3
Alport Cl Belper DE56 .... 179 D3
  Hulland Ward DE6 .... 175 F2
Alport Dr S12 .... 44 C3
Alport Gr S12 .... 44 C3
Alport La Spout DE56 .... 166 B2
  Youlgreave DE45 .... 125 E3
Alport Pl S12 .... 44 C3
Alport Rd S12 .... 44 C3
Alport Rise S18 .... 56 B1
Alport Cl DE21 .... 206 A1
Alsager Cl DE21 .... 206 A1
Alsfeld Way SK22 .... 33 D4
Alsop Gr S17 .... 85 F4
Alsop Pl SK17 .... 85 F4
Alsop Way SK17 .... 85 F4
Alston Cl Chesterfield S40 ... 114 A4
  Sheffield S20 .... 204 B2
Alston Hill S42 .... 130 B3
Alston La S45 .... 130 B2
Alston Rd DE56 .... 179 E2
Alton Cl Derby DE22 .... 204 C2
  Dronfield S18 .... 75 E4
Alts Nook Way DE72 .... 234 C1
Alum Chine Cl S41 .... 115 E4
Alum Cl DE24 .... 233 E4
Alvaston Inf Sch DE24 ...... 233 E3
Alvaston Jun Com Sch
  DE24 .... 233 D4
Alvaston St DE24 .... 233 D4
Alvenor St DE7 .... 194 C1
Alverton Cl DE21 .... 217 E1
Alward's Cl DE24 .... 233 D3
Ambaston La
  Elvaston DE72 .... 234 A3
  Shardlow DE72 .... 234 C2
Amber Cl DE55 .... 95 E1
Amber Cres S40 .... 95 E3
Amber Croft S43 .... 97 E4
Amber Ct Belper DE56 .... 179 D3
  Heanor DE75 .... 181 F1
Amber Dr NG16 .... 182 A1
Amber Gdns DE75 .... 181 F2
Amber Hill DE4 .... 168 A4
Amber Hts DE5 .... 169 E1
Amber La S45 .... 129 E2
Amber Pl S45 .... 131 D2
Amber Rd Bullbridge DE56 ... 168 A3
  Derby DE22 .... 204 C2
Amber St DE24 .... 232 B4
Amber View Rd DE56 .... 168 A4
Amberdene DE4 .... 143 E3
Ambergate Prim Sch
  DE56 .... 167 F2
Ambergate Sta DE56 .... 167 F2
Ambergrove DE56 .... 168 A4
Amberley Dr Buxton SK17 ... 85 E3
  Derby DE24 .... 231 F3
Amberwood DE11 .... 256 A3
Amblesicde Cl
  Chesterfield S41 .... 95 E4
  Mosborough S20 .... 59 F3
Ambleside Dr NG16 .... 182 B2
Ambrose Terr DE1 .... 218 C3
Amen Alley DE1 .... 267 B3
**American Adventure
  Theme Pk The** DE75 ...... 194 A3
Amesbury Cl S41 .... 95 F4
Amesbury La DE21 .... 205 F1
Ameycroft La DE4 .... 143 D4
Amilda Ave DE7 .... 208 C4
Amy St DE22 .... 218 C2
Anchor Ave SK23 .... 47 E3
Anchor Fold S43 .... 82 E3
Anchor Rd DE55 .... 182 B1
Anchor Row DE7 .... 208 C4
Anchor Sq DE4 .... 109 E3
Anderby Gdns DE24 .... 231 E1
Anderson Cl S41 .... 77 F2
Anderson Sch The SK17 ... 85 D4
Anderson St DE24 .... 209 D4
Andrew Ave DE7 .... 209 D4
Andrew Cl DE23 .... 230 C4
Andrew St SK6 .... 15 D1
Andrews Dr
  Langley Mill NG16 .... 182 A2
  Stanley DE7 .... 193 D1
Andwell La S10 .... 42 C3
Angel Row DE1 .... 268 B1

Angel Yd S40 .... 266 B3
Angerford Ave S8 .... 43 D2
Anglers' La DE21 .... 220 C2
Anglesey Rd
  Burton u T DE14 .... 254 A4
  Dronfield S18 .... 76 A4
Anglesey St DE21 .... 219 E4
Angleton Ave S2 .... 44 B4
Angleton Cl S2 .... 44 B4
Angleton Gdns S2 .... 44 B4
Angleton Gn S2 .... 44 B4
Ankerbold Rd S42 .... 131 E4
Ann St S80 .... 81 F1
Anncroft Rd SK17 .... 84 B3
Anne Potter Cl DE72 .... 221 E3
Annesley Cl
  Chesterfield S41 .... 115 E4
  Sheffield S8 .... 56 C4
Annesley Gr NG1 .... 268 B2
Annesley Rd S8 .... 56 C4
Anns Rd S2 .... 43 D4
Anns Rd N S2 .... 43 D4
Annwell La LE65 .... 257 F1
Anslow La DE13 .... 240 A1
Anslow Rd DE13 .... 238 A1
Anson Wlk DE7 .... 194 C2
Anston La S80 .... 236 B3
Anstey Cl DE21 .... 206 A1
Anstey Rise NG2 .... 268 C2
Anthony Bek Prim Sch
  NG19 .... 134 C3
Anthony Cres DE24 .... 232 C3
Anthony Dr DE24 .... 232 C3
Anthony Fell Sch DE21 ...... 165 F4
Antill St NG9 .... 223 E3
Apiary Gate DE74 .... 247 D2
Apperknowle Jun Sch S18 ... 58 A1
Appian Cl DE72 .... 221 E1
Appian Way
  Clay Cross S45 .... 131 E1
  Derby DE24 .... 233 E3
Apple Ave S8 .... 56 B4
Apple Tree Rd SK22 .... 24 A1
Appleby Cl DE7 .... 208 C3
Appleby Ct DE22 .... 218 C2
Appleby Glade DE11 .... 255 E1
Appleby Rd NG19 .... 136 A2
Appledore Dr DE21 .... 206 A1
Applegarth Cl S12 .... 44 A3
Applegarth Dr S12 .... 44 A3
Applegate Cl DE21 .... 220 A4
Appleton Cl Derby DE3 ...... 217 E1
  Swadlincote DE11 .... 255 F3
Appleton Dr Belper DE56 ... 179 D3
  Glossop SK13 .... 17 F4
Appletree Cl DE21 .... 221 E1
Appletree Dr S18 .... 57 D3
Appletree Rd Bolsover S44 ... 99 D1
  Hatton DE65 .... 227 E1
Applewood Cl
  Belper DE56 .... 179 D3
  Uttoxeter ST14 .... 210 A1
Appleyard Cl [⑫] DE5 ...... 269 E4
Aquinas St ST4 .... 269 E2
Arbor Cl DE22 .... 267 A2
Arbor Gr SK17 .... 84 C3
Arbor Low DE45 .... 123 F2
Arboretum Prim Sch
  DE23 .... 219 D1
Arboretum Sch NG1 .... 268 A2
Arboretum Sq DE23 .... 267 C1
Arboretum St Derby DE23 ... 267 C1
  Nottingham NG1 .... 268 A2
Arbour Cl S41 .... 115 E3
Arbour Hill DE7 .... 207 F1
Arbourthorne Cotts S2 ...... 43 E4
**Arbourthorne Fst &
  Mid Sch** S2 .... 43 E4
Arbourthorne Rd S2 .... 43 E4
Arcadia Ave NG20 .... 119 F3
Archdale Cl S2 .... 44 A4
Archdale Pl S2 .... 44 A4
Archdale Rd S2 .... 44 A4
Archer Rd NG9 .... 223 F3
Archer St Derby DE24 .... 219 F1
  Ilkeston DE7 .... 194 C4
Arden Cl Chesterfield S40 ... 95 E3
  Derby DE23 .... 218 C1
  Glossop SK13 .... 17 D4
Arden St S2 .... 33 E4
Ardleigh Cl DE23 .... 230 B4
Ardsley Cl Heanor DE75 ...... 182 A1
  Stapleford NG9 .... 223 E3
Ardsley Dr S20 .... 44 C1
Ardsley Gr S20 .... 44 C1
Ardsley Rd S40 .... 95 D2
Argyle Cl
  Market Warsop NG20 .... 120 C2
  Sheffield S8 .... 43 D3
Argyle Rd S8 .... 43 D3
Argyle St Derby DE22 .... 218 C2
  Langley Mill NG16 .... 182 B2
Argyll Cl DE21 .... 205 E1
Argyll Rd DE5 .... 169 F1
Arkendale Wlk DE24 .... 233 E3
Arklow Cl S41 .... 115 D4
Arkwright Ave DE56 .... 179 D3
Arkwright Cl DE56 .... 178 C2
Arkwright Dr SK6 .... 23 D3
Arkwright Prim Sch S44 ... 97 E2
Arkwright St Derby DE24 ... 232 B4
  Wirksworth DE4 .... 165 F4
Arleston La DE24 .... 231 E1

Arleston St DE23 .... **231** F4
Arlington Ave NG19 .... **136** C2
Arlington Dr Derby DE24 .... **232** C3
  Swanwick DE55 .... **169** F4
Armitage Dr DE23 .... **218** B1
Armitage Dr NG10 .... **237** D4
Arms Grove Prim Sch S2 .... **43** D4
Arms Park Dr S20 .... **59** F3
Armscote Cl DE21 .... **206** A1
Armstrong Ave ST16 .... **269** F4
Armstrong Rd NG19 .... **268** A4
Armytage Ind Est S41 .... **77** D1
Arnfield La SK13 .... **9** F4
Arnhem Terr DE21 .... **220** C2
Arnold Ave
  Long Eaton NG10 .... **236** A2
  Sheffield S12 .... **44** A1
Arnold & Carlton
  Coll of F Ed NG **268** B1
Arnold Cl DE11 .... **261** F4
Arnold Cres NG10 .... **236** A2
Arnold St DE22 .... **218** B3
Arnside NG9 .... **223** F3
Arnside Cl
  Chesterfield S41 .... **76** B1
  Swadlincote DE11 .... **256** B1
Arran Cl Derby DE24 .... **231** F2
  Stapleford NG9 .... **209** F1
Arran Ct DE55 .... **159** D3
Arridge Rd DE23 .... **219** F3
Arrowscroft Way SK14 .... **9** E3
Arthington St S8 .... **43** D3
Arthur Ave NG9 .... **223** F4
Arthur Ct DE23 .... **219** D1
Arthur Hind Cl DE22 .... **218** C4
Arthur Mee Ctr
  (Coll of F Ed) The NG9 .... **223** E4
Arthur Mee Rd NG9 .... **223** F3
Arthur Short Cl S80 .... **82** A3
Arthur St Alfreton DE55 .... **159** D3
  Derby DE1 .... **267** B5
  Draycott DE72 .... **234** C4
  Linton DE11 .... **261** F4
  Mansfield NG18 .... **268** C3
  Nottingham NG7 .... **268** A2
  Pinxton NG16 .... **160** B2
Arthurs Ct DE13 .... **240** C1
Artic Way NG16 .... **195** E4
Artisan View S8 .... **43** D3
Arun Dale NG19 .... **136** B1
Arundel Ave DE3 .... **217** F1
Arundel Cl Chesterfield S41 .... **95** F4
  18 Sandiacre NG10 .... **56** B1
  Sandiacre NG10 .... **223** D2
Arundel Dr Derby DE21 .... **220** C3
  Mansfield NG19 .... **268** A4
Arundel Grange SK13 .... **17** D4
Arundel St Derby DE22 .... **218** B2
  Glossop SK13 .... **10** B1
  Nottingham NG7 .... **268** A2
Ascot Ave NG16 .... **195** F4
Ascot Cl
  Burton u T DE15 .... **248** A2
  West Hallam DE7 .... **207** E4
Ascot Dr DE24 .... **232** B4
Ascot Park Est NG10 .... **223** E4
Ascot Pl DE7 .... **208** B3
Ascott Dr DE11 .... **256** A4
Ash Acre DE56 .... **179** E2
Ash Cl Aston-on-T DE72 .... **246** A4
  Derby DE22 .... **204** B2
  Killamarsh S21 .... **60** B3
  Mottram in L SK14 .... **9** D2
  Pinxton NG16 .... **160** B1
Ash Cres Eckington S21 .... **59** D1
  Ripley DE5 .... **180** B4
Ash Croft Prim Sch
  DE24 .... **231** F1
Ash Gr Brinsley NG16 .... **182** B4
  Chinley SK23 .... **34** C1
  Long Eaton NG10 .... **236** B3
  Mansf Moor S43 .... **79** D2
  Sandiacre NG10 .... **223** D4
  Selston NG16 .... **171** F4
  Shirebrook NG20 .... **119** E3
  Stapleford NG9 .... **223** E3
Ash Grove La DE65 .... **241** E3
Ash La Eckington S18 .... **57** F2
  Hilton DE65 .... **228** C4
  Sutton on t H DE65 .... **228** C4
  Unstone S18 .... **57** F2
Ash Mount Rd NG16 .... **182** A2
Ash St Buxton SK17 .... **85** D3
  Ilkeston DE7 .... **194** C2
  Mosborough S20 .... **59** E4
  Shaw SK17 .... **85** E4
Ash Tree Cl
  Breadsall DE21 .... **205** F2
  Chesterfield S40 .... **95** E2
  Duffield DE56 .... **190** C3
  Swadlincote DE11 .... **255** F3
Ash Tree Cres NG19 .... **136** B3
Ash Tree Rd S43 .... **80** C1
Ash Vale S40 .... **95** D3
Ash View Cl DE65 .... **229** D2
Ashbourne Ave S45 .... **131** D3
Ashbourne Cl **4** S40 .... **95** D3
Ashbourne Ct
  Derby DE22 .... **218** C3
  Glossop SK13 .... **17** F4
Ashbourne Dr DE11 .... **256** A1
Ashbourne La
  Alstonefield DE6 .... **149** D1
  Chapel-en-le-F SK23 .... **47** E3

Ashbourne Rd
  Alstonefield DE6 .... **149** D2
  Belper DE56 .... **178** B2
  Burton u T DE15 .... **85** E2
  Church Broughton DE65 .... **213** F2
  Derby DE22 .... **218** B4
  Kirk Langley DE6 .... **202** B2
  Mackworth DE22 .... **217** F4
  Mayfield DE6 .... **184** B4
  Rocester ST14 .... **196** C2
  Shottle DE56 .... **177** E2
  Turnditch DE56 .... **177** E2
  Uttoxeter ST14 .... **210** A1
Ashbourne St
  Nottingham NG7 .... **268** A2
  Scarcliffe NG20 .... **119** F2
Ashbrook DE15 .... **248** A1
Ashbrook Ave DE72 .... **221** E1
Ashbrook Cl DE22 .... **204** B2
Ashbrook Inf & Jun Sch
  DE72 .... **221** D1
Ashbury Dr S8 .... **43** E1
Ashby Ave S8 .... **43** E1
Ashby Rd NG19 .... **136** B3
Ashby La DE11 .... **257** E1
Ashby Rd
  Blackfordby DE11, LE65 ... **257** E1
  Breedon on t H DE73 ...... **252** C1
  Burton u T DE15 .... **248** A1
  Melbourne DE73 .... **252** A3
  Moira DE12 .... **262** C2
  Ticknall DE73 .... **250** C1
Ashby Rd E DE15 .... **248** C1
Ashby St DE24 .... **232** C3
Ashcombe Gdns DE21 .... **206** A1
Ashcroft Cl DE24 .... **232** C4
Ashcroft Dr S41 .... **77** D1
Ashdale Cl DE15 .... **255** D4
Ashdale Rd DE7 .... **209** D3
Ashdown Dr S40 .... **95** E1
Ashe Pl DE23 .... **218** C1
Asher La DE5 .... **169** E3
Ashes Ave DE6 .... **175** F2
Ashes La
  Fenny Bentley DE6 .... **162** A1
  Glossop SK13 .... **10** A1
Ashfield Ave
  Derby DE21 .... **219** F4
  Mansfield NG18 .... **268** B4
  Somercotes DE55 .... **159** E1
Ashfield Cl S12 .... **43** F2
Ashfield Dr S12 .... **43** F2
Ashfield Gr SK6 .... **15** D1
Ashfield Rd
  Chapel-en-le-F SK23 .... **47** E3
  Chesterfield S41 .... **115** E4
  Hadfield SK13 .... **9** F2
  Nottingham NG2 .... **268** C1
Ashford Ave S42 .... **132** A4
Ashford CE Prim Sch
  DE45 .... **108** C4
Ashford Cl S18 .... **75** E4
Ashford Ct DE7 .... **207** E4
Ashford La DE45 .... **89** E1
Ashford Mews SK13 .... **9** E1
Ashford Pl DE7 .... **194** C3
Ashford Rd S18 .... **75** E4
Ashford Rise DE56 .... **179** E3
Ashford St ST4 .... **269** F2
Ashforth Ave DE75 .... **182** A2
Ashforth St NG3 .... **268** B2
Ashfurlong Cl S17 .... **55** F4
Ashfurlong Dr S17 .... **55** F4
Ashfurlong Rd S17 .... **55** F4
Ashgate Ave S42 .... **95** E2
Ashgate Croft Sch S40 .... **95** E2
Ashgate Inf & Jun Sch
  DE22 .... **218** B3
Ashgate Rd
  Chesterfield S40 .... **95** E2
  Old Brampton S40 .... **95** E2
Ashgate Valley Rd S40 .... **95** E2
Ashgrove Ct DE21 .... **206** A1
Ashland Rd S21 .... **59** F2
Ashlands Ave ST14 .... **269** D2
Ashlands Cres ST14 .... **269** D2
Ashlands Rd ST14 .... **269** D2
Ashlea Dr DE6 .... **184** B4
Ashlea Wlk S43 .... **81** D3
Ashleigh Ave
  Glossop SK13 .... **10** A1
  Sheffield S12 .... **43** F3
  Swadlincote DE11 .... **255** F3
Ashleigh Cl S41 .... **77** D2
Ashleigh Croft S12 .... **43** F3
Ashleigh Ct S21 .... **59** E3
Ashleigh Dr Derby DE73 ... **232** C1
  Sheffield S12 .... **43** F3
Ashleigh Pl S12 .... **43** F3
Ashleigh Rd S43 .... **80** A4
Ashley Cl Kilnmarsh S21 .... **60** B3
  Overseal DE12 .... **262** A2
  Tansley DE4 .... **144** A2
Ashley Ct DE15 .... **248** A2
Ashley La S21 .... **60** B3
Ashley St Derby DE22 .... **218** B3
  Nottingham NG3 .... **268** C2
Ashlyn Rd DE21 .... **267** D3
Ashmeadow Dr DE72 .... **221** D1
Ashmeadow Ct DE6 .... **185** E4
Ashmore Ave S21 .... **59** D1
Ashop Rd DE56 .... **179** E3
Ashopton Ave DE23 .... **231** D4
Ashopton Dr S33 .... **40** A2
Ashopton Rd S33 .... **40** A2
Ashover Cl DE21 .... **219** F4
Ashover New Rd DE55 .... **145** E4
Ashover Prim Sch S45 .... **129** F2

Ashover Rd Alton S45 .... **130** C3
  Ashover S45 .... **129** F2
  Clay Cross S42 .... **130** C3
  Derby, Allestree DE22 ...... **204** B1
  Derby, Chaddesden DE21 ... **219** F4
  Staveley S43 .... **97** E3
  Swadlincote DE11 .... **255** F3
  Tupton S42 .... **131** D4
Ashton Cl Chesterfield S40 .. **114** B4
  Derby DE3 .... **217** E2
  Killamarsh S21 .... **60** B3
  Swanwick DE55 .... **170** A4
Ashton Gdns Clay Cross S42 **131** D3
  Glossop SK13 .... **17** E4
Ashton St S43 .... **17** E4
Ashton Way DE56 .... **179** E2
Ashtree Ave DE24 .... **232** A3
Ashurst Cl S40 .... **95** D3
Ashwin Cl NG10 .... **236** A4
Ashwater Cl DE24 .... **231** F1
Ashwell Ave NG19 .... **136** C3
Ashwood Buxton SK17 ...... **85** E4
  Mansfield Woodhouse NG19 **136** C3
Ashwood Rd Buxton SK17 .. **66** C1
  Disley SK12 .... **32** B3
Ashworth Ave
  Burton u T DE15 .... **248** B1
  Derby DE21 .... **219** F3
Ashworth La SK14 .... **9** D2
Ashworth St ST4 .... **269** F1
Asker La DE4 .... **143** E3
Askerfield Ave DE22 .... **204** B2
Askew Gr DE65 .... **242** B1
Asline Rd S2 .... **43** D4
Aspen Cl Buxton SK17 ...... **66** A1
  Killamarsh S21 .... **60** B3
Aspen Ct NG19 .... **136** C1
Aspen Dr DE21 .... **220** B2
Aspen Rd S21 .... **59** D1
Aspen Rise DE55 .... **146** B1
Aspen Way SK6 .... **32** A4
Aspenshaw Rd SK22 .... **24** C2
Aspley Cl S41 .... **95** F3
Astcote Cl DE75 .... **182** A1
Asterdale Prim Sch DE21 . **220** C2
Asterdale View DE21 .... **220** C2
Astil St DE15 .... **254** C4
Astlow Dr DE56 .... **179** E3
Aston Cl Derby DE73 .... **245** D4
  Dronfield S18 .... **57** E2
Aston Ct Ilkeston DE7 .... **194** C1
  Staveley S43 .... **78** C1
Aston Gn NG9 .... **223** F2
Aston Hall Dr DE72 .... **246** A4
Aston Hall Hospl DE72 .... **246** A3
Aston La Derby DE73 .... **233** D1
  Hope S33 .... **39** D2
  Shardlow DE72 .... **234** C1
  Sudbury DE6 .... **226** A3
  Wensley DE4 .... **142** B4
Aston Rd DE23 .... **231** E3
Aston-on-Trent Prim Sch
  DE72 .... **246** A4
Astonville Park Rd DE72 ... **232** C1
Astwith Cl S44 .... **116** C1
Astwith La S44, S45 .... **133** D3
Atchison Gdns DE21 .... **220** A4
Atherfield Gdns NG16 .... **182** C2
Atherton Ave SK14 .... **9** D2
Atherton Cl S2 .... **43** F3
Atherton Gr SK14 .... **9** D2
Atherton Rd Ilkeston DE7 .. **194** B2
  Sheffield S2 .... **43** F3
  Shipley DE7 .... **194** B2
Athlestan Way DE13 .... **240** B1
Athlone Cl DE21 .... **219** E4
Athol Cl Chesterfield S40 ... **114** A4
  Derby DE24 .... **231** E2
Atkin Pl S2 .... **43** D4
Atkins Way ST14 .... **196** C2
Atlantic Dr S8 .... **56** C3
Atlantic Rd S8 .... **56** B3
Atlantic Way S8 .... **56** C3
Atlantic Wlk S8 .... **56** C3
Atlow Brow DE6 .... **173** E2
Atlow Cl S40 .... **95** D3
Atlow La DE6 .... **175** D3
Atlow Rd DE21 .... **219** F4
Attenborough Nature
  Reserve NG9 .... **237** E4
Attewell Cl DE72 .... **235** D4
Attewell Rd NG16 .... **195** D3
Attlebridge Cl DE21 .... **219** E4
Attlee Rd S43 .... **97** D4
Atworth Gr DE23 .... **230** C3
Auburn Cl DE7 .... **207** D4
Auckland Cl DE7 .... **217** F2
Auden Cl DE65 .... **227** D4
Audens Way DE11 .... **256** B3
Audley Cl DE7 .... **194** B2
Audrey Cres NG19 .... **136** B3
Audrey Dr DE21 .... **220** A4
Aughton Cl S13 .... **44** B4
Aughton Cres S13 .... **44** B4
Aughton Dr S13 .... **44** B4
Augusta St DE23 .... **219** D1
Aukland Dr S20 .... **59** F3
Aukland Rise S20 .... **59** F3
Aukland Way S20 .... **59** F3
Ault Hucknall La S44 .... **134** A4
Aults Cl DE65 .... **230** B1
Austen Ave Derby DE23 ... **231** D4
  Long Eaton NG10 .... **236** C4
Austin Friars ST17 .... **269** E3
Austin Sq DE23 .... **231** F4

Austin St NG20 .... **120** A2
Austins Dr NG10 .... **223** D2
Austwick Gr ST4 .... **269** D1
Autumn Gr DE21 .... **219** F3
Avarne Pl **8** ST16 .... **269** E4
Avenue 1 S41 .... **115** D4
Avenue 2 S41 .... **115** D4
Avenue 3 S41 .... **115** D4
Avenue 4 S41 .... **115** D4
Avenue 5 S41 .... **115** D4
Avenue 6 S41 .... **115** D4
Avenue 7 S41 .... **115** D4
Avenue 8 S41 .... **115** D4
Avenue Cl S32 .... **72** A2
Avenue Rd Chesterfield S41 **96** A4
  Duffield DE56 .... **190** C3
Avenue The Bakewell DE45 **109** E3
  Belper DE56 .... **178** C1
  Chapel-en-le-F SK23 .... **46** C1
  Derby, Chaddesden DE21 ... **219** F3
  Derby, The Holmes DE1 .... **267** B2
  Dronfield S18 .... **57** D1
  Hadfield SK13 .... **10** A2
  Northwood DE4 .... **127** D3
  Spinkhill S21 .... **60** B1
  Stoney Middleton S32 ...... **72** A2
  Tissington DE6 .... **162** A3
  Weston-on-T DE72 .... **245** F3
Averham Cl Derby DE21 ... **206** A1
  Swadlincote DE11 .... **256** A2
Aviemore Way DE24 .... **231** F2
Avis Ave DE75 .... **193** F4
Avocet Ct **2** DE24 .... **231** E2
Avon Cl Derby DE24 .... **231** E1
  Dronfield S18 .... **57** D2
  Swadlincote DE11 .... **256** A3
Avon Rise ST 16 .... **269** F4
Avon St DE24 .... **232** C4
Avon Way Burton u T DE15 . **248** A2
  Hilton DE65 .... **228** C1
Avondale Cl NG10 .... **236** A3
Avondale Rd Bolsover S44 . **118** A4
  Chesterfield S40 .... **266** A4
  Derby, Rose Hill DE23 ...... **267** B1
  Derby, Spondon DE21 ...... **220** B3
  Ilkeston DE7 .... **208** B3
  Staveley S43 .... **97** E4
Avonlea Cl DE7 .... **209** D3
Avonmouth Dr DE24 .... **232** C4
Awdishaw La DE6 .... **213** E3
Awsworth Inf Sch NG16 .. **195** E2
Awsworth Jun Sch NG16 .. **195** E2
Awsworth La
  Awsworth NG16 .... **195** E3
  Cossall Marsh NG16 .... **195** E2
  Kimberley NG16 .... **195** E3
Awsworth Rd DE7 .... **194** C1
Aycliffe Gdns DE24 .... **232** C2
Aylesbury Ave DE21 .... **219** F4
Aylward Cl S2 .... **43** F4
Aylward Rd S2 .... **43** F4
Ayncourt Rd S42 .... **132** A4
Ayr Cl DE21 .... **220** B2
Ayr St NG7 .... **268** A2
Azalea Ave DE55 .... **170** A4
Azalea Cl DE55 .... **159** F2
Azalea Ct NG16 .... **195** E4

Babbacombe Cl DE24 .... **233** E4
Babbington Cl DE13 .... **239** E3
Babbington La NG16 .... **195** F2
Babbington St DE55 .... **148** A3
Babbs La DE6 .... **211** E1
Babington Cl DE73 .... **233** D4
Babington Hospl DE56 .... **178** C1
Babington La DE1 .... **267** B2
Babworth Ct NG18 .... **268** C4
Bacchus Way DE55 .... **147** D3
Back Bridge St SK22 .... **24** B1
Back Browning St ST16 ... **269** D4
Back Croft S45 .... **131** F1
Back Jodrell St S22 .... **24** B1
Back La Alderwasley DE56 . **166** C4
  Biggin SK17 .... **138** A2
  Brackenfield DE55 .... **146** A1
  Calow S44 .... **96** C3
  Castle Donington DE74 .... **247** D3
  Darley Dale DE4 .... **127** F2
  Derby DE73 .... **233** D1
  Elton DE4 .... **140** C3
  Glapwell S44 .... **118** A1
  Glossop SK13 .... **16** C2
  Hartshorne S17 .... **55** F4
  Hathersage S32 .... **53** D4
  Hilton DE65 .... **228** B1
  Ilkeston DE7 .... **194** B2
  Mottram in L SK14 .... **9** D2
  Palterton S44 .... **118** A3
  Pentrich DE5 .... **169** E3
  Pinxton NG16 .... **132** B1
  Roston DE6 .... **197** D4
  Spout DE56 .... **166** B2
  Sutton in A NG17 .... **148** B2
  Thorpe Salvin S80 .... **63** D3
  Thurvaston DE6 .... **215** D2
  Tibshelf DE55 .... **147** F3
  Unstone S18 .... **57** F1
  Wessington DE55 .... **157** F4
  Youlgreave DE45 .... **125** D3
Back Mellor Rd SK22 .... **24** B1
Back Moor SK14 .... **9** D2
Back Sitwell St DE1 .... **267** B2
Back South St S43 .... **78** C2
Back St Bakewell DE45 ...... **109** D3
  Winster DE4 .... **141** D3
Back Union Rd SK22 .... **33** C4

Back Wyver La DE56 .... **178** C3
Backhill La DE6 .... **151** D1
Backhouse La DE72 .... **221** D4
Backmoor Cres S8 .... **43** E1
Backmoor Rd S8 .... **43** E1
Bacon Cl NG16 .... **195** D4
Bacon La DE5 .... **169** D3
Baden Powell Ave S40 .... **266** B1
Baden Powell Rd S40 ...... **266** B1
Badger Cl Chesterfield S40 **114** A4
  Derby DE21 .... **220** C3
Badger La Ashover DE55 .. **145** E4
  Stretton DE55 .... **145** E4
Badgery Cl ST14 .... **210** A1
Bag La Marchington ST14 .. **224** C1
  Roston DE6 .... **197** F4
Bage Hill S42 .... **113** F3
Baggaley Cres NG19 .... **136** A1
Bagot St DE7 .... **207** E4
Bagshaw Hill DE45 .... **109** E3
Bagshaw La S21 .... **48** A3
Bagshaw St Derby DE24 ... **232** C4
  Pleasleyhill NG19 .... **135** D3
Bagshaw's Rd S12 .... **44** A3
Bagshawe Ave S43 .... **46** C3
Bagshawe Cavern S33 .... **51** D3
Bagthorp La S42 .... **94** A2
Bagthorpe La S42 .... **262** A2
Bailey Ave DE12 .... **262** A4
Bailey Brook Bsns NG16 .. **182** A2
Bailey Brook Dr NG16 ...... **182** A2
Bailey Brook Ind Est
  DE75, NG16 .... **182** A1
Bailey Brook Wlk NG16 ... **182** A2
Bailey Cres NG19 .... **268** A4
Bailey Dr S13 .... **60** C4
Bailey Gr SK17 .... **85** F4
Bailey Grove Rd NG16 .... **182** B1
Bailey St Derby DE22 ...... **267** A1
  Stafford ST17 .... **269** D3
  Stapleford NG9 .... **223** E3
Bainbridge Rd S44 .... **98** C2
Bainbridge St DE23 .... **219** D2
Baines Wood Cl S41 .... **95** D4
Bains Dr DE72 .... **221** E1
Bakeacre La DE65 .... **230** C2
Baker Ave DE75 .... **194** A4
Baker Cl Somercotes DE55 . **170** B4
  Stanley DE7 .... **193** D1
Baker Dr S21 .... **60** B3
Baker Rd NG16 .... **136** B3
Baker St Burton u T DE15 ... **254** C4
  Creswell S80 .... **81** F1
  Derby DE24 .... **232** C4
  Ilkeston DE7 .... **194** C1
  Swadlincote DE11 .... **256** B2
Baker's La Cromford DE4 .. **155** D3
  Doveridge DE6 .... **211** E1
Bakers Hill DE56 .... **168** C1
Bakers La DE4 .... **156** A4
Bakestone Moor S80 .... **81** F3
Bakewell CE Inf Sch
  DE45 .... **109** E3
Bakewell Cl DE21 .... **217** F2
Bakewell Dr DE14 .... **247** D1
Bakewell Gn DE11 .... **255** F3
Bakewell Meth Jun Sch
  DE45 .... **109** E2
Bakewell Mews SK13 .... **9** E1
Bakewell Rd Baslow DE45 .. **91** E2
  Buxton SK17 .... **85** E4
  Darley Dale DE4 .... **142** C4
  Long Eaton NG10 .... **236** C3
  Matlock DE4 .... **143** D3
  Over Haddon DE45 .... **109** D1
Bakewell St Derby DE22 ... **218** B3
  Stoke-on-T ST4 .... **269** D1
Balaclava Rd DE23 .... **232** A4
Balderton Ct NG19 .... **268** A4
Baldwin St NG7 .... **268** A2
Balfour Rd Derby DE23 .... **232** A4
  Stapleford NG9 .... **223** E3
Balham Wlk DE22 .... **218** A3
Balk Pas ST16 .... **269** D4
Ball Hill DE55 .... **160** B3
Ball La DE7 .... **234** A3
Ballacraine Dr DE5 .... **169** F1
Ballards Way DE72 .... **221** E2
Ballater Cl DE24 .... **231** F2
Ballery Cl DE21 .... **205** F1
Balmoak La S41 .... **96** B3
Balmoral Cl Derby DE23 .... **231** E2
  Mansfield Woodhouse NG19 **136** C2
  Swadlincote DE11 .... **223** D2
Balmoral Cres S18 .... **56** B1
Balmoral Dr NG9 .... **135** F1
Balmoral Rd
  Borrowash DE72 .... **221** E1
  Burton u T DE15 .... **248** A2
  Ilkeston DE7 .... **208** B3
  Nottingham NG4 .... **268** A2
Balmoral Way S43 .... **77** F2
Baltimore Cl DE11 .... **256** A4
Bamburgh Cl DE24 .... **231** E2
Bamford Ave Derby DE23 .. **231** F4
  North Wingfield S42 .... **131** F4
Bamford La SK13 .... **9** F1
Bamford Mews SK13 .... **9** F1
Bamford Prim Sch S33 .... **40** A2
Bamford St S43 .... **97** E3
Bamford St
  Chesterfield S43 .... **77** E2
  Newton DE55 .... **148** A2
  Ripley DE5 .... **180** B4
Bamford Sta S33 .... **40** A1

amsbrook La S43 ... 80 B1
anbury Ave NG9 ... 223 F2
ancroft Cl DE65 ... 228 B1
ancroft Dr DE22 ... 204 B2
ancroft La NG18 ... 268 A4
ancroft The DE65 ... 229 D2
angor St DE21 ... 219 F4
ank Cl Bolsover S44 ... 99 D2
  Creswell S80 ... 100 B4
  Shirebrook NG20 ... 119 F2
Tibshelf DE55 ... 147 F3
ank Gdns DE4 ... 10 A4
ank La S43 ... 80 C4
ank Pas 5 S18 ... 269 E4
ank Rd Chesterfield S41 ... 96 A3
  Matlock DE4 ... 143 D3
ank Side Derby DE22 ... 204 C1
  Hartington S017 ... 137 E3
ank St Brimington S43 ... 96 B4
  Broadbottom SK14 ... 16 A4
  Chesterfield S40 ... 95 D2
  Glossop SK13 ... 10 A3
  Hadfield SK13 ... 9 F2
  Hayfield SK22 ... 25 E2
  Langley Mill NG16 ... 182 B2
  Long Eaton NG10 ... 236 C4
  Somercotes DE55 ... 170 B4
  Swadlincote DE11 ... 262 A4
ank The Bonsall DE4 ... 142 B1
  Glossop SK13 ... 17 E4
  Stoney Middleton S32 ... 71 F2
ank Top La S32 ... 72 B4
ank Vale Rd SK22 ... 25 E2
ank View SK17 ... 69 D3
ank View Rd Derby DE22 ... 218 C4
  Nether Heage DE56 ... 168 B1
ank Wood Cl S40 ... 95 D3
  Swadlincote DE11 ... 10 A3
ankenvall La DE6 ... 183 E4
ankfield Dr Derby DE21 ... 220 C2
  Ilkeston DE7 ... 208 A3
ankgate SK14 ... 16 A4
ankholmes Cl DE24 ... 231 F1
anks Rd NG9 ... 223 F1
anksburn Cl DE75 ... 181 E1
ankside DE45 ... 125 D3
ankside Cl SK6 ... 15 C1
ankwood Cl S40 ... 10 A2
ankwood Cl S14 ... 43 E3
ankwood Prim Sch S14 ... 43 E3
ankwood Rd S14 ... 43 E3
anmoor La S32 ... 52 C4
annell's La DE73 ... 229 F4
annels Ave DE23 ... 231 D4
anton's La DE73 ... 251 D2
anwell Cl DE7 ... 217 E2
ar Croft S40 ... 95 E3
ar gate S33 ... 38 B1
ar Rd Baslow DE45 ... 91 F3
  Burbage S017 ... 72 C1
arber Cl DE7 ... 194 C2
arber St SK13 ... 10 A3
arbon Cl S40 ... 95 E3
arber's La S21 ... 60 B4
archester Cl DE21 ... 206 A1
arclay Ct DE7 ... 194 B2
arden Dr DE22 ... 204 C2
ardolph Cl DE11 ... 255 F2
ardsey Cl DE21 ... 206 A2
are La DE72 ... 221 E3
arf Cl DE3 ... 217 F1
argate Cl DE56 ... 179 E1
argate La DE55 ... 242 A3
argate Rd DE56 ... 179 D1
arker Fold S40 ... 95 E2
arker Gate Ilkeston DE7 ... 194 C1
  Nottingham NG1 ... 95 E2
arker St NG17 ... 148 C2
arklam Cl DE12 ... 262 C1
arlborough Hall Sch S43 ... 61 D1
arlborough Prim Sch ... 80 A4

Barnard Ave S18 ... 57 E2
Barnard Rd DE21 ... 205 E1
Barnes Ave S18 ... 56 C1
Barnes Gn DE22 ... 218 A4
Barnes La S18 ... 96 C1
Barnes Rd S41 ... 96 C1
Barnfield ST4 ... 269 D1
Barnfield Cl
  Holmewood S42 ... 132 C4
  Staveley S43 ... 78 C1
Barnfield Wlk S43 ... 78 C1
Barnfields S32 ... 52 C4
Barnham Cl S40 ... 114 A4
Barnfield Gr DE23 ... 231 D4
Barnsfold Ct SK22 ... 25 E2
Barnsley La
  Idridgehay DE56 ... 165 F1
  Spout DE56 ... 165 F1
Barnstaple Cl DE21 ... 206 A1
Barnston Rd NG2 ... 268 C2
Barnwell Cl ST14 ... 210 A2
Barnwell La DE4 ... 155 D3
Barnwood Cl DE3 ... 217 E1
Baron Cl DE21 ... 206 B2
Barrack Rd S18 ... 58 A1
Barrack Yd DE55 ... 170 B4
Barracks Sq S40 ... 268 B2
Barratt Rd S21 ... 59 E1
Barrett St DE24 ... 233 D4
Barrie Dr DE21 ... 231 F3
Barringer Rd NG19 ... 136 B1
Barrington Cl DE13 ... 240 B2
Barron's Way DE72 ... 221 E1
Barroon The DE74 ... 247 D2
Barrow Hill Prim Sch S43 ... 78 A2
Barrow La DE73 ... 244 B3
Barrow St S41 ... 78 C1
Barrows Hill La NG16 ... 171 E3
Barry Rd S43 ... 96 C2
Barson Gr SK17 ... 85 F1
Bartle Ave S12 ... 43 F2
Bartle Dr S12 ... 43 F2
Bartle Rd S12 ... 43 F2
Bartle Way S12 ... 43 F2
Barton Cl S21 ... 220 C3
Barton Cres S40 ... 95 D3
Barton Hill DE4 ... 126 B1
Barton Knoll DE56 ... 179 E2
Barton Knowle DE56 ... 179 E2
Barton Rd
  Long Eaton NG10 ... 237 D3
  Sheffield S8 ... 43 E4
Barton St Burton u T DE14 ... 254 B4
  Clowne S43 ... 80 C2
Barton Turn DE13 ... 44 A2
Basegreen Ave S12 ... 44 B2
Basegreen Cl S12 ... 44 B2
Basegreen Cres S12 ... 44 B2
Basegreen Dr S12 ... 44 B2
Basegreen Pl S12 ... 44 B2
Basegreen Rd S12 ... 44 B2
Basegreen Way S12 ... 44 B2
Basildon Cl DE24 ... 232 C3
Basingwerke Ct SK22 ... 25 E2
Baslow Ave DE55 ... 148 B2
Baslow Cl NG10 ... 236 A3
Baslow Dr DE22 ... 204 C2
Baslow Gn DE22 ... 255 F3
Baslow Gr DE21 ... 85 F3
Baslow Gr SK17 ... 85 F3
Baslow Mews SK13 ... 9 E1
Baslow Rd Bakewell DE45 ... 109 E4
  Curbar S32 ... 72 B1
  Holymoorside S42 ... 94 B1
  Totley S17 ... 55 E2
Bass St DE22 ... 218 B3
Bass's Cres DE11 ... 256 A1
Bassett Cl NG16 ... 195 F4
Bassett La S10 ... 42 C3
Bassett Rd NG16 ... 195 F4
Bassett The NG20 ... 119 E3
Bassettbarn La S45 ... 145 E1
Bassford Ave DE75 ... 181 F1
Bassingham Cl DE21 ... 206 A1
Bassledene Rd S2 ... 224 A4
Batch La DE6 ... 224 A4
Bateman St S43 ... 77 E2
Bateman St DE23 ... 219 E2
Batemoor Cl S8 ... 57 D3
Batemoor Dr S8 ... 57 D3
Batemoor Pl S8 ... 57 D3
Batemoor Rd S8 ... 57 D3
Batemoor Wlk S8 ... 57 D3
Bath La Ashover S45 ... 129 F3
  Mansfield NG18 ... 268 C4
  Market Warsop NG20 ... 120 B1
  Moira DE12 ... 262 B2
Bath Rd DE21 ... 217 F1
Bath St Bakewell DE45 ... 109 E3
  Derby DE1 ... 267 B4
  Ilkeston DE7 ... 194 C1
  Mansfield NG18 ... 268 B3
  Nottingham NG1 ... 268 B2
  Stoke-on-T ST4 ... 269 E2
Bath Terr ST4 ... 269 E2
Batham Gate Bradwell SK17 ... 50 A2
  Peak Forest SK17 ... 48 C1
Batham Gate Rd SK17 ... 67 D2
Bathurst Rd S44 ... 118 A4
Bathurst Terr NG20 ... 119 D2
Batley La NG19 ... 135 E1
Baum's La NG18 ... 268 B3
Bauk La Beeston NG9 ... 223 F4
  Hathersage S32 ... 41 D1
Baverstock Cl DE73 ... 232 C2
Baxter Hill NG19 ... 134 C2

arlborough Rd S43 ... 80 B3
arley Cl DE7 ... 232 C1
  South Normanton DE55 ... 160 B2
arley Cl DE21 ... 179 D1
arley Croft DE56 ... 179 D1
arley Dale Dr NG9 ... 223 E1
arley La DE4 ... 95 D3
arleycroft Cl
  Burton u T DE15 ... 248 A1
  Derby DE21 ... 206 A1
arleycroft S12 ... 194 B1
arling Dr Ilkeston DE7 ... 194 B1
  Stapleford NG9 ... 195 D2
arlow Dr N NG16 ... 195 D2
arlow Dr S NG16 ... 195 D2
arlow Lees La S18 ... 75 F4
arlow Rd Barlow S42 ... 94 C4
  Chapel-en-le-F SK23 ... 47 E3
  Staveley S43 ... 267 D1
arlow St DE7 ... 194 C1
arlow View S18 ... 76 A4
arlow Wood Dr SK6 ... 23 D2
arms Way SK17 ... 66 B1
arn Cl
  Castle Donington DE74 ... 247 D2
  Chesterfield S40 ... 95 E3
  Glossop SK13 ... 17 E4
  Quarndon DE22 ... 204 B3

Baxter Sq DE23 ... 231 F3
Bay Ct S21 ... 60 B3
Baycliffe Dr S40 ... 95 E2
Beacon Dr DE21 ... 206 A2
Baydale Croft S20 ... 59 E4
Bayswater Cl DE22 ... 217 F3
Bayswater Rd NG16 ... 195 F4
Bazley Rd S2 ... 43 F3
Beacomfold SK6 ... 15 D2
Beacon Dr DE13 ... 240 A2
Beacon Hill Rise NG3 ... 268 C2
Beacon Rd DE21 ... 206 A2
Beaconsfield St NG10 ... 236 C4
Bean Cl DE13 ... 240 A1
Beard Cres SK22 ... 33 E4
Beardall St 5 NG18 ... 268 B4
Beardmore Cl DE21 ... 205 F1
Beards Rd DE21 ... 256 A3
Bearwood Hill Rd DE15 ... 248 A3
Beast Market Hill NG1 ... 268 B1
Beatrix Dr SK13 ... 9 F2
Beatty St DE24 ... 232 C4
Beatty Wlk DE7 ... 194 C2
Beauchief Abbey La S8 ... 56 B4
Beauchief Dr S17 ... 56 B4
Beauchief Gdns DE55 ... 170 B4
Beaufit La NG16 ... 160 C1
Beaufort Ct Ind Est DE21 ... 219 E4
Beaufort Inf & Jun Schs ... 219 E4
Beaufort Rd
  Burton u T DE15 ... 248 A1
  Derby DE21 ... 219 E4
Beaufort St DE21 ... 219 E4
Beaulieu Way DE55 ... 170 A4
Beaumaris Ct DE21 ... 220 C3
Beaumont Cl
  Barrow u T DE73 ... 244 A3
  Belper DE56 ... 179 E2
  Stapleford NG9 ... 209 F1
Beaumont St NG2 ... 268 C1
Beaumont Wlk DE23 ... 231 F3
Beauvale Dr DE7 ... 194 C3
Beaurepaire Cres DE56 ... 179 D3
Beauvale Rd NG2 ... 268 A4
Beaver Cl DE7 ... 194 C3
Becher St DE23 ... 219 D1
Beck Cl S44 ... 99 E1
Beck Cres NG19 ... 268 A4
Beck St NG3 ... 268 C2
Beckenham Way DE22 ... 218 A3
Becket Ave S8 ... 56 B3
Becket Cres S8 ... 56 B3
Becket Rd S8 ... 56 C3
Becket St DE1 ... 267 B3
Becket Well La DE1 ... 267 B3
Becket Wlk S8 ... 56 C3
Beckett Ave NG19 ... 135 F1
Beckford Rd NG2 ... 268 A4
Beckingham Ct NG19 ... 268 A4
Beckitt Cl DE24 ... 233 D4
Becksitch La DE56 ... 178 C1
Bedehouse La S44 ... 155 D3
Bedford Ave S17 16 ... 269 F4
Bedford Cl DE21 ... 205 F1
Bedford Ct NG9 ... 209 F1
Bedford St DE22 ... 218 B2
Bedgrave Cl S21 ... 60 C4
Bee Hives The DE11 ... 255 F4
Beech Ave Alfreton DE55 ... 159 D3
  Borrowash DE72 ... 235 D4
  Breaston DE72 ... 235 E4
  Creswell S80 ... 81 F1
  Derby DE21 ... 233 D4
  Glossop SK13 ... 17 C4
  Holbrook DE56 ... 191 E4
  Hulland Ward DE6 ... 175 F2
  Long Eaton NG10 ... 236 B4
  Mansfield NG18 ... 268 A3
  Melbourne DE73 ... 252 A4
  New Mills SK22 ... 24 B1
  Pinxton NG16 ... 160 C2
  Quarndon DE22 ... 204 B3
  Sandiacre NG10 ... 223 D4
  Willington DE65 ... 242 B3
Beech Cl Belper DE56 ... 179 D2
  Kilburn DE56 ... 192 A4
Beech Cres Eckington S21 ... 59 D1
  Glapwell S44 ... 134 A4
  Killamarsh S21 ... 60 B3
Beech Ct DE21 ... 220 B3
Beech Dr Ashbourne DE6 ... 185 D1
  Derby DE22 ... 204 C1
  Etwall DE65 ... 229 E2
  Findern DE65 ... 230 C1
  Long Duckmanton S44 ... 97 E1
  Woodville DE11 ... 256 B3
Beech Gdns DE24 ... 233 D4
Beech Gr
  Long Duckmanton S44 ... 98 A2
  South Normanton DE55 ... 160 A3
  Swadlincote DE11 ... 255 F4
Beech Hill Ave NG19 ... 135 F1
Beech Hill Cres NG19 ... 135 F1
Beech Hill Dr NG19 ... 135 F1
Beech Hill Sch NG19 ... 135 F1
Beech La Burton u T DE13 ... 240 C1
  Dove Holes SK17 ... 66 C4
  Hartshorne DE11 ... 257 D4
Beech Rd SK23 ... 45 E3
Beech Rise SK23 ... 45 E3
Beech St S43 ... 80 C3
Beech Tree Ave NG19 ... 136 A3
Beech Tree Dr S43 ... 80 C4
Beech Way Clay Cross S45 ... 131 F1
  Dronfield S18 ... 57 D2

Beech Wlk Cromford DE4 ... 155 D3
  Derby DE23 ... 218 B1
Beechcroft DE21 ... 205 E2
Beechcroft Ave ST17 ... 269 D3
Beechdale Cl S40 ... 95 E2
Beechdale Rd NG19 ... 136 C1
Beeches Ave Derby DE21 ... 220 B3
  Sheffield S2 ... 43 E4
Beeches Dr S2 ... 43 E4
Beeches The Crich DE4 ... 156 C1
  Heanor DE75 ... 193 E4
Beechfield Rd SK13 ... 9 F2
Beechley Dr DE21 ... 206 A1
Beechwood SK13 ... 16 C4
Beechwood Cl DE23 ... 231 E4
Beechwood Cres DE23 ... 23 D3
Beechwood Dr DE18 ... 56 C1
Beehive Yd S40 ... 95 E1
Beeley Cl Belper DE56 ... 179 E3
  Creswell S80 ... 81 E1
  Derby, Allestree DE22 ... 204 B1
  Derby, Oakwood DE22 ... 205 F1
  North Wingfield S42 ... 132 A4
  Staveley S43 ... 97 E3
Beeley La DE4 ... 112 A2
Beeley La DE4 ... 114 A4
Beeley Way S43 ... 97 E3
Beelow Cl SK17 ... 47 F1
Beeston S18 ... 56 B1
Beestone Cl S18 ... 56 B1
Beetwell St S40 ... 266 B2
Beggarway La DE45 ... 90 A3
Beighton St DE5 ... 169 F1
Beldon Cl S2 ... 43 E4
Beldon Pl S2 ... 43 E4
Beldon Rd DE21 ... 220 A2
Belfield St DE7 ... 181 E2
Belfield Rd Etwall DE65 ... 229 E2
  Swadlincote DE11 ... 256 A3
Belfit Dr DE22 ... 114 C1
Belfry Cl DE3 ... 82 A3
Belfry Cl DE13 ... 217 F1
Belfry The DE13 ... 240 B1
Belgrave Ave DE23 ... 34 C1
Belgrave Cl DE56 ... 179 E3
Belgrave Rd S8 ... 43 D4
Belgrave St DE23 ... 267 B1
Belklane Dr S21 ... 60 C4
Bell Ave DE72 ... 246 A4
Bell La Bonsall DE4 ... 142 B1
  Doveridge DE6 ... 224 B4
Belland La S33 ... 268 B1
Belle Acre Cl DE56 ... 178 C2
Belle Gate NG1 ... 173 D1
Belle Vue Ave DE5 ... 169 F4
Belle Vue Cl S43 ... 96 B4
Belledere Cl DE55 ... 169 F4
Bellevue Cl NG3 ... 268 C2
Bellhouse La S43 ... 78 C2
Bellingham Ct DE22 ... 204 B1
Bells End Rd DE12 ... 253 E1
Bellsfield Cl S80 ... 82 A3
Belmont Ave DE72 ... 235 F4
Belmont Dr
  Borrowash DE72 ... 221 D1
  Marple SK6 ... 15 D1
  Sandiacre S43 ... 78 C1
Belmont Prim Sch DE11 ... 256 B2
Belmont Rd DE11 ... 256 B2
Belmont St DE7 ... 239 D2
Belmont Terr 2 SK17 ... 85 D3
Belond La S45 ... 178 C3
Belper La DE56 ... 178 C3
Belper Rd Ashbourne DE6 ... 173 F1
  Derby DE21 ... 218 C4
  Holbrook DE56 ... 191 E4
  Kilburn DE56 ... 179 F1
  Morley DE7 ... 192 C1
  Shirland DE55 ... 146 B1
  Stanley DE7 ... 193 D1
  West Hallam DE7 ... 207 F4
Belper Sch DE56 ... 179 D1
Belper Sports Ctr DE56 ... 179 E2
Belper St Ilkeston DE7 ... 208 C4
  Mansfield NG18 ... 268 B3
Belper Sta DE56 ... 179 D2
Belper Way NG18 ... 268 C4
Belsize Cl DE22 ... 217 F3
Belton Cl Dronfield S18 ... 56 B1
  Sandiacre NG10 ... 223 D2
Belton Dr DE5 ... 169 F4
Belvedere Ave S40 ... 114 C4
Belvedere Cl
  Chesterfield S40 ... 114 A4
  Derby DE21 ... 217 E2
Belvedere Rd DE11 ... 256 C1
Belvedere St NG18 ... 268 B3
Belvoir Cl Breaston DE72 ... 235 E4
  Ilkeston DE7 ... 208 B3
  Long Eaton NG10 ... 236 C3
Belvoir Cres DE11 ... 256 A3
Belvoir Cl DE15 ... 248 A3
Belvoir Rd DE11 ... 256 C1
Belvoir St DE55 ... 159 D3
Belvoir Way DE55 ... 159 E1
Bemrose Com Sch DE22 ... 218 B2
Bemrose Gate S33 ... 40 A3
Bemrose Mews DE22 ... 218 B2
Bemrose Rd DE24 ... 232 C4
Benbow Ave DE73 ... 252 A4
Bench Rd SK17 ... 15 F2
Bend Oak Dr DE15 ... 248 B2
Bend Oak Jun Sch DE15 ... 248 B2
Bendall Gn DE23 ... 231 E3
Benenden Cl ST17 ... 269 D3

Beninmoor Way S40 ... 114 C4
Benjamin Outram
  Bsns Ctr DE5 ... 180 C4
Benmore Ct DE21 ... 206 A2
Benner Ave DE7 ... 209 D3
Bennerley Ave DE7 ... 194 C2
Bennerley Fields Sch
  DE7 ... 194 C2
Bennerley Sch DE7 ... 194 C2
Bennett St Buxton SK17 ... 85 E3
  Derby DE24 ... 9 E3
  Long Eaton NG10 ... 223 E1
  Sandiacre NG10 ... 223 D3
Bennetts La DE4 ... 168 A4
Bennington Wlk NG19 ... 136 C2
Bensington Gdns S45 ... 131 E2
Bensley Cl DE73 ... 233 D1
Benson St DE24 ... 232 C4
Bent La
  Church Broughton DE65 ... 227 E3
  Darley Dale DE4 ... 127 E3
  Derby DE4 ... 143 D4
  Netherthorpe S43 ... 79 D2
  Northwood DE4 ... 127 E3
  Spout DE56 ... 166 B3
  Tissington DE6 ... 162 B3
Bent The S32 ... 72 C2
Bent's La S18 ... 57 E1
Bentfield Rd DE56 ... 95 F3
Bentham Rd S40 ... 95 E3
Bentinck St NG18 ... 268 C4
Bentinck Dr S43 ... 81 D2
Bentinck Rd S44 ... 98 C4
Bentink Cl S80 ... 81 E1
Bentley Brook DE65 ... 228 C1
Bentley Cl Alfreton DE55 ... 159 D2
  Matlock DE4 ... 143 E4
Bentley Fields Open Farm
  DE6 ... 199 E1
Bentley Rd
  Castle Donington DE74 ... 246 C2
  Uttoxeter ST14 ... 210 A1
Bentley St DE24 ... 232 C3
Benton Dr SK6 ... 23 E4
Bents Cres S18 ... 57 E2
Bents La S17 ... 55 E2
Bentside Rd SK12 ... 32 B3
Beowulf Covert S14 ... 240 A1
Beresford Ave
  Ashbourne DE6 ... 173 E1
  Chapel-en-le-F SK23 ... 47 E3
Beresford Cl S45 ... 131 E1
Beresford Dale DE11 ... 255 F1
Beresford Dr Derby DE21 ... 204 C2
  Ilkeston DE7 ... 194 C3
Beresford La S43 ... 137 E1
Beresford PI DE56 ... 168 A3
Beresford Rd
  Chapel-en-le-F SK23 ... 47 E3
  Derby DE23 ... 236 A3
  Mansfield Woodhouse
  NG19 ... 136 B3
Beresford St NG18 ... 268 C3
Berkeley Ave NG10 ... 236 A3
Berkeley Cl DE23 ... 231 E4
Berkshire St DE21 ... 219 E4
Berle Ave DE7 ... 181 F1
Bermuda Ave DE21 ... 205 E3
Bernard Ave NG19 ... 96 C4
Bernard Cl S43 ... 268 A4
Bernard Rd NG19 ... 268 A4
Bernard St Glossop SK13 ... 10 B1
  Swadlincote DE11 ... 256 B2
Bernard Walker Ct SK6 ... 15 D1
Berners Cl S2 ... 43 F3
Berners Dr S2 ... 43 F3
Berners PI S2 ... 43 F3
Berners Rd S2 ... 43 F3
Berridge La S45 ... 145 E4
Berrisford La DE55 ... 160 B4
Berry Ave S21 ... 59 E2
Berry Gdns DE15 ... 248 B2
Berry Hedge La DE15 ... 248 B2
Berry Hill Rd NG18 ... 268 C3
Berry Park Cl DE22 ... 204 C1
Berry St North Wingfield S42 ... 131 F3
  Stoke-on-T ST4 ... 269 E2
Bertrand Ave S45 ... 131 E2
Berwick Ave
  Chesterfield S40 ... 114 B4
  Derby DE21 ... 219 E4
Berwick Cl DE24 ... 233 D3
Berwick Dr DE24 ... 231 E2
Berwick Rd SK17 ... 85 E2
Berwin Cl NG10 ... 223 D1
Berwyn Cl S40 ... 95 E3
Bessalone Dr S18 ... 179 D3
Bessell La Beeston NG9 ... 223 E3
  Stapleford NG9 ... 223 E3
Bessie La S18 ... 51 D3
Best Ave DE15 ... 248 A1
Besthill Cotts SK14 ... 16 A4
Besthorpe Cl DE21 ... 206 A1
Beswick La DE6 ... 184 B2
Bestwood Dr S45 ... 131 E2
Bestwood Pk S45 ... 131 E2
Bestwood Rd NG16 ... 160 C1
Bethel Terr S80 ... 82 A4
Bethulie Rd DE23 ... 232 A4
Betjeman Sq DE24 ... 232 A3

Betlingspring La DE6 .... 184 B2
Betony Cl S21 .... 60 A3
Bevan Dr S43 .... 97 D4
Bevan Rd S45 .... 131 E1
Bevan St DE55 .... 146 C1
Beverley Dr NG16 .... 195 F4
Beverley Rd DE14 .... 254 A4
Beverley St DE24 .... 219 E1
Beverleys Rd S8 .... 43 D2
Bewdley Cl DE73 .... 233 D2
Bexley Cl SK13 .... 10 B2
Bicester Ave DE24 .... 231 E1
Bickley Moss DE21 .... 206 A1
Bideford Cl DE55 .... 169 E1
Bideford Dr DE23 .... 231 E3
Bidston Cl DE4 .... 143 E4
Bidworth La SK13 .... 9 E1
Biggin CE Prim Sch
  SK17 .... 138 B2
Biggin Cl S45 .... 131 E1
Biggin La DE6 .... 176 A2
Biggin The DE74 .... 247 D2
Bigginmill La DE56 .... 176 B3
Bilby La S43 .... 77 F1
Billam St S21 .... 59 D2
Billingsley Ave NG16 .... 160 B2
Bilton St S14 .... 269 E1
Bingham St DE24 .... 232 C3
Bings Rd SK23 .... 45 F4
Bingswood Ave SK23 .... 45 F4
Bingswood Ind Est SK23 .... 45 F4
Bingswood Rd SK23 .... 45 F4
Binscombe La DE21 .... 205 F2
Birch Ave Ilkeston DE7 .... 209 D4
  Swadlincote DE11 .... 256 A4
  Toadmoor DE56 .... 167 F2
Birch Cl Alfreton DE55 .... 159 D3
  Branston DE14 .... 254 A4
  Buxton SK17 .... 66 A1
  Denstone ST14 .... 196 B3
  Grassmoor S42 .... 115 F2
  Killamarsh S21 .... 60 B3
  Ripley DE5 .... 180 B4
  Wessington DE55 .... 157 F4
Birch Farm Ave S8 .... 57 D4
Birch Gn S43 .... 10 C1
Birch Gr Hatton DE65 .... 227 E1
  Shirebrook NG20 .... 119 E3
Birch Hall Cl SK22 .... 25 D1
Birch Holt Gr S18 .... 76 C3
Birch Kiln Croft [5] S43 .... 96 C4
Birch La S43 .... 78 A1
Birch Rd S80 .... 82 B3
Birch St NG20 .... 120 C3
Birch View Ct DE1 .... 218 C4
Birchen Cl
  Chesterfield S40 .... 95 E3
  [11] Dronfield S18 .... 56 B1
Birchen Holme DE55 .... 160 A2
Birches Ave DE55 .... 157 F3
Birches Fold S18 .... 57 E2
Birches La Dronfield S18 .... 57 E2
  South Wingfield DE55 .... 158 A3
Birches Rd DE22 .... 204 B2
Birches The SK22 .... 25 E1
Birchfield Cl DE73 .... 232 C1
Birchfield Pk DE75 .... 193 F4
Birchfield Rd DE15 .... 254 C3
Birchills The S80 .... 81 E1
Birchitt Cl S17 .... 56 B3
Birchitt Pl S17 .... 56 B3
Birchitt Rd S17 .... 56 B3
Birchitt View S18 .... 57 D2
Birchlands NG19 .... 136 C1
Birchlands Dr S21 .... 60 B3
Birchover Edge DE4 .... 141 D4
Birchover La DE4 .... 141 D4
Birchover Pl DE7 .... 194 C3
Birchover Rd
  Birchover DE4 .... 126 B2
  Stanton in P DE4 .... 126 B2
Birchover Rise DE21 .... 205 F1
Birchover Way DE22 .... 204 C1
Birchside Ave SK13 .... 10 A1
Birchvale Rd S12 .... 44 C2
Birchview Cl DE56 .... 179 D1
  Heanor DE75 .... 181 E2
Birchwood Ave
  Derby DE23 .... 231 E3
  Long Eaton, Breaston
    NG10 .... 236 A4
  Long Eaton, New Sawley
    NG10 .... 236 B3
Birchwood Cl
  [22] Mosborough S20 .... 59 F4
  South Normanton DE55 .... 160 A2
Birchwood Cres
  Chesterfield S40 .... 114 C4
  Somercotes DE55 .... 170 B4
Birchwood Croft [23] S20 .... 59 F4
Birchwood Dr DE56 .... 168 A2
Birchwood Gdns S20 .... 59 F4
Birchwood Gr S20 .... 59 F4
Birchwood La
  Pinxton DE55 .... 159 F2
  Somercotes DE55 .... 159 F2
  South Normanton DE55 .... 159 F2
Birchwood Rise [7] S20 .... 59 F4
Birchwood View
  Ashbourne DE6 .... 173 E2
  Mosborough S20 .... 59 F4
Birchwood Way
  [4] Mosborough S20 .... 59 F4
  Somercotes DE55 .... 159 E1

Bircumshaw's Rd DE75 .... 181 F1
Bird St S43 .... 78 C1
Birdcage Wlk DE22 .... 217 F3
Birdcroft La DE7 .... 208 C3
Birdholme Cres S40 .... 115 D4
Birdholme Inf Sch S40 .... 115 D4
Birding St NG19 .... 136 A1
Birdsgrove La
  Mayfield DE6 .... 172 B2
  Swinscoe DE6 .... 172 B2
Birdwood St DE23 .... 218 C1
Birk Hill Inf Sch S21 .... 59 D1
Birkdale Cl Derby DE21 .... 218 A1
  Ilkeston DE7 .... 194 B1
Birkdale Dr S40 .... 114 B4
Birkin Ave S42 .... 115 E1
Birkin La Grassmoor S42 .... 115 F1
  Temple Normanton S42 .... 116 A2
  Wingerworth S42 .... 114 B1
Birkin La W S42 .... 115 F1
Birkinstyle Ave DE55 .... 146 C2
Birkinstyle La DE55 .... 146 C2
Birkland Ave
  Mansfield Woodhouse
    NG19 .... 136 B2
  Nottingham NG1 .... 268 B2
Birkland St NG18 .... 268 C4
Birks Cl S80 .... 82 B3
Birks St S14 .... 268 F1
Birley Brook Dr S40 .... 95 D4
Birley Comp Sch S12 .... 44 B2
Birley La S12 .... 44 C1
Birley Moor Ave S12 .... 44 C2
Birley Moor Cl S12 .... 44 C1
Birley Moor Cres S12 .... 44 C1
Birley Moor Dr S12 .... 44 C1
Birley Moor Pl S12 .... 44 C1
Birley Moor Rd S12 .... 44 C1
Birley Moor Way S12 .... 44 C1
Birley Spa Inf & Jun Sch
  S12 .... 44 C2
Birley Spa La S12 .... 44 C2
Birley St NG9 .... 223 E3
Birley Vale Ave S12 .... 44 B3
Birley Vale Cl S12 .... 44 B2
Biscay Ct DE21 .... 206 B1
Bishop Lonsdale CE Prim
  Sch DE22 .... 218 C2
Bishop Pursglove CE Prim
  Sch SK17 .... 69 E2
Bishop St Alfreton DE55 .... 159 D3
  Eastwood NG16 .... 182 C1
  Mansfield NG18 .... 268 B3
Bishop's Ct DE73 .... 252 A4
Bishop's Dr DE73 .... 252 A4
Bishopdale Cl NG10 .... 236 A3
Bishopdale Dr S20 .... 59 D4
Bishopdale Rise S20 .... 59 D4
Bishops Ct S8 .... 43 D3
Bishops House Mus S8 .... 43 D2
Bishops La S17 .... 84 C4
Bishopscourt Rd S8 .... 43 D3
Bispham Dr NG9 .... 223 F1
Bitham Ct DE13 .... 240 B1
Bitham La DE13 .... 240 B1
Bitham Sch DE13 .... 240 B1
Blaby Cl DE23 .... 231 F3
Black Harry La S32 .... 71 D1
Black Hills Dr DE7 .... 208 C3
Black Tor Rd DE4 .... 143 D4
Blacka Moor Cres S17 .... 55 E3
Blacka Moor Rd S17 .... 55 E3
Blacka Moor View S17 .... 55 E3
Blackberry Flats S20 .... 59 F4
Blackberry La S116 .... 269 D4
Blackberry Way DE56 .... 179 F1
Blackbird Row DE56 .... 179 E1
Blackbrook La SK23 .... 47 F3
Blackburn Pl DE7 .... 194 C2
Blackcliff Field Cl S80 .... 82 A3
Blackden Cl DE56 .... 179 F2
Blackdown Ave S40 .... 95 D3
Blackfordby CE Prim Sch
  DE11 .... 257 E1
Blackmore St DE23 .... 231 F4
Blackmount Cl [7] DE24 .... 231 E2
Blackpit La DE6 .... 224 A4
Blackpool St DE14 .... 254 B4
Blackrocks Ave DE4 .... 142 C4
Blacks La S42 .... 131 F4
Blackshaw Rd SK13 .... 10 C1
Blacksmith La S14 .... 97 D2
Blacksmith's La
  Eggington DE65 .... 241 D3
  Newton Solney DE15 .... 248 C4
  Woodville DE11 .... 256 C2
Blacksmiths Yd DE4 .... 127 F1
Blackstock Cl S14 .... 43 E1
Blackstock Dr S14 .... 43 E1
Blackstock Rd S14 .... 43 E2
Blackstone Cl DE55 .... 170 B4
Blackthorn Cl
  Chesterfield S41 .... 115 E4
  Derby DE73 .... 205 F1
  Melbourne DE73 .... 252 A4
Blackthorn Rd DE15 .... 254 C3
Blackthorne Cl DE56 .... 179 F1
Blackwall La DE6 .... 176 A4
Blackwell La
  Melbourne DE73 .... 252 A4
  Monyash DE45 .... 107 D2
Blackwell Prim Sch
  DE55 .... 147 F1
Blackwell Rd NG17 .... 148 C2
Bladon House Sch
  DE15 .... 248 A3
Bladon St DE15 .... 248 B3

Bladon View DE13 .... 241 D1
Blagdon Cl DE4 .... 127 E2
Blagreaves Ave DE23 .... 231 E3
Blagreaves La DE23 .... 231 E3
Blair Cl NG10 .... 223 D2
Blake Cres NG18 .... 268 C4
Blake Ct NG10 .... 236 A3
Blake Rd NG9 .... 223 F3
Blake St Ilkeston DE7 .... 194 C1
  Mansfield Woodhouse
    NG19 .... 136 A1
Blakebrook Dr DE73 .... 233 D2
Blakeley La DE65 .... 229 D1
Blakelow Dr DE65 .... 229 D2
Blakelow La DE4 .... 142 A2
Blakemere La DE4 .... 141 F1
Blakemore Ave DE73 .... 252 A4
Blakeney Ct Derby DE21 .... 206 B1
  Mansfield Woodhouse
    NG19 .... 136 C2
Blakiston St S116 .... 269 E4
Blanch Croft DE73 .... 252 A4
Blandford Ave NG10 .... 236 A3
Blandford Cl DE24 .... 233 E3
Blanford Dr S41 .... 95 F4
Blankney Cl DE24 .... 231 E1
Bleasby St NG2 .... 268 C1
Blencathra Dr DE3 .... 230 C4
Blenheim Ave DE55 .... 170 A4
Blenheim Cl
  Burton u T DE15 .... 248 B2
  [4] Hadfield SK13 .... 10 A3
  Mansfield NG19 .... 136 B1
  Swadlincote DE11 .... 256 A4
Blenheim Dr DE22 .... 204 B2
Blenheim Mews DE65 .... 229 C2
Blenheim Pl NG17 .... 148 C2
Blenheim Rd DE6 .... 185 F4
Blenheim St S114 .... 269 F1
Blenheim Ct NG10 .... 223 D2
Blessed William Howard
  RC High Sch ST17 .... 269 D3
Blind La Bolsover S44 .... 98 C2
  Breaston DE72 .... 235 E4
  Darley Dale DE4 .... 127 F1
  Kirk Ireton DE6 .... 165 D1
  Wirksworth DE4 .... 165 F4
Blissworth Way DE55 .... 169 F4
Blithfield Gdns DE73 .... 233 D1
Bloom St DE1 .... 267 B2
Bloomfield Cl Derby DE1 .... 267 C1
  Hilton DE65 .... 228 B1
Bloomfield Rd DE55 .... 170 A4
Bloomfield St DE1 .... 267 D1
Bloomgrove Rd DE7 .... 194 C1
Blore Cl DE6 .... 185 E4
Blossom Cres S12 .... 44 A2
Blue Bell Hill Jun & Inf
  Schs NG3 .... 268 C2
Blue Bell Hill Rd NG3 .... 268 C2
Blue John Cavern S33 .... 37 F2
Bluebank View S43 .... 77 E2
Bluebell Cl Derby DE24 .... 231 E1
  Underwood Green NG16 .... 171 F1
Bluebell Croft DE4 .... 143 D2
Bluebell Hill DE55 .... 146 B2
Bluebird Cl DE24 .... 231 E2
Bluecoat Cl NG1 .... 268 B2
Bluecoat St NG1 .... 268 B2
Bluestone Cty Prim Sch
  S2 .... 43 E4
Bluestone La DE15 .... 255 D4
Blundestone La DE4 .... 156 A1
Blunt Ave S43 .... 79 E2
Blunt St DE7 .... 193 D1
Blyth Cl Chesterfield S40 .... 114 A4
  Mansfield NG19 .... 135 E1
Blyth Pl DE21 .... 205 E1
Boam La DE4 .... 142 C4
Boardman Cres S116 .... 269 D4
Boardman Ind Est
  DE11 .... 255 F2
Boardman Rd DE11 .... 255 F1
Boarslack La SK17 .... 69 F1
Boarstones La SK17 .... 85 E4
Boat La NG16 .... 182 A4
Boatmans Cl DE7 .... 194 C1
Bobbin Mill La S40 .... 95 E1
Bobbinmill Hill DE56 .... 168 A4
Bochum Parkway S8 .... 57 E4
Bocking La S8 .... 56 C4
Bocking Rise S8 .... 56 C4
Boden St ST4 .... 269 E1
Bodmin Cl DE24 .... 231 E2
Bodmin Way [5] S40 .... 95 E3
Boggard La S13 .... 16 B3
Boggard La SK6 .... 24 A3
Boggy La DE65 .... 227 D4
Bohem Rd NG10 .... 223 E2
Boiley La S21 .... 60 B2
Boland Rd S8 .... 56 B3
Bold La DE1 .... 267 B3
Bole Hill S8 .... 43 D1
Bolehill La Eckington S21 .... 59 D1
  Marsh Lane S21 .... 58 C1
  Northedge S42 .... 130 B4
  Wingerworth S42 .... 114 B1
Bolehill Rd Buxton SK17 .... 85 E3
Bolsover CE Jun Sch S44 .... 99 D1
Bolsover Cl NG16 .... 171 F3
Bolsover Inf Sch S44 .... 99 D1
Bolsover Rd Bolsover S44 .... 98 C3
  Mastin Moor S43 .... 79 E2
Bolsover St S44 .... 99 D1
Bolsover St NG18 .... 268 C3
Bolton St DE5 .... 169 E4

Boman's La DE56 .... 177 F4
Bonchurch Cl DE24 .... 233 E3
Bond La DE56 .... 168 C1
Bond St Nottingham NG2 .... 268 C1
  Staveley S43 .... 97 E4
Bondfield Rd S43 .... 97 E4
Bondgate DE74 .... 247 D2
Bondhay La S80 .... 62 B1
Bonington Rd NG19 .... 268 A3
Bonner's Rd NG16 .... 195 E2
Bonnington Cres S116 .... 269 E1
Bonnington Dr DE55 .... 170 B4
Bonnington Rise SK6 .... 23 D4
Bonnyrigg Dr DE21 .... 206 A1
Bonsall CE Prim Sch
  DE4 .... 142 C1
Bonsall Cl [2] S41 .... 95 E4
Bonsall Dr DE3 .... 217 F2
Bonsall La Alfreton DE55 .... 158 C2
  Bonsall DE4 .... 141 E2
  Winster DE4 .... 141 E2
Bonsall St NG10 .... 236 C4
Bonsallmoor La DE4 .... 141 F1
Bonsalt Dr DE55 .... 170 B4
Bonser Cres NG17 .... 148 C1
Boon Ave S14 .... 269 E2
Boot Hill DE65 .... 242 B2
Booth Ave NG19 .... 135 D3
Booth Cl NG13 .... 268 B2
Booth Cres NG19 .... 135 E1
Booth St Derby DE24 .... 232 C4
  Hollingworth SK14 .... 9 E3
  Mansfield Woodhouse
    NG19 .... 136 A2
  Ripley DE5 .... 169 F1
  Stoke-on-T ST4 .... 269 E1
Booth's Ct SK13 .... 10 B1
Boothby Ave DE6 .... 173 E1
Boothby Meadows Sch
  DE6 .... 173 E1
Boothen CE Prim Sch
  ST4 .... 269 E1
Boothen Old Rd ST4 .... 269 E1
Boothen Rd ST4 .... 269 E1
Boothenwood Terr ST4 .... 269 E1
Boothgate DE56 .... 179 F4
Boots Yd NG17 .... 148 C2
Border Cl S43 .... 80 C2
Border Dr DE24 .... 233 D3
Border La S80 .... 80 C1
Borlace Cres NG9 .... 223 F3
Borough St DE74 .... 247 D2
Borrow Wood Inf & Jun
  Schs DE21 .... 220 C3
Borrowash By-pass
  Borrowash DE72 .... 221 E2
  Derby DE72 .... 220 B2
  Risley DE72 .... 221 E2
Borrowash Rd DE21 .... 220 C2
Borrowdale Ave S20 .... 59 F3
Borrowdale Cl S20 .... 59 F3
Borrowdale Dr
  Long Eaton NG10 .... 236 A3
  Mosborough S20 .... 59 F3
Borrowdale Rd S20 .... 59 F3
Borrowfield Rd DE21 .... 220 C2
Borrowfields DE72 .... 221 D1
Boscastle Rd DE24 .... 233 D3
Boscovan Ct NG7 .... 194 C2
Bosley La DE6 .... 184 C3
Bosley Mews DE56 .... 178 C3
Bosnall Ave DE23 .... 231 E4
Bostock Rd SK14 .... 16 A4
Bostock's La Risley NG10 .... 222 C2
  Sandiacre NG10 .... 223 D2
Boston Cl DE21 .... 220 B3
Boston St NG1 .... 268 B2
Boswell Sq DE23 .... 231 F4
Bosworth Ave DE23 .... 231 F3
Bosworth Rd DE74 .... 246 C2
Bosworth Way NG10 .... 236 C3
Botany Ave NG18 .... 268 B4
Botany Commercial Pk
  NG18 .... 268 A3
Botany Dr DE7 .... 194 C3
Bothe Cl NG10 .... 236 B3
Bottle La NG1 .... 268 B1
Bottom Cliff S32 .... 71 F2
Bottom Lons DE56 .... 176 A4
Bottom Rd S42 .... 114 C1
Bottomhill Rd SK17 .... 69 F1
Bough La S32 .... 72 A1
Boughey Rd ST4 .... 269 F2
Boughey St ST4 .... 269 E1
Boughton La S43 .... 80 B2
Bould St NG19 .... 135 F1
Boulevard The SK14 .... 9 E2
Boulton Cl S40 .... 95 D3
Boulton Dr DE24 .... 233 D3
Boulton Inf Sch DE24 .... 233 D3
Boulton Jaun Sch DE24 .... 233 D3
Boulton La
  Derby, Allenton DE24 .... 232 C3
  Derby, Boulton DE24 .... 233 D3
Boundary Ct
  Netherthorpe S43 .... 79 D2
  Shirebrook NG20 .... 119 F3
Boundary Gdns DE55 .... 147 F3
Boundary La NG16 .... 182 B2
Boundary Rd Derby DE22 .... 218 C2
  Eggington DE65 .... 241 D3
  Nottingham NG2 .... 268 C1
Boundary Wlk NG20 .... 100 C1
Bourne Cl S43 .... 96 C4
Bourne Dr NG16 .... 182 A3
Bourne Mill Cl S43 .... 80 A4
Bourne Sq DE72 .... 235 F4
Bourne St DE72 .... 267 B2

Bournebrook Ave DE4 .... 165 F
Bow St NG19 .... 136 C
Bowbridge Ave DE23 .... 231 E
Bowden Cres SK22 .... 33 E
Bowden La S012 .... 47 E
Bowden Rd SK13 .... 10 B
Bowdon Ave S43 .... 80 A
Bower Farm Rd S41 .... 77 D
Bower St DE24 .... 232 C
Bowes Well Rd DE7 .... 194 C
Bowland Cl DE3 .... 217 F
Bowland Dr S40 .... 114 A
Bowland Rd SK13 .... 17 A
Bowless Cn DE23 .... 230 D
Bowler Dr DE56 .... 192 A
Bowler Rd DE4 .... 127 E
Bowler St DE5 .... 180 B
Bowling Alley DE56 .... 168 C
Bowling Alley La
  Marston Montgomery DE6 .... 212 A
  Sudbury DE6 .... 212 A
Bowling Cl DE7 .... 222 C
Bowling Gn DE4 .... 153 D
Bowling Green La DE4 .... 154 C
Bowling La NG16 .... 268 C
Bowman Dr S12 .... 43 F
Bowmer La DE56 .... 168 A
Bowmer Rd DE24 .... 219 F
Bowne St DE55 .... 146 C
Bowness Cl
  Chesterfield S41 .... 95 E
  [2] Dronfield S18 .... 56 C
Bowness Rd S41 .... 95 E
Bowns Hill DE4 .... 157 D
Bowshaw Ave S8 .... 57 D
Bowshaw Cl S8 .... 57 D
Bowshaw View S8 .... 57 D
Bowstead St ST4 .... 269 E
Boxmoor Cl DE23 .... 230 C
Boyd Gr DE73 .... 245 D
Boyer St DE22 .... 267 A
Boyer Wlk DE22 .... 267 A
Boylestone Rd DE23 .... 231 E
Boythorpe Ave S40 .... 266 A
Boythorpe Cres S40 .... 266 A
Boythorpe Mount S40 .... 266 A
Boythorpe Rd S40 .... 266 A
Boythorpe Rise S40 .... 95 F
Brabyns Brow SK6 .... 23 D
Bracken Ave S44 .... 116 C
Bracken Cl
  Hollingworth SK14 .... 9 E
  Long Eaton NG10 .... 223 D
  Marple SK6 .... 23 E
Bracken La
  Barlborough S43 .... 80 A
  Holloway DE4 .... 156 A
Bracken Rd NG10 .... 223 D
Bracken Way SK13 .... 17 F
Bracken's La DE24 .... 232 C
Brackendale Cl
  Brimington S43 .... 96 B
  Clay Cross S45 .... 131 F
Brackendale La DE6 .... 163 F
Brackendale Rd DE55 .... 169 E
Brackenfield Ave NG19 .... 136 C
Brackenfield Dr NG16 .... 195 D
Brackenfield Gr S12 .... 44 B
Brackenfield La
  Brackenfield DE55 .... 145 E
  Wessington DE55 .... 157 E
Brackenfield Specl Sch
  NG10 .... 223 D
Brackens Ave DE24 .... 232 C
Brackensdale Ave DE22 .... 218 A
Brackensdale Inf Sch
  DE22 .... 218 A
Brackenwood Rd DE15 .... 254 C
Brackhills Cl NG19 .... 136 C
Brackley DE56 .... 179 F
Brackley Dr DE21 .... 220 C
Brackley Gate DE7 .... 192 A
Bracknell Dr DE24 .... 232 C
Bracton Dr NG3 .... 268 C
Bradbourne Cl S43 .... 97 F
Bradbourne Ct DE22 .... 218 C
Bradbury Cl
  Borrowash DE72 .... 221 E
  Chesterfield S40 .... 95 E
Bradbury Dr S42 .... 114 C
Bradbury St S8 .... 43 D
Bradden Ave NG9 .... 209 E
Bradder Way NG18 .... 268 A
Bradgate Cl NG10 .... 223 D
Bradgate Ct DE23 .... 231 E
Bradgate Dr DE5 .... 169 E
Brading Cl DE24 .... 233 E
Bradley CE Prim Sch
  DE6 .... 186 C
Bradley Cl [3] Birchover DE4 .... 126 A
  [4] Brimington S43 .... 96 C
Bradley Dr DE56 .... 179 E
Bradley St
  Burton u T DE15 .... 254 C
  Derby DE22 .... 218 C
  Sandiacre NG10 .... 223 E
Bradley View DE6 .... 173 E
Bradley Way S43 .... 96 C
Bradmoor Gr DE73 .... 233 E
Bradshaw Ave DE23 .... 170 C
Bradshaw Cres SK6 .... 23 D
Bradshaw Croft DE56 .... 178 C
Bradshaw Dr DE56 .... 191 H
Bradshaw La S32 .... 72 A

Bradshaw Meadow DE65 227 E1
Bradshaw Rd Marple SK6 23 D4
Staveley S43 97 D3
Bradshaw St NG10 236 A3
Bradshaw Way DE1 267 C2
Bradway Cl S17 56 A3
Bradway Cty Prim Sch S8 56 C3
Bradway Dr S17 56 A3
Bradway Grange Rd S17 56 B3
Bradway Rd S17 56 B3
Bradwell CE Inf Sch S33 51 D4
Bradwell Cl Derby DE3 217 F1
8 Dronfield S18 56 B1
Eastwood NG16 195 E4
Bradwell Gr S45 131 E1
Bradwell Head Rd S33 51 D4
Bradwell Jun Sch S33 51 D4
Bradwell Pl S43 97 E4
Bradwell St S2 43 D3
Bradwell Way DE56 179 D3
Braefield Cl DE7 208 B3
Braemar Ave NG16 182 C1
Braemar Cl Chesterfield S43 77 E2
12 Derby DE24 231 E2
Brafield Cl DE56 179 E2
Brailsford Ave DE11 255 F3
Brailsford CE Prim Sch DE6 201 F4
Brailsford Rd DE21 219 F4
Braintree Cl DE21 205 E1
Braithwell Cl DE22 204 C1
Bramah Edge Ct SK13 9 F4
Bramall La S2 43 D4
Bramble Cl
Holmewood S44 116 C1
Long Eaton NG10 223 D1
Shirebrook NG20 119 F3
Bramble Mews DE3 217 E1
Bramble St DE1 267 A3
Bramble Way DE56 179 F1
Brambleberry Ct DE21 206 A2
Brambling Ct S41 96 B1
Bramell Cl DE14 253 F4
Bramfield Ave DE22 218 C2
Bramfield Ct DE22 218 C2
Bramham Rd SK6 23 D2
Bramley Ave S13 44 C4
Bramley Cl Derby DE21 206 B2
Mosborough S20 59 E4
Bramley Ct Hatton DE65 227 E1
Kimberley NG16 195 F3
Bramley Dale DE11 255 F1
Bramley Hall Rd S13 44 C4
Bramley La Baslow DE45 91 E4
Hassop DE45 91 E4
Sheffield S13 44 C4
Bramley Park Cl S13 44 C4
Bramley Park Rd S13 44 C4
Bramley Rd
Bramley-Vale S44 117 F1
Marsh Lane S21 58 C1
Bramley St DE55 170 C4
Bramley Vale Prim Sch S44 117 F1
Bramleymoor La S21 58 C1
Bramlyn Cl S43 80 B3
Bramlyn Ct S43 80 B3
Brampton Ave DE75 182 A1
Brampton Cl DE3 217 E2
Brampton Ct DE56 179 E2
Brampton Dr NG9 223 F3
Brampton Inf & Jun Sch S40 95 F2
Bramshill Rise S40 95 E1
Branch La S45 132 C3
Brancliffe La S81 63 F4
Brandelhow Ct DE21 206 B2
Brandene Cl S44 97 D2
Brandreth Dr NG16 195 D4
Branklene Cl NG16 195 F4
Branksome Ave DE24 233 E4
Branksome Chine Ave S41 115 E4
Bransdale Cl NG10 236 A3
Branston Rd
Branston DE13 253 E4
Burton u T DE14 254 B4
Branston Water Pk DE14 253 E3
Branton Cl S40 266 A1
Brassington Cl
Eastwood NG16 195 D4
West Hallam DE7 207 F4
Youlgreave DE45 125 E3
Brassington Cres SK13 9 E1
Brassington Ct NG19 136 C2
Brassington La S45 131 E3
Brassington Prim Sch DE4 153 D1
Brassington Rd DE21 205 D4
Brassington St S45 131 E2
Braybrook Cl DE55 169 F4
Brayfield Ave DE23 231 E4
Brayfield Rd DE23 231 E4
Breach La Hatton DE65 227 E2
Scropton DE6 226 B3
Stanton by B DE73 244 C1
Breach Rd Denby DE5 181 D2
Heanor DE75 194 A4
Breadsall CE Prim Sch DE21 205 F2
Breadsall Ct DE7 194 C2
Breadsall Hill Top Inf & Jun Sch DE21 205 F1
Breamfield La DE56 166 A4
Brearley Ave S43 77 E2
Brearley St S41 77 E2
Breaston La DE72 222 B2
Brechin Ct NG19 136 A3
Breck La S21, S43 78 B3
Breckbank NG19 136 C1
Breckland Rd S40 114 A4
Brecon Cl
Chesterfield S40 95 E3
Derby DE21 220 C3
6 Long Eaton NG10 236 A4
Bredon Cl 7 NG10 236 A4
Breedon Ave DE23 231 E3
Breedon Hill Rd DE23 218 C2
Breedon on the Hill CE Sch DE73 252 C2
Breedon St NG10 223 E1
Bren Way DE65 228 C1
Brenden Ave DE55 170 B4
Brenden Cl DE55 170 B4
Brendon Ave S40 95 E2
Brendon Cl SK13 17 D4
Brendon Dr NG16 195 F4
Brendon Way NG10 223 D1
Brent Cl S40 95 E3
Brentford Dr DE22 218 A3
Brentwood Ave S33 40 A2
Brentwood Rd S33 40 A2
Bretby Bsns Pk DE15 255 F4
Bretby Hall Hospl DE15 249 E1
Bretby La DE15 248 C2
Bretby Rd
Chesterfield S40 95 D3
Swadlincote DE11 255 F4
Bretby Sq DE23 231 E3
Bretby View DE11 257 D2
Bretlands Way DE15 255 D3
Bretton Ave Bolsover S44 99 E1
Derby DE23 218 B1
Bretton Cl S40 95 D3
Bretton Gr S12 44 B2
Bretton Rd DE56 179 F3
Brewery St
Chesterfield S41 266 C3
Kimberley NG16 195 F3
Breydon Cl DE24 232 B2
Briar Ave NG10 223 D2
Briar Briggs Rd S44 98 C2
Briar Cl Alfreton DE55 159 E2
Borrowash DE72 221 E1
Chesterfield S40 95 F3
Derby DE21 220 A2
Swadlincote DE11 255 F3
Briar Gate NG10 223 D1
Briar Lea Cl DE24 231 F2
Briar Rd NG16 195 D4
Briar View S43 96 C4
Briar's La DE4 168 A4
Briardene Cl S40 94 C3
Briargrove Rd SK22 24 B2
Briars Cl S21 60 B3
Briars Way DE5 180 B4
Briarsgate DE22 204 B1
Briarwood Cres SK6 23 D2
Briarwood Way DE23 231 E3
Brick Kiln La
Mansfield NG19 268 A4
Rolleston DE13 240 A2
Brick Row DE22 205 D1
Brick St DE1 218 C3
Brick-kiln La
Brailsford DE6 186 C1
Hulland Ward DE6 175 E3
Brickbridge Rd SK6 23 D3
Brickfield St SK13 10 A3
Brickfields Cl DE4 155 D2
Brickhouse La S17 55 E4
Brickhouse Yd S40 95 F2
Brickkiln La DE7 206 B4
Bricky Cl S43 80 B3
Brickyard Cotts DE6 185 E4
Brickyard La
Kilburn DE56 179 F1
Ripley DE5 169 F1
South Normanton DE55 160 A3
Brickyard Rd DE56 168 B3
Brickyard The DE7 193 D1
Bridge Bank Cl S40 95 E3
Bridge Cl
Swadlincote DE11 256 B1
Whitwell S80 82 A3
Bridge End Ave NG16 171 F4
Bridge Farm DE13 240 C1
Bridge Field DE72 235 E4
Bridge Foot DE56 178 C3
Bridge Hill DE56 178 C3
Bridge St Bakewell DE45 109 E3
Belper DE56 178 C2
Bradwell S33 51 D4
Burton u T DE13 240 C1
Buxton SK17 85 E4
Chesterfield S40 266 B1
Clay Cross S45 131 E2
Derby DE1 218 C3
Ilkeston DE7 194 C2
Killamarsh S21 60 B4
Langley Mill NG16 182 B2
Linton DE11 261 F4
Long Eaton NG10 223 E1
Mansfield NG18 268 C4
New Mills SK22 24 B1
Pilsley S45 132 B1
Sandiacre NG10 223 E3
Stafford ST16 269 E3
Swadlincote DE11 256 B1
Tupton S42 115 E1
Tutbury DE13 239 E4
Whaley Bridge SK23 45 F4
Bridge View DE56 191 D4
Bridgend Cl NG9 223 E3
Bridgend Ct DE21 206 B1
Bridgeness Rd DE23 230 C3
Bridgeport Rd DE21 220 B3
Bridgeside DE13 240 C1
Bridgett Cl ST4 269 D1
Bridgewater St S42 115 E1
Bridgeway SK23 47 D2
Bridgford Ave DE14 253 F4
Bridgnorth Way NG9 223 F2
Bridgwater Cl DE24 233 E4
Bridle Cl DE73 233 D1
Bridle La
Ripley, Greenwich DE5 169 F1
Ripley, Upper Hartshay DE5 169 D1
Somercotes DE55 170 A4
Swadlincote DE15 255 D3
Bridle Rd Bolsover S44 80 A1
Woodthorpe S43 79 D1
Bridle Stile S20 59 E4
Bridle Stile Cl S20 59 E4
Bridle Stile Gdns S20 59 D4
Bridlesmith Gate NG1 268 B1
Bridleway The NG19 136 C1
Brierfield Ave S12 44 A2
Brierfield Cres S12 44 A2
Brierfield Rd S12 44 A2
Brierfield Way DE3 230 C4
Brierley Cl S43 78 C1
Brierley Pk SK23 34 A1
Brierley Rd
Stonebroom DE55 146 C2
Unstone S18 76 C3
Brierlow Bar SK17 105 D4
Brigden Ave DE24 232 C4
Brigg Inf Sch DE55 160 A3
Bright Meadow S20 60 A3
Bright Sq NG19 135 E1
Bright St Derby DE22 218 B3
Ilkeston DE7 194 C2
North Wingfield S42 131 F3
South Normanton DE55 159 F3
Brightmoor St 10 NG1 268 B1
Brighton Rd DE24 232 C4
Brighton St ST4 269 E2
Brightstone Cl DE24 233 E3
Brigmor Wlk DE22 218 B3
Brimington Ct NG19 136 C2
Brimington Jun Sch S43 96 C4
Brimington Rd S41 96 A3
Brimington Rd N S41 96 A4
Brimmesfield Cl S2 43 F4
Brimmesfield Dr S2 43 F4
Brimmesfield Rd S2 43 F4
Brincliffe Cl S40 95 D1
Brindley Cl S8 43 D2
Brindley Cres S8 43 D2
Brindley Ct S21 60 B3
Brindley Rd S41 96 A3
Brindley Wlk DE24 231 F1
Brinkburn Cl S17 55 F3
Brinkburn Ct S17 55 F3
Brinkburn Dr S17 55 F3
Brinkburn Vale Rd S17 55 F3
Brinks Rd S33 39 D4
Brinsley Hill NG16 171 E1
Brinsley Prim Sch NG16 182 B4
Brisbane Cl NG19 136 B3
Brisbane Dr NG9 209 F1
Brisbane Rd DE3 217 F2
Briset Cl DE24 231 F1
Brisley Hill ST4 269 D1
Bristol Dr DE3 217 F1
Bristol Rd DE7 194 C1
Britannia Ave DE5 181 D4
Britannia Dr DE13 240 B1
Britannia Rd
Chesterfield S40 115 D4
Long Eaton NG10 223 E1
Brittain Dr DE5 170 A1
Britten Gdns NG3 268 C2
Brizlincote La DE15 248 B1
Broad Bank DE22 218 C4
Broad Eye ST16 269 D4
Broad La Brinsley NG16 182 C4
Elvaston DE72 233 F2
Hodthorpe S80 82 B3
Broad Oak Dr
Brinsley NG16 182 C4
Stapleford NG9 223 E3
Broad Pavement S40 266 B3
Broad Pl S80 82 B3
Broad St Long Eaton NG10 236 B4
Nottingham NG1 268 B2
Stafford ST16 269 D4
Broad Way DE56 176 A4
Broad Wlk Buxton SK17 85 D4
Darley Dale DE4 127 E2
Broadbottom CE Prim Sch SK14 15 F4
Broadbottom Rd SK14 9 D2
Broadbottom Sta SK14 16 A4
Broadfield Rd S8 43 D4
Broadfields Cl DE22 218 C4
Broadgorse Cl S40 114 C4
Broadholme La DE56 179 D4
Broadlands
Sandiacre NG10 223 D2
South Normanton DE55 160 A2
Broadleaf Cl DE21 205 F1
Broadleys S45 131 E2
Broadmeadow DE4 127 E2
Broadoaks Cl S41 266 C3
Broadstairs Rd NG9 223 F1
Broadstone La DE73 251 E2
Broadway Derby DE22 218 C4
Duffield DE56 190 C1
Heanor DE75 181 F1
Ilkeston DE7 194 C2
7 Nottingham NG1 268 B1
Broadway continued
Ripley DE5 169 F1
Swanwick DE55 169 F4
Broadway Ave DE5 169 F1
Broadway Park Cl DE22 218 C4
Broadway St DE14 254 B4
Broadway The NG18 268 C3
Brockhall Rise DE75 182 A1
Brockholes SK13 16 C4
Brockhurst Gdns NG3 268 C2
Brockhurst La S45 129 E3
Brocklehurst Ave S8 57 E4
Brocklehurst Piece S40 95 E1
Brockley DE21 220 C3
Brockley Ave S44 98 C3
Brockley Prim Sch S44 98 C4
Brockway Cl S45 131 E1
Brockwell Inf & Jun Sch S40 95 E2
Brockwell La S40 95 F2
Brockwell Pl S40 95 F2
Brockwell Terr S40 95 F2
Brockwell The DE55 160 A2
Bromehead Way S41 95 E4
Bromley Hough ST4 269 D1
Bromley Pl NG1 268 A1
Bromley St DE22 218 C4
Brompton Rd DE22 217 F3
Bromyard Dr DE73 233 D2
Bronte Cl NG10 236 A4
Bronte Pl DE23 231 D4
Bronte St DE55 146 B3
Brook Ave DE55 159 D2
Brook Bottom Rd SK22 33 D4
Brook Cl Alfreton DE55 159 D2
Doveridge DE6 224 B4
Findern DE65 230 B1
Hatton DE65 227 E1
Holymoorside S42 113 E4
Long Eaton NG10 236 C3
Quarndon DE22 204 B2
Brook Cotts DE7 194 C2
Brook Ct NG16 182 A1
Brook End DE65 242 B2
Brook House Mews DE11 256 A4
Brook La Alfreton DE55 159 D2
Clowne S43 80 C2
Crich DE56 168 B3
Hatton DE65 227 E2
Ripley DE5 180 B4
Sutton on t H DE6 228 A4
Brook Lea DE4 143 E2
Brook Meadow SK13 10 C1
Brook Rd Borrowash DE72 221 E1
Elvaston DE72 233 F2
Sheffield S8 43 D3
Brook Sch S13 44 B4
Brook Side DE45 109 E3
Brook St Clay Cross S45 131 D2
Derby DE1 267 A4
Glossop SK13 10 B1
Hartshorne DE11 257 D4
Heage DE56 168 C1
Heanor DE75 181 D3
Nether Heage DE56 168 B1
Nottingham NG1 268 B2
Renishaw S21 79 E4
Stoke-on-T ST4 269 E2
Swadlincote, Church Gresley DE11 256 A2
Swadlincote, Newhall DE11 255 F3
Tibshelf DE55 148 A3
Brook Vale Cl S18 75 E2
Brook Vale Rd NG16 182 B1
Brook Wlk DE1 267 A4
Brook Yd S40 266 A3
Brookbank Ave S40 95 E2
Brookbank Rd S43 80 C2
Brookdale Ave SK6 23 D2
Brookdale Rd DE11 257 D2
Brooke Dr S43 96 C3
Brooke St Ilkeston DE7 209 D3
Sandiacre NG10 223 D3
Brookfield DE73 244 A3
Brookfield Ave
Chesterfield S40 95 D1
Derby, Chaddesden DE21 220 A4
Derby, Littleover DE23 231 E3
Brookfield Cl DE5 170 A1
Brookfield Com Sch S40 95 D1
Brookfield Cres NG20 119 F3
Brookfield Ind Est SK13 9 F2
Brookfield La DE45 109 F4
Brookfield Park Ind Est DE4 143 F2
Brookfield Prim Sch
Derby DE3 230 B4
Shirebrook NG20 119 F3
Brookfield Rd
Bolsover S44 118 A4
Stoke-on-T ST4 269 D1
Brookfield Way DE4 143 F2
Brookfields Calver S32 72 B1
Horsley DE56 191 F4
Brookfields Dr DE21 205 E2
Brookhill S43 80 C2
Brookhill Ave NG16 160 B2
Brookhill Ind Est NG16 160 B1
Brookhill La NG16 160 C3
Brookhill Leys Rd NG16 182 C1
Brookhill Rd NG16 160 B1
Brookhill St NG9 223 E3
Brookhouse Ct SK22 25 E2
Brookhouse St DE24 232 B3
Brookland Ave NG18 268 A4
Brooklands SK17 85 E4
Brooklands Ave
Chapel-en-le-F SK23 47 E3
Heanor DE75 181 F1
Wirksworth DE4 165 F4
Brooklands Bank DE45 109 F3
Brooklands Dr DE23 231 E4
Brooklands Inf Sch NG10 236 B3
Brooklands Jun Sch NG10 236 B4
Brooklands Rd SK23 47 E3
Brookleton DE45 125 E3
Brooklyn Dr S40 95 E2
Brooklyn Pl S8 43 D3
Brooklyn Rd S8 43 D3
Brooks Hollow DE21 205 E4
Brooks Rd S43 78 A2
Brookside Ashbourne DE6 173 E1
Beeley DE4 111 D2
Belper DE56 178 C2
Bradwell S33 51 D4
Burton u T DE15 248 A3
Buxworth SK23 34 A1
Eastwood NG16 182 C2
Glossop SK13 17 D4
Rolleston DE13 240 A2
Rowarth SK22 24 C4
Brookside Ave NG19 136 B3
Brookside Bar S40 94 C1
Brookside Cl Derby DE1 218 C4
Hadfield SK13 9 F2
Long Eaton NG10 236 A4
Repton DE65 242 B1
Brookside Glen S40 94 C1
Brookside Gr SK17 84 B3
Brookside Rd
Breadsall DE21 205 F2
Chapel-en-le-F SK23 47 D3
Brookside Specl Sch DE21 205 F2
Brookvale Ave Codnor DE5 181 D4
Denby DE5 180 A1
Brookvale Rd DE5 180 A1
Brookvale Rise DE5 180 A1
Brookview Ct S18 57 D2
Broom Ave Pilsley S45 132 B1
Swanwick DE55 169 F4
Broom Cl Belper DE56 178 C3
Chesterfield S41 95 E4
Derby, Chellaston DE73 232 C1
Derby, Sinfin DE73 231 F1
Duffield DE56 190 B2
Broom Dr S42 115 F1
Broom Gdns S43 96 C4
Broom La DE6 175 F4
Broom's La DE6 226 A1
Broombank Pk S18 76 B2
Broombank Rd S18 76 B2
Broome Acre DE55 160 B2
Broomfield Ave S41 115 E4
Broomfield Cl NG10 223 D3
Broomfield Coll (Derbyshire Coll of Ag) DE7 206 A3
Broomhill Ave DE7 209 D3
Broomhill Cl Derby DE3 217 E2
Eckington S21 59 D2
Broomhill Fst Sch NG19 268 A4
Broomhill La NG19 268 A4
Broomhill Rd S41 76 C1
Broomhills La DE65 242 B1
Broomyclose La ST14 210 A2
Broscroft SK13 10 A3
Broscroft Village SK13 10 A3
Brough La Bradwell S33 51 E4
Shatton S33 51 E4
Brough Rd DE15 248 B2
Brough St DE22 218 B3
Brougham Ave NG19 135 E1
Broughton Ave DE23 218 B1
Broughton Cl
Church Broughton DE65 227 D4
Ilkeston DE7 194 B1
Broughton Rd S41 95 E4
Brow Cres S20 59 F4
Brown Ave NG19 136 A2
Brown Edge Rd SK17 66 B1
Brown Hills La S10 42 B4
Brown La Ashover S45 145 D4
Barton in F NG11 237 F3
Dronfield S18 57 E2
Brown St NG19 268 A4
Brown's Flats NG16 195 F3
Brown's La DE56 191 E4
Brown's Rd NG10 236 C4
Brown's Yd DE55 170 B4
Brownhill La HD7 3 D4
Brownhills La S42 130 B2
Browning Cir DE23 231 F4
Browning Rd DE11 256 B3
Browning St Derby DE23 231 F4
3 Mansfield NG18 268 B4
Stafford ST16 269 D4
Brownlow Rd NG19 135 F1
Broxtowe Ave NG16 195 E3
Broxtowe Dr NG18 268 C3
Brun La Kirk Langley DE6 217 D4
Mackworth DE22 217 D4
Brunnen The DE55 160 A2
Brunner Ave NG20 119 F2
Brunswick Dr NG9 223 F3
Brunswick St
Chesterfield S41 266 B4
Derby DE23 231 F4
Pilsley S45 132 B1
Brunswick Terr ST17 269 D3

Brunswood Cl DE21 .... 220 C3
Brunswood La DE6 .... 187 E4
Brunswood Rd DE4 .... 143 D1
Brunt St NG18 .... 268 C3
Brunton Cl DE3 .... 217 E1
Brunts Sch The NG19 .... 136 B1
Brushes Rd SK15 .... 4 A2
Brushfield Gr S12 .... 44 B2
Brushfield Rd S40 .... 94 C3
Brussels Terr 🅱 DE7 .... 194 C1
Bryn Lea S41 .... 96 B1
Brynsmoor Rd NG16 .... 182 C4
Bryony Cl Derby DE21 .... 206 A1
  Killamarsh S21 .... 60 A3
Bubnell Rd DE45 .... 91 E3
Buchan St DE24 .... 232 B4
Buchanan St DE1 .... 267 B4
Buck Wood View S12 .... 43 E3
Buckden Cl S40 .... 95 E2
Buckfast Cl DE55 .... 169 E4
Buckford La DE65 .... 242 C4
Buckhazels La DE6 .... 203 D4
Buckingham Ave DE21 ...... 219 E4
Buckingham Cl
  🅱 Dronfield S18 .... 56 B1
  Mansfield Woodhouse
  NG19 .... 136 C3
  Swanwick DE55 .... 170 A4
Buckingham Ct
  Burton u T DE15 .... 248 B2
  Sandiacre NG10 .... 223 D2
Buckingham Rd NG10 .... 223 D2
Buckland Cl DE1 .... 218 C3
Buckland Gr SK14 .... 15 D4
Buckleather La S18 .... 74 B1
Buckley Cl DE11 .... 256 C1
Buckminster Cl DE21 .... 205 F1
Buckminster Rd DE7 .... 208 B2
Bull Farm Fst & Mid
  Sch NG19 .... 135 E1
Bull Hill S18 .... 269 E4
Bull La DE4 .... 143 E3
Bullace Cl NG19 .... 136 C1
Bullbridge Hill DE56 .... 168 A3
Buller St Derby DE23 .... 218 C1
  Ilkeston DE7 .... 209 D3
Bullhill La DE56 .... 176 C2
Bullhurst La DE4 .... 188 C2
Bulling La DE4 .... 156 C1
Bullivant Ave S80 .... 100 B4
Bullivant St NG3 .... 268 B2
Bullock Cl NG19 .... 136 A3
Bullock La Brailsford DE6 .. 201 F4
  Ironville NG16 .... 170 C3
  Somercotes DE55 .... 170 C3
Bullpit La DE56 .... 205 D4
Bullsmoor DE56 .... 179 E2
Bumpmill La DE55 .... 146 C4
Bun Alley DE45 .... 91 E2
Bungalows The
  Chesterfield, Brampton S40 .. 95 E2
  Chesterfield, Hady S41 .... 266 C2
  🅱 Chesterfield, Newbold
  S41 .... 95 F4
  Chesterfield, Whittington Moor
  S41 .... 96 A4
  Killamarsh S21 .... 60 B3
  Stonebroom DE55 .... 146 C2
Bunker S Hill S21 .... 60 C3
Bunker's Hill S80 .... 62 B4
Bunting Cl Chesterfield S40 .. 95 D1
  Ilkeston DE7 .... 208 B3
  Sheffield S8 .... 43 D1
Bunting Ho S41 .... 77 D2
Bunting Nook S8 .... 43 D1
Buntingfield La S45 .... 129 D4
Buntings Cl DE3 .... 218 A2
Bunyan Cres DE55 .... 146 C2
Bunyan Green Rd NG16 .... 171 E4
Burbage Cl Belper DE56 .... 179 E3
  🅱 Dronfield S18 .... 56 B1
Burbage Gr S12 .... 44 B3
Burbage Pl DE24 .... 232 C4
Burbage Prim Sch SK17 .... 84 C3
Burbage Rd S43 .... 97 E4
Burcot Cl DE7 .... 194 C3
Burdekin Cl SK23 .... 47 E3
Burdett Way DE65 .... 242 B2
Burdock Cl DE21 .... 205 F1
Burgess Cl S41 .... 115 E4
Burghley Cl DE73 .... 232 C1
Burghley Way DE23 .... 230 C3
Burke Dr DE55 .... 170 B4
Burkitt Dr S43 .... 79 D2
Burland Green La DE6 .... 189 D2
Burleigh Cres DE55 .... 159 E4
Burleigh Dr DE22 .... 218 C4
Burleigh St 🅱 DE7 .... 194 C1
Burley Cl S40 .... 115 D4
Burley Dr DE22 .... 204 C4
Burley Hill DE22, DE56 .... 205 D4
Burley La DE22 .... 204 C4
Burlington Ave NG16 .... 119 F3
Burlington Dr DE72 .... 235 E4
Burlington Dr NG19 .... 135 F1
Burlington Glen S17 .... 55 F4
Burlington Gr S17 .... 55 F4
Burlington Rd
  Buxton SK17 .... 85 D4
  Derby DE22 .... 217 F3
  Dore S17 .... 55 F4
Burlow Ave S40 .... 266 B3
Burlington Way DE7 .... 217 E1
Burlow Rd SK17 .... 85 E2
Burlow Rd SK17 .... 85 E1

Burnaby St DE24 .... 232 C4
Burnage Cl DE22 .... 218 C2
Burnaston Cl S18 .... 56 B1
Burnaston La NG19 .... 136 C2
Burnaston La DE65 .... 229 E3
Burnbridge Rd S41 .... 77 E2
Burncroft DE7 .... 207 F4
Burnell St S43 .... 96 C4
Burnell St S41 .... 143 D4
Burney La
  Breedon on t H DE73 .... 252 B1
  Lount DE73 .... 252 B1
Burnham Cl DE7 .... 207 E4
Burnham Dr DE3 .... 217 E1
Burnham Way NG2 .... 268 B1
Burns Ave
  Mansfield Woodhouse
  NG19 .... 136 B1
  Nottingham NG2 .... 268 B1
Burns Cl Chesterfield S40 .. 114 C4
  Derby DE23 .... 231 E4
Burns Dr Dronfield S18 ..... 76 B4
  Grassmoor S42 .... 115 F2
Burns St Ilkeston DE7 .... 208 C4
  Mansfield NG18 .... 268 B4
  Nottingham NG7 .... 268 A2
Burnshaw St DE55 .... 146 B3
Burnside Hadfield SK13 .... 9 F4
  Rolleston DE13 .... 240 A2
Burnside Ave Sheffield S8 .. 43 D3
  Shirland DE55 .... 146 B1
Burnside Cl DE24 .... 231 E2
Burnside Dr DE22 .... 204 C2
Burnside St DE24 .... 233 D4
Burnt House Rd DE75 ...... 181 E1
Burnt Oaks Cl NG19 .... 136 B2
Burr La DE7 .... 194 C1
Burre Cl DE45 .... 91 F3
Burrfields Rd SK23 .... 47 D3
Burrowfield Mews DE21 .. 220 C1
Burrows La
  Brailsford DE6 .... 201 F1
  Middleton (Nr Wirksworth)
  DE4 .... 154 B3
  Trusley DE6 .... 201 F1
Burrows The DE11 .... 255 F3
Burrs Wood Croft S40 .... 95 E4
Bursdon Cl S41 .... 77 D1
Burton Close Dr DE45 ..... 109 F2
Burton Edge DE45 .... 109 E2
Burton Rd Branston DE14 .. 254 A4
  Coton in t L DE12 .... 260 B2
  Derby DE23 .... 218 B1
  Findern DE65 .... 230 B2
  Linton DE11 .... 255 E1
  Overseal DE12 .... 262 A2
  Repton DE65 .... 242 A1
  Swadlincote DE11 .... 255 F4
  Ticknall DE73 .... 250 C2
  Tutbury DE13 .... 239 E2
  Willington DE65 .... 241 F4
Burton St Heanor DE75 .... 181 F1
  Mansfield NG18 .... 268 B2
  Tutbury DE13 .... 239 E3
Burton Tech Coll
  (Annexe) DE13 .... 240 B2
Burwell Cl SK13 .... 17 D4
Burwell St NG7 .... 268 A2
Bush Vale DE56 .... 178 C3
Bushey Wood Rd S17 .... 55 F3
Bushton La
  Burton u T DE13 .... 239 D1
  Tutbury DE13 .... 239 D1
Bushy Cl NG10 .... 236 A3
Buskeyfield La NG20 ...... 101 F2
Butcher's La DE4 .... 127 F2
Bute St S43 .... 78 C1
Butler Cres NG19 .... 135 E1
Butler St S14 .... 43 E2
Butler Way S21 .... 60 B3
Butt Hill S80 .... 81 F3
Butt Hill S80 .... 81 F3
Butt La Blackfordby DE11 .. 257 D1
  Mansfield Woodhouse
  NG19 .... 136 B1
Butt St NG10 .... 223 D3
Butterfield Cres DE55 ..... 169 F4
Butterfield La DE55 .... 145 F1
Butterhall Cl S80 .... 82 A3
Butterley Croft Bsns Ctr
  DE5 .... 180 C4
Butterley Hill DE5 .... 169 F2
Butterley La Ashover S45 .. 144 C3
Butterton Cl DE7 .... 209 D4
Butterton Dr 🅱 S40 .... 95 D4
Buttonoak Dr DE73 .... 233 D2
Butts Hill S17 .... 55 E2
Butts Rd Ashover S45 ...... 129 F2
  Bakewell DE45 .... 109 E3
  Darley Dale DE4 .... 127 D2
Butts Terr DE45 .... 109 E3
Butts The DE75 .... 179 D2
Butts View DE45 .... 109 E3
Buxton Ave DE75 .... 193 F4
Buxton Cl DE24 .... 256 A4
Buxton Com Sch SK17 .... 85 D3
Buxton Ct DE7 .... 194 B1
Buxton Ctry Pk SK17 ...... 84 C3

Buxton & District Cottage
  Hospl SK17 .... 85 E3
Buxton Dr Derby DE3 ...... 217 F2
  Little Eaton DE7 .... 191 E1
Buxton Inf Sch SK17 .... 85 D3
Buxton Jun Sch SK17 ...... 85 D3
Buxton Mews SK13 .... 9 F1
Buxton Micrarium Mus
  SK17 .... 85 E3
Buxton Old Rd SK12 .... 32 C2
Buxton Rd
  Alstonefield DE6 .... 149 D3
  Ashbourne DE6 .... 173 D1
  Ashford in t W DE45 ...... 108 C4
  Bakewell DE45 .... 109 D4
  Chapel-en-le-F SK23 ..... 47 E3
  Chinley SK23 .... 34 C1
  Derby DE21 .... 219 F4
  Disley SK12 .... 32 C3
  Dove Holes SK17 .... 66 C4
  Furness Vale SK23 .... 32 A3
  High Lane SK6 .... 32 A3
  Longnor SK17 .... 121 D2
  Mansfield NG19 .... 135 E1
  New Mills SK23 .... 33 E2
  Tideswell SK17 .... 69 E2
Buxton Rd W SK12 .... 32 A3
Buxton Terr SK14 .... 9 E3
Buxworth Prim Sch SK23 .. 34 A1
Byfield Cl DE21 .... 206 A1
Byng Ave DE23 .... 231 F4
Byron Ave Alfreton DE55 .. 159 D2
  Burton u T DE15 .... 254 C4
  Long Eaton NG10 .... 223 D2
  Mansfield Woodhouse
  NG19 .... 136 B1
Byron Cl Dronfield S18 .... 76 B4
  Grassmoor S42 .... 115 F2
Byron Cres NG16 .... 195 E2
Byron Gr NG9 .... 209 F1
Byron Gr DE55 .... 146 C2
Byron Rd Chesterfield S40 .. 115 D4
  Swadlincote DE11 .... 256 B1
Byron St Buxton SK17 ...... 85 E3
  Chesterfield S40 .... 266 B1
  Derby DE23 .... 218 C1
  Ilkeston DE7 .... 194 C1
  Mansfield NG18 .... 268 B4
  Shirebrook NG20 .... 119 F2
  Shirland DE55 .... 146 B1
Bywell La DE56 .... 179 F1

Cacklehill La DE6 .... 184 B1
Cadeby Cl DE55 .... 170 B3
Cadgwith Dr DE22 .... 204 C2
Cadley Hall Ind Est DE11 .. 255 F2
Cadley Hill Rd DE11 .... 255 F2
Cadman St S20 .... 59 E3
Cadman St S20 .... 59 E3
Cadwell Cl DE24 .... 233 E3
Caerhays Ct DE24 .... 231 E2
Caernarfon Cl DE55 .... 170 A4
Caernarvon Cl
  🅱 Chesterfield S40 .... 95 E1
  Derby DE21 .... 220 C3
Caernarvon Rd S18 .... 76 A4
Caesar St DE1 .... 219 D4
Cairngorm Cl DE22 .... 204 C1
Cairn Dr S12 .... 77 E2
Cairngorm Dr DE24 .... 231 E2
Cairns Cl
  Burton u T DE15 .... 248 B2
  Derby DE21 .... 217 F2
Cairns St NG2 .... 268 B2
Cairnsmore Cl NG10 .... 223 D1
Caldene Terr SK23 .... 45 F4
Calder Cl Derby DE24 ..... 204 C2
  Hilton DE65 .... 228 B2
Calderdale Dr NG10 .... 236 A3
Caldermill Dr DE21 .... 206 A1
Caldey Rd S18 .... 76 A4
Caldwell Hall Sch DE12 .. 260 C4
Calesdale Cl S41 .... 85 D3
Calf Croft S80 .... 82 A3
Calgary Cres DE15 .... 248 B2
California Gdns DE22 ...... 218 B2
California La S43 .... 80 A4
Calke Abbey DE65 .... 251 E1
Calke Rise S43 .... 169 F1
Calladine La
  Horsley Woodhouse DE7 .. 192 B3
  Shottle DE56 .... 177 E3
Calladine Rd DE75 .... 181 E1
Callan's La LE65 .... 258 B4
Callow Dr S2 .... 43 E3
Callow Hill Way DE23 .... 231 D4
Callow La Callow DE4 ...... 165 E3
  Wirksworth DE4 .... 165 E3
Callow Mount S14 .... 43 E3
Callow Pl S14 .... 43 E3
Callow Rd S14 .... 43 E3
Callowfield La S18 .... 57 E1
Callow Brook Dr S41 .... 115 D3
Callow CE Prim Sch S44 .. 96 C1
Callow La Callow DE4 ...... 165 E3
Callside Ave DE23 .... 231 D4
Calstock Cl DE24 .... 233 E2
Calton Ave S43 .... 109 E3
Calver Ave S42 .... 132 A4
Calver Cl Belper DE56 .... 179 D2
  Derby DE21 .... 220 C2
Calver Cres S43 .... 97 E4
Calver Mews S43 .... 97 E4
Calvert Cl DE24 .... 232 C2
Calverton Cl DE24 .... 232 C2
Calvert St DE1 .... 267 D2

Calverton Cl DE24 .... 232 C2
Calvin Cl DE24 .... 233 D3
Camberwell Ave DE22 .... 218 A3
Camborne Cl DE21 .... 205 F1
Cambria Rd NG19 .... 135 E2
Cambrian Cl S40 .... 95 E3
Cambrian Way DE11 .... 256 A2
Cambridge Cres
  Bramley-Vale S44 .... 117 F1
  Stapleford NG9 .... 209 E1
Cambridge Rd
  🅱 Brimington S43 .... 96 C4
  Sheffield S8 .... 43 D3
Cambridge St
  Blackwell DE55 .... 147 F1
  Derby, Rose Hill DE23 ... 219 D1
  Derby, Spondon DE21 ... 220 C2
  Mansfield NG18 .... 268 B3
  Stafford ST16 .... 69 F4
Camdale Rise S12 .... 44 C1
Camdale View S12 .... 44 C1
Camden Cl DE22 .... 268 C1
Camden St DE22 .... 218 C2
Camellia Cl DE3 .... 217 E2
Cameron Cl DE13 .... 240 C1
Cameron Rd DE23 .... 231 F4
Cammas Way S43 .... 77 E3
Camms Cl S21 .... 59 E2
Camms Endowed CE
  Prim Sch S21 .... 59 E2
Camp St DE1 .... 219 D4
Camp Wood Cl DE11 ...... 255 E4
Campbell Dr S43 .... 78 A2
Campbell Pl S14 .... 209 E4
Campbell St Belper DE56 .. 178 C2
  Derby DE24 .... 232 B4
  Langley Mill NG16 .... 182 B2
  Nottingham NG3 .... 268 B2
Campion Hill DE74 .... 247 D2
Campion Pl DE24 .... 256 C2
Campion St S42 .... 218 B3
Campsie Ct 🅱 DE24 ...... 231 E2
Canal Bank DE7 .... 235 D1
Canal Bridge DE65 .... 242 A3
Canal Mus NG1 .... 268 B1
Canal Side Cl DE72 .... 221 E1
  Ilkeston DE7 .... 195 D1
  Long Eaton NG10 .... 223 E1
  Marple SK6 .... 23 D3
  Nottingham NG1 .... 268 B1
  Sandiacre NG10 .... 223 E3
  Whaley Bridge SK23 .... 45 F4
Canal Wharf S41 .... 96 A3
Canberra Cl Derby DE3 .. 217 F1
  Stapleford NG9 .... 223 D3
Canberra Dr ST16 .... 269 F4
Candlemass Ct NG19 ...... 136 B1
Cannell Cl S45 .... 131 D2
Canner Cl DE21 .... 257 D1
Canning Cir NG7 .... 268 A2
Cannock Way NG10 .... 237 D4
Cannon Fields S32 .... 72 C2
Cannon St SK14 .... 9 E3
Canon Cl DE7 .... 194 C3
Canon's Wlk DE22 .... 204 C1
Cantelupe Rd DE7 .... 209 D4
Canterbury Cl
  Duffield DE56 .... 190 C2
  Mansfield Woodhouse
  NG19 .... 136 B3
Canterbury Rd
  Burton u T DE15 .... 248 B2
  Sheffield S8 .... 43 D3
  Wirksworth DE4 .... 165 F4
Canterbury St DE21 .... 219 F4
Canterbury Terr DE4 ..... 165 F4
Cantley Cl DE24 .... 232 B2
Cantley Rd DE55 .... 170 B3
Cape St NG18 .... 268 A4
Capel Rise S43 .... 96 B4
Capthorne Cl S40 .... 94 C3
Car Rd S17 .... 71 F4
Car Vale Dr S13 .... 44 B4
Car Vale View S13 .... 44 B4
Cardale Rd NG19 .... 135 E2
Carder Cl DE65 .... 230 B1
Cardean Cl DE1 .... 219 D4
Carder Gn SK17 .... 121 D3
Cardiff St NG3 .... 268 C2
Cardigan St DE21 .... 219 E4
Cardington Cl DE3 .... 217 E1
Cardlemere La SK17 .... 138 C1
Cardrona Cl DE21 .... 205 F1
Cardwell Ave S13 .... 44 C4
Cardwell Dr S13 .... 44 C4
Carfield Ave S8 .... 43 D3
Carfield La S8 .... 43 D3
Carfield Prim Sch S8 .... 43 D3
Carisbrooke Dr DE21 ..... 240 C1
Carlin Cl DE72 .... 235 E4
Carlin St S13 .... 44 C3
Carlisle Ave DE23 .... 231 E4
Carlisle Cl S41 .... 76 C2
Carlisle Gr S41 .... 77 D1
Carlisle Rd SK17 .... 84 C4
Carlton Ave Derby DE24 .. 232 C2
  Northwood DE4 .... 127 D1
Carlton Cl Clay Cross S45 .. 131 E1
  Heanor DE75 .... 181 E1
  Mosborough S20 .... 59 F4
Carlton Dr DE24 .... 232 C2
Carlton Gdns DE24 .... 232 C2

Carlton Rd
  Chesterfield S40 .... 115 D3
  Derby DE21 .... 218 C1
  Long Eaton NG10 .... 236 A3
  Nottingham NG3 .... 268 C2
  Stoke-on-T ST4 .... 269 F2
Carlton St
  Mansfield Woodhouse
  NG19 .... 136 B1
  Nottingham NG1 .... 268 B1
Carlyle Inf Sch DE23 ...... 231 D4
Carlyle Rd S42 .... 146 C2
Carlyle St Derby DE24 .... 232 B4
  Heanor DE75 .... 181 E2
Carlyon Gdns S40 .... 114 C4
Carnarvon Rd NG17 .... 148 C1
Carnegie St DE23 .... 232 A4
Carnfield Cl DE55 .... 159 E3
Carnfield Hill DE55 .... 159 E3
Carnforth Cl Derby DE3 .. 217 F1
  Stapleford NG9 .... 223 E3
Carnoustie Ave S40 .... 114 B4
Carnoustie Cl DE3 .... 217 E1
Carol Cres DE21 .... 219 F3
Caroline Cl DE24 .... 233 E4
Caroline Ct DE7 .... 209 D3
Carpenter Ave
  Mansfield NG19 .... 135 E1
  Mastin Moor S43 .... 79 D2
Carpenter Cl DE55 .... 248 B1
Carpenter Croft S12 .... 44 B3
Carpenter Gdns S12 .... 44 B3
Carpenter Mews S12 ...... 44 B3
Carper La DE6 .... 187 F1
Carr Brow S46 .... 43 D3
Carr La DE45 .... 160 A4
Carr Fields DE7 .... 192 B4
Carr La
  Brackenfield DE55 .... 145 E2
  Crich DE4 .... 156 C1
  Matlock DE4 .... 143 F1
  Scarcliffe S44 .... 117 F4
  South Normanton DE55 .. 160 A4
  Shireoaks S81 .... 63 E3
  Thornhill S33 .... 39 E3
Car Vale Rd S44 .... 98 C2
Carrbrook Ind Est SK15 ... 4 A3
Carfield Ave NG16 .... 223 F1
Carfield Ct S8 .... 43 D3
Carfield Cl S8 .... 43 D3
Carfield Gr S8 .... 43 D3
Carfield La S8 .... 43 D3
Carfield St S8 .... 43 D3
Carhouse La S14 .... 9 E2
Carriage Dr The SK13 .... 9 F3
Carriers Rd DE65 .... 241 E3
Carrington St Derby DE1 .. 267 C2
  Nottingham NG1 .... 268 B1
Carron Cl DE24 .... 231 F2
Carrs Cl DE7 .... 247 D2
Carrwood Rd
  Chesterfield S41 .... 76 A2
  Renishaw S21 .... 79 D4
Carsington Cl S40 .... 95 D3
Carsington Ct DE22 .... 204 B1
Carsington Dr NG19 ...... 136 C2
Carsington & Hopton CE
  Prim Sch S44 .... 164 C4
Carsington Mews DE22 .. 204 C1
Carsington Water
  Visitor Ctr DE6 .... 164 B2
Carson Croft DE4 .... 143 E3
Carson Mount S12 .... 44 A2
Carson Rd DE21 .... 220 A3
Carson Way ST16 .... 269 D4
Carter La
  Shirebrook NG20 .... 119 F2
  Warsop Vale NG20 .... 120 B2
Carter La E DE55 .... 160 B3
Carter La W
  Shirebrook NG20 .... 119 F2
  South Normanton DE55 .. 159 E4
Carter Pl S8 .... 43 D3
Carter Rd Beeston NG9 ... 223 F3
  Sheffield S8 .... 43 D3
Carter St DE24 .... 232 B3
Carterhall La S12 .... 44 B1
Carterhall Rd S12 .... 44 A1
Cartledge La S18 .... 57 D4
Cartmel Cl S18 .... 56 C1
Cartmel Cres S42 .... 115 F2
Cartwright St S81 .... 63 F4
Carver Cl S26 .... 61 F3
Carver Way S26 .... 61 F3
Cary Rd Eckington S21 ..... 59 F2
  Sheffield S2 .... 44 A4
Cascade Gr DE23 .... 231 D4
Casson Ave DE24 .... 233 D3
Casson Dr S26 .... 61 F4
Casson St S21 .... 59 E2
Casson St NG16 .... 182 B4
Castings Rd DE23 .... 232 A4
Castle Bvd NG7 .... 268 A1
Castle Cl DE45 .... 109 D4
Castle Ct Elvaston DE72 .. 234 C3
  Glossop SK13 .... 17 D4
  Mastin Moor S43 .... 79 D2
  Sheffield S2 .... 44 A4
Castle Croft DE24 .... 233 E3
Castle Dr Bakewell DE45 .. 109 D4
  Codnor NG16 .... 181 F3
  Somercotes DE55 .... 170 B4
Castle Gate DE13 .... 239 E2
Castle Green Dr SK22 .... 24 A1
Castle Gn S40 .... 266 B3
Castle Gate S40 .... 118 A4
Castle Gr DE11 .... 256 B3
Castle Gresley Inf Sch
  DE11 .... 261 F4
Castle Hayes La DE13 .... 239 D3

Castle Hill
Castle Donington DE74 — 247 D2
Duffield DE56 — 190 C2
Eckington S21 — 59 E2
Glossop SK13 — 10 C1
Castle Hill Cl S41 — 59 E2
Castle Ho DE1 — 267 D2
Castle La
Bolsover S44 — 99 D1
Ironville NG16 — 170 C1
Melbourne DE73 — 252 A4
Castle Meadow Rd NG7 — 268 A1
Castle Mews
Mansfield Woodhouse NG19 — 136 A2
Melbourne DE73 — 252 A4
Castle Mews The DE11 — 256 A4
Castle Mills DE73 — 252 A4
Castle Mount Cres DE45 — 109 E4
Castle Mount Way DE45 — 109 F4
Castle Mus & Art Gall NG1 — 268 A1
Castle Orch DE56 — 190 C2
Castle Pl NG1 — 268 A1
Castle Quay NG7 — 268 A1
Castle Rd Nottingham NG1 — 268 B1
Swadlincote DE11 — 255 F1
Castle Row S17 — 56 A3
Castle St Bakewell DE45 — 109 E3
Bolsover S44 — 99 D1
Castleton S33 — 38 A1
Derby DE1 — 267 C2
Hadfield SK13 — 10 A2
Mansfield NG18 — 268 B4
Mansfield Woodhouse NG19 — 136 A2
Melbourne DE73 — 252 A4
Nottingham NG2 — 268 C1
Stafford ST16 — 269 D4
Tutbury DE13 — 239 E3
Castle View Aldercar NG16 — 182 A4
Eckington S21 — 59 E2
Stafford ST16 — 269 D4
Castle View Dr DE4 — 156 B3
Castle View S Dr S18 — 269 D3
Castle Way The DE56 — 241 F3
Castle Yd S40 — 266 B2
Castlebeck Ave S2 — 44 B4
Castlebeck Dr S2 — 44 B4
Castledale Croft S2 — 44 A4
Castledale Gr S2 — 44 A4
Castledale Pl S2 — 44 A4
Castledene Dr ST16 — 269 D3
Castlefields Ironville NG16 — 170 C2
Stafford ST16 — 269 D3
Castlegate La DE45 — 89 E3
Castlering Way ⑤ S18 — 56 C1
Castlerow Cl S17 — 56 A3
Castlerow Dr S17 — 56 A3
Castleshaw Dr DE23 — 230 C4
Castleton Ave Derby DE23 — 231 F4
Ilkeston DE7 — 194 C3
Somercotes DE55 — 170 B3
Castleton CE Prim Sch S33 — 38 B1
Castleton Cl S20 — 59 E1
Castleton Cres SK13 — 9 F1
Castleton Gr S43 — 97 D3
Castleton Rd
Hathersage S32 — 52 C4
Hope S33 — 38 C2
Castleview DE55 — 239 E4
Cat & Fiddle La DE7 — 207 F3
Cat La S8 — 43 E3
Catchford View S40 — 95 D4
Catcliff DE45 — 109 E2
Catcliff Cotts DE45 — 109 E2
Cathedral Rd DE1 — 267 B4
Cathedral View DE22 — 218 B1
Catherine Ave
Ilkeston DE7 — 208 C3
Mansfield Woodhouse NG19 — 136 B2
Catherine St
Alfreton DE55 — 159 E2
Chesterfield S40 — 95 F2
Derby DE23 — 219 D1
Catholme La DE13 — 259 D2
Catkin Dr NG16 — 135 E2
Cator Rd NG3 — 45 E2
Catterick Dr DE3 — 217 E1
Catterwood Dr S6 — 15 D1
Catton La Rosliston DE12 — 260 A3
Walton-on-T DE12 — 260 A3
Caudwell Cl S42 — 131 E4
Cauldon Dr S40 — 95 D3
Cauldwell Rd
Caldwell DE12 — 261 D3
Linton DE12 — 261 D3
Caunton Cl NG18 — 268 A3
Causeway DE22 — 204 C1
Causeway Gdns S17 — 55 E4
Causeway Head Rd S17 — 55 E4
Causeway La DE4 — 143 E3
Causeway The
Bamber S45 — 129 E2
Dore S17 — 55 E4
Eyam S32 — 71 F3
Wirksworth DE4 — 165 F4
Cavan Dr DE21 — 220 A2
Cavell Dr S45 — 131 F1
Cavendish Ave
Buxton SK17 — 84 C3
Derby DE22 — 204 C2
Dore S17 — 55 F4
Cavendish Cir SK17 — 85 D4

Cavendish Cl
Castle Donington DE74 — 247 D1
Doveridge DE6 — 211 E1
Duffield DE56 — 190 B1
Holmewood S42 — 116 C1
Shardlow DE72 — 235 D1
Swadlincote DE11 — 256 A4
Cavendish Close Inf & Jun Schs DE21 — 220 A4
Cavendish Cres NG9 — 209 E1
Cavendish Cres N NG7 — 268 A1
Cavendish Cres S NG7 — 268 A1
Cavendish Ct Derby DE21 — 257 D1
Shardlow DE72 — 235 D1
Cavendish Dr
Ashbourne DE6 — 185 E4
Clowne S43 — 81 D2
Ripley DE5 — 169 E1
Cavendish Hospl The SK17 — 85 D4
Cavendish Jun Sch S41 — 95 F4
Cavendish Pk DE4 — 143 E4
Cavendish Pl S43 — 78 A2
Cavendish Rd
Bolsover S44 — 99 D1
Ilkeston DE7 — 208 C3
Long Eaton NG10 — 223 E1
Matlock DE4 — 143 E3
Cavendish Rd E NG7 — 268 A1
Cavendish Rd W NG7 — 268 A1
Cavendish Rise S18 — 75 F4
Cavendish Sq S21 — 77 D4
Cavendish St
Chesterfield S40 — 266 B3
Derby DE1 — 267 A3
Langwith NG20 — 119 F4
Mansfield NG18 — 268 C3
Mansfield Woodhouse NG19 — 136 A2
Staveley S43 — 97 E4
Cavendish St N S41 — 77 D1
Cavendish Way DE3 — 217 F1
Caversfield Cl DE23 — 231 D4
Caversham Way DE7 — 207 F4
Cavill Rd S8 — 43 D2
Cawdor Rd S2 — 43 F3
Caxton Cl S43 — 77 E2
Caxton St
Derby, Littleover DE23 — 231 F3
Derby, Normanton DE23 — 231 F4
Caythorpe Ct NG19 — 136 C2
Ceal The SK6 — 15 D1
Cecil Ave S41 — 77 D1
Cecil Rd Dronfield S18 — 57 D1
Swadlincote DE11 — 255 F3
Cecil St DE22 — 218 B3
Cedar Ave Alfreton DE55 — 159 D3
Long Eaton NG10 — 236 B3
Mansfield Woodhouse NG19 — 136 B3
Cedar Cl Ashbourne DE6 — 185 E4
Eckington S21 — 59 D1
Glapwell S44 — 118 A1
Glossop SK13 — 10 A1
Killamarsh S21 — 60 B3
Sandiacre NG10 — 223 D4
Cedar Croft DE56 — 192 A4
Cedar Dr Ockbrook DE72 — 221 E2
Selston NG16 — 171 F4
Shirland DE55 — 210 A2
Cedar Gr Belper DE56 — 179 D1
Linton DE12 — 261 E3
South Normanton DE55 — 160 A2
Swadlincote DE11 — 256 A4
Cedar Park Dr S44 — 99 E1
Cedar Pk DE7 — 208 C4
Cedar Rd
Castle Donington DE74 — 247 D1
Linton DE11 — 261 F4
Cedar St Brimington S43 — 78 A1
Derby DE22 — 218 C4
Mansfield NG18 — 268 C3
Shirland DE55 — 146 B3
Cedarwood Ct DE21 — 205 F1
Celandine Cl DE21 — 206 A1
Celandine Ct 11 S17 — 56 A3
Celandine Gdns S17 — 56 A3
Celandine Pl DE11 — 256 C2
Celanese Rd DE21 — 220 B2
Cemetery La Ripley DE5 — 169 F1
Staveley S43 — 78 C1
Wirksworth DE4 — 154 C1
Cemetery Rd Belper DE56 — 179 D3
Dronfield S18 — 96 B1
Clay Cross S45 — 131 F1
Dronfield S18 — 76 A4
Glossop SK13 — 10 B2
Somercotes DE55 — 170 B4
Swadlincote DE11 — 223 F4
Cemetery Terr S43 — 96 C4
Central Cl
Shirebrook NG20 — 119 F2
Unstone S18 — 76 C3
Central Dr Blackwell DE55 — 147 F1
Buxton SK17 — 85 E3
Calow S44 — 96 C3
Chesterfield S41 — 96 B1
Shirebrook NG20 — 119 F2

Central Dr continued
Wingerworth S42 — 114 C2
Central Pavement S40 — 266 B3
Central Rd DE55 — 159 D2
Central St Chesterfield S41 — 96 B1
Holmewood S42 — 116 C1
Nottingham NG3 — 268 C2
Central Wlk S43 — 96 B4
Centre Ct DE1 — 267 C1
Centre St S44 — 117 E1
Centurion Wlk DE1 — 219 D4
Chaddesden Cl S18 — 56 B1
Chaddesden Cres NG7 — 268 A1
Chaddesden La DE21 — 220 A3
Chaddesden Lane End DE21 — 219 F3
Chaddesden Park Inf & Jun Schs DE21 — 220 A4
Chaddesden Park Rd DE21 — 219 F4
Chadfield Rd DE56 — 190 C3
Chadwick Ave DE24 — 232 C3
Chadwick Hill DE4 — 141 D3
Chadwick Nick La DE4 — 167 F4
Chadwick Rd S13 — 44 B4
Chadwick St S13 — 17 D4
Chaffinch Cl DE21 — 220 C3
Chain La DE23 — 218 A1
Chalfont Sq DE21 — 206 A1
Challacy Cl DE24 — 232 C4
Challands Cl S41 — 115 E4
Challands Way S41 — 115 E4
Challis Ave DE21 — 220 A4
Challoner Gn ⑧ S20 — 59 F4
Challoner Way DE7 — 208 C4
Chalons Cl DE7 — 194 C1
Chalons Way DE7 — 208 C4
Chamberlain Ave ST4 — 269 E1
Chambers Ave DE7 — 209 D4
Chambers Ct S4 — 9 D2
Chambers St DE24 — 219 F1
Champion Ave DE7 — 194 B2
Champion Cres NG19 — 268 A4
Champion Dr S21 — 60 B3
Champion Hill DE56 — 190 C2
Chancel Pl DE22 — 267 A1
Chancery La DE22 — 218 A3
Chancet Wood Cl S8 — 56 C4
Chancet Wood Dr S8 — 56 C4
Chancet Wood Rd S8 — 56 C4
Chancet Wood View S8 — 56 C4
Chander Hill La S42 — 113 E4
Chandlers Ford DE21 — 205 F1
Chandos Cres S21 — 60 B3
Chandos Pole St DE22 — 218 B3
Chandres Ct DE22 — 204 C2
Chaneyfield Way S40 — 95 D4
Channel The DE1 — 267 C3
Chantrey Ave S41 — 96 A3
Chantrey Rd S8 — 43 D2
Chantry Cl Derby DE21 — 217 E1
Disley SK12 — 32 C3
Long Eaton NG10 — 236 A4
Chantry Ct SK17 — 69 E2
Chantry Fold SK12 — 32 C3
Chantry La SK17 — 69 E2
Chantry Rd SK12 — 32 B3
Chapel Bar NG1 — 268 A1
Chapel Brow
Charlesworth SK13 — 16 C3
Tintwistle SK13 — 10 A4
Chapel Cl Clowne S43 — 80 C2
Moira DE11 — 256 B3
Willington DE65 — 242 A3
Youlgreave DE45 — 125 D3
Chapel Croft Elton DE4 — 140 C3
Middleton (Nr Wirksworth) DE4 — 154 B3
Chapel Ct DE6 — 224 B4
Chapel Hill Ashover S45 — 129 F2
Beeley DE4 — 111 D2
Cromford DE4 — 155 D4
Chapel Houses SK6 — 23 D3
Chapel La Apperknowle S18 — 58 A1
Bakewell DE45 — 109 E3
Barrow u T DE73 — 244 A3
Boylestone DE6 — 213 D4
Church Broughton DE65 — 227 D4
Crich DE4 — 168 A4
Derby, Chaddesden DE21 — 220 A4
Derby, Chellaston DE73 — 233 D1
Derby, Spondon DE21 — 220 C3
Hadfield SK13 — 9 F3
Hanbury DE13 — 238 A1
Holloway DE4 — 156 A3
Middleton (Nr Wirksworth) DE4 — 154 B3
Rolleston DE13 — 240 A2
Stanton DE6 — 162 A3
Totley S17 — 55 E2
Wirksworth DE4 — 154 C1

Chapel St continued
Chesterfield S41 — 96 A4
Coton in t E DE12 — 260 B2
Derby, Spondon DE21 — 220 C3
Derby, The Holmes DE1 — 267 B1
Donisthorpe DE12 — 265 F4
Duffield DE56 — 190 C2
Eastwood NG16 — 182 C1
Fritchley DE56 — 168 A3
Glossop SK13 — 10 B1
Glossop SK13 — 25 E1
Hayfield SK22 — 25 C1
Heanor DE75 — 194 A4
Holbrook DE56 — 191 E4
17 Ilkeston DE7 — 194 C1
Kilburn DE56 — 192 A4
Kimberley NG16 — 195 F3
Linton DE11 — 261 F4
Long Eaton NG10 — 236 C4
Longnor SK17 — 121 D3
Melbourne DE73 — 252 A4
Monyash DE45 — 107 C2
Mosborough S20 — 59 E3
New Mills SK22 — 33 D3
Ripley DE5 — 169 E1
Rowarth SK22 — 24 A1
Smisby LE65 — 257 F2
Somercotes DE55 — 170 B4
Stafford ST16 — 269 E4
Stonebroom DE55 — 147 D2
Stretton en le F DE12 — 265 F3
Swadlincote, Church Gresley DE11 — 256 A1
Swadlincote, Newhall DE12 — 255 F3
Swanwick DE55 — 169 F4
Ticknall DE73 — 251 D3
Whaley Bridge SK23 — 45 F4
Whaley Thorns NG20 — 101 D2
Woodville DE11 — 256 C1
Chapel Terr ST16 — 269 E4
Chapel Way S42 — 115 E1
Chapel Wlk S32 — 72 C1
Chapel Yd Dronfield S18 — 57 D1
Harthill S26 — 61 F3
Chapel-en-le-Frith CE Inf Sch SK23 — 47 D3
Chapel-en-le-Frith High Sch SK23 — 47 D3
Chapel-en-le-Frith Sta SK23 — 47 D2
Chapman Ave DE24 — 233 D3
Chapman La S21 — 115 F2
Chapter Cl DE21 — 205 E1
Chardin Ave S46 — 23 E4
Charing Ct DE1 — 267 C5
Charingworth Rd DE21 — 206 A1
Chariot Cl DE24 — 219 E2
Charity La DE45 — 170 B3
Charlbury Cl DE23 — 231 D4
Charles Ashmore Rd S8 — 57 D4
Charles Ave Derby DE21 — 220 B3
Sandiacre NG10 — 223 D3
Stapleford NG9 — 209 F3
Charles Cl DE7 — 209 D3
Charles La S13 — 10 C2
Charles St Alfreton DE55 — 159 D3
Chesterfield S40 — 95 F4
Glossop SK13 — 10 B1
Long Eaton NG10 — 236 B3
Mansfield NG19 — 136 A1
Charlesworth CE Prim Sch SK13 — 16 B3
Charlesworth Cl S43 — 33 E2
Charlesworth Cres NG19 — 136 C2
Charlesworth Rd SK13 — 33 E2
Charlesworth St S44 — 117 F4
Charley La SK23 — 45 D3
Charlotte Inf Sch DE7 — 194 C1
Charlotte St S41 — 51 D4
Charlotte Rd S2 — 43 D4
Charlotte St DE23 — 219 D1
Charlton Ave NG10 — 223 E1
Charlton Cl DE12 — 261 E3
Charlton St DE14 — 269 E2
Charnock Ave S12 — 44 A1
Charnock Cres S12 — 44 A1
Charnock Dale Rd S12 — 44 A2
Charnock Gr S12 — 44 A2
Charnock Hall Cty Prim Sch S12 — 44 A1
Charnock Hall Rd S12 — 44 A1
Charnock View Rd S12 — 44 A1
Charnock Wood Rd S12 — 44 A1
Charnwood Ave
Belper DE56 — 179 D2
Borrowash DE72 — 221 E2
Castle Donington DE74 — 247 E2
Charnwood Cres DE55 — 148 A2
Charnwood Dr DE55 — 169 E1
Charnwood Gr NG19 — 136 A3
Charnwood St Derby DE1 — 267 B1
Charter Pk DE7 — 208 C4
Charterhouse Dr DE21 — 205 F2

Charterhouse Dr ST17 — 269 F3
Charterstone La DE22 — 204 C2
Chartwell Ave S42 — 114 B3
Chartwell Dr DE21 — 219 E3
Chase Rd DE56 — 167 F2
Chase The Derby DE24 — 231 F2
Hilton DE65 — 192 A4
Little Eaton DE21 — 191 E1
Chase View DE4 — 156 C1
Chasecliff Cl S40 — 95 E3
Chatfield Cl DE15 — 248 B1
Chatham Cl DE56 — 159 E2
Chatham Ct DE56 — 179 E2
Chatham St Derby DE22 — 232 A4
Nottingham NG1 — 268 B2
Chatsworth Ave
Chesterfield S40 — 95 D1
Clowne S43 — 80 C2
Crich DE4 — 156 C1
Darley Dale DE4 — 142 C4
Long Eaton NG10 — 237 D3
Shirebrook NG20 — 119 F3
Chatsworth Cl
Alfreton DE55 — 158 C2
Bolsover S44 — 99 E1
Sandiacre NG10 — 223 D2
Chatsworth Cres
Bullbridge DE56 — 168 A3
Derby DE22 — 204 C2
Chatsworth Ct Derby DE24 — 231 F2
Staveley S43 — 97 E4
West Hallam DE7 — 207 F4
Chatsworth Dr Derby DE3 — 217 F2
Little Eaton DE21 — 191 E1
North Wingfield S42 — 132 A3
Tutbury DE13 — 239 E3
Chatsworth Lodge SK17 — 85 D4
Chatsworth Park Ave S12 — 44 A3
Chatsworth Park Dr S12 — 44 A3
Chatsworth Park Gr S12 — 44 A3
Chatsworth Park Rd S12 — 44 A3
Chatsworth Park Rise S12 — 44 A3
Chatsworth Pl
27 Dronfield S18 — 56 B1
Ilkeston DE7 — 208 A3
Chatsworth Rd Buxton SK17 — 85 D4
Chesterfield S40 — 95 E3
Creswell S80 — 81 E1
Dore S17 — 55 F3
Rowsley DE4 — 111 D1
Swadlincote DE11 — 256 A3
Chatsworth St Derby DE23 — 218 C1
Tibshelf DE55 — 148 A3
Chatteris Dr DE21 — 205 E1
Chatterton La SK6 — 24 A4
Chaucer Dr S18 — 76 B4
Chaucer Inf Sch DE7 — 208 C2
Chaucer Jun Sch DE7 — 194 C1
Chaucer Rd S41 — 95 F4
Chaucer St Ilkeston DE7 — 194 C1
Mansfield NG18 — 268 C3
Nottingham NG1 — 268 A2
Chavery Rd S45 — 131 F2
Cheadle Cl DE23 — 218 A1
Cheadle Rd ST14 — 210 A1
Cheam Cl DE22 — 217 F3
Cheapside Belper DE56 — 178 C2
Derby DE1 — 267 B3
Nottingham NG1 — 268 B1
Chedworth Cl NG3 — 268 C2
Chedworth Dr DE24 — 233 E3
Cheedale Ave S40 — 95 E3
Cheedale Cl
Burton u T DE15 — 248 A3
Chesterfield S40 — 95 E3
Cheetham Ave S18 — 76 C3
Chellaston Inf Sch DE73 — 233 D1
Chellaston Jun Sch DE73 — 232 C1
Chellaston La DE73 — 232 C1
Chellaston Park Ct DE73 — 232 C1
Chellaston Rd DE24 — 232 C2
Chellaston St DE24 — 232 C1
Chelmarsh Cl DE73 — 233 D2
Chelmorton Cl NG19 — 136 C2
Chelmorton Pl DE21 — 219 F4
Chelmsford Cl DE13 — 217 E2
Chelmsford Way S43 — 78 A2
Chelsea Cl DE22 — 217 F3
Chelsea Way ST16 — 269 D3
Cheltenham Cl NG9 — 223 F1
Chelwood Rd DE73 — 232 C1
Chepstow Cl S40 — 114 C4
Chepstow Gdns S40 — 114 C4
Chequer La DE56 — 219 E3
Chequers La DE21 — 219 E3
Chequers Rd DE21 — 219 E3
Cherrybough Rd DE21 — 247 D2
Cheriton Cl NG19 — 135 F1
Cheriton Dr DE7 — 194 B2
Cheriton Gdns DE23 — 231 E4
Cherry Bank Rd S8 — 43 D2
Cherry Cl Breaston DE72 — 235 F4
Shirebrook NG20 — 119 F3
South Normanton DE55 — 160 A4
Cherry Garth DE55 — 160 A4
Cherry Gr NG18 — 268 A3
Cherry Leys DE15 — 248 B2
Cherry St S2 — 43 D4
Cherry St S2 — 43 D4
Cherry Tree Ave
Belper DE56 — 179 D3
Ripley DE5 — 180 B4

Cherry Tree Ave continued
Shireoaks S81 .... 63 F4
Cherry Tree Dr
Barlborough S43 .... 80 A4
Bolsover S44 .... 99 E1
Brinsley NG16 .... 182 C4
Hilton DE65 .... 228 B1
Ilkeston DE7 .... 208 B3
Mansfield Woodhouse
NG19 .... 136 A2
Risley NG10 .... 222 C2
Swadlincote DE11 .... 255 F3
Cherry Tree Dr
Buxton SK17 .... 66 B1
Killamarsh S21 .... 60 B3
Long Duckmanton S44 .... 98 A2
Cherry Tree Gr
Mastin Moor S43 .... 79 E2
North Wingfield S42 .... 131 F3
Cherry Tree Hill Inf & Jun
Schs DE21 .... 220 A3
Cherry Tree Mews DE21 .... 220 A2
Cherry Tree Sq SK17 .... 69 E2
Cherrybrook Dr DE21 .... 206 A2
Cherrytree Ave DE55 .... 170 A4
Cherrytree Rd DE15 .... 254 C4
Chertpit La DE45 .... 89 E3
Chertsey Cl S40 .... 114 C4
Chertsey Ct DE7 .... 207 E4
Chertsey Rd DE23 .... 217 E1
Cherwell Cl S43 .... 77 F1
Chesapeake Rd DE21 .... 220 A3
Chesham Cl S43 .... 10 A3
Cheshire St DE24 .... 232 C3
Cheshire Way NG16 .... 171 E2
Chess Burrow NG19 .... 136 B1
Chessel Cl S8 .... 43 D2
Chester Ave DE22 .... 205 D3
Chester Ct DE21 .... 220 C2
Chester Gdns DE11 .... 256 A1
Chester Gn NG9 .... 223 F1
Chester Green Rd DE1 .... 219 D4
Chester St
Chesterfield S40 .... 95 E2
Mansfield NG19 .... 135 F1
Chesterfield Ave
Chesterfield S43 .... 77 F2
Long Eaton NG10 .... 236 C4
Swadlincote DE11 .... 255 F3
Chesterfield Coll S41 .... 266 B4
Chesterfield Coll
(Tapton House Campus)
S41 .... 96 B3
Chesterfield Dr DE12 .... 261 E3
Chesterfield Midland Sta
S41 .... 266 C3
**Chesterfield & North
Derbyshire Royal Hospl**
S44 .... 96 C2
Chesterfield Rd
Alfreton DE55 .... 158 C3
Barlborough S43 .... 80 A3
Beeley DE4 .... 111 D2
Belper DE56 .... 179 D2
Bolsover S44 .... 98 C3
Brimington, Middlecroft S43 ...... 97 D4
Brimington, Tapton S43 .... 96 B4
Calow S44 .... 96 C1
Darley Dale DE4 .... 127 E1
Dronfield S18 .... 57 D1
Eckington S21 .... 59 D1
Grassmoor S42 .... 115 F1
Hardstoft DE55 .... 133 D1
Heage DE56 .... 168 C2
Holmewood S42 .... 116 B1
Long Duckmanton S44 .... 98 B2
Matlock DE4 .... 143 E4
New Houghton NG19 .... 134 C4
North Wingfield S42 .... 132 A4
Pleasley NG19 .... 135 D3
Rowsley DE4 .... 111 D1
Sheffield S8 .... 43 D3
Shirland DE55 .... 146 B2
Sutton in A NG17 .... 148 C2
Unstone S21 .... 59 D1
Chesterfield Rd N NG19 ...... 135 E2
Chesterfield Rd S
Mansfield NG18 .... 268 B4
Sheffield S8 .... 57 D3
Chesterfield Small Bsns
Ctr S41 .... 96 A4
Chesterfield Trad Est S18 ..... 76 B2
Chesterford Ct DE23 .... 230 C3
Chesterman Ct NG16 .... 195 D2
Chesterton Ave DE23 .... 231 F4
Chesterton Cl S43 .... 96 C2
Chesterton Rd DE21 .... 220 C3
Chestnut Ave Belper DE56 .... 179 D1
Derby, Chellaston DE73 .... 232 C2
Derby, Mickleover DE73 .... 217 E2
Derby, Rose Hill DE23 .... 219 D1
Eckington S21 .... 59 D1
Holbrook DE56 .... 191 E4
Killamarsh S21 .... 60 B3
Ripley DE5 .... 180 B4
Somercotes DE55 .... 170 B3
Swadlincote DE11 .... 256 A3
Chestnut Bank DE75 .... 181 E1
Chestnut Cl
Buxton SK17 .... 66 A1
Dronfield S18 .... 57 D1
Duffield DE56 .... 190 C1
Horsley Woodhouse DE7 .... 192 B4
New Mills SK22 .... 24 C1
Chestnut Ctr SK23 .... 47 F4

Chestnut Dr
Ashbourne DE6 .... 185 E4
Clowne S43 .... 80 B4
Creswell S80 .... 81 F1
Repton DE65 .... 243 E1
Selston NG16 .... 171 F4
Shirebrook NG20 .... 119 E2
South Normanton DE55 .... 160 A2
Chestnut Gn DE11 .... 256 A1
Chestnut Gr
Borrowash DE72 .... 221 E2
Etwall DE65 .... 229 D2
Mansfield Woodhouse
NG19 .... 136 A3
Sandiacre NG10 .... 223 D4
Tibshelf DE55 .... 147 F3
Chestnut La
Barton in F NG11 .... 237 F3
Clifton Campville B79 .... 263 F1
Chestnut Rd
Burton u T DE15 .... 254 C4
Langley Mill NG16 .... 182 A2
Chestnut Way Repton DE65 .. 242 B1
Swanwick DE55 .... 170 A4
Chestnuts The NG10 .... 236 A4
Chevely Ct DE21 .... 219 E4
Cheverton Cl DE24 .... 233 E3
Chevin Ave
Borrowash DE72 .... 221 E1
Derby DE72 .... 217 F1
Chevin Bank DE56 .... 178 C3
Chevin Pl DE1 .... 218 C4
Chevin Rd
Belper, Chevinside DE56 .... 178 C1
Belper, Milford DE56 .... 190 C4
Derby DE1 .... 218 C4
Duffield DE56 .... 190 C3
Chevin The DE13 .... 240 B1
Chevin Vale DE56 .... 190 C3
Chevin View DE56 .... 178 C2
Cheviot Ave NG16 .... 170 C2
Cheviot Cl DE11 .... 256 A2
Cheviot Rd NG10 .... 223 D1
Cheviot St DE22 .... 218 B3
Cheviot Way ■ S40 .... 95 E3
Chew Rd OL3 .... 5 E4
Chewton St NG16 .... 182 C1
Cheyenne Gdns DE21 .... 220 B3
Cheyne Wlk DE22 .... 218 A3
Chichester Cl DE7 .... 209 D4
Chilson Dr DE23 .... 217 E2
Chiltern Cl
Chesterfield S40 .... 95 E2
Grassmoor S42 .... 115 F2
Chesterfield ■ DE7 .... 207 F4
Chiltern Gdns NG10 .... 223 D1
Chiltern Rd DE21 .... 256 A2
Chilton Cres NG19 .... 136 B3
Chilton Ct S41 .... 95 F4
Chime Ct DE21 .... 205 F1
Chine The DE55 .... 160 A2
Chingford Ct DE22 .... 218 A3
Chinley Prim Sch SK23 .... 35 D1
Chinley Rd DE21 .... 206 A1
Chinley Sta SK23 .... 34 B1
Chippinghouse Rd S8 .... 43 D4
Chiswick Cl DE22 .... 217 F3
Chisworth Ct NG19 .... 136 C2
Chiverton Cl S18 .... 57 D1
Chorlton Terr ST14 .... 210 B1
Christ Church CE
Prim Sch S41 .... 96 A3
Christ the King RC
Prim Sch DE55 .... 159 D3
Christchurch Ct DE1 .... 267 B4
Christie Ave S51 .... 269 D4
Christopher Terr ST17 .... 269 F3
Chrysalis Way NG16 .... 182 B2
Chrysanthemum Ct DE11 ... 256 A3
Chunal La SK13 .... 17 E3
Church Alley DE45 .... 109 E3
Church Ave Clay Cross S45 ... 131 F2
Hatton DE65 .... 239 E4
Long Eaton NG10 .... 236 A2
Peak Dale SK17 .... 67 D3
Swadlincote DE11 .... 256 A2
Tideswell SK17 .... 69 E2
Church Bank S32 .... 53 D4
Church Banks DE6 .... 173 D1
Church Bk SK23 .... 45 E4
Church Broughton CE
Prim Sch DE65 .... 227 D4
Church Broughton Rd
DE65 .... 227 E2
Church Brow
Chapel-en-le-F SK23 .... 47 D3
Mottram in L SK14 .... 9 D2
Church Cl
Blackfordby DE11 .... 257 D1
Blackwell DE55 .... 147 E1
Burton u T DE15 .... 248 A2
Clowne S43 .... 80 C2
Derby DE73 .... 233 D1
Glossop SK13 .... 10 C1
Marchington ST14 .... 224 C1
Nottingham NG3 .... 268 B2
Peak Forest SK17 .... 49 D2
Renishaw S21 .... 79 D4
Staveley S43 .... 97 E4
Trowell NG9 .... 209 E2
Willington DE65 .... 242 A3
Wingerworth S42 .... 115 D2
Church Cnr DE6 .... 165 D1
Church Croft
Coton in t E DE12 .... 260 B2
Ripley DE5 .... 169 E1
Church Dr Ilkeston DE7 .... 194 B2
Sandiacre NG10 .... 223 D4
Shirebrook NG20 .... 119 F2

Church Farm ST14 .... 210 A2
Church Fold SK13 .... 16 B4
Church Gresley Inf Sch
DE11 .... 256 A1
Church Gresley
St George's CE
Prim Sch DE11 .... 256 A1
Church Hill Derby DE21 .... 220 B2
Etwall DE65 .... 229 D3
Kimberley NG16 .... 195 F3
Newton DE55 .... 148 A1
Church Hill Ave NG19 .... 136 B2
Church Hill Ctr Broxtowe
Coll of F Ed NG16 .... 195 F3
Church Hill St DE15 .... 248 A2
Church La
Bakewell DE45 .... 109 E3
Barrow u T DE73 .... 244 A3
Barton in F NG11 .... 237 F3
Baslow DE45 .... 91 F3
Beeley DE4 .... 111 D2
Belper DE56 .... 179 D2
Brackenfield DE55 .... 145 E1
Brailsford DE6 .... 201 F4
Breadsall DE21 .... 205 F2
Brinsley NG16 .... 182 C4
Caldwell DE12 .... 260 C4
Calow S44 .... 97 D2
Castle Donington DE74 .... 247 D2
Chapel-en-le-F SK23 .... 47 D3
Chelmorton SK17 .... 106 A4
Chesterfield S40 .... 266 B3
Chilcote DE12 .... 264 C2
Clowne S43 .... 80 C2
Cossall NG16 .... 195 E1
Derby, Chaddesden DE21 .... 220 A3
Derby, Darley Abbey DE22 ...... 205 D1
Dore S17 .... 55 E3
Doveridge DE6 .... 211 D1
Ellastone DE6 .... 183 D2
Fritchley DE56 .... 168 A3
Great Longstone DE45 .... 90 A2
Hanbury DE13 .... 238 A2
Heath S44 .... 117 D2
Hemington DE74 .... 247 F2
Horsley Woodhouse DE7 .... 192 C3
Killamarsh S21 .... 60 D3
Kirk Langley DE6 .... 202 C1
Little Eaton DE21 .... 205 E4
Mackworth DE22 .... 217 F4
Mansfield NG18 .... 268 C3
Marchington ST14 .... 224 C1
Marple SK6 .... 23 D3
Mayfield DE6 .... 184 B3
Morley DE7 .... 206 C3
New Mills SK22 .... 33 E4
Newton Solney DE15 .... 248 C4
Ockbrook DE72 .... 221 E2
Osmaston DE6 .... 186 A3
Peak Forest SK17 .... 49 D2
Pleasley NG19 .... 135 D3
Rocester ST14 .... 197 D2
Roston DE6 .... 197 E4
Rowsley DE4 .... 110 C1
Selston NG16 .... 171 E4
Shirley DE6 .... 200 B4
South Wingfield DE55 .... 157 F2
Stanton-by-D DE7 .... 208 C1
Stapleford NG9 .... 223 E4
Stockley S44 .... 117 E2
Sutton on t H DE6 .... 215 D1
Temple Normanton S42 .... 116 B2
Thorpe DE6 .... 161 E1
Thrumpton NG11 .... 237 E2
Tibshelf DE55 .... 147 F3
Ticknall DE73 .... 251 D2
Tideswell SK17 .... 69 E2
Weston Underwood DE6 .... 188 C1
Church La N
Chesterfield S41 .... 77 D2
Derby DE22 .... 204 C2
Church Level DE6 .... 165 D1
Church Mead NG17 .... 148 C2
Church Meadows
Calow S44 .... 96 C2
North Wingfield S42 .... 131 F3
Church Mews
Derby DE21 .... 220 B2
Hatton DE65 .... 227 E1
Killamarsh S21 .... 60 C4
Mosborough S20 .... 59 E4
Rowsley DE4 .... 110 C1
Church Rd
Bolsover, Shuttlewood S44 .... 99 D3
Bolsover, Stanfree S44 .... 99 D4
Branston DE14 .... 253 F4
Brimington S43 .... 96 C4
Church Broughton DE65 .... 227 D4
Darley Dale DE4 .... 127 D1
Eggington DE65 .... 241 D3
Fritchley DE56 .... 168 A3
Hollingworth SK14 .... 9 F2
Marple SK6 .... 23 E4
New Mills SK22 .... 33 E4
Nottingham NG3 .... 268 A2
Quarndon DE22 .... 204 B3
Snelston DE6 .... 184 B2
Swadlincote DE11 .... 256 A3
Church Rise DE55 .... 160 B3
Church Side Calow S44 .... 96 C2
Derby DE21 .... 220 B2
Church Sq Heanor DE75 .... 181 F1
Melbourne DE73 .... 252 A3

Church St Alfreton DE55 ...... 158 C2
Alstonefield DE6 .... 149 F2
Ashbourne DE6 .... 173 D1
Ashford in t W DE45 .... 108 C4
Ashover S45 .... 129 F2
Barlborough S43 .... 80 A4
Baslow DE45 .... 91 F3
Belper DE56 .... 179 D2
Bolsover S44 .... 99 D1
Bonsall DE4 .... 142 B1
Bradwell S33 .... 51 D4
Brassington DE4 .... 153 D1
Brimington S43 .... 96 C4
Buxton SK17 .... 85 D3
Calow S44 .... 96 C2
Clifton Campville B79 .... 263 F1
Clowne S43 .... 80 C2
Coton in t E DE12 .... 260 B2
Denby DE5 .... 180 B1
Derby, Alvaston DE24 .... 233 E4
Derby, Littleover DE23 .... 218 B1
Derby, Rose Hill DE23 .... 219 D1
Derby, Spondon DE21 .... 220 B3
Donisthorpe DE12 .... 262 C1
Dronfield S18 .... 57 D1
Eastwood NG16 .... 182 C1
Eckington S21 .... 59 F2
Eyam S32 .... 71 F3
Fritchley DE56 .... 168 A3
Glossop SK13 .... 10 B1
Hadfield SK13 .... 10 A2
Hartington SK17 .... 137 E3
Hartshorne DE11 .... 257 D3
Hayfield SK22 .... 25 E1
Heage DE56 .... 168 C2
Heanor DE75 .... 181 F1
Holbrook DE56 .... 191 E3
Holloway DE4 .... 156 A3
Horsley DE21 .... 191 F3
Ilkeston DE7 .... 194 C2
Kilburn DE56 .... 191 F4
Lockington DE74 .... 247 F2
Longnor SK17 .... 121 D3
Mansfield NG18, NG19 .... 268 B4
Mansfield Woodhouse
NG19 .... 136 B2
Marple SK6 .... 23 D3
Matlock DE4 .... 143 E2
Melbourne DE73 .... 252 A4
Monyash DE45 .... 107 E1
Netherseal DE12 .... 264 C3
Ockbrook DE72 .... 221 E2
Pilsley S45 .... 132 B1
Pleasleyhill NG19 .... 135 D2
Ripley, Greenwich DE5 .... 169 E1
Ripley, Waingroves DE5 .... 181 D4
Sandiacre NG10 .... 223 D4
Shirland DE55 .... 146 B1
Somercotes DE55 .... 170 B3
South Normanton DE55 .... 160 A3
Stapleford NG9 .... 223 E4
Staveley S43 .... 78 C1
Stoke-on-T S14 .... 269 E2
Stretton on le F DE12 .... 265 F1
Swadlincote, Church Gresley
DE11 .... 256 A1
Swadlincote, Lower Midway
DE11 .... 256 B2
Swadlincote, Newhall DE11 ..... 256 A3
Tansley DE4 .... 144 A2
Tideswell SK17 .... 69 E2
Tintwistle SK13 .... 10 A4
Tutbury DE13 .... 239 E4
Unstone S18 .... 76 C4
Whaley Thorns NG20 .... 101 D1
Wirksworth DE4 .... 165 F4
Youlgreave DE45 .... 125 E3
Church St N NG16 .... 160 B2
Church St W 77 D2
Church S S
Chesterfield S40 .... 115 D4
Glossop SK13 .... 10 C1
Church St W
Chesterfield S40 .... 95 E1
Pinxton NG16 .... 160 B2
Church View
Barlborough S43 .... 80 A4
Breaston DE72 .... 235 E4
Chesterfield S40 .... 95 E1
Clowne S43 .... 80 C2
Glapwell S44 .... 134 A4
Heanor DE75 .... 181 D2
Ilkeston DE7 .... 208 C4
New Houghton NG19 .... 134 C4
Church View Dr DE45 .... 91 F3
Church Way S40 .... 266 B3
Church Wlk Brinsley NG16 ... 182 C4
Chesterfield S40 .... 266 B3
Derby DE1 .... 205 D2
Duffield DE56 .... 190 C1
Eastwood NG16 .... 182 C1
Glossop SK13 .... 10 C1
Somercotes DE55 .... 170 B3
Churchdale Ave NG19 .... 209 F1
Churchdale Rd S12 .... 44 B2
Churchdown Cl DE21 .... 206 A1
Churchgate DE6 .... 173 D1
Churchill Ave DE45 .... 154 B3
Churchill Cl DE72 .... 235 E4
Churchill Dr Hilton DE65 ..... 228 C1
Stapleford NG9 .... 223 E4
Churchill Gdns NG19 .... 136 B2
Churchland Ave S42 .... 132 A4
Churchside Grassmoor S41 .. 115 E3
Wingerworth S42 .... 115 E3
Churchside La S41 .... 115 E3

Churston Rd S40 .... 95 E2
Cinder Bank NG16 .... 170 C2
Cinder La Killamarsh S21 .... 60 C4
Wirksworth DE4 .... 165 F3
Cinder Rd DE55 .... 170 B4
Cinderhill La S8 .... 57 E4
Circle The Derby DE24 .... 231 F3
Mansfield Woodhouse
NG19 .... 136 A2
Sheffield S2 .... 44 A4
Circular Dr S21 .... 79 D4
Circular Rd
Chesterfield S40 .... 115 D4
Staveley S43 .... 78 B1
City Link NG1 .... 268 C1
City Rd Derby DE1 .... 219 D4
Fenton ST4 .... 269 F1
Sheffield S2 .... 43 F4
Stoke-on-T ST4 .... 269 F1
City Rd Ind Pk DE1 .... 219 D4
City Sch S13 .... 44 C3
City The Woodville DE11 .... 256 C1
Woodville DE11 .... 257 D1
Civic Way DE11 .... 256 A2
Clamp Dr DE11 .... 256 A2
Clapgun St DE74 .... 247 D2
Clara Mount Rd DE75 .... 182 A1
Clare Valley NG7 .... 268 A1
Clarehaven NG9 .... 223 F3
Clarence Rd
Chesterfield S40 .... 266 A3
Derby DE23 .... 218 C1
Long Eaton NG10 .... 236 B3
Clarence St
Chesterfield S40 .... 266 A3
Mansfield NG18 .... 268 B3
Nottingham NG3 .... 268 C2
Pleasleyhill NG19 .... 135 E2
Stonebroom DE55 .... 147 D2
Clarendon Coll NG1 .... 268 A2
Clarendon Rd
Mansfield NG19 .... 268 A4
Staveley S43 .... 97 E4
Clarendon St
Derby DE1 .... 267 D3
Nottingham NG1, NG3 .... 268 A2
Clark St ST16 .... 269 E4
Clarke Ave DE75 .... 181 E1
Clarke Dr NG10 .... 236 A2
Clarke St S40 .... 267 C4
Clarke's Cl ST14 .... 210 A1
Clarkes La DE72 .... 246 A4
Clarkson Ave S40 .... 181 E1
Clatterway DE4 .... 154 C4
Clavehouse Rd DE55 .... 248 A1
Claxton St DE75 .... 181 E1
Claxton Terr DE75 .... 181 E1
Clay Cross Com Hospl
S45 .... 131 D2
Clay Cross Inf & Jun Sch
S45 .... 131 D1
Clay La Clay Cross S45 .... 131 D1
Heanor DE75 .... 181 F1
Clay St
Burton u T DE15 .... 248 A1
Draycott DE72 .... 235 D4
Shirland DE55 .... 146 C1
Clay St E DE15 .... 248 A1
Claye St NG10 .... 236 C4
Clayfields S21 .... 60 C4
Claylands Gr S80 .... 81 F3
Claylands Pl S80 .... 81 F3
Claylands Rd S80 .... 81 F3
Claymar Dr DE11 .... 256 A4
Claymills Rd DE13 .... 241 D1
Claypit La S42 .... 112 C4
Clays La DE14 .... 253 F4
Clayton Gr DE75 .... 181 E2
Clayton St S41 .... 266 C2
Cleave Rd DE14 .... 254 A4
Clegg Hill Dr NG17 .... 148 C2
Clematis Cres DE55 .... 255 D4
Clement La S33 .... 50 B3
Clement Rd
Horsley Woodhouse DE7 .... 192 B4
Heanor DE75 .... 23 E4
Clerkson St ■ NG18 .... 268 B3
Clerkson's Alley NG18 .... 268 B4
Cleve Ave Beeston NG9 .... 223 F2
Darley Dale DE4 .... 127 D1
Cleveland Ave Derby DE21 ... 220 A3
Draycott DE72 .... 235 D4
Long Eaton NG10 .... 223 F1
Cleveland Cl DE11 .... 256 A2
Cleveland Rd DE55 .... 146 C2
Cleveland Way S40 .... 95 E3
Cleveleys Rd NG9 .... 223 F2
Clewley Rd DE14 .... 253 F4
Cliff Bvd NG16 .... 195 F4
Cliff Coll S32 .... 91 F4
Cliff La Curbar S32 .... 272 C1
Elton DE4 .... 140 B4
Kirby-in-A NG16 .... 160 C2
Tideswell SK17 .... 69 E2
Cliff Nook DE55 .... 160 A2
Cliff Rd Buxton SK17 .... 85 E4
Holme HD7 .... 2 C4
Nottingham NG3 .... 268 B1
Cliff St NG18 .... 268 C4
Cliffash La DE56 .... 176 C3
Cliffe Field Rd S8 .... 43 D2
Cliffe Hill Ave NG9 .... 223 E4
Cliffe La S32 .... 52 C4
Cliffe Rd SK13 .... 17 E4
Cliffe View Rd S8 .... 43 D3
Clifford Cl
Chesterfield S40 .... 95 D1
Long Eaton NG10 .... 236 A2

Clifford St Derby DE24 .... 219 E1
Long Eaton NG10 .... 236 C4
Clifton Ave
Barlborough S43 .... 80 A4
Long Eaton NG10 .... 237 D4
Clifton CE Prim Sch
DE6 .... 184 C3
Clifton Cl Overseal DE12 .... 262 A2
Stafford ST 16 .... 256 A1
Swadlincote DE11 .... 256 A1
Clifton Dr Buxton SK17 .... 85 E2
Derby DE3 .... 217 F2
Stafford ST 16 .... 269 F4
Clifton Pl NG18 .... 268 B4
Clifton Rd Ashbourne DE6 .... 185 D4
Buxton SK17 .... 85 E4
Clifton St 184 C3
Derby DE22 .... 204 C2
Matlock Bath DE4 .... 155 D4
Nethersea DE12 .... 264 B3
Clifton St
Chesterfield S40 .... 95 F2
Derby DE1 .... 267 D1
Clifton Terr NG7 .... 268 A1
Clinthill La S80 .... 81 F4
Clipstone Ave NG16 .... 182 B3
Clinton Cl SK22 .... 219 E3
Clinton St E NG1 .... 268 B2
Clinton St W NG1 .... 268 B2
Clipstone Ave
Mansfield NG18 .... 268 C4
Nottingham NG1 .... 268 A2
Clodhall La Curbar S32 .... 72 C1
Old Brampton S32, S42 .... 93 D3
Cloonmore Croft S8 .... 43 E1
Cloonmore Dr S8 .... 43 E1
Close Bank DE13 .... 239 E3
Close The
Derby, Allestree DE24 .... 204 C1
Derby, Rose Hill DE23 .... 218 B1
Great Longstone DE45 .... 89 F2
Linton DE12 .... 261 E3
Marple SK6 .... 15 D1
Matlock DE4 .... 143 D3
Moira DE11 .... 262 B4
Shirebrook NG20 .... 119 F3
Stafford ST16 .... 269 D3
Tutbury DE13 .... 239 D3
Cloud Ave NG9 .... 223 F4
Cloudside Ct NG10 .... 223 D4
Cloudside Jun Sch NG10 .... 223 D4
Cloudside Rd NG10 .... 223 D4
Cloudwood Cl DE23 .... 218 A1
Clough Ave SK6 .... 43 D4
Clough Bank S7 .... 42 C3
Clough La Buxover DE4 .... 141 E4
Little Hayfield SK22 .... 25 E3
Lodge Moor S10 .... 42 C3
Wensley DE4 .... 141 E4
Clough Side SK6 .... 85 D4
Clough St S1 .... 96 C1
Clough The S41 .... 96 C1
Cloughside S12 .... 32 C3
Clover Cl DE21 .... 234 C1
Clover Ct Shardlow DE72 .... 234 C1
Sheffield S8 .... 43 E1
Clover Nook Ind Est
DE55 .... 159 F2
Clover Nook Rd
Pinxton DE55 .... 159 F2
Somercotes DE55 .... 159 F2
South Normanton DE55 .... 159 F2
Clover Rise NG16 .... 195 D4
Clover St 256 A4
Cloverdale Dr DE24 .... 231 F1
Cloves Hill Morley DE7 .... 192 B1
Smalley DE7 .... 192 B1
Clowne Jun & Inf Schs
S43 .... 80 C2
Clowne Rd
Barlborough S43 .... 80 B3
Bolsover S44 .... 99 D4
Club La DE73 .... 244 A3
Club St ST4 .... 269 E1
Clumber Terr NG7 .... 95 F2
Clumber Ave NG16 .... 171 F1
Clumber Cl S43 .... 80 C2
Clumber Cres N NG7 .... 268 A1
Clumber Cres S NG7 .... 268 A1
Clumber Ct Ilkeston DE7 .... 194 C3
Mansfield NG19 .... 135 F1
Nottingham NG7 .... 268 A1
Clumber Dr NG19 .... 135 F1
Clumber Pl S43 .... 97 E3
Clumber Rd E NG7 .... 268 A1
Clumber Rd W NG7 .... 268 A1
Clumber St
Long Eaton NG10 .... 236 B4
Mansfield NG18 .... 268 B4
S Nottingham NG1 .... 268 B2
Clun Ct NG19 .... 136 B1
Clune St S1 .... 81 D3
Cluster Rd DE56 .... 178 C2
Clusters The DE56 .... 178 C2
Co-operative St
Derby DE23 .... 218 C1
Long Eaton NG10 .... 236 C3
Coach Dr Eastwood NG16 .... 182 C2
Quarndon DE22 .... 204 B4
Coach Rd Hollingworth SK14 .... 9 E3
Cromville DE5 .... 170 B2
Cromville NG16 .... 170 B2
Ripley DE5 .... 169 F2
Somercotes DE55 .... 170 B2
Coach Way DE65 .... 242 B3
Coachhouse Mews DE11 .... 256 A4

Coachways DE7 .... 193 F2
Coal La Hartshorne DE11 .... 257 E4
Ticknall DE11 .... 257 E4
Coalpit La
Coton in t E DE12 .... 260 C2
Youlgreave DE45 .... 125 E3
Coastguard Sch 156 C1
Coatsby Rd NG16 .... 195 F4
Cobden Pl NG19 .... 135 F1
Cobden Rd
Chesterfield S40 .... 266 A4
Matlock DE4 .... 143 E3
Cobden St Derby DE22 .... 218 B3
Long Eaton NG10 .... 236 C4
Ripley DE5 .... 169 E1
Cobham Cl DE24 .... 231 E2
Cobnar Ave S8 .... 43 D1
Cobnar Dr Chesterfield S41 .... 95 E4
Sheffield S8 .... 43 D1
Cobnar Rd S8 .... 43 D1
Cobnar Wood Cl S18 .... 76 A2
Cobthorn Dr DE22 .... 204 B2
Cock Brow SK14 .... 15 E4
Cock Hill DE45 .... 91 F3
Cock Pitt The DE1 .... 267 C3
Cockayne Cl NG10 .... 223 D2
Cockayne La S14 .... 164 A1
Cockayne St N DE24 .... 232 C3
Cockayne St S DE24 .... 232 C3
Cockerhouse Rd NG16 .... 182 C2
Cockleys NG10 .... 236 B3
Cockshead La DE6 .... 198 B4
Cockshut La
Holbeck NG20 .... 101 D2
Melbourne DE73 .... 251 F4
Whaley Thorns NG20 .... 101 D2
Cockshutt Dr S8 .... 56 B4
Cockshutt Dr S8 .... 56 B4
Cockshutt La S8 .... 170 C4
Cockshutt Rd S8 .... 56 B4
Cod Beck Cl DE24 .... 233 E3
Codnor CE Prim Sch
DE5 .... 181 D4
Codnor Denby La
Codnor DE5 .... 181 D3
Denby DE5 .... 181 D3
Codnor Gate Ind Est DE5 .... 170 A1
Codnor Gate Ind Est DE5 .... 170 B1
Coffin La DE6 .... 165 D1
Coggers La S32 .... 52 C4
Coisley Hill S13 .... 44 C3
Cokayne Ave S18 .... 57 E3
Coke St DE22 .... 218 B3
Coldharbour La S45 .... 145 D2
Coldstream Wlk DE24 .... 231 F2
Cole St DE4 .... 154 C1
Cole Dr S18 .... 56 C3
Cole La DE7 .... 221 E2
Coleman St DE24 .... 232 C4
Coleraine Cl DE21 .... 220 A2
Coleridge St
Derby, Littleover DE23 .... 231 F3
Derby, Normanton DE23 .... 231 F4
Colin Ave DE5 .... 181 D4
Colin St DE55 .... 159 D2
Colindene Gr S18 .... 269 E1
Coliseum Ctr The DE1 .... 267 C2
Colledge St DE55 .... 170 B3
College Mews DE1 .... 218 C3
College Pl DE1 .... 267 B4
College St Buxton SK17 .... 85 D3
Denstone ST14 .... 196 B3
Spinkhill S21 .... 60 B1
College St
Long Eaton NG10 .... 223 E1
Nottingham NG1 .... 268 A1
College Way SK17 .... 85 E1
Collier Ave NG19 .... 136 A3
Collier La DE72 .... 221 E2
Collier St S43 .... 17 E4
Colliery La S45 .... 131 D2
Colliery Rd Alfreton DE55 .... 158 C1
Blackwell DE55 .... 147 F1
Colliery Row DE55 .... 159 D3
Collin Ave NG10 .... 223 D2
Collin St NG1 .... 268 B1
Collingham Gdns DE22 .... 218 A3
Collingwood Cres DE4 .... 143 D3
Collingwood Gr ST4 .... 269 D2
Collingwood Rd NG10 .... 236 C3
Collins Ave DE55 .... 160 A4
Collis Cl DE24 .... 232 C4
Collishaw Cl S41 .... 115 E4
Collumbell Ave DE72 .... 221 E3
Colne Ct NG19 .... 136 B1
Colombo St DE23 .... 219 D1
Colonnade The ①③ SK16 .... 269 E4
Colonsay Ct NG19 .... 136 B1
Colton Cl S41 .... 76 C4
Coltsfoot Dr DE4 .... 80 C4
Coltsworth La S43 .... 127 E1
Columbell Way DE4 .... 127 E1
Columbia St NG17 .... 148 C2
Columbine Cl DE21 .... 206 A3
Colver Rd S2 .... 43 D4
Colvile St DE72 .... 218 B3
Colville Cl NG1 .... 268 A2
Colville St S2 .... 43 D4
Colwick Cl NG19 .... 135 F1
Colwyn Ave DE23 .... 218 B1
Colyear St DE1 .... 267 B3
Combs Cl SK22 .... 33 D4

Combs Inf Sch SK23 .... 46 C1
Combs La SK23 .... 46 C1
Combs News SK13 .... 9 E1
Combs Rd SK23 .... 46 C2
Comfrey Cl DE23 .... 230 C3
Commerce St Derby DE24 .... 232 C4
Melbourne DE73 .... 252 A4
Commercial Gate NG18 .... 268 B3
Commercial Rd SK17 .... 69 E2
Commercial Row S32 .... 72 B4
Commercial St ④ NG18 .... 268 B3
Common La
Chelmorton SK17 .... 87 D1
Mansfield Woodhouse
NG19 .... 136 A2
Old Brampton S42 .... 94 C4
Pleasley NG20 .... 119 E2
Scarcliffe NG20 .... 119 E2
Shirebrook NG20 .... 119 E2
Stanley DE7 .... 207 D4
Sutton on t H DE6 .... 228 A4
Common Piece La DE65 .... 230 C1
Common Rd Harthill S26 .... 62 A3
Sutton in A NG17 .... 148 C1
Swadlincote DE11 .... 256 B1
Thorpe Salvin S80 .... 62 C3
Common Side
Selston NG16 .... 171 F4
Swadlincote DE11 .... 256 B1
Common The Crich DE4 .... 168 A4
Quarndon DE22 .... 204 B4
South Normanton DE55 .... 160 A3
Common Wood DE4 .... 143 D2
Commonpiece La DE6 .... 215 D1
Commonpiece Rd S45 .... 131 E2
Commons CI NG16 .... 195 D4
Commonside Rd S18 .... 75 E1
Compass Cres S41 .... 77 E2
Compstall Mills Est SK6 .... 15 D1
Compstall Rd Compstall SK6 .... 15 D2
Marple SK6 .... 15 D1
Compton Ave DE72 .... 246 A4
Compton Cl DE24 .... 233 E3
Compton Gr SK17 .... 85 D3
Compton St DE1 .... 267 A3
Compton St SK17 .... 85 D3
Compton St
Ashbourne DE6 .... 173 E1
Chesterfield S40 .... 266 A4
Holmewood S42 .... 116 C1
Langwith NG20 .... 119 F4
Comyn Gdns NG3 .... 268 B2
Conalan Ave S17 .... 56 A3
Concert Pl ⑤ SK17 .... 85 D4
Condiff Rd SK17 .... 69 D3
Conduit St SK14 .... 9 F4
Coniston Ave DE21 .... 220 C3
Coniston Cres DE21 .... 205 E1
Coniston Dr
Clay Cross S45 .... 131 D1
Ilkeston DE7 .... 208 B3
Coniston Rd
Chesterfield S41 .... 95 F4
Dronfield S18 .... 56 C1
Long Eaton NG10 .... 223 D1
Coniston Way S45 .... 95 F4
Conksbury Ave DE45 .... 125 E3
Conksbury La DE45 .... 125 E3
Connaught Ct DE55 .... 159 D2
Connaught Rd DE22 .... 218 B2
Connelly Ct S40 .... 95 F2
Consett Cl DE21 .... 205 E1
Consort Gdns DE21 .... 206 B2
Consort St ST4 .... 269 E2
Constable Ave DE23 .... 218 B1
Constable Cl Dronfield S18 .... 56 C1
Sheffield S14 .... 43 F1
Constable Dr Derby DE23 .... 218 A1
Marple SK6 .... 23 D4
Sheffield S14 .... 43 E1
Constable La DE23 .... 218 B2
Constable Pl S14 .... 43 E1
Constable Rd S14 .... 43 E1
Constable Way S14 .... 43 E1
Convent Ct
Burton u T ST4 .... 254 C3
Stoke-on-t ST4 .... 269 E2
Convent St ⑤ NG1 .... 268 B2
Conway Ave DE72 .... 221 E1
Conway St
Long Eaton NG10 .... 236 C4
Stoke-on-t ST4 .... 269 E2
Congreve La DE7 .... 184 B4
Cook Cl Belper DE56 .... 179 F3
Clay Cross S42 .... 131 D3
Cook Dr DE7 .... 209 D3
Cook La DE6 .... 173 E1
Cookfield DE56 .... 179 F4
Cookham Cl DE3 .... 217 E1
Cooks Ave DE4 .... 247 D2
Coombes La SK13 .... 16 B3
Coombes View SK14 .... 15 F4
Coombe Rd DE45 .... 109 F3
Co-op Dr DE22 .... 218 B3
Glossop SK13 .... 10 A1
Ripley DE5 .... 169 E1
Cooper's Cl DE6 .... 173 E1
Cooper's Cl DE72 .... 221 E1
Cooperage DE72 .... 227 E1
Cope Ct DE24 .... 232 A3
Cope St DE24 .... 269 E4
Copeland Ave NG9 .... 223 F4
Copeland St Derby DE1 .... 267 C2
Copes Way Derby DE21 .... 220 A4
Uttoxeter ST14 .... 210 A1
Copley Croft DE6 .... 173 E2
Coplow La DE65 .... 226 B3

Copper Beech Dr SK13 .... 9 F1
Copper Glade S16 .... 269 F4
Copper Yd DE5 .... 180 C1
Copperas Rd DE11 .... 255 E3
Coppice Ave DE7 .... 194 B3
Coppice Cl
Chesterfield S41 .... 115 E3
Derby DE22 .... 204 C1
Disley SK12 .... 32 A3
Kilburn DE56 .... 192 A4
Coppice Dr Disley SK12 .... 32 A3
Eastwood NG16 .... 182 B2
Heanor DE75 .... 193 F4
Coppice La
Clifton Campville B79 .... 263 F1
Disley SK12 .... 32 A3
Coppice Prim Sch DE75 .... 193 F4
Coppice Side DE11 .... 256 B2
Coppice The
Shirebrook NG20 .... 119 E2
Swadlincote DE11 .... 256 B2
Willington DE65 .... 45 F3
Coppice View DE55 .... 160 A2
Copse Cl DE4 .... 165 F4
Copse Gr DE23 .... 231 D4
Copse Rise DE11 .... 256 A4
Copse The Ilkeston DE7 .... 194 B3
Marple SK6 .... 23 D4
Copseside Cl ⑥ NG10 .... 236 A4
Copsewood DE55 .... 160 A2
Copthorne Inf Sch DE55 .... 159 D3
Copthurst Rd HD7 .... 3 F3
Coral Way S45 .... 131 E2
Corbar Rd SK17 .... 66 A1
Corbarwoods La SK17 .... 66 A1
Corbel Cl DE21 .... 205 F1
Corbridge Gr DE23 .... 231 D4
Corden Ave DE3 .... 218 A1
Corden St DE23 .... 219 D1
Cordville Cl DE21 .... 220 A3
Cordwell Ave S41 .... 95 E4
Cordwell Cl
Castle Donington DE74 .... 246 C2
Staveley S43 .... 97 E4
Cordwell La S18 .... 74 C3
Corfe Cl DE23 .... 231 E3
Corfield Ave DE75 .... 193 F4
Coriander Gdns DE23 .... 231 E2
Corinium Cl DE24 .... 233 E3
Corker Rd S12 .... 32 C3
Corley La DE6 .... 174 B1
Corley La DE6 .... 174 B1
Corn Cl DE55 .... 160 A3
Corn Mkt DE1 .... 267 B3
Corn St SK13 .... 10 B1
Corner Farm DE6 .... 201 F4
Cornfield Ave DE55 .... 160 A2
Cornfield CE Inf Sch
DE75 .... 181 E1
Cornfield Rd NG16 .... 195 F4
Cornflower Dr DE21 .... 206 A2
Cornhill DE22 .... 204 C2
Cornhill Dr DE55 .... 159 D2
Cornmill Cl Bolsover S44 .... 99 D1
Derby DE21 .... 220 B3
Cornmill La DE13 .... 239 F3
Cornwall Ave
Brimington S43 .... 96 C4
Buxton SK17 .... 85 F4
Cornwall Cl
Brimington S43 .... 96 C4
Westwood NG16 .... 171 E2
Cornwall Dr Brimington S43 .... 96 C4
Grassmoor S42 .... 115 F2
Cornwall Rd
Burton u T DE15 .... 254 C3
Derby DE21 .... 219 E3
Shireoaks S81 .... 63 F4
Cornwallis Cl NG10 .... 236 B3
Cornwell Cl S41 .... 269 E1
Coronation Ave
Belper DE56 .... 179 D3
Derby DE24 .... 233 E3
New Houghton NG19 .... 134 C4
Sandiacre NG10 .... 223 D4
Coronation Cl DE73 .... 252 A4
Coronation Cres ST14 .... 197 D2
Coronation Dr
Shirebrook NG20 .... 119 F1
Swadlincote DE11 .... 160 A3
Coronation La DE12 .... 265 F3
Coronation Rd
Brimington S43 .... 96 C4
Cossall NG16 .... 195 D1
Mapperley DE7 .... 193 F2
Stanley DE7 .... 207 E3
Stoke-on-t ST4 .... 269 D2
Coronation St
Derby DE23 .... 232 A4
Ilkeston DE7 .... 208 C4
Mansfield NG18 .... 268 C3
Overseal DE12 .... 262 A2
Swadlincote DE11 .... 256 A3
Whitwell S80 .... 82 A3
Corporation Rd DE7 .... 208 B2
Corporation St
Chesterfield S41 .... 266 C3
Derby DE1 .... 267 B3
⑥ Mansfield NG18 .... 268 B4
Stafford ST16 .... 269 E4
Stoke-on-t ST4 .... 269 D2
Cosby Way NG2 .... 268 C1
Cossall Rd Cossall NG9 .... 209 D2
Trowell NG9 .... 209 E3

Cote Bottom La DE65 .... 227 D4
Cote Green La SK6 .... 15 E1
Cote Green Rd SK6 .... 15 E1
Cote Hilloc DE4 .... 127 D3
Cote La SK22 .... 25 E2
Cotes Park Ind Est DE55 .... 159 E1
Cotes Park La DE55 .... 159 E1
Cotgrave Rd NG19 .... 135 F1
Cotman Dr SK6 .... 23 E4
Cotmanhay Inf & Jun Sch
DE7 .... 194 C3
Cotmanhay Rd DE7 .... 194 C2
Coton Ave ST 16 .... 269 F4
Coton Cl NG19 .... 136 C2
Coton in the Elms CE
Prim Sch DE12 .... 260 B2
Coton La DE12 .... 260 B3
Coton Pk DE11 .... 255 E1
Coton Rd Derby DE23 .... 219 D1
Walton-u-T DE12 .... 259 F3
Cotswold Cl
② Chesterfield S40 .... 95 E3
Derby DE23 .... 231 E4
Glossop SK13 .... 17 D4
④ Long Eaton NG10 .... 236 A4
Swadlincote DE11 .... 256 A2
Cotswold Dr S42 .... 115 F2
Cotswold Rd DE14 .... 253 F4
Cottage Cl Ilkeston DE7 .... 194 B2
Poolsbrook S43 .... 98 A4
Swadlincote DE11 .... 256 A4
Cottage Garden La DE75 .... 181 E1
Cottage La S43 .... 9 F1
Cottam Cres S6 .... 23 D4
Cotterhill La S43 .... 96 C4
Cottesmore Rd DE15 .... 248 A1
Cottisford Cl DE23 .... 231 D4
Cotton La DE24 .... 219 E1
Cotton Mill Hill S42 .... 113 F4
Cotton St S44 .... 99 D1
Conduitt Rd S44 .... 118 A4
Coupe La S42, S45 .... 131 D3
Coupe St DE5 .... 159 E1
Cupland Pl DE55 .... 159 E1
Court Farm La DE14 .... 253 F4
Court La DE45 .... 108 C4
Court Pl S43 .... 97 E4
Court St DE11 .... 256 C2
Court View S48 .... 80 C2
Courtland Dr DE24 .... 233 D3
Courtland Gdns DE24 .... 233 D4
Courtland Rd DE65 .... 229 E2
Courtney Way DE56 .... 179 E3
Courtyard The
Darley Dale DE4 .... 127 E2
Hollingworth SK14 .... 9 E3
Coventry Cl DE55 .... 256 B3
Coventry La NG9 .... 209 F1
Coverdale Wlk DE24 .... 233 E4
Coverley Pl S14 .... 269 D1
Covert Pl DE21 .... 262 B4
Covert The DE21 .... 220 C2
Cow La S43 .... 77 F1
Cowan Dr ST16 .... 269 F4
Cowan St NG1 .... 268 B2
Cowbrook Ave SK13 .... 10 C1
Cowburn Dr SK22 .... 24 B1
Cowdray Cl DE24 .... 231 E1
Cowdry Cl DE24 .... 159 E2
Cowley Bottom S18 .... 75 F4
Cowley Gdns ④ S20 .... 59 F4
Cowley La S18 .... 75 E4
Cowley St DE22 .... 218 C4
Cowlow Cl DE7 .... 194 C2
Cowlow La SK17 .... 47 E1
Cowper Rd NG16 .... 195 D4
Cowper St DE24 .... 232 A3
Cowrington La S43 .... 79 F3
Cowsell Dr S45 .... 131 F1
Cowsley Rd DE21 .... 219 E4
Cox Green Cl DE23 .... 230 C4
Cox Green Ct DE23 .... 230 C4
Cox's La NG19 .... 136 A3
Coxbench Rd DE21 .... 220 C3
Coxon St DE21 .... 220 A3
Coxon's Yd DE6 .... 173 D1
Coyt Rd S43 .... 45 F3
Crab Tree Hill DE21 .... 205 E4
Crabbery St ST16 .... 269 E4
Crabtree Ave S12 .... 32 C3
Crabtree Cl
Castle Donington DE74 .... 247 D1
Derby DE22 .... 204 B2
Wirksworth DE4 .... 165 F4
Crabtree Hill DE21 .... 204 B2
Cracken Cl SK23 .... 34 B1
Craddock Ave DE21 .... 220 C2
Craddock Rd S2 .... 43 E4
Cragdale Gr S20 .... 59 E4
Cragg La DE55 .... 148 A1
Craggon Dr S43 .... 77 E2
Craggs Dr S43 .... 80 C2
Craggs Rd S44 .... 99 D3
Craglands Gr S40 .... 95 D3
Crags Rd S80 .... 82 A1
Crags View S80 .... 81 F1
Craig Dr SK14 .... 9 E3
Craig St NG10 .... 236 C4
Craiglee Ct DE24 .... 231 E2
Craigs Gn NG18 .... 268 A3
Cramer St S17 .... 269 E3

Cranborne Rd S41 .... 95 F4
Cranbourne Cl NG9 .... 209 E1
Cranbrook St NG1 .... 268 B1
Cranfield Way NG10 .... 236 A4
Cranhill Cl DE23 .... 230 C3
Cranleigh Rd S43 .... 79 D2
Cranmer Gr NG19 .... 135 E2
Cranmer Rd DE21 .... 267 D3
Cranmer St Ilkeston DE7 .. 194 C1
  Long Eaton NG10 .... 223 E1
  Stoke-on-T S18 .... 269 E2
Craven Rd S41 .... 95 F3
Crawford Ave NG9 .... 223 E4
Crawford Rd S8 .... 43 D2
Crawford St NG9 .... 82 A3
Crawley Rd DE24 .... 232 C3
Crawshaw Ave S8 .... 56 B4
Cray's Hill DE55 .... 170 A4
Crayford Rd DE24 .... 233 D3
Craythorne Cl DE11 .... 256 A4
Craythorne Rd
  Burton u T DE13 .... 240 B2
  Rolleston DE13 .... 240 B2
Creamery La DE6 .... 151 E1
Crecy Cl DE22 .... 218 B2
Creighton La ST14 .... 210 A3
Crescent S26 .... 61 F3
Crescent Dr SK23 .... 33 E1
Crescent Rd Selston NG16 . 171 E3
  Stafford ST17 .... 269 D3
Crescent The
  Alfreton DE55 .... 159 D2
  Barlborough S43 .... 80 B3
  Bradwell S33 .... 51 D4
  Breaston DE72 .... 235 E4
  Breedon on t H DE73 ..... 252 C1
  Brimington S43 .... 96 B4
  Buxton SK17 .... 85 D4
  Chapel-en-le-F SK23 ...... 47 E4
  Clay Cross S45 .... 131 E1
  Derby, Boulton DE24 ..... 232 C3
  Derby, Chaddesden DE21 . 219 F3
  Holmesfield S18 .... 75 D4
  Holymoorside S42 .... 113 E4
  Horsley Woodhouse DE7 .. 192 B4
  Mayfield DE6 .... 184 B4
  New Mills SK22 .... 33 D4
  Repton DE65 .... 242 B1
  Shirebrook NG20 .... 119 F3
  Shirley DE6 .... 200 B4
  Stanley DE7 .... 207 D4
  Stapleford NG9 .... 209 F1
  Swadlincote DE11 .... 255 F3
  Totley S17 .... 55 F3
Cressbrook Ave S42 .... 132 A4
Cressbrook Way DE21 ..... 206 A2
Cresswell Ave SK22 .... 33 E4
Cresswell St S22 .... 34 C4
Cresswellpart La S33 ..... 50 C4
Cressy Rd DE55 .... 159 D2
Crest Cl DE13 .... 240 C1
Crest The Derby DE22 .... 204 C1
  Linton DE12 .... 261 E3
Creswell CE Inf Sch S80 .. 81 F1
Creswell CE Jun Sch S80 . 81 F1
Creswell Crags Visitor Ctr
  S80 .... 82 A1
Creswell Ct NG19 .... 136 C2
Creswell Rd S43 .... 80 C2
Creswick Cl S40 .... 114 A4
Crewe St DE23 .... 218 C1
Crewton Way DE24 .... 232 C4
Crich Ave DE23 .... 218 B1
Crich Carr CE Prim Sch
  DE4 .... 156 B1
Crich CE Inf Sch DE4 .... 156 C1
Crich Cir DE23 .... 218 B1
Crich Jun Sch DE4 ...... 157 D1
Crich La Belper DE56 .... 179 D4
  Ridgeway DE56 .... 168 A2
Crich Pl S42 .... 131 F3
Crich Rd S43 .... 97 E4
Crich View
  Bolsover S44 .... 118 A4
  Heage DE56 .... 179 F4
  Newton DE55 .... 148 A2
Crich Way DE11 .... 255 F3
Cricket Cl DE15 .... 248 C4
Cricket View S43 .... 80 C1
Cricketers Cl DE15 ..... 254 C4
Cricketers Ct DE23 .... 231 E4
Cricklewood Rd DE22 .. 218 A3
Cringle Mews DE21 .... 205 F1
Cripton La S45 .... 129 F3
Crispin Cl S12 .... 44 A2
Crispin Dr S12 .... 44 A2
Crispin Gdns S12 ...... 44 A2
Crispin Rd S12 .... 44 A2
Critch's Flats NG16 ... 195 F3
Critchley St DE7 ...... 194 C1
Croft Ave DE6 .... 51 E4
Croft Cl Dale DE7 ..... 207 F1
  Derby DE21 .... 220 C3
  Nethersea DE12 .... 264 C4
  Ockbrook DE72 .... 221 E2
  Pinxton NG16 .... 160 B2
  Stanley DE7 .... 240 A2
Croft Cres
  Awsworth NG16 .... 195 E3
  Stoke-on-T S44 .... 269 E1
Croft Ct NG17 .... 148 C2
Croft End DE21 .... 205 E4
Croft Gr ST14 .... 210 B1
Croft Inf Sch DE55 ... 159 D2
Croft La DE21 .... 205 E2

Croft Lea S18 .... 56 B1
Croft Manor SK13 ...... 10 C1
Croft Rd
  Great Longstone DE45 ... 90 A2
  Sheffield S12 .... 44 A3
Croft The Belper DE56 ... 179 E1
  Burton u T DE15 .... 254 C4
  Derby DE72 .... 231 E4
  Draycott DE72 .... 235 D3
  Hadfield SK13 .... 10 A3
  Heage DE56 .... 168 C1
  Morley DE7 .... 192 B1
  Somercotes DE55 ..... 170 B4
  South Normanton DE55 . 160 A3
  Stoke-on-T ST4 ...... 269 D1
  Swadlincote DE11 .... 255 F3
Croft View S43 .... 97 E3
Croft Wlk S80 .... 82 A3
Crofters Ct DE21 .... 205 F1
Crofton Cl S18 ...... 56 C1
Crofton Rise S18 .... 56 C1
Crofts The S32 ...... 53 D4
Croftstead Ave ST14 . 196 B3
Cromarty Cl DE24 .... 231 F2
Cromarty Rise S18 ... 56 B1
Cromdale Ave S43 .... 77 E2
Cromer Cl DE3 ...... 217 E1
Cromford CE Prim Sch
  DE4 .... 155 D3
Cromford Cl
  Aldercar NG16 .... 182 A2
  Long Eaton NG10 .... 236 A3
  North Wingfield S42 .. 132 A4
Cromford Ct
  🅱 Chesterfield S41 ... 95 E4
  Whaley Bridge SK23 .. 45 F3
Cromford Dr Derby DE3 . 217 F2
  Staveley S43 .... 97 E4
Cromford Hill DE4 .... 155 D3
Cromford La Buxton SK17 . 85 E4
  Wirksworth DE4 ...... 154 C1
Cromford Mews DE55 . 45 F3
Cromford PI SK17 ..... 85 F4
Cromford Rd
  Aldercar NG16 .... 181 F3
  Clay Cross S45 ...... 131 D3
  Crich DE4 .... 156 C1
  Duffield DE56 .... 190 C2
  Langley Mill NG16 ... 182 A2
  Ripley DE5 .... 169 E1
Cromford Sta DE4 .... 155 E4
Cromford Wharf DE4 . 155 E4
Crompton Rd
  Ilkeston DE7 .... 209 D2
  Radmanthwaite NG19 . 135 E2
Crompton St Derby DE1 . 267 B2
  New Houghton NG19 .. 134 C4
Cromwell Ave
  Blackwell DE55 ...... 147 F1
  Chapel-en-le-F SK23 . 47 D2
  Findern DE65 .... 230 B1
  Ilkeston DE7 .... 209 D3
Cromwell Cl DE13 .... 239 E3
Cromwell Dr DE55 ... 169 E4
Cromwell Rd Bolsover S44 . 118 A4
  Chesterfield S40 .... 266 A4
  Derby DE23 .... 218 C1
Cromwell St
  Culworth DE55 ...... 195 E4
  Mansfield NG18 ..... 268 C3
  Nottingham NG7 .... 268 A2
Crook Stile S40 ...... 143 D4
Crook's Ave NG19 ... 136 B2
Crooked Bridge Rd ST16 . 269 E4
Crookes Ave NG19 .. 135 D3
Cropton Cl DE24 .... 215 D2
Cropton Cl DE24 .... 233 E3
Cropwell Ct NG18 ... 268 C4
Cropwell Gn NG3 .... 268 C4
Crosby St DE22 ..... 218 B2
Cross Chantrey Rd S8 . 43 D2
Cross Cl DE23 ...... 231 E4
Cross Cliffe SK13 .... 17 F4
Cross Keys Row SK23 . 47 D4
Cross La Calver S32 .. 72 A1
  Codnor DE5 .... 181 D4
  Dore S17 .... 55 E4
  Dronfield, Coal Aston S18 . 57 E2
  Dronfield, Quoit Green S18 . 57 D2
  Flagg SK17 .... 106 C4
  Ible DE4 .... 153 F4
  Monyash DE45 ...... 107 D1
  Rolleston DE13 ..... 240 A1
  Sutton DE55 .... 158 C4
  Sutton in A NG17 ... 148 C1
  Wessington DE55 ... 157 F4
Cross Lanes DE4 .... 144 B1
Cross London St S43 . 77 E2
Cross Myrtle Rd S2 .. 43 D4
Cross Park Rd S8 .... 43 D3
Cross Rd SK14 ...... 210 A1
Cross Rise S13 ...... 17 F4
Cross Side DE6 ..... 184 C4
Cross St Bolsover S44 . 118 A4
  Bramley-Vale S44 ... 117 E1
  Breedon on t H DE73 . 252 C1
  Brimington S43 ..... 96 C4
  Broadbottom SK14 ... 16 A4
  Buxton SK17 .... 85 D3
  Castleton S33 ...... 38 A1
  Chapel-en-le-F SK23 . 47 D2
  Chesterfield S40 .... 266 A4
  Clay Cross S45 ..... 131 E2
  Derby DE22 .... 218 B3
  Grassmoor S42 ..... 115 F2
  Hadfield SK13 ...... 10 A3
  Hollingworth SK14 .. 9 E2
  Killamarsh S21 ..... 60 C4

Cross St continued
  Linton DE11 .... 261 F4
  Long Eaton NG10 ..... 236 C4
  Mansfield Woodhouse NG19 . 136 A1
  New Mills SK22 .... 33 E4
  North Wingfield S42 .. 131 F3
  Sandiacre NG10 ...... 223 E3
Cross The 🄱 SK13 ... 10 A3
Cross Wellington St S43 . 77 E2
Crossdale Gr DE21 ... 206 B2
Crossfield Gr SK6 .... 15 D1
Crossgate La SK13 .... 9 F4
Crosshill DE5 .... 181 D3
Crosshill Dr DE7 ..... 208 B3
Crossings Ave SK23 .. 47 D3
Crossings Rd SK23 ... 46 C3
Crossland Dr S12 .... 44 A2
Crossland Rd S32 .... 53 D4
Crosslands Cl SK13 ... 17 E4
Crossley St DE55 .... 169 E1
Crosslow La DE6 ..... 150 C3
Crossway S16 .... 268 C2
Crossways La DE6 ... 176 A1
Crossways The S2 .... 44 A4
Crow Croft Rd S45 ... 132 B1
Crow Hill NG19 ...... 135 D3
Crow Hill Ct NG18 ... 268 B4
Crow Hill Dr NG18 ... 268 B4
Crow Hill La NG19 ... 136 A1
Crow La Chesterfield S41 . 96 B2
  Stretton DE55 ...... 146 A3
  Unstone S18 .... 76 C4
Crowcroft Way NG10 . 223 D1
Crowestones SK17 ... 85 E3
Crowfoot La DE55 ... 226 C4
Crowhill La DE45 .... 109 D3
Crown Cl Chesterfield S43 . 77 E2
  Long Eaton NG10 ... 236 A4
Crown Hill Way DE7 . 207 D4
Crown Mews DE22 .. 218 C2
Crown Rd S41 ...... 96 A3
Crown Specl Sch The
  DE3 .... 240 B1
Crown Sq DE4 ...... 143 D3
Crown St Clowne S43 . 80 C2
  Derby DE22 .... 218 C2
  Duffield DE56 ...... 190 C2
Crown Terr DE56 .... 178 C2
Crown Yd DE4 ..... 154 C1
Crownland Dr DE73 . 233 D1
Crowshaw St DE24 . 232 A4
Crowstones Rd DE4 . 127 D2
Crowther St ST4 ... 269 F2
Croxton Cl NG19 ... 136 C2
Croydon Wlk DE22 . 217 F3
Cruck Cl S18 ...... 56 C1
Cubley La Great Cubley DE6 . 198 B1
  Marston Montgomery DE6 . 198 B1
Cuckmere Cl DE22 . 205 D3
Cuckoostone La DE4 . 128 C1
Cuillin Cl NG10 .... 223 D1
Cull Ave S18 ...... 269 F4
Culdaine Rd S12 ... 44 A4
Culland View DE4 .. 168 A4
Cullen Ave DE6 .... 173 E1
Cullumbell La S45 . 129 D4
Culworth Cl DE55 . 129 F2
Culworth Ct DE21 . 206 A1
Cumberhills Rd DE56 . 190 B1
Cumberland Ave DE21 . 219 F3
Cumberland Cl NG16 . 171 E2
Cumberland Cres DE72 . 221 D1
Cumberland Dr SK17 . 85 E2
Cumberland Pl 🅱 NG1 . 268 A1
Cumberland Rd DE15 . 254 B3
Cumbria Wlk DE3 ... 217 E1
Cumming St S14 .... 268 B2
Cummings St DE23 .. 219 D1
Cundy Rd S44 ...... 99 D2
Cunliffe St S18 ..... 57 E2
Cunnery La DE4 .... 144 A2
Cunnery The DE4 ... 202 C1
Curbar Cl S42 ..... 132 A4
Curbar Curve S43 .. 97 E3
Curbar Hill S32 .... 72 B1
Curbar Prim Sch S32 . 72 B1
Curborough Dr DE24 . 233 E3
Curlew Ave S21 .... 60 C3
Curlew Cl 🄵 DE24 .. 231 E2
Curtis Gr SK13 .... 10 A3
Curzon Ave S18 .... 75 F4
Curzon CE Prim Sch The
  DE22 .... 204 B3
Curzon Cl Derby DE22 . 204 B2
  Killamarsh S21 .... 60 B3
Curzon Ct Duffield DE56 . 190 C2
  Nottingham NG3 ... 268 B4
Curzon La Derby DE24 . 233 D4
  Duffield DE56 ..... 190 C2
Curzon Rd Buxton SK17 . 85 E4
  Long Eaton NG10 .. 223 D1
  Nottingham NG3 ... 268 B4
Curzon Terr SK17 ... 88 B4
Cuscas La DE6 ..... 187 F2
Cut La DE1 .... 219 D4
Cutholme Cl S40 ... 95 D2
Cutler Cl S21 ..... 60 A4
Cuttholme Rd S40 .. 95 D2
Cuttholme Way S40 . 95 D2
Cutthorpe Grange S40 . 95 D3
Cutthorpe Prim Sch S42 . 94 B4
Cutthorpe Rd S40 .. 95 D2
Cuttlebrook Cl DE23 . 231 F3
Cypress Ave S8 .... 43 E1

Cypress Cl S21 ...... 60 B3
Cypress Wlk DE21 ... 220 A3
Cyprus Rd S8 .... 43 D3
Cyprus Way SK6 .... 32 A4
Cyril Ave NG9 ...... 223 E4

D H Lawrence Mus NG16 . 182 C2
Dade Ave S43 ...... 97 E3
Dag La DE12 .... 263 F4
Dagnall Gdns DE45 . 109 E3
Dagnall Terr DE45 .. 109 E3
Dagnam Cl S2 ..... 43 F3
Dagnam Cres S2 ... 43 F3
Dagnam Dr S2 ..... 43 F4
Dagnam Pl S2 ..... 43 F3
Dagnam Rd S2 .... 43 F4
Dahlia Ave DE55 ... 160 A4
Dahlia Dr DE21 .... 206 B2
Dairy House Rd DE23 . 219 D1
Daisy Farm Rd NG16 . 195 D4
Daisymere La SK17 . 67 D1
Dakeyne Cl DE4 .... 127 F1
Dakeyne St NG3 .... 268 C2
Dakin Ave SK17 ... 88 C4
Dakin Cl S43 ..... 66 C1
Dalbury Rd S18 ... 56 B1
Dalbury Wlk DE23 . 231 E3
Dale Abbey Rd NG10 . 223 E1
Newton DE55 ..... 148 C2
Somercotes DE55 . 170 B3
Dale Bank Cres S43 . 77 E2
Dale Brook DE65 .. 228 C1
Dale Cl Breaston DE72 . 235 E4
  Fritchley DE56 .... 168 A3
  Langwith NG20 ... 119 F4
  Staveley S43 ..... 97 E4
  Stonebroom DE55 . 147 D2
  Whaley Thorns NG20 . 100 C1
Dale Cres Hathersage S32 . 53 D4
  Tupton S42 ...... 115 E1
Dale Dale DE56 ... 191 F4
Dale End Brassington DE4 . 153 D1
  Wirksworth DE4 .. 154 C1
Dale End Rd DE65 . 228 B1
Dale Gr NG2 ..... 268 C1
Dale La Ault Hucknall S44 . 134 B4
  Buxton SK17 ..... 85 F4
Dale Park Ave DE56 . 192 A4
Dale Prim Sch DE23 . 218 C1
Dale Rd Buxton SK17 . 85 E4
  Dale DE21 .... 221 D3
  Derby, Alvaston DE24 . 233 D4
  Derby, Rose Hill DE23 . 218 C1
  Derby, Spondon DE21 . 220 C3
  Dove Holes SK17 .. 66 C4
  Dove Holes S17 .. 67 D4
  Dronfield S18 .... 76 A4
  Killamarsh S21 ... 60 A4
  Kimberley NG16 ... 195 F3
  Matlock Bath DE4 . 143 D2
  New Mills SK22 ... 33 E4
  Over Haddon DE45 . 109 D1
  Stanley DE7 ..... 207 E2
  Stanton-by-D DE7 . 208 B1
  Tupton S42 ...... 115 E1
Dale Rd N Darley Dale DE4 . 127 D3
  Northwood DE4 .. 127 D3
  Rowsley DE4 ..... 126 C4
Dale Side SK17 ... 85 D4
Dale St Ilkeston DE7 . 208 C4
  Mansfield NG19 .. 136 A1
  Nottingham NG2 .. 268 C1
Dale Terr SK17 ... 85 D3
Dale The Bonsall DE4 . 142 B1
  Hathersage S32 .. 53 D4
  Stoney Middleton S32 . 71 F2
  Wirksworth DE4 .. 154 C1
Dale View
  Earl Sterndale SK17 . 105 D2
  Ilkeston DE7 ..... 208 C4
  Litton SK17 ...... 69 F2
  Shirland DE55 ... 146 B2
Dale View Gdns DE56 . 132 A2
Dale View Rd S45 . 132 A2
Daleacre Ave DE74 . 247 F3
Dalebank La S45 .. 145 D4
Dalebrook Rd DE15 . 248 A3
Dalefield Dr DE11 . 256 A4
Dales Cl DE11 .... 188 C3
Dalesfield DE4 ... 143 D3
Daleside DE15 ... 248 A3
Dalestorth Ave NG19 . 135 E1
Daleswood Cres DE55 . 160 A2
Dalewood Cl S41 .. 96 B4
Dalkeith Ave DE24 . 232 C3
Dallas St NG18 ... 268 B3
Dalley Cl NG9 .... 223 D4
Dalley La DE56 ... 178 B3
Dallimore Prim Sch DE7 . 208 B2
Dallimore Rd DE7 . 208 B2
Dalness Ct 🄵 DE24 . 231 E2
Dalston Rd DE11 .. 256 A3
Dalton Ave
  Burton u T DE15 .. 248 A1
  Derby DE22 ..... 218 B2
Dalton Cl NG9 .... 209 F1
Dalvey Way S43 ... 77 E3
Daleyn St DE4 .... 143 D3
Dam La Alsop en le D DE6 . 150 C1
  Shirland DE55 .. 146 C1
Dame Flogan St 🄸 NG18 . 268 B3
Damon Cl S43 .... 82 B3
Damon Dr S43 .... 82 B3
Dan La DE55 ..... 151 D1
Danbury Gr S42 .. 115 F2

Danby Ave S41 .... 77 D1
Dane Bank Dr SK12 . 32 B3
Dane Cl NG1 ..... 268 B2
Dane Gr SK17 .... 85 E2
Dane Hill Cl SK12 . 32 B3
Danebridge Cres DE21 . 206 A1
Danesby Cres DE5 . 180 A1
Danesby Rise DE5 . 180 A1
Danesmoor Inf Est S45 . 131 F2
Danesmoor Inf Sch S45 . 131 F2
Danesway SK23 ... 47 D2
Danewood Ave S2 . 44 B4
Daniel Cres NG18 . 268 A4
Dannah Cres DE5 . 169 F2
Dannah St DE5 ... 169 F1
Darby St DE23 ... 218 C1
Darcy Rd S21 .... 59 E2
Darfield Ct DE7 .. 43 E1
Daresbury Cl S2 . 43 E3
Daresbury Dr S2 . 43 E3
Daresbury Pl S2 . 43 E3
Daresbury Rd S2 . 43 E3
Daresbury View S2 . 43 E3
Darfield Ave S20 . 44 C1
Darfield Dr DE75 . 182 A3
Darfield La DE6 .. 162 B3
Dark La Ashbourne DE6 . 173 D3
  Ashover DE55 ... 145 E3
  Bradley DE6 .... 175 D2
  Callow DE4 ..... 165 E1
  Calow S44 ...... 96 C1
  Chesterfield S44 . 96 C1
  Cromford DE4 ... 154 C1
  Holbrook DE56 .. 191 D4
  North Wingfield S42 . 132 A4
  Youlgreave DE45 . 125 E1
Darley La NG9 .... 223 F3
Darklands La DE11 . 256 A4
Darley Abbey Dr DE22 . 204 C2
Darley Ave Beeston NG9 . 223 E4
  Darley Dale DE4 . 127 E2
  North Wingfield S42 . 132 A4
Darley Churchtown CE
  Prim Sch DE4 .. 127 D2
Darley Cl Harthill S26 . 61 E4
  Staveley S43 .... 78 C2
  Swadlincote DE11 . 256 A4
Darley Dale DE11 . 255 F4
  Dale DE21 ...... 221 D3
Darley Dale Sta DE4 . 127 E1
Darley Dr
  Long Eaton NG10 . 236 A3
  Ripley DE5 ..... 169 E1
Darley Gr Buxton SK17 . 85 E3
  Derby DE1 ...... 219 D4
Darley House Est DE4 . 142 C4
Darley La DE1 ... 267 B4
Darley Lodge Dr DE4 . 142 C4
Darley Park Dr DE22 . 204 C2
Darley Park Rd DE22 . 204 C1
Darley Rd S45 .... 113 D1
Darley Sq DE7 ... 194 C3
Darley St DE22 ... 205 D1
Darley Way Buxton SK17 . 85 E3
  North Wingfield S42 . 132 A4
Darlton St NG19 .. 268 A3
Darnley St ST4 .. 269 E2
Darsway DE74 ... 246 C2
Dartford Pl DE24 . 233 D3
Dartmouth St ST16 . 269 E4
Dartnall Cl SK12 . 32 A3
Darwent Rd S41 .. 96 B4
Darwin Ave Buxton SK17 . 85 E3
  Chesterfield S40 . 266 A4
  Derby DE24 ..... 232 B4
  Ilkeston DE7 .... 208 B3
Darwin Cl DE21 .. 248 A4
Darwin Pl DE1 ... 267 C3
Darwin Rd
  Chesterfield S40 . 266 A4
  Derby DE3 ..... 217 F3
  Long Eaton NG10 . 236 B3
Darwood La S44 .. 118 A4
Dashwood St DE23 . 267 A1
Datchet Cl DE23 . 231 D4
Daveham Ave SK17 . 85 E3
Davenport Rd Derby DE24 . 232 B4
  Tupton S42 ..... 131 D4
Davey Ct S44 .... 98 C2
Davian Way S40 .. 114 A4
David's Cl DE73 .. 233 D2
Davids Dr S42 ... 114 B1
Davidson Cl NG2 . 268 C1
Davies Cl NG10 .. 236 C4
Davis Cl ST16 ... 269 D4
Davis Rd DE11 ... 256 A3
Davis St DE24 ... 232 C4
Dawlish Ct DE21 . 206 A1
  Eastwood NG16 . 182 C2
Dawn View NG9 .. 209 E1
Dawsmere Cl DE21 . 205 F1
Dawver Rd NG16 . 195 F3
Dayfield Rd DE23 . 231 E4
Daylesford Cl DE23 . 231 F3
Days Mill Cl DE4 . 143 D4
Days Mill Ct DE4 . 143 D4
De Sutton Pl S26 . 61 F4
De Warren Pl S26 . 61 F4
Deacon Cl Derby DE21 . 205 F1
  Swanwick DE55 . 169 E4

Dead La NG16 ..... 195 E1
Deadman's La DE24 ..... 219 E1
Deamon St DE55 ..... 147 F1
Dean Cl DE23 ..... 218 A1
Dean Rd DE56 ..... 167 F1
Dean St Derby DE22 ..... 218 C2
 Langley Mill NG16 ..... 182 B2
 Nottingham NG1 ..... 268 B1
Deanhead Dr S20 ..... 44 C1
Deans Dr DE72 ..... 221 D1
Deansgate NG19 ..... 135 D3
Deanshill Cl ST16 ..... 269 D3
Debdale Gate NG19 ..... 136 A1
Debdale La NG19 ..... 136 A1
Deben Cl S40 ..... 114 B4
Deborah Dr DE21 ..... 220 A4
Dee Cl DE24 ..... 231 F2
Dee La DE65 ..... 229 F3
Deep Dale La
 Barrow u T DE73 ..... 244 A4
 Derby DE24, DE73 ..... 231 F1
Deep La S45 ..... 133 D2
Deepdale NG16 ..... 170 C2
Deepdale Ave
 Borrowash DE72 ..... 221 E1
 Stapleford NG9 ..... 223 E3
Deepdale Cl DE15 ..... 248 A3
Deepdale Ct DE75 ..... 181 F1
Deepdale La DE6 ..... 184 A1
Deepdale Rd
 Belper DE56 ..... 179 D3
 Bolsover S44 ..... 98 C2
 Derby DE21 ..... 220 C2
 Long Eaton NG10 ..... 236 A3
 Mansfield NG19 ..... 136 C1
Deepsick La S44 ..... 97 E1
Deepwell Ave
 Killamarsh S20 ..... 60 A3
 Mosborough S20 ..... 59 F3
Deepwell Bank S20 ..... 59 F3
Deepwell Ct S20 ..... 59 F3
Deepwell View S20 ..... 59 F3
Deer Park Prim Sch S42 ..... 114 C2
Deer Park View DE21 ..... 220 C3
Deerlands Rd
 Chesterfield S42 ..... 95 D2
 Wingerworth S42 ..... 114 C1
Deerleap La S42 ..... 130 B2
Deerpark Cres S42 ..... 114 C2
Degge St DE1 ..... 267 B2
Deincourt Cl DE21 ..... 221 D3
Deincourt Cres S42 ..... 131 F4
Deincourt Sch S42 ..... 131 F4
Delamere Cl
 Breaston DE72 ..... 235 E4
 Derby DE21 ..... 206 A1
 Swanwick DE55 ..... 169 F4
Delamere Dr NG18 ..... 268 C3
Delhi Cl DE15 ..... 248 B2
Dell The S40 ..... 95 D2
Delph Bank S40 ..... 114 C4
Delph Cl S32 ..... 71 E3
Delph St S2 ..... 43 D4
Delph The DE73 ..... 252 C1
Delven La DE74 ..... 247 D2
Delves Bank Rd DE55 ..... 170 A4
Delves Cl S40 ..... 95 E1
Delves Rd Heanor DE75 ..... 193 E4
 Shipley DE75 ..... 193 E4
Delves Specl Sch DE55 ..... 169 F4
Delves The DE55 ..... 169 F4
Denacre Ave NG10 ..... 223 F1
Denacre La DE4 ..... 127 F2
Denarth Ave DE24 ..... 232 C2
Denbigh St DE21 ..... 219 F4
Denby Comm DE5 ..... 180 C2
Denby Free CE Prim Sch
 DE5 ..... 180 B1
Denby La DE5 ..... 180 B1
Denby Rd S43 ..... 97 E4
Dene Fields Ct DE4 ..... 143 E3
Denefield Cl SK6 ..... 15 D1
Denham St S45 ..... 131 E2
Denison Cl S8 ..... 43 D3
Denison Gdns DE21 ..... 220 A3
Denman Cres S32 ..... 53 D3
Denmark Rd S2 ..... 43 D3
Dennett Cl NG3 ..... 268 C2
Dennis Cl DE23 ..... 230 C4
Dennor Dr NG19 ..... 136 C3
Denstone Coll ST14 ..... 196 A3
Denstone Dr DE24 ..... 233 D3
Denstone La ST14 ..... 196 B4
Denstone Rd NG3 ..... 268 C2
Dent La S12 ..... 44 C1
Dentdale Cl DE24 ..... 233 E4
Denton Ave DE24 ..... 233 D3
Denton Cl NG19 ..... 136 C1
Denton Way NG16 ..... 169 F4
Denver Ct NG9 ..... 209 F1
Denver Rd DE3 ..... 217 E2
Depedale Ave DE7 ..... 208 B3
Depot St DE23 ..... 219 D1
Derby Cath DE1 ..... 267 B4
Derby City Hospl DE23 ..... 218 A1
Derby High Sch DE23 ..... 218 A1
Derby Ind Gram Sch for
 Boys DE23 ..... 230 C4
Derby La Brailsford DE6 ..... 201 D4
 Derby DE23 ..... 231 F4
 Great Cubley DE6 ..... 198 C1
 Monyash DE45 ..... 123 E4
 Thurvaston S 200 C4
Derby Moor Com Sch
 DE23 ..... 231 D4
Derby Pl S2 ..... 43 E3
Derby Rd
 Alderwasley DE56 ..... 167 F1

Derby Rd continued
 Alfreton DE55 ..... 158 C2
 Ambergate DE56 ..... 167 F2
 Ashbourne DE6 ..... 185 F4
 Aston-on-T DE72 ..... 234 A1
 Belper DE56 ..... 190 C4
 Borrowash DE21, DE72 ..... 221 D1
 Burton u T DE13 ..... 241 D1
 Chesterfield S45 ..... 115 D3
 Clay Cross S45 ..... 131 E3
 Cromford DE4 ..... 155 E3
 Dale DE21 ..... 206 C2
 Derby DE65 ..... 180 B2
 Derby, Chellaston DE23 ..... 232 C1
 Derby, Spondon DE21 ..... 220 B2
 Doveridge DE6 ..... 211 E1
 Draycott DE72 ..... 234 C4
 Duffield DE56 ..... 190 C1
 Eastwood NG16 ..... 182 C1
 Egginton DE65 ..... 241 E2
 Elvaston DE72 ..... 234 A1
 Hatton DE65 ..... 227 F1
 Heanor DE75 ..... 181 E1
 Hilton DE65 ..... 228 C2
 Horsley DE21 ..... 191 E3
 Ilkeston DE7 ..... 208 B4
 Kilburn DE56 ..... 179 F1
 Langley Mill NG16 ..... 182 B2
 Long Eaton NG10 ..... 236 A4
 Marston on D DE65 ..... 228 A1
 Melbourne DE73 ..... 252 A4
 New Mills SK22 ..... 24 B1
 Nottingham NG7 ..... 268 A2
 Ripley DE5 ..... 180 B2
 Risley DE72 ..... 222 B2
 Sandiacre NG10 ..... 223 D3
 Smisby LE65 ..... 258 A2
 Stanley DE7 ..... 207 D2
 Stapleford NG9 ..... 223 E3
 Swadlincote DE11 ..... 256 B2
 Swanwick DE5, DE55 ..... 169 F3
 Ticknall DE11 ..... 257 F4
 Tupton S45 ..... 131 E3
 Uttoxeter ST14 ..... 210 B1
 Wingerworth S42 ..... 115 D3
 Wirksworth DE4 ..... 165 F3
Derby Rd Ind Est NG10 ..... 223 D3
Derby Road Ind Est
 DE75 ..... 181 E1
Derby Small Bsns Ctr
 DE1 ..... 267 C2
Derby St Glossop SK13 ..... 17 E4
 Ilkeston DE7 ..... 208 C4
 Mansfield NG18 ..... 268 C3
 Nottingham NG1 ..... 268 A2
 Sheffield S2 ..... 43 E3
 Stafford ST16 ..... 269 D4
Derby Sta DE1 ..... 219 E2
Derby Terr S2 ..... 43 E3
Derby Trad Est DE21 ..... 219 D4
Derby Univ
 (Mickleover Site) DE3 ..... 217 F2
Derbyshire Ave
 Trowell NG9 ..... 209 E2
 West Hallam DE7 ..... 207 F4
Derbyshire Cl DE7 ..... 207 F4
Derbyshire Cty
 Cricket Gd DE21 ..... 219 E3
Derbyshire Dr
 Ilkeston DE7 ..... 208 C3
 Westwood NG16 ..... 171 E2
Derbyshire La S8 ..... 43 D2
Derbyshire Level SK13 ..... 17 F3
Derbyshire Royal Infmy
 DE1 ..... 267 C1
Derrington Leys DE24 ..... 233 E3
Derventio Cl DE1 ..... 219 D4
Derwent Ave
 Belper DE56 ..... 179 D1
 Borrowash DE72 ..... 221 E2
 Derby DE72 ..... 205 D2
 Grindleford S32 ..... 72 B4
 Ilkeston DE7 ..... 194 B1
 West Hallam DE7 ..... 207 F4
Derwent Cl Derby DE22 ..... 205 D2
 Dronfield S18 ..... 57 D3
 Glossop SK13 ..... 9 F2
 Grindleford S32 ..... 72 B4
 Swadlincote DE11 ..... 256 A1
Derwent Com Sch DE21 ..... 219 E4
Derwent Cres S41 ..... 95 E4
Derwent Croft DE65 ..... 242 A3
Derwent Ct S17 ..... 56 A3
Derwent Dr Baslow DE45 ..... 91 E3
 Chinley SK23 ..... 34 C1
 Darley Dale DE4 ..... 127 E2
 Derby DE24 ..... 232 C1
 Tibshelf DE55 ..... 147 F3
Derwent Gdns DE6 ..... 185 E4
Derwent Gr DE55 ..... 158 C1
Derwent La Derwent S33 ..... 30 A4
 Hathersage S32 ..... 52 C4
Derwent Pl S45 ..... 131 D3
Derwent Rd
 Burton u T DE15 ..... 248 A1
 Buxton SK17 ..... 85 E3
 Derby DE21 ..... 220 B2
 Dronfield S18 ..... 57 D2
 Ripley DE5 ..... 169 E1
Derwent Rise DE21 ..... 220 C2
Derwent Sq S23 ..... 34 C1
Derwent St Belper DE56 ..... 178 C2
 Derby DE1 ..... 267 B3
 Draycott DE72 ..... 235 D4
 Long Eaton NG10 ..... 236 B3
Derwent Street Ind Est
 NG10 ..... 236 B3
Derwent Vale DE56 ..... 178 C1

Derwent View
 Belper DE56 ..... 178 C3
 Mastin Moor S43 ..... 79 E2
Desborough Rd NG16 ..... 171 E4
Dethick La DE4 ..... 144 B1
Dethick Way S42 ..... 132 A4
Devas Gdns DE21 ..... 220 B3
Deveron Cl DE13 ..... 240 B1
Deveron Rd S20 ..... 59 F4
Devizes Cl S40 ..... 114 C4
Devon Cl Burton u T DE15 ..... 254 C3
 Derby DE21 ..... 219 E3
 Grassmoor S42 ..... 115 F1
 Sandiacre NG10 ..... 223 D3
Devon Dr Brimington S43 ..... 96 C4
 Mansfield NG19 ..... 268 A4
Devon Park View S43 ..... 96 C4
Devon St Ilkeston DE7 ..... 209 D3
 Nottingham NG3 ..... 268 C2
Devonish Royal Hospl
 The SK17 ..... 85 D4
Devonshire Ave
 Borrowash DE72 ..... 221 E1
 Darley Dale DE4 ..... 142 C4
 Derby DE22 ..... 204 C2
 Long Eaton NG10 ..... 237 D4
Devonshire Ave E S41 ..... 115 E4
Devonshire Ave N S43 ..... 77 F2
Devonshire Cl
 Chesterfield S41 ..... 95 F4
 Dore S17 ..... 55 F3
 Dronfield S18 ..... 75 F4
 Ilkeston DE7 ..... 194 B3
 Staveley S43 ..... 78 C1
Devonshire Ct S43 ..... 96 B4
Devonshire Dr Chinley SK23 ..... 34 B1
 Creswell S80 ..... 81 E1
 Derby DE3 ..... 217 F2
 Dore S17 ..... 55 F3
 Duffield DE56 ..... 190 B1
 Eastwood NG16 ..... 182 C1
 Langwith NG20 ..... 119 F4
 Rowsley DE4 ..... 110 C1
 Somercotes DE55 ..... 170 A4
 Stapleford NG9 ..... 209 E1
Devonshire Glen S17 ..... 55 F3
Devonshire Gr S17 ..... 55 F3
Devonshire Rd Buxton SK17 ..... 85 D4
 Dore S17 ..... 55 F3
Devonshire Rd E S41 ..... 115 E4
Devonshire Rd N S43 ..... 77 F2
Devonshire Sq DE4 ..... 111 D2
Devonshire St
 Brimington S43 ..... 96 C4
 Chesterfield S41 ..... 266 B3
 New Houghton NG19 ..... 135 D4
 Staveley S43 ..... 78 C1
 Toadmoor DE56 ..... 167 F2
Devonshire Terr S42 ..... 116 C1
Devonshire Terrace Rd
 S17 ..... 55 F4
Devonshire Villas
 Barrow Hill S43 ..... 78 B2
 [13] Chesterfield S41 ..... 95 F4
Devonshire Way S40 ..... 81 D2
Dew Pond La S42 ..... 85 E4
Dewchurch Dr DE23 ..... 231 F3
Dewint Ave SK6 ..... 23 D4
Dewsnap La SK14 ..... 9 D3
Dewy La Ashover DE4 ..... 144 C3
 Crich DE4 ..... 144 C1
Dexter St DE23 ..... 219 E1
Dialstone S33 ..... 51 D4
Diamond Dr DE21 ..... 205 F2
Diamond Jubilee Cotts
 DE6 ..... 184 C4
Dibble Rd DE14 ..... 254 A4
Dickens Dr Holmewood S42 ..... 116 B1
 Swadlincote DE11 ..... 256 B3
Dickens Sq DE23 ..... 231 F4
Dickenson Rd S41 ..... 266 C1
Dickinson St DE24 ..... 219 E1
Dickinson's La DE6 ..... 215 D1
Dicklant La S45 ..... 145 D4
Didcot Cl S40 ..... 114 C4
Didsbury Terr SK22 ..... 25 F1
Dig St Ashbourne DE6 ..... 173 E1
 Hartington SK17 ..... 137 E3
Digby St Cossall DE7 ..... 195 D1
 Kimberley NG16 ..... 195 E4
Diglands Ave SK22 ..... 24 B1
Diglands Cl SK22 ..... 24 B1
Diglee Rd SK23 ..... 33 E2
Digmire La DE6 ..... 161 E1
Dimple Cres DE4 ..... 143 D3
Dimple La DE4 ..... 143 D4
Dingle Cl SK13 ..... 17 D4
Dingle La S44 ..... 96 C1
Dingle The DE15 ..... 248 A3
Dinmore Grange DE11 ..... 257 D3
Dinting CE Prim Sch SK13 ..... 10 A1
Dinting La SK13 ..... 10 A1
Dinting Lane Trad Est SK13 ..... 10 A1
Dinting Lodge Ind Est SK13 ..... 9 F1
Dinting Rd SK13 ..... 10 A1
Dinting Sta SK13 ..... 10 A1
Dinting Vale SK13 ..... 10 A1
Diseworth Rd DE74 ..... 247 D1
Dish La DE65 ..... 228 A3
Dishwell La S26 ..... 61 E3
Disley Cty Prim Sch SK12 ..... 32 B3
Disley Sta SK12 ..... 32 B3
Ditch The SK17 ..... 105 F4
Division Rd NG20 ..... 119 F2
Division St S43 ..... 97 D4

Dix Ave DE7 ..... 192 C3
Dixie St NG16 ..... 171 D2
Dixon's Rd S41 ..... 266 C2
Dobbin La S18 ..... 75 E3
Dobbinhorse La DE6 ..... 185 D3
Dobholes La DE7 ..... 192 C3
Dobson Pl S43 ..... 97 D3
Dock Wlk S40 ..... 266 A2
Dockholm Rd NG10 ..... 223 E1
Doctor La S26 ..... 61 F3
Doctor's La DE4 ..... 252 C1
Dodburn Ct DE24 ..... 231 E2
Dodford Cl DE75 ..... 182 A1
Dodslow Ave DE13 ..... 240 A2
Doe Hill La DE55 ..... 147 E3
Doehole La DE4 ..... 144 C2
Dog La
 Breedon on t H DE73 ..... 252 C3
 Hulland Ward DE6 ..... 175 E2
 Nethersea DE12 ..... 264 C3
 Stonebroom DE55 ..... 146 C1
Doghole La DE4 ..... 154 B2
Dogkennel La DE6 ..... 186 C4
Dolby Rd SK17 ..... 85 E1
Doles La Findern DE65 ..... 230 B2
 Whitwell S80 ..... 82 A4
Dolly La Brierley Green SK23 ..... 34 A1
 Whaley Bridge SK23 ..... 33 F2
Dolly Wood Cl SK23 ..... 34 A1
Dolphin Cl DE21 ..... 221 D3
Dominic St ST4 ..... 269 E2
Dominion Rd DE11 ..... 256 A3
Don Ave DE22 ..... 204 C3
Donald Hawley Way DE56 ..... 190 C2
Doncaster Ave NG10 ..... 223 D3
Doncaster Gr NG10 ..... 223 F1
Doncaster La ST4 ..... 269 D2
Donegal Wlk DE21 ..... 220 A2
Donington Park Motor
 Racing Circuit DE74 ..... 246 B1
Donisthorpe La DE12 ..... 262 C1
Donner Cres DE7 ..... 194 C3
Donnington Cl DE23 ..... 231 F3
Donnington Dr DE23 ..... 231 F3
Donnington La DE74 ..... 247 E4
Dorchester Ave DE21 ..... 219 F4
Dorchester Rd NG16 ..... 195 F4
Dore Cl S17 ..... 56 A4
Dore Hall Croft S17 ..... 55 F4
Dore La S17 ..... 53 D4
Dore Prim Sch S17 ..... 55 E3
Dore Rd S17 ..... 55 F4
Dore & Totley Sta S17 ..... 56 A4
Doris Rd DE7 ..... 209 D4
Dorking Rd DE22 ..... 218 A3
Dormy Cl NG10 ..... 223 D1
Dorothy Ave
 Mansfield Woodhouse
 NG19 ..... 136 B1
 Sandiacre NG10 ..... 223 D3
Dorothy Dr NG19 ..... 136 C1
Dorothy Vale S40 ..... 95 E2
Dorrien Ave DE23 ..... 232 A4
Dorset Ave [2] S43 ..... 96 C4
Dorset Cl Brimington S43 ..... 77 F1
 Burton u T DE15 ..... 254 C3
 Buxton SK17 ..... 85 E2
Dorset Dr S43 ..... 96 C4
Dorset St DE21 ..... 219 E3
Dorterry Cres DE7 ..... 209 D3
Douglas Ave
 Awsworth NG16 ..... 195 E3
 Heanor DE75 ..... 181 E1
 Stoke-on-T ST4 ..... 269 D1
Douglas Rd
 Chesterfield S41 ..... 96 B3
 Long Eaton NG10 ..... 223 D1
 Somercotes DE55 ..... 170 B4
Douglas St DE23 ..... 219 D1
Douse Croft La S10 ..... 42 C3
Dove Bk SK6 ..... 23 F3
Dove Cl Derby DE23 ..... 218 A2
 Kilburn DE56 ..... 192 A4
 Woodville DE11 ..... 256 C2
Dove Farm Sch ST4 ..... 197 D2
Dove Gr DE65 ..... 241 D3
Dove Holes CE Prim Sch
 SK17 ..... 47 F1
Dove Holes Sta SK17 ..... 47 F1
Dove House Gn DE6 ..... 173 D1
Dove La Long Eaton NG10 ..... 236 B3
 Rocester ST14 ..... 197 D2
Dove Lea DE13 ..... 240 A2
Dove Rd DE65 ..... 169 E1
Dove Rise DE65 ..... 228 B1
Dove Side DE65 ..... 239 D4
Dove St DE6 ..... 183 D1
Dove Valley Pk DE65 ..... 227 D3
Dove View DE13 ..... 239 E3
Dovecliff Cres DE13 ..... 240 C1
Dovecliff Rd
 Burton u T DE13 ..... 240 C2
 Rolleston DE13 ..... 240 C2
Dovecote DE74 ..... 247 D2
Dovecote Dr DE72 ..... 221 D1
Dovecote The
 Breedon on t H DE73 ..... 252 C1
 Horsley DE21 ..... 191 F3
Dovecotes S45 ..... 129 F2
Dovedale Ave
 Ashbourne DE6 ..... 173 E1
 Derby DE23 ..... 218 A1
 Long Eaton NG10 ..... 236 A3
 Staveley S43 ..... 97 D3
Dovedale Cir DE7 ..... 194 C3
Dovedale Cl
 Burton u T DE15 ..... 248 A3
 Ripley DE5 ..... 180 B3

Dovedale Cres
 Belper DE56 ..... 179 D3
 Buxton SK17 ..... 84 C3
Dovedale Ct Belper DE56 ..... 179 D2
 [4] Chesterfield S41 ..... 95 F4
 Glossop SK13 ..... 10 C1
 Long Eaton NG10 ..... 236 A3
Dovedale Prim Sch NG10 ..... 236 A3
Dovedale Rd DE21 ..... 220 C2
Dovedale Rise DE22 ..... 204 B1
Dovefields ST14 ..... 196 C2
Dover Cl DE23 ..... 219 D1
Dover St Creswell S80 ..... 81 F1
 Derby DE23 ..... 219 D1
Doveridge Cl DE15 ..... 248 A1
Doveridge Cty Jun Mix &
 Inf Sch DE6 ..... 211 D1
Doveridge Gr SK17 ..... 85 F3
Doveridge Prim Sch DE6 ..... 224 B4
Doveridge Wlk DE23 ..... 231 E3
Doveside DE6 ..... 184 B4
Dowcarr La S26 ..... 61 E3
Dowdeswell St S41 ..... 266 B4
Dower Cl DE22 ..... 205 D2
Downham Cl DE3 ..... 217 F1
Downing Cl DE21 ..... 217 F3
Downing Rd Derby DE21 ..... 219 E3
 Sheffield S8 ..... 56 C4
Downing St DE55 ..... 160 A3
Downings The S26 ..... 61 F3
Downlands S43 ..... 96 B4
Downlee Cl SK23 ..... 46 C3
Downmeadow DE56 ..... 179 F4
Dowson St NG3 ..... 268 C2
Doxey Rd ST16 ..... 269 D4
Dr John Bingham Prim
 Sch S8 ..... 57 D3
Drabbles Rd DE4 ..... 143 D3
Drage St DE1 ..... 219 D4
Drake Terr S43 ..... 96 B4
Draycott Cl DE75 ..... 181 E2
Draycott Dr DE3 ..... 217 E2
Draycott Pl S18 ..... 75 E4
Draycott Prim Sch DE72 ..... 235 D4
Draycott Rd
 Borrowash DE72 ..... 221 E1
 Breaston DE72 ..... 235 E4
 Long Eaton NG10 ..... 236 A2
 North Wingfield S42 ..... 131 F4
Drayton Ave Derby DE22 ..... 217 F3
 Mansfield NG19 ..... 135 E1
Drayton St DE11 ..... 256 B2
Dresden Cl DE3 ..... 217 E1
Drewery La DE22 ..... 218 C2
Drewry Ct DE1 ..... 218 C3
Dreyfus Cl DE21 ..... 220 C3
Drive The DE56 ..... 177 F2
Dronfield Inf & Jun Sch
 S18 ..... 57 D1
Dronfield Pl DE7 ..... 194 C3
Dronfield Rd S21 ..... 59 D1
Dronfield Sch
 (Gosforth Site) The S18 ..... 56 C1
Dronfield Sch The S18 ..... 57 D1
Dronfield Sta S18 ..... 57 D1
Drovers Way DE56 ..... 168 A3
Drovers Wlk SK13 ..... 10 B1
Drummond Rd DE7 ..... 194 C1
Drury Ave DE21 ..... 220 B2
Drury La Biggin SK17 ..... 138 B1
 Dore S17 ..... 55 F3
 Dronfield S18 ..... 57 E2
Dryden Ave S40 ..... 115 D4
Dryden Cres ST17 ..... 269 D3
Dryden Ct NG9 ..... 209 F1
Dryden St Derby DE23 ..... 231 F4
 Nottingham NG1 ..... 268 A2
Dryhurst Dr SK12 ..... 32 B3
Dryhurst La SK12 ..... 32 B3
Drysdale Rd DE3 ..... 217 E2
Duchess St Creswell S80 ..... 81 F1
 Whitwell S80 ..... 82 A3
Duck St DE45 ..... 241 D3
Duckmanton Prim Sch
 S44 ..... 98 A3
Duckmanton Rd S44 ..... 98 A3
Duckworth Sq DE1 ..... 267 B3
Dudwood La DE4 ..... 140 C4
Duesbury Cl DE24 ..... 232 C4
Duesbury The DE55 ..... 160 A2
Duewell Ct S43 ..... 78 A2
Duffield Bank DE56 ..... 191 D2
Duffield Cl NG10 ..... 236 A3
Duffield Rd
 Derby, Allestree DE22 ..... 205 D3
 Derby, Darley Abbey DE22 ..... 204 C1
 Little Eaton DE21 ..... 205 D3
Duffield Sta DE56 ..... 190 C2
Duke of Norfolk's CE
 Prim Sch Glossop SK13 ..... 10 B1
 Glossop, Old Glossop SK13 ..... 10 C1
Duke St Buxton SK17 ..... 85 E3
 Chesterfield S41 ..... 96 A4
 Clowne S43 ..... 81 D2
 Creswell S80 ..... 81 F1
 Derby DE1 ..... 267 B4
 Ilkeston DE7 ..... 194 C2
 Middleton (Nr Wirksworth)
 DE4 ..... 154 B3
 Mosborough S20 ..... 59 E3
 South Normanton DE55 ..... 160 A3
 Staveley S43 ..... 78 C1
 Whitwell S80 ..... 82 A3

Duke William Mount NG7 ... 268 A1
Duke's Dr
  Ault Hucknall S44 ... 134 A4
  Buxton SK17 ... 85 E3
Duke's Dr The DE45 ... 108 C4
Dukeries Ct S43 ... 80 C1
Dukeries La DE21 ... 206 A1
Dukes Cl S42 ... 116 C1
Dukes Dr Chesterfield S41 ... 95 F3
  Curbar S32 ... 72 B1
Dukes Pl DE7 ... 194 C2
Dukes St SK13 ... 17 E4
Duluth Ave DE21 ... 220 A4
Dulverton Ave DE24 ... 231 E1
Dulwich Rd DE22 ... 217 F3
Dumb Hall La
  Shireoaks S80 ... 63 D2
  Thorpe Salvin S80 ... 63 D2
Dumble Wood Grange S40 ... 95 E4
Dumbles Cl DE7 ... 208 B3
Dumbles La DE5 ... 180 C1
Dumbles Rd S44 ... 98 C2
Dumbleton Rd S21 ... 60 C3
Dunbar Cl DE24 ... 231 F1
Duncan Cl DE56 ... 179 D3
Duncan Rd DE22 ... 231 F4
Duncliffe La DE73 ... 252 A4
Duncombe Dr DE6 ... 185 E4
Dundas Cl NG1 ... 268 B2
Dundee Dr NG19 ... 136 A3
Dundee Rd DE11 ... 256 B3
Dundonald Rd S40 ... 266 B1
Dunedin Cl DE3 ... 217 F2
Dunedin Cres DE15 ... 248 B1
Dunedin Glen S20 ... 59 F3
Dunedin Gr S20 ... 59 F3
Dungley Hill DE56 ... 168 B1
Dungreave Ave DE4 ... 127 D3
Dunkery Ct DE21 ... 206 A1
Dunkirk DE22 ... 267 A2
Dunlow La S32 ... 71 E3
Dunnett Rd NG18 ... 268 A4
Dunnsmoor La DE11 ... 256 C4
Dunoon Cl DE24 ... 231 F2
Dunoon Rd NG18 ... 268 A3
Dunsa La DE45 ... 91 E1
Dunsford Rd DE55 ... 159 D3
Dunshill Wlk S45 ... 131 F2
Dunsil Rd NG16 ... 160 B1
Dunsmore Dr DE21 ... 205 F1
Dunsmore Way DE11 ... 256 B3
Dunstall Brook DE15 ... 248 A1
Dunstall Park Rd DE24 ... 232 B4
Dunston Cl NG18 ... 236 C4
Dunston Ct S41 ... 76 C1
Dunston La S41 ... 95 E4
Dunston Pl S41 ... 76 C1
Dunston Prim Sch S41 ... 95 E4
Dunston Rd S41 ... 76 B1
Dunston Trad Est S41 ... 76 C1
Dunton Cl DE21 ... 267 D3
Dunvegan Ave S45 ... 131 F1
Dunvegan Cl DE24 ... 231 E1
Duper La S32 ... 71 F1
Durban Rd DE15 ... 248 B2
Durham Ave
  Chesterfield S43 ... 77 E2
  Derby DE21 ... 219 F3
  Grassmoor S42 ... 115 F1
  Nottingham NG2 ... 268 C1
Durham Cl
  Chesterfield S43 ... 77 E2
  Mansfield Woodhouse
  NG19 ... 136 B2
  Nottingham NG2 ... 268 C1
  Swadlincote DE11 ... 256 C3
Durham St DE7 ... 194 C1
Durley Chine Dr S41 ... 115 E4
Durley Cl DE24 ... 233 E4
Durlstone Cl S12 ... 44 A3
Durlstone Cres S12 ... 44 A3
Durlstone Dr S12 ... 44 A3
Durlstone Gr S12 ... 44 A3
Durrant Rd S41 ... 266 B3
Durvale Ct S17 ... 55 F3
Durward Cl DE24 ... 232 B4
Dyche Cl S8 ... 57 D3
Dyche Dr S8 ... 57 D3
Dyche La Dronfield S18 ... 57 D3
  Sheffield S8 ... 57 D3
Dyche Pl S8 ... 57 D3
Dyche Rd S8 ... 57 D3
Dye House La SK22 ... 33 E4
Dyke Vale Rd S12 ... 44 C3
Dykes Cl S44 ... 99 D1
Dymond Gr S42 ... 115 F2
Dystelegh Rd SK12 ... 32 B3

Earlswood Cl DE72 ... 235 E4
Earlswood Dr DE3 ... 217 F2
Earnshaw St SK14 ... 9 F2
Easedale Cl S40 ... 94 C3
East Ave Bolsover S44 ... 80 A1
  Derby DE3 ... 217 F2
East Bank Cl S2 ... 43 E3
East Bank Cl S2 ... 43 E3
East Bank Pl S2 ... 43 E3
East Bank Rd S2 ... 43 E3
East Bank View S2 ... 43 E3
East Bank Way S2 ... 43 E3
East Circus St **2** NG1 ... 268 A1
East Cl DE22 ... 204 C2
East Cres Holbrook DE56 ... 191 E4
  Long Duckmanton S44 ... 98 A3
East Croft Ave DE23 ... 231 E1
East Dr DE6 ... 211 D1
East End DE11 ... 256 B2
East End Dr DE11 ... 256 B2
East Glade Ave S12 ... 44 C2
East Glade Cl S12 ... 44 C2
East Glade Cres S12 ... 44 C2
East Glade Pl S12 ... 44 C2
East Glade Rd S12 ... 44 C2
East Glade Sq S12 ... 44 C2
East Glade Way S12 ... 44 C2
East Hill Sch S2 ... 43 E4
East Lawn DE65 ... 230 B1
East Midlands Airport
  DE74 ... 247 E1
East Midlands Nuffield
  Hospl DE23 ... 230 C3
East Nelson St DE75 ... 181 F1
East Rd S2 ... 43 D4
East Service Rd DE21 ... 220 A2
East St Bramley-Vale S44 ... 117 E1
  Burton u T DE15 ... 248 B2
  Clay Cross S45 ... 131 E2
  Clowne S43 ... 81 D3
  Creswell S80 ... 81 E1
  Derby DE1 ... 267 B3
  Heanor DE75 ... 194 A4
  Ilkeston DE7 ... 208 C4
  Long Eaton NG10 ... 236 C4
  Nottingham NG1 ... 268 B2
  Renishaw S21 ... 79 D4
  Scarcliffe S44 ... 118 C3
East Vale S45 ... 23 D3
East View Chesterfield S40 ... 266 B2
  Shirebrook NG20 ... 119 F3
East View Ave S21 ... 59 E1
East View Rd DE56 ... 168 C1
Eastbrae Rd DE23 ... 231 E4
Eastbrook Cl SK23 ... 47 D3
Eastcliffe Ct S2 ... 43 E4
Eastcliffe S2 ... 43 E4
Eastcroft Cl S20 ... 59 F4
Eastcroft Dr S20 ... 59 F4
Eastcroft Glen **5** S20 ... 59 F4
Eastcroft View **11** S20 ... 59 F4
Eastern Ave Bolsover S44 ... 118 A4
  Sheffield S2 ... 43 E4
Eastern Cres S2 ... 43 E3
Eastern Dr S2 ... 43 E4
Eastern Wlk S2 ... 43 E4
Eastfield Dr DE55 ... 160 A3
Eastfield Rd Dronfield S18 ... 76 B4
  Ripley DE5 ... 170 A1
  Swadlincote DE11 ... 256 B3
Eastgate DE22 ... 267 D4
Eastgate St S16 ... 269 E4
Eastham Cl NG3 ... 268 C2
Eastleigh Ct S41 ... 115 E4
Eastleigh Dr Derby DE21 ... 217 F1
  Mansfield Woodhouse
  NG19 ... 136 A3
Eastmoor Rd S43 ... 96 C2
Eastway DE74 ... 247 D2
Eastwood Ave DE23 ... 218 B1
Eastwood Cl S41 ... 115 E4
Eastwood Comp Sch
  NG16 ... 182 C2
Eastwood Cotts S32 ... 53 D4
Eastwood Dr Callow S44 ... 97 D1
  Derby DE21 ... 218 B1
Eastwood Jun & Inf Schs
  NG16 ... 182 C2
Eastwood La S45 ... 130 A1
Eastwood Park Dr S41 ... 115 E4
Eastwood Rd NG16 ... 195 F3
Easy Par S80 ... 82 A3
Eather Ave NG19 ... 136 B2
Eaton Ave Derby DE22 ... 205 D3
  Ilkeston DE7 ... 208 B3
Eaton Bank DE56 ... 191 D1
Eaton Cl Derby DE65 ... 205 D3
  Hatton DE65 ... 227 E1
Eaton Ct DE7 ... 175 F2
Eaton Ct Derby DE1 ... 218 C3
  Duffield DE56 ... 190 C1
Eaton Dr DE45 ... 91 F3
Eaton Fold S32 ... 71 F2
Eaton Grange Dr NG10 ... 236 A4
Eaton Hill DE45 ... 91 F3
Eaton Pl DE45 ... 91 F3
Eaton Rd
  Castle Donington DE74 ... 247 D2
  Rocester ST14 ... 196 C2
Eaton St S14 ... 210 B1
Eatons Rd NG9 ... 223 E3
Eaves Knoll Rd SK22 ... 33 D4
Ebenezer St Glossop SK13 ... 17 E4
  Langley Mill NG16 ... 182 A2
Eccles Cl High Lane SK23 ... 39 D2
  Whaley Bridge SK23 ... 45 E4

Eccles Fold SK23 ... 47 D3
Eccles Rd
  Chapel-en-le-F,
  Higher Crossings SK23 ... 47 D3
  Chapel-en-le-F, Hilltop SK23 ... 46 B4
  Whaley Bridge SK23 ... 45 F3
Eccles Terr SK23 ... 46 A4
Ecclesbourne Ave DE56 ... 190 C2
Ecclesbourne Cl
  Duffield DE56 ... 190 C2
  Wirksworth DE4 ... 165 F4
Ecclesbourne Dr SK17 ... 85 D3
Ecclesbourne Sch DE56 ... 176 C3
Ecclesbourne Sch DE56 ... 190 C2
Eckington Cl DE7 ... 207 F4
Eckington Jun Sch S21 ... 59 E2
Eckington Rd Dronfield S18 ... 57 E2
  Eckington S18 ... 57 E2
  Mosborough S20 ... 59 F4
  Staveley S43 ... 78 C2
  Unstone S43 ... 77 E3
Eckington Sch S21 ... 59 D2
Eckington Way S20 ... 59 F4
Eclipse Yd NG18 ... 268 B4
Edale Ave
  Derby, Alvaston DE24 ... 233 D4
  Derby, Mickleover DE3 ... 217 E1
  Derby, Rose Hill DE23 ... 218 C1
Edale CE Prim Sch S33 ... 37 E4
Edale Cl Derby DE22 ... 204 B1
  Long Eaton NG10 ... 236 A3
Edale Cres SK13 ... 9 F1
Edale Ct 1 S41 ... 95 F4
Edale Dr DE21 ... 220 C2
Edale Gr SK17 ... 85 F4
Edale Rd Hayfield SK22 ... 26 A1
  Hope S33 ... 38 C4
  Mastin Moor S43 ... 79 E2
Edale Rise NG9 ... 223 F2
Edale Sq DE7 ... 194 C3
Edale Sta S33 ... 37 E4
Edale Way DE56 ... 179 D3
Eden Bank DE56 ... 167 F1
Eden Low NG19 ... 136 C2
Eden Rd DE21 ... 220 A2
Eden St Derby DE24 ... 233 D4
  Wingerworth S42 ... 114 C2
Edenhall Rd S2 ... 43 F4
Edensor Ave SK17 ... 85 F4
Edensor Cl S41 ... 131 F3
Edensor Ct S41 ... 97 E4
Edensor Dr DE56 ... 179 E3
Edge Farm Dr ST14 ... 196 C2
Edgar Ave NG18 ... 268 C4
Edge Hill DE73 ... 232 C2
Edge Hill Ct NG10 ... 236 B2
Edge Hill Jun Sch DE15 ... 254 C4
Edge Rd Eyam S32 ... 71 F4
  Matlock DE4 ... 143 D3
Edge View Cl S32 ... 72 B4
Edge View Dr DE45 ... 90 A2
Edgecote Dr DE11 ... 256 A4
Edgefold Rd DE4 ... 143 D3
Edgehill Gr NG19 ... 136 B1
Edgelaw Ct **10** DE24 ... 231 E2
Edgewood Rd NG16 ... 195 F3
Edgware Rd DE22 ... 217 F3
Edinburgh Cres DE22 ... 232 C2
Edinburgh Ct DE55 ... 170 A4
Edinburgh Rd
  Chesterfield S41 ... 95 F3
  Nottingham NG2 ... 114 C2
Edision St S14 ... 269 F1
Edith Wood Cl DE24 ... 233 D3
Edlaston La DE6 ... 185 D1
Edmonton Pl DE15 ... 248 B1
Edmund Ave S17 ... 56 B3
Edmund Cl S17 ... 56 B3
Edmund Dr S17 ... 56 B3
Edmund Rd Derby DE22 ... 220 C2
  Sheffield S2 ... 43 D4
Edmund St S41 ... 95 F4
Edmund's Sq DE3 ... 230 A4
Ednaston Ave DE23 ... 231 E3
Edward Ave Derby DE21 ... 220 A3
  Westwood NG16 ... 171 D2
Edward Rd NG10 ... 236 B4
Edward St Aldercar NG16 ... 182 A2
  Belper DE56 ... 179 D2
  Derby DE1 ... 267 B4
  Eckington S21 ... 59 E2
  Glossop SK13 ... 10 B1
  Hartshorne DE11 ... 257 D2
  Marple SK6 ... 15 D1
  Moira DE11 ... 256 B1
  Overseal DE12 ... 262 A2
  Stapleford NG9 ... 223 E4
  Staveley S43 ... 97 E4
Edward Wlk S42 ... 115 E1
Edwards Cres DE56 ... 192 A4
Edwards Dr S18 ... 56 C3
Edwin Ave S40 ... 114 B4
Edwin Rd S2 ... 43 E3
Edwinstowe Rd DE21 ... 206 A1
Egerton Dr NG9 ... 209 E1
Egerton Rd Dronfield S18 ... 57 D1
  Stoke-on-T ST4 ... 269 D2
Eggesford Rd DE24 ... 231 E1
Eggington Prim Sch
  DE65 ... 241 D3
Eggington Rd DE65 ... 228 C1
Egginton Rd DE65 ... 229 D1
Egmanton Cl DE21 ... 206 A1
Egreaves Ave DE75 ... 181 E2
Egstow Pl S45 ... 131 E2
Egstow St S45 ... 131 E2
Ehlinger Ave SK13 ... 10 A3

Eider Cl NG20 ... 119 E2
Eland Cl DE21 ... 221 D3
Eland Rd NG20 ... 119 F3
Elder Cl DE55 ... 170 A4
Elder Cl DE55 ... 170 A4
Elder St S21 ... 60 B3
Elder Way S40 ... 266 B3
Eldon Cl SK23 ... 47 E3
Eldon La SK17 ... 49 D3
Eldon St Burton u T DE15 ... 248 A2
  Clay Cross S45 ... 131 E2
Eleanor Ave DE7 ... 209 D3
Eleanor Cres NG9 ... 223 F4
Elenora St S14 ... 269 E2
Eley Cl DE7 ... 194 B1
Eley Wlk DE22 ... 267 A1
Elford Rise NG2 ... 268 C2
Elgar Dr NG10 ... 236 A3
Elgin Ave DE23 ... 218 A1
Elgin Cl S40 ... 114 B4
Eliot Cl Calow S43 ... 96 C3
  Long Eaton NG10 ... 236 A3
Eliot Dr DE7 ... 208 B3
Eliot Rd DE23 ... 231 D4
Eliot Way ST17 ... 269 D3
Elizabeth Ave Buxton SK17 ... 85 E4
  Disley SK12 ... 32 B3
  Rollerston DE13 ... 240 A1
Elizabeth Cl Derby DE21 ... 220 A3
  West Hallam DE7 ... 207 F4
Elizabeth Ct DE7 ... 194 B1
Elizabeth Pk NG10 ... 170 C3
Elkstone Ct DE21 ... 206 A1
Elkstone Rd S40 ... 95 D3
Ella Bank Rd DE75 ... 182 A1
Ellandale Gdns DE24 ... 233 D4
Ellastone Gr ST14 ... 269 D1
Ellendale Rd DE21 ... 220 A4
Ellerslie Gr NG10 ... 223 D3
Ellesmere Ave
  Alfreton DE55 ... 159 D2
  Derby DE24 ... 219 E1
Ellesmere Dr NG9 ... 209 E3
Ellington Ave ST16 ... 269 F4
Elliot Ave S33 ... 51 D4
Elliott Dr S43 ... 97 E3
Elliott St NG7 ... 268 A2
Ellis Cl NG10 ... 236 B3
Ellis Cl NG3 ... 268 B2
Ellison Ave DE72 ... 246 A4
Ellison Cl SK14 ... 9 E3
Ellison St SK13 ... 10 B1
Elm Ave Belper DE56 ... 179 D1
  Darley Dale DE4 ... 142 C4
  Long Eaton NG10 ... 236 B4
  Sandiacre NG10 ... 223 D4
Elm Cl Bolsover S44 ... 99 F1
  Chesterfield S41 ... 95 F4
  Doveridge DE6 ... 224 B4
  Killamarsh S21 ... 60 B3
  Mottram in L SK14 ... 9 D2
  Pinxton NG16 ... 160 B2
Elm Cres S20 ... 59 F4
Elm Dr Hilton DE65 ... 228 B1
  Killamarsh S21 ... 60 B3
Elm Gr Clay Cross S45 ... 131 E2
  Derby, Allestree DE22 ... 204 B3
  Derby, Cherrytree Hill DE21 ... 220 A3
  Glossop SK13 ... 10 B1
Elm Lodge Farm Cl S41 ... 95 F4
Elm Park S DE1 ... 267 A5
Elm Rd Eckington S21 ... 59 E2
  Pilsley S45 ... 132 B1
Elm St Borrowash DE72 ... 221 D1
  Brimington S43 ... 97 D4
  Temple Normanton S42 ... 116 A2
Elm Tree Ave Kilburn DE56 ... 192 A4
  Mansfield Woodhouse
  NG19 ... 136 A2
  Shirebrook NG20 ... 119 E2
  Shirland DE55 ... 146 B1
Elm Tree Cres S18 ... 57 D2
Elm Tree Dr S44 ... 118 C4
Elm Tree St NG18 ... 268 C4
Elm View S14 ... 196 C3
Elma La NG20 ... 101 E3
Elmfield S43 ... 47 D3
Elmhurst Rd DE65 ... 241 D3
Elmhurst Cl DE55 ... 160 A2
Elmhurst Cl DE55 ... 160 A2
Elmore Ct NG7 ... 268 A2
Elms Ave Alfreton DE55 ... 159 D2
  Derby DE23 ... 218 A1
  Ripley DE5 ... 180 B4
Elms Cl DE55 ... 159 D2
Elms Dr DE23 ... 218 A1
Elms Gr DE65 ... 229 E2
Elms Rd Burton u T DE15 ... 248 A1
  Coton in t E DE12 ... 260 B2
Elms St 1 ... 218 C4
Elms The NG16 ... 195 F4
Elmsdale Rd DE11 ... 257 D2
Elmsfield Ave DE75 ... 182 A1
Elmslea Ave DE12 ... 260 B2
Elmsleigh Cl DE11 ... 256 A3
Elmsleigh Dr DE11 ... 256 A3
Elmsleigh Gr DE11 ... 256 A3
Elmsleigh Inf Sch DE11 ... 256 A3
Elmton Cl Clowne S43 ... 80 C2
  Creswell S80 ... 100 B4
Elmton La S44 ... 99 E2
Elmton Rd S80 ... 81 F1
Elmtree Ave Derby DE24 ... 232 A4
  Selston NG16 ... 171 F4
Elmtree Cl S81 ... 63 F4
Elmwood Dr Derby DE21 ... 205 E1
  Mosborough S20 ... 59 E3
Elnor Ave SK23 ... 45 F3

Elnor La SK23 ... 45 F2
Elnor St NG16 ... 182 B2
Elsecar Cl DE56 ... 179 E3
Elsing St S14 ... 269 F1
Elstead La DE11 ... 257 D3
Elston Cl NG19 ... 135 E2
Elstree Dr S12 ... 44 A2
Elstree Rd S12 ... 44 A2
Elton CE Prim Sch DE4 ... 140 C2
Elton Cl NG9 ... 223 E4
Elton Gr S42 ... 85 F2
Elton Rd Derby DE24 ... 232 A4
  Winster DE4 ... 141 D1
Elton St S44 ... 266 B2
Elton View S43 ... 77 F1
Elvaston Castle DE21 ... 233 F4
Elvaston Castle Ctry Pk
  DE21 ... 233 F2
Elvaston Cl S18 ... 56 A3
Elvaston Dr NG10 ... 236 A2
Elvaston La DE24 ... 233 E4
Elvaston Rd DE7 ... 131 F2
Elvaston St DE72 ... 235 D4
Elveden Dr DE7 ... 194 B2
Elvin Way S42 ... 131 E4
Elwood Rd S17 ... 56 B1
Elwyn Cl DE13 ... 240 B1
Ely Cl
  Mansfield Woodhouse
  NG19 ... 136 B2
  Swadlincote DE11 ... 256 B3
Elyn Ave S42 ... 132 A4
Embankment Cl DE22 ... 217 F4
Ember La DE4 ... 142 C3
Embridge Causeway
  SK10, SK17 ... 64 A3
Emerald Cl Derby DE21 ... 206 A3
  Mansfield NG19 ... 135 F3
Emerson Sq DE23 ... 231 F3
Emery Cl DE12 ... 261 E3
Emmas Williams Ct DE5 ... 169 E3
Emmet Field Cl S40 ... 114 C4
Emmett Carr Cl S21 ... 79 E4
Emmett Carr La S21 ... 79 E4
Empire Pas S14 ... 269 E1
Empire Rd DE15 ... 248 B2
Empire St Mansfield NG18 ... 268 C3
  Down-st ST4 ... 269 F1
Empress Rd DE23 ... 267 A3
Emsworth Cl DE7 ... 194 B2
Ena Ave NG2 ... 268 C2
End The DE15 ... 248 C4
Endcliff Rd S40 ... 114 A4
Endsleigh Gdns DE22 ... 217 F3
Enfield Cl DE65 ... 228 C1
Enfield Rd Chesterfield S41 ... 96 A1
  Derby DE22 ... 218 A3
England Cres DE75 ... 182 A2
English Martyrs RC Prim
  Sch NG10 ... 223 D3
Englishe Rd DE4 ... 143 D2
Ennerdale Ave S20 ... 59 F3
Ennerdale Cl S18 ... 56 C1
Ennerdale Cres S41 ... 95 E4
Ennerdale Dr S20 ... 59 F3
Ennerdale Rd NG10 ... 223 D1
Ennerdale Wlk DE21 ... 205 E1
Ennis Cl DE21 ... 220 B4
Enoch Stone Dr DE21 ... 220 A2
Enslet La DE6 ... 164 A2
Enterprise Dr S42 ... 116 B3
Epping Cl DE22 ... 217 F3
Epsley's Yd S18 ... 269 E3
Epsom Rd NG9 ... 223 F2
Epworth Dr DE24 ... 233 D2
Epworth St S14 ... 269 E2
Erdington Way NG9 ... 223 F2
Erewash Cl DE7 ... 194 B1
Erewash Dr DE7 ... 209 D3
Erewash Gr NG9 ... 223 F1
Erewash Mus DE7 ... 208 C4
Erewash Rd NG16 ... 160 C1
Erewash Sq DE7 ... 209 D3
Erewash St Aldercar DE55 ... 171 D3
  Long Eaton NG10 ... 236 C4
Erica Dr DE55 ... 160 A4
Erin Rd S43 ... 98 A4
Ernest Hall Way DE11 ... 256 B2
Ernocroft La SK6 ... 15 F1
Ernocroft Rd SK6 ... 15 D1
Errill Cl S14 ... 269 E1
Errington Ave S2 ... 43 F3
Errington Cl S2 ... 43 F3
Errington Cres S2 ... 43 F3
Errington Rd S2 ... 43 F3
Errington Way SK17 ... 85 D3
Errwood Ave SK17 ... 85 D3
Erskine Cres S2 ... 43 E4
Erskine Rd S2 ... 43 E4
Erskine St S2 ... 15 D2
Erskine View S2 ... 43 E4
Esdaile Cl Dronfield S18 ... 56 C1
  Long Eaton NG10 ... 236 A3
Esdaile Wlk DE24 ... 233 E3
Essendine Cres S8 ... 43 D2
Essex Rd DE15 ... 254 B3
Essex St Derby DE21 ... 219 E3
  4 Ilkeston DE7 ... 194 C1
Estwic Ave NG16 ... 182 C2
Ethel Wainwright Fst &
  Mid Schs NG19 ... 268 A4
Etherow Brow SK14 ... 16 A4
Etherow Ctry Pk SK6 ... 15 E2
Etherow Ctry Pk Visitor
  Ctr SK6 ... 15 E2
Etherow Way SK13 ... 9 F3

on Ct DE7 .... 207 E4
on St DE24 .... 219 F1
ruria Gdns DE11 .... 267 B5
ta's Way DE65 .... 229 D2
trick Cl 6 S40 .... 95 E3
trick Dr DE24 .... 231 F1
wall Cl S40 .... 95 D3
wall La DE65 .... 229 F3
wall Prim Sch DE65 .... 229 F2
wall Rd Derby DE2 .... 217 E1
  Eggington DE65 .... 241 D4
  Willington DE65 .... 229 D2
wall St DE22 .... 218 C3
Airbank La S43 .... 96 B3
areka Prim Sch DE11 .... 256 B3
areka Rd DE11 .... 256 B3
aston Dr DE7 .... 207 C5
aston Rd DE22 .... 205 D3
vans St DE24 .... 232 C3
anston Gdns DE21 .... 220 A3
velyn Devonshire Cotts
  S45 .... 132 C1
velyn Gr DE21 .... 220 A3
velyn St Fenton S14 .... 269 F1
  Nottingham NG2 .... 268 C1
erard Ave S17 .... 56 A3
erard Dr S17 .... 56 A3
erard Glade 3 S17 .... 56 A3
erest Dr DE55 .... 170 B4
erett Cl S43 .... 96 C4
ergreen Cl DE21 .... 206 A2
ershill Cl DE55 .... 146 C3
ershill La DE55 .... 146 C3
ersleigh Rise DE4 .... 142 A4
verton St NG19 .... 135 F1
esham Ave SK13 .... 10 A3
esham Cl DE21 .... 205 F1
vart La DE55 .... 158 C2
ve Dale La DE6 .... 149 D2
ve Lamb Cl NG9 .... 209 F1
ve Lamb La NG9 .... 209 F1
xcelsior Ave DE24 .... 232 C3
xchange St DE1 .... 267 B3
le Fold NG19 .... 136 B1
xeter Cl DE11 .... 256 C3
xeter Pl DE1 .... 267 C3
xeter St DE1 .... 267 C4
lowmere La DE4 .... 140 C3
port Dr NG17 .... 160 C4
om Ct E Prim Sch S32 .... 71 E3
ram Cl S42 .... 132 A4
ram (Hall) S32 .... 71 E3
ram La SK13 .... 9 F1
ram Mews SK13 .... 9 F1
ram Wlk DE56 .... 179 D3
res Ct DE56 .... 190 C2
res Gdns S40 .... 266 A4
re St Clay Cross S45 .... 131 E2
re's Cl DE7 .... 81 E1
  Nottingham NG2 .... 268 C1
re's St E S41 .... 115 E4
re's Gdns DE7 .... 194 C1
rie The
  Burton u T DE15 .... 248 B2
  Derby DE24 .... 231 F1
abis Cl DE11 .... 256 A2
abric View S42 .... 132 B4
actory La Disley SK12 .... 32 C4
  Ilkeston DE7 .... 194 C1
actory St S40 .... 95 E1
ir Lea Cl NG10 .... 236 B3
ir View Chesterfield S40 .... 95 F2
  Mayfield DE6 .... 184 A4
airbank Ave S14 .... 269 E1
airbourne Dr DE21 .... 217 E2
airburn Croft Cres S43 .... 80 E3
aircroft Ave NG10 .... 223 D3
airdene DE23 .... 218 C2
ire St DE22 .... 218 C2
ires Cl DE72 .... 221 E1
airfax Dr S2 .... 44 A4
airfax Rd DE23 .... 218 C1
airfield Ave
orrnway NG17 .... 221 E2
  Hilcote DE55 .... 148 B1
  Rolleston DE13 .... 240 B2
  Stonebroom DE55 .... 147 D2
airfield Cl Brimington S43 .... 96 B4
airfield Terr DE11 .... 256 C2
airford Cl S40 .... 114 C4
airham Rd DE13 .... 240 C1
airholme Dr NG10 .... 135 F1
airholmes DE4 .... 143 E3
airisle Cl DE21 .... 206 B2
airleigh S2 .... 44 A4
airmeadows Prim Sch
  DE11 .... 255 D3
airview Ave NG16 .... 171 F1
airview Cl Derby DE23 .... 231 E4
  Kilburn DE56 .... 192 A4
airview Grange DE56 .... 192 A4
airview Rd S18 .... 57 D2

Fairview Rise DE4 .... 168 A4
Fairway Branston DE14 .... 254 A4
  Stafford ST8, ST17 .... 269 F3
Fairway Cl DE22 .... 204 B1
Fairway Cres DE22 .... 204 B1
Fairway The Clifton DE6 .... 184 C3
  Swadlincote DE11 .... 255 F3
Fairways Cl S21 .... 10 C1
Fairways The
  Clay Cross S45 .... 131 F2
  Mansfield Woodhouse
  NG19 .... 136 B3
Fairwinds Cl S18 .... 57 D1
Fairwood Dr DE24 .... 233 E3
Fairy Bank Cres S22 .... 25 E2
Fairy Bank Rd S22 .... 25 E2
Fal Paddock NG19 .... 136 B1
Falcon Cl S20 .... 33 E4
Falcon Ct DE7 .... 194 B1
Falcon Rd S18 .... 57 E2
Falcon Rise DE56 .... 179 D2
Falcon Way Derby DE24 .... 231 F1
  Woodville DE11 .... 256 C2
Falcon Yd S40 .... 266 B3
Falcons Rise DE56 .... 179 E3
Faldo Cl DE14 .... 254 A3
Falkland Rise S18 .... 76 A4
Fal Rd DE75 .... 181 F2
Fallow Rd DE21 .... 220 C3
Fallowfield Rd S43 .... 77 E2
Falmouth Rd DE24 .... 233 E3
Fan Rd S43 .... 78 C1
Fan Road Ind Est S43 .... 78 C1
Fanny Ave S21 .... 60 C3
Fanshaw Ave S21 .... 59 E1
Fanshaw Bank S18 .... 57 D1
Fanshaw Cl S21 .... 59 E1
Fanshaw Dr S21 .... 59 E1
Fanshaw Gate La S18 .... 55 F1
Fanshaw Rd Dronfield S18 .... 57 D1
  Eckington S21 .... 59 E1
Fanshaw Way S21 .... 59 E1
Far Croft DE72 .... 235 E4
Far Cross DE4 .... 143 E4
Far Green DE4 .... 143 D3
Far Hill S33 .... 51 D4
Far La Common Side S18 .... 75 D2
  Ockbrook DE72 .... 221 E3
Far Laund DE56 .... 179 D3
Far New Cl NG10 .... 223 D3
Far Woodseats La SK13 .... 15 F3
Faraday Ave DE13 .... 240 A1
Faraday Cl NG9 .... 209 F1
Faraday Pl S14 .... 269 D2
Farfield Rd DE7 .... 209 D4
Farish Pl S2 .... 43 D3
Farley Hill DE4 .... 143 D4
Farley La DE4 .... 128 A1
Farley Rd DE23 .... 218 B1
Farm Cl Belper DE56 .... 179 E2
  Chesterfield S40 .... 114 C3
  Dronfield S18 .... 57 D2
  Ilkeston DE7 .... 208 C4
  Kilburn DE56 .... 192 A4
  Long Eaton NG10 .... 236 C3
  Pentrich DE5 .... 169 D3
  Sheffield S12 .... 44 A1
Farm Cres S20 .... 59 E3
Farm Croft Rd NG19 .... 136 B3
Farm Dr DE24 .... 233 D3
Farm La Disley SK12 .... 32 A3
  Matlock DE4 .... 143 E4
  Newton Solney DE15 .... 248 C4
Farm Side DE11 .... 255 F3
Farm St DE22 .... 218 C2
Farm View S42 .... 131 E4
Farm Wlk S20 .... 59 E4
Farmfields Cl S44 .... 98 C2
Farmhouse Rd DE24 .... 231 F1
Farmilo Cres NG19 .... 135 E1
Farmilo Fst Sch NG19 .... 135 E2
Farmlands La DE23 .... 231 D3
Farmstead Cl S14 .... 43 E3
Farmway NG19 .... 136 B1
Farnah Green Rd DE56 .... 178 B4
Farnborough Gdns DE22 .... 205 D2
Farncombe La DE21 .... 205 F2
Farndale Ave S40 .... 114 A4
Farndale Cl NG10 .... 236 A3
Farndale Ct DE24 .... 233 E3
Farndon Dr NG9 .... 223 F2
Farndon Way NG19 .... 268 A4
Farnsworth Rd DE21 .... 217 E1
Farnham Cl DE3 .... 217 E1
Farnham Wlk DE7 .... 207 E4
Farningham Cl DE21 .... 220 C3
Farnon Cl S40 .... 266 C1
Farnsley La S32 .... 72 A1
Farnsworth St S41 .... 115 E4
Farnway DE22 .... 204 C1
Farrendale Cl NG19 .... 136 B1
Farrier Gdns DE23 .... 231 D4
Farriers Croft DE7 .... 194 B2
Farringdon Cl DE22 .... 217 F3
Farthing Ct NG10 .... 236 A4
Farwater Cl S18 .... 76 A4
Farwater La S18 .... 56 C1
Fauld Ind Pk DE13 .... 238 C3
Fauld La Hanbury DE13 .... 238 B4
  Tutbury, Fauld DE13 .... 238 B4
  Tutbury, Owen's Bank DE13 .... 239 D3
Fauvel Pl SK13 .... 10 B1
Fauvel Rd SK13 .... 10 B1
Faversham Cl DE24 .... 232 C3
Fawn Cl S42 .... 114 C2
Fay Gdns SK13 .... 9 F2
Faywood Dr SK6 .... 23 D3

Fearn Ave DE5 .... 169 F1
Fearn Cl
  Church Broughton DE65 .... 227 D4
  Long Eaton DE72 .... 236 A4
Featherbed La
  Bolsover S44 .... 99 D3
  Worksop S80 .... 81 E4
Featherstone Gr ST4 .... 269 E2
Felkin St S41 .... 266 C3
Fellbrigg Rd S2 .... 43 E4
Fellowlands Way DE73 .... 233 D1
Fellside Belper DE56 .... 179 D2
  Derby DE21 .... 220 C3
Fellview Cl S32 .... 53 D4
Fenchurch Wlk DE22 .... 218 A4
Fenland Way S40 .... 114 C4
Fennel St DE45 .... 108 C4
Fenton Ave S21 .... 257 D1
Fenton Rd DE3 .... 217 E1
Fenton St S21 .... 59 E1
Fenwick St DE24 .... 232 B4
Ferguson Ave NG19 .... 136 A2
Fern Ave Staveley S43 .... 97 E4
  Willington DE65 .... 242 B3
Fern Bank Ave DE55 .... 147 F3
Fern Cl Eckington S21 .... 59 D2
  Holmewood S44 .... 116 C1
  Shirebrook NG20 .... 119 F3
  Willington DE65 .... 242 B3
Fern Cres NG16 .... 182 B2
Fern Lea Hollingworth SK14 .... 9 E3
  Shirland DE55 .... 146 A4
Fern Rd SK17 .... 85 D3
Fern Royd S32 .... 53 D4
Fern Way S21 .... 59 D2
Fernbank S33 .... 51 D4
Fernbank Dr S21 .... 59 D2
Ferncroft Ave S20 .... 59 F4
Ferndale Ave SK17 .... 67 E2
Ferndale Cl S18 .... 57 E2
Ferndale Rd Dronfield S18 .... 57 E2
  Peak Dale SK17 .... 67 E2
Ferndale Rise S18 .... 57 E2
Ferndene Dr NG10 .... 236 A4
Ferneydale Ave SK17 .... 85 E2
Fernhill SK6 .... 23 D3
Fernhill Cl SK13 .... 10 B2
Fernhill Ct DE73 .... 233 D2
Fernilee Cl New Mills SK22 .... 24 B3
  West Hallam DE7 .... 207 F4
Fernilee Cty Inf Sch SK23 .... 45 F2
Fernleys Gdns DE21 .... 205 D4
Fernlea Cl SK13 .... 9 F2
Fernleigh Rise NG19 .... 136 A2
Fernway SK17 .... 85 E2
Fernwood SK6 .... 23 E4
Fernwood Cl
  Chesterfield S41 .... 115 F4
  Derby DE23 .... 231 E4
  Shirland DE55 .... 146 B2
Ferrers Ave DE13 .... 239 D3
Ferrers Cl DE74 .... 247 E4
Ferrers Cres DE56 .... 190 E2
Ferrers Way Derby DE22 .... 204 C1
  Ripley DE5 .... 169 E2
Ferry Gn DE65 .... 242 A3
Ferry St DE15 .... 254 C4
Ferry Vale Cl DE15 .... 254 C4
Festival Ave Branston DE14 .... 253 F4
Festival Rd Branston DE14 .... 253 F4
  Ilkeston DE7 .... 208 B3
Festus Cl NG3 .... 268 B2
Fiddle St SK17 .... 84 C3
Fiddler's La DE13 .... 239 F2
Fidlers Cl S33 .... 40 A2
Fidlers Well S33 .... 40 A2
Field Ave Hatton DE65 .... 239 E4
  Renishaw S21 .... 79 D4
Field Cl Borrowash DE72 .... 221 E2
  Breaston DE72 .... 235 F4
  Dronfield S18 .... 56 B1
  Hilton DE65 .... 228 B1
Field Cres DE55 .... 233 D3
Field Ct DE56 .... 192 A4
Field Dr DE24 .... 233 D3
  Rolleston DE13 .... 240 A2
  Shirebrook NG20 .... 119 F3
Field End DE4 .... 153 D1
Field Head Way DE21 .... 206 B2
Field House Inf Sch DE7 .... 208 C3
Field La Belper DE56 .... 178 C2
Field La
  Ault Hucknall NG19, S44 .... 134 B3
  Belper DE56 .... 178 C2
  Blackfordby DE11 .... 257 E1
  Derby, Boulton DE24 .... 233 D3
  Derby, Chaddesden DE21 .... 220 A4
  Kirk Ireton DE56 .... 176 A4
  Stanton DE6 .... 183 E4
Field Rd DE7 .... 208 C4
Field Rise DE23 .... 231 E4
Field Row DE56 .... 178 C2
Field St DE5 .... 181 D4
Field Terr DE55 .... 169 E1
Field The DE75 .... 194 A3
Field View Clowne S43 .... 80 C2
  South Normanton DE55 .... 160 A4
  Whaley Thorns DE55 .... 101 D1
Field Way DE11 .... 255 F3
Fielden Ave NG19 .... 135 E1
Fieldfare Ho S41 .... 77 D2
Fieldgate Dr DE21 .... 205 F1
Fieldhead Rd S8 .... 43 D4
Fieldhead Way S41 .... 96 C1
Fielding St ST4 .... 269 E1

Fieldings Rd S80 .... 81 F1
Fieldon Cl DE6 .... 202 C1
Fields Cres SK14 .... 9 E3
Fields Farm Rd NG10 .... 236 C3
Fields Gr SK14 .... 9 E3
Fields La Killamarsh S21 .... 60 A3
  Linton DE11 .... 261 F3
Fields The DE4 .... 154 B2
Fieldsway Dr DE21 .... 205 F1
Fife St DE24 .... 232 C4
Finch Cl DE11 .... 256 C2
Fincham Cl DE21 .... 205 E1
Finchley Ave DE22 .... 217 F3
Findern Cl Belper DE56 .... 179 E3
  Derby DE22 .... 204 B1
Findern La
  Burnaston DE65 .... 230 A2
  Willington DE65 .... 242 A3
Findern Prim Sch DE65 .... 242 C4
Finistere St DE22 .... 218 B3
Finley Way DE55 .... 160 A2
Finmere Cl DE23 .... 231 D4
Finningley Dr DE22 .... 204 C1
Finny La DE6 .... 200 A3
Finsbury Ave Derby DE22 .... 218 A3
  Nottingham NG2 .... 268 C1
Finsley Wlk DE23 .... 231 D4
Fir Cl NG20 .... 119 E3
Fir Pl S21 .... 60 B3
Fir Rd S21 .... 59 E1
Fir St S43 .... 78 A1
Fir Tree Ave DE55 .... 146 B2
Firestone DE56 .... 178 B1
Firfield Ave DE72 .... 235 F4
Firfield Prim Sch DE72 .... 235 F4
Firlawns DE56 .... 190 B2
Firs Ave Alfreton DE55 .... 159 D3
  Hulland Ward DE6 .... 175 F2
  Ripley DE5 .... 169 E1
Firs Cres DE22 .... 204 C2
Firs Estate Prim Sch
  DE22 .... 218 B1
Firs Gdns DE55 .... 159 D2
Firs Par DE4 .... 143 E3
Firs St NG10 .... 236 A2
First Ave NG10 .... 223 D1
Firthwood Ave S18 .... 57 E2
Firthwood Cl S18 .... 57 E2
Firthwood Rd S18 .... 57 E2
Firtree Gr DE21 .... 206 A1
Firvale S26 .... 61 F3
Firvale Rd S40 .... 114 A4
Fish Pond Dr NG7 .... 268 A1
Fisher Cl Chesterfield S40 .... 114 C4
  Repton DE65 .... 242 B1
Fisher Ct DE7 .... 194 C2
Fisher Gate NG1 .... 268 B1
Fisher La Duffield DE56 .... 190 C4
  Mansfield NG18 .... 268 C3
Fisher St DE24 .... 232 C3
Fishers Bridge SK22 .... 25 E1
Fishpond La DE65 .... 241 D3
Fishponds Cl S42 .... 115 D2
Fishponds Rd S18 .... 44 B4
Fishponds Rd W S13 .... 44 B4
Fiskerton Way DE21 .... 206 A1
Fitzalan St SK13 .... 10 B1
Fitzherbert CE Prim Sch
  DE6 .... 162 A1
Fitzhubert Rd S2 .... 44 A4
Fitzroy Rd S2 .... 43 D3
Five Lamps Ct DE1 .... 218 C3
Five Lands Rd DE15 .... 254 C4
Five Trees Ave 1 S17 .... 56 A3
Five Trees Cl 3 S17 .... 56 A3
Five Trees Dr 2 S17 .... 56 A3
Flackets La Doveridge DE6 .... 225 D4
  Sudbury DE6 .... 225 D4
Flagg La DE6 .... 106 C4
Flagshaw La DE6 .... 202 C2
Flake La DE7 .... 208 C1
Flamstead Ave DE75 .... 181 D1
Flamstead La DE5 .... 180 C1
Flamstead Rd DE7 .... 194 C1
Flamstead St DE24 .... 232 C3
Flamsteed Cres S42 .... 96 A3
Flash CE Prim Sch SK17 .... 103 D2
Flash La DE4 .... 128 A4
Flat La SK17 .... 137 F4
Flat The DE6 .... 191 F4
Flatts La NG16 .... 171 E2
Flax Croft DE65 .... 227 E1
Flax St S14 .... 269 E1
Flaxholme Ave S18 .... 190 C1
Flaxpiece Rd S45 .... 131 E2
Fleet Cres DE56 .... 178 C2
Fleet Pk DE56 .... 179 D2
Fleet St DE23 .... 219 D1
Fleet The DE56 .... 178 C2
Fleming Rd S14 .... 269 D2
Fletcher Ave S18 .... 57 D1
Fletcher Gate NG1 .... 268 B1
Fletcher Rd S41 .... 96 B3
Fletcher St Heanor DE75 .... 181 F1
  Long Eaton NG10 .... 236 B2
Fletcher's Row DE5 .... 169 F1
Fletches The DE13 .... 240 A1
Flewitt Gdns NG3 .... 268 C2
Flint La DE6 .... 136 C1
Flint La DE4 .... 142 A4
Flint St DE24 .... 232 B3
Flintson Ave S43 .... 77 E2
Flixton Rd NG16 .... 195 F4
Flood St DE72 .... 221 E2
Florence Ave NG10 .... 223 D2
Florence Cl S40 .... 114 C3
Florence Ct DE7 .... 194 C1

Florence Dr DE6 .... 211 E1
Florence Gladwin Cl DE4 .... 141 E3
Florence Rd
  Clay Cross S45 .... 131 F2
  Wingerworth S42 .... 114 C2
Florence Way SK14 .... 9 E3
Florin Gdns NG10 .... 236 A4
Flowery Leys La DE55 .... 159 E2
Floyd St S14 .... 269 E2
Fluery Cl S14 .... 43 F2
Fluery Cres S14 .... 43 F2
Fluery Pl S14 .... 43 F2
Fluery Rd S14 .... 43 F2
Fluery Rise S14 .... 43 F2
Fly Hill DE45 .... 109 E3
Foden St S14 .... 269 E1
Foggs Entry DE4 .... 165 E4
Fold The S32 .... 71 F2
Folds La SK23 .... 45 F2
Folds Yd S14 .... 156 C1
Foljambe Ave S40 .... 114 B4
Foljambe Rd S43 .... 96 C4
Folkestone Dr DE24 .... 233 D3
Folly Rd DE22 .... 205 D1
Fontaine Pl ST4 .... 269 E1
Foolow Ave S40 .... 266 A1
Forbes Cl NG10 .... 236 C3
Ford Ave DE75 .... 181 E2
Ford Cl Dronfield S18 .... 56 C1
  Ripley DE5 .... 180 B4
Ford La DE56 .... 9 D2
Ford La Derby DE65 .... 205 D3
  Ford S12 .... 58 C3
  Willington DE65 .... 242 B3
Ford Rd S21 .... 58 C2
Ford St Belper DE56 .... 178 C2
  Burton u T DE15 .... 254 C4
  Derby DE1 .... 218 C3
  Tupton S42 .... 131 E4
Fordbridge La DE55 .... 160 A4
Fordwells Cl DE23 .... 231 D4
Foregate Ct S14 .... 269 E4
Foregate St S16 .... 269 D4
Foremark Ave DE23 .... 231 F4
Forest Cl Buxton SK17 .... 85 E3
  Mansfield NG18 .... 268 C3
Forest Cl DE56 .... 179 D3
Forest Ct S43 .... 80 A3
Forest Dr S45 .... 132 B1
Forest Fields Coll NG3 .... 268 C2
Forest La S17 .... 50 B1
Forest Rd NG16 .... 268 A2
Forest Rd E NG1 .... 268 C2
Forest Rd W NG7 .... 268 A2
Forester St DE1 .... 267 B2
Foresters Way DE5 .... 169 E1
Forge La Burton u T DE13 .... 241 D1
  Killamarsh S21 .... 60 A4
Forge Rd S21 .... 45 F4
Forge Terr SK23 .... 34 C1
Forge The NG9 .... 209 D3
Forman Cl DE11 .... 256 A2
Forman St Derby DE1 .... 267 A3
  Nottingham NG1 .... 268 B2
Forrester Ave DE72 .... 245 F3
Forrester's La DE18 .... 57 E2
Forth Ave S18 .... 185 E4
Forth Ave S18 .... 56 B1
Forties La LE65 .... 257 F2
Forty Horse Cl DE56 .... 170 A1
Forum Cl DE24 .... 233 E3
Fosbrook Dr DE74 .... 246 C2
Fosbrooke Dr NG10 .... 236 B3
Fosse Cl DE72 .... 221 E1
Fossett's Ave NG16 .... 171 F4
Foster Rd DE11 .... 256 C3
Foston Cl NG65 .... 239 E4
Foston Dr S40 .... 95 D3
Foundry La DE56 .... 190 C4
Foundry St S41 .... 96 A4
Foundry Street Ind Est
  S41 .... 96 A4
Fountain Sq DE22 .... 32 B3
  Tideswell SK17 .... 69 E2
Fountain St SK17 .... 85 D4
Fountains Cl DE22 .... 205 D2
Four Lane Ends DE4 .... 127 F1
Four Lanes S14 .... 9 D2
Fowler Ave DE21 .... 220 B2
Fowler St Chesterfield S41 .... 76 C1
  Derby DE22 .... 218 C3
  Draycott DE72 .... 235 D4
Fox Cl Derby DE24 .... 231 E1
  Long Eaton NG10 .... 236 B3
Fox Croft DE55 .... 147 F3
Fox Hill S44 .... 74 A3
Fox La Holmesfield S18 .... 74 A3
  Sheffield, Frecheville S12 .... 44 B2
  Sheffield, Lower Bradway
  S18 .... 56 B3
Fox Rd
  Castle Donington DE74 .... 246 C2
  Whitwell S80 .... 82 A3
Fox St DE21 .... 267 C4
Foxbrook Cl S40 .... 94 C3
Foxcote Way S40 .... 114 A4
Foxcroft Chase S21 .... 60 B3
Foxcroft Dr S21 .... 60 B3
Foxcroft Gr S21 .... 60 B3
Foxdale Ave S12 .... 44 A3
Foxdell Way DE73 .... 233 D1
Foxes Cl DE7 .... 268 A1
Foxes Wlk DE22 .... 204 C2

Foxes Yd SK17 .... 66 B1
Foxfields Dr DE21 .... 205 F1
Foxglove Ave DE15 .... 255 D4
Foxglove Cl S44 .... 97 D2
Foxglove Rd NG16 .... 195 D4
Foxhall La S10 .... 42 C3
Foxholes La Kniveton DE6 .. 174 A3
  Tansley DE4 .... 144 A4
Foxlands Ave DE22 .... 204 C1
Foxlea SK13 .... 16 C4
Foxley Ct DE21 .... 206 A1
Foxlow Ave SK17 .... 85 E2
Foxpark View DE55 .... 147 F3
Foxstone Cl S43 .... 97 E4
Foxwood Ave S12 .... 44 A3
Foxwood Cl
  Chesterfield, Hasland S41 .... 115 E3
  Chesterfield, Sheepbridge
  S41 .... 76 C1
Foxwood Dr S12 .... 44 A3
Foxwood Gr S12 .... 44 A3
Foxwood End Pk S41 .... 76 C1
Foxwood Rd
  Chesterfield S41 .... 76 C1
  Sheffield S12 .... 44 A3
Foxwood Way S41 .... 76 C1
Foyle Ave DE21 .... 220 A2
Framlingham Pl S2 .... 43 E4
Framlingham Rd S2 .... 43 E4
Frampton Gdns DE23 .... 230 C3
Frances Dr S42 .... 114 C2
Frances St NG16 .... 171 E1
Franchise St DE22 .... 218 C2
Francis Rd S43 .... 96 B4
Francis St Derby DE21 ...... 219 E3
  Nottingham NG7 .... 268 A2
Frank Ave NG16 .... 268 A3
Frank Merifield Ctr S41 ..... 96 B2
Frank St S14 .... 269 E1
Franklin Ave S80 .... 81 F3
Franklin Cl DE15 .... 248 A1
Franklin Cres S80 .... 81 F3
Franklin Rd
  Stoke-on-T S14 .... 269 D2
  Westwood NG16 .... 171 D2
Franklyn Dr Derby DE24 ... 233 D3
  Staveley S43 .... 78 C2
Franklyn Rd S40 .... 95 F2
Fraser Cl DE21 .... 220 C3
Frecheville Inf Sch S12 ...... 44 B2
Frecheville Sch S12 .... 44 B2
Frecheville St S43 .... 78 B1
Freckingham St NG1 .... 268 B1
Frederic Ave DE75 .... 193 F4
Frederick Ave Derby DE24 .. 232 C3
  Ilkeston DE7 .... 209 D3
  Stoke-on-T ST4 .... 269 E2
Frederick Gent Sch DE55 .. 160 A3
Frederick Harrison Inf
  Sch NG9 .... 223 F4
Frederick Rd NG9 .... 223 E4
Frederick St Alfreton DE55 .. 159 D3
  Burton u T DE15 .... 254 C4
  Derby DE22 .... 218 B3
  Grassmoor S42 .... 115 F2
  Long Eaton NG10 .... 236 C4
  Mansfield NG18 .... 268 C3
  Somercotes DE55 .... 170 B3
  Swadlincote DE11 .... 256 C2
Freebirch View S40 .... 95 D4
Freeby Ave NG19 .... 136 B3
Freehold St DE22 .... 218 C2
Freeland Cl NG9 .... 223 F2
Freeman Ave DE23 .... 231 F3
Freemantle Rd DE3 .... 217 F2
Freesia Cl DE3 .... 217 F1
Freetown SK13 .... 17 E4
French La DE21 .... 191 F3
French St Derby DE23 .... 218 C1
  Ilkeston DE7 .... 209 D3
French Terr NG20 .... 101 D1
Fresco Dr DE23 .... 230 C4
Fresh Ct SK13 .... 16 C4
Freshfield Cl SK6 .... 15 D1
Fretson Rd S2 .... 44 A4
Frew Cl ST16 .... 269 F4
Freydon Way S44 .... 97 D2
Friar Gate DE1 .... 218 C3
Friar Gate Ct DE1 .... 218 C3
Friar Gate House Sch
  DE1 .... 218 C3
Friar Gr SK17 .... 85 E3
Friar La NG1 .... 268 A1
Friar St NG10 .... 236 B4
Friars Cl DE22 .... 205 D1
Friars Ct Ilkeston DE7 .... 208 B3
  Nottingham NG7 .... 268 A1
Friars' Rd ST17 .... 269 E3
Friars' Terr ST17 .... 269 E3
Friars' Wlk ST17 .... 269 E3
Friary Ave DE24 .... 232 C3
Friary Croft DE11 .... 256 A4
Friary St DE1 .... 267 A3
Friesland Dr NG10 .... 222 C3
Friesland Sch NG10 .... 222 C3
Frinton Cl S40 .... 114 C4
Frisby Ave NG10 .... 236 C3
Fritchley CE Prim Sch
  DE56 .... 168 A3
Fritchley Cl DE21 .... 206 A1
Fritchley La DE56 .... 168 A4
Frith Cl S12 .... 44 A3
Frith Gr NG19 .... 268 A4
Frith Rd S12 .... 44 A3
Frith View SK23 .... 47 D3

Frithall La S42 .... 94 B1
Frithwood La S80 .... 100 B4
Frizams La DE65 .... 242 C4
Froggatt Cl Derby DE22 .... 205 D3
  Staveley S43 .... 97 E3
Froggett Cl DE55 .... 170 B4
Frogmore St NG1 .... 268 B2
Front St DE56 .... 168 A3
Frost Ave NG16 .... 182 A2
Fryar Rd NG16 .... 182 C2
Fulbrook Rd DE23 .... 231 D4
Fulford Cl S40 .... 114 B4
Fulforth St NG1 .... 268 B2
Fulham Rd DE22 .... 218 A3
Full St DE1 .... 267 B3
Fuller Dr S41 .... 96 B3
Fullwood Ave DE7 .... 194 C1
Fullwood St [B] DE7 .... 194 C1
Fulmar Cl DE3 .... 218 A2
Fulwood Dr NG10 .... 236 A4
Fulwood Head Rd S10 .... 42 B4
Fulwood La S10 .... 42 C3
Fulwood Rd N NG17 .... 148 C1
Fulwood Rd S NG17 .... 160 C4
Furlong Cl NG9 .... 223 E4
Furlong La
  Alstonefield DE6 .... 149 E2
  Atlow DE6 .... 175 D4
Furnace Cl S42 .... 115 F1
Furnace La Barlow S18 .... 75 F2
  Heanor DE75 .... 181 E2
  Moira DE12 .... 262 C2
Furnace La Ind Est DE12 .. 262 C2
Furnace Mus The DE12 .... 262 C2
Furnace Rd DE7 .... 209 D3
Furnace Row DE55 .... 170 C4
Furnall Ave DE45 .... 90 A2
Furness Cl SK13 .... 17 E4
Furness Lodge Cl SK23 ..... 33 E2
Furness Row SK23 .... 33 E2
Furness Vale Prim Sch
  SK23 .... 33 E2
Furness Vale Sta SK23 .... 33 E2
Furniss Ave S17 .... 55 E3
Furrows Cl DE21 .... 206 B2
Fyfield Rd DE15 .... 254 C3
Fylde Cl NG9 .... 223 F1

Gable Ct DE3 .... 230 C4
Gable St ST4 .... 269 E1
Gables Cl S42 .... 132 B4
Gables The DE11 .... 255 F3
Gadley Cl SK17 .... 84 C4
Gadley La SK17 .... 84 C4
Gadsby Rise DE56 .... 168 B1
Gag La DE6 .... 161 E3
Gainborough Cl DE21 .... 206 A1
Gainsborough Ave SK6 ..... 23 D4
Gainsborough Cl
  Long Eaton NG10 .... 236 C3
  Stapleford NG9 .... 223 F3
Gainsborough Rd S18 .... 75 F4
Gainsborough Way DE15 .. 248 A2
Gairloch Cl DE24 .... 231 E1
Galahad Dr DE13 .... 240 C1
Gale Rd SK22 .... 33 E4
Gallery La S42 .... 113 E4
Gallery The DE6 .... 173 E1
Gallows Inn Cl DE7 .... 209 D3
Gallowtree La DE6 .... 184 B4
Galway Ave DE21 .... 220 A2
Gamble St NG7 .... 268 A2
Gamesley Cty Prim Sch
  SK13 .... 9 F1
Gang La S44 .... 118 C3
Gannow Cl S21 .... 60 C4
Gaol Rd ST16 .... 269 E4
Gaol Sq ST16 .... 269 E4
Gaolgate St [B] ST16 .... 269 E4
Gapsick La S43 .... 81 D3
Garden Ave Ilkeston DE7 ... 208 C3
  New Houghton NG19 .... 134 C4
  Renishaw S21 .... 79 D4
  Shirebrook NG20 .... 119 F2
Garden Cl S43 .... 77 E2
Garden Cr DE55 .... 159 F2
Garden Cres DE74 .... 247 D2
Garden Pl Stafford ST17 ... 269 E3
  Stoke-on-T ST4 .... 269 D1
Garden Rd Eastwood NG16 . 182 C2
  [B] Mansfield NG18 .... 268 B3
Garden Row S44 .... 117 E1
Garden St
  Broadbottom SK14 .... 16 A4
  Derby DE1 .... 267 A4
  Stafford ST17 .... 269 E3
  Stoke-on-T ST4 .... 269 D1
Gardens The Heanor DE75 . 181 E2
  Ripley DE5 .... 180 B4
Gardner Pl ST14 .... 210 A1
Gardom Cl [B] S18 .... 56 B1
Garfield Ave DE7 .... 235 D4
Garfield Cl Derby DE23 ..... 231 E3
  Stapleford NG9 .... 209 F1
Garland Cl [B] S20 .... 59 F4
Garland Croft S20 .... 59 F4
Garland Mount [2] S20 ..... 59 F4
Garland Way S20 .... 59 F4
Garner La DE4, DE55 .... 157 E1
Garnet Cl NG3 .... 268 C2
Garnett Ave DE75 .... 181 F1
Garnon St NG18 .... 268 A3
Garratt Ave NG18 .... 268 C4
Garrett La S45 .... 131 E1
Garrick St DE24 .... 233 D3
Garry Cl DE24 .... 231 E1
Garsdale Ct DE24 .... 233 E3
Gartan Rd DE14 .... 254 A4

Garth Cres DE24 .... 233 D3
Garth Rd S6 .... 23 D3
Garth Way S18 .... 56 C1
Garth Way Cl S18 .... 56 C1
Garthorpe Ct DE21 .... 205 F1
Gartrice Gdns S20 .... 60 A3
Gary Cl DE23 .... 231 E3
Gas St Hollingworth SK14 ... 9 E3
  Sandiacre NG10 .... 223 E3
  Uttoxeter ST14 .... 210 B1
Gascoine Dr DE21 .... 220 B2
Gashouse La Eckington S21 .. 59 E3
  Mosborough S21 .... 59 E3
Gaskell Ave DE23 .... 231 F4
Gasny Ave DE74 .... 247 D3
Gatcombe Cl
  Burton u T DE13 .... 240 B1
  Derby DE21 .... 206 A1
Gatcombe Gr NG10 .... 223 D2
Gate Brook Cl DE5 .... 170 A1
Gatefield Cl S41 .... 95 E4
Gateland La S18 .... 75 F3
Gateway Christian Sch
  DE7 .... 207 F1
Gattrice Gdns S20 .... 60 A3
Gauledge La SK17 .... 121 D3
Gaunt Cl Killamarsh S21 ... 60 B3
  Sheffield S31 .... 43 E2
Gaunt Dr S14 .... 43 E2
Gaunt Pl S14 .... 43 E2
Gaunt Rd S14 .... 43 E2
Gaunt Way S14 .... 43 E2
Gawain Gr DE13 .... 240 C1
Gawsworth Cl SK13 .... 10 A3
Gayton Ave DE23 .... 231 E3
Gayton Com Jun Sch
  DE23 .... 231 E3
Gayton Thorpe Cl DE23 ... 230 C4
Geary La DE15 .... 248 C1
Gebbs Gdns S40 .... 95 E1
Gedling Gr NG7 .... 268 A2
Gedling St NG1 .... 268 B1
Geen St S14 .... 269 E2
Geer La S12 .... 58 B3
Gelderd Pl S18 .... 76 A4
Gema Cl DE22 .... 205 D2
Genista Cl DE15 .... 255 D4
Gentshill Ave S45 .... 131 F1
George Ave NG10 .... 223 F1
George Baily Ct ST17 .... 269 E3
George Cres DE55 .... 170 B3
George Dutton Ind Est
  DE6 .... 185 F4
George Holmes Way DE11 . 256 A2
George Percival Pl S45 ..... 131 D2
George Rd DE4 .... 143 E3
George Spencer Comp
  Sch NG9 .... 223 F3
George St Alfreton DE55 .. 159 D2
  Ashbourne DE6 .... 185 D4
  Belper DE56 .... 178 C2
  Brimington S43 .... 96 C4
  Buxton SK17 .... 85 D4
  Chesterfield S43 .... 76 C1
  Compstall SK6 .... 15 D1
  Derby DE1 .... 267 A3
  Glossop SK13 .... 17 E4
  Langley Mill NG16 .... 182 A2
  Mansfield NG18, NG19 .... 268 A4
  Mansfield Woodhouse
  NG19 .... 136 B2
  Market Warsop NG20 ..... 120 C1
  Melbourne DE73 .... 252 A4
  North Wingfield S42 .... 131 F4
  Nottingham NG1 .... 268 B2
  Pinxton NG16 .... 160 B2
  Riddings DE55 .... 170 B3
  Somercotes DE55 .... 170 B4
  South Normanton DE55 .. 159 F3
  Swadlincote DE11 .... 256 A1
  Whaley Bridge SK23 .... 45 F4
  Whaley Thorns NG20 ...... 101 D1
Gerard Cl
  [B] Chesterfield S40 .... 95 E1
  Derby DE21 .... 220 C3
  Sheffield S8 .... 43 D3
Gerard Ct DE1 .... 267 A2
Gerard Gr DE65 .... 229 E2
Gerard St Derby DE1 .... 267 A2
  Sheffield S8 .... 43 D3
Gerrard St S14 .... 269 E2
Gertrude Rd Derby DE21 .. 220 A4
  Draycott DE72 .... 235 D4
Gervase Ave S8 .... 56 C3
Gervase Dr S8 .... 56 C3
Gervase Pl S8 .... 56 C3
Gervase Rd S8 .... 56 C3
Gervase Wlk S8 .... 56 C3
Gibb La Marple SK6 .... 23 F3
  Sudbury DE6 .... 225 F3
Gibb St NG10 .... 236 C4
Gibbons Ave NG9 .... 223 E3
Gibbons Dr S14 .... 43 F1
Gibbons Rd NG18 .... 268 A3
Gibbons Way S14 .... 43 F1
Gibfield La Belper DE56 ... 178 C1
  Hognaston DE6 .... 175 E3
  Kirk Ireton DE6 .... 175 E3
Gifford Pl S14 .... 269 D1
Gifford Rd S8 .... 43 D4
Gilbert Ave S40 .... 114 A4
Gilbert Cl DE21 .... 220 B2
Gilbert Cres DE56 .... 190 C1
Gilbert Heathcote Inf Sch
  S41 .... 96 A4
Gilbert St DE24 .... 233 D3
Gilcroft St NG18 .... 268 C3
Gildersdale Way DE21 ...... 206 A2

Gill La DE4 .... 127 E2
Gill St NG1 .... 268 A2
Gill's La S42 .... 115 F1
Gillamoor Ct DE24 .... 233 E3
Gilleyfield Ave S17 .... 55 F4
Gillies The NG19 .... 268 A3
Gilliver Gdns DE72 .... 235 D4
Gillot St DE75 .... 194 A4
Gilt Hill NG16 .... 195 E4
Gilt Hill Prim Sch NG16 ... 195 E4
Giltbrook Cres NG16 .... 195 E4
Giltway NG16 .... 195 E4
Gimson Cl DE7 .... 194 C1
Gin Close Way
  Awsworth NG16 .... 195 E3
  Kimberley NG16 .... 195 E3
Gink La S42 .... 144 C4
Gipsy La Alstonefield DE6 .. 149 F2
  Apperknowle S18 .... 58 A1
  Chesterfield S41 .... 77 D1
Gipsyhill La S80 .... 81 D4
Gird La SK6 .... 15 F1
Girdon Cl SK17 .... 84 C3
Gisborne Cl DE3 .... 217 F2
Gisborne Cres DE22 .... 204 C2
Gisborne Gn DE1 .... 218 C3
Gisbourne Dr SK23 .... 47 D3
Glade Cl S40 .... 95 F3
Glade Croft S12 .... 44 A2
Glade Lea S12 .... 44 A2
Glade The Buxton SK17 ...... 85 D4
  Chesterfield S40 .... 95 E2
Gladstone Ave
  Blackwell DE55 .... 147 F1
  Heanor DE75 .... 181 F1
Gladstone Cl DE73 .... 232 C2
Gladstone Dr NG16 .... 182 C4
Gladstone Pl S14 .... 269 D1
Gladstone Rd
  Alfreton DE55 .... 158 C2
  Chesterfield S40 .... 266 A4
  Derby DE21 .... 220 C3
Gladstone St Derby DE23 .. 218 C1
  Glossop SK13 .... 17 E4
  Hadfield SK13 .... 10 A2
  Heanor DE75 .... 181 F1
  Ilkeston DE7 .... 208 C4
  Langley Mill NG16 .... 182 B2
  Long Eaton NG10 .... 236 B3
  Mansfield NG18 .... 268 C4
  South Normanton DE55 .. 160 A3
  Stanton Hill NG17 .... 148 B4
  Swadlincote DE11 .... 256 B2
Glaisdale Nook DE24 .... 233 E3
Glamis Cl DE21 .... 206 A1
Glapwell La S44 .... 118 A1
Glasshouse Hill DE5 .... 181 D4
Glasshouse La S43 .... 77 E2
Glasshouse St NG1 .... 268 B2
Glastonbury Cl NG19 .... 136 B2
Glastonbury Rd DE24 ...... 233 E4
Glaven Cl NG19 .... 136 B1
Gleadless Ave S12 .... 44 A2
Gleadless Bank S12 .... 43 F2
Gleadless Comm S12 .... 44 A3
Gleadless Cres S12 .... 43 F3
Gleadless Ct S12 .... 43 D2
Gleadless Dr S12 .... 43 F2
Gleadless Fst Sch S12 .... 44 A3
Gleadless Mid Sch S12 ..... 44 A3
Gleadless Mount S12 .... 44 A2
Gleadless Rd S2 .... 43 E3
Glebe Ave
  Great Longstone DE45 ..... 90 A2
  Harthill S26 .... 61 F4
  Pinxton NG16 .... 160 B2
  Ripley DE5 .... 169 E1
  Smalley DE7 .... 192 C3
Glebe Cl Cotton in t E DE12 . 260 B2
  Doveridge DE6 .... 224 A4
  Holmewood S42 .... 132 B4
  Rolleston DE13 .... 240 A2
  South Normanton DE55 .. 160 A3
  Thurvaston DE6 .... 201 F1
Glebe Cres Ilkeston DE7 ... 209 D4
  Stanley DE7 .... 207 D3
Glebe Ct ST4 .... 269 F2
Glebe Farm Cl S26 .... 61 F4
Glebe Jun Sch DE55 .... 160 A3
Glebe Rd SK17 .... 85 E4
Glebe Rise DE23 .... 218 B1
Glebe St Stoke-on-T S14 .. 269 E2
  Swadlincote DE11 .... 256 A2
Glebe The
  Awsworth NG16 .... 195 D2
  Rosliston DE12 .... 260 B3
Glebe Way The S41 .... 77 D1
Gledhill Cl S18 .... 57 D1
Glen Ave DE56 .... 191 E4
Glen Cl DE55 .... 148 A2
Glen Rd DE4 .... 156 B1
Glen View DE56 .... 178 C1
Glen View Rd S8 .... 56 C4
Glen Vine DE5 .... 170 A1
Glenavon Cl S43 .... 77 E3
Glenbrook Hill S13 .... 10 B1
Glencoe Way S40 .... 95 D2
Glencroft Cl DE14 .... 254 A4
Glencroft Dr DE24 .... 232 C1
Glendale Dr DE21 .... 220 C3
Glendon Rd Derby DE24 ... 231 E2
  Ilkeston DE7 .... 208 B2
Glendon St DE7 .... 193 D1

Gleneagles Dr DE13 .... 240 ...
Glenfield Ave NG16 .... 195 ...
Glenfield Cres
  Chesterfield S41 .... 96 ...
  Derby DE3 .... 217 ...
Glenfield Rd NG10 .... 236 ...
Glengarry Way DE24 .... 231 ...
Glenholme Dr S13 .... 44 ...
Glenholme Pl S13 .... 44 ...
Glenholme Way S13 .... 44 ...
Glenmoor Rd SK17 .... 66 ...
Glenmore Croft S12 .... 44 ...
Glenmore Dr DE24 .... 231 ...
Glenmoy Cl DE23 .... 231 ...
Glenn Way DE72 .... 239 ...
Glenorchy Ct DE21 .... 206 ...
Glenthorn Cl S41 .... 63 ...
Glenthorne Cl S40 .... 95 ...
Glenwood Rd DE73 .... 245 ...
Glinton Ave DE55 .... 147 ...
Glossop Brook Rd SK13 .... 10 ...
Glossop Central Sta SK13 .. 10 ...
Glossop Rd
  Charlesworth SK13 .... 16 ...
  Gamesley SK13 .... 9 ...
  Little Hayfield SK22 .... 25 ...
  Marple SK6 .... 15 ...
Glossop St DE24 .... 232 ...
Glossop's Croft S41 .... 77 ...
Glossopdale Comm Coll
  Glossop SK13 .... 10 ...
  Hadfield SK13 .... 10 ...
Gloster St DE24 .... 219 ...
Gloucester Ave
  Chesterfield S41 .... 95 ...
  Sandiacre NG10 .... 223 ...
Gloucester Rd S41 .... 95 ...
Gloucester Way
  Burton u T DE15 .... 248 ...
  Glossop SK13 .... 17 ...
Glover Rd Sheffield S8 .... 43 ...
  Totley S17 .... 55 ...
Glover St ST16 .... 269 ...
Gloves La DE55 .... 147 ...
Glumangate S40 .... 266 ...
Goathland Rd DE24 .... 231 ...
Goddard La Hadfield SK13 .. 10 ...
  Rowarth SK22 .... 24 ...
Goddard Rd SK13 .... 10 ...
Godfrey Dr DE7 .... 208 ...
Godfrey St DE75 .... 181 ...
Godkin Dr NG16 .... 182 ...
Godward Rd SK22 .... 33 ...
Gold Cl DE4 .... 142 ...
Gold La DE22 .... 217 ...
Goldcrest Dr DE21 .... 220 ...
Goldcrest Ho S41 .... 77 ...
Golden Valley
  Horsley Woodhouse DE7 .. 192 ...
  Somercotes DE55 .... 170 ...
Golders Green Wlk DE22 . 218 ...
Goldhill DE4 .... 144 ...
Goldsmith St
  Mansfield NG18 .... 268 ...
  Nottingham NG1 .... 268 ...
Golf Club Rd DE7 .... 209 ...
Golf La DE56 .... 190 ...
Gomersal La S18 .... 57 ...
Goodacre St NG18 .... 268 ...
Goodale St DE23 .... 219 ...
Goodhand Cres NG18 ...... 268 ...
Goodman Cl NG16 .... 195 ...
Goodrington Rd DE21 ..... 206 ...
Goods Rd DE56 .... 178 ...
Goods Yd DE56 .... 178 ...
Goodsmoor Rd DE23 ...... 231 ...
Goodwin Cl NG10 .... 223 ...
Goodwin Dr NG16 .... 195 ...
Goodwin Rd S8 .... 43 ...
Goodwin St NG7 .... 268 ...
Goodwin's La DE56 .... 178 ...
Goodwood Cl DE13 .... 240 ...
Goodwood Cres DE7 .... 208 ...
Goodwood Dr
  Beeston NG9 .... 223 ...
  Derby DE24 .... 233 ...
Gooker La DE55 .... 158 ...
Goole Ave DE7 .... 208 ...
Goose Gate NG1 .... 268 ...
Goose Green La DE55 ..... 146 ...
Goose Green View DE45 .... 91 ...
Goose La DE5 .... 181 ...
Gordon Ave S8 .... 43 ...
Gordon Cres DE55 .... 160 ...
Gordon Rd
  Borrowash DE72 .... 221 ...
  Derby DE23 .... 218 ...
  Nottingham NG3 .... 268 ...
  Swanwick DE55 .... 169 ...
  Tideswell SK17 .... 69 ...
Gordon St DE7 .... 195 ...
Gordondale Rd NG19 ...... 136 ...
Gore La S33 .... 51 ...
Gorman Cl S41 .... 95 ...
Gorse Bank S44 .... 116 ...
Gorse Cl Derby DE23 .... 231 ...
  Eastwood NG16 .... 195 ...
  Long Eaton NG10 .... 223 ...
Gorse Dr S21 .... 60 ...
Gorse La Bradley DE6 ...... 175 ...
  Lodge Moor S10 .... 42 ...
Gorse Ridge Dr DE45 .... 91 ...
Gorse Valley Rd S41 .... 115 ...
Gorse Valley Way S41 ...... 115 ...
Gorse Way S43 .... 17 ...
Gorsebank La DE45 .... 91 ...
Gorses Alderwasley DE56 .. 178 ...
  Idridgehay DE56 .... 176 ...

rsey Bank DE4 .... 165 F4
rsey Brigg S8 .... 9 D1
rsey Brow SK14 .... 9 D1
rsey Cl DE56 .... 178 C3
rsey Intakes SK14 .... 16 A4
rsey La Kirk Ireton DE6 .. 165 D1
lethersd DE12 .... 265 D4
rseybrigg Rd Sch S18 ... 56 B1
rseybrigg Jun Sch S18 ... 56 B1
rsty Leys DE5 .... 230 B1
sber Rd S21 .... 59 F2
sber St S21 .... 59 E2
seley Ave DE11 .... 257 D2
seley Cres DE11 .... 257 D2
sforth Cl S18 .... 56 C1
sforth Cres S18 .... 56 C1
sforth Dr S18 .... 56 C1
sforth Gn S18 .... 56 C1
sforth Rd DE24 .... 232 C4
wer Cres S40 .... 95 E3
wer St S21 .... 267 B2
yt SK23 .... 45 F4
yt Rd Disley SK12 .... 32 B3
lew Mills SK22 .... 33 E3
yt Side Rd S40 .... 95 F1
yt Valley Ind Est SK23 .... 33 E2
yt View SK22 .... 33 D3
yt's La SK17 .... 65 D2
ytlands SK17 .... 84 C3
ace Cres DE75 .... 181 F1
afham Cl DE73 .... 233 D2
afton Rd DE15 .... 248 A1
afton St DE22 .... 218 C1
aham Cl DE14 .... 254 B4
aham Dr SK12 .... 32 B3
aham St DE7 .... 208 C1
ammer St DE5 .... 181 D2
ampian Cres S40 .... 95 D2
ampian Prim Sch DE24 . 231 E2
ampian Way

erby DE24 .... 231 F2
ong Eaton NG10 .... 236 A4
ansfield NG18 .... 268 B4
anby Ave Chinley SK23 .. 34 C1
ansfield NG18 .... 268 B4
anby Cl S45 .... 132 B1
anby Croft DE45 .... 109 E3
anby Jun Sch DE7 .... 194 C3
anby Rd Bakewell DE45 . 109 E3
radwell S33 .... 50 C4
uxton SK17 .... 85 E4
anby St DE7 .... 194 C3
andfield St DE75 .... 181 E2
andstand Rd DE21 ...... 219 F3
ange Ave Breaston DE72 . 235 E4
chapel-en-le-F SK23 ...... 47 D3
erby DE72 .... 221 E3
anfield S18 .... 56 C1
ulland Ward DE6 .... 175 F2
ransfield S18 .... 56 C1
ange Cl Melbourne DE73 . 252 A4
omercotes DE55 .... 159 F1
ricknall DE73 .... 251 D2
ange Cl DE65 .... 241 D3
ange Dale DE4 .... 153 E4
ange Dr

Castle Donington DE74 .. 247 D2
ong Eaton NG10 .... 236 C4
ange La Barlow S18 .... 75 D1
Darley Dale DE4 .... 127 F1
ble DE4 .... 153 E4
ange Park Ave

Calow S43 .... 96 C2
chapel-en-le-F SK23 ...... 47 D3
ange Park Rd SK23 .... 47 D3
ange Rd Buxton SK17 .... 85 E4
erby DE24 .... 233 D3
ong Eaton NG10 .... 236 C4
Pilsley S45 .... 132 B1
atton DE65 .... 255 F3
Littoxeter ST14 .... 210 A1
ange Rd S SK14 .... 15 D4
ange St Alfreton DE55 ... 159 D2
erby DE23 .... 219 D1
ange The

Old Brampton S40 .... 94 C2
Smalley DE75 .... 193 E4
south Normanton DE55 . 160 A2
ange View NG16 .... 182 C2
ange Wlk S42 .... 115 F1
angemill Pl S43 .... 97 E4
angewood Ave DE7 ..... 208 C4
angewood Rd NG16 ... 191 D4
angewood Rd S40 ...... 114 C4
ansden Way S40 .... 114 B4
ant Ave DE21 .... 220 A3
ant St ST14 .... 269 F2
ant Way NG16 .... 182 C2
antham Ave DE21 ...... 205 F1
antham Cl NG16 .... 195 E4
anville Ave NG10 .... 223 E1
anville Cl

chesterfield S41 .... 115 E4
duffield DE56 .... 190 C2
atton DE65 .... 227 E1
anville Com Sch DE7 .... 256 C2
anville St Derby DE1 .... 218 C3
swadlincote DE11 .... 256 C2
asmere Ave

Clay Cross S45 .... 131 D2
Jerby DE21 .... 220 C3
asmere Cl

urton u T DE15 .... 248 A1
chesterfield S41 .... 95 E4
asmere Cres DE24 ...... 231 F2

Grasmere Rd
[11] Dronfield S18 .... 56 B1
Long Eaton NG10 .... 223 D1
Grasmere St S6 .... 194 C2
Grass St DE7 .... 208 C1
Grasscroft Cl [8] S40 ...... 95 E3
Grassdale View S12 .... 44 C2
Grassmoor Cl S12 .... 43 F3
Grassmoor Cres SK13 ..... 9 E1
Grassmoor Ctry Pk S42 .. 116 A2
Grassmoor Prim Sch S42 . 115 F1
Grassthorpe Cl DE21 ...... 206 A1
Grassthorpe Rd S12 .... 44 A2
Gratton Ct S43 .... 78 C2
Gratton La DE4 .... 140 B4
Gravel Pit Hill DE6 .... 249 F4
Gravel Pit La DE21 .... 220 C2
Gravelly Bank Mews DE6 . 199 E3
Graves Tennis & L Ctr S8 . 57 D4
Graves Trust Homes S8 ... 57 D4
Gray Fallow DE55 .... 160 A2
Gray St Clowne S43 .... 80 C2
Mosborough S20 .... 59 E4
Grayling St DE23 .... 219 D1
Grayswood Cl DE55 ...... 170 A4
Great Central Rd NG8 .... 268 B3
Great Common Cl S43 ..... 80 A3
Great Croft S18 .... 56 B1
Great Freeman St NG3 .... 268 B4
Great Hucklow Prim Sch

SK17 .... 51 D1
Great Longstone Ind Est

DE45 .... 90 A2
Great Northern Cl The

NG2 .... 268 B1
Great Northern Rd

Derby DE1 .... 218 C3
Eastwood NG16 .... 182 B1
Greatbatch Ave DE4 ...... 269 D2
Greatorex Ave DE24 ...... 232 C3
Greaves La DE45 .... 108 C4
Greaves St Ripley DE5 .... 169 E1
Shirland DE55 .... 146 C1
Greek St NG7 .... 268 A2
Green Ave DE73 .... 233 D1
Green Bank SK13 .... 9 E2
Green Chase S21 .... 59 E2
Green Cl Matlock DE4 .... 143 D3
Newton DE55 .... 148 A2
Staveley S43 .... 97 E3
Unstone S18 .... 76 C3
Willington S18 .... 242 A3
Green Cres NG16 .... 171 F3
Green Cross S18 .... 57 D1
Green Farm Cl S40 .... 95 E3
Green Farm Rd NG16 ..... 171 E3
Green Glen S40 .... 95 D1
Green Hill DE4 .... 154 C1
Green Inf Sch The DE55 . 160 A3
Green La Bakewell DE45 . 108 B2
Barlborough S21 .... 60 B2
Barrow u T DE73 .... 244 B3
Belper DE56 .... 178 C2
Bonsall DE4 .... 153 F4
Breedon on t H DE73 .... 252 C3
Burnaston DE65 .... 230 A2
Buxton SK17 .... 85 D4
Chelmorton SK17 .... 106 B4
Chesterfield S41 .... 96 B2
Chinley SK23 .... 34 C1
Clifton DE6 .... 184 C4
Darley Dale DE4 .... 233 D4
Derby, Alvaston DE24 ... 233 E4
Derby, The Holmes DE1 . 267 B2
Disley SK12 .... 32 B2
Dronfield S18 .... 57 D1
Glossop SK13 .... 15 D4
Hackingmirle SK14 .... 9 F2
Hadfield SK13 .... 9 F3
Hodthorpe S80 .... 82 B3
Hognaston DE6 .... 164 A1
Hollingworth SK14 .... 9 F3
Ilkeston DE7 .... 209 D4
Killamarsh S21 .... 60 B2
Mansfield NG19 .... 135 D1
Marchington ST14 .... 225 D1
Ockbrook DE7 .... 221 E3
Old Brampton S42 .... 93 F3
Overseal DE12 .... 261 F2
Pilsley S45 .... 132 B2
Pleasley S44 .... 134 B4
Roston DE6 .... 198 A4
Tansley DE4 .... 144 B3
Tissington DE6 .... 150 B1
Tupton S42 .... 115 E1
Tutbury DE13 .... 239 D3
Water Swallows SK17 ..... 67 E1
Weston Underwood DE6 . 188 C1
Green Lands DE11 .... 256 A4
Green Lea S18 .... 56 B1
Green Lea DE72 .... 246 A4
Green Oak Ave S17 .... 55 F2
Green Oak Cres S17 ...... 55 F2
Green Oak Dr S17 .... 55 F2
Green Oak Gr S17 .... 55 F2
Green Oak Rd S17 .... 55 F2
Green Park Dr S23 .... 47 D3
Green Pk DE22 .... 218 A3
Green Rd The DE6 .... 173 E2
Green St Barton in F NG1 . 237 F3
Chesterfield S41 .... 96 B1
Green The Alfreton DE55 . 159 D2
Aston-on-T DE72 .... 246 A4
Bamford S33 .... 40 A2
Belper DE56 .... 178 C3
Birchover DE4 .... 126 A1
Bradwell S33 .... 51 D3
Brailsford DE6 .... 201 F4

Green The continued
Breaston DE72 .... 235 E4
Breedon on t H DE73 .... 252 C1
Burton u T DE13 .... 240 C1
Castle Donington DE74 . 247 D2
Chesterfield S41 .... 115 E4
Clowne S43 .... 80 C2
Curbar S32 .... 72 C1
Derby, Allestree DE22 ... 204 B1
Derby, Mickleover DE7 .. 217 E1
Draycott DE72 .... 235 D4
Findern DE65 .... 230 B1
Fritchley DE56 .... 168 A3
Froggatt S32 .... 72 B3
Glapwell S44 .... 118 B3
Glossop SK13 .... 17 D4
Hardstoft S45 .... 133 D2
Kirk Langley DE6 .... 202 B1
Mansfield Woodhouse

NG19 .... 136 A3
Marple SK6 .... 23 D2
Middleton (Nr Wirksworth)

DE4 .... 154 B3
Stoke-on-T ST4 .... 269 D2
Sutton in A NG17 .... 148 C3
Swanwick DE55 .... 169 F4
Tissington DE6 .... 162 A3
Totley S17 .... 55 E2
Willington DE65 .... 242 A3
Green Way Findern DE65 . 230 C1
Wingerworth S42 .... 115 E1
Greenacre Ave DE75 ..... 182 A2
Greenacre The DE4 ...... 184 C4
Greenacres DE23 .... 231 D4
Greenacres Cl S18 .... 76 B4
Greenacres Dr

South Normanton DE55 . 160 A3
Uttoxeter ST14 .... 210 A1
Greenaway Rd DE44 ...... 127 F1
Greenbank DE21 .... 220 B2
Greenbank Dr S40 .... 95 E2
Greenbank Rd SK6 .... 15 D1
Greenburn Cl DE23 .... 231 E3
Greendale Ave S42 .... 113 F4
Greendale Cl S18 .... 57 D1
Greendale Sh Ctr S18 .... 57 D1
Greenfell Ave DE22 ...... 231 F3
Greenfield Ave S80 .... 82 B3
Greenfield Cl

New Mills SK22 .... 33 D4
Sheffield S8 .... 56 C4
Greenfield Dr Linton DE12 . 261 E3
Sheffield S8 .... 56 C4
Greenfield Rd S8 .... 56 C4
Greenfield St SK13 .... 10 A3
Greenfields Aldercar NG16 . 182 A2
Denstone ST14 .... 196 B3
Eckington S21 .... 59 E2
Fritchley DE4 .... 168 A3
Greenfields Ave DE23 ... 231 D4
Greenfinch Cl DE21 ...... 220 C3
Greengate Cl S40 .... 95 E3
Greengate St S16 .... 269 E4
Greenhall Rd S21 .... 59 E2
Greenhead S33 .... 40 A2
Greenhead Cres SK17 ... 138 B1
Greenhead Pk S33 .... 40 A2
Greenhill Ave Ripley DE5 . 180 C4
Sheffield S8 .... 56 C4
Greenhill Ind Est DE55 . 170 A3
Greenhill Inf & Jun Sch

S8 .... 56 C3
Greenhill La DE55 .... 170 B3
Greenhill Main Rd S8 .... 56 C3
Greenhill Parkway S8 .... 56 C3
Greenhill Wlk SK12 .... 32 B3
Greenhills Rd NG16 ..... 182 C3
Greenhouse La S10 .... 42 C3
Greenland Ave DE22 ..... 218 A3
Greenland Cl S42 .... 132 A4
Greens Ct DE7 .... 194 B1
Greens La NG16 .... 195 F3
Greenshall La SK12 .... 32 C3
Greenside Ave S41 .... 96 C1
Greenside Cl

Donisthorpe DE12 .... 262 C1
Long Eaton NG10 .... 236 C4
Greenside Cl DE63 .... 217 E1
Greensquare Rd NG16 .. 160 C1
Greenvale Cl DE15 .... 254 C4
Greenview DE4 .... 153 D1
Greenway Ashbourne DE6 . 173 D2
Brassington DE4 .... 153 D2
Burton u T DE15 .... 248 A2
Hulland Ward DE6 .... 175 F2
Stafford St S16 .... 269 F4
Whitwell S80 .... 81 F3
Greenway Cl DE72 .... 221 D2
Greenway Croft DE4 ..... 154 C1
Greenway Dr S44 .... 118 A4
Greenway The

Sandiacre NG10 .... 223 D3
Sheffield S8 .... 56 C4
Greenways S40 .... 114 B4
Sheffield S8 .... 56 C4
Greenwich Dr N DE22 ... 218 B3
Greenwich Dr S DE22 .. 218 A3
Greenwood Ave

Derby DE21 .... 219 F4
Ilkeston DE7 .... 209 D4
Mansfield Woodhouse

NG19 .... 136 A2
Sutton in A NG17 .... 148 C3
Greenwood Cl DE24 ..... 232 B3
Greenwood Ct DE1 .... 267 B4
Greenwood Rd DE15 .... 248 B3
Greer La S44 .... 118 B1
Gregg Ave DE75 .... 181 F1
Greggs Ave SK23 .... 46 C3

Gregory Ave
Aldercar NG16 .... 182 A2
Breaston DE72 .... 235 E4
Langley Mill NG16 .... 182 A2
Gregory Cl Brimington S43 . 96 B4
Stapleford NG9 .... 223 F4
Gregory La S43 .... 77 E1
Gregory Rd S8 .... 43 D3
Gregory St DE7 .... 208 C4
Gregory Wlk DE23 ...... 230 C4
Gregorys Way DE56 ...... 179 E3
Gregson Cl DE11 .... 256 A4
Grenville Dr Ilkeston DE7 . 194 C2
Stapleford NG9 .... 223 F4
Grenvoir Dr DE5 .... 170 A1
Gresham Rd DE24 .... 232 B4
Gresley Dr NG2 .... 268 C1
Gresley Rd Ilkeston DE7 . 194 C1
Sheffield S8 .... 56 C3
Gresley Wlk S8 .... 56 C3
Gresley Wood Rd DE11 . 256 A1
Gresley Woodlands DE11 . 256 A1
Gresty St ST4 .... 269 E2
Gretton Ave DE13 .... 240 C1
Gretton Rd SK17 .... 85 E4
Grey Friars' Pl ST14 ..... 269 D4
Grey St DE22 .... 267 A2
Greyfriar Gate NG1 ..... 268 B1
Greystones Ct S26 .... 61 E3
Grice Rd ST4 .... 269 D2
Griffin Cl Derby DE24 ... 232 C4
New Mills SK22 .... 33 E3
Griggs Gdns DE4 .... 165 F4
Grimshaw Ave DE24 .... 233 D4
Grin Low Rd SK17 .... 85 D2
Grindleford Prim Sch S32 . 72 B4
Grindleford St S32 .... 53 F1
Grindley S4 ST4 .... 269 D1
Grindlow Ave S40 .... 266 A1
Grindlow Cl S14 .... 43 E3
Grindlow Dr S2 .... 43 E3
Grindon Rd DE21 .... 220 A4
Grindon Cl S40 .... 95 E3
Grindslow Ave DE7 ..... 207 F4
Grinlow Cl SK17 .... 85 E2
Grisedale Rd E DE45 ..... 90 A2
Grisedale Rd W DE45 .... 90 A2
Grisedale Wlk S18 .... 56 C1
Gritstone Rd DE4 .... 143 E4
Groome Ave DE75 .... 181 E2
Grosvenor Ave

Breaston DE72 .... 235 F4
Long Eaton NG10 .... 236 A2
Grosvenor Rd

Eastwood NG16 .... 182 C1
Marple SK6 .... 23 A3
Ripley DE5 .... 169 E1
Grosvenor St DE24 ...... 232 B4
Grove Ave

Nottingham NG7 .... 268 A2
Sheffield S8 .... 56 C4
Grove Cl DE72 .... 233 F2
Grove Ct S40 .... 180 C4
Grove Farm Cl S43 .... 96 C3
Grove Gdns S43 .... 96 C3
Grove Hospl The DE72 .. 234 B1
Grove House Ct S17 ...... 55 F3
Grove La Buxton SK17 ... 85 E3
Darley Dale DE4 .... 127 F1
Doveridge DE6 .... 224 C4
Old Brampton S42 .... 94 A2
Somersal Herbert DE6 .. 211 F1
Grove Mews DE11 .... 182 C1
Grove Pk DE65 .... 229 D1
Grove Pl DE45 .... 125 D3
Grove Rd Calow S43 ...... 96 C3
Totley S17 .... 55 E3
Grove St Chesterfield S41 . 115 E4
Derby DE23 .... 267 B1
[5] Mansfield NG18 .... 268 B3
Mansfield Woodhouse NG19 . 136 A2
New Mills SK22 .... 33 D4
Swadlincote DE11 .... 256 A2
Grove The Breaston DE72 . 235 F4
Derby DE72 .... 9 F2
Poolsbrook S43 .... 98 A4
Totley S17 .... 55 E3
Grove Way Calow S43 .... 96 C3
Mansfield Woodhouse NG19 . 136 A2
Grovebury Dr DE23 ...... 231 E3
Groves Nook DE72 .... 232 C1
Grundy Ave NG16 .... 171 E4
Grundy Nook S80 .... 82 A3
Grundy Rd S45 .... 131 E2
Grunmore Dr DE13 .... 240 C1
Guernsey Rd S2 .... 43 D4
Guide Post DE56 .... 168 B1
Guildford Ave

Chesterfield S40 .... 114 B4
Mansfield Woodhouse NG19 . 136 B3
Sheffield S2 .... 43 E4
Swadlincote DE11 .... 256 C3
Guildford Cl S2 .... 43 E4
Guildford Dr S2 .... 43 E4
Guildford Rise S2 .... 43 E4
Guildford St S14 .... 269 F2
Guildford View S2 .... 43 E4
Guildford Way S2 .... 43 E4
Guilford S45 .... 131 F2
Guilford La S45 .... 131 E2
Guinea Cl NG10 .... 236 A4
Guinevere Ave DE13 .... 240 C1
Gulliver's Kingdom DE4 . 143 D3
Gun La DE56 .... 168 B1
Gun Rd Charlesworth SK6 . 16 B1
Marple SK6 .... 16 B1
Gunby Hill DE12 .... 261 F1

Gunhills La DE56 .... 189 F3
Gunnel Cl ST16 .... 269 D3
Gurney Ave DE23 .... 231 E3
Guterstoh Cl NG9 .... 223 F4
Guy Cl NG9 .... 223 F3
Gypsy La Creswell S80 .... 81 F1
Draycott DE72 .... 221 F1

H

Hackney La S18 .... 75 F1
Hackney Rd DE4 .... 58 B3
Hackthorne Rd S8 .... 43 D2
Haddon Ave S43 .... 81 D2
Haddon Cl Alfreton DE55 . 158 C2
Bullbridge DE56 .... 168 A2
Chesterfield S40 .... 95 E1
Derby DE22 .... 204 B2
Dronfield S18 .... 56 B4
West Hallam DE7 .... 207 F4
Haddon Ct DE6 .... 185 E4
Haddon Dr Bakewell DE45 . 109 F2
Derby, Allestree DE22 ... 204 B2
Derby, Mickleover DE3 . 217 F2
Derby, Spondon DE21 ... 220 C2
Little Eaton DE21 .... 191 E2
Haddon Hall DE45 .... 110 A1
Haddon Nurseries DE7 . 194 C2
Haddon Pl Shirebrook NG20 . 119 E3
Staveley S43 .... 97 E4
Haddon Rd Bakewell DE45 . 109 F2
Buxton SK17 .... 85 E4
Mansfield NG18 .... 268 B4
North Wingfield S42 ..... 132 A4
Haddon St Derby DE23 . 218 C1
Ilkeston DE7 .... 194 C2
Tibshelf DE55 .... 148 A3
Haddon Way NG10 .... 235 F2
Hade La SK17 .... 106 C4
Hadfield Ind Est SK13 .... 9 F3
Hadfield Inf Sch SK13 ..... 9 F3
Hadfield Pl SK13 .... 17 E4
Hadfield Rd SK13 .... 9 F2
Hadfield Sq SK13 .... 17 E4
Hadfield St SK13 .... 17 E4
Hadfield St Andrew's CE

Jun Sch SK13 .... 9 F2
Hadfield St Charles RC

Prim Sch SK13 .... 10 A3
Hadfield Sta SK13 .... 10 A3
Hadfields Ave SK14 .... 9 E3
Hadleigh Cl NG9 .... 223 F1
Hadley La DE6 .... 186 C4
Hadley Dr DE7 .... 209 D3
Hadstock Cl NG10 .... 223 D2
Hady Cres S41 .... 96 B2
Hady Hill S41 .... 96 B1
Hady La S41 .... 96 B1
Hady Prim Sch S41 .... 96 B1
Hag Bank La S12 .... 32 B4
Hagg La Dale DE7 .... 207 E2
Windley DE56 .... 177 E1
Hague Bar S21 .... 79 D4
Hague Barr Prim Sch S12 . 32 C4
Hague Bar Rd S22 .... 23 F4
Hague Fold SK22 .... 32 C4
Hague La S21 .... 79 D3
Hague Rd SK14 .... 16 A4
Hague St SK13 .... 17 E4
Haig Meml Homes S8 .... 57 D4
Haig St DE24 .... 232 C4
Haigh Moor Rd S13 .... 44 C4
Haighton Way S13 .... 44 C4
Hailsham Cl DE3 .... 217 E2
Haines Cl DE24 .... 231 F2
Halcyon App S42 .... 115 E1
Halcyon Cl S12 .... 81 F1
Haldane Ct S80 .... 81 F1
Haldane Cres S44 .... 98 C1
Halesworth Cl S40 .... 114 A4
Haley Cl NG16 .... 195 E3
Half Acre La S18 .... 76 B4
Half Croft S43 .... 96 C4
Hallam Fields La Callow DE6 . 165 D2
Kirk Ireton DE4 .... 165 D2
Halfway Ctr S20 .... 59 F4
Halfway Dr S20 .... 59 F4
Halfway Gdns S20 .... 59 F4
Halfway Inf Sch S20 .... 59 F3
Halfway Jun Sch S20 ...... 59 F3
Halifax Cl Derby DE65 .. 205 E1
Hilton DE65 .... 228 C1
Halifax Pl [6] NG1 .... 268 B1
Hall Bank Buxton SK17 ... 85 D4
Hartington SK17 .... 137 F3
Hall Cl Dronfield S18 ...... 56 B1
Mottram in L SK14 .... 9 D3
Hall Ct DE7 .... 194 C2
Hall Dale View DE4 ...... 127 E2
Hall Dr Doveridge DE6 .. 211 D1
Mottram in L SK14 .... 9 D3
Sandiacre NG10 .... 223 D3
Hall Dyke DE21 .... 220 B3
Hall End La DE11 .... 108 C4
Hall Farm Cl

Castle Donington DE74 . 247 D2
Swadlincote DE11 .... 256 B2
Hall Farm Rd

Duffield DE56 .... 190 C1
Swadlincote DE11 .... 256 B2
Hall Gate View S33 .... 51 D4
Hall Green Ave DE13 .... 240 C1
Hall La Ashbourne DE6 .. 173 E1
Brailsford DE6 .... 182 B3
Brinsley NG16 .... 182 C4
Donisthorpe DE12 .... 265 F4
Doveridge DE6 .... 224 A4

Hall La continued
Litton SK13 .... 69 F2
Nether Heage DE56 ...... 168 B2
Newton DE55 .... 148 A2
Shirley DE6 .... 200 B4
Stanton DE6 .... 183 D3
Staveley S43 .... 78 B2
Willington DE65 .... 242 A3
Hall Leys La DE73 .... 245 E1
Hall Meadow Croft S20 ... 59 F3
Hall Meadow Dr S20 .... 59 F3
Hall Meadow Gr S20 ...... 59 F3
Hall Meadow Rd SK13 ... 10 B1
Hall Pk DE73 .... 244 A3
Hall Rd Aldercar NG16 ... 182 B2
  Brimington S43 .... 96 C4
  Marchington ST14 .... 224 C1
  Rolleston DE13 .... 239 F2
Hall Rise Ashbourne DE6 ... 173 E2
  Darley Dale DE4 .... 127 E2
Hall St Alfreton DE55 .... 159 D2
  Derby DE24 .... 233 D4
  New Mills SK22 .... 33 D4
  Swadlincote DE11 .... 256 A1
Hall Terr S45 .... 131 E2
Hall The DE4 .... 154 B3
Hall View S41 .... 95 F3
Hall Wlk S42 .... 115 E1
Hall's Ct S13 .... 10 B1
Hall's Row [1] S40 .... 95 E1
Hallahan Gr S14 .... 269 E2
Hallam Ct S18 .... 76 A4
Hallam Fields DE74 .... 247 D1
Hallam Fields Jun Sch
  .... 208 C3
Hallam Fields Rd DE7 ... 209 D2
Hallam St S14 .... 269 F1
Hallam Way DE7 .... 207 E4
Hallamway NG19 .... 136 B1
Hallcliff La S42 .... 93 F1
Hallcroft Rd DE12 .... 262 A2
Hallcroft Rd DE7 .... 208 C4
Halldale La DE4 .... 127 E2
Hallfield Cl S42 .... 115 D2
Hallfield Rd DE55 .... 148 A2
Hallfieldgate La DE55 ... 146 B1
Hallfields Rd
  Swadlincote, Newhall DE11 ... 255 F2
  Swadlincote, Stanton DE11 ... 255 E2
Hallflash La S44 .... 116 A4
Hallgate La S41 .... 132 A1
Hallington Dr DE75 .... 181 E1
Hallmoor Rd DE4 .... 127 E2
Hallowes Ct S18 .... 57 D1
Hallowes Dr S18 .... 76 B4
Hallowes La S18 .... 76 B4
Hallowes Rise S18 .... 76 B4
Halls La NG16 .... 195 D4
Halls Rd NG9 .... 223 E3
Hallsteads SK17 .... 47 F1
Hallsteads Cl SK17 .... 47 F1
Hallum Ct DE7 .... 194 C2
Hallworth Wlk S21 .... 58 C1
Hallyburton Cl S2 .... 43 E3
Hallyburton Dr S2 .... 43 E3
Hallyburton Rd S2 .... 43 E3
Halstead's The DE6 .... 163 D1
Halstock Dr DE24 .... 233 E4
Halton Cl S41 .... 76 C1
Hambledon Cl S40 .... 95 E3
Hambledon Dr DE24 ...... 231 E1
Hambleton Ave S42 .... 131 F3
Hambleton Cl NG10 .... 223 D1
Hamblin Cres DE24 .... 231 F2
Hamill Cl S42 .... 131 F4
Hamilton Cl Beeston NG9 ... 223 F1
  Derby DE3 .... 217 F2
Hamilton Dr
  Nottingham NG7 .... 268 A1
  Swadlincote DE11 .... 256 B3
Hamilton Fields DE15 .... 248 A1
Hamilton Gr DE21 .... 256 B3
Hamilton Rd
  Burton u T DE15 .... 248 A1
  Derby, Rose Hill DE23 ... 218 C1
  Derby, Spondon DE21 ... 220 C3
  Long Eaton NG10 .... 223 E1
Hamilton St S14 .... 269 F1
Hamilton Terr DE65 ...... 242 A3
Hamlet La DE55 .... 160 A3
Hamlet The Heanor DE75 ... 181 F2
  South Normanton DE55 ... 160 A3
Hammersmith DE5 .... 169 E2
Hammonds Ct DE4 .... 165 F4
Hampden St Derby DE23 ... 232 A4
  Eastwood NG16 .... 195 E4
  Nottingham NG1 .... 268 A2
Hampshire Cl SK13 .... 17 F4
Hampshire Ct NG16 .... 171 D2
Hampshire Dr NG10 .... 223 D3
Hampshire Rd DE21 ...... 219 E4
Hampstead Dr DE22 ...... 218 A3
Hampton Cl Beeston NG9 ... 223 F2
  Derby DE21 .... 220 C3
  West Hallam DE7 .... 207 E4
Hampton St S41 .... 115 E4
Hanbury Ave DE65 .... 227 E1
Hanbury Cl
  Chesterfield S40 .... 95 D3
  Dronfield S18 .... 56 C1
Hanbury Hill DE13 .... 238 A3
Hanbury Rd DE21 .... 219 F3
Hancock St S14 .... 269 F2
Hand's Rd DE75 .... 182 A1
Handby St S41 .... 115 E4

Handel St Derby DE24 ... 232 B4
  Nottingham NG3 .... 268 C2
Handford Cl DE22 .... 218 B3
Handford St DE22 .... 218 B3
Handley La
  Clay Cross S45 .... 131 D1
  Edensor DE45 .... 91 D1
  Stretton DE55 .... 145 F4
Handley Rd S43 .... 77 E3
Handsacre Cl DE11 .... 255 F2
Handyside St DE1 .... 267 B4
Hangar Hill S80 .... 82 A3
Hanger Bank DE72 .... 246 A4
Hanley Cl S42 .... 32 B3
Hanley St [1] NG1 .... 268 A2
Hanover Sq DE2 .... 127 D2
Hansard Gate DE21 ...... 267 D3
Hanslynn DE72 .... 233 F2
Hanstubbin Rd NG16 ..... 171 F3
Hanwell Way DE22 .... 218 A3
Harbin Rd DE12 .... 253 E1
Harborough Ave S2 .... 44 A4
Harby Ave NG19 .... 136 B3
Harcourt Pl DE14 .... 247 D2
Harcourt Rd DE14 .... 253 F4
Harcourt St Derby DE1 ... 267 B2
  Mansfield NG18 .... 268 A3
Hard La S26 .... 61 F4
Hardcare Cl DE73 .... 252 A4
Hardhurst Rd Derby DE24 ... 233 D3
  Unstone S18 .... 76 C3
Hardie Ave DE55 .... 160 A3
Hardie Pl S43 .... 97 E4
Hardince St S14 .... 269 F1
Harding Terr S14 .... 269 E1
Harding's La SK17 .... 138 A3
Hardmeadow La S45 ..... 130 A1
Hardstoft Rd
  Holmewood S45 .... 132 C1
  Pilsley S45 .... 132 C1
Hardwick Ave
  Chesterfield S43 .... 77 E2
  Derby DE22 .... 204 B2
  Shirebrook NG20 .... 119 F2
  West Hallam DE7 .... 207 F4
Hardwick Cl Clowne S43 ... 81 D2
  Dronfield S18 .... 57 E1
  Holmewood S42 .... 132 C4
  Ripley DE5 .... 169 E2
Hardwick Ct NG10 .... 235 F2
Hardwick Dr Derby DE3 ... 217 F1
  Long Duckmanton S44 ... 97 E2
Hardwick Hall S44 .... 133 F2
Hardwick Inf & Jun Schs
  S44 .... 133 F3
Hardwick La
  DE55 .... 219 D1
Hardwick La S45 .... 129 E3
Hardwick Mount SK17 .... 85 E4
Hardwick Old Hall S44 ... 133 F2
**Hardwick Park Nature
  Wlk** S44 .... 133 E2
Hardwick Pl DE7 .... 208 B3
Hardwick Rd NG7 .... 268 A1
Hardwick Sq E SK17 .... 85 E4
Hardwick Sq N SK17 ...... 85 E4
Hardwick Sq S SK17 ...... 85 D4
Hardwick Sq W SK17 ...... 85 E4
Hardwick St Buxton SK17 ... 85 D4
  Chesterfield S41 .... 266 B4
  Derby DE24 .... 232 B4
  Langwith NG20 .... 119 F4
  Mansfield NG18 .... 268 C4
  Shirebrook NG20 .... 120 A2
  Tibshelf DE55 .... 148 A4
Hardwick View Rd S42 ... 132 C4
Hardwick's Yd S40 .... 95 F1
Hardy Barn DE75 .... 194 A4
Hardy Cl Kimberley NG16 ... 195 E4
  Long Eaton NG10 .... 236 B3
Hardy Cres DE5 .... 181 D4
Hardy Pl NG19 .... 268 A4
Hardy St Alfreton DE55 ... 158 C3
  Kimberley NG16 .... 195 F4
  Nottingham NG7 .... 268 A2
Hardybarn La SK17 .... 86 B4
Harebell Cl DE21 .... 206 A2
Harehedge La DE13 ...... 240 A1
Harehill Cres S42 .... 114 B2
Harehill Rd S40 .... 114 C4
Hareholme St NG19 ...... 268 B4
Harepit Cl DE24 .... 233 D3
Harewood Cres S42 ...... 131 D3
Harewood Ct NG10 .... 223 D2
Harewood Rd Derby DE22 ... 204 B2
  Holymoorside S42 .... 113 E3
Hargate Hill La SK13 .... 16 C4
Hargate Rd SK17 .... 84 C3
Hargrave Ave DE72 ...... 221 E3
Hargreaves La ST17 ...... 269 D3
Harlaxton Dr
  Long Eaton NG10 .... 237 D4
  Nottingham NG7 .... 268 A1
Harlech Cl Derby DE21 ... 221 D3
  Ilkeston DE7 .... 194 B2
Harlequin Cl NG16 .... 182 B2
Harlesden Ave DE22 ..... 218 A4
Harlesthorpe Ave S43 ... 80 C3
Harlesthorpe La S43 .... 80 C3
Harlow Cl Derby DE24 ... 232 C2
  Mansfield Woodhouse NG19 ... 136 B3
Harlow DE7 .... 207 E4
Harold Ave NG16 .... 182 A2
Harold St NG2 .... 268 C1
Harpenhill Cl S40 .... 114 C4
Harpfield Rd S14 .... 269 D1
Harpole Cl DE55 .... 169 F4
Harport Dr S45 .... 131 F1

Harpswell Cl DE22 .... 204 C1
Harpur Ave Derby DE73 ... 231 D4
  Ticknall DE73 .... 251 D2
Harpur Hill Prim Sch SK17 ... 85 E2
Harpur Hill Rd SK17 .... 85 E2
Harrier Way DE24 .... 231 F2
Harrier Rd DE14 .... 179 E3
Harriet St DE23 .... 219 D2
Harriett St NG9 .... 223 E4
Harrimans Dr DE72 ...... 235 F4
Harringay Gdns DE22 ... 218 B3
Harrington Ave DE72 .... 221 E1
Harrington Jun Sch
  NG10 .... 223 D1
Harrington Rd Derby DE23 ... 218 B1
  Sheffield S2 .... 43 D4
Harrington St
  Derby, Allenton DE24 ... 232 C3
  Derby, Normanton DE23 ... 232 A4
  Draycott DE72 .... 235 D4
  Long Eaton NG10 .... 236 A3
  Mansfield NG18 .... 268 B3
Harris Ave DE5 .... 169 F4
Harris Cl DE5 .... 169 E1
Harris Rd Buxton SK17 .... 85 E2
  Stafford ST16 .... 269 F4
Harrison St S14 .... 269 E2
Harrison Cl DE14 .... 254 A4
Harrison Dr DE14 .... 154 C1
Harrison La
  Lodge Moor S10 .... 42 C4
  Tibshelf DE55 .... 147 F3
Harrison Rd
  Mansfield NG18 .... 268 A3
  Stapleford NG9 .... 223 E4
Harrison St DE22 .... 218 C2
Harrogate Cres DE21 .... 205 E1
Harrop La S10 .... 42 C3
Harrop White Rd NG19 ... 268 A4
Harrots La SK17 .... 137 E3
Harrow Dr DE14 .... 254 B4
Harrow Rd DE11 .... 256 A4
Harrow St DE24 .... 219 F1
Harrowby St ST16 .... 269 F4
Hart Ave NG10 .... 223 D3
Hartfield Cl S41 .... 115 D4
Hartford Cl S8 .... 43 D2
Hartford Rd S8 .... 43 D2
Harthill Field Rd S26 ..... 62 A2
Harthill Inf & Jun Sch S26 ... 61 F3
Harthill La S43 .... 61 F1
Harthill Rd Sheffield S13 ... 44 A4
  Thorpe Salvin S80 .... 62 B4
Hartill St S14 .... 269 F2
Hartington CE Prim Sch
  SK17 .... 137 E3
Hartington Cl DE7 .... 207 F4
Hartington Ct Clowne S43 ... 81 D2
  Dronfield S18 .... 57 D1
Hartington Dr Chinley SK23 ... 34 C1
  Creswell S80 .... 81 E1
Hartington Ind Est S43 ... 78 C2
Hartington Pl DE7 .... 194 C3
Hartington Rd Buxton SK17 ... 85 D4
  Chesterfield S41 .... 96 B1
  Dronfield S18 .... 57 D1
Hartington St Derby DE23 ... 267 B1
  Langwith NG20 .... 119 F4
Hartington View S43 .... 78 C2
Hartington Way DE22 .... 217 F4
Hartland Dr DE12 .... 231 F3
Hartland Way S41 .... 77 D1
Hartley St S2 .... 43 D4
Hartopp Ave S2 .... 43 E3
Hartopp Cl S2 .... 43 E3
Hartopp Dr S2 .... 43 E3
Hartopp Rd S2 .... 43 E3
Hartshay Hill DE5 .... 169 E1
Hartshill Rd
  Hartshorne DE11 .... 257 D2
  Stoke-on-T S14 .... 264 C4
Hartshorne CE Prim Sch
  DE11 .... 257 D3
Hartshorne Rd Derby DE23 ... 231 E3
  Repton DE65 .... 249 F4
  Woodville DE11 .... 256 C2
Hartside Cl [1] S40 .... 95 E3
Hartside Gdns [1] NG10 ... 236 A4
Hartwell St NG3 .... 268 B2
Hartwood Dr NG9 .... 209 F1
Harvest Hill DE11 .... 256 A4
Harvest Way Derby DE21 ... 206 B2
  [2] Old Brampton S40 ... 95 D3
Harvey Close Mews S8 .... 43 D2
Harvey Clough Rd S8 ...... 43 D2
Harvey Croft NG9 .... 209 E3
Harvey Ct S44 .... 98 C1
Harvey Pl ST14 .... 210 A1
Harvey Rd Branston S14 ... 254 A4
  Castle Donington DE74 ... 247 D1
  Derby DE24 .... 232 C3
Harwood Ave DE14 ...... 253 F4
Harwood Cl S2 .... 43 D4
Harwood St S2 .... 43 D4
Haslamg Cl DE21 .... 206 B2
Haslam Cres S8 .... 56 C3
Haslam St NG7 .... 268 A1
Haslam La DE22 .... 205 D1
Hasland Hall Com Sch
  S41 .... 115 E4
Hasland Inf Sch S41 ..... 115 E4
Hasland Jun Sch S41 .... 115 E4
Hasland Rd S41 .... 115 E4
Haslemere Ct DE23 ...... 219 D1
Haslemere Rd NG10 ...... 236 A4
Haslin Rd SK17 .... 85 E1

Hassall Rd DE65 .... 227 E1
Hassock La N DE75 .... 194 A4
Hassock La S DE75 .... 194 B3
Hassocky La Calow S44 ... 116 A3
  Temple Normanton S44 ... 116 A3
Hassop Rd Calver S32 ..... 72 A1
  Derby DE21 .... 220 A4
  Hassop DE45 .... 90 B1
  Staveley S43 .... 78 C2
Hastilar Cl S2 .... 44 A4
Hastilar Rd S2 .... 44 A4
Hastilar Rd S S13 .... 44 B4
Hasting St DE74 .... 247 D1
Hastings Cl
  Breedon on t H DE73 ... 252 C1
  Chesterfield S40 .... 95 E3
Hastings Rd Buxton SK17 ... 85 E2
  Swadlincote DE11 .... 256 A2
Hastings St DE23 .... 219 D1
Haston Dr DE55 .... 170 B4
Hatchmere Cl DE21 ...... 206 A1
Hatfield Ave NG10 .... 223 D2
Hatfield Cl DE24 .... 232 C3
Hathaway Cl S42 .... 131 D2
Hathern Cl Calow S43 ...... 96 C2
  Derby DE23 .... 231 F3
  Long Eaton NG10 .... 236 B3
Hathersage Ave
  Derby DE23 .... 231 F4
  Long Eaton NG10 .... 235 F3
Hathersage Cres SK13 ..... 9 F1
Hathersage Dr
  Glossop SK13 .... 17 F4
  Somercotes DE55 .... 170 A4
Hathersage Rd Bamford S33 ... 40 A1
  Totley S11 .... 54 B3
Hathersage Sta S32 .... 53 D4
Hatherton St ST16 .... 269 F4
Hatton Cl S18 .... 75 E4
Hatton Crofts NG10 ...... 236 B3
Hatton Ct DE73 .... 252 A4
Hatton Dr S40 .... 95 D3
Haulton Dr DE74 .... 247 D2
Havelock Gdns NG3 ...... 268 B2
Havelock Rd DE23 .... 232 A4
Havelock St Ilkeston DE7 ... 208 C4
  Ripley DE5 .... 169 F1
Haven Baulk Ave DE23 ... 230 C4
Haven Baulk La DE23 .... 230 C4
Haven Ct DE24 .... 233 E3
Havercroft Tr S21 .... 60 A4
Hawfield La
  Burton u T DE15 .... 248 B2
  Newton Solney DE15 .... 248 C2
Hawk Green Rd SK6 ...... 23 D2
Hawk Rd SK22 .... 33 F4
Hawk's Dr DE15 .... 248 B2
Hawke St DE22 .... 218 B3
Hawkeshead Ave S18 ...... 56 C1
Hawkhill Rd S32 .... 71 E3
Hawking La S44 .... 133 D4
Hawkins Ct DE7 .... 194 C2
Hawkins Dr DE56 .... 168 A2
Hawkins St S14 .... 269 F1
Hawkshead Ave DE21 .... 205 E1
Hawksley Ave S40 .... 95 F2
Hawksley Dr
  Darley Dale DE4 .... 127 D2
  Rolleston DE4 .... 240 A2
Hawksway S21 .... 59 D2
Hawksworth St NG3 ..... 268 C2
Hawley St S18 .... 58 A1
Hawleys Cl DE4 .... 143 F3
Hawthorn Ave
  Breaston DE72 .... 235 F4
  Creswell S80 .... 81 F1
  Derby DE24 .... 233 D4
  Glapwell S44 .... 134 A4
  Mastin Moor S43 .... 79 E2
  Netherseal DE12 .... 264 C4
  Ripley DE5 .... 180 B4
  Stapleford NG9 .... 223 E3
Hawthorn Bank Hadfield SK13 ... 9 F2
  New Mills SK22 .... 33 D3
Hawthorn Cl Ashbourne DE6 ... 185 E4
  Chinley SK23 .... 34 C1
  Clowne S43 .... 80 B2
  Denstone ST14 .... 196 C3
  Doveridge DE6 .... 211 D1
  Hilton DE65 .... 228 B1
  Hope S33 .... 39 D2
Hawthorn Cr DE65 .... 228 B1
Hawthorn Cres DE15 .... 254 C4
Hawthorn Dr DE4 .... 155 D3
Hawthorn Gr S43 .... 9 E3
Hawthorn Rd
  Castle Donington DE74 ... 247 D3
  Eckington S21 .... 59 D1
Hawthorn Rise DE11 ..... 255 F4
Hawthorn St DE24 .... 232 B4
Hawthorn Way S17 .... 269 F3
Hawthorne Ave
  Borrowash DE72 .... 221 E1
  Dronfield S18 .... 57 D2
  Long Eaton NG10 .... 236 B3
  Shirebrook NG20 .... 119 E2
  Shirland DE55 .... 146 B3
  Stoke-on-T S14 .... 269 D1
  Tibshelf DE55 .... 148 A4
Hawthorne Cl
  Barlborough S43 .... 80 A3
  Kilburn DE56 .... 179 F1
  Stretton DE55 .... 145 E4

Hawthornes Ave DE55 ... 159 F3
Hawthorns The
  Belper DE56 .... 179 D3
  Chapel-en-le-F SK23 ...... 47 D3
  Little Eaton DE21 .... 205 D4
Hawton Cl NG19 .... 135 D1
Hawtrey Gdns DE24 ..... 233 E3
Haxby Cl S13 .... 44 B3
Haxby Pl S13 .... 44 B3
Haxby St S13 .... 44 B3
Hay La Ashover S45 ...... 145 D2
  Scropton DE6 .... 226 C3
  Spout DE56 .... 166 C2
  Wirksworth DE56 .... 166 C2
Hay Wain La DE11 .... 256 A3
Haybrook Ct S17 .... 56 A4
Haycroft Cl NG19 .... 136 F1
Hayden Fold SK13 .... 16 B4
Haydn Rd DE21 .... 219 F4
Haydock Cl NG16 .... 195 F4
Haydock Park Rd DE24 ... 232 C4
Hayes Ave Breaston DE72 ... 235 F4
  Derby DE72 .... 231 E3
Hayes Cl Pinxton NG16 ... 160 B3
  West Hallam DE7 .... 207 E4
Hayes Con Ctr The DE55 ... 170 B1
Hayes Cres DE55 .... 169 F4
Hayes Ct S20 .... 59 F4
Hayes Dr S20 .... 59 F4
Hayes Farm Ct DE73 ..... 251 D1
Hayes La DE55 .... 169 F4
Hayes The DE65 .... 230 B4
Hayes Wood Rd DE7 ..... 193 F4
Hayfield Cl Belper DE56 ... 179 D3
  Sheffield S8 .... 56 C3
  Staveley S43 .... 78 B2
  Wingerworth S42 .... 114 C2
Hayfield Cres S12 .... 44 B3
Hayfield Dr S12 .... 44 B3
Hayfield Pl S12 .... 44 B3
Hayfield Prim Sch SK22 ... 25 D3
Hayfield Rd
  Chapel-en-le-F SK23 .... 47 D3
  Chinley SK23 .... 35 D1
  New Mills SK22 .... 24 B3
Hayfield Rd E SK23 .... 47 D3
Hayfield View S21 .... 59 E3
Hayford Way S43 .... 78 B2
Hayley Croft DE56 .... 190 D4
Hayling Cl DE7 .... 194 C2
Haynes Ave NG9 .... 209 F4
Hays Cl DE7 .... 194 C2
Hays La DE6 .... 164 C2
Hays The DE65 .... 227 D1
Haywards Cl SK13 .... 10 C1
Haywood Cl DE24 .... 233 E4
Haywood St NG2 .... 268 C2
Hayworth Rd NG10 .... 223 D4
Hazel Ave Derby DE22 ... 205 D3
  Killamarsh S21 .... 60 C4
  Lower Pilsley S45 .... 132 B4
Hazel Cl Ashbourne DE6 ... 185 E4
  Dronfield S18 .... 76 A4
  Findern DE65 .... 230 B2
  Heanor DE75 .... 181 F2
  Stoke-on-T S14 .... 269 D1
  Swadlincote DE11 .... 256 B2
Hazel Cres NG20 .... 119 E2
Hazel Ct S18 .... 76 A4
Hazel Dr Chesterfield S40 ... 114 C4
  Derby DE21 .... 221 D3
  Wingerworth S42 .... 114 C1
Hazel Gr Calver S32 .... 72 C3
  Duffield DE56 .... 190 D4
  Mansfield Woodhouse NG19 ... 136 C4
  Mastin Moor S43 .... 79 E3
  South Normanton DE55 ... 160 A3
Hazel Rd S21 .... 60 C4
Hazelbadge Cres S12 ...... 44 C4
Hazelby Rd S80 .... 100 C3
Hazeldene Cl DE56 .... 190 D3
**Hazelhurst S41 .... 115 E4
Hazelhurst Ave S41 .... 96 C4
Hazelhurst La S41 .... 96 C4
Hazelmere Rd S80 .... 81 F4
Hazelrigg Cl DE74 .... 246 C4
Hazeltree Cl DE5 .... 169 D2
Hazelwood Cl [1] S18 ...... 56 C1
Hazelwood Hill DE56 ..... 190 B4
Hazelwood Rd
  Burton u T DE15 .... 254 C4
  Derby DE21 .... 219 F3
  Duffield DE56 .... 190 D2
  Hazelwood DE56 .... 190 B3
Hazlebarrow Cl S8 .... 57 D4
Hazlebarrow Cres S8 .... 57 D4
Hazlebarrow Ct S8 .... 57 D4
Hazlebarrow Dr S8 .... 57 D4
Hazlebarrow Gr S8 .... 57 D4
Hazlebarrow Rd S8 .... 57 D4
Hazlebarrow St S8 .... 57 D4
Hazlearrow Prim Schs
  S8 .... 57 D4
Headingley Ct S43 .... 231 F1
Headland Cl S43 .... 78 B2
Headland Rd S43 .... 78 B2
Heage La DE65 .... 229 D1
Heage Prim Sch DE56 ... 168 B2
Heage Rd DE5 .... 169 E1
Healaugh Way S40 .... 114 C4
Heale St S43 .... 80 A4
Heanor Gate Ind Est
  DE75 .... 193 D3
Heanor Gate Rd
  Heanor DE75 .... 193 E4
  Shipley DE75 .... 193 D3
Heanor Gate Sch DE75 ... 181 E4

eanor Langley Mill &
District Meml Hospl
DE75 .... 181 F1
eanor Rd Codnor DE5 .... 181 D2
Denby DE5 .... 181 D2
eanor Rd, DE75 .... 181 E1
eanor Rd
Heanor, Loscoe DE75 .... 181 E2
Ilkeston DE7 .... 194 B2
Smalley DE7 .... 193 D4
earthcote Rd DE11 .... 256 A2
earthstone La DE4 .... 143 E1
eath Ave Derby DE23 .... 218 B1
Killamarsh S21 .... 60 B3
eath Cross ST14 .... 210 A1
eath La DE7 .... 231 F2
eath Fields Prim Sch
DE65 .... 227 E1
eath Gdns DE72 .... 236 A4
eath St S43 .... 85 E3
eath La Blackfordby DE11 .. 257 F1
Findern DE65 .... 242 B4
Hartshorne DE11 .... 257 F2
Smisby LE65 .... 258 A3
Ticknall LE65 .... 258 A3
eath Park Rd SK17 .... 85 E3
eath Prim Sch S44 .... 116 C1
eath Rd Burton u T DF15 ... 254 C4
Glossop SK13 .... 10 B1
Hollmewood S44 .... 116 C1
Williamthorpe S42 .... 132 C4
Ripley DE5 .... 169 F1
Uttoxeter ST14 .... 210 A1
eath St SK17 .... 85 D3
eath The NG16 .... 195 D4
eath View SK17 .... 85 F1
eath Way DE65 .... 227 E1
eathcoat St NG1 .... 268 B2
eathcote Cl DE24 .... 233 E3
eathcote Dr S41 .... 115 F4
eather Ave S44 .... 116 C1
eather Bank Cl SK13 .... 9 F7
eather Cl Calow S44 .... 97 D2
Derby DE24 .... 231 E1
Mansfield NG18 .... 268 B3
South Normanton DE55 ..... 160 A2
Swanwick DE55 .... 170 A4
eather Cres
Breaston DE72 .... 235 F4
Heage DE56 .... 179 E1
Heritage La NG18 .... 268 C1
eather Gr SK14 .... 9 E3
eather Lea Ave S17 .... 55 E4
eather Lea Pl S17 .... 55 E4
eather La S41 .... 115 F4
eather Way S42 .... 113 E4
eatherley Dr NG19 .... 136 C1
eatherley Prim Sch
NG19 .... 136 C1
eathervale Rd S41 .... 115 E4
eathfield Dr4 .... 143 E4
eathfield Ave
Chesterfield S40 .... 95 E2
Ilkeston DE7 .... 209 D4
eathfield Cl Dronfield S18 .. 75 F3
Wingerworth S42 .... 114 C3
eathfield Gdns DE55 .... 148 A4
eathfield Nook Rd SK17 ..... 85 F1
eathfield Rd S12 .... 44 B2
eathlands Dr ST14 .... 210 A1
eaton C 🖂 S18 .... 56 B1
eaton St S40 .... 95 E1
eavygate La DE56 .... 177 F4
ebden Cl DE23 .... 230 C3
ebden Dr S13 .... 17 F4
ebrides Cl DE24 .... 231 E2
ebdon Bar NG19 .... 136 C2
edge Gr DE11 .... 256 A4
edgebank Ct DE21 .... 206 B2
edgerow Gdns DE21 .... 206 B2
edingham Way DE3 .... 230 B4
edley Cl DE55 .... 170 B4
edley Dr S43 .... 96 B4
edley Arches S8 .... 43 D4
eeley Bank Inf & Jun Sch
S8 .... 43 D4
eeley Bank Rd S2 .... 43 D4
eeley Grn S2 .... 43 D4
eigham Ct DE4 .... 232 B2
eights of Abraham DE4 ..... 143 D1
eimsdale Cl NG18 .... 268 A3
elmsley Ave S9 .... 59 F4
elmton Dr S8 .... 43 D3
elmton Rd S8 .... 43 D3
elston Cl
Chesterfield S41 .... 115 D4
Derby DE24 .... 233 D3
Linton DE12 .... 261 E3
elvellyn Way NG10 .... 223 D1
eming Ave S45 .... 132 B1
emington Cty Sch DE74 .... 247 E3
emington Hill DE74 .... 247 E2
emington La DE74 .... 247 F3
emlock Ave
Long Eaton NG10 .... 223 E1
Stapleford NG9 .... 223 F4
emlock Cl DE21 .... 206 A2
emlock La DE7 .... 208 B3
emp Yd DE6 .... 165 D1
emper La S8 .... 56 B4
emper La S8 .... 56 B3
emsley Dr NG16 .... 182 B2
emsworth Prim Sch S8 ...... 43 E1
emsworth Rd S8 .... 43 E1
endon Way DE7 .... 218 A3
enley Ave S45 .... 131 F3
enley Gdns NG9 .... 209 F1
enley Gn DE22 .... 217 F3
enley Way DE7 .... 207 E4

Henmore Pl DE6 .... 173 E1
Henmore Trad Est DE6 .... 173 D1
Hennymoor Cl S80 .... 82 A3
Hennymoor La S80 .... 82 B1
Henry Ave
Mansfield Woodhouse
NG19 .... 136 A3
Matlock DE4 .... 143 E3
Henry Bradley Inf Sch
S13 .... 96 C4
Henry Cres DE55 .... 159 F3
Henry Prince CE Fst Sch
The DE6 .... 184 B4
Henry St Chesterfield S41 ... 267 A4
Derby DE1 .... 267 A4
Eckington S21 .... 59 E2
Glossop SK13 .... 10 B1
Grassmoor S42 .... 115 F2
Nottingham NG2 .... 268 C1
Ripley DE5 .... 169 E1
Henshaw Ave DE7 .... 208 B3
Henshaw Pl DE7 .... 194 C2
Herbert Rd ST17 .... 269 E3
Herbert St Burton u T DE15 .. 248 A2
Derby DE1 .... 269 F1
Mansfield NG18 .... 268 B3
Herbert Strutt Prim Sch
S41 .... 178 C1
Herdings Cl S12 .... 44 A2
Herdings Prim Sch S14 .... 43 F1
Herdings Rd S12 .... 44 A2
Herdings View S12 .... 44 A2
Hereford Ave NG19 .... 136 B3
Hereford Cl SK17 .... 85 E2
Hereford Cres S43 .... 256 B3
Hereford Dr S43 .... 96 C4
Hereford Rd Buxton SK17 .... 85 E2
Derby DE21 .... 219 E4
Hereward's Rd S8 .... 43 F1
Herewood Cl NG20 .... 119 F2
Heritage Con Sch S43 .... 80 B2
Heritage Dr S43 .... 80 B3
Heritage Mint Sch DE4 ...... 143 E2
Heritage Way DE15 .... 248 A1
Hermitage Ave
Borrowash DE72 .... 221 E1
Mansfield NG18 .... 268 A3
Somercotes DE55 .... 170 B3
Hermitage Ct DE21 .... 206 A1
Hermitage La S42 .... 268 A3
Hermitage Park Way
DE11 .... 256 A4
Hermitage Sq NG2 .... 268 C1
Hermitage Wlk
Ilkeston DE7 .... 208 C3
Nottingham NG7 .... 268 A2
Hermon St NG7 .... 268 A2
Hernstone La SK17 .... 49 D1
Heron Dr DE11 .... 256 C2
Heron Way DE3 .... 218 A1
Heronswood Dr DE21 .... 220 B3
Herriot Dr S40 .... 266 C1
Heskey Cl NG3 .... 268 B2
Hessey St S13 .... 44 C3
Hewers Holt S43 .... 80 A3
Hewett St NG20 .... 120 B3
Hewitt Pl S26 .... 61 F3
Hexham Ave DE7 .... 209 D2
Hexham Wlk DE7 .... 205 F1
Hey St NG10 .... 236 B2
Heydon Ct DE56 .... 179 D3
Heyford Ct DE75 .... 182 A1
Heysbank Rd SK12 .... 32 B3
Heyward St NG18 .... 268 C4
Heywood St Brimington S43 .. 96 C4
Mansfield NG18 .... 268 A3
Heyworth Rd SK23 .... 47 E3
Heyworth St DE22 .... 218 B3
Hibbert Rd NG18 .... 268 C4
Hibbert St SK22 .... 33 D3
Hickings La NG9 .... 223 F4
Hickingwood La S43 .... 81 D3
Hickinwood Cres S43 .... 80 C3
Hickleton Ct DE5 .... 169 E1
Hickling Cl DE24 .... 232 B2
Hickling Ct NG18 .... 268 C4
Hickton Rd DE55 .... 169 F1
Hide St S14 .... 137 F4
Hide St ST4 .... 269 E2
Hides Gn S44 .... 99 D1
Higg La DE4, DE56 .... 167 D3
Higger La S32 .... 52 C4
Higgins Rd DE11 .... 255 F3
High Bank DE5 .... 180 C1
High Bank Rd DE15 .... 248 A2
High Cross Biggin SK17 ...... 138 A1
Hartington SK17 .... 137 F3
High Cross St 🖂 NG1 .... 268 B2
High Edge Dr DE56 .... 179 E4
High Edge Mews DE56 .... 179 D3
High Hazel Cl S45 .... 131 F2
High Hazel WlkS45 .... 131 F2
High Hazels Rd S43 .... 80 A3
High Hill Rd SK22 .... 24 B1
High Holborn DE7 .... 194 C2
High Holborn Rd
Codnor DE5 .... 170 A1
Ripley DE5 .... 170 A1
High La Charlesworth SK13 .. 16 C4
Glossop SK13 .... 16 C4
Highlane S12 .... 44 C1
Holloway, Dethick Common
DE4 .... 144 C3
Holloway, Upper Holloway
DE4 .... 156 B3
Holymoorside S42 .... 113 F3
High La Central DE7 .... 193 F1
High La E DE7 .... 208 A4

High La W DE7 .... 193 F1
High Lea Rd SK22 .... 33 D4
High Lees Rd S43 .... 80 C1
High Meadow Cl DE5 .... 180 B4
High Pavement
Belper DE56 .... 179 D2
Nottingham NG1 .... 268 B1
High Peak Coll of F Ed
SK17 .... 85 E2
High Pk SK16 .... 269 D3
High Rd DE55 .... 157 F2
High Ridge
Mansfield NG19 .... 136 C1
Matlock DE4 .... 143 E4
High Spania NG16 .... 195 F4
High St Alfreton DE55 .... 159 D2
Apperknowle S18 .... 58 A1
Barlborough S43 .... 80 A4
Belper DE56 .... 179 D2
Bolsover S44 .... 99 D1
Bonsall DE4 .... 142 B1
Brimington S43 .... 96 C4
Brinsley NG16 .... 171 E1
Buxton SK17 .... 85 D4
Calver S32 .... 72 A1
Castle Donington DE74 ...... 247 D2
Chapel-en-le-Fr SK23 .... 47 D3
Chesterfield, New Whittington
S41 .... 77 E2
Chesterfield, Stonegravels
S40 .... 266 B3
Clay Cross S45 .... 131 E2
Clowne S43 .... 80 B2
Codnor DE5 .... 181 D4
Derby DE73 .... 233 D1
Dore S17 .... 55 E4
Doveridge DE6 .... 211 D1
Dronfield S18 .... 57 D1
Eckington S21 .... 59 E2
Heanor, Loscoe DE75 .... 181 F1
Heanor, Newlands DE75 ..... 181 F1
Ilkeston DE7 .... 208 C4
Kilburn DE56 .... 192 A4
Killamarsh S21 .... 60 B3
Kimberley NG16 .... 195 F3
Linton DE12 .... 261 E3
Long Eaton NG10 .... 236 C4
Longnor SK17 .... 121 B3
Mansfield NG18 .... 268 B3
Mansfield Woodhouse
NG19 .... 136 B2
Marchington ST14 .... 224 C1
Melbourne DE73 .... 252 A4
Mosborough S20 .... 59 E4
New Mills SK22 .... 33 E4
Nottingham NG1 .... 268 B1
Pleasleyhill NG19 .... 135 D3
Repton DE65 .... 242 B1
Riddings DE55 .... 170 B3
Ripley DE5 .... 169 E1
Rocester ST14 .... 196 C2
Somercotes DE55 .... 170 B4
South Normanton DE55 ..... 160 A4
Stapleford NG9 .... 223 F4
Staveley S43 .... 78 C1
Stonebroom S45 .... 147 D2
Stoney Middleton S32 .... 71 F2
Stretton, Church Gresley
DE11 .... 256 B2
Swadlincote, Newhall DE11 .. 255 F3
Swanwick DE55 .... 169 F4
Tibshelf DE55 .... 148 A4
Ticknall DE73 .... 251 D2
Tideswell SK17 .... 69 E2
Tutbury DE13 .... 239 E3
Whaley SK13 .... 81 F3
Woodville DE11 .... 256 C1
High St E S43 .... 100 B4
High St W SK13 .... 10 B1
High Tor DE4 .... 143 D1
High Tor Rd DE4 .... 143 D1
High Trees S17 .... 55 E4
High View Cl S41 .... 96 B1
High View Rd DE5 .... 180 B4
High View Sch & Tech Ctr
DE55 .... 205 F1
High Wood Fold SK6 .... 23 E4
Higham La
Hackingknife SK14 .... 15 D4
Morton DE55 .... 146 C2
Highashes La S45 .... 113 F1
Highbank S43 .... 9 F4
Highbank Rd SK13 .... 17 F4
Highbury Cl DE22 .... 217 F3
Highbury Rd S41 .... 96 A3
Highcliffe Ave NG20 .... 119 E2
Highcroft CI NG10 .... 236 C3
Higher Albert St S41 .... 266 B4
Higher Barn Rd SK13 .... 9 F2
Higher Halsteads SK17 .... 67 F2
Higher Sq SK13 .... 10 A4
Highfield S45 .... 108 C4
Highfield Ave
Chesterfield S41 .... 95 F3
Dove Holes SK17 .... 47 F1
Mansfield NG18 .... 136 A1
Shirebrook NG20 .... 119 E3
Highfield Cl Bakewell DE45 .. 109 E3
Heanor DE75 .... 181 D3
Mansfield NG18 .... 136 A1
Highfield Cotts DE21 .... 219 F3
Highfield Dr
Bakewell DE45 .... 109 E3
Ilkeston DE7 .... 208 A3
Matlock DE4 .... 143 E4
South Normanton DE55 ..... 160 B4
Highfield Gdns Derby DE22 .. 218 C4
Hollingworth SK14 .... 9 E3

Highfield Hall Sch S41 .... 95 F3
Highfield La Biggin SK17 .... 138 A2
Chesterfield S41 .... 95 F3
Derby DE21 .... 219 F3
Hartington SK17 .... 137 F3
Weston Underwood DE6 .... 188 C3
Highfield Mews DE21 .... 219 F3
Highfield Pl S2 .... 43 D4
Highfield Prim Sch NG10 .. 223 E1
Highfield Rd
Ashbourne DE6 .... 185 D4
Belper DE56 .... 178 C1
Bolsover S44 .... 99 D1
Chesterfield S41 .... 266 A4
Clay Cross S45 .... 131 E2
Derby, Little Chester S41 .. 218 C4
Derby, Littleover DE23 .... 231 E4
Glossop SK13 .... 17 E4
Hayfield SK22 .... 25 E2
Hulland Ward DE6 .... 175 F2
Kilburn DE56 .... 191 E4
Little Eaton DE21 .... 205 E4
Marple SK6 .... 23 D3
Swadlincote DE11 .... 256 A2
Swanwick DE55 .... 169 E4
Highfield St
Long Eaton NG10 .... 223 E1
Swadlincote DE11 .... 256 A2
Highfield Terr
Chesterfield S41 .... 95 F3
Mansfield NG18 .... 268 B3
New Mills SK22 .... 33 E4
Highfield View Rd S41 .... 95 F3
Highfield Way
Mansfield NG18 .... 268 B3
Ripley DE5 .... 180 B4
Highfields Codnor DE5 ...... 181 D4
Peak Dale SK17 .... 67 D3
Highfields Cres S18 .... 56 A3
Highfields Dr
Holmewood S42 .... 132 B4
Linton DE12 .... 261 E3
Highfields Lower Sch DE4 . 143 E2
Highfields Rd S18 .... 76 A4
Highfields S18 .... 143 F4
Highfields Way S42 .... 132 B4
Highgate Dr Dronfield S18 ... 76 A4
Shipley DE7 .... 194 B2
Highgate Gn DE22 .... 218 A3
Highgate La S18 .... 76 B4
Highgate Rd SK22 .... 25 F1
Highgrove Cl DE13 .... 240 B1
Highgrove Dr DE73 .... 232 C1
Highland Bsns Ctr DE56 ...... 80 B3
Mansfield Woodhouse NG19 136 B2
Highland Rd S43 .... 77 E2
Highlands DE15 .... 248 A2
Highlands Pl S41 .... 76 C1
Highlidge La S18 .... 75 E3
Highlow Cl S40 .... 95 E3
Highstairs La DE55 .... 146 B4
Highstool La SK17 .... 106 A3
Highthorpe St NG7 .... 17 D4
Highway La S18 .... 151 F1
Highwood Ave DE56 .... 179 E1
Highwood Cl SK13 .... 17 D4
Highwood La S80 .... 81 E3
Highwood Rd SK21 .... 59 E2
Higson Ave ST4 .... 269 E2
Hilary Cl DE56 .... 179 F3
Hilcote La DE55 .... 148 A1
Hilcote St DE55 .... 146 B4
Hilderstone Cl DE24 .... 233 E3
Hill Brow DE1 .... 267 B2
Hill Cl Derby DE21 .... 220 C2
Stanley DE7 .... 193 D1
Turnditch DE56 .... 177 D1
Hill Crest Crich DE4 .... 157 D1
Shirebrook NG20 .... 119 E2
Hill Crest Rd DE21 .... 219 E4
Hill Cross DE45 .... 108 C4
Hill Cross Ave DE23 .... 231 D4
Hill Cross Dr DE23 .... 231 D4
Hill Fields DE55 .... 160 A2
Hill Gr S43 .... 78 A2
Hill Green Cl DE12 .... 260 B2
Hill Nook Cl DE73 .... 233 D1
Hill Park Cl DE23 .... 218 A1
Hill Rd Ashover S45 .... 129 F2
Hill The Derby DE22 .... 204 C2
Eckington S21 .... 59 F2
Heanor DE75 .... 181 E1
Hill Rise NG9 .... 209 E2
Hill Rise Cl DE23 .... 231 D1
Hill Sq The DE22 .... 205 D1
Hill St Burton u T DE15 ..... 254 C4
Clay Cross S45 .... 131 E2
Donisthorpe DE12 .... 262 C1
Pleasleyhill NG19 .... 135 D3
Ripley DE5 .... 169 E1
Sheffield S2 .... 43 D4
Stoke-on-T S4 .... 269 E2
Swadlincote, Church Gresley
DE11 .... 256 B2
Swadlincote, Newhall DE11 255 F3
Hill Top Bolsover S44 .... 99 D1
Castle Donington DE74 ...... 247 D1
Derby DE21 .... 220 C2
Hill Top La NG20 .... 119 F2
Hill Top Inf Sch DE56 .... 185 E4
Hill Top Rd DE55 .... 170 B3
Hill Top Rise SK23 .... 45 E4
Hill View DE55 .... 146 B3
Hill View Duffield DE56 ..... 190 E2
Repton DE65 .... 242 C1
Whaley Bridge SK23 .... 45 F4
Hill View Ct DE7 .... 192 A4
Hill View Gr DE21 .... 220 C3

Hill View Rd S43 .... 96 C4
Hilary Pl DE7 .... 208 A3
Hillberry Cl S43 .... 170 A1
Hillberry Rise S40 .... 114 C3
Hillcliff La DE56 .... 176 C3
Hillclose Ct DE23 .... 239 D3
Hillcrest Ave
Burton u T DE15 .... 248 A2
Hulland Ward DE6 .... 175 F2
South Normanton DE55 ..... 160 A2
Hillcrest Dr for Codnor DE5 .. 181 D4
Kilburn DE56 .... 192 A4
Hillcrest Gr S41 .... 78 C2
Hillcrest Rd S41 .... 115 E4
Hillcrest Dr DE73 .... 221 E2
Hillcroft Dr DE72 .... 221 E2
Hilland SK14 .... 9 D1
Hilland S14 .... 9 D1
Hillfield La DE13 .... 240 C1
Hillfield Rd NG9 .... 209 F1
Hillfoot Rd S17 .... 55 E3
Hillhead La SK17 .... 85 F1
Hillhouses La S42 .... 114 C2
Hillman Dr S43 .... 97 E4
Hillmoor St NG19 .... 135 E2
Hillock The S32 .... 72 C1
Hills Croft DE6 .... 164 A1
Hills Rd DE72 .... 235 E4
Hills The S33 .... 51 D3
Hillsdale Rd DE15 .... 248 A3
Hillside Ashover S45 .... 130 A2
Buxton SK17 .... 85 E2
Castle Donington DE74 ...... 247 D2
Findern DE65 .... 230 B1
Holloway DE4 .... 156 A3
Langley Mill NG16 .... 182 A2
Middleton (Nr Wirksworth)
DE4 .... 154 B2
Mosborough S20 .... 59 E4
Tutbury DE13 .... 239 E3
Whitwell S80 .... 81 F3
Hillside Ave Ashbourne DE6 220 A3
Whitwell S80 .... 76 A4
Hillside Gr Marple SK6 .... 15 D1
Sandiacre NG10 .... 223 D3
Hillside La DE4 .... 152 C1
Hillside Rd Derby DE21 ..... 220 C2
Linton DE12 .... 261 E4
Hillside S18 .... 178 C1
Hillside View SK22 .... 33 D4
Hillsway
Derby, Chellaston DE73 ..... 232 C2
Derby, Littleover DE23 ...... 218 A1
Shirebrook NG20 .... 119 E2
Hilltop La S18 .... 168 A4
Hilltop Cl S44 .... 98 B1
Hilltop Rd DE4 .... 215 E3
Hilltop Way S18 .... 76 A4
Hilton Cl DE3 .... 143 E3
Hilton Cl Derby DE23 .... 217 E1
Long Eaton NG10 .... 236 C3
Swadlincote DE11 .... 256 A4
Hilton Park Dr DE55 .... 170 B4
Hilton Prim Sch DE65 ...... 228 B1
Hilton Rd Eggington DE65 .. 241 D4
Etwall DE65 .... 229 D3
New Mills S44 .... 32 A4
Stoke-on-T S14 .... 269 D2
Hinckley Ct DE4 .... 110 C1
Hind Ave DE4 .... 235 E4
Hinderstich La DE4 .... 217 F1
Hinton Gr SK14 .... 15 D4
Hindscarth Cres DE23 ...... 217 F1
Hipley Cl S40 .... 95 D3
Hipper St S40 .... 266 B2
Hipper St S W S40 .... 266 B2
Hipper St W S40 .... 95 D3
Hoades La DE4 .... 131 E4
Hoargate La DE56 .... 200 C1
Hoades St S40 .... 190 A4
Hob La Kirk Ireton DE56 ... 176 B4
Totley S18 .... 55 F1
Hobart Cl Burton u T DE15 .. 248 B1
Derby DE21 .... 217 F1
Hobart Dr NG9 .... 209 F1
Hobhouse Rd NG19 .... 135 D3
Hobkirk Dr S43 .... 231 F1
Hobsic Cl NG16 .... 182 B4
Hobsic La NG16 .... 171 F4
Hobson Dr DE7 .... 208 C3
Hobson Moor Rd SK14 .... 9 D4
Hockerley Ave SK23 .... 45 E4
Hockerley Cl SK23 .... 45 E4
Hockerley La SK23 .... 45 E4
Hockley NG1 .... 268 B1
Hockley La Fallgate S45 .... 130 A1
Wingerworth S42 .... 115 D2

Hockley Way DE55 .... 159 D1
Hodge Beck Cl DE24 .... 233 E3
Hodge Fold SK14 .... 15 F4
Hodge La Ashover S45 ..... 128 C4
  Broadbottom SK14 .... 15 C4
  Marchington ST14 .... 224 A1
Hodmire La S44 .... 133 F4
Hodthorpe Cl DE21 .... 206 A1
Hodthorpe Prim Sch S80 .... 82 B3
Hogarth Cl NG9 .... 223 F3
Hogarth Rd S46 .... 23 D4
Hogarth Rise S18 .... 75 F4
Hogarth St NG3 .... 268 C2
Hoggbarn La NG16 .... 181 E3
Hoggs Field NG16 .... 182 C1
Hogshaw Villas Rd
  ⚫ SK17 .... 85 E4
Hoillant Sq DE6 .... 175 F2
Holbeach Dr S40 .... 114 C4
Holbeck Ave S44 .... 99 E1
Holbeck Cl S41 .... 266 C4
Holbeck La S80 .... 101 E4
Holbeck St S80 .... 81 E1
Holbein Cl S18 .... 75 F4
Holborn Ave NG2 .... 268 C1
Holborn Dr DE22 .... 218 A4
Holborn View DE5 .... 170 A1
Holbrook Ave
  Mosborough S20 .... 59 F4
  North Wingfield S42 .... 132 A4
Holbrook CE Prim Sch
  DE56 .... 191 E4
Holbrook Cl
  Chesterfield S40 .... 114 B4
  Long Eaton NG10 .... 135 D3
Holbrook Dr S13 .... 44 A3
Holbrook Gn S20 .... 60 A4
Holbrook Pl S43 .... 97 F3
Holbrook Rd Belper DE56 .. 178 C1
  Derby DE24 .... 233 D3
  Sheffield S13 .... 44 A4
Holbrook St DE75 .... 182 A1
Holbrook View DE56 .... 192 A4
Holbrook Way S42 .... 132 A4
Holburn Ave S18 .... 57 D1
Holcombe St DE23 .... 219 D1
Holden Ave DE72 .... 246 A4
Holden Gdns NG9 .... 223 F3
Holden St Mansfield NG18 ... 268 B3
  Nottingham NG7 .... 268 A2
Holderness Cl DE24 .... 231 E1
Holdings The DE11 .... 256 A1
Holdon Croft DE12 .... 260 B3
Holestone Gate Rd S45 ... 129 E1
Holker Ave SK17 .... 85 E4
Holkham Cl DE7 .... 194 B2
Holland Cl DE55 .... 146 C3
Holland Meadow NG10 .... 236 B3
Holland Pl S2 .... 43 D4
Holland Rd Chesterfield S41 .. 76 C1
  Sheffield S2 .... 43 D4
Hollens Way S40 .... 95 D3
Hollies Cl Clifton DE6 ...... 184 C3
  Dronfield S18 .... 76 B4
  Newton Solney DE15 .... 248 C4
Hollies Dr S46 .... 23 D3
Hollies La Great Cubley DE6 .. 198 B2
  Roston DE6 .... 198 B2
Hollies Rd DE22 .... 204 B2
Hollies The
  Eastwood NG16 .... 182 C1
  Sandiacre NG10 .... 223 D3
Hollin Cl S41 .... 95 E4
Hollin Cross La SK13 .... 17 E4
Hollin Dr SK23 .... 47 D3
Hollin Hill S43 .... 81 D2
Hollindale Dr S12 .... 44 B3
Hollington Cl DE21 .... 219 F4
Hollingwood Cres S43 .... 78 A1
Hollingwood Prim Sch
  S43 .... 78 A1
Hollingworth Ave NG10 ... 223 D2
Hollingworth Prim Sch
  SK14 .... 9 E3
Hollinhey Terr SK14 .... 9 E3
Hollins Ave SK17 .... 85 D4
Hollins La Crich DE4 .... 157 D2
  Gamesley SK13 .... 9 E1
  Marple SK6 .... 23 E4
Hollins Mews SK13 .... 9 E1
Hollins Mt SK6 .... 23 E4
Hollins Spring Ave S18 ..... 76 A4
Hollins Spring Rd S18 ...... 76 A4
Hollins St SK17 .... 85 D4
Hollins The DE4 .... 156 A3
Hollins Wood Cl DE4 ...... 156 A3
Hollinsclough CE
  Prim Sch SK17 .... 104 B1
Hollinsclough Rake SK17 ... 104 A1
Hollinsend Ave S12 .... 44 B3
Hollinsend Pl S12 .... 44 B3
Hollinsend Rd S12 .... 44 A3
Hollinsmoor Rd SK22 ...... 24 B4
Hollinwood Rd Disley SK12 .. 32 B3
  Marple SK6 .... 23 D1
Hollis La Chesterfield S41 ... 266 C2
  Denstone ST14 .... 196 A3
Hollis St DE24 .... 233 D4
Hollow Cres DE15 .... 248 B2
Hollow Gate S33 .... 51 D4
Hollow La Burton u T DE15 .. 248 B2
  Mayfield DE6 .... 172 B1
  Mosborough S20 .... 59 F3
Hollow Of The Moor SK17 .. 87 F2

Hollow Rd DE73 .... 252 C2
Hollow Stone ⚫ NG1 ...... 268 B1
Hollow The Bamford S33 .... 40 A2
  Castle Donington DE74 .. 247 D2
  Derby, Littleover DE74 .... 231 E4
  Derby, Mickleover DE3 .... 230 B4
  Holloway DE4 .... 156 A3
  Roston DE6 .... 197 F2
Holloway Rd Derby DE24 .. 232 C3
  Duffield DE56 .... 190 C2
Hollowford Rd S33 .... 38 A2
Hollowford Training &
  Conference Ctr S33 .... 38 B2
Hollowood Ave DE23 .... 231 E4
Hollows The NG10 .... 237 D4
Holly Ave Breaston DE72 ... 222 C1
  Ripley DE5 .... 180 B4
Holly Bank S14 .... 9 E3
Holly Brook Way DE23 .... 230 C3
Holly Bush La DE56 .... 191 D3
Holly Cl Ashbourne DE6 .. 185 E4
  Draycott DE72 .... 235 D4
  Killamarsh S21 .... 60 B3
Holly Ct Derby DE1 .... 217 E1
  Mansfield NG19 .... 136 C1
  Woodville DE11 .... 256 C1
Holly Gdns S12 .... 44 B3
Holly Gn DE15 .... 254 C4
Holly Gr Sheffield S12 ...... 44 B3
  Swanwick DE55 .... 169 F4
Holly Hill Rd NG16 .... 171 F3
Holly House Sch S41 .... 77 D2
Holly La Alderwasley DE56 ... 167 E2
  Tansley DE4 .... 144 A2
Holly Rd Kimberley NG16 .. 195 F4
  Mansfield NG19 .... 136 C1
  Uttoxeter ST14 .... 210 A1
Holly St DE15 .... 254 C4
Hollybank Ave S12 .... 44 B3
Hollybank Cl Sheffield S12 .. 44 B3
  Swadlincote DE11 .... 256 A4
Hollybank Cres
  Sheffield S12 .... 44 B3
  Stoke-on-T ST4 .... 269 E1
Hollybank Dr S12 .... 44 B3
Hollybank Rd S12 .... 44 B3
Hollybank Way S12 .... 44 B3
Hollybrook Way DE23 ..... 230 C3
Hollybush Cl DE12 .... 264 C4
Hollyhouse Dr DE55 .... 160 A3
Hollyhurst La DE6 .... 212 A3
Hollyhurst Row DE55 ...... 170 C3
Hollymoor Dr DE73 .... 232 C1
Hollythorpe Cl S41 .... 115 E4
Hollythorpe Cres S41 .... 43 D2
Hollythorpe Rd S8 .... 43 D2
Hollythorpe Rise S8 .... 43 D2
Hollywell Ave DE5 .... 181 D4
Hollywell Prim Sch NG16 .. 195 F4
Hollywell St S41 .... 266 B3
Hollywood Rd SK6 .... 23 F4
Holm Ave DE21 .... 205 D4
Holm Cl S18 .... 56 B1
Holm La DE55 .... 158 A2
Holme Cl Hatton DE65 ..... 227 E1
  Holloway DE4 .... 156 A3
  Ilkeston DE7 .... 194 B1
Holme Croft DE7 .... 207 F4
Holme Farm Ave DE15 .... 254 C4
Holme Hall Cres S40 .... 95 D3
Holme Hall Prim Sch S40 .. 95 D3
Holme La Bakewell DE45 .. 109 E4
  Derby DE21 .... 220 B2
Holme Park Ave S40 .... 95 D4
Holme Rd Chesterfield S41 .. 96 A3
  Matlock Bath DE4 .... 143 D1
Holme Woods La HD7 .... 2 C2
Holmebank Cl S40 .... 95 F2
Holmebank E S40 .... 95 F2
Holmebank W S40 .... 95 F2
Holmefield Cres DE7 .... 209 D4
Holmefield Rd S80 .... 82 A3
Holmes Bank DE6 .... 184 B4
Holmes Cl NG16 .... 182 A2
Holmes Rd DE72 .... 235 E4
Holmes St Derby DE23 .... 219 D1
  Heanor DE75 .... 181 E1
Holmesdale Cl S18 .... 57 E2
Holmesdale Inf Sch S18 .... 57 E1
Holmesdale Rd S18 .... 57 E2
Holmesfield Cl DE4 .... 144 A3
Holmesfield Dr Derby DE3 .. 217 F1
  Shipley DE75 .... 194 A4
Holmesfield Rd S18 .... 56 A1
Holmewood Dr NG16 ...... 195 D4
Holmewood Ind Pk S42 ... 116 B1
Holmfield Buxton SK17 ...... 84 C3
  Derby DE23 .... 231 E4
Holmgate Prim Sch S45 ... 131 D2
Holmgate Rd S42 .... 130 C2
Holmley Bank S18 .... 57 D2
Holmley La S18 .... 57 D2
Holmoak Cl DE21 .... 206 A2
Holmshaw Dr S13 .... 44 C4
Holmshaw Gr S13 .... 44 C4
Holmwood Terr ⚫ SK17 .... 85 E4
Holroyd Ave NG2 .... 268 C1
Holt Ave DE24 .... 233 E3
Holt Dr DE4 .... 142 C4
Holt La Holloway DE4 ...... 156 A3
  Matlock DE4 .... 143 D2
Holt Rd DE4 .... 127 F1
Holt's La DE13 .... 239 D3
Holtlands Dr DE24 .... 232 C3
Holy Rosary RC Prim Sch
  The DE15 .... 248 A2
Holyhead Dr DE24 .... 206 A2
Holymoor Rd S42 .... 113 F4

Holymoorside Prim Sch
  S42 .... 113 E4
Holyoake Ave S13 .... 44 C4
Holyrood Cl DE21 .... 221 D3
Holywell DE45 .... 109 E3
Holywell Cl S44 .... 118 A3
Home Farm Cl DE72 .... 221 E3
Home Farm Dr DE22 ...... 205 D2
Home Fm Ct NG16 .... 171 E3
Homecroft Dr NG16 .... 171 F4
Homeport Mews S41 .... 266 B4
Homer Dr SK6 .... 23 D4
Homestead NG16 .... 182 A2
Homestead Rd SK12 .... 32 B3
Honeycroft Ct DE55 .... 179 D1
Honeycroft Ct DE55 .... 160 A2
Honeyfield Dr DE5 .... 180 C4
Honeysuckle Cl DE11 ...... 256 A3
Honeysuckle View DE15 .. 255 D4
Honeywall S14 .... 9 E4
Honeywall La DE6 .... 183 F4
Honingham Rd DE7 .... 194 B2
Hook La S13 .... 210 A3
Hoole St S41 .... 115 E4
Hooley Cl NG10 .... 236 A3
Hooley St NG16 .... 171 F3
Hoon Rd DE65 .... 227 F4
Hoonwell La DE6 .... 175 F3
Hooton St NG2 .... 268 C2
Hop Inge The S26 .... 61 F3
Hope Ave DE3 .... 217 E1
Hope Dr NG7 .... 268 A1
Hope Prim Sch S33 .... 39 D2
Hope Rd Hope S33 .... 39 E1
  Thornhill S33 .... 39 E1
Hope St Chesterfield S40 ... 95 F2
  Derby DE1 .... 267 C2
  Glossop SK13 .... 10 C1
  Ilkeston DE7 .... 208 C4
  Mansfield NG18 .... 268 C3
  Melbourne DE73 .... 252 A4
Hope Sta S33 .... 39 E2
Hope Terr DE4 .... 143 D1
Hope Valley Coll S33 .... 38 C2
Hopedale Rd S12 .... 44 A2
Hopefield Ave S12 .... 44 B2
Hopetoun St DE23 .... 232 A4
Hopewell Rd DE4 .... 143 E3
Hopewell Wlk DE7 .... 194 C3
Hopkins Ct NG16 .... 182 C2
Hopping Hill DE56 .... 190 C4
Hopping Hill Terr E DE56 . 191 D4
Hopping Hill Terr W DE56 . 191 D4
Hopping La DE45 .... 125 D2
Hopton Cl DE21 .... 206 A1
Hopwell Rd DE72 .... 222 A2
Hopwell Sch DE72 .... 221 F3
Horace Ave NG9 .... 223 E3
Hordern La SK23 .... 47 D3
Horderns Park Rd SK23 ..... 47 D3
Horderns Rd SK23 .... 47 D3
Horeston Cotts DE7 .... 192 A4
Hornbeam Cl Derby DE21 . 205 F1
  Ilkeston DE7 .... 209 D4
Hornbeams The ST14 ...... 210 A1
Hornby Row ST4 .... 269 F2
Horncastle Rd DE21 .... 205 E1
Horner Rd S8 .... 43 D4
Hornscroft Rd S44 .... 99 D1
Hornsea Rd DE21 .... 205 E1
Hornthorpe Rd S21 .... 59 E1
Horridge St DE7 .... 194 C2
Horse Fair Ave SK23 .... 47 D3
Horse Shoes The DE74 .... 247 E2
Horsecroft Cl DE7 .... 194 B1
Horsehead La S44 .... 99 E1
Horseshoe Ave SK17 .... 47 F1
Horsewood Rd S40 .... 114 A4
Horsley CE Prim Sch
  DE21 .... 191 F3
Horsley Cl S40 .... 95 D3
Horsley Cres
  Holbrook DE56 .... 191 E4
  Langley Mill NG16 .... 182 A2
Horsley La DE21 .... 191 F3
Horsley Rd Horsley DE21 . 191 F3
  Kilburn DE56 .... 191 F3
Horsley Woodhouse Prim
  Sch DE7 .... 192 B3
Horsleygate La S18 .... 74 C4
Horsleygate Rd S17, S18 ... 74 A4
Horton Dr S20 .... 59 F4
Horton St DE23 .... 219 E1
Horwood Ave DE23 .... 218 B1
Hoselett Field Rd NG10 ... 236 C3
Hospital La DE3 .... 230 A3
Hoten Rd NG2 .... 268 C1
Houfton Cres S44 .... 98 C2
Houfton Rd S44 .... 98 C2
Hough La Heanor DE7 ..... 194 B2
Houghton Ct DE21 .... 205 F1
Houldsworth Cres S44 ...... 98 C1
Houldsworth Dr S41 .... 96 C1
Hoult St DE22 .... 218 B2
Houndkirk Rd S11 .... 54 B4
Hounds Gate NG7 .... 268 A1
Hounslow Rd DE22 .... 218 A3
Houston Cl DE21 .... 220 A3
Hoveton Cl DE24 .... 232 B2
How La S33 .... 38 B3
Howard Cl Glossop SK13 ... 10 A1
  Long Eaton NG10 .... 223 F1
Howard Dr Chesterfield S41 . 77 D1
  North Wingfield S42 ...... 131 F3

Howard Rd NG19 .... 268 A4
Howard St Derby DE24 .... 218 C1
  Glossop SK13 .... 10 B1
  Nottingham NG3 .... 268 B2
Howden Cl Derby DE3 ..... 217 E1
  Staveley S43 .... 78 C2
Howden Rd SK22 .... 24 B1
Howe St DE22 .... 218 B3
Howells Pl S43 .... 79 D2
Howitt Cres ST14 .... 210 A1
Howitt St Heanor DE75 .... 181 F1
  Long Eaton NG10 .... 236 C4
Howth Cl DE21 .... 220 A2
Hoylake Ave S40 .... 114 B4
Hoylake Cl NG19 .... 136 C3
Hoylake Ct DE3 .... 217 E2
Hoylake Dr DE3 .... 217 E2
Hubert Shaw Cl DE24 ..... 232 C2
Huckerby Rd DE7 .... 194 B1
Hucklow Ave
  Chesterfield S40 .... 266 A1
  North Wingfield S42 .... 132 A4
  Staveley S43 .... 97 E4
Hucklow Ct DE21 .... 206 A2
Hucknall Ave S40 .... 95 E2
Hudson Cl S26 .... 61 F4
Hudson Mount S44 .... 118 A4
Hudson St NG3 .... 268 C2
Hufton's Ct DE75 .... 194 A4
Hufton's Dr DE75 .... 194 A4
Hugh La S33 .... 51 D4
Hugh St SK13 .... 10 A1
Hulland CE Prim Sch DE6 . 175 F2
Hulland St DE1 .... 267 D1
Hulland View DE22 .... 204 B1
Hulme St S8 .... 269 D2
Humber Rd DE24 .... 233 E3
Humber Rd NG10 .... 223 E1
Humbleton Dr DE22 .... 218 A3
Humphrey Rd S8 .... 56 C4
Hundall La Chesterfield S41 . 77 D2
  Unstone S18 .... 77 D4
Hunger La DE6 .... 188 C2
Hungerhill La S42, S45 .... 113 D2
Hungry La Bradwell S33 .... 51 D3
  Hathersage S32 .... 53 D4
Hunloke Ave S40 .... 95 F1
Hunloke Cres S40 .... 95 F1
Hunloke Park Prim Sch
  S42 .... 115 D2
Hunloke Rd S42 .... 132 C4
Hunloke View S42 .... 115 D2
Hunsdon Rd S21 .... 59 E2
Hunstone Ave S8 .... 57 D4
Hunt Ave DE75 .... 181 F1
Hunt La S45 .... 145 D4
Hunter Dr DE56 .... 191 F4
Hunter Rd DE56 .... 179 E3
Hunter's La S13 .... 44 B3
Hunters Croft DE24 .... 231 F1
Hunters Dr S14 .... 269 D1
Hunters Gn SK23 .... 34 B4
Hunters La S13 .... 16 C4
Hunters Way S14 .... 269 E1
Huntingdon Ave NG9 .... 99 D1
Huntingdon Ct DE73 ...... 252 A4
Huntingdon Dr
  Castle Donington DE74 .. 247 D2
  Nottingham NG7 .... 268 A1
Huntingdon Gn DE21 ...... 219 E3
Huntingdon Jun & Inf
  Schs NG3 .... 268 C2
Huntingdon Rd DE15 ...... 254 B4
Huntingdon St NG3 .... 268 B2
Huntingdon Way NG9 ..... 223 F1
Huntingdon Wlk NG10 ... 223 D3
Huntley Ave Derby DE21 . 220 C3
Huntley-Cl S14 .... 269 E1
Huntley Cl S43 .... 97 D4
Hunts La DE12 .... 264 C4
Huntsman Rd S43 .... 78 C1
Huntspill Rd DE65 .... 228 C1
Hurd Dr S12 .... 44 C3
Hurley Ct DE7 .... 207 F4
Hurlfield Ave S12 .... 44 A3
Hurlfield Campus S2 .... 43 F3
Hurlfield Ct S12 .... 44 A3
Hurlfield Dr S12 .... 43 F3
Hurlfield Hill S2 .... 43 F3
Hurlfield Rd S12 .... 44 A3
Hurst Dr Burton u T DE13 . 240 C1
  Stanley DE7 .... 207 E3
Hurst La DE55 .... 146 A3
Hurst Lea Rd SK22 .... 33 E4
Hurst Rd SK13 .... 10 A1
Hurst Rise DE4 .... 143 E3
Hurstbrook Cl SK13 .... 10 A1
Hurstclough La
  Bamford S32 .... 40 B1
  Hathersage S33 .... 40 B1
Huss's La NG10 .... 236 C4
Hut La S21 .... 60 C2
Hutchings Cres S43 .... 80 A4
Hutchinson Gn NG3 .... 268 B2
Hawthorne CE Inf Sch
  NG7 .... 148 C1
Huthwaite La DE55 .... 148 B1
Hutmoor Butts DE45 ...... 107 D2
Hutton St Derby DE24 ..... 232 C3
  Nottingham NG2 .... 268 C1
Hyde Bank Rd SK22 .... 33 E4
Hyde Park Rd DE22 .... 218 A3
Hyde Rd SK14 .... 9 D2
Hyde Way SK14 .... 9 D2

Hydro Cl DE45 .... 91 F2
Hylton Cl DE14 .... 254 A4
Hyndley Rd S44 .... 98 C2

Ian Ave DE4 .... 165 F4
Ians Way S40 .... 95 E2
Ibbotsons Croft S32 .... 53 D4
Ibsley Cl DE24 .... 233 E3
Ida's Rd S21 .... 59 E2
Ilam Cl S43 .... 97 E1
Ilam Ct DE6 .... 185 E4
Ilam Sq DE7 .... 194 C3
Ilford Cl DE7 .... 194 C3
Ilford Ct DE7 .... 194 B2
Ilford Rd DE22 .... 218 A3
Ilford Wlk DE22 .... 218 A3
Ilion St NG19 .... 135 F2
Ilkeston Com Hospl DE7 . 194 B2
Ilkeston Rd Heanor DE75 . 193 F4
  Nottingham NG7 .... 268 A2
  Sandiacre NG10 .... 223 E4
  Sandiacre NG10 .... 223 E4
  Smalley DE7 .... 192 C2
  Stanton-by-D DE7 .... 208 C2
  Stapleford NG9 .... 209 F3
  Trowell NG9 .... 209 E2
Ilkeston Sch DE7 .... 208 B4
Immingham Gr S43 .... 78 B3
Imperial Ct DE22 .... 204 B3
Imperial Rd DE4 .... 143 D3
Inchwood Cl NG9 .... 223 F1
Independent Hill DE55 .... 158 C2
Industrial St DE23 .... 219 D1
Infirmary Rd S41 .... 266 C4
Ingestre Rd S17 .... 269 E1
Ingham Dr DE3 .... 230 B4
Ingham Rd NG10 .... 223 E3
Ingle Cl DE21 .... 220 C2
Ingle's Channel DE56 ...... 178 C2
Ingleborough Gdns
  ⚫ NG10 .... 236 A4
Ingleby Ave DE23 .... 231 F4
Ingleby Cl
  ⚫ Dronfield S18 .... 56 B3
  Swadlincote DE11 .... 256 A2
Ingleby La DE73 .... 251 D1
Ingleby Rd NG10 .... 235 F2
Inglefield Rd DE7 .... 209 D1
Ingleton Rd S41 .... 115 D4
Inglewood S17 .... 269 D1
Inglewood Ave DE23 ...... 217 E3
Inglis St ST4 .... 269 D1
Ingliston Cl DE24 .... 233 E1
Inkerman Rd NG16 .... 171 F3
Inkerman St NG16 .... 171 F3
Inkersall Dr S20 .... 59 F4
Inkersall Green Rd S43 ..... 97 E4
Inkersall Prim Sch S43 ...... 97 E4
Inkersall Rd S43 .... 97 F4
Inn La DE22 .... 204 A4
Inns La DE55 .... 157 F3
Institute La DE55 .... 159 D2
Instow Dr DE23 .... 231 E3
Instow Rise NG3 .... 268 B2
Intake Ave NG18 .... 268 C4
Intake Farm Fst Sch
  NG18 .... 268 A4
Intake Fst & Mid Sch S12 .. 44 A2
Intake La Bakewell DE45 . 109 F1
  Cromford DE4 .... 155 D2
  Holloway DE4 .... 155 F3
Intakes La DE6 .... 188 B4
Inveraray Cl DE24 .... 231 F1
Invernia Cl DE23 .... 231 F1
Iona Cl Derby DE24 .... 231 E1
  Tibshelf DE55 .... 147 F3
Iona Dr NG9 .... 209 E1
Ireland Cl S43 .... 78 C1
Ireland St S43 .... 78 C1
Ireton St NG7 .... 268 A2
Iron Cliff Rd S44 .... 98 A3
Iron Gate DE1 .... 267 B3
Irongate S40 .... 266 B3
Ironside Cl S14 .... 43 E2
Ironside Pl S14 .... 43 F2
Ironside Rd S14 .... 43 F2
Ironside Wlk S14 .... 43 F2
Ironville & Codnor Park
  Prim Sch NG16 .... 170 C3
Ironwalls La DE13 .... 239 E3
Irvine Cl DE24 .... 231 E1
Irving Pl DE24 .... 232 C2
Isaac's La NG9 .... 223 E3
Isabella St NG1 .... 268 B1
Islay Cl NG9 .... 209 E1
Islay Rd DE24 .... 231 E1
Isleworth Dr DE22 .... 217 F3
Ismay Rd DE21 .... 219 F4
Ivan Brook Cl ⚫ S18 .... 56 B1
Ivanhoe Cl S41 .... 77 D1
Ivatt Dr S2 .... 43 D4
Iveagh Wlk DE55 .... 147 F3
Ivonbrook Cl DE4 .... 142 A4
Ivonbrook Gr DE4 .... 142 A4
Ivy Cl Chesterfield S41 ...... 77 D1
  Donisthorpe DE12 .... 265 D4
Ivy Ct DE7 .... 242 A2
Ivy Ct Derby DE23 .... 218 C2
  Hilton DE65 .... 228 B2
  Sheffield S8 .... 43 E1
Ivy Gr DE55 .... 169 D3
Ivy House Specl Sch
  DE23 .... 219 E1
Ivy La Eastwood NG16 ..... 182 C3
  Elton DE4 .... 140 A2
Ivy Lodge Cl DE15 .... 254 C4
Ivy Spring Cl S42 .... 115 D2
Ivy Sq DE23 .... 219 D1
Ivybridge Cl DE21 .... 206 B2
Ivycroft SK13 .... 9 F3

-yside CI S21 .... 60 B3
-yside Gdns S21 .... 60 B3

ack's La ST14 .... 224 C1
ackass La DE56 .... 167 D2
acklin CI DE14 .... 254 A3
acksdale CI DE22 .... 204 B1
acksdale Prim Sch
.... 171 D2
ackson Ave Derby DE3 .... 218 A1
  Ilkeston DE7 .... 208 C4
  Sandiacre NG10 .... 223 D3
  Tupton S42 .... 131 E4
ackson Rd
  Bramley-Vale S44 .... 117 F1
  Clay Cross S45 .... 131 F2
  Matlock DE4 .... 143 D3
ackson St Derby DE22 .... 218 C2
  Glossop SK13 .... 17 E4
  Mottram in L SK14 .... 9 D2
  Padfield SK13 .... 10 B3
ackson Tor Rd DE4 .... 143 D3
agger's La S32 .... 72 B1
aggers La Ashover S45 .... 128 C3
  Darley Dale DE4 .... 128 C3
Jago Ave S43 .... 81 D2
James Andrew CI S8 .... 56 C4
James Andrew Cres S8 .... 56 C4
James Andrew Croft S8 .... 56 C4
James CI DE1 .... 218 C3
James St Chesterfield S41 .... 96 A3
  Glossop SK13 .... 17 E4
  Kimberley NG16 .... 195 F3
  Somercotes DE55 .... 170 B4
  Stoke-on-t ST4 .... 269 E1
  Swadlincote DE11 .... 256 B3
James's La DE6 .... 215 E1
Jane La SK23 .... 34 A1
Jap La DE6 .... 110 C4
Jarnett The SK17 .... 107 D4
Jarvey's La DE22 .... 217 F4
Jarvis Rd DE24 .... 231 F1
Jasmin CI NG20 .... 119 E3
Jasmine Ct
  Burton u T DE15 .... 255 D4
  Derby DE21 .... 220 A3
  Swanwick DE55 .... 169 F4
Jaspers La S43 .... 153 D1
Jaunty Ave S12 .... 44 B2
Jaunty CI S12 .... 44 A2
Jaunty Cres S12 .... 44 B2
Jaunty Dr S12 .... 44 A2
Jaunty La S12 .... 44 A2
Jaunty Mount S12 .... 44 A2
Jaunty PI S12 .... 44 A2
Jaunty Rd S12 .... 44 B2
Jaunty View S12 .... 44 B2
Jaunty Way S12 .... 44 A2
Jaw Bones Hill S40 .... 115 D4
Jawbone La DE73 .... 252 B4
Jebb's La Idridgehay DE56 .... 176 C4
  Shottle DE56 .... 177 D4
Jedburgh CI Derby DE24 .... 231 F1
  Nottingham NG3 .... 268 B2
Jefferson PI DE24 .... 232 C4
Jeffery St S2 .... 43 D3
Jeffrey La S33 .... 51 D3
Jeffries Ave DE4 .... 156 C1
Jeffries La DE4 .... 156 C1
Jellicoe St NG20 .... 120 C3
Jemison CI DE23 .... 230 C4
Jenford St NG18 .... 268 A3
Jennison St NG19 .... 136 A1
Jenny's Ct DE56 .... 179 E3
Jephson Rd DE14 .... 254 A4
Jeremy CI ST4 .... 269 D1
Jermyn Ave S12 .... 44 C2
Jermyn CI S12 .... 44 C2
Jermyn Cres S12 .... 44 C2
Jermyn Dr S12 .... 44 C2
Jermyn Way S12 .... 44 C2
Jermyngham St ST16 .... 269 D4
Jersey Gdns NG3 .... 268 C2
Jersey Rd S2 .... 43 D4
Jervis Ct DE7 .... 194 C2
Jervis St DE1 .... 97 D3
Jesses La DE56 .... 178 B4
Jessop Ave NG16 .... 170 C2
Jessop Dr DE24 .... 231 F1
Jessop St Codnor DE5 .... 181 D4
  Ripley DE5 .... 181 D4
Jimmy CI DE65 .... 239 E4
Joan Ave DE75 .... 181 F1
Joan La S33 .... 40 B2
Jodrell Ave DE56 .... 179 E2
Jodrell Meadow SK23 .... 45 E4
Jodrell Rd SK23 .... 45 E4
Jodrell St S22 .... 33 D4
John Bank La DE45 .... 108 C4
John Berrysford CI DE21 .... 219 F3
John Dalton St DE1 .... 9 F3
John Davies Prim Sch
  NG7 .... 148 C2
John Duncan Sch SK17 .... 66 A1
John Eaton's Almshouses
  S8 .... 43 D1
John F Kennedy Gdns
  DE21 .... 220 B3
John Flamsteed Com Sch
  DE5 .... 180 A1
John Kennedy Gdn SK14 .... 9 D4

John Kennedy Rd SK14 .... 9 D2
John King Inf Sch NG16 .... 160 B2
John King Workshop Mus
  NG16 .... 160 B2
John Lombe Dr DE1 .... 219 D4
John O'Gaunts Way DE56 .... 179 E2
John of Rolleston
  Prim Sch DE13 .... 240 A2
John Port Cl DE65 .... 229 E2
John Port L Ctr DE65 .... 229 D2
John Port Sch DE65 .... 229 D2
John St Alfreton DE55 .... 159 D2
  Brimington S43 .... 96 C4
  Chesterfield S40 .... 95 F2
  Clay Cross S45 .... 131 E2
  Clowne S43 .... 80 B2
  Compstall SK6 .... 15 D2
  Creswell S80 .... 81 F1
  Derby DE1 .... 267 C2
  Eckington S21 .... 59 E2
  Glossop SK13 .... 17 E4
  Heanor DE75 .... 181 E1
  Ilkeston DE7 .... 194 C1
  Marple SK6 .... 23 D3
  Matlock DE4 .... 143 D3
  North Wingfield S42 .... 131 F4
  Somercotes DE55 .... 170 B4
  Stafford ST16 .... 269 F4
  Swadlincote, Albert Village
  DE11 .... 256 B1
  Swadlincote, Lower Medway
  DE11 .... 256 B3
  Swadlincote, Newhall DE11 ...... 255 F3
John Turner Rd DE4 .... 127 E2
John Wright La DE56 .... 75 D2
Johnson Ave DE24 .... 232 C4
Johnson Dr DE75 .... 181 F1
Johnson La
  Idridgehay DE56 .... 176 C4
  Sheldon DE45 .... 107 F3
Johnson Rd ST14 .... 210 A1
Johnson St SK23 .... 45 F4
Johnson Way SK23 .... 47 E3
Johnstone CI S40 .... 266 A1
Jolly La DE6 .... 175 D4
Jones St S43 .... 10 A3
Jordan Ave DE13 .... 240 C1
Jordan St S13 .... 10 C1
Jordanthorpe Gn S8 .... 57 E3
Jordanthorpe Parkway
  S8 .... 57 E3
Jordanthorpe Sch S8 .... 57 D3
Jordanthorpe View S8 .... 57 E4
Joseph St Belper DE56 .... 179 D1
  Derby DE23 .... 219 D1
  Eckington S21 .... 59 E2
  Marple SK6 .... 23 D3
Joseph Wright Terr DE1 .... 267 B4
Joyce Ave NG7 .... 268 A2
Jubalton CI DE24 .... 232 C3
Jubilee Ave DE5 .... 169 E1
Jubilee CI DE73 .... 252 A4
Jubilee Cres Clowne S43 .... 81 D2
  Killamarsh S21 .... 60 B3
  Whitwell S80 .... 81 F3
Jubilee Ct Belper DE56 .... 179 D1
  Wirksworth DE4 .... 165 F4
Jubilee Gdns
  New Mills SK22 .... 33 E4
  Whitwell S80 .... 81 F3
  Jubilee PI S80 .... 81 F3
Jubilee Rd
  Chapel-en-le-F SK23 .... 47 D3
  Derby DE24 .... 232 C2
  Whitwell S80 .... 81 F3
Jubilee St
  Kimberley NG16 .... 195 F4
  New Mills SK22 .... 33 E4
  Nottingham NG2 .... 268 C2
Jubilee Terr DE12 .... 262 C1
Judith Gr ST4 .... 269 F1
Judy Hill DE4 .... 127 F1
Julia Cres DE55 .... 146 C2
Julian CI DE7 .... 209 D3
Julie Ave DE75 .... 182 A1
Jumble Rd S11 .... 42 C1
Junction Rd NG10 .... 237 D3
Junction St DE1 .... 218 C2
Juniper CI NG16 .... 195 E4
Juniper Rise S21 .... 60 B3
Jura Ave DE5 .... 169 E1
Jury St DE1 .... 267 A3

Katherine St NG9 .... 223 F2
Katrine Wlk DE24 .... 231 F2
Kay Dr DE11 .... 255 F3
Kean PI DE24 .... 232 C4
Kearsley Rd S2 .... 43 D4
Kearyn St ST14 .... 269 E1
Keats Ave DE23 .... 218 A3
Keats CI NG10 .... 236 A3
Keats Dr DE11 .... 256 B3
Keats Rd Chesterfield S41 .... 95 F4
  Stonebroom DE55 .... 146 C2
Keats Way S42 .... 115 F2
Keble CI Burton u T DE15 .... 248 B1
  Derby DE1 .... 267 C1
Kedleston CI
  Burton u T DE13 .... 240 B1
  Derby DE22 .... 204 B1
  Long Eaton NG10 .... 236 A3
  Ripley DE5 .... 169 E2
Kedleston Dr DE7 .... 194 B2
Kedleston Gdns DE1 .... 267 A4
Kedleston Hall DE22 .... 203 F3
Kedleston Old Rd DE22 .... 218 B4

Kedleston Rd Buxton SK17 .... 85 E4
  Derby DE22 .... 204 A3
  Quarndon DE22 .... 204 A3
  Weston Underwood DE22 .... 203 F4
Kedleston St DE1 .... 267 A4
Keeling La DE4 .... 156 B2
Keepers La S18 .... 75 F2
Kegworth Ave DE23 .... 231 E3
Keilder Ct S40 .... 95 E1
Kelburn Ave S40 .... 95 E1
Keldholme La DE24 .... 233 E3
Kelham Gn NG3 .... 268 C2
Kelham Rd NG19 .... 268 A4
Kelmoor Rd DE24 .... 233 D4
Kelsons Ave SK17 .... 85 E3
Kelstedge La S45 .... 129 F3
Kelvedon Gdns NG3 .... 268 C2
Kelvin CI NG0 .... 223 E3
Kemble PI DE24 .... 232 C4
Kemp CI S21 .... 60 B3
Kemp Rd SK6 .... 23 E4
Kempton CI NG16 .... 195 F4
Kempton Park Rd DE24 .... 232 B4
Kempton Rd DE15 .... 248 A2
Kendal CI SK17 .... 85 E2
Kendal Dr S18 .... 56 C1
Kendal Rd S41 .... 95 F4
Kendal Wlk DE21 .... 205 E1
Kendon Ave DE23 .... 231 F3
Kendray CI DE56 .... 179 E3
Kendricks CI DE11 .... 257 D4
Kenilworth Ave DE23 .... 231 F4
Kenilworth Dr DE7 .... 208 B3
Kenilworth Rd
  Nottingham NG7 .... 268 A1
  Ripley DE5 .... 169 E1
Kenmere CI S45 .... 131 E1
Kenmore CI NG19 .... 268 A3
Kenmore Gdns NG3 .... 268 B2
Kennack CI DE55 .... 160 B3
Kennedy Ave
  Long Eaton NG10 .... 236 B3
  Mansfield Woodhouse
  NG19 .... 136 B2
Kennedy CI DE22 .... 220 A4
Kennedy Dr NG9 .... 209 F1
Kennet Paddock NG19 .... 136 B2
Kennet Vale S40 .... 95 E3
Kenning St S42 .... 84 C3
Kenning St S45 .... 131 E2
Kenninghall Cl S2 .... 43 E4
Kenninghall Dr S2 .... 43 E4
Kenninghall PI S2 .... 43 E4
Kenninghall Rd S2 .... 43 E4
Kensal Rise DE22 .... 218 A3
Kensington Ave DE75 .... 181 E1
Kensington CI NG19 .... 136 C3
Kensington Dr DE7 .... 208 C4
Kensington Jun Sch DE7 .... 209 D4
Kensington Rd
  Burton u T DE15 .... 248 A2
  Sandiacre NG10 .... 223 D2
Kensington St Derby DE1 .... 267 A3
  Ilkeston DE7 .... 208 C3
Kent Ave NG16 .... 171 D2
Kent House CI S12 .... 58 C4
Kent Rd Burton u T DE15 .... 254 C3
  Eastwood NG16 .... 195 E4
  Glossop SK13 .... 43 D3
Kent St Chesterfield S41 .... 115 E4
  Derby DE21 .... 219 F4
  Nottingham NG2 .... 268 B2
Kent's Bank Rd SK17 .... 85 E3
Kentmere CI S18 .... 56 C1
Kentwood Rd NG2 .... 268 C1
Kenwell Dr S17 .... 56 A3
Kenyon Rd S41 .... 96 C1
Keppel CI DE7 .... 180 C4
Kepple Gate DE5 .... 180 B4
Kernel CI DE23 .... 231 D4
Kerry Dr DE7 .... 192 C3
Kerry St DE21 .... 219 F4
Kerry's Yd DE56 .... 191 F4
Kershaw St SK13 .... 17 E4
Kershope Dr DE21 .... 206 A2
Kerwin CI S17 .... 55 E4
Kerwin Dr S17 .... 55 E4
Kerwin Rd S17 .... 55 E4
Kestrel Ave DE11 .... 256 C2
Kestrel CI Ilkeston DE7 .... 208 C2
  Killamarsh S21 .... 60 A4
  Marple SK6 .... 23 D2
Kestrel Dr S21 .... 59 D2
Kestrel Hts NG16 .... 170 C2
Kestrel Way DE15 .... 248 B2
Kestrels Croft DE24 .... 231 F2
Keswick Ave DE23 .... 231 F3
Keswick CI DE7 .... 208 B3
Keswick Ct NG10 .... 223 E2
Keswick Dr S41 .... 95 E4
Keswick PI S18 .... 56 C4
Keswick St NG2 .... 268 C1
Ketton Ave S8 .... 43 D2
Kevin CI DE21 .... 220 A4
Kew Cres Heanor DE75 .... 182 A1
  Sheffield S12 .... 44 A1
Kew Gdns DE22 .... 218 A3
Key St NG2 .... 268 C2
Keyhaven CI DE21 .... 219 F4
Keynsham CI DE24 .... 232 C4
Keys Rd DE55 .... 159 D1
Keys St DE1 .... 267 C4
Keyworth CI NG19 .... 268 A4
Kibworth CI DE21 .... 220 A4
Kidd Rd SK13 .... 9 D3
Kidsley CI ▯ NG40 .... 268 B2
Kilburn St NG40 .... 268 B2

Kilburn Inf & Jun Schs
  DE56 .... 191 F4
Kilburn La DE56 .... 179 F2
Kilburn Rd Belper DE56 .... 179 E2
  Sheffield S8 .... 56 C4
Kilburn Toll Bar DE56 .... 179 F1
Kilburn Way DE11 .... 255 F3
Kildale Gdns S20 .... 59 E4
Kildare Rd DE21 .... 220 A3
Kildonan Gr S12 .... 44 B2
Kilhallam Inf Sch S21 .... 60 C4
Kilhallam Jun Sch S21 .... 60 C4
Kilhallam La S21 .... 61 D3
Killingworth Ave DE24 .... 231 F2
Killis La Belper DE56 .... 179 E1
  Holbrook DE56 .... 191 E4
Kiln Bent Rd HD7 .... 3 D3
Kiln CI DE7 .... 193 F1
Kiln Croft DE65 .... 229 E2
Kiln La Hadfield SK13 .... 10 A3
  Parwich DE6 .... 151 E1
Kiln Way DE11 .... 256 B2
Kilnsey Ct DE23 .... 230 C3
Kilvington Ave S13 .... 44 A4
Kilvington Cres S13 .... 44 A4
Kilvington Rd S13 .... 44 A4
Kimberley CI NG16 .... 195 F3
Kimberley Dr DE15 .... 248 B2
Kimberley Prim Sch
  NG16 .... 195 F3
Kimberley Rd DE72 .... 221 D1
Kinder CI S13 .... 17 D4
Kinder Cres DE56 .... 168 A3
Kinder Dr SK6 .... 23 D3
Kinder Gr SK17 .... 85 D3
Kinder Rd Hayfield SK22 .... 25 E1
  Staveley S43 .... 97 D3
Kinder Row SK22 .... 25 F1
Kinder View SK22 .... 33 E4
Kinder Way SK17 .... 85 E4
Kinder Wlk DE22 .... 218 A3
King Alfred St DE22 .... 267 A2
King Charles Ct S13 .... 17 E4
King Charles St
  ▯ NG1 .... 268 A1
King Ecgbert Lower Sch
  S17 .... 55 E3
King Ecgbert Rd S17 .... 55 F3
King Ecgbert Upper Sch
  S17 .... 55 F3
King Edward Ave SK13 .... 10 B1
King Edward Fst Sch
  NG18 .... 268 C3
King Edward Gdns
  NG10 .... 223 D3
King Edward St
  Nottingham NG1 .... 268 B2
  Sandiacre NG10 .... 223 D3
  Shirebrook NG20 .... 119 F2
  Wirksworth DE4 .... 166 A4
King Edward VI High Sch
  ST17 .... 269 D3
King George Ave DE7 .... 208 C4
King George St
  Wessington DE55 .... 157 F4
  Wirksworth DE4 .... 165 F4
King St Alfreton DE55 .... 159 D2
  Ashbourne DE6 .... 173 E1
  Bakewell DE45 .... 109 E3
  Belper DE56 .... 178 C2
  Brimington S43 .... 77 F1
  Broadbottom SK14 .... 254 B4
  Burton u T DE14 .... 254 A4
  Clay Cross S45 .... 131 E2
  Clowne S43 .... 80 C2
  Derby DE1 .... 267 B4
  Duffield DE56 .... 190 C1
  Eastwood NG16 .... 182 C1
  Glossop SK13 .... 17 E4
  Hodthorpe S80 .... 82 B3
  Hollingworth SK14 .... 9 E3
  Ilkeston DE7 .... 194 C1
  Long Eaton NG10 .... 236 B4
  Mansfield NG18 .... 268 C4
  Mansfield Woodhouse
  NG19 .... 136 B1
  Middleton (Nr Wirksworth)
  DE4 .... 154 B3
  Nottingham NG1 .... 268 B2
  Pinxton NG16 .... 160 B2
  South Normanton DE55 .... 159 F3
  Tibshelf DE55 .... 148 A4
  Warsop Vale NG20 .... 120 B3
King St N S41 .... 96 A4
King St S S41 .... 115 D4
King William Ctr NG16 .... 170 C2
King William St NG16 .... 170 C2
King's CI SK17 .... 85 E2
King's Mead CI DE1 .... 267 A4
King's Mead Wlk DE1 .... 267 A4
King's Mills La DE72 .... 245 F3
King's PI NG1 .... 268 B1
King's Rd SK17 .... 85 E2
Kingfisher Ave DE11 .... 256 C2
Kingfisher CI DE3 .... 217 F2
Kingfisher Wlk DE24 .... 231 F1
Kings CI Carsington DE4 .... 164 C4
  Clowne S43 .... 80 C2
  Creswell S80 .... 81 F1
Kings Croft DE45 .... 108 C4
Kings Ct S17 .... 55 E3
Kings Ct DE22 .... 204 C2
Kings Ct DE1 .... 267 B4
Kings Dr Brinsley NG16 .... 182 C4
  Derby DE22 .... 218 A1
Kings Gate DE4 .... 247 F2
Kings Hill Hill DE4 .... 153 D1
Kings Mews S21 .... 59 F2

Kings Rd Sandiacre NG10 .... 223 D3
  Swadlincote DE11 .... 256 A3
Kings Way S80 .... 82 B3
Kingsbury CI DE15 .... 248 A2
Kingsbury Rd DE22 .... 218 A3
Kingsclere Ave DE21 .... 206 A1
Kingscroft Cl S17 .... 55 E4
Kingsdale CI NG10 .... 236 A3
Kingsfield Ind Est DE4 .... 165 F3
Kingsfield Rd DE4 .... 165 F4
Kingsgate S32 .... 72 B1
Kingsland Ave ST4 .... 269 D1
Kingsland CI DE21 .... 205 F1
Kingsley Ave
  Chesterfield S40 .... 114 C4
  Mansfield Woodhouse NG19 ..... 136 B3
Kingsley CI NG19 .... 136 B2
Kingsley Cres
  Long Eaton NG10 .... 236 A2
  Stonebroom DE55 .... 146 C2
Kingsley Ct NG19 .... 136 A3
Kingsley Rd DE22 .... 204 B2
Kingsley St DE24 .... 231 F3
Kingsmead Ave NG9 .... 209 E1
Kingsmead Hospl ST16 .... 269 E4
Kingsmead Ind Est DE22 .... 218 B3
Kingsmead Wlk DE22 .... 95 E1
Kingsmoor Fields SK13 .... 10 B2
Kingsmoor Rd SK13 .... 10 B1
Kingsmuir Rd DE3 .... 217 E2
Kingsthorpe CI NG19 .... 136 C1
Kingston Ave Ilkeston DE7 .... 209 D2
  Stafford ST16 .... 269 F4
Kingston Ct DE7 .... 207 E4
Kingston Rd
  Burton u T DE15 .... 248 B1
  Mansfield NG18 .... 268 C4
Kingston St DE1 .... 218 C4
Kingsway Derby DE22 .... 218 A3
  Heanor DE75 .... 181 E1
  Ilkeston DE7 .... 209 D3
  Stafford ST16 .... 269 D3
  Stoke-on-t ST4 .... 269 E2
Kingsway Cres DE56 .... 192 A4
Kingsway Hospl DE3 .... 218 A2
Kingsway Ind Est DE22 .... 218 B3
Kingsway Park Ct DE22 .... 218 B3
Kingsway Ret Pk DE22 .... 218 B3
Kingswood Ave DE56 .... 179 E3
Kingswood CI S41 .... 95 E4
Kinross Ave DE21 .... 219 E4
Kintyre Dr ▯ DE24 .... 231 E2
Kipling CI S18 .... 76 B4
Kipling Dr DE3 .... 217 E1
Kipling Rd S41 .... 95 F4
Kipling St ▯ NG18 .... 268 B4
Kirby La DE4 .... 142 A4
Kirk CI DE55 .... 180 B4
Kirk Dale Ave DE21 .... 220 C2
Kirk Hallam Com Sch
  DE7 .... 208 B3

Kirk Ireton CE Prim Sch
  DE6 .... 165 D1
Kirk Langley CE Prim Sch
  DE6 .... 202 C1
Kirk Leys Ave N DE21 .... 220 C2
Kirk Leys Ave S DE21 .... 220 C2
Kirk St DE1 .... 219 D4
Kirk's La DE56 .... 179 D2
Kirkby Ave Ilkeston DE7 .... 208 C3
  Sheffield S12 .... 44 A2
Kirkby Rd S12 .... 44 A2
Kirkby Way S12 .... 44 A2
Kirkby Way S12 .... 44 A2
Kirkcroft Ave S21 .... 60 B4
Kirkcroft Dr S21 .... 60 B3
Kirkcroft La S21 .... 60 B4
Kirkdale CI S40 .... 115 D4
Kirkdale Gdns NG10 .... 236 A3
Kirkdale Rd NG10 .... 236 A3
Kirkewhite Ave NG10 .... 236 B4
Kirkfield Dr DE72 .... 235 E4
Kirkham CI DE75 .... 181 E1
Kirkham Dr NG9 .... 223 F1
Kirkham La DE56 .... 168 A4
Kirkham St ST4 .... 269 E1
Kirkhill Sch S2 .... 43 E4
Kirkistown CI DE24 .... 233 A3
Kirkland Ave NG18 .... 268 A3
Kirkland Cl DE74 .... 247 D2
Kirkland La S14 .... 269 E1
Kirkland Way ▯ DE24 .... 231 E2
Kirkman Rd DE75 .... 206 A4
Kirkstead CI Derby DE21 .... 206 A1
  Pinxton NG16 .... 160 B2
Kirkstead Jun Sch S42 .... 160 B2
Kirkstead Rd NG16 .... 160 B2
Kirkstone CI NG10 .... 223 D1
Kirkstone Rd Buxton SK17 .... 85 E2
  Chesterfield S41 .... 95 E4
Kirton Ave NG10 .... 236 B4
Kishfield La S23 .... 45 D3
Kissingate L Ctr NG20 .... 119 F2
Kitchener Ave DE23 .... 231 F4
Kitchener Dr NG18 .... 268 C3
Kitchener Terr NG20 .... 101 D1
Kitson Ave NG16 .... 171 E2
Knab Rd DE4 .... 127 F2
Knabhall La DE4 .... 144 B3
Knapp Ave NG16 .... 182 C1
Knifesmithgate S40 .... 266 B3
Knight Ave ST16 .... 269 F4
Knight's La Bretby DE15 .... 249 D3
  Repton DE15 .... 249 D3

Knighton St S80 .... 131 F3
Knights Cl DE24 .... 231 F1
Knights Ct DE13 .... 240 C1
Knightsbridge DE22 .... 218 A3
Knightwake Rd SK22 .... 33 D4
Kniveton CE Prim Sch
DE6 .... 163 E1
Kniveton La DE6 .... 174 B2
Kniveton Pk DE7 .... 208 B4
Knob Fields DE11 .... 261 F4
Knob La DE56 .... 166 B3
Knoll Cl DE23 .... 231 D4
Knoll St S012 .... 23 C3
Knoll The Chesterfield S40 .... 94 C1
Dronfield S18 .... 57 E2
Mansfield NG18 .... 268 A3
Shirebrook NG20 .... 119 E2
Swadlincote DE11 .... 256 A3
Tansley DE4 .... 144 A3
Knowes Cl SK17 .... 85 E4
Knowes Cres SK17 .... 85 E4
Knowl Ave DE56 .... 178 C3
Knowl St S14 .... 269 E2
Knowle Ave SK23 .... 47 D3
Knowle Rd Sk6 .... 23 C3
Knowle Top S20 .... 59 F4
Knowles Hill DE13 .... 240 A2
Knowles Ind Est SK13 .... 33 E2
Knowleston Pl DE4 .... 143 E2
Knutsford La DE21 .... 205 E1
Kye La S26 .... 61 F3
Kyle Gr DE21 .... 206 A2
Kynance Cl Derby DE24 .... 233 E3
South Normanton DE55 .... 160 B3

Laburnam Cl S80 .... 81 F1
Laburnham Ct S44 .... 97 D2
Laburnum Ave NG20 .... 119 F3
Laburnum Cl Bolsover S44 .... 99 E1
Darley Dale DE4 .... 127 D2
Sandiacre NG10 .... 223 D4
South Normanton DE55 .... 160 A4
Laburnum Cres Derby DE22 .... 204 B2
Swanwick DE55 .... 170 A4
Laburnum Gr Derby DE22 .... 218 A3
Killamarsh S21 .... 60 B3
Mansfield Woodhouse
NG19 .... 136 A2
Laburnum Rd
Burton u T DE15 .... 254 C3
Swadlincote DE11 .... 256 A3
Laburnum St S14 .... 78 A1
Laburnum Way DE65 .... 229 E2
Laceby Cl NG19 .... 136 C2
Lacey Cl DE7 .... 194 B2
Lacey Fields Rd DE75 .... 182 A1
Ladbroke Gdns DE22 .... 217 F3
Ladies Spring Dr S17 .... 56 A4
Ladies Spring Gr S17 .... 56 A4
Ladle End La DE12 .... 253 E1
Lady Field Rd S80 .... 62 B4
Lady Grove Rd DE4 .... 127 F1
Lady Lea Rd DE21 .... 192 A3
Lady Ley Hill DE21 .... 192 A3
Lady Manners Sch DE45 .... 109 E2
Lady Mantle Cl DE73 .... 232 C1
Ladybank Rd Derby DE3 .... 217 E1
Mosborough S20 .... 59 C2
Ladybank View S21 .... 59 E2
Ladybower Cl DE11 .... 256 A1
Ladybower Ct ⑨ S17 .... 56 A3
Ladybower Dr S32 .... 53 D4
Ladybower La S43 .... 97 E4
Ladybower Rd DE21 .... 220 C2
Ladybrook La NG18 .... 268 A4
Ladybrook Pl NG19 .... 268 A4
Ladycroft Paddock DE22 .... 204 C2
Ladycross Inf Sch NG10 .... 223 D3
Ladyfields DE11 .... 256 B3
Ladyflatts Rd DE4 .... 165 F4
Ladygrove Cotts DE23 .... 219 D2
Ladylea Rd NG10 .... 236 A2
Ladypit Rd SK23 .... 33 F2
Ladysmith Rd DE22 .... 221 D1
Ladythorne Ave SK6 .... 23 D3
Ladywell Cl DE13 .... 240 C1
Ladywell Ct DE56 .... 179 D3
Ladywood Dr DE56 .... 179 D3
Ladywood Dr S40 .... 95 E4
Ladywood Prim Sch DE7 .... 208 B3
Ladywood Rd Dale DE7 .... 208 B3
Ilkeston DE7 .... 208 B3
Lake Ave Heanor DE75 .... 181 E2
Mansfield NG19 .... 268 A4
Lake Dr Derby DE24 .... 231 F4
Doveridge DE6 .... 211 D1
Lake Side Doveridge DE6 .... 211 D1
Hatfield SK13 .... 10 A3
Lakeside Ashbourne DE6 .... 173 F1
Bakewell DE45 .... 109 D4
Wingerworth S42 .... 114 C1
Lakeside Ave NG10 .... 236 B3
Lakeside Cres NG10 .... 236 B3
Lakeside Dr DE23 .... 231 D4
Lakeside Inf Sch NG10 .... 236 B3
Lamartine St NG3 .... 268 B2
Lamb Cres DE5 .... 169 F1
Lamb Hill Cl S13 .... 44 B4
Lambcroft Rd NG16 .... 160 B2
Lambe Ct DE23 .... 267 C1
Lambgates SK13 .... 10 A3
Lambhouse La DE56 .... 177 F3
Lambley Dr DE22 .... 204 B1
Lambourn Ct DE22 .... 205 D2

Lambourn Dr DE22 .... 205 D2
Lambourne Ave DE6 .... 185 E4
Lambpart La S33 .... 51 D4
Lambrook Cl DE13 .... 217 E1
Lambton Cl DE7 .... 194 C2
Lammascote Rd ST16 .... 269 E4
Lampad Cl DE73 .... 252 A4
Lampeter Cl DE21 .... 206 A1
Lanark St DE21 .... 219 F4
Lancaster Ave
Sandiacre NG10 .... 223 D2
Stapleford NG9 .... 223 F4
Lancaster Dr DE13 .... 239 D3
Lancaster Rd S41 .... 95 F4
Lancaster Sports Ctr DE1 .... 267 B4
Lancaster St S44 .... 117 F1
Lancaster Wlk DE21 .... 221 D3
Lancelot Cl S40 .... 114 A4
Lancelot Dr DE13 .... 240 C1
Lancing Rd S2 .... 43 D4
Landau Forte Coll DE1 .... 267 C4
Lander La DE56 .... 179 D2
Landmere Cl DE7 .... 194 B2
London Cl S40 .... 114 A4
Lansdowne Gr NG10 .... 223 F1
Landseer Cl Dronfield S18 .... 56 C1
Sheffield S14 .... 43 E1
Landseer Pl S14 .... 43 E1
Landseer Wlk S14 .... 43 E1
Lane Head Longnor SK17 .... 121 D4
Stoney Middleton S32 .... 71 E2
Lane Head Rd Totley S17 .... 55 E2
Whaley Bridge SK23 .... 45 E3
Lane The Awsworth NG16 .... 195 E2
Spinkhill S21 .... 60 B1
Lanes The DE4 .... 155 D2
Lanesend Cotts SK23 .... 46 A4
Laneside Ave NG9 .... 223 F1
Laneside Cl SK23 .... 47 D3
Laneside Rd New Mills SK22 .... 33 F4
Rowarth SK22 .... 24 C3
Laneward Cl DE7 .... 194 B2
Lang Rd DE24 .... 232 C3
Langdale Cl S40 .... 94 C3
Langdale Dr Derby DE21 .... 205 E1
Dronfield S18 .... 57 E2
Long Eaton NG10 .... 236 A3
Langdale Sq S43 .... 96 B4
Langdon Cl NG10 .... 223 D1
Langer Cl DE14 .... 254 A3
Langer Field Ave S40 .... 115 D4
Langer La
Chesterfield S40, S42 .... 114 C3
Wingerworth S40, S42 .... 114 C3
Langford Rd Derby DE3 .... 217 E2
Mansfield NG19 .... 268 A3
Langham Pl NG18 .... 268 A4
Langhurst Rd S40 .... 95 E2
Langley Ave Ilkeston DE7 .... 194 B3
Somercotes DE55 .... 170 B4
Langley Cl
⑧ Chesterfield S40 .... 95 D3
Mansfield NG19 .... 135 F1
Langley Ct SK13 .... 10 A3
Langley Dr SK13 .... 17 F4
Langley Inf Sch DE75 .... 182 A1
Langley Mill CE Inf Sch
NG16 .... 182 A2
Langley Mill Jun Sch
NG16 .... 182 A2
Langley Mill Sta NG16 .... 182 A2
Langley Pk NG16 .... 182 A2
Langley Rd DE21 .... 220 C2
Langley St DE22 .... 218 B3
Langsett Dr DE73 .... 233 D1
Langsett La S14 .... 43 F1
Langstone Ave S44 .... 99 E1
Langton Hollow NG16 .... 171 E3
Langtree Ave S41 .... 77 D1
Langwith Bassett Prim
Sch NG20 .... 100 C3
Langwith Ctry Pk NG20 .... 100 C1
Langwith Dr NG20 .... 100 C1
Langwith Maltings NG20 .... 119 F4
Langwith Rd Bolsover S44 .... 118 B4
Shirebrook NG20 .... 119 F3
Lansbury Ave
Mastin Moor S43 .... 79 D2
Pilsley S45 .... 132 B1
Lansbury Dr DE55 .... 160 A3
Lansbury Rd S21 .... 59 E2
Lanscombe Park Rd
DE22 .... 204 C1
Lansdowne Ave S41 .... 95 F3
Lansdowne Rd
Branston DE14 .... 253 F4
Brimington S43 .... 96 B4
Buxton SK17 .... 66 A1
Swadlincote DE11 .... 256 A2
Lansing Gdns DE21 .... 220 A3
Lant La DE4 .... 144 A4
Lantern View SK22 .... 24 A1
Lapwing Cl DE24 .... 231 F1
Larch Ave Killamarsh S21 .... 60 B3
Mansfield Woodhouse
NG19 .... 136 A3
Ripley DE5 .... 169 E1
Shirebrook NG20 .... 119 E2
Larch Cl DE22 .... 204 B2
Larch Cres NG16 .... 182 C1
Larch Rd Eckington S21 .... 59 D1
Kilburn DE56 .... 192 A4
Swadlincote DE11 .... 255 F3
Larch Way Chesterfield S40 .... 95 E3
Glossop SK13 .... 17 F4

Larchdale Cl DE55 .... 160 A2
Larges St DE1 .... 218 C3
Lark Cl DE13 .... 253 E3
Larkdale St NG7 .... 268 A2
Larkhill DE55 .... 169 F4
Larkhill Cl DE55 .... 169 F4
Larkhill Cres DE24 .... 231 F2
Larkin Cl DE24 .... 232 A3
Larklands Ave DE7 .... 209 D4
Larklands Inf Sch DE7 .... 209 D4
Larkspur Cl
Mansfield NG19 .... 136 B1
South Normanton DE55 .... 160 A2
Larkspur Ct DE21 .... 206 A2
Larkstone La DE6 .... 149 D1
Larpit Gn S80 .... 82 A3
Lascelles Rd SK17 .... 85 D4
Lashley Cl DE21 .... 205 F1
Latham Cl DE15 .... 248 B1
Lathbury Cl DE21 .... 205 E1
Lathkil Dr DE55 .... 159 F3
Lathkil Gr SK17 .... 85 E4
Lathkill Ave Derby DE24 .... 233 E4
Ilkeston DE7 .... 194 C3
Staveley S43 .... 97 E3
Lathkill Cl Sheffield S13 .... 44 B4
West Hallam DE7 .... 207 F4
Lathkill Dale DE11 .... 255 F1
Lathkill Dr Ashbourne DE6 .... 185 D4
Ripley DE5 .... 180 B3
Selston NG16 .... 171 E4
Lathkill Gr Clay Cross S45 .... 131 E1
Tibshelf DE55 .... 147 F3
Lathkill Rd Derby DE21 .... 219 F4
Sheffield S13 .... 44 B4
Lathkilldale Cres NG10 .... 236 A3
Latimer Cl DE23 .... 230 C4
Latimer St DE24 .... 232 B3
Latrigg Cl DE7 .... 217 F1
Lauder Cl DE24 .... 231 E1
Launceston Rd DE24 .... 233 D3
Laund Ave DE56 .... 179 D3
Laund Cl DE56 .... 179 D3
Laund Hill DE56 .... 179 D3
Laund Nook DE56 .... 179 D3
Launds Ave NG16 .... 171 E4
Laurel Ave
Long Duckmanton S44 .... 97 E2
Mansfield NG19 .... 136 C1
Mansfield NG18 .... 268 C3
Ripley DE5 .... 169 F1
Laurel Cl Eckington S21 .... 59 E1
Shirebrook NG20 .... 119 E3
Swanwick DE55 .... 170 A4
Laurel Cres Brimington S43 .... 78 A1
Long Eaton NG10 .... 236 B3
Smalley DE7 .... 192 C3
Laurel Dr S21 .... 60 B3
Laurel Garth Cl S41 .... 77 D2
Laurel Gr Burton u T DE15 .... 254 C3
South Normanton DE55 .... 160 A3
Laurence Cl S41 .... 77 D1
Laurie Pl DE24 .... 232 C4
Lavender Cl DE55 .... 170 A4
Lavender Row ⑦ DE22 .... 204 C1
Laverdene Ave S17 .... 55 F2
Laverdene Cl S17 .... 55 F2
Laverdene Dr S17 .... 55 F2
Laverdene Rd S17 .... 55 F2
Laverdene Way S17 .... 55 F2
Laverick Rd NG16 .... 171 C2
Lawn Ave Derby DE65 .... 204 B1
Etwall DE65 .... 229 E3
Lawn Cl DE75 .... 181 F1
Lawn Heads Ave DE23 .... 218 B1
Lawn Mill Rd NG16 .... 195 F4
Lawn Prim Sch DE22 .... 204 B1
Lawn Rd DE17 .... 269 D3
Lawn The S18 .... 57 D1
Lawn Villas S44 .... 97 D1
Lawnfold SK13 .... 9 F2
Lawnlea Cl DE23 .... 231 F3
Lawns Dr DE11 .... 256 A4
Lawns The
Aston-on-T DE72 .... 246 A4
Rolleston DE13 .... 240 A2
Uttoxeter ST14 .... 210 A1
Lawnside DE21 .... 220 C3
Lawnswood Cl DE23 .... 231 E4
Lawrence Ave
Awsworth NG16 .... 195 E2
Breaston DE72 .... 235 F4
Derby DE21 .... 220 A4
Eastwood NG16 .... 182 C1
Holmewood S42 .... 116 B1
Mansfield Woodhouse NG19 .... 136 A2
Ripley DE5 .... 180 B4
Lawrence Dr NG16 .... 182 B4
Lawrence St Derby DE23 .... 231 F4
Long Eaton NG10 .... 236 B4
Sandiacre NG9 .... 223 D3
Stafford ST17 .... 269 E3
Stapleford NG9 .... 223 F3
Lawson Ave NG10 .... 236 C4
Lawson St NG7 .... 268 A2
Laxfield Cl S40 .... 114 B4
Layton Ave NG18 .... 268 B4
Layton Burroughs
⑩ NG18 .... 268 B4
Layton Dr S41 .... 77 D1
Lea Cl DE22 .... 204 C2
Lea Cres DE55 .... 170 B3
Lea Dr
Derby, Chaddesden DE21 .... 219 F3
Derby, Mickleover DE3 .... 217 F2
Lea La NG16 .... 171 F3
Lea Main Rd DE4 .... 156 A4
Lea Moor Rd DE4 .... 156 C4

Lea Prim Sch DE4 .... 156 A4
Lea Rd Cromford DE4 .... 155 F3
Dronfield S18 .... 57 D1
Hayfield SK22 .... 26 C2
Holloway DE4 .... 156 A4
Lea St SK22 .... 33 D4
Lea Vale DE55 .... 160 A2
Lea Wood Croft DE4 .... 156 A3
Leabrook Rd S18 .... 56 B1
Leabrooks Ave NG19 .... 136 B3
Leabrooks Rd DE55 .... 170 B4
Leacroft Rd Derby DE22 .... 219 D1
Winster DE4 .... 141 E3
Leadale Ave DE55 .... 170 A4
Leadale Cres NG19 .... 136 C3
Leadbeater Ave ST4 .... 269 D1
Leadbeater Rd S12 .... 44 A2
Leafenden Cl DE22 .... 205 D2
Leafgreen La DE23 .... 231 E3
Leafield Rd SK12 .... 32 B3
Leafy La DE75 .... 181 F1
Leake St DE22 .... 218 B3
Leam Glen NG19 .... 136 B1
Leamington Cl DE23 .... 218 B1
Leamington Dr DE55 .... 160 A3
Leamington Rd DE14 .... 253 F4
Leamington St DE5 .... 169 F1
Leamoor Ave DE55 .... 170 A4
Lean Town SK13 .... 17 E3
Leander Cl DE23 .... 231 E4
Leander Rise DE15 .... 255 D4
Leaper St DE1 .... 218 C3
Leapley La Alkmonton DE6 .... 199 E2
Yeaveley DE6 .... 199 E2
Leas Ave NG19 .... 136 B3
Leas Park Jun Sch NG19 .... 136 B2
Leas Rd NG19 .... 136 B2
Leashaw Crich DE4 .... 156 B2
Leashaw Rd Crich DE4 .... 156 B2
Holloway DE4 .... 156 B2
Leaside Rd S14 .... 269 D1
Leason St ST4 .... 269 D2
Leathersley La
Scropton DE6 .... 226 B1
Sudbury DE6 .... 226 B1
Leaway The NG20 .... 119 E2
Leawood Gdns DE21 .... 206 A2
Leawood Pump Ho DE4 .... 155 F2
Leawood Rd DE11 .... 256 B4
Leche Cft DE56 .... 179 E2
Lechlade Cl DE7 .... 207 E4
Ledbury Chase DE24 .... 231 E1
Ledbury Pl DE21 .... 205 E1
Ledo Ave DE5 .... 169 E1
Lee Cres DE7 .... 209 D4
Lee Dale S17 .... 85 E2
Lee Farm Cl DE23 .... 232 C1
Lee Head SK13 .... 16 B3
Lee La DE75 .... 182 A1
Lee Mount SK13 .... 17 E4
Lee Rd S41 .... 96 A3
Lee Vale Dr S13 .... 16 B4
Leebangs Rd SK14 .... 16 A4
Leech Cl NG16 .... 195 F4
Leedhams Croft DE12 .... 259 E4
Leeds Pl DE1 .... 267 D2
Leeds Rd S81 .... 63 F4
Leefield Rd SK23 .... 47 D3
Leek Rd Buxton SK17 .... 84 C3
Longnor SK17 .... 121 D3
Stoke-on-T ST4 .... 269 D2
Leeming La NG19, NG20 .... 136 C4
Leeming La N NG19 .... 136 C3
Leeming La S NG19 .... 136 B1
Leeming Pk NG19 .... 136 B2
Leeming St NG18 .... 268 B4
Leen Valley Dr NG20 .... 119 F2
Lees Brook Com Sch
DE21 .... 220 A4
Lees Hall Ave S8 .... 43 D2
Lees Hall Pl S8 .... 43 D3
Lees Hall Rd S8 .... 43 D3
Lees Hill St NG2 .... 268 C1
Lees House Ct S8 .... 43 D2
Lees La DE55 .... 159 F3
Lees Nook S8 .... 43 D2
Lees Rd DE4 .... 126 C2
Lees Row SK13 .... 10 A3
Lees The DE24 .... 233 E3
Leese St ST4 .... 269 E2
Leeside Rd S33 .... 40 B2
Leeswood Cl S41 .... 95 F4
Leeway DE21 .... 220 B2
Leicester Dr SK13 .... 17 F4
Leicester St
Burton u T DE14 .... 254 B4
Derby DE22 .... 218 C2
Long Eaton NG10 .... 236 C3
Leigh Rd Beeston NG9 .... 223 F2
Disley SK12 .... 32 A3
Leigh Way S42 .... 114 B2
Leighton Dr Marple SK6 .... 23 E4
Sheffield S14 .... 43 F2
Leighton Pl S14 .... 43 F2
Leighton St S43 .... 44 A2
Leighton View S2 .... 43 F3
Leisure La SK17 .... 137 F3
Leman St DE22 .... 218 C2
Lemont Rd S17 .... 55 F2
Leniscar Ave DE75 .... 181 E2
Lennox St NG3 .... 268 B2
Lens Rd DE22 .... 204 B1
Lenthall Inf Sch S18 .... 57 D2
Lenton Ave Derby DE21 .... 219 F3
Nottingham NG7 .... 268 A1
Lenton Rd NG7 .... 268 A1
Lenton St NG10 .... 223 E4
Leominster Dr DE21 .... 206 A1
Leonard Cl Derby DE23 .... 267 B1
Sheffield S2 .... 44 A4
Leonard St DE23 .... 267 C1
Leonard Way NG16 .... 182 B1
Leopold St Derby DE1 .... 267 B2
Long Eaton NG10 .... 236 B4
Leslie Ave NG16 .... 195 F3
Leslie Cl DE23 .... 230 C4
Lesser La SK17 .... 85 F4
Level La SK17 .... 84 B3
Leven Cl DE24 .... 231 F1
Levens Way S41 .... 95 F4
Leveret Cl DE73 .... 233 D1
Leverton Rd NG19 .... 268 A4
Lewcote La DE7 .... 194 C3
Lewis Cl NG3 .... 268 B2
Lewis St Derby DE23 .... 218 C1
Stoke-on-T ST4 .... 269 E2
Lexington Rd DE21 .... 220 B3
Ley Ave DE55 .... 159 D2
Ley Croft Hatton DE65 .... 227 E1
Mansfield Woodhouse
NG19 .... 136 B3
Ley Gdns DE55 .... 159 D2
Ley La
Mansfield Woodhouse
NG19 .... 136 B2
Marple SK6 .... 23 E4
Leyburn Cl S40 .... 95 F3
Leycote Way DE56 .... 179 D3
Leyfield Rd S17 .... 55 E4
Leygate View SK22 .... 33 D4
Leyland Cl NG9 .... 223 F1
Leyland Cres DE7 .... 218 C4
Leyland Ct DE1 .... 218 C4
Leyland Gdns DE1 .... 218 C4
Leyland St DE1 .... 218 C4
Leylands DE22 .... 218 C4
Leylands La S14 .... 15 F4
Leys Ct DE56 .... 179 E2
Leys Field Gdns DE73 .... 233 D1
Leys Jun Sch DE55 .... 159 E2
Leys La DE4 .... 154 A4
Leys The Little Eaton DE21 .... 191 E1
Swadlincote DE11 .... 255 F3
Leytonstone Dr DE22 .... 218 A3
Lichfield Ave DE11 .... 256 C3
Lichfield Cl NG9 .... 223 F2
Lichfield Ct ST17 .... 269 E4
Lichfield Dr DE24 .... 233 D4
Lichfield Rd
Burton u Turn DE14 .... 253 E2
Branston DE14 .... 253 E2
Chesterfield S40 .... 114 B4
Stafford ST17 .... 269 E3
Lichford Rd S2 .... 44 A4
Lickpenny La DE4 .... 144 C2
Lid La DE6 .... 197 F4
Liddle St S14 .... 269 E1
Lidgate Cl DE3 .... 217 E1
Liffs Rd Alsop en le D DE6 .... 150 B4
Biggin SA17 .... 138 B1
Light Alders La S12 .... 32 A3
Lightfoot Rd S14 .... 210 A1
Lightwood Ave ⑧ SK17 .... 85 E4
Lightwood House Hospl
S8 .... 43 F1
Lightwood La
Middle Handley S21 .... 77 F4
Sheffield S8 .... 43 F1
Lightwood Rd Buxton SK17 .... 66 A1
Marsh Lane S21 .... 58 C1
Lilac Ave DE22 .... 218 A3
Lilac Cl Derby DE24 .... 233 D3
Holmewood S44 .... 116 C1
Lilac Gr Bolsover S44 .... 99 E1
Burton u T DE15 .... 254 C3
Glapwell S44 .... 134 A4
Heanor DE75 .... 181 F1
Market Warsop NG20 .... 120 C4
Shirebrook NG20 .... 119 F3
South Normanton DE55 .... 160 A2
Lilac Mews DE7 .... 194 B2
Lilac St S43 .... 78 A1
Lilac Way Derby DE22 .... 204 B1
Shirland DE55 .... 146 B1
Lilian Prime Cl DE24 .... 233 D4
Lilley St DE24 .... 233 D3
Lillymede Cl S40 .... 114 C3
Lilybank Cl DE4 .... 143 E3
Lilypools The DE73 .... 252 A4
Limb La S17 .... 55 E4
Limbersitch La DE55 .... 227 F3
Lime Ave
Derby, Breadsall Hilltop
DE21 .... 205 E1
Derby, Rose Hill DE1 .... 267 A1
Duffield DE56 .... 190 C3
Langley Mill NG16 .... 182 B1
New Mills SK22 .... 24 B1
Ripley DE5 .... 169 E1
Staveley S43 .... 78 C1
Lime Cl Calow S44 .... 97 D2
Doveridge DE6 .... 224 B4
Hatton DE65 .... 227 E1
Pinxton NG16 .... 160 B2
Lime Cres Belper DE56 .... 179 D3
Mansfield NG19 .... 120 C4
Lime Gr Ashbourne DE6 .... 185 E4
Burton u T DE13 .... 254 C3
Darley Dale DE4 .... 127 E2
Derby DE21 .... 220 A3
Draycott DE72 .... 234 C4
Long Eaton NG10 .... 236 A3
Sandiacre NG10 .... 223 D3
South Normanton DE55 .... 160 A3
Stapleford NG9 .... 223 E3

ime Grove Ave DE4 ..... 143 E3
ime Grove Wlk DE4 ..... 143 E3
ime Kiln La Marple SK6 ..... 23 D3
Turnditch DE56 ..... 189 D4
ime La Derby DE21 ..... 206 A2
Morley DE7 ..... 206 B3
ime Rd S21 ..... 59 D1
ime St Ilkeston DE7 ..... 208 C4
Stoke-on-T ST4 ..... 269 E1
ime Terr NG10 ..... 236 B4
ime Tree Ave
Darley Dale DE4 ..... 127 D2
Glapwell S44 ..... 134 A4
Killamarsh S21 ..... 60 B3
Mansfield Woodhouse
NG19 ..... 136 A3
Swadlincote DE11 ..... 256 A4
ime Tree Gr
Clay Cross S45 ..... 131 F1
Long Duckmanton S44 ..... 97 E2
ime Tree Pl NG18 ..... 268 C3
ime Tree Rd DE4 ..... 143 E3
ime Wlk DE23 ..... 218 B1
imecroft View S42 ..... 115 D2
medale Ave DE21 ..... 206 A2
imekiln Fields Rd S44 ..... 99 D2
imerick Rd DE21 ..... 220 A2
imes Av Derby DE3 ..... 217 E1
Nether Langwith NG20 ..... 101 D1
imes Cl The DE4 ..... 143 E3
imes Cres NG20 ..... 119 E3
imes Pk DE5 ..... 169 E1
imes The DE7 ..... 193 F2
imestone Terr NG19 ..... 136 A2
imetree Cl S43 ..... 96 C3
imetree Rise DE7 ..... 208 B3
immen Gdns NG3 ..... 268 C2
impenny St NG7 ..... 268 A4
inacre Ave S45 ..... 131 E1
inacre Rd Chesterfield S40 ..... 95 D3
Old Brampton S40 ..... 95 D3
inacre Way S13 ..... 17 F4
inacres Dr DE73 ..... 233 D1
inbery Cl DE55 ..... 158 A2
incoln Ave Derby DE24 ..... 233 D4
Sandiacre NG10 ..... 223 C4
incoln Cir NG7 ..... 268 A1
incoln Cl Stapleford NG9 ..... 209 F1
Tibshelf DE55 ..... 148 A3
incoln Dr NG19 ..... 136 B2
incoln Gn DE73 ..... 232 C1
incoln Rd DE15 ..... 254 B4
incoln St Alfreton DE55 ..... 158 C2
Chesterfield S40 ..... 115 D4
Nottingham NG3 ..... 268 B2
Tibshelf DE55 ..... 148 A3
incoln Way Glossop SK13 ..... 17 F4
Swadlincote DE11 ..... 256 C3
indale Rd S41 ..... 76 B1
inden Ave
Chesterfield S40 ..... 95 D1
Clay Cross S45 ..... 131 E1
Dronfield S18 ..... 57 D2
inden Cl DE56 ..... 192 A4
inden Ct S45 ..... 131 E1
inden Dr S41 ..... 115 E3
inden Gr Matlock DE4 ..... 143 D2
Sandiacre NG10 ..... 223 D4
Shirebrook NG20 ..... 119 F2
Stapleford NG9 ..... 223 F3
inden Park Gr S40 ..... 95 E2
inden Rd S80 ..... 81 F1
inden St Mansfield NG19 ..... 136 A1
Shirebrook NG20 ..... 119 F2
inden Way S46 ..... 32 A4
indford Cl DE21 ..... 205 F2
indisfarne Cl ■ DE24 ..... 231 E2
indisfarne Ct ■ S40 ..... 95 E1
indisfarne Rd S18 ..... 76 A4
indley St Mansfield NG18 ..... 268 B4
Selston NG16 ..... 171 E3
indon Dr DE24 ..... 233 E3
indrick Cl Derby DE21 ..... 217 F1
Mansfield Woodhouse
NG19 ..... 136 B3
indrick Gdns S40 ..... 114 B4
indsay Cl NG18 ..... 268 B3
indsey Cl DE21 ..... 219 F3
indum Gr S42 ..... 268 C1
indway La
Brackenfield DE55 ..... 145 D1
Crich DE55 ..... 145 D1
ng La S44 ..... 114 B4
ng Rd S40 ..... 114 B4
ngfield Rd DE4 ..... 253 F4
ngfield Rise DE7 ..... 217 E2
ngfoot Cl S8 ..... 57 D3
ngfoot Cl S8 ..... 57 D3
ngfoot Cres S8 ..... 57 D3
ngfoot Dr S8 ..... 57 D3
ngfoot Pl S8 ..... 57 D3
ngfoot Rd S8 ..... 57 D3
nglongs Ave SK23 ..... 45 E3
nglongs Rd SK23 ..... 45 E3
ngs Cres S42 ..... 132 A4
nkmel Rd NG16 ..... 182 B2
nks Cl DE24 ..... 231 F2
nks Rd
Chapel-en-le-F SK23 ..... 46 C3
Dronfield S18 ..... 76 A4
nley La S12 ..... 44 B3
nley Way S41 ..... 269 D2
nmell St NG3 ..... 268 C2
nnet Cl DE21 ..... 220 C3
nnet Ho S41 ..... 77 D2
nscott Cl S41 ..... 95 E4
nshaws Rd HD7 ..... 3 F3
nslin Prim Sch DE12 ..... 261 E3

Linton Rd Chesterfield S40 ..... 114 B4
Linton DE11 ..... 261 F4
Rosliston DE12 ..... 260 C3
Linwood Cres NG16 ..... 182 C1
Linwood Ct NG19 ..... 136 C2
Linwood La DE7 ..... 269 E2
Lionel Gr ST4 ..... 269 D1
Lipp Ave S21 ..... 60 B4
Liskeard Dr DE22 ..... 204 B2
Lismore Ct ■ DE24 ..... 231 E2
Lismore Gr SK17 ..... 85 D4
Lismore Park SK17 ..... 85 D4
Lismore Rd Buxton SK17 ..... 85 D4
Sheffield S8 ..... 43 D3
Lissett Ave DE7 ..... 208 C4
Lister Ave S12 ..... 44 A2
Lister Cl Derby DE21 ..... 218 A2
Sheffield S12 ..... 44 A2
Lister Cres S12 ..... 44 A2
Lister Gate NG1 ..... 268 B1
Lister Pl S12 ..... 44 A2
Lister Way S12 ..... 44 A2
Liston Dr DE22 ..... 218 C4
Litchen Cl DE7 ..... 194 C1
Litchfield Cl NG16 ..... 237 D4
Lithurch La DE24 ..... 219 E1
Lithurch St DE7 ..... 267 C1
Little Acre NG19 ..... 136 C3
Little Bolehill DE4 ..... 155 D1
Little Breck DE55 ..... 160 A2
Little Bridge St DE1 ..... 218 C3
Little Brind Rd S40 ..... 95 D4
Little Debdale La NG19 ..... 135 F1
Little Eaton Prim Sch
DE21 ..... 205 E4
Little Fen DE55 ..... 147 F3
Little Hallam Hill DE7 ..... 208 C3
Little Hallam La DE7 ..... 209 D3
Little La
Ashford in t W DE45 ..... 89 F1
Kimberley NG16 ..... 195 F3
Litton SK17 ..... 69 F2
Pleasleyhill NG19 ..... 135 D3
Sheffield S12 ..... 44 A3
Shirebrook NG20 ..... 119 F2
Sutton in A NG17 ..... 148 C1
Thorpe Salvin S80 ..... 63 D3
Little London DE1 ..... 156 A3
Little Longstone Cl DE3 ..... 217 F1
Little Lunnon NG11 ..... 237 F3
Little Meadow Rd DE73 ..... 233 D1
Little Morton Rd S42, S45 ..... 132 A3
Little Norton Ave S8 ..... 57 D4
Little Norton Dr S8 ..... 57 D4
Little Norton La S8 ..... 57 D4
Little Norton Way S8 ..... 57 D4
Little Thorn Ind Est
DE11 ..... 256 C1
Little Wood Dr S12 ..... 44 A2
Little Wood Rd S12 ..... 44 A2
Little Woodbury Dr DE23 ..... 230 C3
Littlebrook Cl S13 ..... 10 A2
Littledale Cl DE22 ..... 206 B2
Littlefield La Ellastone DE6 ..... 183 D1
Snelston DE6 ..... 184 A2
Littlefield Rd DE65 ..... 241 F4
Littlefields S14 ..... 9 D2
Littlemoor Chesterfield S41 ..... 95 E4
Eckington S21 ..... 59 F2
Littlemoor Cres S41 ..... 95 E4
Littlemoor Ctr ■ S41 ..... 95 F4
Littlemoor La DE4 ..... 143 F1
Littlemoor Rd S14 ..... 9 D1
Littleover Com Sch DE23 ..... 230 C4
Littleover Cres DE23 ..... 218 B1
Littleover La DE23 ..... 231 F4
Littleton Cl ST16 ..... 269 F4
Littlewell La DE7 ..... 208 C1
Littlewood La NG19 ..... 136 A3
Littleworth NG18 ..... 268 C3
Litton CE Prim Sch SK17 ..... 69 F2
Litton Cl Belper DE56 ..... 179 D3
Ilkeston DE7 ..... 194 C2
Staveley S43 ..... 97 E4
Litton Dr DE21 ..... 220 C2
Litton Mews SK13 ..... 9 F1
Litton Rd NG19 ..... 136 C2
Liverpool Rd S14 ..... 269 E2
Liverpool St Derby DE21 ..... 219 F4
Nottingham NG3 ..... 268 C2
Liversage Pl DE1 ..... 267 C2
Liversage Rd DE1 ..... 267 C2
Liversage St DE1 ..... 267 C2
Livingstone Rd DE23 ..... 218 C1
Lloyd St Derby DE22 ..... 218 B3
Stafford DE5 ..... 269 E4
Loads Rd S42 ..... 113 D4
Loadshead La S42 ..... 112 B4
Lochinvar Cl DE21 ..... 220 C4
Lock Cl DE7 ..... 208 B3
Lock La Long Eaton NG10 ..... 236 B2
Sandiacre NG10 ..... 223 C4
Locke Way S16 ..... 269 F4
Lockington Cl DE73 ..... 232 C4
Lockington Rd DE74 ..... 247 E3
Locko Ct DE21 ..... 220 B3
Locko La S45 ..... 132 C2
Locko Rd Dale DE21 ..... 220 C4
Derby DE21 ..... 220 C4
Pilsley S45 ..... 132 B2
Lockoford La
Chesterfield, Stonegravels
S41 ..... 96 A3
Chesterfield, Tapton S41 ..... 96 B3
Lockoford Rd S41 ..... 96 A3
Lockside S45 ..... 23 D3
Lockton Ave DE75 ..... 193 F4

Lockwood Rd DE22 ..... 204 B2
Lode La DE6 ..... 149 F2
Lodge Ave DE6 ..... 185 D4
Lodge Bank S43 ..... 10 A3
Lodge Cl Calow S43 ..... 97 D2
Duffield DE56 ..... 190 C2
Etwall DE65 ..... 229 E2
Lodge Ct S14 ..... 9 D2
Lodge Dr Belper DE56 ..... 178 C3
Wingerworth S42 ..... 115 D2
Lodge Est DE7 ..... 222 B4
Lodge Farm Cl S40 ..... 114 B4
Lodge Hill DE13 ..... 239 F3
Lodge La Aldercar NG16 ..... 181 F4
Alstonefield DE6 ..... 149 D2
Derby, Little Chester DE1 ..... 267 A4
Derby, Spondon DE21 ..... 220 B2
Mackworth DE6, DE22 ..... 203 E3
Stoke-on-T ST4 ..... 269 D2
Lodge Mews DE7 ..... 246 A4
Lodge Moor Rd S10 ..... 42 C4
Lodge Pl S43 ..... 97 E3
Lodge Rd Eastwood NG16 ..... 195 D4
Long Eaton NG10 ..... 236 B3
Mapperley DE7 ..... 193 F2
Nethersea DE21 ..... 261 E1
Stoke-on-T ST4 ..... 269 D2
Lodge St DE7 ..... 235 D4
Lodge Wlk S43 ..... 97 E3
Lohengrin Ct DE13 ..... 240 C1
Lombard St DE22 ..... 217 F3
Lomond Ave DE24 ..... 231 F1
London Rd Buxton SK17 ..... 85 E3
Castle Donington DE74 ..... 247 D4
Derby DE24 ..... 219 E1
Nottingham NG2 ..... 268 B1
Stoke-on-T ST4 ..... 234 C1
Sheffield, Heeley S8 ..... 43 D3
Sheffield, Highfield S2 ..... 43 D4
Stoke-on-T S14 ..... 269 E1
London Rd S S2 ..... 43 D4
London St S43 ..... 77 D1
Long Acre View S20 ..... 60 A4
Long Bridge La DE24 ..... 232 B4
Long Causeway DE72 ..... 246 A4
Long Croft
Chapel-en-le-F SK23 ..... 47 D2
Charlesworth SK13 ..... 16 B4
Killamarsh S21 ..... 60 C3
Kirk Langley DE6 ..... 202 A1
Lees DE65 ..... 228 A2
Longford DE6 ..... 200 C1
Shipley DE75 ..... 194 B3
Shirebrook NG20 ..... 119 F2
Taddington SK17 ..... 87 F3
Thurvaston DE6 ..... 201 E1
Trusley DE6 ..... 201 E1
West Handley S21 ..... 77 E4
Whaley Bridge SK23 ..... 46 B2
Long Lane CE Prim Sch
DE6 ..... 201 F1
Long Meadow
Great Cubley DE6 ..... 198 C1
Mansfield Woodhouse NG19 ..... 136 B3
Mansfield Woodhouse NG18 ..... 158 C2
Long Rake SK45 ..... 123 E2
Long Row Belper DE56 ..... 178 C2
Nottingham NG1 ..... 268 B2
Shardlow DE72 ..... 235 D1
Long Row Prim Sch
DE56 ..... 178 C2
Long Row W NG1 ..... 268 B1
Long Shambles S40 ..... 266 B3
Long Stl S45 ..... 254 C4
Longacre Rd S18 ..... 76 A4
Longacre Way S20 ..... 60 A4
Longbow Cl DE13 ..... 240 B1
Longbow Cl DE13 ..... 240 B1
Longbridge La
Heanor DE75 ..... 181 E2
Peak Dale SK17 ..... 67 D2
Longclough Dr SK13 ..... 17 D4
Longcourse La S44 ..... 98 A1
Longcroft Ave S18 ..... 56 B1
Longcroft Cl S42 ..... 131 F4
Longcroft Cres ■ S18 ..... 56 B1
Longcroft Rd S18 ..... 56 B1
Longcroft View S80 ..... 82 A3
Longdale NG19 ..... 136 C1
Longdale Dr S14 ..... 9 D2
Longdale Gdns S14 ..... 9 D2
Longdon Cl NG19 ..... 209 F1
Longdon St S43 ..... 268 C2
Longdendale High Sch
SK14 ..... 9 E4
Longedge Gr S42 ..... 115 D2
Longedge La S42 ..... 114 C2
Longedge Rise S42 ..... 115 D2
Longfield Cres DE7 ..... 208 C3
Longfield La DE7 ..... 208 C3
Longfield Rd S14 ..... 266 A2
Longford CE Prim Sch DE6 ..... 204 B1
■ Sheffield S17 ..... 56 A3
Longford Cres S17 ..... 56 A3
Longford Dr S17 ..... 55 F2
Longford La DE6 ..... 214 C4

Longford Parochial CE
Prim Sch DE6 ..... 214 B4
Longford Rd S17 ..... 56 A2
Longford Spinney S17 ..... 55 F2
Longford St DE22 ..... 218 C4
Longhedge La
Burton u T DE13 ..... 239 F1
Pleasley NG19 ..... 134 C3
Longhurst La SK6 ..... 23 E3
Longhurst View S80 ..... 81 F3
Longlands DE55 ..... 158 A4
Longlands Dr SK22 ..... 33 D4
Longlands La DE65 ..... 230 B1
Longlands Rd
New Mills SK22 ..... 33 D4
Swadlincote DE11 ..... 256 B4
Longley La DE21 ..... 220 B3
Longload La DE4 ..... 154 C3
Longmeade Dr SK23 ..... 47 D2
Longmoor Gdns NG10 ..... 223 C1
Longmoor La
Breaston DE72 ..... 222 C1
Sandiacre NG10 ..... 222 C2
Longmoor Prim Sch
NG10 ..... 223 E2
Longmoor Rd Glossop SK13 ..... 17 D4
Long Eaton NG10 ..... 223 D1
Longmoor Mews SK13 ..... 9 E1
Longnor Mews SK13 ..... 90 B2
Longrose La DE6 ..... 163 E1
Longshaw Cl
Northwild S42 ..... 131 F3
Staveley S43 ..... 97 E4
Longshaw Ctry Pk S32 ..... 54 A2
Longside La DE55 ..... 112 C3
Longson Rd S43 ..... 47 E3
Longster La NG20 ..... 120 B2
Longstock Cl DE21 ..... 205 F1
Longstone CE Prim Sch
DE45 ..... 89 F2
Longstone Cres S12 ..... 44 B2
Longstone La DE45 ..... 89 F1
Longstone Rise DE56 ..... 179 D3
Longstone Wlk DE1 ..... 267 D3
Longwalls La DE56 ..... 178 B3
Longwood Inf Sch NG16 ..... 160 B1
Longwood Rd NG16 ..... 160 C1
Lons Inf Sch S41 ..... 96 B2
Lonsdale Dr NG9 ..... 223 F1
Lonsdale Gr DE4 ..... 142 C4
Lonsdale Pl DE22 ..... 218 B2
Lonsdale Rd
Branston DE14 ..... 254 A4
Pilsley S45 ..... 132 A1
Lonscale St S14 ..... 269 E1
Loosemore Dr S12 ..... 43 F3
Lord Haddon Rd DE7 ..... 194 C1
Lord Nelson St NG2 ..... 268 C1
Lord Roberts Rd S40 ..... 266 B3
Lord St Derby DE24 ..... 232 B3
Glossop SK13 ..... 10 B1
Hollingworth SK14 ..... 9 E2
Mansfield NG18 ..... 268 B3
Nottingham NG2 ..... 268 C1
Lords Cl S44 ..... 99 D1
Lordship La S14 ..... 269 E2
Lordsmill St S41 ..... 266 C2
Lorne Cl S8 ..... 56 B1
Lorne St S14 ..... 218 C2
Lorraine Cl DE24 ..... 232 C2
Loscoe CE Prim Sch
DE75 ..... 181 E2
Loscoe Grange DE75 ..... 181 E2
Loscoe Rd Derby DE21 ..... 206 A1
Heanor DE75 ..... 181 E1
Loscoe-denby La
DE5, DE75 ..... 181 D2
Losk Cnr S44 ..... 118 B2
Losk La S44 ..... 118 B2
Lothian Pl
Castle Donington DE74 ..... 247 D2
Derby DE21 ..... 219 F4
Lothlorien Cl DE21 ..... 231 D4
Loudon St DE23 ..... 219 D2
Loudoun Pl DE74 ..... 247 D2
Loughborough Ave NG2 ..... 268 C1
Lounds Rd S18 ..... 76 C3
Loundsley Ct S40 ..... 94 C2
Loundsley Green Rd S40 ..... 95 E3
Lount La DE13 ..... 239 F1
Lousie Greaves La DE21 ..... 207 D3
Louvain Rd DE23 ..... 218 B1
Louvil Ave NG10 ..... 136 C3
Lovatt Cl DE13 ..... 240 C4
Lovatt St S41 ..... 269 E2
Love La DE55 ..... 147 E2
Low Cl DE6 ..... 189 D1
Low Comm S21 ..... 79 E4
Low Lea Rd SK6 ..... 23 D3
Low Leighton Rd SK22 ..... 33 E4
Low Meadow SK23 ..... 45 E4
Low Pavement
Chesterfield S40 ..... 266 B3
■ Nottingham NG1 ..... 268 B1
Low's La DE7 ..... 209 D1
Lowburn Rd S13 ..... 44 B4
Lowdham St NG3 ..... 268 C2
Low Se S9 Derby DE24 ..... 232 C3
Lowedges Cres S8 ..... 56 C3
Lowedges Dr S8 ..... 56 C3
Lowedges Pl S8 ..... 57 D3
Lowedges Prim Sch S8 ..... 56 C3
Lowedges Rd S8 ..... 56 C3
Lower Bagthorpe NG16 ..... 171 F2
Lower Bank DE4 ..... 17 E4
Lower Barn Rd SK13 ..... 9 F2

Lower Bloomsgrove Rd
DE7 ..... 194 C1
Lower Brook St NG10 ..... 236 C4
Lower Chapel St
■ Ilkeston DE7 ..... 194 C1
Stonebroom DE55 ..... 147 D2
Lower Clara Mount Rd
DE75 ..... 182 A1
Lower Cres ST4 ..... 269 C2
Lower Dale Rd DE23 ..... 218 C2
Lower Dunstead Rd
Aldercar NG16 ..... 182 A2
Langley Mill NG16 ..... 182 A2
Lower Eaves View S43 ..... 47 E3
Lower Eldon St NG2 ..... 268 C1
Lower Eley St DE1 ..... 267 A1
Lower Fold S43 ..... 23 D4
Lower Gladstone St DE75 ..... 181 F1
Lower Gm DE65 ..... 230 B1
Lower Granby St DE7 ..... 194 C1
Lower Greenshall La S12 ..... 32 C3
Lower Grove Rd S40 ..... 266 A3
Lower Hague S42 ..... 32 C4
Lower Hall Cl DE56 ..... 192 A1
Lower Hardwick St ■ SK17 ..... 85 D4
Lower High St DE13 ..... 239 E4
Lower La S23 ..... 34 B1
Lower Macclesfield Rd
S23 ..... 45 F3
Lower Mantle S145 ..... 131 E2
Lower Maples DE75 ..... 194 A4
Lower Market St S14 ..... 16 A4
Lower Middleton St DE1 ..... 195 D1
Lower Nelson St DE75 ..... 181 F1
Lower Orchard St NG9 ..... 223 E4
Lower Park St NG9 ..... 223 E3
Lower Parliament St NG1 ..... 268 B1
Lower Rd DE22 ..... 217 F4
Lower Somercotes DE55 ..... 170 C4
Lower St DE6 ..... 224 A4
Lower Stanton Rd DE7 ..... 208 C3
Lower Strines Rd SK6 ..... 23 D3
Lower Terr Rd SK17 ..... 69 E4
Lower Whitworth Rd
DE7 ..... 208 C3
Lowerlea S12 ..... 32 B3
Lowery Dr SK6 ..... 23 D4
Lowes Hill DE5 ..... 169 E2
Lowes La DE73 ..... 244 B4
Lowfield Ave S12 ..... 58 C4
Lowfield Cl S12 ..... 43 D4
Lowfield Prim Sch S2 ..... 43 D4
Lowfields S43 ..... 79 D1
Lowgates S43 ..... 79 D2
Lowlands Lea DE75 ..... 181 F1
Lowlands Rd DE56 ..... 179 D2
Lowndes Cl ST4 ..... 269 D1
Lowry Ct S14 ..... 9 D2
Lowry Dr S18 ..... 56 C1
Lowside S32 ..... 72 B1
Lowside Cl S32 ..... 72 A1
Loxley Cl Chesterfield S40 ..... 95 D2
Derby DE21 ..... 206 A1
Loxton Cir DE3 ..... 217 E2
Loyne Cl DE24 ..... 231 F1
Lucas La DE65 ..... 228 C1
Lucas Rd S41 ..... 95 F3
Lucas Terr SK22 ..... 25 E2
Luccombe Dr DE24 ..... 233 E3
Lucerne Rd DE21 ..... 206 B2
Ludborough Wlk NG19 ..... 136 C2
Ludgate St DE13 ..... 239 E3
Ludgate Wlk DE22 ..... 217 F3
Ludham Cl S41 ..... 95 F4
Ludham Gdns S41 ..... 95 F4
Ludlam Ave NG16 ..... 195 D4
Ludlow Cl DE21 ..... 220 C3
Ludworth Prim Sch SK6 ..... 23 D4
Luke La DE6 ..... 201 F4
Lukesland Ave S14 ..... 269 D1
Lullington Rd
Clifton Campville B79 ..... 263 F2
Overseal DE12 ..... 262 A2
Lulworth Cl DE23 ..... 231 E3
Lulworth Ct NG16 ..... 195 F4
Lum's Hill Rise DE4 ..... 143 E3
Lumb La Hazelwood DE56 ..... 178 A2
Northwood DE4 ..... 127 D3
Lumber La DE6 ..... 176 B1
Lumsdale Cres DE4 ..... 143 E3
Lumsdale Rd Matlock DE4 ..... 143 F3
Sheffield S43 ..... 97 E4
Luna Croft S12 ..... 43 F1
Lundie Cl DE24 ..... 231 E1
Lune Meadow NG19 ..... 136 C2
Lunn La DE12 ..... 266 B2
Lupin Way S44 ..... 97 D2
Lupton Cres S8 ..... 56 C3
Lupton Dr S8 ..... 56 C3
Lupton Rd S8 ..... 57 D3
Lupton Wlk S8 ..... 56 C3
Lych Bank DE21 ..... 205 E3
Lychgate Cl DE21 ..... 205 E1
Lydden Cl S41 ..... 96 C4
Lydford Ave S41 ..... 77 D1
Lydford Rd DE55 ..... 159 E2
Lydgate S32 ..... 71 F3
Lydgate Dr S42 ..... 114 C2
Lydia Gdns NG16 ..... 182 B1
Lydstep Cl DE21 ..... 206 B1
Lye La DE56 ..... 177 F4
Lyle Cl NG16 ..... 195 F4
Lyme Hall SK12 ..... 32 A1

Lyme Park Cntry Pk SK12 ...... 32 A1
Lyme Pk SK23 .... 34 C1
Lyme Rd SK12 .... 32 A3
Lymefield Terr SK14 .... 16 A4
Lymewood Dr SK12 .... 32 B3
Lynam Cl S45 .... 131 F2
Lynam Rd Fritchley DE56 ...... 168 B4
  South Wingfield DE56 .... 168 B4
Lynam St S14 .... 269 E2
Lyncroft Ave NG10 .... 169 F1
Lyndale Dr DE5 .... 181 D4
Lynden Ave NG10 .... 236 B3
Lyndhurst Gr DE21 .... 220 A3
Lyndhurst Rd NG2 .... 268 C1
Lyndhurst St DE23 .... 219 D1
Lyne Ave SK13 .... 17 D4
Lynholmes Rd DE4 .... 143 E3
Lynmouth Dr DE7 .... 194 B2
Lyne Cl SK13 .... 17 F4
Lynton Cl DE5 .... 169 E2
Lynton Rd DE56 .... 168 A2
Lynton St DE22 .... 218 C2
Lywood Cl
  Branston DE14 .... 253 F4
  🔟 Dronfield S18 .... 56 B1

Lynwood Rd
  Branston DE14 .... 253 F4
Lytham Cl DE21 .... 205 E1
Lyttelton St DE22 .... 218 B3
Lyttel Cl NG3 .... 268 C2
Lytton St ST4 .... 269 F2

Macaulay St DE24 .... 232 A3
Macclesfield Main Rd SK17 ... 84 B3
Macclesfield Old Rd SK17 ..... 84 B3
Macclesfield Rd
  Buxton SK17 .... 85 D3
  Whaley Bridge SK23 .... 45 E3
Macdonald Cl S42 .... 115 F2
Macdonald Sq DE7 .... 208 B3
Machins Ct S18 .... 57 D1
Mackenzie St DE22 .... 218 B3
Mackinley Ave NG9 .... 209 F1
Macklin St DE1 .... 267 B3
Mackworth Coll DE1 .... 267 B2
Mackworth Tertiary Coll
  DE22 .... 218 A3
Maclagan St S14 .... 269 E1
Macready Pl DE24 .... 232 C4
Macworth Rd DE1 .... 218 C3
Maddock La DE4 .... 153 D1
Madehurst Gdns S2 .... 43 D4
Madehurst Rd S2 .... 43 D4
Madehurst Rise S2 .... 43 D4
Madehurst View S2 .... 43 D4
Madeley Ct DE7 .... 217 E1
Madeley St DE23 .... 219 D1
Madin Dr S43 .... 97 D3
Madin St Chesterfield S41 .... 266 B4
  Tupton S42 .... 131 E4
Madison Ave DE21 .... 219 F4
Madras Rd DE15 .... 248 B2
Mag La Idridgehay DE56 ...... 176 B3
  Whaley NG20 .... 100 B3
Magnolia Way DE55 .... 170 A4
Magson St NG3 .... 268 C2
Maguere Ave SK13 .... 10 A3
Maid Marian Way NG1 .... 268 B1
Maidstone Dr DE24 .... 232 C3
Maidwell Cl DE56 .... 179 E3
Main Ave Derby DE22 .... 204 C3
  Totley S17 .... 55 F2
Main Rd Aston DE6 .... 226 A2
  Bamford S33 .... 40 A2
  Bradwell S33 .... 51 D4
  Brailsford DE6 .... 201 F4
  Crich DE4 .... 156 B1
  Elvaston DE72 .... 234 A3
  Flagg SK17 .... 106 C3
  Grindleford S32 .... 72 B4
  Hathersage S32 .... 53 D4
  Heath S44 .... 117 D1
  Holmesfield S18 .... 75 D4
  Marsh Lane S21 .... 58 C2
  Morton DE55 .... 147 D3
  Nether Langwith NG20 .... 101 D1
  Old Brampton S42 .... 94 C4
  Pentrich DE5 .... 169 E3
  Renishaw S21 .... 79 D4
  Ridgeway S12 .... 58 A2
  Ripley DE5 .... 169 D2
  Shirland DE55 .... 146 B1
  Smalley DE7 .... 192 C2
  Somercotes DE55 .... 170 C3
  Stretton DE55 .... 146 B3
  Stretton DE55 .... 146 B3
  Sudbury DE6 .... 225 F3
  Taddington SK17 .... 88 A2
  Underwood Green NG16 ...... 171 F1
  Unstone S18 .... 76 C4
  Wensley DE4 .... 127 E1
  West Handley S21 .... 77 E4
  Westwood NG16 .... 171 D2
Main St Awsworth NG16 ...... 195 E3
  Blackfordby DE11 .... 257 E1
  Bolsover S44 .... 117 F4
  Branston DE14 .... 253 F4
  Breaston DE72 .... 235 E4
  Breedon on t H DE73 .... 252 C1
  Brinsley NG16 .... 171 E1
  Burnaston DE65 .... 229 F3
  Burton u T, Stapenhill DE15 . 254 C4
  Burton u T, Stretton DE13 .... 240 C1
  Caldwell DE12 .... 260 C4

Main St continued
Calver S32 .... 72 B1
Chelmorton SK17 .... 106 A4
Church Broughton DE65 ...... 227 D4
Clifton Campville B79 .... 263 F1
Coton in t E DE12 .... 260 B2
Eastwood NG16 .... 182 C1
Eggington DE65 .... 241 D3
Elvaston DE72 .... 234 B3
Etwall DE65 .... 229 D2
Findern DE65 .... 230 B1
Great Longstone DE45 .... 90 A2
Hartshorne DE11 .... 257 D3
Hemington DE74 .... 247 E3
Hilton DE65 .... 228 B1
Horsley Woodhouse DE7 ..... 192 B3
Kimberley NG16 .... 195 F3
Kirk Ireton DE6 .... 165 D1
Linton DE12 .... 261 E3
Lockington DE74 .... 247 F3
Long Eaton NG10 .... 236 C4
Mapperley DE7 .... 193 F2
Melbourne DE73 .... 245 E1
Middleton (Nr Wirksworth)
  DE4 .... 154 B2
Milton DE65 .... 243 D1
Moira DE11 .... 256 B1
Nethersead DE12 .... 264 C4
Newton DE55 .... 148 A2
Newton Solney DE15 .... 248 C4
Over Haddon DE45 .... 109 D1
Overseal DE12 .... 262 A2
Palterton S44 .... 118 A3
Repton DE65 .... 242 B1
Rosliston DE12 .... 260 B3
Scarcliffe S44 .... 118 C3
Shirebrook NG20 .... 119 F2
Smisby LE65 .... 257 F2
South Normanton DE55 ...... 160 A3
Stanton-by-D DE7 .... 222 C4
Sutton in A NG17 .... 148 C2
Swadlincote DE12 .... 255 F3
Tatenhill DE13 .... 253 D4
Ticknall DE73 .... 251 D3
Walton-on-T DE12 .... 253 E1
Weston-on-T DE72 .... 245 F3
Whaley Thorns S44 .... 101 D1
Wilson DE73 .... 252 C3
Winster DE4 .... 141 E3
Maine Dr DE21 .... 220 A3
Mais Cl DE4 .... 144 A3
Makeney Rd Belper DE56 ..... 191 D3
  Duffield DE56 .... 190 C1
  Holbrook DE56 .... 191 E3
Malbon's Yd DE1 .... 173 E1
Malcolm Gr DE23 .... 230 C4
Malcolm St DE23 .... 219 D1
Malham Cl S40 .... 95 E3
Malham Gdns S20 .... 59 F4
Malham Gr S20 .... 59 F4
Malham Rd DE23 .... 230 C3
Malia Rd S41 .... 96 B3
Malin Cl DE24 .... 233 D3
Mainscommon La DE56 ...... 166 B2
Malkin St S41 .... 266 C3
Mallard Cl Killamarsh S21 ..... 60 A4
  Shirebrook NG20 .... 119 F2
Mallatratt Pl NG19 .... 136 A3
Malmesbury Ave DE21 .... 256 B3
Malpas Rd DE4 .... 143 D3
Malson Way S41 .... 95 F3
Malt Hall La ST16 .... 269 E4
Maltby Ave DE55 .... 146 C3
Maltby Cl DE22 .... 204 C1
Malthouse Cl
  Eastwood NG16 .... 182 C1
  Wirksworth DE4 .... 154 C2
Malthouse La DE6 .... 173 E1
Malthouse La Ashover S45 ... 129 F2
  Froggatt S32 .... 72 B3
  Hatton DE65 .... 227 E2
  Nether Heage DE56 .... 168 A1
Malthouse Rd S80 .... 82 A3
Maltings The
  Burton u T DE15 .... 248 A1
  Shardlow DE72 .... 235 D1
Maltmill La NG1 .... 268 B1
Malton Pl DE21 .... 205 E1
Malvern Ave DE15 .... 248 A1
Malvern Cl Derby DE3 .... 217 E2
  Stafford ST17 .... 269 F3
Malvern Gdns
  🔟 Long Eaton NG10 .... 236 A4
  Matlock DE4 .... 143 D3
Malvern Rd S40 .... 95 F2
Malvern Rise SK13 .... 10 A3
Malvern Way DE21 .... 205 E1
Manchester La DE11 .... 257 E3
Manchester Rd Buxton SK17 . 85 E3
  Chapel-en-le-f S23 .... 46 C3
  Tideswell SK17 .... 69 D3
  Tintwistle SK13 .... 9 F4
Manchester St Derby DE22 .. 218 B3
  Long Eaton NG10 .... 236 B3
Manifold Ave
  Ashbourne DE6 .... 173 E1
  Staveley S43 .... 97 E4
Manifold Dr Derby DE24 ..... 233 D4
  Selston NG16 .... 171 F4
Manitoba Way NG16 .... 171 F4
Mankwell Rd S41 .... 96 A4
Manners Ave DE7 .... 194 B1
Manners Cl SK23 .... 34 B1
Manners Ind Est DE7 .... 194 C1
Manners Rd DE7 .... 194 C1
Manners St DE7 .... 209 D3
Manning View DE7 .... 194 C1
Mannion Cres NG10 .... 236 A3

Manor Ave Brimington S43 .... 96 C4
Derby DE23 .... 218 B2
Stapleford NG9 .... 223 E4
Manor Bglws S18 .... 56 C1
Manor Cl Brassington DE4 ... 153 D1
  Newton DE55 .... 148 A2
  Pilsley S45 .... 132 B1
  Swadlincote DE15 .... 255 D3
Manor Coll S40 .... 266 A3
Manor Comp Lower Sch
  NG19 .... 136 A1
Manor Comp Mid Sch
  NG19 .... 136 B3
Manor Comp Upper Sch
  NG19 .... 136 B3
Manor Court Rd S44 .... 98 C2
Manor Cres
  Burton u T DE15 .... 255 D3
  Chesterfield S40 .... 95 E2
  Dronfield S18 .... 56 C1
Manor Croft DE55 .... 147 E2
Manor Ct Barrow u T DE73 .. 244 A3
  Breaston DE72 .... 235 E4
  Clowne S43 .... 80 C2
Somercotes DE55 .... 170 C3
Manor Ct St S14 .... 269 D1
Manor Dr Brimington S43 .... 96 C4
  Chesterfield S40 .... 95 E2
  Nethersead DE12 .... 264 C3
Manor Farm Cl S80 .... 81 F1
Manor Farm Mews
  Burnaston DE65 .... 229 F3
  Long Duckmanton S44 ...... 98 A2
Manor Farm Rd DE72 .... 246 A4
Manor Fields Dr DE7 .... 208 B4
Manor Gr S43 .... 80 A4
Manor House Rd NG10 .... 236 C3
Manor Inf Sch S43 .... 96 C3
Manor Leigh DE72 .... 235 F4
Manor Park Ct S41 .... 266 C4
Manor Park View SK13 .... 10 C1
Manor Park Way DE3 .... 218 A2
Manor Pk DE72 .... 221 D1
Manor Rd Ashbourne DE6 .. 173 E2
  Barlborough S43 .... 80 A4
  Barton in H NG11 .... 237 F3
  Belper DE56 .... 178 C2
  Borrowash DE72 .... 221 D1
  Calow S43 .... 96 C3
  Chesterfield S40 .... 95 E2
  Derby, California DE23 ...... 218 B1
  Derby, Chaddesden DE21 ... 220 A4
  Eastwood NG16 .... 182 C1
  Harthill S26 .... 61 F4
  Ilkeston DE7 .... 194 C1
  Killamarsh S21 .... 60 C3
  Mansfield Woodhouse
    NG19 .... 136 A2
  South Wingfield DE55 .... 158 B3
  Swadlincote DE15 .... 255 D3
Manor St Glossop SK13 ...... 10 B1
  Nottingham NG2 .... 268 C1
Manor View S20 .... 59 F4
Manse Ave S80 .... 100 B4
Manse Cl S80 .... 100 B4
Mansell Cl ST16 .... 269 D3
Mansfeld Cres S41 .... 95 F3
Mansfeldt Rd S41 .... 95 F3
Mansfield Comm Hospl
  NG18 .... 268 B3
Mansfield Dr S12 .... 44 B3
Mansfield Gr NG1 .... 268 A2
Mansfield Rd
  Alfreton DE55 .... 159 D2
  Bramley-Vale S44 .... 117 F1
  Brinsley NG16 .... 182 C2
  Chesterfield S44 .... 115 F3
  Clowne S43 .... 80 C1
  Creswell S80 .... 81 F1
  Derby DE1 .... 219 D4
  Eastwood NG16 .... 182 C2
  Glapwell S44 .... 134 B4
  Heanor DE75 .... 182 A1
  Heath S44 .... 117 D2
  Killamarsh S21, S26 .... 60 C3
  Mansfield Woodhouse NG19 136 B1
  Market Warsop NG20 .... 120 C1
  Nottingham NG1 .... 268 B2
  Palterton S44 .... 118 A3
  Scarcliffe S44 .... 118 B3
  Selston NG16 .... 171 F4
  Sheffield S12 .... 44 B3
  South Normanton DE55 ..... 160 B3
  Temple Normanton S42 ..... 116 B2
  Tibshelf DE55 .... 148 A4
  Worksop S80 .... 82 C4
Mansfield St Derby DE1 ...... 267 B5
Somercotes DE55 .... 170 B4
Mansfield Woodhouse Sta
  NG19 .... 136 A2
Mansfields Croft DE65 .... 229 D2
Manton Cl DE11 .... 255 F3
Manvers Ave DE5 .... 169 F1
Manvers Ct NG20 .... 120 A2
Manvers Rd S44 .... 97 D2
Manvers St
  🔟 Mansfield NG18 .... 268 B4
  Mansfield Woodhouse NG19 136 A2
  Market Warsop NG20 .... 120 A2
  Nottingham NG2 .... 268 C1
  Ripley DE5 .... 169 F1
Manystones La DE4 .... 153 D2
Maple Ave Derby DE23 .... 218 B3
  Disley SK12 .... 33 D3
  Ripley DE5 .... 180 B4
  Sandiacre NG10 .... 223 D3

Maple Cl Doveridge DE6 ...... 211 D1
  Mansfield NG19 .... 136 C1
Maple Dr Ashbourne DE6 .... 185 E4
  Belper DE56 .... 179 D1
  Creswell S80 .... 81 F1
  Derby, Boulton DE24 .... 233 D3
  Derby, Chellaston DE73 ..... 233 D1
  Killamarsh S21 .... 60 B3
  South Normanton DE55 ..... 160 A2
Maple Gdns DE75 .... 181 E1
Maple Gr Breaston DE72 ..... 235 F4
  Burton u T DE15 .... 254 C3
  Derby DE22 .... 204 B3
  Glapwell S44 .... 134 A4
  Swadlincote DE11 .... 255 F3
Maple St S43 .... 97 D4
Maple Way DE14 .... 254 A4
Maplebeck Ct DE1 .... 267 B5
Maplotoft Ave NG19 .... 136 A3
Mapleton Ave DE21 .... 205 F1
Mapleton Rd
  Ashbourne DE6 .... 173 D1
  Draycott DE72 .... 235 D4
Mapperley CE Prim Sch
  DE7 .... 193 F2
Mapperley La DE7 .... 193 F1
Mapperley Rd 🔟 S18 .... 56 B1
Marchington Cl DE22 .... 204 C2
Marchington Ind Est
  ST14 .... 224 C1
Marchwood Cl S40 .... 95 F2
Marchwood Ct S14 .... 269 D1
Marcus St DE1 .... 219 D4
Mardale Cl S41 .... 76 C1
Maree Cl DE24 .... 231 F2
Marfleet Cl DE3 .... 217 E2
Margaret Ave Derby DE21 ... 219 F3
  Ilkeston DE7 .... 208 C4
  Long Eaton NG10 .... 223 D2
  Sandiacre NG10 .... 223 D2
Margaret St DE1 .... 267 B5
Margreave Rd DE21 .... 219 F4
Marham Cl NG2 .... 268 C1
Marigold Cl DE21 .... 206 A2
Marina Dr
  Derby, Allenton DE24 .... 232 C3
  Derby, Spondon DE21 .... 220 B3
Marina Rd DE7 .... 194 B1
Marion Cl SK17 .... 85 E3
Marjorie Rd DE21 .... 219 F4
Marjory La DE6 .... 213 E2
Mark's Cl NG10 .... 223 E3
Mark's Cl DE21 .... 231 E3
Markeaton La DE22 .... 204 B2
Markeaton Prim Sch
  DE22 .... 218 C4
Markeaton St DE22 .... 218 C3
Market Cl Shirebrook NG20 . 119 F2
  South Normanton DE55 ..... 160 A3
Market Pl Ashbourne DE6 ... 173 E1
  Belper DE56 .... 179 D2
  Bolsover S44 .... 99 D1
  🔟 Buxton SK17 .... 85 D4
  Castleton S33 .... 38 B1
  Chapel-en-le-F S23 .... 47 D3
  Chesterfield S40 .... 266 B3
  Codnor DE5 .... 181 D4
  Crich DE4 .... 156 C1
  Cromford DE4 .... 155 D3
  Ilkeston DE7 .... 208 C4
  Ironville NG16 .... 170 C2
  Long Eaton NG10 .... 236 C4
  Longnor SK17 .... 121 D3
  Mansfield NG18 .... 268 B3
  Mansfield Woodhouse
    NG19 .... 136 B2
  Melbourne DE73 .... 252 A4
  Mottram in L SK14 .... 9 D2
  Ripley DE5 .... 169 E1
  Somercotes DE55 .... 170 B4
  Staveley S43 .... 78 C1
  Sutton in A NG17 .... 148 C2
  Tideswell SK17 .... 69 E2
  Wirksworth DE4 .... 165 F4
Market Sq Stafford ST16 .... 269 E4
  Tideswell SK17 .... 69 E2
Market St Bakewell DE45 .... 109 F3
  Broadbottom SK14 .... 16 A4
  Buxton SK17 .... 85 D4
  Castle Donington DE74 ...... 247 D2
  Chapel-en-le-F SK23 .... 47 D3
  Clay Cross S45 .... 131 E2
  Disley SK12 .... 32 B3
  Draycott DE72 .... 235 D4
  Eckington S21 .... 59 E2
  Glossop SK13 .... 10 B1
  Hayfield SK22 .... 25 D3
  Heanor DE75 .... 181 F1
  Hollingworth SK14 .... 9 E3
  Ilkeston DE7 .... 194 C1
  Ironville NG16 .... 170 C2
  Mansfield NG18 .... 268 B4
  Mottram in L SK14 .... 9 D2
  New Mills SK22 .... 33 D4
  Nottingham NG1 .... 268 B1
  Shirebrook NG20 .... 119 F2
  South Normanton DE55 ..... 160 A3
  Stafford ST16 .... 269 D4
  Staveley S43 .... 78 C1
  Sutton in A NG17 .... 148 C2
  Swadlincote DE11 .... 256 A2
  Swadlincote, Church Gresley
    DE11 .... 256 A1
  Whaley Bridge SK23 .... 45 F4
Markham Cres S43 .... 78 C1
Markham Ct DE21 .... 205 F1

Markham La S44 .... 98 A2
Markham Rd
  Chesterfield S40 .... 266 B2
  Long Duckmanton S44 ...... 98 A3
Markham Rise S45 .... 131 D2
Markland Ave S43 .... 81 D2
Markland View S80 .... 81 E2
Markland S S80 .... 81 D1
Markland View DE15 .... 254 C4
Marlborough Cl DE15 .... 255 D4
Marlborough Dr DE56 .... 179 E3
Marlborough Rd
  Breaston DE72 .... 235 E4
  Buxton SK17 .... 85 D4
  Derby DE24 .... 232 B4
  Long Eaton NG10 .... 223 F1
  Mansfield NG19 .... 135 F1
Marlborough St S14 .... 269 F1
Marlow Brow S13 .... 10 A2
Marlow Cres DE7 .... 207 E4
Marlow St 🔟 Buxton SK17 ... 85 E4
  🔟 Hadfield SK13 .... 10 A3
Marlpit La Bolsover S44 .... 99 E2
  Denstone ST14 .... 196 B3
  Ellastone DE6 .... 183 D1
  Sutton on t H DE6 .... 215 D2
Marlpool Inf Sch DE75 ...... 194 A4
Marlpool Jun Sch DE75 ..... 182 A1
Marple Rd SK13 .... 16 A3
Marple Sta SK6 .... 23 D4
Marples Ave NG19 .... 136 C3
Marriott Ave NG18, NG19 .. 268 A4
Marrison Dr S21 .... 60 B3
Marsden Cl DE56 .... 190 C2
Marsden Pl 🔟 S40 .... 95 E1
Marsden St
  Chesterfield S40 .... 266 B3
  Derby DE24 .... 232 C4
  Hadfield SK13 .... 10 A2
Marsh Ave Dronfield S18 .... 57 D2
  Hope S33 .... 38 C2
Marsh Cl S20 .... 59 F2
Marsh Green La S45 .... 129 F2
Marsh Hall La SK23 .... 46 C3
Marsh Hollow DE6 .... 200 C3
Marsh La Belper DE56 .... 179 D3
  New Mills SK22 .... 33 E3
Marsh Lane CE Prim Sch S21 58 C2
Marsh Lane Prim Sch S21 .. 58 C2
Marsh View S21 .... 59 D1
Marshall St Alfreton DE55 .. 159 D2
  Heanor DE7 .... 181 F1
Marsham Dr S6 .... 23 D3
Marshaw Cl DE3 .... 217 F1
Marshes The S33 .... 38 C2
Marshfield Gr S43 .... 78 C1
Marshgreen Cl DE24 .... 233 E3
Marston St S17 .... 106 A4
Marston Brook DE65 .... 228 C1
Marston Cl Belper DE56 ..... 179 E3
  Derby DE23 .... 231 E3
  Dronfield S18 .... 75 E4
Marston Cres S17 .... 55 F3
Marston La Doveridge DE6 .. 211 E2
  Hatton DE65 .... 239 E4
  Marston on D DE65 .... 228 B1
  Rolleston DE13 .... 240 A2
Marston Montgomery
  Prim Sch DE6 .... 211 F4
Marston Old La DE65 .... 239 E4
Marston Rise DE15 .... 254 C4
Martin Ct S21 .... 59 F2
Martin Dr Derby DE21 .... 220 A4
  Stafford ST16 .... 269 D4
Martin Rise S21 .... 59 E2
Martin St S14 .... 269 E4
Martindale Cl DE56 .... 179 E2
Martinez La S42 .... 131 D4
Martlet Ave SK12 .... 32 B2
Mary Ann St S41 .... 76 C1
Mary Howitt Inf Com Sch
  DE75 .... 181 E1
Mary St Eckington S21 .... 59 E2
  Whaley Thorns NG20 .... 101 D3
Mary Swanwick Prim Sch
  S41 .... 77 D1
Maryfield Wlk S41 .... 95 F3
Maryland Ct
  Stapleford NG9 .... 209 F1
  Swadlincote DE11 .... 256 A4
Maryland Rd DE21 .... 220 A3
Marylebone Cres DE22 ...... 218 A4
Masefield Ave Derby DE23 . 231 F4
  Holmewood S42 .... 116 B2
  Swadlincote DE11 .... 256 B2
Masefield Dr ST17 .... 269 D3
Masefield Rd S13 .... 44 B8
Mason Cres S13 .... 44 B7
Mason Gr S13 .... 44 B8
Mason Rd DE7 .... 194 B3
Masonic Pl NG1 .... 268 A2
Masons Gr SK13 .... 10 A4
Massey Gdns NG3 .... 268 C2
Masson Cl S40 .... 95 D3
Masson Rd DE4 .... 143 D3
Masterson St S14 .... 269 F1
Mastin Ave S43 .... 80 A4
Mather's Way S42 .... 115 F2
Matlock Ave NG18 .... 268 B4
Matlock Bath Holy Trinity
  CE Prim Sch DE4 .... 155 D1
Matlock Bath Sta DE4 .... 143 D1
Matlock Cl NG10 .... 223 D1
Matlock Dr S43 .... 97 E3
Matlock Gn DE4 .... 143 E1

Matlock Inf & Jun Sch
DE4 .... 143 E3
Matlock Rd
Ambergate DE56 .... 167 F2
Ashover S45 .... 113 F2
Belper DE56 .... 178 C4
Brackenfield DE55 .... 145 E1
Brackenfield DE55 .... 145 E1
Derby DE21 .... 205 F1
Holymoorside S42 .... 114 A4
Wessington DE55 .... 157 F4
Matlock St DE45 .... 109 E3
Matlock Sta DE4 .... 143 D3
Mattersey Ct NG17 .... 136 A1
Matthew Cl SK13 .... 9 F4
Matthew Holland Comp
Sch NG16 .... 171 F4
Matthew St DE24 .... 232 C3
Matthew Way DE24 ...... 230 C4
Matthews St NG9 .... 209 F1
Matthews Fold S8 .... 43 E1
Matthews La S8 .... 43 E1
Maude St S21 .... 59 E2
Maugerhay S8 .... 43 E1
Maunleigh NG19 .... 136 C1
Mawfa Ave S14 .... 43 E1
Mawfa Cres S14 .... 43 E1
Mawfa Dr S14 .... 43 E1
Mawfa Rd S14 .... 43 E1
Mawkin La NG16 .... 160 C3
Maws La NG16 .... 195 F4
Mawstone La DE45 .... 125 D2
Max Rd DE21 .... 220 A3
Maxey Pl S8 .... 43 D3
Maxtoke Rd NG7 .... 268 A1
Maxwell Ave DE22 .... 218 B4
Maxwell Pl S14 .... 269 D2
Maxwell St DE72 .... 235 F4
May Ave S41 .... 77 E2
May South DE7 .... 194 B2
May St Derby DE22 .... 218 C2
Ilkeston DE7 .... 194 C2
Maybank Cl S43 .... 35 D1
Mayfair DE11 .... 255 F3
Mayfair Ave NG18 .... 268 C3
Mayfair Cres DE22 .... 217 F3
Mayfield Ave Heanor DE75 . 181 F1
Kilburn DE56 .... 192 A4
Swadlincote DE11 .... 184 B4
Mayfield Dr
Burton u T DE13 .... 255 D4
North Wingfield S42 .... 131 F3
Stapleford NG9 .... 209 D1
Mayfield Gr NG10 .... 223 F1
Mayfield Place E S14 .... 269 D1
Mayfield Place W S14 ... 269 D1
Mayfield Rd
Ashbourne DE6 .... 173 D1
Burton u T DE15 .... 248 A2
Chesterfield S40 .... 95 E1
Derby DE21 .... 219 F4
Lodge Moor S10 .... 42 C4
Marple SK6 .... 15 D1
Mayfield Terr
Hathersage S32 .... 53 D4
Mayfield DE6 .... 184 B3
Mayflower Ct NG20 ...... 119 F2
Mayflower Rd NG16 ...... 195 D4
Mayhall Ave NG16 .... 136 A2
Maylands DE72 .... 221 D1
Maylands DE72 .... 235 F4
Maynard Rd
Chesterfield S40 .... 266 A1
Nether Padley S32 .... 53 E1
Maypole Hill DE11 .... 256 A3
Maypole La DE23 .... 230 C4
McAdam Cl DE15 .... 248 A1
McGough Mews DE24 ... 232 A3
McMahon Ave S43 .... 97 D3
McNeil Gr DE72 .... 235 D4
Mead Cl DE24 .... 231 F2
Mead Cres DE15 .... 255 D3
Mead Wlk DE15 .... 255 D3
Meadow Ave Codnor DE5 . 181 D4
Mansfield NG18 .... 268 C3
Peak Dale SK17 .... 67 D3
Meadow Bank Glossop SK13 . 16 C4
Hollingworth SK14 .... 9 E3
Mansfield Woodhouse
NG19 .... 136 C3
South Normanton DE55 .... 160 A4
Meadow Cl Bolsover S44 . 118 A4
Breaston DE72 .... 235 F4
Chesterfield S43 .... 77 E1
Derby DE21 .... 220 C2
Dove Holes SK17 .... 47 F1
Draycott DE72 .... 235 D4
Dronfield S18 .... 182 C2
Findern DE65 .... 230 B1
Horsley Woodhouse DE7 ... 192 B3
Repton DE65 .... 242 C1
Stoney Middleton S32 .... 148 A4
Tibshelf DE55 .... 148 A4
Whaley Bridge SK23 .... 45 E4
Meadow Cotts NG19 .... 136 B2
Meadow Cres DE74 .... 247 D1
Meadow Croft DE4 .... 143 E3
Meadow Ct Belper DE56 . 178 C2
Chesterfield S43 .... 77 E2
Kilburn DE56 .... 192 A4
South Normanton DE55 .... 159 F2
Meadow Farm Com
Prim Sch DE22 .... 220 A2
Meadow Gr Newton DE55 . 148 A2
Totley S17 .... 55 E2
Meadow Grove Rd S17 .. 55 E2

Meadow Head Ave S8 .... 56 C4
Meadow Head Dr S8 ...... 56 C4
Meadow La
Burton u T DE13 .... 248 A4
Derby, Chaddesden DE21 ... 219 F3
Derby, The Holmes DE1 ... 267 D3
Disley SK12 .... 32 B3
Dove Holes SK17 .... 47 F1
Long Eaton NG10 .... 236 C4
Newton DE55 .... 159 F4
Repton DE65 .... 243 D2
Roston DE6 .... 197 E4
Swadlincote DE11 .... 256 A3
Tideswell SK17 .... 69 D1
Meadow Lane Ind Est
DE55 .... 159 D3
Meadow Nook DE24 ..... 233 E3
Meadow Rd
Awsworth NG16 .... 195 E3
Clay Cross S45 .... 131 D3
Derby, The Holmes DE1 ... 267 D3
Derby, Wilmorton DE24 ... 219 F1
Ripley DE5 .... 169 F1
Meadow Rise
Brassington DE4 .... 153 D1
Church Broughton DE65 ... 227 D4
Glossop SK13 .... 16 C4
Old Brampton S40 .... 94 C2
Meadow St Ilkeston DE7 . 194 C1
Ironville NG16 .... 170 C3
New Mills SK22 .... 33 E4
Meadow Vale DE56 ...... 190 B2
Meadow View
Bolsover S43 .... 80 C2
Chesterfield S40 .... 114 A4
Darley Dale DE4 .... 142 C4
Doveridge DE6 .... 224 B4
Holmewood S42 .... 132 B4
Rolleston DE13 .... 240 B2
South Wingfield DE55 ...... 157 F3
Meadow View Rd DE21 . 206 A2
Meadow View Rd
Sheffield S8 .... 56 C4
Swadlincote DE11 .... 255 F3
Meadow Way Derby DE73 . 233 D1
Swadlincote DE11 .... 256 A3
Meadowbank Way NG16 . 182 B2
Meadowbrook Ind Est
S20 .... 60 A4
Meadowcroft SK14 .... 9 D2
Meadowcroft Gdns S20 . 59 F4
Meadowcroft Glade S20 . 59 F4
Meadowcroft Rise S20 ... 59 F4
Meadowfield S43 .... 45 E4
Meadowfield Cl SK13 ...... 9 F2
Meadowgrass Cl DE23 ... 231 D3
Meadowhead S8 .... 57 D4
Meadowhead Sec Sch S8 . 57 D4
Meadowhill Rd S41 .... 115 E4
Meadowlands S44 .... 99 E1
Meadowlark Gr DE21 .... 206 A1
Meadows Com Sch S41 ... 77 D2
Meadows Croft DE56 .... 190 B2
Meadows Ind Est The
DE21 .... 219 E3
Meadows Prim Sch The
DE56 .... 190 B2
Meadows The
Chesterfield S40 .... 94 C3
Heanor DE75 .... 181 F1
Old Brampton S40 .... 95 E4
Swanwick DE55 .... 169 F4
Uttoxeter ST14 .... 210 A1
Meadowside Disley SK12 . 33 D3
Mayfield DE6 .... 184 B3
Whaley Bridge SK23 .... 45 E4
Meadowside Cl
Shirley DE6 .... 200 B4
Wingerworth S42 .... 115 D2
Meads The S8 .... 57 D4
Meadway Dr S17 .... 55 E4
Meadway The S17 .... 55 E4
Meakin St S41 .... 115 E4
Meal Hill Rd HD7 .... 2 C4
Meal St SK22 .... 33 E4
Mear Dr DE72 .... 221 D1
Mear Greaves La DE15 .. 248 A2
Mease La B79 .... 263 D1
Mease The DE65 .... 228 C1
Measham Rd
Donisthorpe DE12 .... 265 E3
Moira DE12 .... 262 C2
Stretton en le F DE12 ...... 265 F1
Meath Ave DE21 .... 220 A2
Meden Ave DE55 .... 134 C4
Meden Bank NG19 .... 135 D3
Meden Cl NG10 .... 135 D3
Meden Rd NG19 .... 136 B2
Meden Sq NG19 .... 135 D3
Medina Cl DE24 .... 233 E3
Medlock Cl S40 .... 114 A4
Medlock Rd S40 .... 114 B4
Medway Dr DE22 .... 205 D3
Meerbrook Cl DE21 .... 206 A1
Meerbrook Pl DE7 .... 208 B3
Meerbrook Park Rd S8 ... 43 D3
Meersbrook Rd S8 .... 43 D3
Megaloughton La DE21 . 220 B2
Melandra DE6 .... 143 D3
Melandra Castle Rd SK13 . 9 E1
Melandra Rd DE13 .... 218 C2
Melandra Rd SK13 .... 9 E1
Melanie Cl SK14 .... 17 D4
Melbourn Cl DE56 .... 190 C2
Melbourne Ave
Burton u T DE15 .... 248 B2
Dronfield S18 .... 56 A1

Melbourne Cl Belper DE56 . 179 D1
Derby, Allestree DE1 .... 204 B1
Derby, Mickleover DE3 .... 217 F2
Melbourne Ct NG18 ...... 235 F2
Melbourne Hall DE73 .... 252 A4
Melbourne Inf Sch DE73 . 252 A4
Melbourne Jun Sch DE73 . 252 A4
Melbourne La
Breedon on t H DE73 ...... 252 C1
Ticknall DE73 .... 251 E3
Melbourne Rd NG9 .... 209 F1
Melbourne St Derby DE1 . 267 B1
Mansfield Woodhouse
NG19 .... 136 B3
Melbreak Cl DE3 .... 217 F1
Melfort Cl DE24 .... 231 F1
Meliden Way ST4 .... 269 D1
Melling Cl S40 .... 114 C4
Mellington Cl S8 .... 43 E1
Mellor Dr ST14 .... 210 A1
Mellor La Barlow S18 .... 75 F1
Chapel-en-le-F SK23 .... 46 C3
Mellor Rd Branston DE14 . 254 A4
New Mills SK22 .... 24 B2
Mellor St DE24 .... 232 C3
Melbay Way S40 .... 115 D4
Mellor's La DE56 .... 191 E3
Melrose Ave NG18 .... 268 C3
Melrose Cl Chesterfield S40 . 95 D2
Derby DE24 .... 231 F1
Meltham La S41 .... 266 C3
Melton Ave Derby DE73 . 231 E3
Melbourne DE73 .... 252 A4
Melton Rd S43 .... 96 C2
Somercotes DE55 .... 170 B3
Melville Cl DE55 .... 170 B3
Melville Cres S43 .... 96 C2
Melville Gdns NG3 .... 268 C2
Melville St NG1 .... 268 B1
Melton Cl DE7 .... 194 B2
Melton Rd DE22 .... 204 B2
Mendip Cl NG10 .... 223 D1
Mendip Cres S40 .... 95 D2
Mendip Ct DE21 .... 205 F1
Menin Rd DE22 .... 204 B1
Mentmore Cl DE55 .... 170 A4
Mercaston Cl S40 .... 95 D3
Mercaston La
Hulland Ward DE6 .... 188 A2
Mackworth DE6, DE22 .... 203 D4
Weston Underwood
DE6, DE22 .... 203 D4
Mercaston Rd DE21 ...... 219 F4
Mercer Cres DE55 .... 159 E2
Merchant Ave DE21 ...... 220 C2
Merchant St Derby DE1 . 218 C3
Shirebrook NG20 .... 120 A2
Mercia Cl DE65 .... 239 E4
Mercia St Dore S17 .... 55 F3
Willington DE65 .... 242 B3
Mercian Mews DE21 ..... 220 B2
Meredith Cl NG9 .... 209 F1
Mereoak La DE21 .... 257 F4
Meridian Cl DE7 .... 194 C2
Merlin Cl DE56 .... 179 E3
Merlin Cres DE14 .... 253 F4
Merlin Gn DE24 .... 231 E2
Merlin Way Ilkeston DE7 . 208 C2
Woodville DE11 .... 256 C2
Merrial Cl DE45 .... 109 E2
Merrick Cl S40 .... 95 E3
Merridale Rd DE23 .... 231 E4
Merrill Coll DE24 .... 232 C2
Merrill Lower Sch DE24 . 232 C3
Merrill Way DE24 .... 232 B3
Merryborver Cl DE24 .... 231 E2
Merrydale Rd DE55 ...... 255 D4
Mersey Bank Rd SK13 ..... 9 F2
Merthyr Ct DE21 .... 206 A1
Merton Cl NG9 .... 209 F1
Mervyn Rd DE15 .... 248 A4
Metcalfe Cl DE24 .... 233 D4
Metcalfe Way S21 .... 60 B3
Meteor Ctr The DE21 .... 205 E1
Methley Cl S21 .... 43 F3
Metro Ave DE55 .... 148 A4
Mettesford DE4 .... 143 E3
Mevrill Rd S43 .... 69 E3
Mevrill Rd S43 .... 45 F3
Mewies Cl DE12 .... 253 E1
Mews The DE7 .... 252 A4
Meynell Cl Burton u T DE15 . 248 A1
Chesterfield S40 .... 95 E1
Meynell Ct DE22 .... 204 B1
Meynell Rd NG10 .... 236 B3
Meynell Rise DE6 .... 173 D2
Meynell St Derby DE23 .. 218 C1
Swadlincote DE11 .... 256 A1
Meynell Way S21 .... 60 B3
Meyrick Rd ST17 .... 269 E3
Michael Cl S42 .... 115 D3
Michael House-Rudolf
Steiner Sch DE6 .... 194 A3
Michael's La DE6 .... 183 E3
Michelle Cl DE24 .... 231 E2
Michigan Cl DE21 .... 220 C3
Michlow Cl S33 .... 51 D4
Michlow La S33 .... 51 D4
Micklebring Cl DE5 .... 169 E1
Micklecroft Gdns DE23 . 230 C4
Mickleton Cl DE11 .... 256 B4
Mickleover Prim Sch DE3 . 217 E1
Micklecross Cl DE3 .... 217 E2
Mickleton Cl DE11 .... 256 A1
Mickley Inf Sch DE55 .... 146 B2
Mickley La Dronfield S17 .. 55 F2
Shirland DE55 .... 146 B3
Totley S17 .... 55 F2

Middle Friars S17 .... 269 E3
Middle Hay Cl S14 .... 43 F2
Middle Hay Pl S14 .... 43 F2
Middle Hay Rise S14 .... 43 F2
Middle Hay View S14 ..... 43 F2
Middle Hill NG1 .... 268 B1
Middle La S45 .... 131 F2
Middle Ox Cl S20 .... 59 F3
Middle Ox Gdns S20 .... 59 F3
Middle Pavement
Chesterfield S40 .... 266 B3
[8] Nottingham NG1 ..... 268 B1
Middle Rd S42 .... 114 C1
Middle Shambles S40 .... 266 B3
Middle St S44 .... 118 B4
Middlebeck Cl DE73 ...... 232 C1
Middlecroft L Ctr S43 ...... 97 E4
Middlecroft Rd S43 .... 97 E3
Middlefield Cl S17 .... 55 E4
Middlefield Croft S17 ...... 55 E4
Middlegate Field Dr S80 . 82 A3
Middleton Ave
Codnor DE5 .... 181 D3
Derby DE21 .... 218 B1
Middleton Dr S43 .... 97 D3
Middleton La S32 .... 71 E2
Middleton Prim Sch DE4 . 154 B2
Middleton Rd
Ilkeston DE7 .... 209 D3
Mansfield Woodhouse
NG19 .... 136 B3
Middleton St
Awsworth NG16 .... 195 E2
Cossall DE7 .... 195 D1
Derby DE23 .... 219 D1
Middleton Top
Visitor's Ctr DE4 .... 154 B2
Midhill Rd S2 .... 223 E3
Midland Ave NG9 .... 223 E4
Midland Cl S41 .... 115 D4
Midland Ct DE1 .... 267 D2
Midland Railway Ctr S45 . 169 F4
Midland Rd Derby DE1 ... 182 C1
Eastwood NG16 .... 182 F1
Heanor DE75 .... 181 F1
Swadlincote DE11 .... 256 A2
Midland Road Ind Est
DE11 .... 256 A3
Midland St NG10 .... 236 C4
Midland Terr
Ambergate DE56 .... 167 F2
Barrow Hill S43 .... 78 A2
Blackwell DE55 .... 147 E1
Chesterfield S41 .... 115 D4
Midland View S43 .... 131 F4
Midland Way S43 .... 80 A3
Midway DE21 .... 220 C3
Midway Ctr S45 .... 131 E2
Midway Rd DE11 .... 256 B3
Midworth St NG18 .... 268 B3
Mikado Rd NG10 .... 236 B3
Milbank Cl DE7 .... 217 F3
Milburn Gdns DE21 ...... 206 A1
Milbury Cl DE21 .... 205 F1
Mile Ash La DE22 .... 204 C1
Milford Cl DE56 .... 109 E3
Milford Ave NG10 .... 223 D2
Milford Dr DE7 .... 194 C3
Milford Prim Sch DE56 ... 190 C4
Milford Rd Duffield DE56 . 190 C2
Staveley S43 .... 97 E3
Milford St DE1 .... 218 C4
Milken La S45 .... 130 A2
Mill Brow Broadbottom SK14 . 16 A4
Marple SK6 .... 23 E4
Mill Brow Rd SK6 .... 23 F4
Mill Cl Borrowash DE72 .. 221 E1
Findern DE65 .... 230 B1
Kilburn DE56 .... 192 A4
Newton Solney DE15 .... 248 C4
Swadlincote DE11 .... 256 B3
Swanwick DE55 .... 169 F4
Mill Cliff SK17 .... 69 E3
Mill Cres Whitwell S80 ..... 82 A3
Wingerworth S42 .... 115 E2
Mill Croft DE7 .... 217 E2
Mill Farm Cl S32 .... 72 B1
Mill Fleam DE65 .... 228 C1
Mill Gn S43 .... 80 B4
Mill Hill Sch DE5 .... 180 C4
Mill Hill Evaston DE24 ... 233 E2
Long Duckmanton S44 .... 117 D3
Mill Hill Dr DE65 .... 222 C1
Mill Hill La Breaston DE72 . 248 A2
Derby DE23 .... 267 A1
Mill Hill Rd DE23 .... 267 A1
Mill Holme DE55 .... 160 A2
Mill La Ashbourne DE6 ... 173 D2
Bolsover, Limekiln Field S44 . 99 D2
Bolsover, Shuttlewood S44 . 98 C4
Bradbourne DE6 .... 163 D3
Castleton S33 .... 38 B2
Chesterfield S40 .... 95 E1
Clay Cross S42, S45 .... 130 C3
Codnor DE5 .... 181 D4
Common Side S18 .... 75 C2
Cossall NG16 .... 195 E1
Crich DE4 .... 157 D2
Doveridge DE6 .... 211 D1
Dronfield S18 .... 57 D1
Eyam S32 .... 71 F3
Foston DE6 .... 226 B4
Grassmoor S42 .... 115 F2
Hartington S17 .... 137 E3
Hathersage S32 .... 52 C4

Mill La continued
Heath S44 .... 117 D1
Hilton DE65 .... 228 B1
Holloway DE4 .... 156 A3
Millthorpe S18 .... 74 C3
Pinxton NG16 .... 160 B1
Renishaw S21 .... 60 A1
Roston DE6 .... 197 E4
Sandiacre NG10 .... 223 E3
Scropton DE65 .... 226 C1
Shirley DE6 .... 200 B4
Stainsby S44 .... 133 E4
Totley S17 .... 55 F3
Whaley SK23 .... 45 E4
Wingerworth S42 .... 115 E2
Mill Meadow Way DE55 . 229 D2
Mill Moor Cl DE73 .... 232 C1
Mill Mus DE4 .... 155 D4
Mill Rd Cromford DE4 .... 155 D3
Heanor DE75 .... 194 A4
Stapleford NG9 .... 223 E4
Mill St Bakewell DE45 .... 109 E3
Belper DE56 .... 179 D2
Chesterfield S41 .... 266 C3
Clowne S43 .... 80 C2
Common Side S18 .... 75 C2
Coton in t E DE12 .... 260 B2
Derby DE1 .... 218 C3
Glossop SK13 .... 10 B1
Hayfield SK22 .... 25 E2
Ilkeston DE7 .... 194 C1
Mansfield NG18 .... 268 C3
Rocester ST14 .... 197 D2
Stafford ST16 .... 269 E4
Stoney Middleton S32 .... 72 A2
Mill Stream Cl S40 .... 95 E1
Mill Wlk Bolsover S44 ...... 99 D2
Whitwell S80 .... 82 A3
Mill Yd DE55 .... 170 B4
Milland La S80 .... 82 A2
Millbank Heanor DE75 ... 194 A4
Stafford ST16 .... 269 E4
Millbank Dr DE7 .... 194 B2
Millbank St S14 .... 197 D2
Millbrook SK14 .... 9 F3
Millcross La S18 .... 75 F2
Milldale Ave S43 .... 84 C3
Milldale Cl Chesterfield S40 . 95 E3
Ripley DE5 .... 180 B3
Milldale Ct Ashbourne DE6 . 185 E4
Belper DE56 .... 179 D2
Milldale Rd Derby DE21 ... 220 C2
Long Eaton NG10 .... 236 A3
Totley S17 .... 55 F3
Milldam La DE6 .... 186 C4
Miller Ave S43 .... 79 E2
Millers Dale DE56 .... 179 E3
Millers Gn DE4 .... 165 F3
Millers La DE55 .... 145 F3
Millersdale Ave DE7 ...... 194 C3
Millersdale Cl DE15 ...... 248 A3
Millersdale Ct SK17 .... 10 C1
Millersdale Way SK17 .... 85 D3
Millfield DE72 .... 235 D1
Millfield Cl DE7 .... 194 B2
Millfield Croft DE11 ...... 256 A4
Millfield Rd Ilkeston DE7 . 209 D4
Kimberley NG16 .... 195 F4
Millfield St DE11 .... 257 D1
Millom Pl DE21 .... 205 E1
Mills Cl DE7 .... 194 C3
Mills Ct DE4 .... 156 C1
Millstone Cl [8] S18 .... 56 B1
Millstone La DE5 .... 169 E4
Millthorpe La S18 .... 75 D3
Millway SK13 .... 10 B1
Millview Cl NG2 .... 268 C1
Millway NG12 .... 136 B1
Millway La DE6 .... 149 F2
Milnbank Ave SK17 .... 85 E4
Milner Ave Codnor DE5 .. 181 D4
Draycott DE72 .... 235 D4
Milner Rd NG10 .... 236 B4
Milnhay Rd Heanor NG16 . 182 B1
Langley Mill NG16 .... 182 B1
Milton Ave Alfreton DE55 . 159 E2
Ilkeston DE7 .... 194 C2
Shirland DE55 .... 146 B2
Swadlincote DE11 .... 256 B3
Milton Cres S40 .... 115 D4
Milton La S42 .... 132 B4
Milton Pl S43 .... 78 C1
Milton Rd Derby DE65 .... 217 D2
Ilkeston DE7 .... 194 C2
Repton DE65 .... 242 B1
Milton St Derby DE22 .... 218 B2
Ilkeston DE7 .... 194 C2
Long Eaton NG10 .... 236 B4
Mansfield NG18 .... 268 B4
Nottingham NG1 .... 181 E1
Milward Rd DE75 .... 181 F2
Mimosa Cres DE23 .... 231 F3
Miners Hill DE4 .... 153 D1
Minimum Terr S40 .... 266 A2
Minshall St S41 .... 266 C3
Minster Rd DE21 .... 205 F1
Minster Way DE55 .... 169 F4
Mint Cl NG10 .... 236 A4
Minton Rd DE74 .... 246 C2
Minton St ST4 .... 269 D2
Mires La
Great Longstone DE45 ...... 90 A2
Litton SK17 .... 70 A2
Mires Rd The Alstonefield DE6 . 149 D2
Birchover DE4 .... 126 A1

Miriam Ave S40 .... 114 A4
Miry La DE65 .... 227 E2
Misterton Cl DE22 .... 204 C1
Misterton Ct NG19 .... 136 A1
Mitcham Wlk DE22 .... 218 A3
Mitchell Ave NG16 .... 182 A2
Mitchell St Clowne S43 .... 80 C2
  Long Eaton NG10 .... 236 C4
Mitchell Terr DE7 .... 209 D3
Mitchell Way S43 .... 77 F2
Mitre Dr DE65 .... 242 B1
Mitre (Repton School)
  The DE65 .... 242 B1
Moat Bank DE15 .... 248 B1
Moat St DE11 .... 256 A1
Moat The DE74 .... 247 D2
Model Village S80 .... 100 C4
Model Village Prim Sch
  NG20 .... 119 F2
Moffatt Rd S2 .... 43 D4
Moira Cl DE21 .... 220 A4
Moira Dale DE74 .... 247 E2
Moira Rd
  Donisthorpe DE12 .... 262 C1
  Moira DE11 .... 262 C4
  Overseal DE12 .... 262 A2
  Woodville DE11 .... 256 C1
Moira St DE73 .... 252 A4
Moisty La
  Marchington ST14 .... 224 B2
  Stoney Middleton S32 .... 71 D2
Molineux Ave S43 .... 78 B1
Molineux St DE23 .... 219 D1
Molloy Pl S8 .... 43 D3
Molloy St S8 .... 43 D3
Monarch Dr DE21 .... 206 B2
Moncrieff Cres DE21 .... 220 A4
Mondello Dr DE24 .... 233 E3
Monk Rd DE55 .... 159 D1
Monk St Derby DE22 .... 267 A2
  Tutbury DE13 .... 239 E4
Monk's Rd SK13 .... 17 F3
Monks Cl Derby DE24 .... 231 E2
  Ilkeston DE7 .... 209 D4
Monks' Rd S13 .... 16 C3
Monks Way S81 .... 63 F4
Monksdale Cl SK17 .... 69 D2
Monksdale La SK17 .... 68 C1
Monkton Cl DE7 .... 194 B2
Monkwood Rd S41 .... 95 E4
Monmouth St DE21 .... 219 E3
Monnies End S43 .... 80 B3
Monpelier Cl DE14 .... 254 A4
Monsal Ave S40 .... 85 E4
Monsal Cres Staveley S43 ..... 97 D3
  Tibshelf DE55 .... 147 F3
Monsal Dr Derby DE21 .... 220 C2
  South Normanton DE55 ...... 159 F3
Monsal Gr S43 .... 85 E4
Monsaldale Cl
  Burton u T DE15 .... 248 A2
  Long Eaton NG10 .... 236 A3
Monsall Ave DE7 .... 194 C3
Monsdale La DE6 .... 151 F1
Monsom La DE65 .... 242 B2
Montagu St SK6 .... 15 D1
Monteith Pl DE74 .... 247 D2
Montford Mews DE74 .... 247 D2
Montfort St NG7 .... 268 A2
Montgomery Cl DE65 .... 228 C1
Montgomery St NG7 .... 268 A2
Montpelier DE22 .... 204 B4
Montpelier Pl SK17 .... 66 B1
Montpelier Rd DE56 .... 167 F2
Montrose Cl DE24 .... 231 E2
Montrose Ct NG9 .... 209 F1
Montrose Pl 12 S18 .... 56 B1
Montrose Sq NG19 .... 136 A3
Monument Hill NG16 .... 170 C2
Monument La NG16 .... 170 C2
Monyash CE Prim Sch
  DE45 .... 107 E1
Monyash Cl Derby DE24 ...... 220 A4
  Ilkeston DE7 .... 194 C2
  Staveley S43 .... 97 E4
Monyash Mews DE45 .... 9 E1
Monyash Rd
  Bakewell DE45 .... 109 E3
  Over Haddon DE45 .... 109 D1
Monyash Way DE56 .... 179 D3
Moonpenny Way S18 .... 57 D1
Moor Cres S20 .... 59 E4
Moor Ct DE24 .... 233 D3
Moor End Rd S46 .... 24 A3
Moor Farm Ave S20 .... 59 D4
Moor Farm Garth S20 .... 59 E4
Moor Farm Rd E DE6 .... 185 F4
Moor Farm Rd W DE6 .... 185 F4
Moor La Aston-on-T DE72 ... 246 A4
  Barrow u T DE73 .... 244 A4
  Bolsover S44 .... 99 D1
  Bonsall DE4 .... 142 B1
  Callow DE4 .... 165 D2
  Darley Dale DE4 .... 116 B4
  Chelmorton SK17 .... 87 F1
  Dale DE7 .... 207 F1
  Darley Dale DE4 .... 142 C4
  Derby DE24 .... 232 B3
  Elton DE4 .... 140 C3
  Flagg DE45 .... 106 C2
  Kirk Ireton DE6 .... 165 D2
  Kirk Langley DE6 .... 202 C1
  Little Eaton DE21 .... 191 F1

Moor La continued
Mansfield NG18 .... 268 A3
  Ockbrook DE72 .... 221 E3
  Osmaston DE6 .... 185 F3
  Scarcliffe S44 .... 119 D4
  Taddington SK17 .... 87 F1
  Youlgreave DE45 .... 125 D3
Moor Lane Fst Sch NG18 .. 268 A3
Moor Rd Ashover S45 .... 129 F2
  Breadsall DE7 .... 205 F3
  Brinsley NG16 .... 182 C4
  Great Longstone DE45 .... 89 F3
Moor Rise DE56 .... 191 E4
Moor St Derby DE21 .... 220 C3
  Mansfield NG18 .... 268 B3
Moor The Brinsley NG16 .... 182 B4
  Middleton (Nr Wirksworth)
  DE4 .... 154 B2
Moor Valley
  Mosborough S20 .... 59 D4
  Sheffield S20 .... 44 C1
Moor View Rd S43 .... 79 D1
Mooracre La S44 .... 99 E1
Moorbridge La NG9 .... 209 E1
Moorbrook La S33 .... 50 C4
Moore Cl S42 .... 116 B1
Moore St DE23 .... 219 D2
Mooredge Dr DE4 .... 143 E3
Mooredge Rd DE4 .... 157 D1
Moorend DE4 .... 142 B4
Moores Ave NG10 .... 223 E4
Moorfield DE4 .... 143 E4
Moorfield Ave Bolsover S44 . 99 D1
  Holbrook DE56 .... 191 E4
Moorfield Cres NG10 .... 223 D3
Moorfield La S44 .... 90 C1
Moorfield La NG10 .... 100 C2
Moorfield Prec SK14 .... 9 E3
Moorfield St S44 .... 99 D1
Moorfield St S14 .... 9 E3
Moorfield Terr S14 .... 9 E3
Moorfields Ave NG16 .... 182 C2
Moorgate DE22 .... 217 F3
Moorgate Ave NG19 .... 134 C4
Moorgate Cres S18 .... 76 A4
Moorgate St Ng7 .... 268 A2
Moorhaigh La NG19 .... 135 D2
Moorhall DE45 .... 109 E3
Moorhead Ave DE24 .... 232 C3
Moorhead Prim Sch DE24 232 C3
Moorings The S42 .... 32 C3
Moorland Ave NG9 .... 223 E3
Moorland Cl NG19 .... 268 A4
Moorland Dr S44 .... 116 C1
Moorland La NG19 .... 268 A4
Moorland Rd Derby DE2 .... 217 E2
  Hathersage S32 .... 53 D4
Moorland View
  Apperknowle S18 .... 58 A1
  Sheffield S12 .... 44 A1
Moorland View Rd S40 ...... 95 E1
Moorlands Cl NG10 .... 223 D1
Moorlands La Bonsall DE4 .. 142 A2
  Froggatt S32 .... 72 B3
Moorlawn Ave S42 .... 113 F4
Moorpark Ave S40 .... 114 B4
Moorpool Cres DE56 .... 191 E4
Moorside Cl Cromford DE4 . 155 D3
  Mosborough S20 .... 59 E4
Moorside Cres DE24 .... 231 F2
Moorside La DE56 .... 191 E4
Moorside Rd S14 .... 269 D1
Moorthorpe Gdns S20 ...... 44 C1
Moorthorpe Gn S20 .... 44 C1
Moorthorpe Way S20 .... 44 C1
Moortop Rd S21 .... 58 A1
Moorview Cl Brimington S43 . 96 B4
  Wingerworth S42 .... 115 D2
Moorview Ct 14 S17 .... 56 A3
Moorway DE21 .... 205 F2
Moorway Croft DE23 .... 231 D4
Moorway La DE23 .... 231 D3
Moorways Sports Ctr
  DE24 .... 232 B3
Moorwood Ave S17 .... 55 E1
Moorwoodmoor La DE55 . 157 E3
Moray Ct NG16 .... 195 F4
Moray Pl S18 .... 56 B1
Mordaunt Rd S2 .... 43 F3
Morden Gn DE22 .... 218 A3
Morden Rd NG16 .... 195 E4
Morefern Dr DE21 .... 205 F1
Moreland St NG2 .... 268 C1
Morland Cl S14 .... 43 F2
Morland Dr S14 .... 43 F2
Morland Rd S14 .... 43 F2
Morland Rd Birch Vale SK22 . 25 D1
  Sheffield S14 .... 43 F2
Morledge DE1 .... 267 C3
Morleston St DE23 .... 267 C1
Morley Almshouses La
  DE7 .... 206 A4
Morley Ave NG3 .... 95 E2
Morley Cl Belper DE56 ...... 179 F3
  Dronfield S18 .... 56 B1
Morley Dr DE7 .... 194 B2
Morley La
  Breadsall DE7, DE21 .... 205 F4
  Little Eaton DE7, DE21 .... 205 F4
  Stanley DE7 .... 207 D3
Morley Prim Sch DE7 .... 206 B4
Morley Rd DE21 .... 206 B1
Morley St Derby DE22 ...... 218 B3
  Glossop SK13 .... 17 E4
Morleyfields Cl DE5 .... 169 F1
Morlich Dr DE24 .... 231 F3
Morningside Cl DE24 .... 232 B2

Mornington Cl NG10 .... 223 E3
Mornington Cres DE22 ..... 218 A3
Mornington Rd S42 .... 132 B4
Mornington Rise DE4 ...... 143 E2
Morpeth Gdns DE21 .... 205 E1
Morrell Wood Dr DE56 .... 179 E3
Morris Ave S41 .... 95 F3
Morris Dr S41 .... 95 F3
Mortimer St DE24 .... 232 B4
Mortimer Wilson Sch
  DE55 .... 159 D2
Morton Ave S44 .... 131 D2
Morton La S21 .... 58 B1
Morton Prim Sch DE55 .... 147 D3
Morton Rd Pilsley S45 ..... 147 E4
  Shirland DE55 .... 146 B3
Morton St NG19 .... 135 F1
Morven Ave Bolsover S44 .. 99 D1
  Mansfield Woodhouse
  DE21 .... 136 A1
Morven St S80 .... 100 C4
Mosborough Inf & Jun Sch
  S20 .... 59 E4
Mosborough Moor S20 .... 59 D4
Mosbrough Rd S13 .... 44 A4
Moscar Cross Rd S6 .... 31 F3
Mosedale Cl DE24 .... 232 C4
Moseley St DE5 .... 169 E1
Moses La DE7 .... 206 C3
Moses View S81 .... 63 F4
Mosley Dr ST14 .... 210 A1
Mosley Rd SK17 .... 85 D3
Moss Dr S21 .... 60 B3
Moss Edge Rd HD7 .... 3 E4
Moss La Broadbottom SK14 . 15 F4
  Hulland Ward DE6 .... 175 F2
  Ripley DE5 .... 169 E2
Moss Rd Ilkeston DE7 ...... 208 C4
  Totley S17 .... 55 D2
Moss Rise PI S21 .... 59 E2
Moss St Derby DE22 .... 218 C2
  Hollingworth SK14 .... 9 E3
Moss View S20 .... 59 E3
Moss View Rd SK23 .... 47 E3
Mossbank Cl S13 .... 9 E3
Mossborough Hall Dr S20 .. 59 F3
Mossbrook Sch S8 .... 57 E4
Mossdale Ave S20 .... 59 E4
Mostyn Ave DE23 .... 218 B1
Mottistone Cl DE24 .... 233 E3
Mottram CE Prim Sch SK14 . 9 D2
Mottram Old Rd SK14 ...... 15 D4
Mottram Rd
  Broadbottom SK14 .... 16 A4
  Mottram in L SK14 .... 9 E3
Mouldridge La
  Aldwark DE4 .... 139 F1
  Ballidon DE4 .... 139 F1
Moult Ave DE21 .... 220 C2
Moulton Cl Belper DE56 .... 179 E3
  Swanwick DE55 .... 169 F4
Mound Rd S40 .... 266 A3
Mount Ave ST4 .... 269 D2
Mount Carmel St DE23 .... 267 A1
Mount Cres DE55 .... 160 A2
Mount Hooton Rd NG7 ... 268 A3
Mount Milner NG18 .... 268 C3
Mount Pleasant
  Ashford in t W DE45 ...... 108 C4
  Castle Donington DE74 .... 247 D2
  Ilkeston DE7 .... 194 C2
  Mansfield NG18 .... 268 B4
  Ripley DE5 .... 169 E1
  Somercotes DE55 .... 170 B3
Mount Pleasant CE Prim
  Sch DE4 .... 269 F1
Mount Pleasant Dr
  Belper DE56 .... 178 C3
  Heage DE56 .... 179 F4
Mount Pleasant La DE12 ... 265 D4
Mount Pleasant Rd
  Grindleford S32 .... 72 B4
  Linton DE11 .... 261 F4
  Repton DE65 .... 242 C1
  Swadlincote DE11 .... 256 B2
Mount Rd Bretby DE15 ..... 249 D2
  Hackinggthorpe SK14 ...... 15 D3
  Hartshorne DE11 .... 257 D2
  Linton DE11 .... 261 E4
Mount Row DE7 .... 269 E4
Mount Sch for the Deaf
  ST4 .... 269 D2
Mount St Breaston DE72 ... 235 F4
  Burton u T DE15 .... 248 A2
  Derby DE1 .... 267 B1
  Heanor DE75 .... 181 F1
  Mansfield NG19 .... 268 B4
  Nottingham NG1 .... 268 A1
  Stafford ST16 .... 269 E4
Mount St Mary's RC Coll
  S21 .... 60 B1
Mount The NG9 .... 223 E3
Mount View Ave S8 .... 43 D2
Mount View Gdns S8 ...... 43 D2
Mount View La S8 .... 43 D2
Mount View Rd S8 .... 43 D2
Mountbatten Cl DE7 ...... 194 C2
Mountcastle St S41 .... 95 F4
Mountfield Ave NG10 ..... 236 A4
Mountfield Ave NG10 ..... 223 D2
Mountfield PI ST4 .... 269 F1
Mountford Ave DE4 .... 233 E2
Mountford Ave DE4 .... 165 E4
Mountford Cl DE21 .... 206 A1
Mountford Croft S17 ...... 55 F3

Mouselow Cl SK13 .... 9 F2
Mowbray St DE24 .... 232 B4
Moy Ave DE24 .... 231 F1
Moyne Gdns DE73 .... 245 D4
Mudhurst La SK12 .... 32 C1
Muggington CE Prim Sch
  DE6 .... 188 C1
Muirfield Cl S41 .... 96 A3
Muirfield Dr DE24 .... 217 F1
Muirfield Way DE16 .... 136 C3
Mulberry Cl Belper DE56 ... 179 D2
  Wingerworth S42 .... 115 D2
Mulberry Mews DE5 .... 180 B3
Mulberry St DE5 .... 59 D1
Mulberry Way Hilton DE65 . 228 C1
  Killamarsh S21 .... 60 A3
Mull Ct DE24 .... 231 E2
Mullberries Ct DE22 .... 204 C2
Mullion PI DE24 .... 233 D3
Munday Cl DE55 .... 159 D1
Mundy CE Jun Sch DE75 . 181 F1
Mundy Cl DE1 .... 218 C3
Mundy St Derby DE1 ...... 218 C3
  Heanor DE75 .... 181 F1
  Ilkeston DE7 .... 194 C1
Mundy's Dr DE75 .... 193 F4
Munro Cl S21 .... 60 B3
Munro St S14 .... 269 E1
Munster Terr S14 .... 269 D1
Murray Park Com Sch DE3 217 F2
Murray Rd Derby DE3 ...... 217 F2
  Killamarsh S21 .... 60 C4
Murray St Derby DE24 ..... 232 C4
  Mansfield NG18 .... 268 B3
Murrayfield Dr S20 .... 59 F3
Musard Pl S21 .... 78 B1
Musard Way S21 .... 60 B3
Muse La Boylestone DE6 ... 213 D1
  Church Broughton DE65 .. 213 D1
Mushroom La DE11 .... 262 B4
Muskham Ave DE7 .... 194 C2
Muskham Ct NG19 .... 136 A1
Musters St NG20 .... 120 A2
Muswell Rd DE22 .... 217 F3
Mycock La DE45 .... 106 C3
Myers Cl DE24 .... 231 F2
Mynd The NG19 .... 136 C3
Mynors St S14 .... 269 F4
Myrtle Ave Long Eaton NG10 236 B3
  Stapleford NG9 .... 223 F3
Myrtle Cl NG20 .... 119 E3
Myrtle Gr S43 .... 78 A1
Myrtle Rd S2 .... 43 D4
Myrtle Springs S12 .... 43 F3
Myrtle Springs Sch S12 .... 43 F2
Mytham Bridge S33 .... 40 A1

Nabb La ST14 .... 196 A2
Nailers Way DE56 .... 179 E3
Nailor La DE4 .... 142 B2
Nairn Cl DE24 .... 231 E2
Nairn Dr S18 .... 56 B1
Namur Cl DE22 .... 218 B2
Nan Gell's Hill DE4 .... 155 D2
Napier Cl DE3 .... 217 F2
Napier St Derby DE22 ..... 218 B3
  Fenton ST4 .... 269 F1
Narlow La DE6 .... 161 F1
Narrow La Denstone ST14 . 196 B3
  Ticknall DE73 .... 250 C2
Narrowleys La S45 .... 129 F2
Naseby Cl DE22 .... 217 E2
Naseby Dr NG10 .... 236 C3
Naseby Rd DE56 .... 179 E2
Nathaniel Rd NG10 .... 236 C3
National Stone Ctr DE4 ... 154 C2
National Tramway Mus
  DE4 .... 156 C1
Navan Rd S2 .... 44 A4
Neal Ct NG16 .... 182 A2
Neale Bank S43 .... 96 B4
Neale St NG10 .... 236 C4
Near Meadow NG10 ...... 236 C3
Nearwell Cl SK23 .... 46 C3
Nearwood Dr DE21 ...... 205 F2
Needham St DE5 .... 181 D4
Needwood Ave NG9 ...... 209 E1
Needwood Cl DE13 .... 239 F3
Neighwood Cl NG9 .... 223 F1
Neilson St DE24 .... 232 C4
Nelper Cres DE7 .... 209 D3
Nelson Cl DE3 .... 217 F2
Nelson Pl DE21 .... 257 F2
Nelson St Burton u T DE15 . 248 B2
  Chesterfield S41 .... 96 A3
  Derby DE1 .... 267 D1
  Ilkeston DE7 .... 194 C1
  Long Eaton NG10 .... 236 B3
  Nottingham NG1 .... 268 B1
  Swadlincote DE11 .... 256 B3
Nene Cl DE13 .... 240 B1
Nesbit St S44 .... 118 A4
Nesfield Cl Chesterfield S41 . 95 F4
  Derby DE24 .... 233 E4
Nesfield Rd DE11 .... 194 C1
Nether Ave S21 .... 60 B3
Nether Blindow La SK17 . 106 A3
Nether Cl Duffield DE56 ... 190 C3
  Eastwood NG16 .... 182 C2
  Swanwick DE55 .... 169 F4
  Wingerworth S42 .... 115 D1

Nether Croft Cl S43 .... 96 C4
Nether Croft Rd 5 S43 ...... 96 C4
Nether Gdns DE4 .... 165 F4
Nether La Brassington DE4 . 163 F4
  Hazelwood DE56 .... 190 A4
  Holbrook DE56 .... 191 E3
  Kirk Ireton DE56 .... 176 A4
Nether Springs Rd S44 ..... 98 C2
Nether Thorpe Rd S80 ...... 63 D3
Nether Way DE4 .... 127 E2
Netherclose St DE23 ...... 219 D1
Nethercroft La S45 .... 131 F2
Netherdene Rd S18 .... 57 D1
Netherfield Cl S43 .... 79 D1
Netherfield La DE74 ...... 247 F4
Netherfield Rd
  Chapel-en-le-F SK23 .... 47 E3
  Chesterfield S40 .... 114 A4
  Long Eaton NG10 .... 236 B2
  Sandiacre NG10 .... 223 D2
Netherfields Cres S18 .... 76 A4
Nethergreen Ave S21 ...... 60 B4
Nethergreen Gdns S21 ..... 60 B4
Netherleigh Ct S40 .... 95 D2
Netherleigh Rd S40 .... 95 D2
Nethermoor Ave S21 .... 60 B4
Nethermoor Cl S21 .... 60 B4
Nethermoor Dr S21 .... 60 B4
Nethermoor La S21 .... 60 B4
Nethermoor Rd
  Nether Moor S42 .... 115 D1
  Tupton S42 .... 131 E4
  Wingerworth S42 .... 115 D1
Netherseal Rd
  Chilcote DE12 .... 264 C2
  Clifton Campville B79 ...... 263 F1
Netherside S33 .... 51 D4
Netherside Dr DE73 .... 233 D1
Netherthorpe S21 .... 79 D1
Netherthorpe Cl
  Killamarsh S21 .... 60 B4
  Staveley S43 .... 78 C1
Netherthorpe La S21 ...... 60 B4
Netherthorpe Prim Sch S43 . 78 C1
Netherthorpe Sch S43 ..... 78 C1
Netherwood Cl DE22 ...... 204 B2
Nettlefold Cres DE73 ...... 245 D1
Nettleton La SK17 .... 85 E2
Nettleworth Inf Sch NG19 . 136 B2
Neville Cl DE13 .... 240 A2
Nevinson Ave DE23 .... 231 E4
Nevinson Dr DE23 .... 231 E4
Nevis Cl Chesterfield S40 ... 95 E2
  Derby DE24 .... 231 E1
New Barlborough Cl S43 ... 80 B3
New Bath Rd DE4 .... 155 D4
New Beetwell St S40 .... 266 B3
New Bolsover Prim Sch
  S44 .... 98 C1
New Breck Rd DE56 .... 179 D2
New Church St S33 .... 51 D4
New Cl S32 .... 71 E3
New Cotts NG20 .... 101 F2
New Derby Rd NG16 ...... 182 B1
New Eaton Rd NG9 .... 223 F3
New England Way NG1 ... 135 E2
New Fall St NG17 .... 148 C2
New Garden St ST17 ...... 269 E3
New Hall Rd S40 .... 95 E1
New High St SK17 .... 85 E4
New Horwich Rd SK23 .... 45 F4
New Inn La DE21 .... 205 E4
New La Bradwell S33 .... 50 C3
  Hilcote DE55 .... 148 B1
New Lawn Rd DE7 .... 208 C4
New Linden St NG20 ...... 120 C2
New Lumford DE45 .... 109 E4
New Market St SK17 ...... 85 D3
New Mill La NG19 .... 136 C2
New Mills Central Sta
  .... 33 D4
New Mills Newtown Sta
  SK22 .... 33 D4
New Mills Prim Sch SK22 . 33 D4
New Mills Rd
  Chisworth SK13 .... 16 A2
  Hayfield SK22 .... 25 D2
New Mills Sch The SK22 .... 33 E4
New Mount Cl DE23 ...... 231 E3
New Queen St S41 .... 266 B4
New Rd Apperknowle S18 .. 58 A3
  Bamford S33 .... 40 A3
  Barlborough S43 .... 80 A4
  Barton in F NG11 .... 237 F3
  Belper DE56 .... 178 C2
  Boylestone DE6 .... 213 D2
  Bradwell S33 .... 51 D2
  Buxworth SK23 .... 34 A1
  Coton in t E DE12 .... 260 B2
  Crich DE4 .... 168 A4
  Derby DE56 .... 205 D3
  Eyam S32 .... 72 A1
  Grindleford S32 .... 72 A2
  Heage DE56 .... 179 E4
  Holbrook DE56 .... 191 E3
  Holmesfield S18 .... 75 D3
  Holymoorside S42 .... 113 E4
  Horwich End SK23 .... 45 F3
  Ironville NG16 .... 170 C2
  Middleton (Nr Wirksworth)
  DE4 .... 154 A1
  Ridgeway DE56 .... 168 B2
  Somercotes DE55, NG16 . 170 B3
  Stapleford NG9 .... 209 E1
  Swadlincote DE11 .... 255 F1
  Tintwistle SK13 .... 10 A3
  Uttoxeter ST14 .... 210 A1
  Weston Underwood DE6 . 188 B3

New Rd continued
Whaley Bridge, Buxworth
SK23 .... 33 F1
Whaley Bridge, Over Leigh
SK23 .... 45 F3
Wingerworth S42 .... 114 C2
Wirksworth DE4 .... 155 D2
Woodville DE11 .... 256 C1
Youlgreave DE45 .... 125 E3
New Rd (Baslow Rd)
DE45 .... 108 C4
New Row NG16 .... 171 D3
New Sq S40 .... 266 B3
New St Alfreton DE55 .. 159 D2
Bakewell DE45 .... 109 E3
Bolsover S44 .... 99 D2
Broadbottom SK14 .... 16 A4
Chesterfield S41 .... 266 B2
Derby DE1 .... 267 C2
Donisthorpe DE12 .... 262 C1
Draycott DE72 .... 235 D4
Grassmoor S42 .... 115 F2
Hilcote DE55 .... 160 B4
Little Eaton DE21 .... 205 E4
Long Eaton NG10 .... 236 C4
Matlock DE4 .... 143 E3
Morton DE55 .... 147 D3
Mosborough S20 .... 60 A4
New Mills SK22 .... 33 E4
Newton DE55 .... 148 A2
North Wingfield S42 ..... 131 F3
Ockbrook DE72 .... 221 E2
Peak Dale SK17 .... 67 D3
Pilsley S45 .... 132 B1
Ripley DE5 .... 169 F1
Rosliston DE12 .... 260 B3
Shirland DE55 .... 146 B1
Somercotes DE55 .... 170 B4
South Normanton DE55 ... 160 A3
Stanley DE7 .... 207 E3
Sutton in A NG17 .... 148 C2
Swadlincote DE11 .... 256 A1
Swanwick DE55 .... 169 F4
Whitwell S80 .... 81 F3
New St Bus Link S20 .. 60 A4
New Station Rd S44 ... 99 D1
New Terr Pleasley NG19 . 134 C3
Sandiacre NG10 .... 223 D3
New Tythe St NG10 .... 236 C4
**New Whittington Prim
Sch** S41 .... 77 E2
New Wye St S41 .... 85 E4
New Zealand La DE56 ... 190 C1
New Zealand Sq DE22 ... 218 B3
Newark S20 .... 59 F4
Newark Cres NG2 ...... 268 C1
Newark Rd DE21 .... 205 E1
Newark St NG2 .... 268 C1
Newbarn Cl NG10 ...... 119 E1
Newbery Ave NG10 ..... 236 C3
Newbold Ave
Borrowash DE72 .... 221 E1
Chesterfield S41 .... 95 F3
Newbold Back La S40 .. 95 E3
Newbold CE Prim Sch
S41 .... 95 F4
Newbold Com Sch
Chesterfield S41 .... 95 F3
Chesterfield, Newbold S40 . 95 E3
Newbold Dr S41 .... 95 F4
Newbold Dr
Castle Donington DE74 ... 247 D3
Chesterfield S41 .... 95 F3
Newbold Rd S40 .... 95 E3
Newborough Rd DE24 ... 233 E3
Newbound La NG17 ..... 134 B1
Newboundmill La NG19 .. 135 D3
Newbridge Cl DE7 ..... 207 E4
Newbridge Cres DE24 .. 232 C2
Newbridge Ct S41 ..... 77 D1
Newbridge Dr S43 ..... 96 B4
Newbridge La S41 ..... 77 D1
Newbridge Rd DE56 .... 168 A1
Newbridge St S41 ..... 77 D1
Newburgh Terr S32 .... 72 B1
Newbury Dr DE13 ...... 240 B1
Newbury St DE24 ...... 232 C4
Newby Rd S41 .... 95 E4
Newcastle Cir NG7 .... 268 A1
Newcastle Dr NG7 ..... 268 A2
Newcastle La S14 ..... 269 D1
Newcastle Rd S14 ..... 269 D1
Newcastle St
2 Mansfield NG18 .... 268 B4
Mansfield Woodhouse
NG19 .... 136 A2
Sutton in A NG17 .... 148 C2
Newchase Bsns Pk DE23 . 219 D1
Newdigate St Derby DE23 . 232 A4
Ilkeston DE7 .... 209 D3
Kimberley NG16 .... 195 F3
Nottingham NG7 .... 268 A2
West Hallam DE7 .... 207 E4
Newell Way DE45 ...... 127 E2
Newfield Cres S17 .... 55 E4
Newfield Croft S17 ... 55 E4
Newfield Farm CI S12 . 43 F3
Newfield Green Rd S2 . 43 E3
Newfield La S17 ...... 55 E4
Newfield Rd DE55 ..... 248 A2
Newfield Sec Sch (Boys)
S8 .... 43 E2
Newfield Sec Sch (Girls)
S8 .... 43 E2
Newgate Cl DE73 ...... 233 D1
Newgate Fst Sch NG18 . 268 C4
Newgate La NG18 ...... 268 C4

Newgates La NG19 ..... 134 C1
Newhall Inf Sch DE11 . 255 F4
Newhall Jun Sch DE11 . 255 F4
Newhall Rd DE11 ...... 256 B3
**Newhall St Edward's RC
Prim Sch** DE11 .... 256 A3
Newham Ave DE55 ...... 169 E1
Newham Cl DE75 .... 182 A1
Newhaven Ave NG19 .... 136 A2
Newhaven Cl S40 ...... 95 D1
Newhaven Rd DE21 ..... 220 A3
Newholme Hospl DE45 .. 109 E4
Newland Dale S41 ..... 266 B4
Newland Gdns S41 ..... 95 F3
Newland St DE11 ...... 267 A3
Newlands Ave
Chesterfield S40 .... 95 E2
Sheffield S12 .... 44 A3
Newlands Cl DE11 ..... 256 A1
Newlands Cres DE55 ... 148 A2
Newlands Dr Hadfield SK13 . 9 F2
Heanor DE75 .... 181 F2
Sheffield S12 .... 44 A3
Newlands Gr S12 ...... 44 A3
Newlands Rd Sheffield S12 . 44 A3
Somercotes DE55 .... 170 B2
Newlyn Dr Derby DE23 .. 231 F4
South Normanton DE55 ... 160 B3
Newlyn Pl S8 .... 43 D2
Newman Dr DE14 .... 254 A4
Newmanleys Rd NG16 ... 194 C4
Newmanleys Rd S NG16 . 194 C4
Newmarket Cl DE24 .... 219 F1
Newmarket Dr DE24 .... 232 C4
Newmarket La S45 ..... 130 C2
Newmarket Way NG9 .... 223 F1
Newport Cres NG19 .... 135 F1
Newport Rd S18 .... 233 E3
Newport St S18 .... 269 D3
Newquay Pl DE24 ...... 233 E3
Newshaw La SK13 ...... 9 F2
Newstead Ave Derby DE21 . 219 F3
.... 44 C2
Newstead Gr
5 Dronfield S18 .... 56 B1
Sheffield S12 .... 44 C2
Newstead Dr S12 ...... 44 C1
Newstead Gr
Nottingham NG1 .... 268 A2
Sheffield S12 .... 44 C2
Newstead Pl S12 ...... 44 C1
Newstead Rd
Long Eaton NG10 .... 223 E2
Sheffield S12 .... 44 C1
Newstead Rd S DE7 .... 194 B2
Newstead Rise S12 .... 44 C1
Newstead Terr SK17 ... 85 D2
Newstead Way S12 ..... 44 C1
Newton Cl Belper DE56 . 179 E3
Newton Solney DE15 ..... 248 C4
Newton Dr NG9 .... 223 F3
Newton La DE15 .... 248 B2
Newton Leys DE15 ..... 248 B2
Newton Park Cl DE11 .. 256 A4
Newton Prim Sch DE55 . 148 A2
Newton Rd
Burton u T DE15 .... 248 A3
Tibshelf DE55 .... 147 F2
**Newton Solney CE Inf
Sch** DE15 .... 248 C4
Newton St NG18 .... 268 C3
Newton's La NG16 ..... 195 D2
Newton's Wlk DE22 .... 218 B4
Newton Croft Cres S43 . 80 A3
Newtons Croft Cres S43 . 80 A3
Newtonwood La DE55 ... 148 A3
Newtown Cty Prim Sch
SK22 .... 33 D3
Nicholas Cl DE21 ..... 220 C3
Nicholas St S41 ...... 115 E4
Nicholls St ST4 ...... 269 E1
Nicholson Cl SK17 .... 69 E2
Nicholson Pl S8 ...... 43 D3
Nicholson's Row NG20 . 119 F2
Nicklaus Cl DE14 ..... 254 A4
Nicola Gdns DE23 ..... 231 E2
Nicolas Cl SK17 ...... 85 E4
Nidderdale Ct DE24 ... 233 E3
Nields Way SK6 .... 23 E2
Nightingale Ave NG19 . 135 D2
Nightingale Cl
Clay Cross S45 .... 131 F1
Holloway DE4 .... 155 F3
Ripley DE5 .... 169 E1
Nightingale Dr
Mansfield NG19 .... 135 F1
Woodville DE11 .... 256 C2
Nightingale Inf Sch DE24 . 232 B4
Nightingale Jun Sch
DE24 .... 232 B4
Nile St NG1 .... 268 B2
Nine Ladies DE4 ...... 126 B2
Ninelands Rd S12 ..... 53 D4
No Man's Heath Rd
DE12 .... 264 C2
No Man's La Risley DE7 . 222 A4
Sandiacre DE7 .... 222 B4
Nobel Cl S80 .... 81 F1
Noble St DE11 .... 267 D1
Nodder Rd S13 .... 44 B4
Nodin Hill La DE56 ... 168 A2
Noel St Derby DE22 ... 218 B3
Mansfield NG18 .... 268 B4
Noel-Baker Com Sch
DE24 .... 232 C2

Nook End Rd DE75 ..... 181 E1
Nook The Barrow u T DE73 . 244 A3
Heanor DE75 .... 181 E2
Holbrook DE56 .... 191 E4
Shirebrook NG20 .... 119 E2
Stoney Middleton S32 ... 72 A2
Nooning La DE72 ...... 234 C4
Norbriggs Prim Sch S43 . 79 F2
Norbriggs Rd S43 ..... 79 E1
Norburn Dr S21 .... 60 B3
Norbury CE Prim Sch
DE6 .... 197 F4
Norbury Cl Chesterfield S40 . 95 D3
Derby DE22 .... 204 C1
Sheffield S8 .... 56 C4
Norbury Cres DE23 .... 231 E3
Norbury Ct DE22 ...... 204 B1
Norbury Hollow DE6 ... 183 E1
Norbury Way DE56 ..... 179 E3
Norfolk Ave S42 ...... 115 F1
Norfolk Cl S40 .... 114 A4
Norfolk Ct NG19 ...... 136 C3
Norfolk Dr NG18 ...... 268 B4
Norfolk Fst Sch S2 ... 43 F4
Norfolk Gdns DE22 .... 218 C4
Norfolk Mid Sch S2 ... 43 F4
Norfolk Rd Burton u T DE15 . 254 B4
Long Eaton NG10 .... 223 F1
Norfolk Sch S2 .... 43 F4
Norfolk Sq SK13 ...... 10 B1
Norfolk St Derby DE23 . 219 D1
Glossop SK13 .... 10 B1
Norfolk Wlk NG10 ..... 223 D3
Norgreave Way S20 .... 59 F4
Norman Ave DE23 ...... 231 F4
Norman Cl NG3 .... 268 B2
Norman Cres DE7 ...... 194 C2
Norman Keep DE13 ..... 239 E3
Norman Rd Ripley DE5 . 169 E1
Somercotes DE55 .... 170 C4
Tutbury DE13 .... 239 E3
Norman St Ilkeston DE7 . 194 C2
Kimberley NG16 .... 195 F4
Normandy Rd DE65 ..... 228 C1
Normanton Ave DE55 ... 159 E2
Normanton Gr S13 ..... 44 C3
Normanton Hill S13 ... 44 B3
Normanton Inf Sch S13 . 231 F4
Normanton Jun Sch
DE23 .... 231 F4
Normanton La DE23 .... 231 E3
Normanton Rd DE1 ..... 267 B1
Normanton Sch S13 .... 44 B3
Normanton Spring Cl S13 . 44 C3
Normanton Spring Rd S13 . 44 C3
**Normanton Village Inf
Sch** DE23 .... 231 F4
North Ave Ashbourne DE6 . 173 D1
Derby, Darley Abbey DE3 . 205 D2
Derby, Mickleover DE3 .. 217 F1
Sandiacre NG10 .... 223 D3
North Brook Rd SK13 .. 9 F2
North Castle St S16 .. 269 D4
North Church St
Bakewell DE45 .... 109 E3
1 Nottingham NG1 ...... 268 B2
North Circus St NG7 .. 268 A2
North Cl Derby DE55 .. 159 F3
North Cres Killamarsh S21 . 60 C4
Long Duckmanton S44 ... 98 A3
**North Derbyshire Tertiary
Coll** S43 .... 80 C2
**North Derbyshire Tertiary
Coll (Markland Campus)**
S80 .... 81 F2
North End DE4 .... 154 C1
North Farm Cl S26 .... 61 F4
North Gr S44 .... 98 A3
North La
Belper, Farnah Green DE56 . 178 B1
Belper, Milford DE56 ... 190 C4
North La DE56 .... 187 F2
North Leys DE6 .... 173 D1
North Moor View S43 .. 96 C4
North Par Derby DE1 .. 267 B4
Matlock Bath DE4 .... 143 D1
North Rd Buxton SK17 . 66 B1
Calow S44 .... 96 C2
Clowne S43 .... 80 C2
Glossop SK13 .... 10 B2
Hayfield SK22 .... 25 E2
Long Eaton NG10 .... 236 B3
Nottingham NG7 .... 268 A2
North Row DE22 .... 205 D1
North Sherwood St NG1 . 268 B2
North Side S42 .... 115 E1
North St Alfreton DE55 . 159 D2
Blackwell DE55 .... 147 F1
Bramley-Vale S44 ...... 117 E1
Burton u T DE15 .... 248 A2
Clay Cross S45 .... 131 D3
Cromford DE4 .... 155 D3
Derby, Little Chester DE1 . 267 B4
Derby, Littleover DE23 . 218 C1
3 Ilkeston DE7 .... 194 C1
Langley Mill NG16 ...... 182 A2
Market Warsop NG20 .... 120 B2
Melbourne DE73 .... 252 A4
North Wingfield S42 .... 132 A3
Nottingham NG2 .... 268 C1
Pinxton NG16 .... 160 B2
Somercotes DE55 .... 170 B3
South Normanton DE55 .. 159 F3
Stoke-on-T ST4 .... 269 E2

North St continued
Swadlincote DE11 .... 256 A3
Whaley Thorns NG20 ..... 101 D1
**North Staffs Hospl Ctr
(Outpatients Dept)** ST4 . 269 D2
North Staffs Royal Infmy
ST4 .... 269 D2
North Terr S41 .... 115 D4
North View DE4 .... 168 A4
North View St S44 .... 98 C2
North Walls ST16 ..... 269 D4
**North Wingfield Inf &
Jun Sch** S42 .... 131 F4
North Wingfield Rd S42 . 115 F2
Northacre Rd DE21 .... 206 A1
Northam Dr DE5 .... 169 E2
Northampton St NG3 ... 268 C2
Northcliffe Rd DE6 ... 173 D1
Northcote Ave Sheffield S2 . 43 D3
Stoke-on-T ST4 .... 269 E2
Northcote Rd S8 ...... 43 D3
Northcote St NG10 .... 236 C4
Northedge La S42 ..... 130 A4
Northern Ave S2 ...... 43 F4
Northern Comm S18 ... 56 A1
Northern Dr NG9 ...... 209 E2
Northern Rd DE75 ..... 181 E1
Northfield Derby DE4 . 231 E2
Kilburn DE56 .... 179 F1
Northfield Ave
Ilkeston DE7 .... 194 C1
Long Eaton NG10 .... 236 A2
Northfield Cl ST14 ... 210 A1
Northfield Cres NG9 .. 223 F2
Northfield Inf & Jun Sch
NG19 .... 136 A3
Northfield Jun Sch S18 . 57 E2
Northfield La
Mansfield Woodhouse
NG19 .... 136 A3
Palterton S44 .... 118 B3
Northfield Pk NG19 ... 136 A3
Northfield Rd NG9 .... 223 F2
Northfields Clowne S43 . 80 C2
Long Eaton NG10 .... 236 A2
Northgate St 6 DE7 .. 194 C1
Northlands S20 .... 61 F4
Northmead Dr DE3 ..... 218 A2
Northmoor Cl 7 S43 .. 96 C4
Northumberland Cl NG3 . 268 B2
Northumberland Rd DE15 . 254 A4
Northumberland St S18 . 218 C1
Northwood Ave
Darley Dale DE4 .... 127 E2
Derby DE21 .... 219 F4
Northwood La
Ellastone DE6 .... 183 E2
Darley Dale DE4 .... 127 D3
Northwood Rise DE6 ... 185 E4
Northwood St NG9 ..... 223 E4
Norton Ave Bolsover S44 . 98 C3
Chesterfield S40 ...... 114 A4
Sheffield S8, S12 ..... 43 D1
Norton Church Glebe S8 . 43 E1
Norton Church Rd S8 .. 43 E1
Norton Coll S8 .... 57 D4
Norton Free Sch S8 ... 43 E1
Norton Green Cl S8 ... 43 E1
Norton La S8 .... 57 D4
Norton Lawns S8 ...... 43 E1
Norton Lees Cl S8 .... 43 D2
Norton Lees Cres S8 .. 43 D2
Norton Lees La S8 .... 43 D2
Norton Lees Rd S8 .... 43 D2
Norton Mews S8 .... 43 E1
Norton Park Ave S8 ... 57 D4
Norton Park Cres S8 .. 57 D4
Norton Park Dr S8 .... 57 D4
Norton Park Rd S8 .... 57 D4
Norton Park View S8 .. 57 D4
Norwell La NG19 ...... 136 A1
Norwich Cl NG19 ...... 136 B3
Norwich St DE21 ...... 219 F4
Norwood Ave S41 ...... 115 F3
Norwood Cl
Chesterfield S41 .... 115 F3
Derby DE22 .... 218 A3
Norwood Cres S21 ..... 60 C4
Norwood High Sch S17 . 55 F3
Norwood Ind Est S21 .. 60 C4
Norwood Pl S21 .... 60 C4
Notintone St NG2 ..... 268 C1
Nottingham Cl S42 .... 115 D2
Nottingham Dr S42 .... 115 D2
Nottingham High Sch
NG1 .... 268 A2
**Nottingham High Sch for
Girls** NG1 .... 268 A2
Nottingham La
Ironville NG16 .... 170 C3
Somercotes DE55 .... 170 C3
Nottingham Midland Sta
NG1 .... 268 B1
Nottingham Rd
Alfreton DE55 .... 159 D1
Ashby-de-la-Z LE65 ..... 258 C1
Belper DE56 .... 179 D2
Borrowash DE72 .... 221 E1
Breedon on t H DE73 ... 252 B1
Codnor DE5 .... 181 D4
Derby, Chaddesden DE21 . 219 F3
Derby, Little Chester DE1 . 267 C4

Nottingham Rd continued
Derby, Spondon DE21 .... 220 C2
Eastwood, Bailey Grove
NG16 .... 182 C1
Eastwood, Giltbrook NG16 . 195 E4
Ilkeston DE7 .... 209 D3
Long Eaton NG10 .... 236 C4
Mansfield NG18 .... 268 B3
Ripley DE5 .... 169 F1
Selston NG16 .... 171 F3
Somercotes DE55 .... 159 D1
Stapleford, Stanton Gate
NG9 .... 223 F4
Stapleford, Trowell NG9 . 209 F3
Tansley DE4 .... 144 A2
Trowell NG9 .... 209 F3
Nottingham Trent Univ
NG1 .... 268 A2
Nowill Cl S8 .... 43 D3
Nowill Pl S8 .... 43 D3
Nugent Gdns NG3 ...... 268 C2
Nun's St DE1 .... 218 C3
Nunbrook Gr SK17 ..... 85 E4
Nunn Brook Rd NG17 ... 148 C1
Nunn Brook Rise NG17 . 148 C1
Nunn Cl NG17 .... 148 C1
Nunsfield Dr DE24 .... 233 D4
Nunsfield Rd SK17 .... 66 B1
Nursery Ave
Sandiacre NG10 .... 222 C3
West Hallam DE7 .... 207 F4
Nursery Cl
Borrowash DE72 .... 221 D1
Glossop SK13 .... 10 A3
Swadlincote DE11 ...... 256 A3
Nursery Croft DE4 .... 165 F3
Nursery Ct NG18 ...... 268 C4
Nursery Dr S43 .... 96 B1
Nursery Gdns DE55 .... 160 B2
Nursery Hollow DE7 ... 208 C3
Nursery La S41 .... 84 C3
Nursery St Mansfield NG18 . 268 C4
Stoke-on-T ST4 .... 269 D2
Nutbrook Cres DE7 .... 208 B2
Nuthall Cir DE7 ...... 208 B2
Nuttall Cl DE55 ...... 158 C2
Nuttall St DE55 ...... 158 C2
Nuttall Terr S44 ..... 117 E1
Nutwood Cl DE22 ...... 205 D2

O

Oadby Rise DE23 ...... 231 F3
Oak Ave Aldercar NG16 . 182 A3
Disley SK12 .... 33 D3
Mansfield NG18 .... 268 C4
Ripley DE5 .... 180 B4
Sandiacre NG10 .... 223 D4
Shirebrook NG20 .... 119 E2
Oak Bank S41 .... 77 D1
Oak Bank Cl NG18 ..... 268 C4
Oak Cl Chapel-en-le-F SK23 . 47 E3
Derby DE22 .... 204 C4
Duffield DE56 .... 190 C1
Killamarsh S21 .... 60 B3
Linton DE11 .... 261 F4
Mottram in L SK14 ..... 9 D2
Pinxton NG16 .... 160 B2
Oak Cres Ashbourne DE6 . 185 E4
Derby DE23 .... 231 E4
Wingerworth S42 .... 114 C2
Oak Dr Alfreton DE55 . 159 D2
Derby, Boulton DE24 ... 233 D3
Derby, Mickleover DE65 . 217 F1
Doveridge DE6 .... 211 D1
Eastwood NG16 .... 182 B1
Hilton DE65 .... 228 C1
Oak La DE6 .... 212 B2
Oak Lodge Dr NG16 .... 195 F4
Oak Rd Denstone ST14 . 196 B3
Elvaston DE72 .... 233 F2
Grassmoor S42 .... 115 F2
Matlock DE4 .... 143 E3
Sheffield S12 .... 44 A1
Oak St Brimington S43 . 78 A1
Derby DE23 .... 219 D1
Glossop SK13 .... 10 B1
Mosborough S20 .... 59 E4
Sheffield S8 .... 43 D4
Swadlincote DE11 ...... 256 A1
Oak Tree Ave S44 ..... 134 A4
Oak Tree Cl S44 ...... 134 A4
Oak Tree Cres NG19 ... 136 A2
Oak Tree Ct DE72 ..... 221 E1
Oak Tree Gdns DE4 .... 144 A2
Oak Tree Rd S43 ...... 80 C1
Oakamoor Cl S40 ...... 95 D3
Oakbank Cl S17 .... 55 F4
Oakdale Cl S43 .... 131 F1
Oakdale Rd NG18 ...... 160 A2
Oakdell S18 .... 57 D2
Oakenthorpe Rd DE4 ... 155 D1
Oakes Park Sch S8 .... 43 F1
Oakes Park View S8 ... 43 E1
Oakes The SK13 .... 17 D4
Oakes's Row NG16 ..... 170 C3
Oakfield Cl DE7 ...... 207 F4
Oakfield Ct DE7 ...... 193 D1
Oakfield Dr NG10 ..... 223 D2
Oakfield Rd Hadfield SK13 . 9 F2
Stapleford NG9 .... 223 E4
Oakfields DE13 .... 238 A2
Oakham Cl DE21 .... 205 E1
Oakham Way DE7 .... 194 C2
Oakhill Rd S18 .... 57 E2

Oakhurst Cl DE56 .... 178 B3
Oakland Ave
  Long Eaton NG10 .... 236 B3
  Sutton in A NG17 .... 148 C1
Oakland Cres DE55 .... 170 B3
Oakland St DE55 .... 159 D2
Oakland Terr NG10 .... 236 B3
Oaklands Ave Derby DE23 .. 231 E3
  Heanor DE75 .... 182 A1
  Marple SK6 .... 23 E4
Oaklands Cl DE5 .... 180 B1
Oaklands Dr ST17 .... 269 D3
Oaklands Rd Etwall DE65 .. 229 E2
  Swadlincote DE11 .... 256 A3
Oaklands The 160 A2
Oaklands Way DE73 .... 252 A4
Oaklea SK17 .... 85 E3
Oaklea Way S42 .... 131 D3
Oakleigh Ave Derby DE21 .. 219 F3
  Swadlincote DE11 .... 255 F3
Oakley Ave S40 .... 95 F2
Oakley's Rd NG10 .... 236 C4
Oakley's Rd W NG10 ...... 236 B3
Oakover Dr DE22 .... 204 B1
Oakridge DE21 .... 220 A4
Oakridge Cl NG19 .... 136 C1
Oaks Ave Creswell S80 .... 100 B4
  Hayfield SK22 .... 25 E1
Oaks Farm La S44 .... 97 D1
Oaks La Ashover S45 .... 129 E3
  Old Brampton S42 .... 94 A4
Oaks Rd DE65 .... 242 A3
Oaks The DE21 .... 205 E4
Oaksedge La DE4 .... 144 A3
Oakside Way DE21 .... 206 A2
Oakstedge La S45 .... 145 D4
Oaktree Ave DE24 .... 232 A4
Oaktree Cl DE55 .... 170 A4
Oaktree Rd DE55 .... 148 B1
Oakwell Cres DE7 .... 208 C4
Oakwell Dr DE7 .... 208 C4
Oakwood SK13 .... 16 C4
Oakwood Cl DE65 .... 231 E1
Oakwood District Ctr
  DE21 .... 206 A1
Oakwood Dr DE21 .... 206 A1
Oakwood Inf Sch DE24 .... 233 D3
Oakwood Jun Sch DE24 .. 233 D3
Oakwood Rd SK12 .... 32 B3
Oakworth Cl S20 .... 59 F3
Oakworth Dr S20 .... 59 E3
Oakworth Gr S20 .... 59 E3
Oakworth View S20 .... 59 E3
Oardale Rd NG18 .... 268 A4
Oarr La S18 .... 56 B1
Oat Hill DE4 .... 165 F4
Oats Orch S20 .... 59 E3
Occupation Cl S43 .... 80 A3
Occupation La
  North Wingfield S42 ...... 131 F4
  Sheffield S12 .... 44 C2
  Woodville DE11 .... 256 C1
Occupation Rd
  Chesterfield S41 .... 95 F4
  Moira DE11 .... 262 B4
  New Houghton NG19 ...... 134 C4
Ochard St DE7 .... 208 C4
Ochbrook Ct DE7 .... 194 C2
Ockbrook Sch DE72 ...... 221 E3
Oddfellows Cotts **B** SK17 .. 85 D4
Oddfellows Rd S32 .... 53 D4
Oddfellows Terr S32 ...... 53 D4
Oddford La DE4 .... 127 E1
Odom Ct S8 .... 43 D3
Offcote Cres DE6 .... 173 E2
Offerton Ave DE23 .... 231 F4
Offridge Cl S43 .... 80 C1
Ogden St SK14 .... 16 A4
Ogle Dr NG7 .... 268 A1
Ogston La
  Brackenfield DE55 ...... 146 A2
  Shirland DE55 .... 146 A2
Ogston New Rd DE55 .... 145 F2
Okeover Ave DE6 .... 173 E1
Oker Ave DE4 .... 127 D2
Oker Dr DE4 .... 127 D2
Oker La DE4 .... 142 B3
Oker Rd DE4 .... 142 A4
Oker Terr DE4 .... 142 A4
Old Bakery Cl S41 .... 77 D1
Old Bank DE6 .... 184 B4
Old Barn Cl DE21 .... 205 E4
Old Chester Rd DE1 ...... 219 D4
Old Church La DE22 ...... 204 B3
Old Coach Rd DE4 ...... 143 F2
Old Coalpit La SK17 ...... 86 C1
Old Colliery La S42 ...... 132 C4
Old Coppice Side DE75 .. 193 F4
Old Dam La SK17 .... 49 E2
Old Derby Rd
  Ashbourne DE6 .... 185 E4
  Eastwood NG16 .... 182 B2
Old End DE12 .... 265 F1
Old Gate HD7 .... 2 C4
Old Gate Ave DE4 .... 245 F3
Old Hackney La DE4 ...... 142 C4
Old Hall Ave
  Derby, Alvaston DE24 .. 233 D4
  Derby, Littleover DE23 .. 218 A1
Duffield DE56 .... 190 C2
  Whaley Bridge SK23 .... 45 F2
Old Hall Cl
  Darley Dale DE4 .... 127 E2
  Glossop SK13 .... 10 B1
Old Hall Dr DE65 .... 242 A3

Old Hall Gdns
  Stoney Middleton S32 .... 72 A2
  Swadlincote DE11 .... 256 A1
Old Hall Jun Sch S40 .... 95 E1
Old Hall La
  Church Broughton DE65 .. 227 D4
  Marple SK6 .... 23 E3
  Mottram in L SK14 .... 9 D3
  Whitwell S80 .... 81 F3
Old Hall Mills Bsns Pk
  DE21 .... 205 E4
Old Hall Rd
  Chesterfield S40 .... 95 E2
  Derby DE23 .... 218 B1
Old Hall Sq **B** SK13 ...... 10 A3
Old Hartshay Hill DE5 .. 169 E1
Old Hay Gdns S17 .... 55 E3
Old Hay La S17 .... 55 E3
Old Highcliff La DE56 .... 177 D2
Old Hill Ashbourne DE6 .. 173 E1
  Bolsover S44 .... 99 D1
Old House Mus DE45 .... 109 E3
Old House Rd S40 .... 95 E3
Old La Derby DE22 .... 205 D1
  Mosborough S20 .... 60 A4
  Shottle DE56 .... 177 D3
  Wirksworth DE4 .... 154 C1
Old Lenton St NG1 .... 268 B2
Old Lime Ct DE4 .... 143 E3
Old Longhill Rd SK17 .... 65 D2
Old Manor Rd NG19 .... 136 B2
Old Mansfield Rd DE21 .. 205 E1
Old Market Pl
  Mansfield NG18 .... 268 B4
  South Normanton DE55 .. 160 A3
Old Market Sq NG1 ...... 268 B1
Old Mill Cl Duffield DE56 . 190 C2
  Pilsley S45 .... 132 B1
Old Mill Dr S40 .... 95 D4
Old Mill La NG19 .... 136 C1
Old Park Ave S8 .... 56 B4
Old Park Rd S8 .... 56 B4
Old Peveril Rd S44 .... 98 A2
Old Pit La DE7 .... 193 D3
Old Pond The DE75 ...... 194 A4
Old Rd Branston DE14 .... 253 F4
  Buxton SK23 .... 45 E3
  Chesterfield S40 .... 95 E2
  Darley Dale DE4 .... 127 E1
  Furness Vale SK23 .... 33 E2
  Heage DE56 .... 179 F4
  Ladder Hill SK23 .... 46 A1
  Mottram in L SK14 .... 9 D3
  Old Brampton S40 .... 95 E2
  Tintwistle SK14 .... 10 A4
  Whaley Bridge SK23 .... 45 F3
Old School Cl S41 .... 117 E1
Old School La
  Chesterfield S44 .... 96 C1
  Pleasley NG19 .... 135 D3
Old St SK14 .... 16 A4
Old Station Cl DE4 ...... 126 C4
Old Station Yd S43 .... 96 B4
Old Storth La DE55 ...... 160 A2
Old Terr NG19 .... 134 C2
Old Vicarage Cl DE21 .... 204 B3
Old Vicarage La DE22 .... 204 B3
Old Vicarage Sch The
  DE22 .... 205 D2
Old Whieldon Rd DE1 .. 269 F1
Old Whittington La S18 .. 76 C3
Oldbury Cl DE21 .... 206 A1
Olde Derwent Ave DE4 .. 143 D2
Oldfield Dr DE11 .... 256 B3
Oldfield La Hilton DE65 .. 241 D4
  Hognaston DE6 .... 164 A1
  Kirk Ireton DE6 .... 164 C1
  Snelston DE6 .... 184 A2
  Wensley DE4 .... 142 A4
Oldhay Cl S17 .... 55 E3
Oldicote La DE11 .... 248 C2
Oldknow Rd SK6 .... 23 D3
Oldmill St S14 .... 269 F2
Oldridge Cl S40 .... 95 D3
Oldwell Cl S17 .... 55 E2
Olga Rd NG3 .... 268 C2
Olive Ave Long Eaton NG10 . 223 F1
  Shirebrook NG20 .... 119 E3
Olive Cres S12 .... 44 A1
Olive Gr DE21 .... 219 F3
Olive Grove Rd S2 .... 43 D4
Olive Rd S20 .... 59 E4
Olive St DE22 .... 218 B3
Oliver Cl S14 .... 16 A4
Oliver Cl T Heanor DE75 . 182 A1
  Nottingham NG7 .... 268 A2
Oliver Rd Ilkeston DE7 .. 208 B3
  Stoke-on-T ST4 .... 269 D2
Oliver St NG2 .... 268 A2
Olivet Rd S8 .... 43 D2
Olivier St DE23 .... 219 D1
Ollersett Ave SK22 ...... 33 E4
Ollersett Dr SK22 .... 24 C1
Ollersett View Hospl
  SK22 .... 33 E4
Olton Rd DE3 .... 217 E2
Onslow Rd DE22 .... 217 F2
Onward Cotts SK17 .... 85 E4
Opal Cl DE21 .... 206 A1
Openacre NG16 .... 170 C2
Openwood Rd DE56 .... 179 F2
Openwoodgate DE56 .... 179 E2
Orange St DE45 .... 109 E3
Orange St S80 .... 159 D2
Orby Cl NG3 .... 268 C2
Orchard Ave
  Castle Donington DE74 .. 247 D2
  Whaley Bridge SK23 .... 45 F4

Orchard Bsns Pk
  Ilkeston DE7 .... 194 B1
  Sandiacre NG10 .... 223 E3
Orchard Cl Barlborough S43 . 80 A4
  Belper DE56 .... 191 D4
  Bolsover S44 .... 99 D1
  Breaston DE72 .... 235 F4
  Clowne S43 .... 80 C2
  Derby DE65 .... 228 B1
  Melbourne DE73 .... 252 A4
  Ockbrook DE72 .... 221 E2
  Ripley DE5 .... 181 D4
  Shirebrook NG20 .... 119 F3
  Uttoxeter ST14 .... 210 A1
  Walton-on-T DE12 ...... 253 E1
  West Hallam DE7 .... 207 F4
  Willington DE65 .... 242 A3
Orchard Cotts DE56 .... 190 C2
Orchard Cres
  Glapwell S44 .... 134 A4
  Swanwick DE55 .... 169 E4
Orchard Ct Derby DE21 .. 220 C3
  Langley Mill NG16 .... 182 A2
Orchard Cty Prim Sch
  DE74 .... 247 D2
Orchard Dr Creswell S80 .. 81 F1
  Gamesley SK13 .... 9 F1
Orchard La
  Darley Dale DE4 .... 142 C4
  Wyaston DE6 .... 185 E1
Orchard Lea S26 .... 61 F3
Orchard Pl S21 .... 60 B3
Orchard Rd Compstall SK6 .. 15 D1
  Matlock Bath DE4 .... 143 D1
  Somercotes DE55 .... 170 B3
  Whaley Bridge SK23 .... 45 E4
Orchard Rise DE75 ...... 181 F1
Orchard St **20** S18 .... 56 B1
Orchard St
  Derby, Little Chester DE1 .. 267 A4
  Derby, Mickleover DE3 .. 217 E1
  Kimberley NG16 .... 195 F3
  Langley Mill NG16 ...... 182 A2
  Long Eaton NG10 ...... 236 C4
  Mansfield NG19 .... 136 A1
  Stafford ST17 .... 269 E3
  Stapleford NG9 .... 223 D4
  Swadlincote DE11 .... 255 F3
Orchard The Belper DE56 .. 179 D2
  Codnor DE5 .... 170 A1
  Horsley Woodhouse DE7 .. 192 B3
  Stanton-by-D DE7 .... 222 C4
  Stramshall ST14 .... 210 A2
  Youlgreave DE45 ...... 125 D3
Orchard View
  Bolsover S44 .... 117 F4
  Mansfield Woodhouse
  NG19 .... 136 A2
Orchard View Rd S40 .... 95 F2
Orchard Way Derby DE21 . 232 C1
  Sandiacre NG10 .... 223 D2
Orchards The
  Derby DE22 .... 204 B2
  Westwood NG16 .... 171 D2
Orchards Way S40 .... 95 E1
Orchid Cl Burton u T DE15 . 255 D4
  Calow S44 .... 97 D2
Ordish Ave DE21 .... 219 F3
Ordley La DE6 .... 183 F4
Oregon Way DE21 .... 220 B3
Orford Ave S12 .... 32 B3
Organ Way S14 .... 9 E3
Oriel Cl ST4 .... 267 C1
Oriel St S14 .... 269 E2
Orkney Cl DE24 .... 231 E2
Orly Ave DE74 .... 247 D1
Orly Cl S18 .... 56 B1
Ormond Cl
  Chesterfield S40 .... 114 A4
  Sheffield S8 .... 57 D3
Ormond Dr S8 .... 57 D3
Ormond Rd S8 .... 57 D4
Ormonde St NG16 ...... 182 A2
Ormonde Terr NG16 .... 182 A2
Orpen Dr S14 .... 43 F1
Ormskirk Rise S20 .... 220 C2
Orpean Way NG9 .... 223 F1
Orpen Dr S14 .... 43 F1
Orpen Way S14 .... 43 F1
Osborne Cl NG10 .... 223 D2
Osborne Croft S26 .... 61 F3
Osborne Rd S11 .... 10 A3
Osborne St DE22 .... 219 E2
Osborne St S40 .... 269 D2
Osborne St DE55 .... 248 A2
Osmaston CE Prim Sch
  DE6 .... 185 F2
Osmaston Cl NG10 ...... 235 F3
Osmaston Park Ind Est
  DE24 .... 232 C4
Osmaston Rd DE23 ...... 219 D1
Osmaston St NG10 ...... 223 E3
Osmond Rd S21 .... 59 E2
Osprey Cl Burton u T DE15 . 248 A2
  Nottingham NG1 .... 231 F1
Ossington Cl NG1 ...... 268 B2
Osterly Gn DE21 ...... 218 A3
Ostrich La DE6 .... 163 D1
Otter St DE1 .... 219 D4
Otterburn Dr DE22 ...... 204 B1
Oulton Cl DE24 .... 232 A2
Oundle Dr Ilkeston DE7 .. 209 D4
  Mansfield NG19 .... 135 E1

Our Lady's RC Prim Sch
  ST4 .... 269 F1
Ousley La DE6 .... 183 E3
Out La S44 .... 132 C3
Outfield Rd DE15 .... 254 C4
Outgang La
  Mansfield Woodhouse
  NG19 .... 136 B2
  Pleasley NG19 .... 135 D3
Outlands Rd S33 .... 50 C3
Outram Ct DE5 .... 169 F1
Outram Rd S41 .... 95 F3
Outram St DE5 .... 169 F1
Outram Way DE24 ...... 231 F1
Outseats Dr S42 .... 159 D2
Oval Ct DE23 .... 231 E4
Oval The ST17 .... 269 E3
Over Haddon Craft Ctr
  DE45 .... 109 D1
Over Hill Rd Buxworth SK23 . 34 A3
  Chinley SK23 .... 34 A3
Over La Baslow DE45 ...... 91 F3
  Belper DE56 .... 179 F3
  Hazelwood DE56 .... 178 A1
Overcroft Rise S17 .... 55 E2
Overdale DE4 .... 143 E3
Overdale Ave SK17 .... 85 E4
Overdale Cl NG10 .... 236 A3
Overdale Gdns S17 ...... 55 E2
Overdale Rd Derby DE23 . 218 C1
  Disley SK12 .... 32 C3
Overdale Rise S17 .... 55 E3
Overend Cl S14 .... 43 E2
Overend Dr S14 .... 43 E2
Overend Way S14 .... 43 E2
Overlees S18 .... 75 E2
Overseal Manor Sch DE12 . 262 A2
Overseal Prim Sch DE12 .. 262 A1
Oversetts Ct DE11 .... 255 F3
Oversetts Rd DE11 ...... 255 F3
Overstone Cl DE56 ...... 179 E2
Overton Cl S43 .... 78 C2
Owen Ave NG10 .... 237 D3
Ower Bar Rd S17 .... 54 A2
Owers Ave DE75 .... 193 F4
Owlcotes View S44 .... 98 B3
Owler Car La S18 .... 57 F3
Owlersptch Dr DE23 .... 230 C1
Owlers La DE23 .... 218 B1
Owlswick Cl DE23 ...... 231 D4
Owlthorpe Ave S20 ...... 59 D4
Owlthorpe Cl S20 .... 59 D4
Owlthorpe Dr S20 .... 59 D4
Owlthorpe Gr S20 .... 59 D4
Owlthorpe La S20 .... 59 D4
Owlthorpe Rise S20 ...... 59 D4
Ox Cl S45 .... 131 E2
Ox Close Ave S17 .... 56 A3
Ox Hill S20 .... 60 A3
Oxbury Rd NG16 .... 195 F4
Oxclose Dr S18 .... 56 B1
Oxclose La
  Alsop en le D DE6 ...... 150 B1
  Dronfield S18 .... 56 B1
  Mansfield Woodhouse
  NG19 .... 136 A2
  Radmanthwaite NG19 .. 135 E2
Oxcroft Est S44 .... 99 E4
Oxcroft La Bolsover S44 .. 99 D3
  Elmton S44 .... 99 F4
Oxcroft Way S43 .... 80 A3
Oxenhope Cl DE23 ...... 230 C4
Oxford Cl S43 .... 96 C4
Oxford Cres ST4 .... 269 E2
Oxford St Blackwell DE55 . 147 F1
  Bramley-Vale S44 .... 117 F1
  Derby, Litchurch DE1 .... 267 C1
  Derby, Spondon DE21 .. 220 C3
  Eastwood NG16 ...... 182 C1
  Ilkeston DE7 .... 208 C4
  Long Eaton NG10 ...... 236 B4
  Mansfield Woodhouse
  NG19 .... 136 B1
  Nottingham NG1 ...... 268 A1
  Ripley DE5 .... 169 F1
  Scropton DE65 .... 227 D3
  Stoke-on-T ST4 .... 119 F2
  Stanley DE7 .... 207 E3
  Uttoxeter ST14 .... 210 A1
Oxley La S21 .... 59 F2
Oxmead DE6 .... 184 B4
Oxpasture La NG20 ...... 100 A3
Oxton Cl NG19 .... 268 A4
Oxwich Ct DE21 .... 206 A1
Ozier Holt NG10 .... 236 B3

Paddocks The
  Mansfield Woodhouse
  NG19 .... 136 C3
Pilsley S45 .... 132 B1
Sandiacre NG10 .... 223 D3
  Swadlincote DE11 .... 255 F3
  Woodthorpe S43 .... 79 E2
Paddocks View NG10 .... 236 A4
Padfield Cty Prim Sch
  SK13 .... 10 A3
Padfield Gate SK13 ...... 17 E4
Padfield Main Rd SK13 .. 10 A3
Padget High Sch DE14 .. 254 A4
Padgett Cl DE11 .... 255 F3
Padley Cl Derby DE22 .... 205 D3
  Ripley DE5 .... 169 E2
Padley Hill Mansfield NG18 . 268 B3
  Nether Padley S32 .... 53 F1
Padley Rd S32 .... 53 F1
Padley Way S42 .... 131 F3
Padley Wood La S45 ...... 147 D4
Padley Wood Rd S45 .... 132 B1
Padstow Cl DE24 .... 231 E2
Padstow Rd DE24 .... 233 E3
Painter's La DE6 .... 186 A2
Painters Way
  Darley Dale DE4 .... 127 E1
  Winster DE4 .... 141 E3
Paisley Cl S43 .... 97 E4
Palace La DE56 .... 166 B1
Palace Rd SK17 .... 85 D4
Palatine Gr DE23 .... 230 C4
Palatine St NG7 .... 268 A1
Palerow La
  Alderwasley DE56 ...... 166 C2
  Spout DE56 .... 166 C2
Pall Mall DE21 .... 205 F2
Palladium Dr DE23 ...... 218 A1
Palm Cl DE23 .... 218 A1
Palmbourne Ind Pk S116 . 269 D4
Palmer Cl Branston DE14 . 254 A4
  Stafford ST 16 .... 269 E4
Palmer Cres S18 .... 57 D1
Palmer Dr Stapleford NG9 . 223 E3
  Swanwick DE55 .... 169 F4
Palmerston Cl DE73 ...... 252 A4
Palmerston Gdns NG3 .. 268 B2
Palmerston St DE23 ...... 218 C1
Universal Green NG16 .. 171 F1
  Westwood NG16 .... 171 F1
Palterton La S44 .... 117 E3
Palterton Prim Sch S44 .. 118 A3
Pamela's Cl DE21 .... 221 D3
Pankhurst Pl S45 .... 131 E2
Panton Cl S14 .... 269 E4
Parade The DE3 .... 217 E1
Paradise St SK13 .... 10 A3
Parcel Terr DE22 .... 218 B3
Pares Way DE72 .... 221 E3
Park Ave Ashbourne DE6 .. 173 E1
  Awsworth NG16 .... 195 D3
  Darley Dale DE74 .... 246 C4
  Castle Donington DE74 .. 127 E2
  Dronfield S18 .... 57 D1
  Eastwood NG16 .... 182 C2
  Furness Vale SK23 .... 33 E2
  Glossop SK13 .... 10 B1
  Heage DE56 .... 179 F4
  Ilkeston DE7 .... 209 D4
  Stafford ST17 .... 269 E3
Park Ct Heanor DE75 ...... 181 F1
  Mansfield NG18 .... 268 C4
  Swadlincote DE11 .... 256 B3
Park Dene Dr SK13 ...... 10 B1
Park Farm Ctr DE22 ...... 204 B1
Park Farm Dr DE22 ...... 204 B1
Park Farm Mews S21 .... 60 B3
Park Gr DE22 .... 218 C4
Park Grange Cl S2 .... 43 E4
Park Grange Dr S2 .... 43 E4
Park Grange Mount S2 .. 43 E4
Park Grange Rd S2 ...... 43 E4
Park Grange View S2 .... 43 E4
Park Hall Ave S40 ...... 114 A4
Park Hall Cl S40 .... 114 A4
Park Hall Gdns
  Chesterfield S40 .... 114 A4
  Mansfield Woodhouse
  NG19 .... 136 B3

ark Hall La DE7 .... 207 E4
ark Hall Rd Denby DE5 .... 180 A2
Mansfield Woodhouse
NG19 .... 136 A3
ark Head Rd DE4 .... 143 D3
ark Hill Ashworth NG16 ... 195 D3
Eckington S21 .... 59 F2
ark Hill Cl SK22 .... 24 B1
ark Hill Dr DE23 .... 231 F4
ark House Prim Sch
S45 .... 132 A2
ark Jun & Inf Schs The
NG20 .... 119 F3
ark La
Castle Donington DE74 .... 246 C2
Chesterfield S41 .... 95 F4
Darley Dale DE4 .... 127 E1
Derby, Allestree DE22 .... 204 C2
Derby, Littleover DE23 ... 218 B1
Holbeck NG20 .... 101 F1
Mansfield NG18 .... 268 B3
Over Haddon DE4 .... 110 B1
Pentrich DE5 .... 169 D4
Pinxton NG16 .... 160 B1
Shirland DE5 .... 159 D4
Shirley DE6 .... 200 B4
South Wingfield DE55 ..... 157 E1
Tutbury DE13 .... 239 D3
Weston-on-T DE72 .... 245 F2
ark Leys Ct DE21 .... 220 C2
ark Mews
Mansfield Woodhouse
NG19 .... 136 B2
Somercotes DE55 .... 170 B3
ark Mill Dr DE55 .... 159 E4
ark Pale The DE13 .... 239 E3
ark Ravine NG7 .... 268 A1
ark Rd Ashbourne DE6 ..... 173 E1
Bakewell DE45 .... 109 C3
Belper DE56 .... 179 D1
Buxton SK17 .... 85 D4
Chapel-en-le-F SK23 ...... 47 D3
Chesterfield S40 .... 266 A1
Chesterfield S40 .... 266 B2
Derby, Mickleover DE3 .... 217 E1
Derby, Spondon DE21 ...... 220 B3
Disley SK12 .... 32 A3
Duffield DE56 .... 190 B2
Hadfield SK13 .... 10 A2
Heage DE56 .... 179 F4
Holmewood S42 .... 116 C1
Ilkeston DE7 .... 208 C4
Linton DE12 .... 262 A3
Mansfield Woodhouse
NG19 .... 136 A2
New Mills SK22 .... 33 E4
Nottingham NG7 .... 268 A1
Ripley DE5 .... 169 F1
Shirebrook NG20 .... 119 F3
Nottingham NG7 .... 223 F4
Swadlincote, Church Gresley
DE11 .... 256 B1
Swadlincote, Newhall DE12 . 255 B1
Tupton S42 .... 131 C2
Whaley Bridge SK23 .... 45 E3
ark Rise S18 .... 75 D4
ark Row Clay Cross S45 ... 131 E2
ark Side DE55 .... 170 B4
ark Spring Cl S2 .... 43 E4
ark Spring Dr S2 .... 43 E4
ark Spring Gr S2 .... 43 E4
ark Spring Pl S2 .... 43 E4
ark Spring Rd S2 .... 43 E4
ark St Alfreton DE55 ..... 158 C2
Barlborough S43 .... 80 A4
Breaston DE72 .... 235 F4
Chesterfield S40 .... 115 D4
Derby DE1 .... 267 D2
Heanor DE75 .... 181 E1
Long Eaton NG10 .... 223 E1
Mansfield Woodhouse
NG19 .... 136 A2
Ripley DE5 .... 169 F1
Stafford ST17 .... 269 E3
Stapleford NG9 .... 223 E3
Swadlincote DE11 .... 256 A3
Uttoxeter ST14 .... 210 B1
Wessington DE55 .... 157 F4
ark Terr Glossop SK13 .... 17 E4
Northwood DE4 .... 127 D3
Nottingham NG7 .... 268 A1
ark The Darley Dale DE4 .. 127 E2
Mansfield NG18 .... 268 A1
Mayfield DE6 .... 184 B4
ark Valley NG7 .... 268 A1
ark View
Aston-on-T DE72 .... 246 A4
Bakewell DE45 .... 109 E3
Barlborough S43 .... 80 A4
Chesterfield S41 .... 115 E4
Clowne S43 .... 80 C3
Heanor DE75 .... 181 E1
Somercotes DE55 .... 170 B3
ark View Ave S20 .... 59 F4
ark View Cl DE22 .... 204 C2
ark View Ct S18 .... 43 D1
ark View Dr SK23 .... 47 D3
ark View Rise SK22 .... 24 B1
ark View Way NG18 .... 268 C3
ark Way DE65 .... 229 E2
arker Ave S44 .... 96 C2
arker Cl DE1 .... 267 A4
arker Ctr DE21 .... 219 E4
arker St DE1 .... 218 C4
arker's Croft Rd ST17 .... 269 E3
arker's La NG19 .... 136 B2

Parkers Cl DE11 .... 257 D1
Parkers La S17 .... 55 E4
Parkfield Cl S12 .... 43 D4
Parkfield Cres DE12 ...... 265 F1
Parkfield Ct SK17 .... 85 D4
Parkfields Cl DE4 .... 184 B2
Parkfields Dr DE22 .... 204 C1
Parkgate Cl S20 .... 59 D4
Parkgate Croft S20 ...... 59 D4
Parkgate Dr S20 .... 59 D4
Parkgate La Staveley S21 . 77 F3
Unstone S21 .... 77 F3
Parkham Rd NG16 .... 195 F4
Parkhill La S17 .... 60 B1
Parkhouse Cl S45 .... 131 D2
Parkhouse Dr DE55 .... 159 F3
Parkhouse Rd S45 .... 132 A2
Parkin St DE55 .... 159 D2
Parkland Ave S42 .... 24 B1
Parkland Dr S42 .... 115 D1
Parklands Dr DE3 .... 245 A4
Parklands Inf Sch NG10 .. 223 D1
Parks Ave DE55 .... 157 F2
Parkside Buxton SK17 .... 85 D4
Heage DE56 .... 179 F4
Parkside Ave NG10 .... 236 A4
Parkside Cl NG16 .... 170 C2
Parkside Com Sch S40 .... 266 A2
Parkside Dr Ironville NG16 . 170 C2
Long Eaton NG10 .... 236 A4
Parkside Jun Sch DE6 .... 173 E1
Parkside La SK6 .... 23 E3
Parkside Rd DE21 .... 220 A3
Parkside Sh Ctr S21 ..... 60 B4
Parkview DE21 .... 205 E4
Parkside S41 .... 85 E3
Parkway Derby DE21 ...... 232 C1
New Mills SK22 .... 24 B1
Whitwell S80 .... 82 A3
Parkway Ct S8 .... 56 C4
Parkway The DE4 .... 127 E2
Parkwood Sch DE55 ...... 158 C2
Parliament Cl DE22 ...... 218 C2
Parliament St NG16 ...... 268 A4
Parliament St Derby DE22 . 218 C2
Swadlincote DE11 .... 255 F3
Parsonage Cl S20 .... 59 F3
Parsonage Croft DE45 .... 109 E3
Parsonage Gdns SK6 ...... 23 D2
Parsons Cl SK17 .... 137 E3
Parsons Gate S33 .... 40 A3
Parsons Gr DE21 .... 180 B1
Partington Cl SK13 ...... 10 C1
Partington Pk SK13 ...... 10 B2
Partridge Cl S21 .... 59 D2
Partridge Dr DE11 .... 256 C2
Partridge Way DE3 .... 218 A2
Parture Gr S21 .... 59 F2
Parwich Cl S40 .... 95 D3
Parwich La DE4 .... 151 E1
Parwich Prim Sch DE6 .... 151 E1
Parwich Rd S42 .... 131 F3
Pasteur Ave DE5 .... 180 A1
Pasture La Brassington DE4 . 152 B1
Flagg SK17 .... 106 B3
Hilcote DE55 .... 148 B1
Long Eaton NG10 .... 237 D3
Stonebroom DE55 .... 147 D2
Pasture Rd NG9 .... 209 E1
Pastures Ave DE23 .... 230 C4
Pastures Hill DE23 ...... 230 C4
Pastures Hospl DE3 ...... 230 A4
Pastures The
Duffield DE56 .... 190 C2
Eastwood NG16 .... 195 D4
Mansfield Woodhouse
NG19 .... 136 C3
Repton DE65 .... 242 B1
Swadlincote DE11 .... 255 F3
Paterson Ave DE21 .... 220 A3
Patmore Sq DE23 .... 231 F4
Paton Gr S43 .... 96 B4
Patrick Cl DE12 .... 261 E3
Patterdale Cl S18 .... 56 C1
Patterson Pl NG18 .... 268 C4
Pattison St S44 .... 98 C3
Paulet High Sch DE15 .... 254 C4
Paulson's Dr NG18 .... 268 B4
Pavilion Cl S43 .... 80 C1
Pavilion Gdns Buxton SK17 . 85 D4
New Houghton NG19 .... 134 C4
Pavilion Rd Derby DE23 .. 231 E4
DE7 .... 194 C3
Pavilion Workshops S42 .. 116 B1
Paxton Cl Derby DE3 ..... 217 E1
Matlock DE4 .... 143 D3
Paxton Ct S14 .... 43 F2
Paxton Gdns NG3 .... 268 C2
Paxton Rd S41 .... 96 B3
Payler Cl S2 .... 44 A4
Payne St DE22 .... 218 B3
Peach Ave Selston NG16 .. 171 F3
South Normanton DE55 .... 160 A4
Peach St Derby DE22 ..... 218 B1
Heanor DE75 .... 181 E1
Peacock St NG1 .... 268 B2
Peacock Pl Hadfield SK13 . 9 F2
Killamarsh S21 .... 60 B3
Peacock Pl DE7 .... 192 B4
Peacock Way DE55 .... 169 F4
Peacroft La DE65 .... 228 B1
Peafield La NG19 .... 136 C2
Peafield Lane Prim Sch
NG19 .... 136 C2

Peak Ave DE55 .... 170 A3
Peak Cavern S33 .... 38 A1
Peak Dale Prim Sch SK17 . 67 D3
Peak Forest CE Prim Sch
SK17 .... 49 D3
Peak Pl S43 .... 97 E4
Peak Railway DE4 .... 143 D3
Peak Rd SK22 .... 33 E4
Peak The NG20 .... 119 F2
Peak View Clowne S43 .... 80 B3
South Normanton DE55 .... 159 F3
Peak View Dr DE6 .... 173 E1
Peak View Rd S40 .... 95 E3
Peakdale Cl
Long Eaton NG10 .... 236 A3
Ripley DE5 .... 180 B3
Peakdale Cres S12 .... 44 C3
Peakdale Rd Hadfield SK13 . 9 F2
Marple SK6 .... 23 A3
Peakland View DE4 ...... 127 D2
Peaknaze Cl SK13 .... 17 D4
Peaktor La DE4 .... 126 C4
Pear Tree Ave Ripley DE5 . 180 B4
South Normanton DE55 .... 159 F3
Pear Tree Cl Brimington S43 . 97 D4
Hadfield SK13 .... 9 F2
Hartshorne DE11 .... 257 D4
Killamarsh S21 .... 60 B3
Wilson DE73 .... 252 C4
Pear Tree Com Jun & Inf
Schs DE23 .... 232 A4
Pear Tree Cres DE23 .... 232 A4
Pear Tree Dr Linton DE12 . 261 E3
Pear Tree Rd DE55 ...... 159 D2
Pear Tree St DE23 ...... 219 D1
Pear Tree Sta DE23 ..... 232 A4
Pearce La S42 .... 114 B2
Pearl Bank DE6 .... 211 F4
Pearl Way SK14 .... 9 D1
Peartree Ave S42 .... 114 C2
Peartree Cl DE7 .... 194 C2
Peartree Cl DE24 .... 205 E1
Peartree La NG17 .... 134 A1
Peartree Schs DE23 ..... 219 D1
Peas Hill Rd NG3 .... 268 B2
Pease Cl S43 .... 159 D2
Pease Hill Rd DE55 ..... 159 D2
Peasehill Rd DE5 .... 180 C4
Peasunhurst La S45 ..... 113 D1
Peat La DE56 .... 166 B2
Peatburn Ave DE75 ...... 181 E1
Peatfield Rd Killamarsh S21 . 60 C4
Stapleford NG9 .... 209 E1
Peats Cl DE6 .... 165 D1
Peckham Gdns DE55 ...... 218 A3
Pedley Ave S20 .... 59 F4
Pedley Dr S20 .... 59 F4
Pedley St DE7 .... 208 C4
Peebles Cl DE24 .... 231 F1
Peel Cres NG19 .... 135 E1
Peel St Long Eaton NG10 . 236 C4
Langley Mill NG16 ...... 182 A2
Long Eaton NG10 .... 236 C4
Nottingham NG1 .... 268 A2
Padfield SK13 .... 10 B3
South Normanton DE55 ... 160 A3
Stafford ST16 .... 269 D4
Peers Cl DE21 .... 206 A1
Peet St DE22 .... 218 C2
Pegasus Way DE65 ...... 228 C1
Pegg's Wlk DE23 .... 231 F4
Pegwell Cl DE23 .... 231 E4
Pelham Ave DE7 .... 194 C1
Pelham Cres NG7 .... 268 A1
Pelham St Derby DE22 ... 218 C2
Mansfield NG18 .... 268 C4
NG1 Nottingham NG1 .... 268 B1
Pemberton St NG1 ...... 268 B1
Pemberton The DE55 .... 160 A2
Pembleton Dr NG19 ..... 135 E1
Pembrey Cl NG9 .... 209 F1
Pembroke Cl S40 .... 95 E1
Pembroke Ct S41 .... 96 B3
Pembroke Rd Dronfield S18 . 76 A4
Shireoaks S81 .... 63 F4
Pembroke St DE21 ...... 219 E4
Pen Cl DE55 .... 148 A2
Penallton Cl DE24 ..... 232 C3
Pendean Cl DE55 .... 147 F1
Pendennis Cl DE24 ..... 233 D3
Pendine Cl DE55 .... 160 B3
Pendlebury Dr DE21 .... 217 F1
Pendleside Way DE24 ... 230 C4
Pendleton La DE56 ..... 166 C4
Penfold Way DE55 ...... 147 F1
Penge Rd DE22 .... 218 A4
Penhallgan's Cl DE73 .. 233 E2
Penine View DE56 ...... 179 F4
Peniston Rise DE73 .... 252 A4
Penistone Gdns S45 .... 131 E1
Penkhull Inf Sch ST4 .. 269 E2
Penkhull New Rd ST4 ... 269 E1
Penkhull Terr ST4 ..... 269 E1
Penkhull St ST4 .... 269 E1
Penmore Cl S41 .... 115 E4
Penmore Gdns S41 ...... 96 B1
Penmore La S41 .... 115 E4
Penmore St S41 .... 115 E4
Penn La DE73 .... 252 A4
Penn St NG3 .... 268 C2
Penncroft Dr S45 ...... 131 E2
Penncroft La S45 ...... 131 E2
Penniment La NG19 ..... 135 D1

Pennine Ave DE55 ...... 170 B4
Pennine Cl
Long Eaton, New Sawley
NG10 .... 236 B2
Long Eaton, Wilsthorpe
NG10 .... 223 D1
Mansfield Woodhouse NG19 . 136 B2
Newton DE55 .... 148 A2
Sutton in a NG17 ...... 148 C2
Tibshelf DE55 .... 147 F3
Pennine Dr Selston NG16 . 171 F4
South Normanton DE55 ... 159 F3
Pennine Rd SK13 .... 17 D4
Pennine View S44 ...... 118 A3
Pennine Way
Chesterfield S40 ...... 95 E3
Grassmoor S42 .... 115 F2
Swadlincote DE11 ...... 256 A1
Pennine Way Jun Sch
DE11 .... 256 A1
Pennine Way S42 .... 43 E3
Pennfoot St NG1 .... 268 C1
Pennytown Ct S55 ..... 159 E1
Pennyunk La DE45 ..... 89 F1
Pennywell Dr S42 ..... 113 E4
Penrhyn Ave DE23 ..... 218 B1
Penrhyn Cl NG3 .... 268 B2
Penrith Pl DE21 ..... 205 E1
Penrose Cres S44 .... 97 E2
Pentagon The DE21 ... 219 E3
Pentewan Cl DE22 .... 204 C1
Penthorpe Cl S12 .... 44 A3
Pentland Cl
Chesterfield S40 .... 95 E3
Derby DE21 .... 206 A1
Pentland Gdns NG10 .. 223 D1
Pentland Rd S18 ..... 56 B1
Pentrich Rd Ripley DE5 . 169 E1
Swanwick DE55 .... 169 E4
Penzance Rd DE24 .... 233 D3
Pepper La DE7 .... 208 C1
Percy St Derby DE22 .. 218 C2
Ilkeston DE7 .... 208 C4
Percy Wood Cl DE65 .. 228 B1
Peregrine Way S26 ... 61 F3
Peregrine Cl
Burton u T DE15 .... 248 B2
S Burton u T DE15 ... 231 E2
Perlethorpe Ave
Nottingham NG3 ..... 136 A1
Northern NG2 .... 268 C1
Perth Cl Burton u T DE15 . 248 B1
Derby DE3 .... 217 F2
Mansfield Woodhouse
NG19 .... 136 A3
Perth Dr NG9 .... 209 F1
Perth St Derby DE21 . 205 E1
Mansfield NG18 ..... 268 B2
Peter Baines Ind Est DE22 . 267 A1
Peter More Hill S80 . 81 F2
Peter St Ashbourne DE6 . 173 E1
Hadfield SK13 ...... 10 A3
Peterborough St DE21 . 219 F4
Peterdale Cl S43 ... 96 C4
Peterdale Rd S43 ... 96 C4
Peterhouse Terr DE23 . 219 D1
Peterlee Pl DE24 ... 233 D3
Peters Ave S45 ..... 131 D2
Peters Ct DE65 ..... 227 E1
Petersgate NG10 .... 223 D1
Petersgate Cl NG10 . 223 D1
Petersham Dr DE24 .. 233 E3
Petersham Rd NG10 .. 223 D1
Petersway NG10 ..... 170 B4
Pettifor Terr DE55 . 147 E1
Petty Close La DE6 . 202 B1
Pettyclose La S41 .. 96 B3
Petworth Ave NG9 ... 223 F2
Pevensey Ave S41 ... 95 F3
Pevensey Ct S41 ... 95 F3
Peveril Ave Borrowash DE72 . 221 E1
New Mills SK22 ..... 24 B1
Peveril Cl Castleton S33 . 38 B1
Darley Dale DE4 .... 127 E2
Somercotes DE55 ... 170 B3
Peveril Cres
Long Eaton NG10 ... 235 F3
West Hallam DE7 ... 207 F4
Peveril Ct Glossop SK13 . 17 F4
Ripley DE5 .... 169 E1
Peveril Mews SK12 .. 33 D3
Peveril Rd Buxton SK17 . 85 E4
Castleton S33 ...... 38 B1
Chesterfield S41 ... 95 F4
Eckington S21 ...... 59 F2
Tibshelf DE55 ...... 147 F3
Peveril St NG1 ..... 268 A2
Pewit Cl S42 .... 132 B4
Pewit La Pilsley DE55 . 147 E3
Tibshelf DE55 ...... 147 E3
Pheasant Field Dr DE21 . 221 D3
Pheasant Hill NG19 . 136 A1
Philip Howard Rd SK13 . 17 E4

Philips Croft DE56 .. 190 C2
Philipway DE55 ...... 170 B4
Phoenix Cl S12 ..... 44 C1
Phoenix Rd S12 ..... 44 C1
Phoenix St DE1 ..... 267 B4
Phyllis Gr NG10 .... 236 C4
Pic Tor La DE4 ..... 143 D2
Piccadilly Cotts S41 . 96 B2
Piccadilly Cl S41 .. 96 B2
Piccadilly Rd S41 .. 96 B2
Pickard La DE56 .... 168 B1
Pickering Ave NG16 . 182 C1
Pickering Rise DE21 . 205 E1
Pickford St DE23 ... 47 D3
Pickleys La DE6 .... 224 B4
Pickton Cl S40 ..... 95 E1
Pictor Gr SK17 .... 85 E4
Pictor Rd SK17 .... 85 E4
Piddocks Rd DE15 .. 255 D3
Pig La DE4 .... 111 D2
Pighills La S18 .... 57 D2
Pike Cl S40 .... 95 D3
Pike View Cl SK23 .. 34 C1
Pike's La SK13 .... 17 C3
Pilgrim Cl S41 .... 266 B1
Pilgrim Ct S81 .... 63 F4
Pilgrim Pl S16 .... 269 E3
Pilgrim St S16 .... 269 E3
Pilgrims Way DE24 .. 231 E2
Pilhough La DE4 ... 126 B3
Pilhough Rd DE4 ... 126 C3
Pilkington's Yd S21 . 59 F2
Pillar Butts DE4 .. 165 F4
Pilsley CE Prim Sch DE45 . 91 E1
Pilsley Cl DE56 ... 179 E3
Pilsley Prim Sch S45 . 132 B1
Pilsley Rd Clay Cross S45 . 131 F2
Morton DE55 .... 147 D3
Pimlico Derby DE22 .. 218 A3
Ilkeston DE7 ...... 208 C4
Pimm's Rd DE6 .... 217 D4
Pinch The DE4 .... 150 A1
Pinchom's Hill Rd DE56 . 179 D2
Pincot Rd DE22 ... 33 E4
Pindale Ave S43 .. 97 E4
Pindale Rd Castleton S33 . 38 C1
Hope S33 .... 38 C1
Pinder St NG1 .... 268 B1
Pine Ave NG16 .... 182 A2
Pine Cl Branston DE14 . 254 A4
Creswell S80 ..... 82 C1
Derby DE21 .... 220 A2
Etwall DE65 ...... 229 E2
Killamarsh S21 ... 60 B3
Mansfield Woodhouse
NG19 .... 136 B3
Ripley DE5 .... 169 E1
Shirebrook NG20 .. 119 F3
Smalley DE7 ...... 192 C3
Pine Croft DE56 .. 185 E4
Pine Gr DE11 ..... 256 A3
Pine St S43 ...... 97 D4
Pine Tree Wlk NG16 . 182 B1
Pine View Chesterfield S40 . 95 D2
Clay Cross S45 ... 131 F2
Pine Wlk DE11 ... 261 F4
Pinecroft Ct DE21 . 206 A1
Pines The DE72 .. 235 D3
Pinewood DE5 .... 181 D4
Pinewood Rd Belper DE56 . 178 C3
Burton u T DE15 .. 254 C3
Matlock DE4 ...... 143 D4
Pinfold SK13 .... 9 F2
Pinfold Cl
Holymoorside S42 .. 113 F4
Repton DE65 ..... 242 B1
Tutbury DE13 .... 239 E3
Pinfold Cres SK17 . 69 E2
Pinfold Hill S32 . 72 C1
Pinfold La Bradley DE6 . 187 D4
Repton DE65 ..... 242 B1
Stapleford NG9 .. 223 F4
Pinfold Rd SK17 . 69 E2
Pinfold St S21 .. 59 E2
Pinfold The Belper DE56 . 179 E3
Elvaston DE72 ... 233 F2
Glapwell S44 .... 118 A1
Lea DE4 .... 156 C1
Pinfold View DE45 . 109 C3
Pingle La DE55 .. 170 B3
Pingle Cres DE56 . 178 C3
Pingle Farm Rd DE11 . 255 F3
Pingle Grange S43 . 96 C4
Pingle La Belper DE56 . 178 C3
Carsington DE4 .. 164 C4
Pingle Rd S21 ... 60 C4
Pingle Sch DE11 . 256 A3
Pingle The Derby DE21 . 220 C2
Long Eaton NG10 . 236 B4
Melbourne DE73 .. 252 A4
Pingott La SK13 . 10 A3
Pintail Dr DE24 . 231 E2
Pinxton Gn NG16 . 160 C2
Pinxton La
Kirby-in-A NG17 . 160 C3
South Normanton DE55 . 160 B3
Piper Ave S45 ... 131 F2
Piper La Holymoorside S42 . 94 C2
Old Brampton S40 . 94 C2
Pipeyard La S21 . 59 E1
Pippenwell Rd SK17 . 106 A4
Pippin Hill DE5 . 180 C1
Pipworth La S21 . 59 F2
Pit Close La DE73 . 233 D1
Pit Farm DE55 ... 170 A2

Pit La Codnor DE5 .... 181 D4
Crich DE4 .... 157 D3
Ripley DE5 .... 169 F1
Sheffield S13 .... 44 A4
Shipley DE75 .... 194 A3
Shirland DE55 .... 158 B4
Pitch Cl S43 .... 80 C1
Pitt Hill NG20 .... 100 C1
Pitt St S21 .... 59 E1
Pittar St DE22 .... 267 A2
Pittlemere La SK17 .... 50 A1
Pittywood Rd DE4 .... 165 F4
Placket La DE4 .... 141 D3
Plackett Cl DE72 .... 235 E4
Plain The DE6 .... 201 F4
Plains La DE56 .... 178 A2
Plainspot Rd NG16 .... 171 F1
Plaistow Green Rd DE4 .... 156 C1
Plant La NG10 .... 236 A2
Plantagenet St NG3 .... 268 B2
Plantain Gdns DE23 .... 231 E3
Plantation Cl S80 .... 81 F3
Plantation Rd S8 .... 43 D3
Plantations The **8** NG10 .... 236 A4
Plantin Rise S20 .... 59 F4
Plantin The S20 .... 59 F4
Platt St Padfield SK13 .... 10 A3
Pinxton NG16 .... 160 B1
Platts Ave DE75 .... 181 E1
Pleasant Ave S44 .... 118 A4
Pleasant Cl S12 .... 44 A3
Pleasant Pl S40 .... 95 E2
Pleasant Rd S12 .... 44 A3
Pleasant View SK6 .... 15 D2
Plimsoll St DE22 .... 218 B3
Plough Gate DE22 .... 204 C1
Plough La NG1 .... 268 C1
Ploughfield Cl DE23 .... 231 D3
Plover Ave DE11 .... 256 C2
Plover Way S44 .... 96 C2
Plowman Ct NG9 .... 223 E3
Plowright Cl S14 .... 43 E3
Plowright Dr S14 .... 43 E3
Plowright Mount S14 .... 43 E3
Plowright Way S14 .... 43 E3
Plucksbridge Rd SK6 .... 23 D2
Plumbley Hall Mews S20 .... 59 E3
Plumbley Hall Rd S20 .... 59 E3
Plumbley La S12 .... 59 D3
Plummer Rd DE11 .... 256 A3
Plumptre NG16 .... 182 A3
Plumptre Cl NG16 .... 182 C1
Plumptre Sq NG1 .... 268 B1
Plumptre St NG1 .... 268 B1
Plumptre Way NG16 .... 182 C1
Plymouth Ave NG16 .... 160 C1
Pocknedge La S42 .... 113 E4
Pole La Marple SK22 .... 24 A2
New Mills SK22, SK6 .... 24 A2
Pole's Rd DE6 .... 217 D4
Pollard Dr NG18 .... 268 C4
Pollards Oaks DE72 .... 221 E1
Polly Froggat La S32 .... 72 A1
Polyfields La S44 .... 118 A4
Pond La Tupton S42 .... 131 E4
Wingerworth S42 .... 114 C2
Pond Rd DE56 .... 191 E4
Pond St S40 .... 266 B2
Pondwell Cnr S43 .... 96 C4
Pondwell Dr S43 .... 96 C4
Ponsonby Terr DE1 .... 218 C3
Pontefract St DE24 .... 232 B4
Pontypool Cl DE21 .... 206 A1
Pool Cl Elvaston DE24 .... 233 E2
Pinxton NG16 .... 160 B1
Pool Rd DE11 .... 252 B3
Pool St DE1 .... 256 B1
Pool's La S21 .... 77 E4
Poole St DE24 .... 232 C3
Poole's Cavern SK17 .... 84 C3
Poolsbrook Ave S43 .... 98 A4
Poolsbrook Cres S43 .... 98 A4
Poolsbrook Prim Sch S43 .... 98 A4
Poolsbrook Rd S44 .... 98 A3
Poolsbrook Sq S43 .... 98 A4
Poolsbrook View S43 .... 98 A4
Pope Carr Rd DE4 .... 143 E3
New Mills SK22 .... 266 B1
Poplar Ave Chesterfield S40 .... 95 D1
Derby DE21 .... 220 C3
Moira DE12 .... 262 C1
New Mills SK22 .... 24 A1
Ripley DE5 .... 180 B4
Sandiacre NG10 .... 223 D4
Swadlincote DE11 .... 256 A3
Poplar Cl Derby DE24 .... 233 D4
Dronfield S18 .... 76 B4
Killamarsh S21 .... 60 B3
Poplar Cres DE6 .... 185 E4
Poplar Dr Glapwell S44 .... 134 A4
Pleasleyhill NG19 .... 135 D2
Poplar Nook DE22 .... 204 C2
Poplar Rd Breaston DE72 .... 235 F4
Eckington S21 .... 59 E1
South Normanton DE55 .... 160 A4
Poplar Row DE22 .... 205 D1
Poplar St
Mansfield Woodhouse
NG19 .... 136 B2
Nottingham NG1 .... 268 C1
Poplar Terr SK23 .... 47 D4
Poplar Way High Lane SK6 .... 32 A4
Ilkeston DE7 .... 208 B3
Poplars The Derby DE22 .... 204 C2
Whitwell S80 .... 82 A3

Porlock Cl **2** NG10 .... 236 A4
Porlock Ct DE21 .... 206 A1
Port Way DE21, DE56 .... 191 E3
Porteous Cl DE4 .... 127 E2
Porter La Matlock Bath DE4 .... 154 C2
Middleton (Nr Wirksworth)
DE4 .... 154 C2
Wirksworth DE4 .... 154 C2
Porter Rd DE23 .... 218 C1
Porter St S43 .... 78 C1
Porter's La Derby DE21 .... 205 F2
Findern DE65 .... 230 B1
Porterhouse Rd DE5 .... 169 F1
Porters Farm ST14 .... 224 C1
Portcharl Pl DE21 .... 206 B1
Portland Ave Bolsover S44 .... 99 D1
Branston DE14 .... 254 A2
Creswell S80 .... 81 F1
Portland Cl DE7 .... 217 E1
Portland Cres Bolsover S44 .... 99 D1
Mansfield Woodhouse
NG19 .... 136 B2
Stapleford NG9 .... 223 F3
Portland Ct Mews NG19 .... 136 B2
Portland Gr SK23 .... 34 C1
Portland Rd Beeston NG9 .... 223 F1
Eastwood NG16 .... 195 D4
Ilkeston DE7 .... 194 C2
Long Eaton NG10 .... 236 A2
New Mills SK22 .... 24 B1
Nottingham NG7 .... 268 A2
Shirebrook NG20 .... 119 F2
Whaley Thorns NG20 .... 101 D1
Portland Sq DE45 .... 109 E3
Portland St Clowne S43 .... 81 D2
Derby DE23 .... 232 A4
Etwall DE65 .... 229 D2
Mansfield Woodhouse
NG19 .... 136 B2
New Houghton NG19 .... 135 D4
Whitwell S80 .... 81 F3
Portman Cl Matlock DE4 .... 143 E4
Portman Chase DE24 .... 231 E1
Portreath Dr DE22 .... 204 C2
Portway DE22 .... 205 D3
Portway Dr DE13 .... 239 E3
Portway Inf & Jun Sch
DE22 .... 204 C2
Post St SK13 .... 10 A3
Postern St **4** NG1 .... 268 A1
Postmans La S44 .... 116 B2
Posy La DE7 .... 246 A4
Potato Pit Hill DE7 .... 208 A1
Potlocks The DE65 .... 242 B3
Potter Rd SK13 .... 9 F2
Potter St Derby DE21 .... 220 B2
Melbourne DE73 .... 252 A4
Potters Cl S41 .... 77 E1
Potters La S44 .... 157 D3
Potters Nook S81 .... 63 F4
Potters Way S40 .... 209 D4
Pottery Cl DE56 .... 179 E3
Pottery La Chesterfield S41 .... 96 A4
Denby DE5 .... 180 B2
Pottery Prim Sch DE56 .... 179 E2
Poulson St ST4 .... 269 E2
Poulter St NG20 .... 100 C1
Poulton Dr NG2 .... 268 C1
Poultry NG1 .... 268 B1
Powell Dr S21 .... 60 B3
Powell St DE23 .... 218 C1
Powtrell Pl DE7 .... 209 D3
Poynter Cl DE75 .... 181 E1
Poynton Wood Cres S17 .... 56 A3
Poynton Wood Glade S17 .... 56 A3
Poyser Ave DE21 .... 220 A4
Poyser La DE6 .... 203 D1
Pratt Cl NG19 .... 135 E1
Pratthall La DE56 .... 166 A3
Premier Ave DE6 .... 185 E4
Prescot Cl DE3 .... 217 E1
Prescott Ave ST 16 .... 269 F4
Press La S42 .... 130 B3
Prestbury Cl DE21 .... 206 A1
Preston Ave DE55 .... 159 D2
Preston Ave DE55 .... 159 D2
Preston St DE58 .... 43 D4
Prestwood Ct ST17 .... 269 E3
Prestwood La ST14 .... 196 C4
Prestwood Park Dr DE11 .... 256 B3
Pretoria St S44 .... 98 C3
Previn Gdns NG3 .... 268 C2
Pride Park Stad
(Derby FC) DE21 .... 219 F2
Pride Parkway DE21 .... 219 E2
Priestcliffe Rd SK17 .... 87 F2
Priestland Ave DE24 .... 232 B4
Priestley Ave DE55 .... 146 B3
Primary Cl DE56 .... 179 D2
Prime Ind Est DE23 .... 219 D1
Prime Ind Pke DE23 .... 219 E1
Primrose Ave NG16 .... 171 F1
Primrose Cl Derby DE21 .... 205 F2
Killamarsh S21 .... 60 C4
South Normanton DE55 .... 160 A4
Primrose Cres SK13 .... 17 D4
Primrose Dr DE7 .... 206 B4
Primrose Hill
Blackwell DE55 .... 147 F1
Glossop SK13 .... 17 D4
Primrose La Glossop SK13 .... 17 D4
Killamarsh S21 .... 60 C4
Little Hayfield SK22 .... 25 E3
Marple SK6 .... 24 A2
Primrose Meadow DE11 .... 256 A4
Primrose Rise NG16 .... 195 D4

Primrose St DE7 .... 194 C2
Primula Way DE23 .... 231 E2
Prince Charles Ave DE7 .... 218 A3
Prince Edward Fst & Mid
Sch S2 .... 44 A4
Prince of Wales Rd S2 .... 44 A4
Prince St Ilkeston DE7 .... 194 C2
Long Eaton NG10 .... 236 B4
Prince's Rd Buxton SK17 .... 85 E4
Stoke-on-T S4 .... 269 D2
Princes Dr DE23 .... 218 A2
Princes Rd S423 .... 34 C1
Princes St Derby DE23 .... 219 D1
Mansfield NG18 .... 268 B3
4 Stafford ST16 .... 269 E4
Princess Ave Linton DE12 .... 261 E3
South Normanton DE55 .... 160 A3
Princess Cl DE11 .... 256 C1
Princess Ct S2 .... 44 A4
Princess Dr
Borrowash DE72 .... 221 D1
Sandiacre NG10 .... 223 D4
Princess Pl S45 .... 131 E1
Princess Rd Dronfield S18 .... 57 D1
Uttoxeter ST14 .... 210 A1
Princess St Brimington S43 .... 96 C4
Chesterfield S40 .... 266 A4
Eastwood NG16 .... 182 C2
Glossop SK13 .... 17 E4
Long Eaton NG10 .... 236 B4
Swadlincote DE11 .... 261 F4
Princess Way DE13 .... 240 C1
Printers Fold SK14 .... 9 E3
Printers Pk SK14 .... 9 F3
Priors Barn Cl DE72 .... 221 E1
Priorway Ave DE72 .... 221 E1
Priorway Gdns DE72 .... 221 E1
Priory Cl Derby DE73 .... 245 D4
Ilkeston DE7 .... 208 B3
Swadlincote DE11 .... 256 A3
Tutbury DE13 .... 239 D3
Yeaveley DE6 .... 199 E3
Priory Ct S26 .... 61 E3
Priory Gdns DE55 .... 170 A4
Priory Lands DE13 .... 240 C1
Priory Rd Alfreton DE55 .... 159 D3
Eastwood NG16 .... 182 C1
Mansfield Woodhouse NG19 .... 136 A2
Priory Sq NG19 .... 136 A2
Pritchard Dr NG9 .... 223 F3
Pritchett Dr DE23 .... 230 C4
Private Dr S43 .... 78 A1
Progress Ct DE45 .... 109 E3
Prospect Cl S18 .... 75 E3
Prospect Ct **3** Sheffield S17 .... 56 A3
Sutton in a NG17 .... 148 C1
Prospect Dr Belper DE56 .... 178 C1
Matlock DE4 .... 143 D3
Sheffield S17 .... 56 A3
Shirebrook NG20 .... 119 F2
Prospect Pl **5** S17 .... 56 A3
Prospect Rd
Chesterfield S45 .... 76 C1
Denby DE5 .... 180 A1
Dronfield S18 .... 57 E2
Heanor DE75 .... 194 A4
Pilsley S45 .... 132 B1
Sheffield, Lowfield S2 .... 43 D4
Sheffield, Totley Rise S17 .... 56 A3
Stafford ST16 .... 269 F4
Prospect St Alfreton DE55 .... 159 D2
Mansfield NG18 .... 268 C3
Prospect Terr
Chesterfield S40 .... 95 F2
Crich DE4 .... 168 A4
Providence Ct DE11 .... 256 C1
Providence Pl **2** DE7 .... 194 C1
Providence Rd NG16 .... 171 D2
Providence St DE5 .... 180 C4
Provident St DE23 .... 219 D1
Pryor Mede S26 .... 61 F3
Pudding Bag La S45 .... 129 F2
Pulborough Gdns DE23 .... 231 D3
Pullman Cl S43 .... 78 C2
Pullman Rd Derby DE21 .... 219 F2
Nottingham NG2 .... 268 C1
Pump Cl DE4 .... 143 E2
Pump La DE55 .... 211 D1
Pump St S43 .... 269 D2
Purbeck Ave S40 .... 95 E2
Purbeck Cl NG10 .... 236 A4
Purchase Ave DE75 .... 181 E1
Purdy Meadow NG10 .... 235 F3
Purseglove Dr SK17 .... 69 E2
Purseglove Rd SK17 .... 69 E2
Putney Cl DE22 .... 217 F3
Pybus St DE22 .... 218 B3
Pye Bridge Ind Est DE55 .... 170 C3
Pye Hill Rd NG16 .... 171 D2
Pyegrove SK13 .... 10 C1
Pyegrove Rd SK13 .... 10 C1
Pykestone Cl DE21 .... 205 F1
Pym La NG10 .... 235 F3
Pym St NG10 .... 236 C2
Pynot Rd S41 .... 77 D1
Pytchley Cl DE56 .... 179 E2

Quadrant The Buxton SK17 .... 85 D4
Sheffield S7 .... 55 F3
Quaker Cl DE73 .... 252 A4
Quaker La NG18 .... 268 B3
Quantock Cl DE24 .... 231 E1
Quantock Rd NG10 .... 223 D1
Quantock Way S40 .... 95 D3
Quarn Dr DE22 .... 204 B2
Quarn Gdns DE1 .... 218 C4
Quarn St DE1 .... 218 C4

Quarn Way DE1 .... 218 C3
Quarndon Hts DE22 .... 204 B2
Quarndon View DE22 .... 204 B1
Quarry Ave S14 .... 269 D2
Quarry Bank DE4 .... 143 D4
Quarry Bank Rd S41 .... 96 B1
Quarry Berry La DE12 .... 264 C1
Quarry Cl SK13 .... 10 B1
Quarry Hill Marsh Lane S21 .... 58 B1
Mosborough S20 .... 59 D4
Stanton-by-B NG10 .... 234 C3
Quarry Hill Ind Pk DE7 .... 208 C2
Quarry Hill Rd DE7 .... 208 C3
Quarry La Alton S42 .... 130 B3
Brackenfield DE55 .... 145 E3
Chesterfield S40 .... 95 E1
Mansfield NG18 .... 268 B3
Matlock DE4 .... 143 F4
Stonebroom DE55 .... 146 C3
Quarry Rd Apperknowle S18 .... 58 A1
Belper DE56 .... 178 C1
Birch Vale SK22 .... 24 C1
Bolsover S44 .... 99 D2
Killamarsh S21 .... 60 B4
Morley DE7 .... 192 A1
New Mills SK22 .... 33 E4
Somercotes DE55 .... 170 B4
Stoke-on-T S4 .... 269 D2
Totley S17 .... 55 F3
Quarry Vale Gr S12 .... 44 B2
Quarry Vale Rd S12 .... 44 B2
Queen Anne St ST4 .... 269 E2
Queen Elizabeth Ct DE1 .... 218 C3
Queen Elizabeth Way DE7 .... 208 B3
Queen Elizabeth's Gram
Sch DE6 .... 173 E2
Queen Elizabeth's Lower
Sch Department DE6 .... 185 E4
Queen Elizabeth's Sch
The NG19 .... 136 A1
Queen Elizabeths Gram
Sch DE6 .... 173 D1
Queen Mary Cl S44 .... 44 A4
Queen Mary Cres S2 .... 44 A4
Queen Mary Ct DE1 .... 218 C3
Queen Mary Rd
Chesterfield S40 .... 95 D1
Sheffield S2 .... 44 A4
Queen St Belper DE56 .... 179 D2
Brimington S43 .... 77 F1
Chesterfield S40 .... 266 A4
Clay Cross S45 .... 131 E2
Creswell S80 .... 81 F1
Derby DE1 .... 267 B4
Eckington S21 .... 59 F2
Glossop SK13 .... 17 D4
Hadfield SK13 .... 10 A2
Ilkeston DE7 .... 208 C4
Ironville NG16 .... 170 C2
Langley Mill NG16 .... 182 B2
Long Eaton NG10 .... 236 C4
Longnor SK17 .... 121 D3
Mansfield NG18 .... 268 B4
Marple SK6 .... 23 D3
Middleton (Nr Wirksworth)
DE4 .... 154 B3
Mosborough S20 .... 59 E4
Pilsley S45 .... 132 B1
Pinxton NG16 .... 160 B2
Ripley DE5 .... 181 D4
Somercotes DE55 .... 170 B4
South Normanton DE55 .... 159 F3
Staveley S43 .... 97 E4
Swadlincote DE11 .... 256 A1
Tideswell SK17 .... 69 E2
Queen St N S41 .... 96 A4
Queen Victoria Rd
New Tupton S42 .... 115 E2
Tutbury S17 .... 55 F3
Queen's Ave SK17 .... 85 E4
Queen's Bridge Rd NG2 .... 268 B1
Queen's Dr Belper DE56 .... 178 C3
Glossop SK13 .... 10 C1
Ilkeston DE7 .... 208 C4
Swadlincote DE11 .... 256 A3
Queen's Park Sports Ctr
S40 .... 266 A2
Queen's Rd Buxton SK17 .... 85 E4
Nottingham NG2 .... 268 B1
Stoke-on-T S4 .... 269 D2
Queen's Sq NG16 .... 182 C1
Queen's Way S11 .... 115 E1
Queen's Wlk
Nether Langwith NG20 .... 101 D1
Tupton S42 .... 115 E1
Queens Ave Heanor DE75 .... 181 E1
Ilkeston DE7 .... 209 D3
Stanley DE7 .... 207 E3
Queens Cl S80 .... 82 B3
Queens Ct Creswell S80 .... 81 F1
Draycott DE72 .... 235 D4
Queens Dr Brinsley NG16 .... 182 C4
Derby DE23 .... 218 B1
Sandiacre NG10 .... 223 D2
Queens Lt Ctr DE1 .... 267 B4
Queens Rd Hadthorpe S80 .... 82 B3
Sheffield S2 .... 43 D4
Queens Rd N NG16 .... 182 C1
Queens Rd S NG16 .... 182 C1
Queens Rd W S80 .... 63 D3
Queensferry Gdns DE24 .... 232 C2
Queensland Cl DE3 .... 217 F2
Queensland Cres DE15 .... 248 B1
Queensview Dr DE5 .... 181 D4
Queensville Ave ST17 .... 269 F3
Queensville Bridge ST17 .... 269 F3

Queensway
Castle Donington DE74 246
Derby DE22 204
Holmewood S42 116
Melbourne DE73 252
Pilsley S45 132
Stafford ST16 269
Stoke-on-T S4 269
Stonebroom DE55 146
Quenby La DE5 169
Quentin Rd SK23 47
Quick Cl DE73 252
Quick Hill Rd DE24 231
Quillings Way DE72 221
Quilow La DE6 185
Quixhill Bank ST14 196
Quoit La S18 57
Quoit Gn S18 57
Quorn Cl DE15 248
Quorn Dr **5** S40 95
Quorn Rise DE23 231
Quorndon Cres NG10 236

Rabown Ave DE23 231
Racecourse Ind Est DE21 219
Racecourse Mount S41 95
Racecourse Rd S41 95
Racecourse Rd E S41 96
Racester Way S42 131
Rad Meadows NG10 236
Radbourne La DE22 217
Radbourne Rd NG2 268
Radbourne St Derby DE22 218
Mansfield Woodhouse
NG19 136
Radburn Ct NG9 209
Radcliffe Ave DE21 219
Radcliffe Dr DE22 218
Radford Rd DE7 192
Radford St Derby DE24 232
1 Mansfield NG18 268
Radmanthwaite Rd NG19 135
Radnor Pl NG19 135
Radnor St DE21 219
Radstock Gdns DE21 205
Radstone Cl DE21 206
Raeburn Cl S14 43
Raeburn Dr Beeston NG9 223
Marple S66 23
Raeburn Pl S14 43
Raeburn Rd S14 43
Raeburn Way S14 43
Raglan Ave DE22 218
Raglan St DE55 159
Railway Ave S80 100
Railway Cotts NG16 195
Railway Row NG16 160
Railway Side DE1 256
Railway St Glossop SK13 10
Hadfield SK13 10
Nottingham NG2 268
Railway Terr Buxton SK17 85
Chesterfield S41 115
Derby DE1 267
Rain's La DE4 154
Rainham Gdns DE24 233
Rainier Dr DE21 220
Rake Head Rd HD7 2
Rake La DE45 124
Rake The DE45 123
Rakes La DE6 162
Rakes Rd DE45 107
Raleigh Cl DE7 194
Raleigh Inf Sch NG7 268
Raleigh St DE7 194
Ramper La NG16 268
Ramsden Cl S18 76
Ramsden Cl SK13 10
Ramsden La S40 8
Ramsden Rd HD7 3
Ramsey Ave S40 95
Ramsey Cl NG9 209
Ramsey St S14 269
Ranby Av **3** S40 95
Ranshaw Rd S18 76
Randal St NG9 223
Randall Dr DE11 256
Randall Pl S2 43
Randolph Rd DE23 231
Ranelagh Gdns DE22 218
Raneld Mount S40 114
Rangemoor La DE6 183
Rangemore Cl DE3 217
Ranmoor Cl S41 115
Ranmoor Hill S32 52
Rannoch Cl
Derby, Allestree DE22 204
Derby, Spondon DE21 220
Rannoch Dr NG19 268
Ranworth Cl DE24 232
Ratcliffe Ave DE14 254
Ratcliffe Gate NG18 268
Ratcliffe St NG16 182
Rauche Ct DE23 267
Raven Ave DE55 147

ven Cl DE55 ... 170 B3
ven Oak Cl DE56 ... 179 D2
ven St DE4 ... 218 C2
vencar Rd S21 ... 59 D2
venscourt Rd DE22 ... 218 B3
venscroft Ave S13 ... 44 C4
venscroft Cl S13 ... 44 C4
venscroft Cres S13 ... 44 C4
venscroft Dr
  Derby DE21 ... 219 F3
  Sheffield S13 ... 44 C4
venscroft Oval S13 ... 44 C4
venscroft Pl S13 ... 44 C4
venscroft Rd S13 ... 44 C4
venscroft Way S13 ... 44 C4
vensdale Ave
  Long Eaton NG10 ... 223 D1
  Mansfield NG18 ... 268 C4
vensdale Cl S43 ... 97 E3
vensdale Inf & Jun Sch
  DE3 ... 217 F2
vensdale Rd
  Derby DE22 ... 204 B2
  Dronfield S18 ... 56 B1
  Mansfield NG18 ... 268 C4
venstor Rd DE4 ... 154 C1
venswood Rd S40 ... 95 D3
vwdon Cl DE7 ... 247 D2
vwdon Rd DE12 ... 262 C3
vwdon St DE23 ... 218 C1
vwlins S18 ... 57 E2
vwlinson Ave DE22 ... 232 A4
vwson Gn DE56 ... 179 F1
vwy St DE75 ... 181 F1
vay's Ave DE75 ... 181 F1
vayleigh Ave S43 ... 96 B4
vaynald Rd S2 ... 44 A4
vaynesham Rd DE7 ... 194 B2
vaynesway DE22 ... 220 A2
vaynesway Park Dr DE21 ... 220 A1
vader St DE21 ... 220 C3
vbecca St ST4 ... 269 E2
vcreation Cl
  Blackwell DE55 ... 147 F1
  Clowne S43 ... 80 C2
vcreation Dr NG20 ... 119 F1
vcreation Gd
(Chesterfield FC) The
  S40 ... 266 A4
vcreation Rd Calow S43 ... 96 E3
  New Houghton NG19 ... 134 C4
  Shirebrook NG20 ... 223 D3
  Tibshelf SK17 ... 69 E2
  Wirksworth DE4 ... 165 F4
vcreation St
  Long Eaton NG10 ... 236 C4
  Mansfield NG18 ... 268 C4
vcreation View NG20 ... 119 F3
vctory Cl
  Breedon on t H DE73 ... 252 C1
  Eckington S21 ... 59 F2
  Long Duckmanton S44 ... 98 A2
vctory Dr S42 ... 114 C2
vctory Farm Mews DE72 ... 245 F2
vctory Gdns
  Aston-on-T DE72 ... 246 A4
  Barthill S26 ... 61 F3
  Killamarsh S21 ... 60 D4
vctory La Breadsall DE21 ... 205 E3
  Kirk Ireton DE6 ... 165 D1
  Stretton en le F DE12 ... 265 F1
vctory Pl NG11 ... 237 F3
vctory La Belper DE56 ... 171 F1
vctory Rd Breaston DE72 ... 235 E4
  Clowne S43 ... 80 C2
  Killamarsh S21 ... 60 D4
  Long Duckmanton S44 ... 98 A2
  Staveley S43 ... 78 C1
vculver Cl DE23 ... 231 E4
Barn Cl DE55 ... 148 A2
Hill DE4 ... 144 B2
Hill La DE4 ... 144 B2
La Belper DE56 ... 191 D3
Grimsley NG16 ... 171 F1
Ilsley SK12 ... 32 B3
Repton DE65 ... 249 F3
South Normanton DE55 ... 159 F2
Lion Hill DE4 ... 153 D1
Lion Sq DE75 ... 181 F1
Lion St ST16 ... 269 E4
dacre Cl S44 ... 99 E1
dbarn La DE55 ... 148 A2
dbrook Ave S41 ... 115 D4
dbury Cl DE1 ... 218 C2
dcar Gdns DE21 ... 205 E1
dcliffe Rd NG18 ... 268 C3
ddish Ave SK23 ... 45 E3
ddish La S43 ... 45 E3
ddish Rd SK23 ... 45 E3
dfern Ave DE5 ... 169 F1
dfern Cl S43 ... 10 A3
dfern Rd ST14 ... 210 A1
dgap La SK17 ... 86 A4
dgate S13 ... 10 B2
dgate Cl NG19 ... 268 A4
dgate Sch NG19 ... 268 A4
dgate St Mansfield NG19 ... 268 A4
  Pinxton NG16 ... 160 B1
dgrave DE75 ... 194 B3
dgrove Way S40 ... 114 A4
dhill La DE13 ... 239 D3
dhill Lodge Rd DE11 ... 256 A4
dhill Prim Sch DE72 ... 221 E3
dhouse Cl S43 ... 77 E2
dhouse La SK12 ... 32 C3

Redland Cl Derby DE24 ... 231 F2
  Ilkeston DE7 ... 194 C4
Redmires Dr DE73 ... 233 D1
Redmires Rd S10 ... 42 A4
Redmoor Cl
  Burton u T DE15 ... 248 A2
  Codnor DE5 ... 170 A1
Redmoor La Disley SK12 ... 33 D2
  New Mills SK22 ... 33 D3
Rednall Cl S40 ... 95 D3
Redruth Pl DE24 ... 233 E3
Redshaw St DE1 ... 218 C2
Redstart Cl DE7 ... 220 C3
Redthorn Rd S13 ... 44 C4
Redvers Buller Rd S40 ... 266 B1
Redway Croft DE73 ... 252 A4
Redwing Croft DE23 ... 231 E4
Reeves Rd DE23 ... 219 D1
Regatta Way S43 ... 96 B4
Regency Cl Derby DE23 ... 231 E4
  Glossop SK13 ... 10 B1
Regent Cl NG16 ... 170 C2
Regent St Clowne S43 ... 80 B2
  Derby DE1 ... 267 C1
  Glossop SK13 ... 10 B1
  Ilkeston DE7 ... 208 C4
  Kimberley NG16 ... 195 F3
  Langley Mill NG16 ... 182 A2
  Long Eaton NG10 ... 236 B4
  Mansfield NG18 ... 268 B4
  Nottingham NG1 ... 268 A1
  Padfield SK13 ... 10 A3
  Stapleford NG10 ... 223 E3
  Stoke-on-T S14 ... 269 E1
  Swadlincote DE11 ... 256 A1
Reginald Rd N DE21 ... 219 F4
Reginald Rd S DE21 ... 219 F3
Reginald St DE23 ... 219 D1
Regis Cl DE21 ... 206 A1
Registry St ST4 ... 269 F2
Reigate Dr DE22 ... 218 A4
Reigate Prim Sch DE22 ... 217 F4
Rembrandt Dr S18 ... 56 C1
Renals St DE22 ... 267 B1
Reney Ave S8 ... 56 B3
Reney Cres S8 ... 56 B3
Reney Dr S8 ... 56 B3
Reney Rd S8 ... 56 C4
Reney Wlk S8 ... 56 B3
Renfrew Ct NG19 ... 268 A3
Renfrew St DE21 ... 219 F4
Renishaw Hall Mus &
Craft Ctr S21 ... 59 F1
Renishaw Prim Sch S21 ... 79 D4
Renishaw Rd S21 ... 79 E2
Renishaw Dr DE11 ... 255 F3
Rent Cl S41 ... 95 F3
Repton Ave DE23 ... 218 B1
Repton Cl S40 ... 95 D3
Repton Ct NG19 ... 136 C2
Repton Dr DE7 ... 209 D4
Repton La 18 S18 ... 56 B1
Repton Prep Sch DE65 ... 243 E1
Repton Prim Sch DE65 ... 242 C1
Repton St Hartshorne DE11 ... 256 C4
  Long Eaton NG10 ... 223 E2
  Newton Solney DE15 ... 248 C4
  Willington DE65 ... 242 A3
Repton Sch DE65 ... 242 B2
Reservoir Hill DE12 ... 262 B4
Reservoir Rd S43 ... 45 E4
Reservoir Terr S40 ... 95 F2
Resthaven DE11 ... 256 A3
Retford Cl DE21 ... 205 E1
Revill Cl DE7 ... 194 B1
Revill Cres DE7 ... 222 A2
Revolution House Mus S41 ... 77 D1
Reynard Cres S21 ... 79 D4
Reynards La S17 ... 137 F2
Reynolds Ave DE5 ... 169 F1
Reynolds Cl S18 ... 75 F4
Rhodes Ave S44 ... 23 D4
Rhodes Ave S41 ... 95 F3
Rhodes Cotts S43 ... 80 C2
Rhodes St SK13 ... 10 A3
Rhodes Wlk NG16 ... 268 A3
Rhodesia Rd S40 ... 95 E1
Rhodeswood Dr SK13 ... 10 A3
Rhuddlan Pl SK23 ... 34 B1
Ribbledale DE7 ... 208 B3
Ribbledale Cl DE22 ... 204 B1
Ribbledale Dr S12 ... 59 D4
Ribbledale Rd NG10 ... 236 A3
Riber Ave DE55 ... 170 B4
Riber Bank SK13 ... 9 F1
Riber Cl Long Eaton NG10 ... 236 B3
  Staveley S43 ... 97 E3
  West Hallam DE7 ... 207 F4
Riber Cres S45 ... 131 D3
Riber Rd Holloway DE4 ... 156 A4
  Matlock DE4 ... 143 E1
Riber Terr S40 ... 266 A2
Riber View Cl DE4 ... 144 A3
Riber Wildlife Pk DE4 ... 143 E2
Richard La SK17 ... 69 E3
Richard Wakefield CE
Prim Sch DE13 ... 239 E3
Richards Ave ST16 ... 269 F4
Richards Ct S8 ... 43 D3
Richards Rd S2 ... 43 D4
Richardson Dr DE7 ... 192 C3
Richardson Endowed
Prim Sch DE7 ... 192 C3
Richardson St DE22 ... 218 B3

Richardsons La DE55 ... 170 B3
Richmond Ave Derby DE72 ... 231 E4
  Ilkeston DE7 ... 194 C2
  Long Eaton DE72 ... 236 A4
  Sandiacre NG10 ... 223 D2
  Sheffield S13 ... 44 C4
Richmond Cl
  Chesterfield S40 ... 114 C4
  Hadfield SK13 ... 10 A3
  West Hallam DE7 ... 207 E4
Richmond Coll of F Ed
  S41 ... 84 B4
Richmond Ct DE65 ... 242 B1
Richmond Dr Duffield DE56 ... 190 B3
  Mansfield Woodhouse
  NG19 ... 136 B1
Richmond Gr S13 ... 44 B4
Richmond Hall Ave S13 ... 44 B4
Richmond Hall Cres S13 ... 44 B4
Richmond Hall Dr S13 ... 44 B4
Richmond Hall Rd S13 ... 44 B4
Richmond Hall Way S13 ... 44 B4
Richmond Park Rd S13 ... 44 B4
Richmond Pl S13 ... 44 B4
Richmond Rd
  Derby, Chaddesden DE21 ... 219 F3
  Derby, Rose Hill DE23 ... 231 D4
  Sheffield S13 ... 44 B4
Richmond St ST4 ... 269 E2
Richworth Rd S13 ... 44 C4
Rick St NG1 ... 268 B2
Riddial Way S42 ... 115 D2
Riddings DE72 ... 204 C2
Riddings Cl S2 ... 44 A4
Riddings Inf Sch DE55 ... 170 B3
Riddings Jun Sch DE55 ... 170 B3
Riddings La S32 ... 72 B2
Riddings St DE22 ... 218 C2
Ridge Ave Sk6 ... 23 D2
Ridge Cl Sk6 ... 9 F2
Ridge Cres Sk6 ... 23 D2
Ridge End Fold Sk6 ... 23 D2
Ridge La SK23 ... 65 E4
Ridge Rd Marple Sk6 ... 23 D2
  Marsh Lane S21 ... 58 C1
Ridge The Blackwell DE55 ... 147 F1
  Marple Sk6 ... 23 D2
Ridge Top La S32 ... 25 E1
Ridgedale Rd S44 ... 118 A4
Ridgedale View S18 ... 169 E1
Ridgehill Ave S12 ... 44 A3
Ridgehill Gr S12 ... 44 A3
Ridgeway Derby DE73 ... 245 D4
  Dronfield S18 ... 57 E2
  Heanor DE75 ... 193 F4
Ridgeway Ave Bolsover S44 ... 99 E1
  Derby DE23 ... 231 E3
Ridgeway Cottage Ind Ctr
  S12 ... 58 C4
Ridgeway Cres S12 ... 44 A4
Ridgeway Dr Ilkeston DE7 ... 208 A3
  Sheffield S12 ... 44 A3
Ridgeway La S12 ... 168 B2
Ridgeway Moor S12 ... 58 C3
Ridgeway Prim Sch S12 ... 58 C4
Ridgeway Rd
  Burton u T DE15 ... 254 C4
  Sheffield S12 ... 44 A3
Ridgeway St NG3 ... 268 C2
Ridgeway The S12 ... 32 B3
Ridgeways SK22 ... 25 E1
Ridgewood Cl DE21 ... 205 F1
Ridgewood Dr DE4 ... 155 E3
Ridgway S43 ... 80 C1
Ridgway W S43 ... 80 B2
Riding Bank DE73 ... 251 F3
Ridings Rd SK13 ... 9 F3
Ridings The
  Mansfield NG19 ... 136 C1
  Ockbrook DE72 ... 221 E3
Ridley St ST4 ... 269 F1
Rigga La DE56 ... 191 D1
Riggotts Way S42 ... 94 C4
Riggs La DE6 ... 212 A4
Rigley St DE1 ... 267 B2
Riley Ave DE55 ... 147 F4
Riley Back La S32 ... 71 F3
Riley La DE5 ... 169 D3
Rimsdale Cl DE24 ... 231 F2
Ring-o-Bells La S42 ... 32 B3
Ringer La S43 ... 80 C2
Ringinglow Rd S11 ... 42 C2
Ringstone Way S43 ... 45 E4
Ringwood Ave
  Chesterfield S41 ... 95 F4
  Hackingknife SK14 ... 9 F4
  Staveley S43 ... 97 E4
Ringwood Cl DE21 ... 219 F4
Ringwood Rd S43 ... 96 C4
Ringwood View 9 S43 ... 96 C4
Ripley Hospl DE5 ... 169 E1
Ripley Inf Sch DE5 ... 180 B4
Ripley Jun Sch DE5 ... 180 B4
Ripley Rd DE56 ... 168 B3
Ripon Cres DE21 ... 205 F1
Ripon Gdns SK17 ... 85 E3
Risborrow Cl DE65 ... 229 E2
Rise The Derby DE22 ... 204 C1
  Swadlincote DE11 ... 255 F3
  Whaley Bridge SK23 ... 45 E3
Rises The SK13 ... 9 F3

Risley Ct DE7 ... 194 C2
Risley La DE72 ... 222 B1
Risley Lower Gram CE
Prim Sch DE72 ... 222 C2
Ritson Cl S43 ... 268 B2
Rivenhall Cl DE23 ... 230 C4
River St DE1 ... 267 C2
River View Aldercar DE55 ... 171 D3
  Belper DE56 ... 190 C4
  Litton SK17 ... 88 B4
Riverbank DE4 ... 110 C1
Riverbank The DE65 ... 242 A3
Riverbank Way S43 ... 17 F4
Riverdale Cl DE15 ... 248 A3
Riversdale DE56 ... 168 A2
Riversfield Dr ST14 ... 196 C2
Riverside DE12 ... 253 E1
Riverside Cl Calver S32 ... 72 B1
  Glossop SK13 ... 10 B1
Riverside Cres DE4 ... 113 F4
Riverside Dr
  Branston DE14 ... 253 F4
  Calver S32 ... 72 B1
Riverside L Ctr ST16 ... 269 E4
Riverside Rd DE21 ... 219 E2
Riverside Way NG16 ... 136 B3
Riverview Cotts S13 ... 17 E4
Riverway ST17 ... 269 F3
Rivington Rd NG9 ... 223 F1
Roadmeadow Cl DE6 ... 185 E4
Roadnook Farm S42 ... 130 A4
Robert Ave NG18 ... 268 A3
Robert Cl S18 ... 76 C3
Robert Rd S8 ... 57 D4
Robert Sherborne Inf Sch
The DE13 ... 240 B2
Robert St DE1 ... 267 C4
Robert Sutton High Sch
DE15 ... 255 D4
Roberts Ave NG17 ... 148 C1
Roberts Dr DE55 ... 159 D2
Roberts St Ilkeston DE7 ... 209 D3
  Nottingham NG2 ... 268 C1
Robertson Rd SK17 ... 85 D3
Robertson's Ave S44 ... 98 A2
Robey Dr NG16 ... 182 C2
Robian Way DE11 ... 256 A2
Robin Croft Rd DE22 ... 204 C2
Robin Hood Chase NG3 ... 268 B2
Robin Hood Cl NG16 ... 182 C1
Robin Hood Ind Est NG3 ... 268 C2
Robin Hood Inf &
Jun Sch NG19 ... 136 A2
Robin Hood Pl DE11 ... 256 B1
Robin Hood St NG3 ... 268 C2
Robin Rd DE1 ... 218 C4
Robin's Cross La DE65 ... 249 F4
Robina Cl DE21 ... 206 B2
Robina Dr NG16 ... 195 E4
Robincroft Rd S42 ... 114 C4
Robincroft Rd S42 ... 114 B2
Robinettes La NG16 ... 195 E1
Robinlands La S33 ... 38 A2
Robins Cl DE24 ... 231 F1
Robinscross DE72 ... 221 D1
Robinson Ind Est DE21 ... 219 D1
Robinson Rd DE11 ... 256 A3
Robinson Way S21 ... 60 B3
Robinson's Hill DE73 ... 251 F3
Robridding Rd S45 ... 129 D2
Robson Cl DE24 ... 233 D4
Roby Lea DE74 ... 246 C2
Roche 9 S20 ... 59 F4
Rochester Cl Derby DE24 ... 233 D3
  Long Eaton NG10 ... 236 A4
Rochley Cl DE21 ... 205 F1
Rock Bank Buxton SK17 ... 85 E2
  Whaley Bridge SK23 ... 45 F3
Rock Cres S45 ... 131 D3
Rock Ct NG18 ... 268 C4
Rock Dr NG7 ... 268 A1
Rock Hill NG18 ... 268 C4
Rock La S44 ... 116 C4
Rock St Mansfield NG18 ... 268 C3
  New Mills SK22 ... 24 C1
Rock Terr Bakewell DE45 ... 109 E3
  Buxton SK17 ... 85 D3
Rock Valley NG18 ... 268 C4
Rockbourne Cl DE24 ... 233 E3
Rockcliffe Cl DE11 ... 256 A1
Rockeries The DE56 ... 168 C1
Rockfield Rd SK17 ... 85 E4
Rockford Ct NG9 ... 209 F1
Rockhall Terr SK22 ... 25 E1
Rockhouse Rd DE24 ... 233 D3
Rockingham 18 S20 ... 59 F4
Rockingham Cl
  Chesterfield S40 ... 95 E2
  Derby DE22 ... 205 D2
  4 Dronfield S18 ... 56 B1
Rocklands The NG20 ... 119 F2
Rockley Cl NG20 ... 114 C4
Rockley Way NG20 ... 119 F2
Rocks The CE4 ... 144 C4
Rockside Stps DE4 ... 143 E3
Rockside View DE4 ... 143 E4
Rod Moor Rd S18 ... 56 A2
Roden St NG3 ... 268 C2
Rodge Croft S41 ... 77 D2
Rodger's La DE55 ... 159 D3
Rodknoll La S42 ... 93 E1
Rodney Cl DE65 ... 228 C1
Rodney Way DE7 ... 194 C2
Rodney Wlk DE24 ... 231 F1
Rodsley La Rodsley DE6 ... 200 C4
  Wyaston DE6 ... 199 F4
  Yeaveley DE6 ... 199 F3
Rodwood Ave S43 ... 80 A4

Roe Cross Rd SK14 ... 9 D3
Roe Farm La DE21 ... 219 F4
Roe Wlk DE23 ... 219 D1
Roe's La DE4 ... 157 D1
Roebuck Pl SK23 ... 47 D3
Roebuck St ST4 ... 269 F2
Roecar Cl S41 ... 77 D1
Roehampton Dr
  Derby DE22 ... 218 A4
  Stapleford NG9 ... 209 E1
Rogers Ave DE21 ... 81 E1
Rogerstone Ave ST4 ... 269 D3
Rolaine Cl NG19 ... 136 B2
Rolleston Cres NG16 ... 195 F4
Rolleston Dr NG16 ... 195 D4
Rolleston La DE13 ... 239 E3
Rollet Cl S2 ... 44 A4
Rollins La S6 ... 15 D1
Roman Bank NG19 ... 136 B2
Roman Way DE72 ... 221 E1
Romeley Cres S43 ... 80 B2
Romford Way S43 ... 78 A2
Romney Dr S18 ... 56 C1
Romney Gdns S2 ... 43 D3
Romsley Cl DE3 ... 217 E2
Rona Cl Derby DE24 ... 231 F2
  Mansfield NG18 ... 268 A3
Ronald Cl DE23 ... 230 C4
Rood La Clowne S43 ... 80 C2
  Idridgehay DE56 ... 176 C3
Rookery The NG18 ... 268 B4
Roosevelt Ave Derby DE21 ... 220 A3
  Long Eaton NG10 ... 236 B3
Rooth St NG18 ... 268 B3
Roper Ave DE75 ... 193 F4
Roper Hill S10 ... 42 B4
Ropewalk Ind Ctr DE7 ... 195 D1
Ropewalk The Heanor DE75 ... 193 F4
  Ilkeston DE7 ... 195 D1
  Nottingham NG7 ... 268 A1
  Stanley DE7 ... 193 D1
Rosamond Ave S17 ... 56 A3
Rosamond Cl S17 ... 56 A3
Rosamond Dr S17 ... 56 A3
Rosamond Glade S17 ... 56 A3
Rosamond Pl S17 ... 56 A3
Rosamond's Ride DE22 ... 231 E4
Rose Ave Borrowash DE72 ... 221 E1
  Burton u T DE13 ... 241 D1
  Calow S43 ... 97 D2
  Ilkeston DE7 ... 208 C4
  Riddings DE55 ... 170 B4
  Ilkeston DE7 ... 194 C1
Rose Bank Cl SK14 ... 9 E3
Rose Cottage Dr NG17 ... 148 C1
Rose Cotts S41 ... 96 B1
Rose Cres S41 ... 79 E2
Rose Ct Clay Cross S45 ... 131 D2
  Long Eaton NG10 ... 223 D1
Rose End Ave DE4 ... 155 D3
Rose Farm Prim Sch DE21 ... 219 F4
Rose Hill Chesterfield S40 ... 266 B2
  Stafford ST16 ... 269 D4
  Swadlincote DE11 ... 256 C2
Rose Hill E S40 ... 266 B3
Rose Hill St DE23 ... 219 D1
Rose Hill W S40 ... 266 A3
Rose La
  Mansfield Woodhouse
  NG19 ... 136 B2
  Ticknall DE73 ... 251 D2
Rose Tree La DE11 ... 255 F4
Rose Valley DE11 ... 256 A3
Rose Way S21 ... 60 B3
Rose Wood Cl S41 ... 95 E4
Roseberry Ct DE21 ... 206 A1
Rosebery Hill NG18 ... 268 C3
Rosecroft Gdns DE11 ... 256 B2
Rosedale Ave
  Chesterfield S40 ... 115 D4
  Derby DE24 ... 233 D3
Rosedale Cl NG10 ... 236 A3
Rosedale View S40 ... 114 A4
Rosedale Way NG19 ... 136 C1
Roseheath Cl DE23 ... 231 F3
Rosehill St ... 99 D1
Rosehill Inf Sch DE23 ... 219 D2
Rosehill Sch NG3 ... 268 C2
Roseleigh Cres DE11 ... 255 F3
Rosemary Ave NG18 ... 268 B4
Rosemary Dr DE23 ... 233 D3
Rosemary St NG18 ... 268 B4
Rosemoor La DE21 ... 206 A1
Rosemount Cl DE22 ... 204 B2
Rosengrave St DE1 ... 267 B2
Rosette Cl DE21 ... 206 B2
Rosewood Cl Derby DE24 ... 233 E4
  South Normanton DE55 ... 160 A4
Rosewood Rd DE15 ... 254 C4
Rosier Cres DE55 ... 170 A4
Rosling Way S44 ... 97 E1
Rosliston CE Prim Sch
DE12 ... 260 B3
Rosliston Rd
  Burton u T DE15 ... 254 C4
  Rosliston DE15 ... 254 B2
  Walton-on-T DE12 ... 259 F4
Rosliston Rd S DE15 ... 254 C3
Roslyn Cres S32 ... 53 D4
Roslyn Rd S32 ... 53 D4
Ross Wlk DE21 ... 205 F1
Rossell Dr NG9 ... 223 F3
Rossendale Cl S40 ... 114 C4
Rossendale Ct DE7 ... 194 C2

Rosser Ave S12 .... 43 F1
Rossington Dr SK13 .... 230 C3
Rossington Rd NG2 .... 268 C2
Rosslyn Gdns DE24 .... 233 D3
Roston Cl 10 S18 .... 56 B1
Rothay Cl S18 .... 75 F4
Rothbourne Croft DE6 ...... 151 E1
Rothbury Ave NG9 .... 209 E1
Rothbury Pl DE21 .... 205 F1
Rother Ave S43 .... 96 B4
Rother Cl S40 .... 114 C4
Rother Croft S42 .... 131 E4
Rother Jun Sch S40 .... 115 D4
Rother Way S41 .... 96 A3
Rotherham Cl S21 .... 60 C4
Rotherham Rd
  Barlborough S43 .... 80 A4
  Killamarsh S21 .... 60 C4
  Clowne S43 .... 80 C3
  Eckington S20 .... 59 F3
  Killamarsh S21 .... 60 C4
  Mosborough S20 .... 59 F3
  New Houghton NG19 ... 134 C4
  Scarcliffe S44 .... 118 B4
  Stony Houghton S44 ..... 118 B2
Rotherham Rd N S20 .... 59 F4
Rotherside Rd S21 .... 59 F2
Rothervale Rd S40 .... 115 D4
Rotherwood Rd S21 .... 60 C4
Rothesay Cl DE24 .... 231 F2
Rothey Gr S40 .... 94 C3
Rothley Ave NG2 .... 268 C2
Rothwell La DE56 .... 179 D2
Rothwell Rd DE3 .... 217 E2
Rothwell St S14 .... 269 D1
Rough Heanor Rd DE3 .... 218 A1
Rough La DE6 .... 186 B3
Roughpiece La DE56 .... 166 B3
Roughton Cl DE3 .... 230 B4
Round Hill Cl SK13 .... 9 F2
Round Way S42 .... 33 E4
Rouse Cl S41 .... 269 D3
Rouse St S45 .... 132 A1
Routh Ave DE74 .... 247 D1
Rowan Ave Ripley DE5 .... 180 B4
  Stapleford NG9 .... 209 F1
Rowan Cl Creswell S80 ...... 81 F1
  Darley Dale DE4 .... 127 D2
  Derby, Cherrytree Hill DE21 220 A3
  Derby, Sinfin DE24 .... 231 E2
  Ilkeston DE7 .... 208 C3
  Mansfield NG19 .... 136 B1
Rowan Croft NG17 .... 148 C2
Rowan Dr Kilburn DE56 ... 192 A4
  Selston NG16 .... 171 E4
  Shirebrook NG20 .... 119 E3
  Shirland DE55 .... 146 B1
Rowan Park Cl DE23 .... 231 E4
Rowan Rd Eckington S21 ... 59 E1
  Martin Moor S43 .... 79 E2
Rowan Sch The S17 .... 55 F3
Rowan Tree Cl
  Ashbourne DE6 .... 185 E4
  Killamarsh S21 .... 60 B3
Rowan Tree Dell S17 .... 55 F2
Rowan Tree Rd S21 .... 60 A3
Rowan Wlk SK13 .... 9 F2
Rowbury Dr DE15 .... 248 A1
Rowdale Cres S12 .... 44 B3
Rowditch Ave DE22 .... 218 B2
Rowditch Pl DE22 .... 218 B2
Rowena Cl DE24 .... 232 C4
Rowland Ct DE55 .... 158 C2
Rowland Rd S2 .... 43 D4
Rowland St Alfreton DE55 . 159 D2
  Derby DE24 .... 232 C3
Rowley Ave S17 .... 269 D3
Rowley Ct DE11 .... 256 A2
Rowley Gdns DE23 .... 231 E4
Rowley Hall Dr ST17 .... 269 D3
Rowley La DE23 .... 231 E4
Rowsley Ave Derby DE22 ... 236 A3
  Long Eaton NG10 .... 223 E1
Rowsley CE Prim Sch
  DE4 .... 126 C4
Rowsley Cres S43 .... 97 E4
Rowsley Mews SK13 .... 9 F1
Rowthorne Ave DE55 .... 170 A4
Rowthorne La
  Ault Hucknall S44 .... 134 A4
  Glapwell S44 .... 134 A4
Rowton Grange Rd SK23 ... 47 D3
Roxburgh Ave DE21 .... 219 F4
Roxton Ave S8 .... 56 C4
Roxton Ct NG16 .... 195 F4
Royal Ave NG10 .... 223 E1
Royal Cl DE72 .... 221 D1
Royal Croft Dr DE45 .... 179 E2
Royal Gate DE56 .... 179 E2
Royal Gr DE21 .... 206 B2
Royal Hill Rd DE21 .... 220 B3
Royal Oak Pl DE45 .... 109 E3
Royal Rd SK12 .... 32 B3
Royal Sch for the Deaf
  DE22 .... 218 B3
Royale Cl S21 .... 59 F2
Royston Cl DE3 .... 217 E2
Royle Ave S K13 .... 10 B1
Royston Cl Ashbourne DE6 . 185 E4
  Chesterfield S40 .... 114 A4
Royston Dr DE56 .... 179 E3
Rubens Cl Dronfield S18 ... 56 C1
  Marple SK6 .... 23 E4

Ruby Paddocks NG16 .... 195 F3
Rudyard Ave DE21 .... 220 C3
Rufford Ave NG18 .... 268 C4
Rufford Cl S40 .... 95 F1
Rufford Dr NG19 .... 136 C2
Rufford Rd NG10 .... 236 A2
Ruffstone Cl DE56 .... 190 E4
Rugby Ave DE55 .... 159 E3
Rugby Cl DE14 .... 254 B4
Rugby St DE24 .... 219 F1
Rugeley Ave NG10 .... 237 D4
Ruislip Cl NG16 .... 195 F4
Rupert Rd DE72 .... 220 A4
Rupert St Ilkeston DE7 ..... 195 D1
  Lower Pilsley S45 .... 132 A2
Rush Leys NG10 .... 236 B3
Rushcliffe Ave DE21 .... 219 F3
Rushdale Ave Sheffield S8 ... 43 D1
  Sheffield S8 .... 43 D1
Rushdale Mount S8 .... 43 D3
Rushdale Rd S8 .... 43 D3
Rushdale Terr S8 .... 43 D3
Rushen Mount S40 .... 114 C3
Rushes The Hadfield SK13 ... 9 F2
  Mansfield Woodhouse NG19 136 B3
Rushleigh Ct S17 .... 55 E4
Rushley Ave S17 .... 55 E4
Rushley Cl S17 .... 55 E4
Rushley Dr S17 .... 55 E4
Rushley Rd S17 .... 55 E4
Rushpool Ave NG19 .... 136 B2
Rushton Cl SK6 .... 23 D3
Rushton Dr SK6 .... 23 D3
Rushup Cl DE27 .... 205 D3
Rushup La SK17 .... 48 B4
Rushy La NG10 .... 222 C3
Rushycroft SK14 .... 9 D2
Ruskin Ave NG10 .... 236 A3
Ruskin Rd Derby DE1 ...... 218 C4
  Mansfield NG19 .... 135 E1
Ruskin Sq S8 .... 43 D3
Russel St ST16 .... 269 D4
Russell Gdns S42 .... 131 D3
Russell Pl NG1 .... 268 A2
Russell St Compstall SK6 ... 15 D2
  Derby DE24 .... 219 E1
  Long Eaton NG10 .... 223 E1
  Nottingham NG2 .... 268 A2
  Swadlincote DE11 .... 256 B2
Russet Cl Derby DE21 ...... 206 A1
  Hatton DE65 .... 227 E1
Ruston Cl Chesterfield S40 . 95 D3
  Swadlincote DE11 .... 256 A2
Rutherford Dr DE21 .... 205 F1
Rutherford Pl S14 .... 269 D2
Ruthyn Ave S43 .... 80 A4
Rutland Ave Bolsover S44 ... 99 D1
  Borrowash DE72 .... 221 E3
  Matlock DE4 .... 143 E1
  Ripley DE5 .... 181 D4
Rutland Cl DE15 .... 254 B3
Rutland Ct DE7 .... 194 B1
Rutland Dr DE3 .... 217 F2
Rutland Pl DE56 .... 168 A3
Rutland Rd Chesterfield S40 266 A3
  Westwood NG16 .... 171 E2
Rutland Sq DE45 .... 109 E3
Rutland St Chesterfield S41 ... 77 D1
  Derby DE23 .... 219 D1
  Ilkeston DE7 .... 194 C1
  Mansfield NG18 .... 268 C3
  Matlock DE4 .... 143 E3
  9 Nottingham NG1 .... 268 A2
Rutland Terr DE7 .... 194 C1
Rutland Way SK23 .... 34 B1
Ryal Cl DE72 .... 221 E3
Ryan Cl DE24 .... 231 F2
Rycroft CE Mid Sch ST14 . 196 C2
Rycroft Rd DE74 .... 247 E3
Rydal Ave NG10 .... 223 D2
Rydal Cl Derby DE22 .... 204 C2
  Dronfield S18 .... 56 B1
Rydal Cres S41 .... 95 F4
Rydal Way S45 .... 131 D2
Ryder Cl DE11 .... 255 F1
Rye Butts DE73 .... 232 C1
Rye Cl DE21 .... 205 F2
Rye Cres S45 .... 131 E2
Rye Flatt La S40 .... 95 E1
Rye Flatts La DE55 .... 227 E1
Ryecroft DE4 .... 127 E1
Ryecroft Glen Rd S17 .... 56 A4
Ryecroft St NG9 .... 223 F4
Ryecroft View S17 .... 55 F4
Ryegrass Cl DE56 .... 179 E2
Ryegrass Rd DE21 .... 206 B1
Ryehill Ave S40 .... 95 D1
Ryemere Cl NG16 .... 182 C1
Rykneld Cl DE23 .... 230 C3
Rykneld Ct S45 .... 131 E2
Rykneld Dr DE23 .... 230 C4
Rykneld Prim Sch DE14 .. 253 F4
Rykneld Rd Derby DE23 .. 230 C3
Rykneld Sq S40 .... 266 B3
Rykneld Rise S42 .... 115 D2
Rykneld Way DE23 .... 230 C3
Rykneld Hill DE55 .... 180 A1
Rykneld Rd DE56 .... 192 A4
Rylah Hill S44 .... 118 A3
Rymill Dr DE21 .... 205 F1

Sabine St ST17 .... 269 E3
Sacheveral La DE4 .... 140 C2
Sacheveral Ave NG16 .... 160 B2
Sachererel St DE1 .... 267 B2

Sackerville Tr S21 .... 60 A4
Sackville Cl S40 .... 114 A4
Sackville St DE23 .... 231 F4
Saddlegate NG19 .... 136 C1
Saddlers Cl NG19 .... 136 C1
Saddleworth Wlk DE24 ... 232 C2
Sadler Gate DE1 .... 267 B3
Sadler St NG19 .... 268 C4
Saffron Dr DE21 .... 206 A1
Sage Dr DE11 .... 256 C2
St Agnes Ave DE22 .... 204 B2
St Aidan's Ave S2 .... 43 E4
St Aidan's Cl S2 .... 43 E4
St Aidan's Dr S2 .... 43 E4
St Aidan's Mount S2 .... 43 E4
St Aidan's Pl S2 .... 43 E4
St Aidan's Rd S2 .... 43 E4
St Aidan's Way S2 .... 43 E4
St Alban's RC Prim Sch
  DE21 .... 219 F3
St Albans Cl S42 .... 132 C4
St Albans Pl SK22 .... 33 E4
St Albans Rd DE22 .... 218 B3
St Albans St SK22 .... 33 E4
St Alkmund's Cl DE56 ..... 190 C2
St Alkmund's Way DE1 .. 267 B4
St Alkmunds Way DE56 .. 190 C2
St Andrew St NG18 .... 268 C3
St Andrew's CE Prim Sch
  DE7 .... 207 D3
St Andrew's CE/Meth
  Prim Sch S18 .... 56 B1
St Andrew's Cl DE55 .... 170 A4
St Andrews Cl SK13 .... 10 A2
St Andrews Rise S40 .... 114 B4
St Andrews Specl Sch
  DE21 .... 205 F1
St Andrews View DE21 ... 205 F1
St Andrews Wlk SK22 .... 33 E4
St Ann's Cl SK13 .... 46 C3
St Ann's St NG1 .... 268 B2
St Ann's Valley NG3 .... 268 B2
St Ann's Way NG3 .... 268 B2
St Ann's Well Rd NG3 ..... 268 B2
St Anne's CE Prim Sch
  DE45 .... 91 F3
St Anne's Cl Baslow DE45 ... 91 F3
  Derby DE1 .... 218 C3
St Anne's La DE74 .... 247 D2
St Annes Rd
  SK17 .... 66 A1
St Annes St SK14 .... 16 A4
St Augustine St DE23 ...... 218 C1
St Augustines Ave S40 ... 115 D4
St Augustines Cl S40 ...... 115 D4
St Augustines Dr S40 ...... 266 B1
St Augustines Mount S40 115 D4
St Augustines Rise S40 .. 115 D4
St Austin's RC Prim Sch
  ST17 .... 269 E3
St Barnabas La S2 .... 43 D4
St Barnabas Rd S2 .... 43 D4
St Barnabus RC Cath NG1 268 A2
St Bartholomew's CE
  Prim Sch SK17 .... 121 D4
St Benedict RC Sch DE22 204 C1
St Benet's Sch S40 .... 266 B4
St Bride's Wlk DE22 .... 218 A3
St Catherine St NG18 ..... 268 C3
St Catherine's Rd DE11 .. 255 F3
St Catherines Prep Sch
  SK6 .... 23 D4
St Cecilia Gdns NG3 ...... 268 B2
St Chad's Cl Inf Sch
  DE23 .... 218 C2
St Chad's Rd
  Denstone ST14 .... 196 B3
  Draycott DE72 .... 235 D4
St Chad's Pl 11 ST16 ...... 269 E4
St Chad's Rd Derby DE23 218 C1
  Nottingham NG3 .... 268 C2
St Charles Cl S13 .... 9 F3
St Charles' RC Sch SK13 .. 9 F3
St Christopher Ave ST4 .. 269 D1
St Christopher St NG2 ... 268 C1
St Clare's Cl DE22 .... 218 B1
St Clare's Sch DE3 .... 218 A1
St Cuthbert's Rd
  Derby DE22 .... 218 B2
  Nottingham NG5 .... 268 C2
St David's Cl DE22 .... 218 B2
St David's Rise S40 .... 114 B4
St Davids Rd B79 .... 263 F1
St Dominic's Jun Sch
  ST4 .... 269 D2
St Edmund's Ave NG19 .. 136 B2
St Edmund's Cl DE22 ..... 204 C2
St Edmunds CE Prim Sch
  DE74 .... 247 D2
St Edward's CE Sch
  DE74 .... 247 D2
St Edward's Rd DE74 ..... 247 D1
St Edwards Ct DE11 .... 255 F3
St Elizabeth Cl S2 .... 43 D4
St Elizabeth's RC Prim
  Sch DE56 .... 178 C3
St Elphins Sch DE4 .... 127 F1
St Francis Ley Ind Pk
  DE23 .... 219 D1
St George's CE Prim Sch
  S22 .... 33 E4
St George's Pl DE56 .... 178 C2

St George's RC Prim Sch
  DE23 .... 231 E4
St George's Rd ST17 .... 269 F3
St Georges Hospl ST16 ... 269 E4
St Georges Rd SK22 .... 33 E4
St Giles CE Prim Sch
  Killamarsh S21 .... 60 B3
  Matlock, Old Matlock DE4 143 E2
  Matlock, Starkholmes DE4 143 E1
St Giles Cl S21 .... 60 B3
St Giles Rd DE23 .... 218 C1
St Giles Spec1 Sch DE21 . 205 E1
St Giles Wlk DE23 .... 218 C1
St Hardulph's Prim Sch
  DE73 .... 252 C1
St Helen's Cl
  Chesterfield S41 .... 266 B4
  Darley Dale DE4 .... 127 D2
  Grindleford S32 .... 72 B4
St Helen's Cres NG9 .... 209 E2
St Helen's Croft S32 .... 72 B4
St Helen's Dr NG16 .... 171 E4
St Helen's La DE56 .... 166 A4
St Helen's St
  Chesterfield S41 .... 266 B4
  Derby DE1 .... 267 A4
St Helen's Sr NG7 .... 268 A2
St Helens Ave NG16 .... 160 B2
St Hugh's Cl DE22 .... 205 D1
St James Ave DE7 .... 209 D4
St James' CE Inf Sch
  DE23 .... 267 C1
St James CE Jun Sch
  DE23 .... 219 D2
St James Cl Belper DE56 . 179 E2
  Chesterfield S41 .... 96 B1
  Glossop SK13 .... 17 E4
  Willington DE65 .... 242 B3
St James Dr NG16 .... 182 B4
St James' Sq SK22 .... 33 E4
St James' St
  5 Buxton SK17 .... 85 D4
  Derby, Rose Hill DE23 ... 219 D1
  Derby, The Holmes DE1 .. 267 B3
  Nottingham NG1 .... 268 A1
  6 Sutton in A NG17 ...... 148 C2
St James's Ct S42 .... 85 E2
St James's St NG9 .... 223 E3
St James' Terr
  5 Nottingham NG1 .... 268 A1
  Nottingham NG9 .... 223 E3
St John Fisher RC Prim
  Sch DE24 .... 233 E4
St John Houghton RC Sch
  DE7 .... 208 B3
St John St Haughmill SK22 . 25 E1
  Mansfield NG18 .... 268 B4
St John's Ave DE21 .... 220 A3
St John's CE Mid Sch
  NG18 .... 268 B4
St John's CE Prim Sch
  Belper DE56 .... 179 D3
  Ripley DE5 .... 169 F1
  Stafford ST16 .... 269 E4
  Stapleford NG9 .... 223 F4
St John's CI Brinsley NG16 171 E1
St John's Cl DE22 .... 204 C1
St John's Dr Derby DE21 .. 220 A3
  Kilburn DE56 .... 192 A4
  Swadlincote DE11 .... 255 F3
St John's Mount S41 .... 95 F4
St John's Pl NG18 .... 268 B4
St John's Rd Belper DE56 . 179 D2
  Buxton SK17 .... 85 D4
  Chesterfield S41 .... 95 F4
  Dronfield S18 .... 76 C4
  Ilkeston DE7 .... 209 D4
  Matlock Bath DE4 .... 143 D2
  Smalley DE7 .... 192 C3
  Tideswell SK17 .... 69 E2
St John's St Ashbourne DE6 173 E1
  Long Eaton NG10 .... 236 B4
  Wirksworth DE4 .... 165 F4
St John's Terr DE1 .... 218 C3
St John's Wlk St 16 .... 269 F4
St Johns Bamford S33 ..... 40 A2
St Johns CE Prim Sch
  Chesterfield S40 .... 114 A4
  Ripley DE5 .... 169 F1
St Johns Pl S43 .... 78 B1
St Johns Rd S41 .... 78 B1
St Jonn's Cres S43 .... 80 C2
St Joseph's Prep Sch NG1 268 A2
St Joseph's RC Prim Sch
  Derby DE73 .... 267 A1
  Matlock DE4 .... 143 E3
  Shirebrook NG20 .... 119 F3
  Staveley S43 .... 97 E4
  Wirksworth DE4 .... 165 F4
St Joseph's St DE4 .... 143 E3
St Katherine's La DE4 ..... 110 C1
St Lawrence CE Prim Sch
  DE23 .... 236 C3
St Lawrence Ave S41 ...... 118 B4
St Lawrence CE Prim Sch
  NG10 .... 236 C3
St Lawrence Cl DE75 ...... 181 F4
St Lawrence Rd S42 .... 131 F3
St Lawrence View S80 ..... 81 F3
St Leonard's Ave S17 ...... 269 F3
St Leonard's Prim Sch
  DE23 .... 269 F3
St Leonards Dr S41 .... 96 B1
St Leonards Pl DE55 .... 146 C1
St Luke's CE Prim Sch
  SK13 .... 10 B1
St Luke's Sch S81 .... 63 F4
St Luke's St NG3 .... 268 C2
St Lukes Ct 7 S41 .... 95 F4

St Lukes Prim Sch SK17 ... 137 D4
St Margaret St NG18 .... 268 C2
St Margaret's RC Prim Sch
  SK13 .... 16 B4
St Mark's Cl DE4 .... 155 D3
St Mark's Rd
  Chesterfield S41 .... 95 F2
  Derby DE21 .... 219 E2
St Marks Ct NG3 .... 268 B2
St Martin's PI S116 .... 269 E4
St Martin's Rd Sk6 .... 23 D3
St Martin's Specl Sch
  DE24 .... 232 C4
St Martin's Wlk S80 .... 82 B3
St Mary's Ave DE7 .... 208 C4
St Mary's Ave DE7 .... 235 D4
St Mary's CE Fst Sch ST14 210 A3
St Mary's CE Inf Sch DE24 233 D2
St Mary's Cl DE11 .... 210 A3
St Mary's Cres S14 .... 210 A3
St Mary's Ct DE1 .... 267 B3
St Mary's Dr S21 .... 240 C3
St Mary's Gate
  Chesterfield S41 .... 266 C3
  Derby DE1 .... 267 B3
  Nottingham NG1 .... 268 B3
  2 Stafford ST16 .... 269 E4
  Wirksworth DE4 .... 165 F4
St Mary's Gr 6 S116 .... 269 E4
St Mary's Inf Sch S18 .... 76 C4
St Mary's Pl 3 S116 .... 269 E4
St Mary's RC Prim Sch
  Chesterfield S40 .... 266 A4
  Derby DE1 .... 267 B3
  Glossop SK13 .... 17 E4
  Marple SK6 .... 23 D4
  New Mills SK22 .... 33 D4
St Mary's RC Sch S40 ..... 95 E1
St Mary's Rd Disley SK12 .. 32 B4
  Glossop SK13 .... 17 E4
  New Mills SK22 .... 33 D3
St Mary's Wlk NG16 .... 171 D4
St Marys Wharf Rd DE1 .. 219 D3
St Matthew's St DE14 .... 254 B3
St Matthew's Wlk DE22 . 204 C1
St Matthias Rd NG3 .... 268 C1
St Mawes Cl DE22 .... 204 B1
St Mellion Cl DE23 .... 217 F1
St Michael's CE Prim Sch
  S32 .... 53 D1
St Michael's Cl
  Holbrook DE56 .... 191 E1
  Shirley DE6 .... 200 B4
  Willington DE65 .... 242 A3
St Michael's Dr
  South Normanton DE55 . 160 A3
St Michael's La DE1 .... 267 B3
St Michaels CE Crich DE4 . 156 C2
  Derby DE24 .... 233 E4
St Michaels View DE21 ... 204 B1
St Nicholas Cl DE22 .... 204 B1
St Nicholas St NG1 .... 268 B2
St Norbert Dr DE7 .... 208 B3
St Oswald Cres DE6 .... 173 E1
St Oswald's CE Inf Sch
  DE6 .... 173 D1
St Oswald's Hospl DE6 .. 173 D1
St Pancras Way DE1 .... 267 C3
St Patrick's Pl 1 S116 .... 269 E4
St Patrick's St 2 S116 .... 269 E4
St Paul's CE Prim Sch
  DE22 .... 269 E2
St Paul's Rd DE1 .... 219 D1
St Pauls Ave S41 .... 115 E1
St Peter & St Paul Sch
  ST14 .... 224 C2
St Peter's CE Fst Sch
  ST14 .... 224 C2
St Peter's CE Jun Sch
  DE23 .... 218 B3
St Peter's Churchyard DE1 267 B3
St Peter's Dr DE56 .... 178 C2
St Peter's Gate NG1 .... 268 B3
St Peter's Rd Buxton SK17 . 66 B3
  Derby DE23 .... 233 D2
St Peter's St NG18 .... 268 B3
St Peter's St DE1 .... 267 B3
St Peter's Way NG18 ...... 268 B3
St Peters CE Sch DE6 ...... 149 E2
St Peters Cl
  Long Duckmanton S44 ... 98 A3
  Stoke-on-T ST4 .... 269 D1
St Peters Croft DE56 ...... 179 D3
St Peters High Sch ST4 .. 269 D1
St Philip Howard RC Sch
  SK13 .... 17 D2
St Philip Neri's with St
  Bede's RC Prim Sch**
  NG18 .... 268 B3
St Philip's Dr S41 .... 115 D1
St Philomena's Convent
  Prim Sch DE1 .... 267 B3
St Quentin Cl Derby DE22 231 F4
  12 Sheffield S17 .... 56 A3
St Quentin Dr S17 .... 56 A3
St Quentin Mount S17 ..... 56 A3
St Quentin Rise S17 .... 56 A3
St Quentin View S17 .... 56 A3
St Ronan's Ave DE56 ...... 190 C2
St Stephen's Ave NG2 .... 268 C1
St Stephen's Cl DE21 ...... 220 C2
St Stephen's Ct DE21 ..... 256 C2

tephen's Rd NG2 .... 268 C1
tephens Cl DE7 .... 221 D1
within's Cl DE22 .... 218 B2
heresa's RC Prim Sch
.... 44 A4
homas Cl DE55 .... 147 F3
homas More RC Sch
17 .... 85 D4
homas of Canterbury
im Sch S8 .... 56 C4
homas Pl S14 .... 269 D1
homas Prim Sch
.... 269 D2
homas RC Prim Sch
.... 208 C3
homas St DE23 .... 219 D1
homas' St S40 .... 95 E1
homas St S16 .... 269 F4
incent Cl NG10 .... 236 C3
Verburgh's CE Prim
h DE21 .... 220 B3
Verburgh's CE Prim
h DE13 .... 238 A2
Verburgh's View DE21 220 B3
Vilfrid's Rd Sheffield S2 .. 43 D4
st Hallam DE7 .... 207 F4
Vystan's Rd DE22 .... 218 B2
Vystans Sch DE65 .... 242 B1
ey Cl NG9 .... 169 F4
ey Dr NG3 .... 209 E1
ey Sq [3] S40 .... 95 E1
combe Rd DE55 .... 159 E3
n DE13 .... 244 A3
y
St DE23 .... 219 D1
s Ave S42 .... 131 E4
s La DE15 .... 248 B2
Gdns NG3 .... 268 B2
sbury Ave
ton LE7 DE5 .... 248 B2
esterfield S41 .... 95 F4
nfield S18 .... 76 A4
sbury Cl NG19 .... 136 B2
sbury Cres S41 .... 95 F4
sbury Dr Stafford ST16 269 F4
adlincote DE11 .... 256 C3
sbury La DE73 .... 252 A4
sbury Rd Dronfield S18 .. 76 A4
nnsfield NG19 .... 268 A4
tford ST16 .... 269 F4
sbury St Derby DE23 ..267 B1
dfield SK13 .... 10 A3
ng Eaton NG10 .... 236 C4
efield La DE6 .... 183 F4
ywood Cl DE24 .... 231 E1
ond Ave ST16 .... 269 F4
 St17 .... 269 E3
Rd S17 .... 269 E3
burn Cl DE21 .... 205 F1
er Cl DE74 .... 246 C2
er St S16 .... 269 E4
ergate S40 .... 266 B3
ergate La S30 .... 40 B1
ers La DE4 .... 142 C2
n Cres S40 .... 80 C2
antha Ct DE21 .... 206 A1
pson's La NG19 .... 135 D2
uel Cl Mansfield NG19 .. 268 A4
uel Cl 43 E4
uel Dr S2 .... 43 E4
uel Pl S2 .... 43 E4
uel Rd S2 .... 43 E4
d La DE16 .... 9 E2
J La DE6 .... 211 D1
dalwood Cl DE4 .... 127 F4
dalwood Rd DE55 .... 254 C3
dbach Cl DE21 .... 206 A1
dbed La DE56 .... 179 E2
dby Croft S14 .... 43 F1
dby Ct S14 .... 43 F1
dby Dr Marple SK6 ..... 23 D4
nfield S14 .... 43 F1
dcliffe Pk DE11 .... 256 B4
dcliffe Rd DE11 .... 256 B3
dcroft Cl DE11 .... 256 B2
dcroft Rd DE21 .... 220 C3
derson Rd DE21 .... 220 A3
dfield Cl DE21 .... 220 A4
dford Ave NG10 .... 236 C4
dbrook DE65 .... 228 C1
dgate Ave NG19 .... 136 B2
dgate Cl DE4 .... 233 D3
dgate Rd NG19 .... 136 B2
dgate La DE56 .... 166 C3
dham La DE55 .... 169 E1
dhill La
arlesworth SK13 .... 16 A1
arple SK6 .... 15 F1
dhills Rd S44 .... 99 E3
diacre Rd NG9 .... 223 E2
diway Chesterfield S40 114 B4
ssop SK13 .... 17 F4
dlands The DE11 .... 256 A4
down Ave DE3 .... 217 E2
down Cl
.... 254 A4
dington S21 .... 59 D2
down Rd Beeston NG9 .. 223 F1
by DE24 .... 232 C4
dringham Ave DE15 .. 248 A1
dringham La S42 .... 94 C2
dringham Pl NG19 ..... 136 A3
dringham Dr
by DE21 .... 220 C3
dfield Woodhouse
.... 136 A3
dringham Pl DE7 .... 208 B3

Sandringham Rd
Calow S44 .... 97 D2
Derby DE21 .... 205 F1
Mansfield Woodhouse
NG19 .... 136 C3
Nottingham NG2 .... 268 C1
Sandiacre NG10 .... 223 D2
Sands Cl S14 .... 43 F2
Sandstone Ave S40 .... 114 A4
Sandwood Cl DE55 .... 148 A2
Sandy Cl S80 .... 81 F3
Sandy La Caldwell DE12 216 B4
Chisworth SK13 .... 16 A2
Crich DE4 .... 167 F4
Horsley DE21 .... 192 A2
Mansfield NG18 .... 268 C4
Matlock DE4 .... 143 E4
Sandybank Cl SK13 ..... 9 F2
Sandybrook Cl DE6 .... 173 E2
Sandycliffe Cl NG19 .. 136 C1
Sandyford La
Alderwasley DE56 .... 166 C2
Spout DE56 .... 166 C2
Sandyhill Cl DE23 ...... 233 D1
Sandypits La DE65 ..... 229 E2
Sanforth St S41 .... 96 A3
Santolina Dr DE21 ..... 205 F1
Sapperton Cl DE23 ..... 231 E3
Sapperton La
Boylestone DE65 .... 213 F1
Church Broughton DE65 .. 213 F1
Sarah Cl DE55 .... 170 B4
Sargent Gdns NG3 ..... 268 C2
Sark Rd S2 .... 43 D4
Sash St ST16 .... 269 E4
Saundby Ave NG19 ..... 135 E1
Saundersfoot Way S20 .. 206 B1
Savage La S17 .... 55 E4
Saville Cl NG9 .... 223 F4
Saville House Sch NG19 136 A2
Saw Pit Ind Est DE55 .. 148 B3
Saw Pit La DE55 .... 148 A3
Sawley Jun & Inf Sch
NG10 .... 236 A3
Sawley Rd Breaston DE72 235 F3
Draycott DE72 .... 235 D4
Sawmills Ind Pk DE75 .. 181 E2
Sawpit La DE65 .... 227 F3
Saxon Cl S41 .... 254 C4
Saxon Croft DE65 .... 242 B1
Saxon Rd S8 .... 43 D4
Saxon St DE15 .... 254 C4
Saxondale Ave DE3 ..... 181 F1
Saxton Ave DE75 .... 181 F4
Scaddows La DE73 .... 250 C2
Scalby Cl NG16 .... 182 B1
Scaliot Cl SK22 .... 33 D4
Scalpcliffe Rd DE15 ... 248 A1
Scarborough Ave DE7 .. 208 C4
Scarborough Rise DE21 .. 205 F1
Scarborough St NG3 ... 268 B2
Scarcliffe Cl DE24 ...... 232 C2
Scarcliffe La DE55 ..... 119 E4
Scarcliffe Prim Sch S44 118 C3
Scarcliffe St NG18 ...... 268 C4
Scarcliffe Terr NG20 .. 101 D1
Scargill CE Prim Sch DE7 207 E4
Scargill Rd DE7 .... 207 F4
Scargill Wlk NG16 ...... 182 C2
Scarsdale Ave
Derby, Allestree DE23 ... 204 B2
Derby, California DE23 .. 218 B1
Scarsdale Cl S18 .... 76 A4
Scarsdale Cres S43 .... 80 A4
Scarsdale Cross S18 .. 57 D1
Scarsdale Hospl S40 .. 266 B4
Scarsdale Pl [7] SK17 .. 85 D4
Scarsdale Rd
Chesterfield S41 .... 96 A4
Dronfield S18 .... 57 D1
Duffield DE56 .... 190 C2
Scarsdale St S44 .... 117 F4
Scarthin DE4 .... 155 D3
Scarthin La DE4 .... 155 D3
Schofield Ct DE11 ...... 110 C1
School Ave S20 .... 59 E3
School Board La S40 .. 95 F2
School Cl Blackwell DE55 .. 147 F1
Fenny Bentley DE6 ...... 162 A1
Moira DE11 .... 256 B1
Mosborough S20 .... 59 F2
Newton DE55 .... 148 A2
Shirland DE55 .... 146 B1
Stonebroom DE55 .... 146 C2
School Croft DE55 ..... 170 B3
School House Hill DE56 148 B4
School La Ashbourne DE6 173 D1
Baslow DE45 .... 91 F3
Beeley DE4 .... 111 D2
Brackenfield DE55 ...... 145 E1
Castle Donington DE74 .. 247 D2
Compstall SK6 .... 15 D2
Crich DE4 .... 157 D1
Derby DE73 .... 233 D1
Dronfield S18 .... 57 D1
Hassop DE45 .... 90 C2
Hatheragge S32 .... 53 D4
Heage DE56 .... 168 B1
Long Duckmanton S44 .. 97 E2
Mansfield Woodhouse NG19 136 B2
Marsh Lane S21 .... 58 C2
Roston DE6 .... 197 D1
Ripley DE5 .... 169 E1
Rolleston DE13 .... 240 B2
Rowsley DE4 .... 126 C4
Sheffield, Greenhill S8 .. 56 C4
Sheffield, Norton S8 ... 56 C3
South Normanton DE55 160 A2

School La continued
Stanton in P DE4 .... 126 B3
Stanton-by-D DE7 .... 222 C4
Sudbury DE6 .... 225 F2
Taddington SK17 .... 87 F2
School Lane DE1 .... 43 E1
School Rd Chesterfield S41 .. 96 A4
Matlock DE4 .... 143 E3
Peak Dale SK17 .... 67 D3
Uttoxeter ST14 .... 210 A1
School Sq DE7 .... 207 F4
School St Eckington S21 .. 59 E2
Moira DE12 .... 262 C1
Mosborough S20 .... 59 E4
Swadlincote DE11 .... 256 A1
Schoolpiece La DE55 .. 227 E4
Scothches The DE56 ... 178 C3
Scotia Cl S2 .... 43 F4
Scotia Dr S2 .... 43 F4
Scotland St S80 .... 81 F3
Scotswood Rd NG19 ... 136 A3
Scott Cl S42 .... 131 D3
Scott Cres DE55 .... 146 C2
Scott Dr Belper DE56 .. 179 F3
Marple S45 .... 23 D4
Somercotes DE55 .... 170 B4
Scott St Derby DE23 ... 218 C2
Whaley Thorns NG20 ... 101 D1
Scotts The DE11 .... 261 E4
Scowerdens Cl S12 ..... 44 C3
Scowerdens Dr S12 .... 44 C3
Scratta La S80 .... 63 D3
Screetham La DE4 ...... 112 B1
Scropton Old Rd DE65 239 E4
Scropton Rd
Hatton DE65 .... 239 D4
Scropton DE65 .... 226 C1
Scropton DE24 .... 232 C2
Sea Breeze Terr S13 .. 44 C4
Seaburn Rd NG9 .... 223 F1
Seaford Way DE7 .... 194 C3
Seagrave Ave S12 .... 44 A2
Seagrave Cl DE21 .... 220 A4
Seagrave Cres S12 ..... 44 A2
Seagrave Dr S12 .... 44 A2
Seagrave Rd S12 .... 44 A2
Seal View DE12 .... 261 E3
Seale St DE1 .... 267 B3
Sealey Cl DE65 .... 242 B3
Seals Rd DE12 .... 262 C1
Sealwood La Linton DE12 .. 261 F3
Overseal DE12 .... 261 F3
Seamer Rd NG16 .... 195 F4
Seanor La S45 .... 132 A2
Searl St DE1 .... 218 C3
Searle Ave DE73 .... 269 D3
Searson Ave S44 .... 99 D1
Searston Ave S42 .... 115 E2
Seascale Cl DE21 .... 205 E1
Seaton Cl DE3 .... 217 E2
Second Ave Derby DE7 .. 245 D4
Risley DE72 .... 222 C3
Sedbergh Cres S41 ..... 95 E4
Sedgebrook Cl DE21 ... 205 F1
Sedgebrook St NG19 .. 136 C2
Sedgefield Gn DE21 .... 217 E1
Sedgemoor Cl S40 ...... 95 D2
Sedgley Ave NG2 .... 268 C2
Sedgwick St
Langley Mill NG16 .... 182 A2
Westwood NG16 .... 171 D2
Seely La NG7 .... 268 A2
Sefton Ave NG9 .... 223 F4
Sefton Cl DE55 .... 248 A1
Sefton Rd DE21 .... 219 F3
Sefton St S13 .... 44 C4
Selborne St DE24 .... 219 E1
Selburst Rd S41 .... 95 F3
Selina Cl DE74 .... 247 D2
Selkirk St DE21 .... 219 F4
Selly Oak Gr S8 .... 57 E3
Selly Oak Rd S8 .... 57 E3
Selmer Cl S43 .... 96 B4
Selston CE Inf Sch NG16 171 F3
Selston Rd NG16 .... 171 D3
Selworthy Cl DE21 ..... 206 A1
Selwyn St Bolsover S44 118 B4
Derby DE1 .... 267 A1
Senners La SK17 .... 87 D1
Serina Ave DE23 .... 231 E4
Serlay La S26 .... 61 F3
Serlby Rise NG3 .... 268 C2
Setcup La S21 .... 59 E1
Sett Cl S32 .... 33 D4
Settlement The DE72 .. 221 E3
Setts Way S42 .... 115 D2
Seven Archers Way ST4 268 P2
Seven Oaks Rd DE7 .... 209 D1
Sevenoaks Ave DE22 .. 217 F3
Severals NG19 .... 223 F4
Severn Cl DE13 .... 240 B1
Severn Cres S42 .... 132 A3
Severn Sq DE55 .... 159 D2
Severn St DE24 .... 232 C4
Severnale Cl DE22 ..... 205 D3
Severnlands Dr DE24 .. 233 E2
Sewell Rd S20 .... 59 F3
Sexton St S43 .... 79 F4
Seymour Cl DE22 .... 218 B3
Seymour La S43 .... 79 E1
Seymour Rd NG16 ...... 182 C1
Seymour St NG3 .... 268 C2
Shacklecross Cl DE72 221 E3
Shady Gr DE65 .... 228 B1

Shaftesbury Ave
Chesterfield S40 .... 95 E2
Long Eaton NG10 .... 236 A2
Mansfield NG19 .... 135 F1
Sandiacre NG10 .... 223 D3
Shaftesbury Cres DE23 219 D1
Shaftesbury St DE23 ... 219 D1
Shaftesbury St S DE23 219 D1
Shafton Cl S45 .... 131 F2
Shafton Wlk S45 .... 131 F2
Shakespeare Ave
Creswell S80 .... 81 E1
Mansfield Woodhouse NG19 136 A2
Shirland DE55 .... 146 B2
Shakespeare Cl
Clay Cross S42 .... 131 D3
Repton DE65 .... 242 B1
Swadlincote DE11 .... 256 B3
Shakespeare Cres S18 .. 76 A4
Shakespeare Dr DE55 .. 159 D2
Shakespeare Rd NG16 .. 195 E3
Shakespeare St
Derby DE24 .... 232 A3
Grassmoor S42 .... 115 F2
Holmewood S42 .... 116 B1
Long Eaton NG10 .... 223 E1
Nottingham NG1 .... 268 B2
Shakespeare Villas NG1 268 B2
Shaldon Dr DE23 .... 218 B1
Shalfleet Dr DE24 .... 233 E3
Shallcross Ave S33 ..... 45 F2
Shallcross Cres S33 ... 45 F2
Shallcross Rd SK23 .... 45 F2
Shambles The S40 ...... 266 B3
Shamrock Pl S43 .... 79 E2
Shamrock St DE23 ...... 218 C1
Shandwick Cl [4] DE24 .. 231 E2
Shanklin Dr NG9 .... 223 E4
Shannon Cl DE23 .... 231 E3
Shap Cl [7] S40 .... 95 E3
Shardlow Prim Sch DE72 .. 234 C1
Shardlow Rd
Aston-on-T DE72 .... 246 B4
Derby DE24 .... 233 E3
Sharley Park L Ctr S45 .. 131 E2
Sharman Cl
Apperknowle S18 .... 58 A1
Stoke-on-T ST4 .... 269 D2
Sharp Cl Ilkeston DE7 .. 208 B3
Long Eaton NG10 .... 236 B3
Sharpe Ave S8 .... 56 C4
Sharpswood Manor S41 256 C2
Sharrard Cl S12 .... 44 A3
Sharrard Dr S12 .... 44 A3
Sharrard Gr S12 .... 44 A3
Sharrard Rd S12 .... 44 A3
Shatton La S33 .... 51 F4
Shaw La Belper DE56 .. 191 D4
Hadfield SK13 .... 9 F2
Holloway DE4 .... 156 B4
Marston Montgomery DE6 .. 198 A1
Shaw St Chesterfield S41 .. 96 A1
Derby DE22 .... 218 C3
Dronfield S18 .... 57 E4
Glossop SK13 .... 17 E4
Holmewood S42 .... 116 B1
Mottram in L SK14 ...... 9 D2
Somercotes DE55 .... 170 B3
Shaw St E DE7 .... 209 D3
Shaw St W DE7 .... 209 D3
Shaw's Row S40 .... 95 E1
Shaw's Yd S45 .... 191 F4
Shawcroft DE6 .... 173 E1
Shawcroft Ave DE55 ... 170 B3
Shawfield Rd SK13 ...... 9 F2
Shaws Gn DE22 .... 218 C3
Shaws Hill DE4 .... 156 B1
Sheaf Bank S2 .... 43 D4
Sheardhall Ave SK12 .. 32 C3
Sheardhall Ave S18 .... 56 C1
Sheards Dr S18 .... 56 C1
Sheards Way S18 .... 56 C1
Shearwater Cl DE23 .... 231 E4
Sheepbridge La
Chesterfield S41 .... 76 C1
Mansfield NG18 .... 268 A3
Sheepcote Rd S21 ...... 60 B3
Sheephill Rd S21 .... 42 C1
Sheeplea La S45 .... 129 F4
Sheepwash La S45 ...... 145 D4
Sheet Stores Ind Est
NG10 .... 236 B3
Sheffield City Poly S17 .. 55 E2
Sheffield Hallam Univ S17 .. 55 E2
Sheffield La DE56 .... 267 D2
Sheffield Rd Baslow DE45 .. 91 F4
Chapel-en-le-F SK23 .... 47 F4
Chesterfield S41 .... 96 A3
Creswell S80 .... 81 E2
Dronfield S18 .... 56 C2
Eckington S21 .... 59 F3
Glossop SK13 .... 10 C1
Hathersage S32 .... 53 D4
Killamarsh S21 .... 60 B4
Mosborough S20 .... 59 F2
Renishaw S21 .... 79 F4
Sheffield S12 .... 44 C1
Unstone S18 .... 76 C2
Unstone S18 .... 76 C2
Whitwell S80 .... 82 C2
Shelburne St ST4 .... 269 E1
Sheldon Cl NG10 .... 223 D2
Sheldon Ct DE24 .... 232 C2
Sheldon Mews SK13 ... 9 E1
Sheldon Rd
Chesterfield S40 .... 95 D3
Heanor DE75 .... 181 E3
Shelford Cl DE3 .... 217 E2

Shelford Hill NG19 ...... 268 A3
Shelley Ave NG19 .... 136 A2
Shelley Dr Derby DE23 .. 231 E3
Dronfield S18 .... 76 B4
Shelley Gr DE55 .... 146 C2
Shelley St S42 .... 116 B1
Shelly Rd DE11 .... 256 B3
Shelmory Cl DE24 .... 232 C3
Shelton Cl NG19 .... 135 F1
Shelton Dr DE24 .... 232 C2
Shelton Jun & Inf Sch
DE24 .... 232 B2
Shelton Old Rd ST4 .... 269 E2
Shelton St NG3 .... 268 B2
Shenington Way DE21 .. 206 A1
Shepherd St DE23 .... 218 B1
Shepherd's La DE73 .... 251 E3
Shepherd's Row
Glossop SK13 .... 10 C1
Hadfield SK13 .... 9 F2
Shepley's Yd S40 .... 266 B3
Sheppard St S14 .... 269 E1
Shepton Cl DE7 .... 194 B2
Sheraton Way SK17 .... 66 A1
Sherbourne Ave S41 ... 95 F4
Sherbourne Dr
Belper DE56 .... 179 E3
Branston DE14 .... 254 A4
Sherbrook Gr SK17 ..... 85 E3
Sherbrooke Rd SK12 ... 32 B3
Sheridan Ct NG9 .... 209 F1
Sheridan St Derby DE24 .. 231 F3
Stafford ST16 .... 269 F4
Sheriff Dr DE4 .... 143 D3
Sheringham Dr NG18 .. 268 C3
Sherman Cl DE65 .... 228 C1
Sherriff's Lea NG9 ...... 223 F1
Sherston Cl DE21 .... 206 A1
Sherwin Cl NG3 .... 268 A2
Sherwin Rd NG9 .... 209 F1
Sherwin St DE22 .... 218 C4
Sherwood Ave
Borrowash DE72 .... 221 E1
Creswell S80 .... 81 E1
Derby, Chaddesden DE21 .. 219 F4
Derby, Littleover DE23 .. 231 E3
Hope S33 .... 39 D2
Pinxton NG16 .... 160 B2
Shirebrook NG20 .... 119 F2
Sherwood Chase S17 .. 69 C2
Sherwood Copse S17 .. 69 C2
Sherwood Dr NG20 ..... 119 F2
Sherwood Fold SK13 ... 16 B4
Sherwood Foresters
Regiment Meml DE4 .. 156 C2
Sherwood Hall L Ctr DE4 143 E2
Sherwood Pl [8] S18 ... 56 B1
Sherwood Rd Buxton SK17 85 E3
Dronfield S18 .... 56 B1
Killamarsh S21 .... 60 C4
Matlock DE4 .... 143 E2
Tideswell SK17 .... 69 E2
Sherwood Rise
Eastwood NG16 .... 182 C1
Mansfield Woodhouse
NG19 .... 136 C2
Sherwood St Bolsover S44 .. 117 F4
Chesterfield S41 .... 266 C1
Derby DE22 .... 218 C2
Mansfield NG18 .... 268 B3
Mansfield Woodhouse
NG19 .... 136 A1
Newton DE55 .... 148 A2
Shirland DE55 .... 146 B3
Somercotes DE55 .... 170 B4
Sutton in A NG17 .... 148 C1
Shetland Cl Derby DE21 .. 219 E4
Mansfield NG19 .... 136 C1
Shetland Rd Dronfield S18 .. 76 A4
Tibshelf DE55 .... 147 F3
Shields Cres DE4 .... 246 C2
Shieling The DE65 ...... 227 E1
Shilling Way NG10 ...... 236 A3
Shiloh Rd SK22, SK6 ... 24 A3
Shilton Cl S14 .... 269 D1
Shinwell Ave S43 .... 97 D4
Shipley Cl DE14 .... 254 A4
Shipley Ctry Pk DE75 .. 194 B1
Shipley Ctry Pk Visitor Ctr
DE75 .... 193 F4
Shipley La Mapperley DE75 .. 193 F3
Shipley DE75 .... 193 F3
Shipley Wlk DE24 .... 232 C2
Shipman Ct S20 .... 59 E4
Shipstone St DE7 .... 209 D3
Shirburn Ave NG18 ..... 268 C4
Shire Hill Hospl SK13 .. 10 C2
Shire La Heath S44 ...... 116 C2
Long Duckmanton S44 .. 116 C2
Shirebrook Com Sch
NG20 .... 119 F3
Shirebrook Dr SK13 .... 17 F4
Shirebrook Rd S8 .... 43 D3
Shireoaks Cl DE55 ...... 178 B3
Shireoaks Rd Dronfield S18 .. 57 E1
Shireoaks S80 .... 63 F3
Shireoaks Row S81 ..... 63 F4
Shireoaks Sta S81 ...... 63 F4
Shires The NG19 .... 136 C1
Shirland Prim Sch DE55 146 B1
Shirland St S41 .... 266 B4

Shirley Cl
Castle Donington DE74 ...... 247 D2
🔟 Chesterfield S40 .... 95 D3
Hope S33 .... 39 D2
Shirley Cres DE72 .... 235 E4
Shirley La Rodsley DE6 .... 200 A3
Shirley DE6 .... 200 A3
Shirley Pk DE72 .... 246 A4
Shirley Rd Derby DE21 .... 205 F1
Ripley DE5 .... 169 E1
Swanwick DE55 .... 169 F4
Shirley St NG10 .... 236 A2
Shop La DE56 .... 168 B1
Shop Stones DE72 .... 221 E3
Shoreham St S2 .... 43 D4
Short Ave DE22 .... 204 C3
Short Brook Fst & Mid Sch
S20 .... 59 F4
Short Cl S42 .... 113 E4
Short Hill
Breedon on t H DE73 .... 252 C3
🔟 Nottingham NG1 .... 268 B1
Short La DE74 .... 246 C2
Short Lands DE56 .... 179 D2
Short Row DE56 .... 178 C2
Short St Belper DE56 .... 179 D2
Burton u T DE15 .... 254 C4
Short Street Inf Sch
DE15 .... 254 C4
Shortbrook Bank 🔟 S20 .... 59 F4
🔟 Nottingham NG1 .... 59 F4
Shortbrook Cl 🔟 S20 .... 59 F4
Shortbrook Dr 🔟 S20 .... 59 F4
Shortbrook Rd S20 .... 59 F4
Shortbrook Way 🔟 S20 ...... 59 F4
Shortbrook Wlk 🔟 S20 ...... 59 F4
Shortheath DE12 .... 262 B2
Shortheath Rd DE12 .... 262 C2
Shortlands The DE44 .... 143 D2
Shorts La S17 .... 55 D3
Shortwood Cl NG1 .... 268 B1
Shorwell Gdns DE24 .... 233 E3
Shottle Wlk DE24 .... 232 C2
Shotwoodhill La DE13 ...... 240 A3
Shrewsbury Cl DE21 .... 206 B1
Shrewsbury Rd
Burton u T DE13 .... 240 C1
Stafford ST17 .... 269 E3
Shrewsbury St SK13 .... 10 B1
Shropshire Ave
Derby DE21 .... 219 F4
Westwood NG16 .... 171 E2
Shropshire Dr SK13 .... 17 F4
Shrubbery The DE11 .... 257 D1
Shuckstone La DE4 .... 156 C3
Shudehill Cl SK22 .... 25 E2
Shuttlewood Rd S44 .... 99 D2
Shutts La DE45 .... 109 E2
Sibthorpe St NG18 .... 268 B3
Sicklebrook La S18 .... 57 F2
Sickleholme S33 .... 40 A1
Siddals La DE22 .... 204 C2
Siddals Rd DE1 .... 267 C2
Siddals St DE15 .... 248 B3
Siddons St DE24 .... 233 D4
Side End La SK23 .... 45 D1
Sides La DE6 .... 184 A3
Sideway Rd ST4 .... 269 E1
Sidings The DE21 .... 220 A2
Sidings Way DE55 .... 147 E1
Sidlaw Cl 🔟 S40 .... 95 E3
Sidmouth Cl DE24 .... 233 E4
Sidney Cl DE3 .... 217 F2
Sidney St Derby DE1 .... 267 C1
Kimberley NG16 .... 195 F3
Long Eaton NG10 .... 236 B3
Siemens Rd ST17 .... 269 E3
Silk Hill SK3 .... 45 F4
Silk Mill La DE13 .... 239 E3
Silk St SK13 .... 17 E4
Silken Holme DE55 .... 160 A2
Silkstone Cres Sheffield S12 ... 44 C2
Swadlincote DE11 .... 256 A1
Silkstone Cres S12 .... 44 C2
Silkstone Pl S12 .... 44 C2
Silkstone Rd S12 .... 44 C2
Sillitoe Pl ST4 .... 269 E1
Silver Birch Cres DE55 .... 159 E4
Silver Hill Rd DE23 .... 219 D1
Silver La Elvaston DE72 .... 234 A3
Marchington ST14 .... 224 C1
Silver Mill Rd S2 .... 43 D4
Silver Spring SK14 .... 15 D4
Silverburn Dr DE21 .... 206 A1
Silverdale NG9 .... 223 F3
Silverdale Ave NG19 .... 136 A2
Silverdale Cl S41 .... 76 C1
Silverhill Cl DE13 .... 240 B1
Silverhill La NG17 .... 148 C4
Silverhill Prim Sch DE13 .. 227 E2
Silverhill Rd DE21 .... 220 C2
Silverlands SK17 .... 85 E4
Silverlands Cl SK17 .... 85 E4
Silverlands Pk SK17 .... 85 E4
Silverton Dr DE24 .... 231 E1
Silvey Gr DE21 .... 220 B2
Simcoe Leys DE73 .... 233 D1
Simcrest Ave S21 .... 60 B3
Simmondley Gr SK13 .... 17 D4
Simmondley La SK13 .... 17 D4
Simmondley New Rd SK13 . 17 D4
Simmondley Prim Sch
SK13 .... 17 D4
Simon Fields Cl DE7 .... 193 D1
Simonhorn Ave ST4 .... 269 D2

Simons Cl SK13 .... 17 D4
Simons Wlk SK13 .... 17 D4
Simpson St DE24 .... 232 C3
Sims Ave DE1 .... 218 C3
Sims Croft S41 .... 77 E2
Sinclair Cl Derby DE24 ...... 231 F2
Heanor DE7 .... 193 E4
Sinfin Ave DE24 .... 232 B3
Sinfin Central Sta DE24 .... 232 A3
Sinfin Com Sch DE24 .... 231 F2
Sinfin Fields Cres DE24 ... 232 B3
Sinfin La Barrow u T DE73 . 244 A3
Derby DE24 .... 231 F2
Sinfin Moor La
Chellaston DE73 .... 232 C1
Derby, Sinfin DE73 .... 231 F2
Sinfin North Sta DE24 ...... 232 A3
Sinfin Prim Sch DE24 .... 231 F3
Sir Frank Whittle Rd DE21 . 219 E4
Sir Harold Jackson Prim
Sch S17 .... 55 D3
Sir Henry's La DE73 .... 252 A2
Sir Josephs La DE4 .... 127 D2
Sir William Hill Rd S32 ..... 71 E4
Siskin Dr DE24 .... 231 E2
Sisley Ave NG9 .... 223 F3
Sister's La DE72 .... 221 E3
Sitch La Callow DE4 .... 165 D2
Thornsett SK22 .... 24 C2
Sitwell Av DE4 .... 127 D2
Sitwell 🔟 S20 .... 59 F4
Sitwell Ave S40 .... 266 A1
Sitwell Cl DE21 .... 220 B2
Sitwell Dr DE56 .... 192 A4
Sitwell Grange La
Pilsley S45 .... 147 E4
Tibshelf S45 .... 147 E4
Sitwell St
Derby, Spondon DE21 .... 220 C2
Derby, The Holmes DE1 ..... 267 B2
Eckington S21 .... 59 E2
Sitwell Villas DE55 .... 146 C3
Skeavington's La DE7 .... 194 C3
Skegby La NG18, NG19 ...... 268 A3
Skegby Mount NG18 .... 268 A3
Skeldale Dr S40 .... 95 D3
Skelton Rd S8 .... 43 D3
Skelwith Cl S41 .... 95 E4
Sketchley St NG3 .... 268 C2
Ski 2000 Ilkeston NG16 .... 195 D1
Skiddaw Cl 🔟 S40 .... 95 E3
Skiddaw Dr DE3 .... 217 F1
Skinner St S80 .... 81 E1
Skipton Cl DE7 .... 194 B2
Skipton Gn DE21 .... 205 E1
Skye Gdns DE55 .... 147 F3
Skylark Way DE24 .... 231 E2
Slack La Ashover S45 .... 129 E1
Brailsford DE6 .... 187 E1
Chesterfield S40 .... 95 D2
Derby, Darley Abbey DE22 .. 204 C1
Derby, New Zealand DE22 .. 218 B1
Hartshorne DE11 .... 257 D3
Mayfield DE6 .... 184 B4
Nether Heage DE56 .... 168 B2
Ripley DE5 .... 169 E1
Shipley DE75 .... 193 F4
Somercotes DE55 .... 170 B3
Wessington DE55 .... 157 E4
Slack's La S45 .... 132 B1
Slackey La DE12 .... 262 B2
Slacks La SK22 .... 25 E3
Slade Cl Etwall DE65 .... 229 E2
South Normanton DE55 ..... 160 A2
Slade Fields ST14 .... 210 A1
Slade Hollow La DE6 .... 201 D2
Slade La DE6 .... 202 A4
Slag La S43 .... 77 E3
Sladburn Cl DE3 .... 217 F1
Slaley La DE4 .... 154 B4
Slaley View Rd S43 .... 80 A3
Slaney Cl DE24 .... 232 C4
Slant Cl SK13 .... 17 E4
Slant La NG19 .... 136 A2
Slant The NG20 .... 119 E2
Slate St S2 .... 43 D4
Slatelands Ave SK13 .... 17 D4
Slatelands Rd SK13 .... 17 D4
Slatepit La
Barlow S32, S42 .... 93 E4
Old Brampton S32, S42 ...... 93 E4
Slater Ave DE22 .... 218 C3
Slater Cres DE4 .... 165 F4
Slater St S45 .... 131 E2
Slayley Hill S43 .... 80 B2
Slayley View S43 .... 80 B3
Slaypit La S80 .... 62 B3
Sledgegate La DE4 .... 156 A4
Sledmere Cl DE24 .... 233 E4
Sleepy La DE73 .... 245 E1
Sleetmoor La
Somercotes DE55 .... 170 A4
Swanwick DE55 .... 170 A4
Sleights La NG16 .... 160 B1
Slindon Croft DE24 .... 233 E3
Slipperlow La SK17 .... 87 F1
Sloade La S12 .... 58 C3
Sloane Rd DE22 .... 218 A3
Sly Rd NG7 .... 268 A2
Small Gate NG19 .... 136 C3
Small Knowle End SK17 .... 67 E3
Small Meer Cl DE72 .... 232 C1
Small Thorn Pl DE11 .... 256 C1
Smalldale Cotts SK17 .... 67 E4
Smalldale Head Rd S33 .... 50 C4
Smalldale Rd Sheffield S12 . 44 B2
Smalldale SK17 .... 67 E4
Smalley Dr DE21 .... 206 A2

Smalley Mill Rd
Horsley DE21 .... 192 A2
Smalley DE7 .... 192 A2
Smallman St ST16 .... 269 E4
Smeath Rd NG16 .... 171 F1
Smeckley Wood Cl S18 ..... 76 B2
Smedley Ave Ilkeston DE7 .. 209 D4
Somercotes DE55 .... 159 E1
Smedley Cl DE65 .... 241 D3
Smedley Pl SK13 .... 10 C1
Smedley St DE4 .... 143 D3
Smedley St E DE4 .... 143 E3
Smedley St W DE4 .... 143 D4
Smedley's Ave NG10 .... 223 D3
Smeeton St DE75 .... 182 A1
Smelter Wood Ave S13 ..... 44 C4
Smelter Wood Cl S13 .... 44 C4
Smelter Wood Cres S13 .... 44 C4
Smelter Wood Ct S13 .... 44 C4
Smelter Wood Dr S13 .... 44 C4
Smelter Wood La S13 .... 44 C4
Smelter Wood Pl S13 .... 44 C4
Smelter Wood Rd S13 ...... 44 C4
Smelter Wood Rise S13 .... 44 C4
Smelter Wood Way S13 .... 44 C4
Smethinghouse La S18 ..... 75 F2
Smisby Rd LE65 .... 258 A1
Smisby Way DE24 .... 232 C2
Smith Ave Codnor DE5 ...... 170 A1
Melbourne DE73 .... 245 D1
Smith Cres S41 .... 96 B1
Smith Dr NG16 .... 182 A2
Smith Rd DE4 .... 143 D3
Smith-Hall La DE6 .... 188 A4
Smithfield Ave
Chesterfield S41 .... 115 E4
Trowell NG9 .... 209 E2
Smithfield Rd S12 .... 44 A2
Smithpool Rd ST4 .... 269 F1
Smithson Ave S44 .... 99 D1
Smithurst Rd NG16 .... 195 D4
Smithy Ave S45 .... 131 E2
Smithy Cl Glossop SK13 .... 10 B1
Parwich DE6 .... 151 E1
Smithy Croft S18 .... 56 B1
Smithy Fold SK13 .... 10 B1
Smithy Hill S33 .... 51 D4
Smithy Knoll Rd S32 .... 72 B1
Smithy La
Clifton Campville B79 .... 263 F1
Marple SK6 .... 15 F1
Smithy Meadows S32 .... 53 D4
Smithy Pl S42 .... 115 F1
Smithy Row NG1 .... 268 B1
Smuse La DE4 .... 143 F2
Snake La DE6 .... 190 C2
Snake Rd S33 .... 38 B3
Snape Hill S18 .... 57 D1
Snape Hill Dr S18 .... 57 D2
Snape Hill La S18 .... 57 D1
Snapehill Cl S18 .... 57 D2
Snapehill Cres S18 .... 57 D2
Snapes La DE6 .... 184 A1
Sneinton Bvd NG2 .... 268 C1
Sneinton CE Prim Sch The
NG2 .... 268 C1
Sneinton Hermitage NG2 .. 268 C1
Sneinton Hollows NG2 ..... 268 C1
Sneinton Rd NG2 .... 268 C1
Snelsmoor La DE73 .... 233 D1
Snelston Cl S18 .... 56 B1
Snelston Cres DE23 .... 218 B1
Snipe Cl S42 .... 113 E4
Snipesmoor La DE6 .... 185 F4
Snitterton Rd DE4 .... 143 D3
Snow Hill ST16 .... 269 E4
Snowberry Ave DE56 .... 179 D2
Snowdon La S21 .... 60 B1
Snowdrop Valley DE4 .... 168 A4
Snowfield View DE4 .... 165 F3
Snows Yd ST16 .... 269 D4
Soaper La S18 .... 57 D1
Soarbank Cl NG16 .... 195 F4
Society Pl DE23 .... 219 D1
Soft Water La S33 .... 51 D4
Solney Cl DE11 .... 255 F2
Soloman Pk NG16 .... 195 D1
Soloman Rd NG16 .... 195 D1
Solomons View SK17 .... 85 E4
Solway Cl DE21 .... 206 A1
Solway Rise S18 .... 56 B1
Somerby Way DE21 .... 205 F1
Somercotes Hill DE55 ...... 170 B4
Somercotes Inf Sch DE55 . 170 B4
Somercotes Rd S12 .... 44 B3
Somerlea Park Jun Sch
DE55 .... 170 B4
Somersal Cl DE24 .... 232 C2
Somersall Cl S40 .... 95 D1
Somersall La S40 .... 95 D1
Somersall Park Rd S40 ..... 95 D1
Somersall St NG19 .... 268 A4
Somersall Willows S40 ..... 95 D1
Somerby Ave S40 .... 114 A4
Somerset Cl Buxton SK17 .. 85 E2
Long Eaton NG10 .... 237 D4
Somerset Dr S43 .... 97 D4
Somerset St DE15 .... 254 B3
Somerset St DE7 .... 219 E4
Somme Rd DE22 .... 204 A2
Sookholme Cl NG20 .... 119 F2
Sookholme La NG20 .... 120 C3
Sookholme Rd
Market Warsop NG20 .... 120 C1
Shirebrook NG20 .... 119 F2
Soresby St S40 .... 266 B3
Sorrel Dr DE11 .... 256 C2

Sough La Bolehill DE4 .... 155 D1
Taddington SK17 .... 87 E1
Wirksworth DE4 .... 154 C1
Sough Rd DE55 .... 160 A4
Soughley La S10 .... 42 B4
South Ave Buxton SK17 ...... 85 D4
Derby, Chellaston DE23 ..... 232 C2
Derby, Darley Abbey DE23 .. 205 D2
Derby, Littleover DE23 .... 218 B1
Derby, Littleover DE23 .... 220 C2
Shirebrook NG20 .... 119 F2
South Brae Cl DE23 .... 231 E4
South Broadway St DE14 .. 254 B4
South Church St DE45 ...... 109 E3
South Cl Tintwistle SK13 .... 9 F4
Unstone S18 .... 76 C1
South Cres Bolsover S44 .... 99 D1
Killamarsh S21 .... 60 C4
Long Duckmanton S44 ...... 98 A3
South Darley CE Prim Sch
DE4 .... 142 A4
South Dr
Derby, Chellaston DE73 ..... 232 C2
Derby, Cherrytree Hill DE21 . 220 A3
Derby, Little Chester DE1 ... 218 C4
Derby, Littleover DE23 .... 218 A1
Swadlincote DE11 .... 255 F3
South East Derbyshire Coll
Heanor DE75 .... 181 F1
Ilkeston DE7 .... 208 C4
South Farm Ave S26 .... 61 F3
South Hill Rolleston DE13 .. 240 B2
Stretton DE55 .... 145 F4
South Hill La DE55 .... 145 F3
South Lodge Ct S40 .... 95 D2
South Marlow St SK13 ...... 10 A2
South Oak St DE14 .... 254 A4
South Par
Matlock Bath DE4 .... 143 D1
🔟 Nottingham NG1 .... 268 B1
South Park Ave DE4 .... 127 E2
South Pl
Chesterfield, Brampton S40 . 95 E1
Chesterfield, Stonegravels
S40 .... 266 B2
Ripley DE5 .... 169 E1
North Wingfield S42 .... 268 A1
South Sherwood St NG1 .... 268 B2
South St
Ashbourne DE6 .... 173 E1
Blackwell DE55 .... 147 F1
Buxton SK17 .... 85 D4
Chesterfield S40 .... 266 B2
Derby DE1 .... 218 C3
Draycott DE72 .... 235 D4
Eastwood, Bailey Grove
NG16 .... 182 C1
Eastwood, Gittbrook NG16 . 195 E4
Ilkeston DE7 .... 208 C4
Long Eaton NG10 .... 236 C4
Melbourne DE73 .... 252 A4
Mosborough S20 .... 59 E4
Pilsley S45 .... 132 B1
Somercotes DE55 .... 170 B3
South Normanton DE55 ..... 160 A3
Stafford ST16 .... 269 D4
South Terr ST4 .... 269 F1
South Uxbridge St DE14 ... 254 A4
South View Bamford S33 .... 40 A2
Mayfield DE6 .... 184 B3
Mosborough S20 .... 60 A4
New Mills SK22 .... 33 D4
Whitwell S80 .... 81 F3
South View Rd SK13 .... 17 F4
South View Wlk ST14 .... 196 C2
South Walls ST16 .... 269 D4
South Wingfield Prim Sch
DE55 .... 157 F2
South Wolfe St ST4 .... 269 E2
Southall St S8 .... 43 D3
Southampton St NG3 .... 268 C2
Southard's La S80 .... 62 C3
Southbrook Cl SK13 .... 9 F2
Southcote Dr S8 .... 43 D1
Southcroft Alfreton DE55 ... 159 D2
Buxton SK17 .... 85 D4
Derby DE23 .... 231 E2
Southdown Ave S40 .... 95 E3
Southdown Cl DE24 .... 231 E1
Southend St S43 .... 78 C1
Southend Sq NG2 .... 268 A2
Southfield Ave S41 .... 115 E3
Southfield Cl S80 .... 81 F3
Southfield Dr Dronfield S18 . 76 B4
South Normanton DE55 ..... 160 B3
Southfield Ind Site S80 ..... 82 A2
Southfield Mount S18 .... 76 B4
Southfields Clowne S43 ..... 80 C2
Long Eaton NG10 .... 236 C4
Southfields Ave NG16 ...... 160 B2
Southgate S21 .... 59 F2
Southgate Cl DE23 .... 217 E2
Southgate Cres S43 .... 80 C3
Southgate Inf Sch S43 ...... 59 F2
Southgate St Sch DE24 ..... 232 C4
Southgate Way S43 .... 78 A2
Southmead Way DE23 ...... 218 A2
Southwark Cl DE22 .... 218 A3
Southwell Rd NG1 .... 268 B1
Southwood Ave S18 .... 76 A4
Southwood Dr S43 .... 266 C3
Southwood House Specl
Sch DE56 .... 191 E3

Southwood St DE24 23
Sovereigh Gr NG10 23
Sovereign Way
Derby DE21 20
Heanor DE75 18
Sowbrook Brook DE7 20
Sowbrook La DE7 20
Sowter Rd DE1 26
Spa Brook Cl S12 4
Spa Brook Dr S12 4
Spa Croft DE55 14
Spa La
Chesterfield, Hady S41 26
Chesterfield, Stonegravels
S41 26
Derby DE1 26
Spa View Ave S12 4
Spa View Dr S12 4
Spa View Pl S12 4
Spa View Rd S12 4
Spa View Terr S12 4
Spa View Way S12 4
Spalden Ave DE6 17
Spalding Rd NG3 26
Spang La NG17 14
Spaniel Row 🔟 NG1 26
Spanker La DE56 16
Spanker Terr S18 16
Spark St ST4 26
Spark Terr S14 4
Sparrow Cl DE24 23
Sparrowbusk Cl S43 7
Speedwell S43 7
Speedwell Cl Derby DE21 .. 20
Tintwistle SK13 ....
Woodville DE11 25
Speedwell Ind Est S43 7
Speedwell Inf Sch S43 7
Speighthill Cres S42 11
Spenbeck Dr DE22 20
Spencer Ave Belper DE56 .. 17
Derby DE24 23
Sandiacre NG10 22
Woodthorpe S43 7
Spencer Cl DE13 24
Spencer Cres NG9 22
Spencer Dr DE55 14
Spencer Gr SK17 ....
Spencer Rd Belper DE56 ... 17
Buxton SK17 ....
Chapel-en-le-F SK23 ....
Sheffield S2 ....
Stoke-on-T ST4 26
Spencer St Bolsover S44 ... 11
Chesterfield S40 26
Derby DE24 23
Mansfield NG18 26
Stanley DE7 19
Spend La Mappleton DE6 ... 18
Thorpe DE6 18
Spender Cl DE6 18
Sperry Cl NG16 17
Spindletree Dr DE21 20
Spinkhill Ave S13 ....
Spinkhill Dr S13 4
Spinkhill Immaculate
Conception Prim Sch S21 ..
Spinkhill La S21 ....
Spinkhill Rd Killamarsh S21 .
Sheffield S13 4
Spinnerbottom SK22 2
Spinners Way DE56 1
Spinney Cl Derby DE22 20
Glossop SK13 ....
Mansfield Woodhouse NG19 1
Spinney Cres NG9 2
Spinney Dr NG10 2
Spinney Hill DE73 2
Spinney Rd Branston DE14 . 2
Derby, Chaddesden DE21 ... 2
Derby, St Luke's DE22 2
Ilkeston DE7 2
Long Eaton NG10 2
Spinney Rise NG9 2
Spinney The Belper DE56 .. 1
Borrowash DE72 2
Castle Donington DE74 2
Ripley DE5 1
Shirebrook NG20 2
Stanton-by-D NG10 2
Spire Hollin SK13 ....
Spital Gdns S41 ....
Spital La S41 ....
Spittalgate La LE18, S32 .. 2
Spittal Dr S2 2
Spittal Gn S44 ....
Spittal Hill DE74 ....
Spode St ST4 2
Spondon Sta DE21 2
Spooner Dr S21 ....
Spooner La S32 ....
Spoonley Wood Ct DE23 .. 2
Sporton Cl DE55 1
Sporton La DE55 1
Spotswood Cl S14 ....
Spotswood Dr S2 ....
Spotswood Mount S14 ....
Spotswood Pl S14 ....
Spout La Spout DE56 1
Tansley DE4 ....
Spridgeon Cl NG10 2
Spring Bank
Great Longstone DE45 ......
Peak Dale SK17 ....
Spring Bank Rd
Chesterfield S40 2
New Mills SK22 ....

ing Cl Belper DE56 .... 178 C3
radwell S33 .... 51 D4
easton DE72 .... 235 E4
inishaw S21 .... 79 E4
wadincote DE11 .... 256 A1
ing Cl Dell S14 .... 43 F2
ing Cl Mount S14 .... 43 F2
ing Cl View S14 .... 43 F2
ing Cottage Rd DE22 ... 262 B3
ing Dale Gdns NG9 .... 209 E2
ing Garden Terr DE7 .... 194 C1
ing Gdns Buxton SK17 .... 85 E4
bedford S21 .... 219 F4
adfield S43 .... 10 A3
ing Hill Kimberley NG16 . 195 F3
ansfield Woodhouse
S19 .... 136 A2
hitwell S80 .... 82 A3
ing Hollow DE56 .... 190 B4
ing House Cl S40 .... 94 C3
ing La Elmton NG20 .... 99 F3
eanor DE75 .... 181 F1
heffield S2 .... 43 F4
hireoaks S80 .... 63 F3
ing Mount SK22 .... 33 E4
ing Pl S40 .... 266 B3
ing Rd DE55 .... 170 C3
ing Rise SK13 .... 16 C4
ing St Broadbottom SK14 .. 16 A4
rootley DE72 .... 218 C2
ossop SK13 .... 10 A1
ollingworth SK14 .... 9 E3
wadincote DE11 .... 262 A4
heffield S8 .... 82 A3
ing The NG10 .... 236 B3
ing Vale Rd
imington S43 .... 96 C4
ayfield SK22 .... 25 F1
ing Water Dr SK13 .... 9 F2
ing Wood Cl S41 .... 95 E4
ingbank SK13 .... 9 F3
ingdale Ct DE3 .... 217 F1
ringfarm Rd DE15 .... 248 A1
ingfield
harlesworth SK13 .... 16 B3
erby DE23 .... 218 A1
ingfield Ave
shbourne DE6 .... 185 E4
ansfield S40 .... 95 E2
ong Eaton NG10 .... 236 C4
wadincote NG10 .... 223 D2
rirebrook NG20 .... 119 F3
ingfield Cl Clowne S43 ..... 80 C2
ckhill DE4 .... 157 D1
ickington S21 .... 59 E2
eadfield S43 .... 9 E2
wadincote DE11 .... 256 A3
ingfield Cres
olsover S44 .... 98 C2
omercotes DE55 .... 170 B4
ingfield Ct NG9 .... 209 F1
ingfield Dr DE56 .... 190 B2
ingfield Gdn DE7 .... 194 C1
ingfield Jun Sch DE11 . 256 B3
ingfield Prim Sch
erby DE21 .... 220 B3
roke-on-T ST4 .... 269 D2
ingfield Rd Bradwell S33 . 51 D4
ommon Side S18 .... 75 F2
erby, Chellaston DE4 ...... 232 C1
erby, Cherrytree Hill DE21 . 220 A3
twall DE65 .... 229 D2
olmewood S42 .... 132 C4
epton DE65 .... 242 B1
wadincote DE11 .... 256 A3
ingfield Rise DE4 .... 143 E3
ingfield Terr
.... 25 E1
ipley DE5 .... 169 F1
ingfield View DE65 .... 229 D2
ing Hollies SK14 .... 9 F3
inghill DE11 .... 257 D4
ringhill Way DE5 .... 181 D4
ingmeadow Sk13 .... 16 A4
ringvale Cl S45 .... 131 E1
ringvale Rd S45 .... 132 E3
ringwell Com Sch S43 .... 77 E4
ingwell Hill S21 .... 77 E4
ingwell St NG17 .... 148 C1
ingwood SK13 .... 16 C4
uare The Bretby DE15 . 249 D2
inalan SK17 .... 85 D4
lay Cross S45 .... 131 F2
erby, Darley Abbey DE3 .. 205 D1
erby, Mickleover DE3 ..... 217 E1
yam S32 .... 71 F3
arrington ST14 .... 224 C1
donyash DE45 .... 107 E1
uiers View S14 .... 269 F2
uires Way DE23 .... 231 D4
uirrel La DE73 .... 252 C2

able Cl DE4 .... 156 A3
able La DE6 .... 149 D1
able Ct S44 .... 99 E1
able Dr DE22 .... 218 B3
acey Rd NG19 .... 135 E1

Staden Bsns Pk SK17 .... 85 F3
Staden La SK17 .... 85 F2
Stadium Ind Pk NG10 ... 236 C4
Stadmoor Ct DE73 .... 232 C1
Staffa Dr DE55 .... 147 F3
Stafford Cl
1 Dronfield S18 .... 56 B1
Glossop SK13 .... 17 F4
Smalley DE7 .... 192 C3
Stafford Coll SK16 .... 269 D4
Stafford Coll
(The Oval Annexe) ST17 . 269 E3
Stafford Ct DE6 .... 165 E4
Stafford St Derby DE1 ... 267 A3
Long Eaton NG10 .... 236 C4
Mansfield NG18 .... 268 A4
New Mills SK22 .... 24 B1
Stafford Sta ST16 .... 269 D3
Staffordshire General
Infmy ST16 .... 269 D4
Staffordshire Univ ST4 ... 269 F2
Staines Cl DE3 .... 217 E1
Stainforth St NG19 .... 136 B1
Stainsbro' La Callow DE4 .. 165 D3
Carsington DE4 .... 165 D3
Stainsby Ave Heanor DE75 . 193 F4
Horsley Woodhouse DE7 . 192 C3
Stainsby Cl S42 .... 132 C4
Staithes Wlk DE21 .... 205 E1
Staker La DE3 .... 230 B3
Stalybridge Ctry Pk SK15 . 4 A2
Stalybridge Rd SK14 .... 9 D2
Stamer St S14 .... 269 E1
Stamford Cl NG10 .... 236 C2
Stamford St
Awsworth NG16 .... 195 E2
Derby DE24 .... 232 B3
Heanor DE75 .... 181 F1
3 Ilkeston DE7 .... 194 C1
Stamps Cl DE15 .... 248 B2
Stanage Gn DE23 .... 217 F1
Stanage Rise S12 .... 44 C3
Stanage Way S40 .... 94 C3
Stancliffe Ave DE4 .... 127 E2
Stancliffe Hall Sch DE4 . 127 D3
Stancliffe View DE4 .... 127 E2
Stand House Fst Sch S2 .. 44 A4
Stand Rd S41 .... 95 F4
Standard Hill 7 NG1 ..... 268 A1
Standard St ST4 .... 269 F1
Standing Butts Cl DE12 . 259 E4
Standlow La DE6 .... 163 E1
Stanedge Rd DE45 .... 109 D3
Stanford Rd S8 .... 56 C4
Stanford St NG1 .... 268 B1
Stanford Way S40 .... 94 C3
Stanhope Glade DE15 ... 256 A4
Stanhope Rd Derby DE3 . 217 F2
Sheffield S12 .... 44 B3
Swadlincote DE11 .... 256 A2
Stanhope St
Bramley-Vale S44 .... 117 F1
Burton u T DE15 .... 248 A2
Derby DE23 .... 219 D1
Ilkeston DE7 .... 209 D3
Long Eaton NG10 .... 236 B4
Nottingham NG1 .... 268 B1
Stanton-by-D NG10 .... 222 C4
Stanier Way DE21 .... 220 A2
Staniforth Ave S21 .... 59 D2
Stanleigh Rd DE12 .... 262 A2
Stanley Ave Ripley DE5 .. 169 F1
Staveley S43 .... 78 C1
Stanley Cl Derby DE22 ... 218 C4
Ilkeston DE7 .... 208 C4
Nethersseal DE12 .... 264 C4
Woodville DE11 .... 256 C1
Stanley Comm Prim Sch
DE7 .... 193 D1
Stanley Cres S14 .... 210 A1
Stanley Dr NG9 .... 209 F1
Stanley Hall La SK12 .... 32 B1
Stanley Matthews Sports
Ctr ST4 .... 269 F2
Stanley Pl DE23 .... 268 A2
Stanley Rd
Derby, Allenton DE24 ..... 232 C3
Derby, Cherrytree Hill DE21 . 220 A3
Sheffield S8 .... 43 D3
Stoke-on-T ST4 .... 269 D2
Stanley St Chesterfield S41 . 96 B1
Derby DE23 .... 218 B3
Ilkeston DE7 .... 208 C4
Killamarsh S21 .... 60 B4
Long Eaton NG10 .... 236 C4
Somercotes DE55 .... 170 B4
Swadlincote DE11 .... 256 A2
Stanton Ave DE56 .... 179 D2
Stanton Cl DE4 .... 127 D2
Stanton Cres S12 .... 44 C3
Stanton Gate DE7 .... 209 E1
Stanton Hill DE73 .... 251 E3
Stanton Moor View DE4 . 142 C4
Stanton Pl Mansfield NG18 . 268 B4
New Houghton NG19 ...... 134 C4
Stanton Prim Sch DE15 . 255 D3
Stanton Rd Ashbourne DE6 . 185 E4
Burton u T DE15 .... 254 C4
Ilkeston DE7 .... 208 C4
Sandiacre NG10 .... 223 D4
Stanton St Derby DE23 . 218 C1
New Houghton NG19 ...... 134 C4

Stanton Vale Specl Sch
DE7 .... 208 C3
Stanton View DE45 .... 109 E2
Stanton-in-Peak CE Prim
Sch DE4 .... 126 B3
Stantonhall La DE4 .... 126 B4
Stanwood Dr S40 .... 114 B2
Stanyforth St SK13 .... 10 A2
Stapleford La NG9 .... 223 F2
Stapleford Rd
Stapleford NG9 .... 209 E2
Trowell NG9 .... 209 E2
Stapleton Rd DE7 .... 194 C2
Starch La NG10 .... 223 E4
Starcross Ct DE3 .... 217 E2
Starkholmes Rd DE4 ...... 143 E1
Starkie Ave DE74 .... 246 C2
Start La SK23 .... 45 D4
Starthe Bank DE7 .... 181 F1
Statham Ave S42 .... 131 E4
Statham St DE22 .... 218 C4
Station App Buxton SK17 . 85 D4
Station Back La S41 .... 266 C3
Station Cl DE21 .... 232 C1
Station Cl DE7 .... 194 C1
Station Dr DE12 .... 262 C2
Station Hill NG19 .... 136 A2
Station La Apperknowle S18 . 58 A1
Chesterfield S43 .... 81 D3
Codnor DE5 .... 181 D3
Pinxton NG16 .... 160 C2
Shatton S33 .... 40 A1
Walton-on-T DE12 .... 253 E1
Station La Ind Est S41 ... 266 C3
Station New Rd S42 .... 131 E4
Station Rd Ambergate DE56 . 167 F2
Ashbourne S6 .... 173 D1
Awsworth NG16 .... 195 E3
Bakewell DE45 .... 109 E3
Bamford S33 .... 40 A1
Barton Turn DE13 .... 253 D1
Birch Vale SK22 .... 25 D1
Bolsover S44 .... 98 C2
Borrowash DE72 .... 221 D1
Breadsall DE21 .... 205 F3
Brimington S43 .... 96 B4
Brimington, New Brimington
S43 .... 78 A1
Buxton SK17 .... 85 E4
Buxworth SK23 .... 34 A1
Chapel-en-le-F SK23 .... 47 D3
Chesterfield, Old Whittington
S41 .... 77 D1
Chesterfield S43 .... 266 C3
Chinley SK23 .... 34 C3
Clowne S43 .... 80 C2
Darley Dale DE4 .... 127 E1
Denby DE5 .... 180 A2
Derby, Chellaston DE4 .... 232 C1
Derby, Mickleover DE3 ... 217 E2
Dove Holes SK17 .... 47 F1
Draycott DE72 .... 235 D4
Duffield DE56 .... 190 C2
Eckington S21 .... 59 F2
Furness Vale SK23 .... 33 E2
Great Longstone DE45 .... 89 F2
Hadfield SK13 .... 10 A3
Hatherssage S32 .... 53 D4
Hatton DE65 .... 227 E1
Heanor NG16 .... 181 F4
Hemmington DE74 .... 247 D3
Hemmington DE74 .... 247 E3
Hope S33 .... 39 E2
Ilkeston DE7 .... 194 C1
Killamarsh S21 .... 60 C4
Kimberley NG16 .... 195 F3
Langley Mill NG16 .... 182 A1
Little Eaton DE21 .... 205 E4
Long Eaton NG10 .... 236 C4
Mansfield NG18 .... 268 B3
Marple SK6 .... 23 D4
Melbourne DE73 .... 252 B4
Morton DE55 .... 147 D3
Mosbrough S20 .... 59 F4
New Mills SK22 .... 33 D4
North Wingfield S42 .... 132 A3
Pilsley S45 .... 132 B1
Rolleston DE13 .... 240 B2
Sandiacre NG10 .... 223 E3
Scarcliffe S44 .... 118 C3
Shirebrook NG20 .... 119 F3
Sponkhill S21 .... 60 B1
Stafford DE55 .... 269 D3
Stanley DE7 .... 207 E3
Strines SK6 .... 23 E3
Tibshelf DE55 .... 147 F3
West Hallam DE7 .... 207 E4
Whitwell S80 .... 82 A3
Woodville DE11 .... 256 C1
Station St Ashbourne DE6 . 173 D1
Cossall DE7 .... 195 D1
Glossop SK13 .... 10 B1
Long Eaton NG10 .... 236 C4
Mansfield NG18 .... 268 B3
Station Terr DE4 .... 155 D4
Staunton Ave DE55 .... 159 E2
Staunton Cl DE74 .... 247 D2
Staunton Harold Hall Craft
& Ferrous Ctr LE65 .... 258 C4

Staunton La DE73 .... 251 D1
Staveley Cl DE24 .... 232 C2
Staveley Jun Sch S43 .... 78 C1
Staveley La Barrow Hill S43 . 78 A3
Eckington S21 .... 59 F1
Staveley Rd
Chesterfield S43 .... 77 F2
Long Duckmanton S44 ..... 97 F2
Poolsbrook S43 .... 98 A4
Sheffield S8 .... 43 D4
Staverton Dr DE3 .... 217 E2
Staveley Cl S43 .... 96 C4
Stead St S21 .... 59 E2
Steam Mill La DE5 .... 181 D4
Steel La S44 .... 99 D1
Steel St ST4 .... 269 D2
Steel's La S44 .... 118 A3
Steele Ave S43 .... 77 F2
Steele Ct SK17 .... 85 D4
Steep La S43 .... 114 A2
Steep Turnpike DE4 .... 143 E3
Steeping Cl S43 .... 96 C4
Steeping Cl S41 .... 205 F1
Steeple Dr DE21 .... 205 F1
Steeple Grange DE4 .... 154 C2
Steetley La Whitwell S80 .. 63 F2
Worksop S80 .... 63 F2
Stella St NG18 .... 231 F3
Stenson Ave DE23 .... 231 F3
Stenson Fields Prim Com
Sch DE24 .... 231 E2
Stenson Rd
Derby, Littlover DE23, DE24 . 231 E2
Derby, Sinfin DE23, DE24 . 231 E2
Stenton Rd S8 .... 56 C4
Stephens Rd DE14 .... 254 A4
Stephenson Pl
Chesterfield S40 .... 266 B3
Clay Cross S45 .... 131 D2
Stephenson Rd S43 .... 78 C1
Stepping Cl DE22 .... 218 C3
Stepping La DE22 .... 218 C3
Sterland St S40 .... 95 F2
Sterndale Cl Sk17 .... 69 F2
Sterndale La SK17 .... 69 F2
Sterndale Moor SK17 ..... 105 F3
Sterndale Rd NG10 .... 236 A3
Sterry Cl S43 .... 80 C1
Steven Cl NG9 .... 223 C2
Stevenage Cl DE24 .... 232 C3
Stevens La DE72 .... 235 E4
Stevens Rd NG10 .... 223 D3
Stevenson Ave DE72 ...... 235 D4
Stevenson Jun Sch NG9 . 223 F3
Stevenson Pl DE23 .... 231 D4
Stevenson Rd DE6 .... 224 A4
Steward Gate S33 .... 40 A3
Stewart Cl Branston DE14 . 253 E4
Derby DE21 .... 220 C2
Stewart St Fenton ST4 ... 269 F1
Somercotes DE55 .... 170 B3
Stile Croft DE4 .... 154 B3
Stiles Cl S43 .... 9 F3
Stiles Rd DE24 .... 233 D4
Stillman Cl S41 .... 115 E4
Stinting La
Mansfield NG19 .... 136 C1
Shirebrook NG20 .... 119 E1
Stirland St DE5 .... 170 A1
Stirling Ave NG19 .... 268 A3
Stirling Cl DE21 .... 219 E4
Stirling Gr NG16 .... 195 F4
Stock La ST14 .... 224 B1
Stockbrook Rd DE22 ...... 218 B2
Stockbrook St DE22 .... 218 C2
Stocker Ave DE24 .... 233 E4
Stockley La S44 .... 117 F1
Stockley View S44 .... 118 A4
Stockport Rd
Broadbottom SK14 .... 15 E4
Marple SK6 .... 23 D4
Stocks Green Ct S17 .... 55 E2
Stocks Green Dr S17 .... 55 E2
Stocks Rd NG16 .... 195 F4
Stocks The S13 .... 10 A4
Stockton Dr SK23 .... 34 C1
Stockwell Gate NG18 ..... 268 B3
Stoddard Dr DE75 .... 181 F1
Stoke Cl DE56 .... 179 F3
Stoke Recn Ctr ST4 .... 269 E2
Stoke-on-Trent Sixth
Form Coll ST4 .... 269 F2
Stoke-on-Trent Sta ST4 .. 269 E2
Stollard St S45 .... 131 E2
Stone Bridge Rd NG3 ..... 268 C2
Stone Cl DE21 .... 220 C3
Stone Cross La DE18 ...... 268 B4
Stone Furlong Rd DE45 ... 91 F3
Stone Hill Rd DE23 .... 218 C1
Stone La S43 .... 77 E2
Stone Meadows NG10 ..... 58 C2
Stone Rd S18 .... 57 D2
Stone Row Chesterfield S40 . 95 F3
Marple SK6 .... 23 D3
Stone St Mosbrough S20 .. 59 F4
Stoke-on-T ST4 .... 269 D2
Stonebench La S17 .... 55 E2
Stonebridge Ct Ind Est
NG3 .... 268 C2
Stoneborn La DE55 .... 147 F3
Stonebroom Prim Sch
DE55 .... 147 D2
Stonebroom Wlk DE24 . 232 C2
Stonechat Cl DE3 .... 218 A2
Stonecliff Terr SK17 .... 85 E4
Stonecroft Rd S17 .... 55 F3
Stonedale Cl S20 .... 59 E4
Stonegravels Croft S20 ... 59 E4
Stonegravels La S41 .... 96 A3
Stonegravels Way S20 ...... 59 F3

Stoneheads Rise SK23 ..... 45 E4
Stonehill DE74 .... 247 D1
Stoneholes Dr S45 .... 131 F1
Stoneleigh St NG7 .... 268 A2
Stoneleigh Way S45 .... 169 F4
Stoneley Cl S12 .... 44 A1
Stoneley Cres S12 .... 44 A1
Stoneley Dell S12 .... 44 A1
Stoneley Rd S12 .... 44 A1
Stonelow Cres S18 .... 57 E1
Stonelow Cty Jun Sch The
S18 .... 57 E1
Stonelow Gn S18 .... 57 E1
Stonelow Rd S18 .... 57 E1
Stonepit La DE6 .... 164 A2
Stoneridge S13 .... 44 C2
Stonerows La DE55 .... 145 E3
Stonesby Cl DE21 .... 205 F1
Stonesdale Ct DE24 .... 233 E3
Stonewall La SK17 .... 137 E3
Stoney Cl DE45 .... 109 E2
Stoney Cross DE21 .... 220 C2
Stoney Flatts Cres DE21 . 220 A4
Stoney Hill DE4 .... 155 D1
Stoney La Brinsley NG16 . 182 B3
Derby DE21 .... 220 C3
Hognaston DE6 .... 164 A2
Littlemoor S42 .... 130 B2
Selston NG16 .... 171 F4
Stretton en le F DE12 ..... 265 F1
Trowell NG9 .... 209 D3
Stoney Middleton CE Prim
Sch S32 .... 71 F2
Stoney St NG2 .... 268 B1
Stoney Way DE4 .... 143 E2
Stoney Wood Dr DE4 ...... 156 B1
Stoneycroft La S42 .... 114 A3
Stoneydale Cl DE11 .... 255 F3
Stoneyland Dr SK22 .... 33 D4
Stony La DE56 .... 191 E3
Stony Ridge Rd S17 .... 54 B3
Stonyhurst Ct DE24 .... 232 C2
Stoodley Pike Gdns DE22 . 204 A1
Stoops Cl S40 .... 95 E3
Stoppard Cl DE7 .... 194 B1
Storer La DE56 .... 166 A2
Stores Rd DE21 .... 219 D4
Storforth La S41 .... 115 E4
Storforth Lane Terr S41 . 115 E4
Storforth Lane Trad Est
S40 .... 115 D4
Stormont Cl DE55 .... 160 A2
Stornoway Cl DE24 .... 231 E2
Storrs Rd S40 .... 95 D1
Stort Sq NG19 .... 136 B1
Storth Bank S13 .... 16 C4
Storth La DE55 .... 160 A2
Storth Meadow Rd SK13 .. 16 C4
Storthfield Way DE55 ..... 160 A2
Stour Cl S43 .... 96 C4
Stourdale Cl NG10 .... 236 A3
Stourport Dr DE73 .... 233 D2
Stowe Av DE72 .... 246 A4
Stow Ct NG19 .... 136 C2
Stowmarket Dr DE21 ..... 219 E4
Stradbroke Ave S13 .... 44 B4
Stradbroke Cl S13 .... 44 C4
Stradbroke Cres S13 .... 44 C4
Stradbroke Dr S13 .... 44 C4
Stradbroke Pl S13 .... 44 C4
Stradbroke Prim Sch S13 . 44 B4
Stradbroke Rd S13 .... 44 C4
Stradbroke Rise S40 .... 114 B4
Stradbroke Way S13 .... 44 C4
Stradbroke Wlk S13 .... 44 B4
Strand DE1 .... 267 B3
Strand Arc DE1 .... 267 B3
Stranfaer Cl DE55 .... 170 A4
Stranrear Cl NG19 .... 136 B3
Stratford Cl DE55 .... 242 B1
Stratford Rd DE21 .... 205 E1
Stratford St DE7 .... 194 C2
Strathallan Cl DE4 .... 127 E2
Strathaven Cl DE21 .... 220 C3
Strathglen Cl NG16 .... 195 F4
Strathmore Ave DE24 .... 233 D3
Stratton Rd S43 .... 99 D1
Straw La DE55 .... 146 B4
Strawberry Bank NG17 . 148 C2
Strawberry La
Blackfordby DE11 .... 257 D1
Rosliston DE12 .... 260 B3
Strawberry Lee La S17 .... 55 E1
Streatham Rd DE22 .... 218 A3
Street Farm Cl S26 .... 61 F3
Street La Denby DE5 .... 180 A3
Ripley DE5 .... 180 A3
Street Laine Prim Sch DE5 . 180 A1
Street The SK17 .... 106 A4
Streetfield Cres S20 .... 59 E3
Streetfield La S20 .... 59 E3
Streetfields S20 .... 59 E3
Strelley Ave DE5 .... 180 B4
Stretfield Rd S33 .... 39 D1
Strettea La DE55 .... 146 B1
Stretton Cl DE3 .... 223 D1
Stretton Handley CE Prim
Sch DE55 .... 145 E4
Stretton Rd Clay Cross S45 . 131 E1
Morton DE55 .... 146 C3
Stretton DE55 .... 146 B4
Stretton View DE12 .... 265 F3
Striding Edge Cl NG10 .. 223 D1
Strines Rd SK6 .... 23 D2
Strines Sta SK6 .... 23 D2
Stroma Cl DE24 .... 231 F2

Strutt St Belper DE56 ... 178 C2
  Derby DE23 ... 219 D1
Stuart Cl S41 ... 96 B3
Stuart St S41 ... 267 B4
Stubben Edge La S45 ... 130 B1
Stubbin Wood Sch NG20 ... 119 F3
Stubbing Rd S40 ... 114 C4
Stubbins La S43 ... 34 B1
Stubbins Wood NG20 ... 119 F3
Stubbins Wood La NG20 ... 119 F3
Stubley Cl S18 ... 56 C2
Stubley Croft S8 ... 56 C4
Stubley Dr S18 ... 56 C1
Stubley Hollow S18 ... 56 C2
Stubley La S18 ... 56 C1
Stubley Pl S18 ... 56 C1
Stubwood Hollow ST14 ... 196 B3
Studbrook Cl DE74 ... 246 C2
Studfarm Cl DE73 ... 252 C3
Sturge Croft S2 ... 43 D3
Sturges La DE72 ... 233 F2
Sturgess St ST4 ... 269 E1
Sturston Rd DE6 ... 173 E1
Stychfields ST17 ... 269 F1
Sudbury Ave Ilkeston DE7 ... 209 D4
  Sandiacre NG10 ... 223 D3
Sudbury Cl Chesterfield S40 ... 95 D3
  Derby DE21 ... 218 C3
Sudbury Hall & Mus DE6 ... 225 E3
Sudbury Mews NG16 ... 182 C1
Sudbury Pk DE6 ... 225 E4
Sudbury Prim Sch DE6 ... 225 F2
Sudbury St DE1 ... 267 A3
Sudhall Cl S41 ... 95 E4
Suff La NG16 ... 160 B2
Suffolk Ave DE21 ... 219 F4
Suffolk Rd DE15 ... 254 B4
Sugworth Rd S6 ... 31 F3
Summer Cross ST17 ... 69 D2
Summer Dr DE4 ... 165 F4
Summer La Totley S17 ... 55 E2
  Wirksworth DE4 ... 165 F4
Summer Leys La NG2 ... 268 B1
Summer St S41 ... 96 B3
Summer Wood Ct DE23 ... 231 E4
Summerbottom SK14 ... 16 A4
Summerbrook Ct DE22 ... 218 C2
Summerfield Cres S43 ... 96 C4
Summerfield Rd
  Chesterfield S40 ... 266 A1
  Dronfield S18 ... 57 D2
Summerfields Way DE7 ... 194 B2
Summerfields Way S DE7 ... 194 B1
Summerley Lower Rd S18 ... 57 F1
Summerley Rd S18 ... 57 F1
Summerskill Gn S43 ... 97 E4
Summerwood La S18 ... 56 C1
Summerwood Pl S18 ... 56 C1
Summit Dr NG20 ... 119 F2
Sumner St S13 ... 17 E4
Sumners Pl S13 ... 10 A1
Sun La DE4 ... 156 C1
Sun St Derby DE22 ... 267 A2
  Woodville DE11 ... 256 C1
Sunart Ct S41 ... 231 F1
Sunbourne Ct NG7 ... 268 A2
Sundew Cl DE21 ... 220 C2
Sundown Ave DE23 ... 231 E3
Sundown Cl SK23 ... 33 D4
Sundown Pl S13 ... 44 C4
Sundown Rd S13 ... 44 C4
Suningdale Cl DE13 ... 240 B1
Sunlaws St SK13 ... 17 D4
Sunlea Cres NG9 ... 223 F3
Sunningdale Ave
  Derby DE21 ... 220 B3
  Heanor DE75 ... 193 F4
Sunningdale Cl S40 ... 114 C4
Sunningdale Dr DE7 ... 208 A3
Sunningdale Rise S40 ... 114 B4
Sunninghill Cl DE7 ... 207 E4
Sunny Bank
  Great Longstone DE45 ... 90 A2
  Tibshelf DE55 ... 147 F3
Sunny Bank Gdns DE56 ... 178 C1
Sunny Bank La S17 ... 69 E2
Sunny Banks SK13 ... 17 D4
Sunny Brook Cl S43 ... 80 C2
Sunny Gr DE21 ... 220 A3
Sunny Hill DE56 ... 190 C4
Sunny Springs S41 ... 266 B4
Sunnybank DE4 ... 110 C1
Sunnyfield SK17 ... 85 F1
Sunnyhill Ave DE23 ... 231 F3
Sunnyside Swadlincote DE11 ... 255 F4
  Whitwell S80 ... 82 A3
Sunnyside Rd ST14 ... 210 A1
Sunnyvale Ave S17 ... 55 F2
Sunnyvale Rd S17 ... 55 E2
Surbiton Cl DE23 ... 218 A3
Surbiton Ct DE7 ... 207 E4
Surgery La DE4 ... 157 D1
Surrey Dr NG19 ... 268 A4
Surrey St Derby DE22 ... 218 B3
  Glossop SK13 ... 10 B1
Sussex Cir DE21 ... 219 F4
Sussex Rd DE15 ... 254 C3
Sussex Way NG10 ... 223 D3
Sutherland Rd DE23 ... 219 D1
Sutherland St ST4 ... 269 F1
Sutton Ave DE73 ... 232 C2
Sutton Cl DE22 ... 218 B3
Sutton Cres S43 ... 97 E4
Sutton Ct NG16 ... 182 C1

Sutton Dr Derby DE24 ... 232 C2
  Stoke-on-T S4 ... 269 D1
Sutton Hall Rd S44 ... 117 F4
Sutton La Etwall DE65 ... 229 D3
  Hatton DE65 ... 227 F2
  Hilton DE65 ... 228 B2
  Long Duckmanton S44 ... 116 C4
Sutton Rd
  Church Broughton DE65 ... 227 E4
  Mansfield NG18 ... 268 A3
  Sutton in a NG17 ... 148 C2
Sutton Road Fst Sch
  NG18 ... 268 A3
Sutton Scarsdale Hall
  S44 ... 117 D3
Sutton View S44 ... 118 A4
Sutton Way SK13 ... 10 B3
Suttons La S44 ... 23 D3
Swaddale Ave S41 ... 96 A3
Swaddale Cl S41 ... 96 A3
Swadlincote La DE11 ... 255 F1
Swadlincote Rd DE11 ... 256 C2
Swadlincote Ski Ctr
  DE11 ... 256 B2
Swalebank Cl S40 ... 115 D4
Swaledale Ct DE24 ... 233 E3
Swallow Cl DE3 ... 218 A2
Swallow House Cres SK22 ... 25 E2
Swallow House La SK22 ... 25 E2
Swallow Rd DE11 ... 256 C2
Swallowdale Rd DE24 ... 231 E2
Swan Cl ST16 ... 269 D3
Swan La NG19 ... 136 A3
Swan St S14 ... 269 E2
Swanbourne Cl S41 ... 96 B1
Swanmore Rd DE21 ... 231 D4
Swann Yd NG17 ... 148 C2
Swanson Ave NG17 ... 148 C2
Swanwick Ave NG20 ... 119 F2
Swanwick Gdns DE21 ... 206 A1
Swanwick Hall Sch DE55 ... 169 F4
Swanwick Hill DE55 ... 169 F4
Swanwick Prim Sch DE55 ... 169 E3
Swanwick Rd DE55 ... 170 A4
Swanwick St S41 ... 77 D1
Swarkestone Dr DE73 ... 231 E3
Swarkestone Rd
  Barrow-u-T DE73 ... 244 A3
  Derby DE73 ... 244 C4
Swathwick Cl S42 ... 114 C2
Swathwick La S42 ... 114 B2
Swayfield Cl DE3 ... 217 E2
Sweetbriar Cl DE24 ... 233 D3
Swift Cl Derby DE3 ... 218 A2
  Woodville DE11 ... 256 C2
Swift Sq NG16 ... 182 C1
Swinburne St Derby DE1 ... 267 B1
  Nottingham NG3 ... 268 C2
Swinderby Dr DE21 ... 206 A1
Swindon Cl NG16 ... 195 E4
Swiney Way NG9 ... 223 F1
Swinger La S45 ... 129 E4
Swinney Bank DE56 ... 179 D3
Swinney La DE56 ... 179 D3
Swinscoe Hill DE6 ... 172 A1
Swinscoe Way S40 ... 95 D3
Swinson Ct ST14 ... 197 D2
Sycamore Ave
  Chesterfield S40 ... 95 F1
  Creswell S80 ... 81 F1
  Derby DE65 ... 204 B2
  Dronfield S18 ... 57 D2
  Findern DE65 ... 230 C1
  Glapwell S44 ... 134 A4
  Ripley DE5 ... 180 B4
  Swadlincote DE11 ... 256 A4
Sycamore Cl Bolsover S44 ... 99 E1
  Buxton SK17 ... 66 A1
  Etwall DE65 ... 229 E2
  Ilkeston DE7 ... 209 D4
  Mapperley DE7 ... 193 F2
  New Mills SK22 ... 24 C1
  Pinxton NG16 ... 160 B2
  Selston NG16 ... 171 E4
  Shirland DE55 ... 146 B2
Sycamore Cotts DE56 ... 151 E1
Sycamore Cres NG10 ... 223 D4
Sycamore Dr Calow S44 ... 96 C2
  Ilkeston DE7 ... 209 D4
  Killamarsh S21 ... 60 B3
Sycamore Jun & Inf Sch
  NG3 ... 268 B2
Sycamore La
  Barlborough S43 ... 80 A3
  Brimington S43 ... 78 A1
Sycamore Rd
  Awsworth NG16 ... 195 E3
  Brimington S43 ... 78 A1
  Burton u T DE15 ... 254 C3
  Castle Donington DE74 ... 247 D3
  Chapel-en-le-f SK23 ... 47 D2
  Long Eaton NG10 ... 236 B3
  Mansfield Woodhouse
  NG19 ... 136 B3
  Matlock DE4 ... 143 D3
  Mayfield DE6 ... 184 B4
  Thornsett SK22 ... 24 C1
Sycamore St
  Market Warsop NG20 ... 120 C1
  Mosborough S20 ... 59 E4
Sycamores The
  Eastwood NG16 ... 182 C1
  Hadfield SK13 ... 9 F2
  South Normanton DE55 ... 160 A3
Syda La S42 ... 93 F1
Syday La S21 ... 79 F4
Sydenham Rd DE22 ... 218 A4
Sydney St NG19 ... 136 B3

Sydney St Chesterfield S40 ... 95 F2
  Draycott DE72 ... 235 D4
Sydnope Hill DE4 ... 128 A3
Syerscote La B79 ... 263 D1
Sylvan Cl S41 ... 266 C1
Sylvan Cliff SK17 ... 85 E4
Sylvan Ct S42 ... 131 D3
Sylvan Pk SK17 ... 85 E4
Sylvester St NG18 ... 268 A3
Sylvia Rd S18 ... 76 B3
Sywell Cl DE55 ... 169 F4

Tabley Gdns SK6 ... 23 D2
Taddington Cl DE21 ... 219 F4
Taddington & Priestcliffe
  CE Prim Sch SK17 ... 87 F2
Taddington Rd
  Chesterfield S40 ... 95 D3
  Derby DE21 ... 205 F1
Taft Ave NG10 ... 223 D3
Tagg La DE45 ... 107 D1
Taggs Knoll S33 ... 40 A2
Taghole La DE6 ... 188 C1
Tailby Dr DE65 ... 242 A3
Talbot Cres S41 ... 115 E4
Talbot Dr NG9 ... 209 E1
Talbot House Sch S41 ... 10 B1
Talbot Pl DE12 ... 265 F4
Talbot Rd Glossop SK13 ... 10 B1
  Stafford ST17 ... 269 E3
Talbot St Chesterfield S41 ... 115 E4
  Derby DE1 ... 218 C3
  Glossop SK13 ... 10 B1
  Nottingham NG1 ... 268 A2
  Pinxton NG16 ... 160 B1
  Swadlincote DE11 ... 256 A1
Talgarth Cl DE21 ... 206 B1
Tamar Ave DE22 ... 204 B2
Tamworth Rd
  Castle Donington DE74 ... 235 F1
  Long Eaton NG10 ... 236 B3
  Stretton en le F DE12 ... 265 F1
Tamworth St DE56 ... 190 C2
Tamworth Terr DE56 ... 190 C2
Tanner's La DE6 ... 242 B2
Tansley Ave DE7 ... 193 D1
Tansley Dr ... 95 D3
Tansley Prim Sch DE4 ... 144 A2
Tansley Rd S42 ... 131 F3
Tansley Rise DE21 ... 205 F1
Tansley Way S43 ... 97 E3
Tants Meadow DE56 ... 191 F3
Tantum Ave DE75 ... 181 E2
Tanyard Cl DE74 ... 247 D2
Tapley La S40 ... 266 A1
Taplow Cl DE3 ... 217 E1
Tapton La S43 ... 266 C3
Tapton Lock Hill S41 ... 96 A3
Tapton Terr S41 ... 266 C4
Tapton Vale S41 ... 96 B3
Tapton View Rd S41 ... 95 F3
Tapton Way S41 ... 96 C2
Tarina Cl DE73 ... 233 D1
Tarnside Fold SK13 ... 17 D4
Tarporley Ct S41 ... 269 D1
Tasman Cl DE24 ... 217 F2
Tatenhill La
  Branston DE14 ... 253 E4
  Tatenhill DE13 ... 253 D4
Tatham's La DE7 ... 194 C1
Tattersall Wlk NG19 ... 136 C2
Tattershall Dr NG7 ... 268 A1
Tattle Hill DE7 ... 207 F1
Taunton Cl DE24 ... 233 E4
Tavern Rd SK13 ... 9 E1
Taverners Cres DE23 ... 231 E4
Tavistock Ave DE5 ... 169 E1
Tavistock Cl DE24 ... 231 E2
Tavistock Sq DE55 ... 159 D3
Tawney Croft DE4 ... 144 A2
Tawny Way DE23 ... 231 D4
Taxal & Fernilee CE Contr
  Prim Sch SK23 ... 45 E3
Taxal Lodge Sch SK23 ... 45 E3
Taxal Moor Rd SK23 ... 45 E2
Tay Cl Derby DE24 ... 231 E1
  Tibshelf DE55 ... 56 B1
Tay Wlk DE22 ... 204 C2
Taylor Cres
  Chesterfield S41 ... 96 B1
  Stapleford NG9 ... 223 F4
Taylor La DE75 ... 181 D2
Taylor St Derby DE24 ... 219 F1
  Hollingworth SK14 ... 9 E2
  Ilkeston DE7 ... 194 C1
Taylor's La Spout DE56 ... 166 A2
  Tideswell SK17 ... 69 D3
Tayside Cl DE24 ... 231 E2
Teal Cl NG20 ... 119 E2
Tealby Wlk NG19 ... 136 C2
Tean Cl DE15 ... 248 A1
Tedder Ave SK17 ... 85 E2
Tedgness Rd S32 ... 53 F1
Tedworth Ave DE24 ... 231 E1
Teesdale Rd
  Long Eaton NG10 ... 236 A3
  Mosborough S12 ... 58 C2
Telegraph St ST17 ... 269 E3
Telford Cl S12 ... 217 F1
Telford Cres S43 ... 78 C1
Telford Rd SK6 ... 23 D2
Telmah Cl DE13 ... 240 B1
Temperance Hill DE55 ... 146 C4
Temperance St SK14 ... 16 A4
Templar Cl DE24 ... 231 E2
Temple Ave S43 ... 10 B3
Temple Normanton Bsns
  Pk S42 ... 116 A2

Temple Normanton Prim
  Sch S42 ... 116 B2
Temple Rd Buxton SK17 ... 85 D3
  Matlock Bath DE4 ... 143 D1
Temple St Derby DE23 ... 219 D2
  Fenton ST4 ... 269 F1
  Padfield SK13 ... 10 B3
Temple View SK17 ... 85 E4
Temple Wlk DE4 ... 143 D1
Ten Foot Cl SK13 ... 10 A3
Tenant St DE1 ... 267 B3
Tennessee Rd DE21 ... 220 A4
Tennis Dr NG7 ... 268 A1
Tennyson Ave
  Chesterfield S40 ... 266 A3
  Mansfield Woodhouse NG19 ... 136 A3
  Swadlincote DE11 ... 256 B3
Tennyson Rd S80 ... 81 E1
Tennyson Sq NG16 ... 195 E2
Tennyson St Derby DE24 ... 232 B4
  Holmewood S42 ... 116 B1
  Ilkeston DE7 ... 194 C2
  Mansfield NG18 ... 268 B4
  Nottingham NG7 ... 268 A2
  Shirland DE55 ... 146 B3
Tennyson Way S42 ... 115 F2
Tenter Cl NG10 ... 236 B3
Tenter La Heage DE56 ... 168 B1
  Mansfield NG18 ... 268 B3
Tenterbanks ST16 ... 269 D4
Tern Ave DE11 ... 256 C2
Terrace La NG19 ... 134 C3
Terrace Rd Buxton SK17 ... 85 D4
  Chapel-en-le-f SK23 ... 47 D3
  Matlock DE4 ... 143 D3
Terrace The DE4 ... 143 F4
Terret Gr SK17 ... 84 B3
Terrey Rd S17 ... 55 F3
Terry St DE24 ... 232 C4
Tetford Wlk NG19 ... 136 C2
Teversal Ave NG19 ... 135 D2
Tevery Cl NG9 ... 223 F4
Teviot Pl DE21 ... 206 A1
Tewkesbury Ave NG19 ... 136 B2
Tewkesbury Cres DE21 ... 219 E4
Tewkesbury Dr NG16 ... 195 F4
Tewkesbury Rd NG10 ... 236 C3
Thackeray Rd DE55 ... 146 C2
Thackeray St DE24 ... 232 A3
Thames Cl DE21 ... 234 B4
Thanet Dr DE24 ... 233 D3
Thanet St S45 ... 131 E2
Thatchers La DE4 ... 144 A2
Theatre La S41 ... 266 C3
Theatre Sq NG1 ... 268 B3
Theatre Sq NG9 ... 268 B3
Thickley Cl NG20 ... 119 F2
Thirlmere Ave DE21 ... 204 C2
Thirlmere Cl NG10 ... 223 D1
Thirlmere Dr S18 ... 57 D1
Thirlmere Rd
  Chesterfield S41 ... 95 E4
  Long Eaton NG10 ... 223 D1
Thirsk Pl DE24 ... 232 B4
Thirteen Row S44 ... 118 A3
Thistle Cl NG16 ... 195 D4
Thistle Green Cl DE75 ... 182 A1
Thistledown Cl DE22 ... 205 D1
Thistley Hough S41 ... 269 D1
Thistley Hough High Sch
  ST4 ... 269 D2
Thomas Cl NG3 ... 268 B2
Thomas Cook Cl DE7 ... 252 A4
Thomas St Compstall SK6 ... 15 D1
  Glossop SK13 ... 10 C1
Thompson Cl S41 ... 96 A4
Thompson St
  Chesterfield S41 ... 96 A4
  Langley Mill NG16 ... 182 A2
Thomson Dr DE5 ... 181 D4
Thoresby Ave NG20 ... 119 F2
Thoresby Cl Derby DE21 ... 206 A1
  Ripley DE5 ... 169 F1
Thoresby Cres DE55 ... 234 C4
Thoresby Pl S43 ... 97 E3
Thoresby Rd
  Long Eaton NG10 ... 236 B3
  Mansfield Woodhouse NG19 ... 136 A3
Thoresby St NG18 ... 268 B4
Thorn Ave NG19 ... 135 F1
Thorn Cl DE22 ... 204 B2
Thorn Dr NG16 ... 195 D4
Thorn St Derby DE23 ... 218 C1
  Woodville DE11 ... 256 C1
Thorn Tree Gdns NG16 ... 182 C2
Thorn Tree La Bretby DE15 ... 255 F4
  Swadlincote DE11 ... 255 E2
Thornborough Cl S2 ... 43 E4
Thornborough Pl S2 ... 43 E4
Thornborough Rd S2 ... 43 E4
Thornbridge Ave S12 ... 44 B2
Thornbridge Ave S12 ... 44 B2
Thornbridge Cl S12 ... 44 B2
Thornbridge Cres
  Chesterfield S40 ... 115 D3
  Sheffield S12 ... 44 B2
Thornbridge Dr S12 ... 44 B2
Thornbridge Gr S12 ... 44 B2
Thornbridge Hall Training
  Coll DE45 ... 89 F1
Thornbridge La S12 ... 44 C2
Thornbridge Pl S12 ... 44 C2
Thornbridge Rise S12 ... 44 C2
Thornbridge Sch S12 ... 44 B1
Thornbridge Way S12 ... 44 C2
Thornbrook Rd SK23 ... 47 D3

Thornburrow Dr ST4 ... 269
Thorncliffe Ave DE4 ... 127
Thorncliffe Rd SK13 ... 10
Thorndene Cl S41 ... 96
Thorndike Ave DE24 ... 232
Thorndon Cl DE3 ... 230
Thorndon Way S40 ... 114
Thorne Cl S40 ... 95
Thornecliffewood SK14 ... 9
Thornell Cl S43 ... 78
Thornescroft Gdns DE14 ... 254
Thorness Cl DE24 ... 231
Thornewill Dr DE13 ... 240
Thorneywood Rd NG10 ... 223
Thornfield Ave S40 ... 95
Thornhill La S33 ... 51
Thornhill Rd
  Derby, California DE21 ... 219
  Derby, Littleover DE23 ... 218
Thornsett S80 ... 82
Thornsett Ave DE7 ... 208
Thornsett Cl SK17 ... 85
Thornsett Gdns S17 ... 55
Thornsett Prim Sch SK22 ... 24
Thornton Pl S18 ... 56
Thornton Rd S14 ... 43
Thorntree Cl DE72 ... 221
Thorntree La DE1 ... 267
Thornway SK6 ... 23
Thornwood Cl SK17 ... 85
Thoroton St NG7 ... 268
Thorp Cl S2 ... 43
Thorpe Ave Dronfield S18 ... 57
  Whitwell S80 ... 82
Thorpe Cl
  Chesterfield S41 ... 96
  Stapleford NG9 ... 223
Thorpe Croft DE4 ... 156
Thorpe Downs Rd DE11 ... 256
Thorpe Dr S21 ... 59
Thorpe Hill Dr DE75 ... 193
Thorpe House Ave S8 ... 43
Thorpe House Rd S8 ... 43
Thorpe House Rise S8 ... 43
Thorpe Leys NG10 ... 236
Thorpe Rd Eastwood NG16 ... 182
  Harthill S26 ... 61
Thorpe St Glossop SK13 ... 10
  Ilkeston DE7 ... 194
Thorpe's Rd Heanor DE75 ... 193
  Shipley DE75 ... 193
Thorpelands Ave DE22 ... 204
Thorpelands Dr DE22 ... 204
Thorpleigh Rd S43 ... 79
Three Gates DE56 ... 176
Throstle Nest Way DE6 ... 260
Thrumpton Ave NG10 ... 237
Thrumpton Hall NG11 ... 237
Thrushton Cl DE65 ... 230
Thruxton Cl DE24 ... 233
Thunderpit La S32 ... 71
Thurcaton Way DE55 ... 148
Thurgarton Ct DE6 ... 173
Thurgarton St NG2 ... 268
Thurland St NG1 ... 268
Thurlby Cl NG19 ... 136
Thurlow Ct DE21 ... 206
Thurman St DE7 ... 209
Thurrows Way DE73 ... 233
Thurstan Ave S8 ... 56
Thurston Ave DE55 ... 170
Thurstone Furlong DE73 ... 232
Thurvaston Rd DE6 ... 197
Thyme Cl DE23 ... 231
Tibbials Cl DE3 ... 230
Tibshelf Inf Sch DE55 ... 147
Tibshelf Rd Blackwell DE55 ... 147
  Holmewood S42 ... 132
Tibshelf Sch DE55 ... 147
Tibshelf Way S42 ... 231
Ticknall La Derby DE55 ... 180
  Hartshorne DE11 ... 257
Ticknall Parochial Sch
  DE73 ... 251
Ticknall Wlk DE23 ... 231
Tideswell Cl S43 ... 97
Tideswell Ct NG18 ... 268
Tideswell Gn DE11 ... 255
Tideswell La S32 ... 71
Tideswell Rd DE21 ... 205
Tiger Yd DE6 ... 173
Tilbury Pl DE24 ... 232
Tillotson Cl S8 ... 43
Tillotson Rise S8 ... 43
Tilson Ave S? ... 269
Tilton Gr DE7 ... 208
Timber La S45 ... 132
Timbersbrook Cl DE21 ... 206
Timsbury Ct DE21 ... 206
Tinderbox La DE65 ... 229
Tinkerley La ... 165
Tinkinswood Cl S26 ... 61
  Kirk Ireton DE56 ... 165
Tinkley La S42 ... 113
Tinsell Brook DE65 ... 228
Tinsley Rd NG16 ... 182
Tintagel Cl
  Burton u T DE13 ... 240
  Derby DE21 ... 206
Tintwistle CE Prim Sch
  SK13 ... 9
Tip Tree Hill DE4 ... 165
Tipnall Rd DE74 ... 247
Tipper's La S26 ... 61
Tippett St NG3 ... 268
Tipping St ST16 ... 269

Tiree Cl Derby DE24 ... 231 F2
Stapleford NG9 ... 209 E1
Tibshelf DE55 ... 147 F3
Tissington Cl S43 ... 95 D3
Tissington Dr DE21 ... 206 A2
Titchfield Ave NG18 ... 136 B2
Titchfield St Creswell S80 ... 81 F1
Mansfield NG19 ... 268 B4
Whitwell S80 ... 81 F3
The Barn Cl SK17 ... 69 E2
Tithe Barn Ct S17 16 ... 269 F4
Tithe Barn Rd S17 16 ... 215 E3
Tithebarn La DE6 ... 269 F4
Titterton St S14 ... 269 F1
Tiverton Cl DE3 ... 217 E2
Tivoli Gdns DE11 ... 256 C4
Tixall Rd ST16, S118 ... 269 F4
Toadmoor La DE56 ... 167 F2
Tobermory Way DE24 ... 231 E2
Todbrook Cl S33 ... 45 E3
Todd St S13 ... 17 E4
Tolkien Way ST4 ... 43 F3
Toll Bar Ave S12 ... 43 F3
Toll Bar Cl S12 ... 43 F3
Toll Bar Dr S12 ... 43 F3
Toll Bar Pl S12 ... 43 F3
Toll Bar Rd S12 ... 43 F3
Tollbridge Rd S43 ... 79 D1
Tollemache Cl S14 ... 9 D3
Tollemache Rd S14 ... 9 D3
Tollhouse Hill 11 NG1 ... 268 A2
Tom La
Chapel-en-le-F SK23 ... 46 B3
Staveley S44 ... 97 F3
Tomlinson Ind Est DE21 ... 205 D1
Tomwood Rise S18 ... 16 B3
Tonbridge Dr DE24 ... 233 D3
Tonge La DE74 ... 252 C2
Tongue La SK17 ... 85 F4
Tongue La West S17 ... 85 F4
Tontine Rd S40 ... 266 B2
Toothill La NG18 ... 268 C4
Toothill Rd NG18 ... 268 C4
Top Farm Ct DE56 ... 191 F4
Top Fingle Cl S43 ... 96 C4
Top Hag La DE56 ... 168 A3
Top La DE4 ... 156 B1
Mansfield NG19 ... 135 D1
Old Brampton S42 ... 93 F2
Shottle DE56 ... 166 B1
Top Lons DE56 ... 176 A4
Top Manor Cl DE72 ... 221 E3
Top Meadow DE11 ... 256 A4
Top Rd Calow S44 ... 96 C2
Wingerworth S42 ... 114 B1
Top Row NG16 ... 171 D3
Tophill La DE4 ... 153 E4
Tophole Rd S33 ... 50 C2
Topley Gdns DE21 ... 205 F1
Toppham Dr S8 ... 56 C3
Toppham Rd S8 ... 56 C3
Toppham Way S8 ... 56 C3
Topshill La DE6 ... 165 D1
Tor Ave DE55 ... 170 B3
Tor Rise DE4 ... 143 D2
Tor View Rise DE4 ... 155 D3
Torksey Wlk NG19 ... 136 C2
Torr St SK17 ... 85 D4
Torr Top St SK22 ... 33 E4
Torrance Cl DE14 ... 254 A3
Torridon Cl DE24 ... 231 F2
Torrs Valley SK22 ... 33 E4
Torrvale Rd SK22 ... 33 D4
Tors The DE4 ... 156 C1
Torside Way SK13 ... 10 A3
Torwood Dr S8 ... 56 B4
Totley All Saints CE Prim
Sch S17 ... 55 E2
Totley Brook Cl S17 ... 55 E3
Totley Brook Croft S17 ... 55 E3
Totley Brook Glen S17 ... 55 E3
Totley Brook Gr S17 ... 55 E3
Totley Brook Rd S17 ... 55 E3
Totley Brook Way S17 ... 55 E3
Totley Cty Inf & Jun Sch
S17 ... 55 E2
Totley Grange Cl S17 ... 55 E2
Totley Grange Dr S17 ... 55 E2
Totley Grange Rd S17 ... 55 E2
Totley Hall La S17 ... 55 E2
Totley La S17 ... 56 A3
Totley Mews SK13 ... 9 F1
Totley Mnt S43 ... 96 B4
Toton Bank Road Int Sch
NG9 ... 223 F1
Toton Cty Jun Sch NG9 ... 223 F2
Toton La Beeston NG9 ... 223 F3
Stapleford NG9 ... 223 F3
Toulmin Dr DE11 ... 256 A2
Tower Bsns Pk S45 ... 131 E2
Tower Cl Sheffield S2 ... 43 E4
Somercotes DE55 ... 170 B4
Tower Cres S44 ... 118 A4
Tower Dr S2 ... 43 E4
Tower Rd Burton u T DE15 ... 248 A1
Hartshorne DE11 ... 257 D3
Tower St DE24 ... 232 B4
Tower View Prim Sch
DE15 ... 248 B2
Towers La S32 ... 40 C1
Towle Cl DE72 ... 221 E1
Town La SK13 ... 236 A2
Towles Pastures DE74 ... 247 D2
Town End
Apperknowle S18 ... 58 A1
Bolsover S44 ... 99 D1
Buxton SK17 ... 66 C1
Shirland DE55 ... 146 B1
Town End Rd DE72 ... 235 D4

Town End Sch DE55 ... 147 F3
Town Fold SK6 ... 23 D4
Town Gate S33 ... 51 D4
Town Hall Yd DE6 ... 173 E1
Town La Bradwell S33 ... 51 D4
Charlesworth SK13 ... 16 B3
Newton DE55 ... 148 A2
Town St Brassington DE4 ... 153 D1
Duffield DE56 ... 190 C2
Holbrook DE56 ... 191 E3
Marple SK6 ... 23 D4
Pinxton NG16 ... 160 C2
Sandiacre NG10 ... 223 D3
Town The DE21 ... 205 E4
Town View NG16 ... 195 F4
Townfield La S33 ... 39 F1
Townhead La S33 ... 39 F2
Townhead Rd S18 ... 55 E4
Townscliffe La SK6 ... 23 E3
Townsend Gr DE73 ... 233 D1
Townside Cl NG10 ... 236 A2
Towson Ave NG16 ... 182 B1
Trade St ST4 ... 269 E2
Trafalgar Rd
Long Eaton NG10 ... 236 B3
Stoke-on-T ST4 ... 269 D2
Trafalgar Sq NG10 ... 236 C4
Traffic St Derby DE1 ... 267 C2
Nottingham NG2 ... 268 B1
Traffic Terr
Barrow Hill S43 ... 78 A2
Chesterfield S41 ... 115 D4
Trafford Way DE23 ... 231 E4
Tranmere Ave S44 ... 131 E2
Transvaal Terr S44 ... 118 A3
Travers Rd NG10 ... 223 D3
Travey Rd S2 ... 44 A4
Tream Cliff Cavern S33 ... 37 F2
Tredcroft St S10 ... 17 D4
Tredegar Dr DE21 ... 206 A1
Treeneuk Cl S40 ... 95 D2
Trefoil Cl DE21 ... 231 D4
Tregaron Cl DE21 ... 206 B1
Tregony Way DE24 ... 231 E2
Trelawney Rd S45 ... 131 E2
Trenchard Ave S17 16 ... 269 F4
Trenchard Dr S17 ... 85 E2
Trent Ave Buxton S17 ... 85 E2
Willington DE65 ... 242 B3
Trent Bridge Ct DE23 ... 231 E4
Trent Cl Derby DE65 ... 268 C1
Nottingham NG2 ... 268 C1
Willington DE65 ... 242 B3
Trent Coll NG10 ... 236 B4
Trent Dr DE23 ... 231 E3
Trent Gr Alfreton DE55 ... 159 D1
Dronfield S18 ... 57 D2
Trent La
Castle Donington DE74 ... 247 D3
Long Eaton NG10 ... 236 C3
Melbourne DE73 ... 245 E3
Newton Solney DE15 ... 248 C4
Weston-on-T DE72 ... 245 F2
Trent Rd Ilkeston DE7 ... 208 B2
Nottingham NG2 ... 268 C1
Trent Rise DE21 ... 220 C2
Trent St Derby DE24 ... 232 C4
Long Eaton NG10 ... 236 C4
Nottingham NG1 ... 268 B1
Trent Valley Rd ST4 ... 269 D1
Trent Wlk NG19 ... 136 C2
Trenton Cl NG9 ... 223 D4
Trenton Dr NG10 ... 237 D4
Trenton Green Dr DE21 ... 220 A3
Trenton Grn DE21 ... 220 A3
Tresillian Cl DE22 ... 204 C1
Tressall Cl DE7 ... 208 B2
Trevelyn Cl DE15 ... 248 B1
Treveris Cl DE21 ... 220 C2
Trevone Ave NG9 ... 223 F3
Trevose Cl S40 ... 114 B4
Triangle The DE7 ... 209 D3
Trickett Cl S33 ... 38 B2
Trinity Cl
Chesterfield S40 ... 266 A4
Ilkeston DE7 ... 194 C2
Trinity Gr DE11 ... 256 B3
Trinity Sq NG1 ... 268 B2
Trinity St DE1 ... 267 C2
Trinkey La S32 ... 72 A2
Tristram Gr DE11 ... 240 C1
Troon Cl Burton u T DE13 ... 240 A1
Chesterfield S40 ... 114 B4
Derby DE23 ... 231 D4
Kimberley NG16 ... 195 F4
Trot La SK17 ... 70 A3
Trough La NG16 ... 195 F4
Troughbrook Hill S43 ... 97 D4
Troughbrook Rd S43 ... 78 A1
Trowbridge Cl DE21 ... 205 F1
Trowell Ave DE7 ... 209 D3
Trowell CE Sch NG9 ... 209 E2
Trowell Gr
Long Eaton NG10 ... 223 E1
Stapleford NG9 ... 209 F2
Trowell Park Dr NG9 ... 209 E1
Trowell Rd NG9 ... 209 E1
Trowels La DE22 ... 218 C3
Trueman St DE7 ... 194 C2
Truman Cl NG3 ... 268 B2
Truman St Cossall DE7 ... 195 D1
Kimberley NG16 ... 195 E4
Truro Cl DE11 ... 256 A3
Truro Cres DE21 ... 219 F4
Trusley Gdns DE23 ... 231 E3
Trusley Wlk NG19 ... 136 C2
Trustley Cl DE14 ... 254 A4
Tuckers La S33 ... 268 A4

Tudor Cl
Long Eaton NG10 ... 223 F1
Stoke-on-T ST4 ... 269 E1
Tudor Falls DE75 ... 181 F2
Tudor Field Cl DE73 ... 233 D1
Tudor Pl DE7 ... 208 B3
Tudor Rd DE21 ... 220 A3
Tudor Rise B79 ... 263 F1
Tudor St S43 ... 78 C1
Tudor Way DE11 ... 256 A3
Tudorhouse Cl DE11 ... 256 A4
Tuffolds Cl S2 ... 44 A4
Tufnell Gdns DE22 ... 218 A4
Tulip Rd NG16 ... 195 D3
Tulla Cl DE24 ... 231 F1
Tullis Cl ST16 ... 269 D3
Tunnel Rd NG7 ... 268 A1
Tunnel Yd DE7 ... 173 D1
Tunstall Gn S40 ... 95 E1
Tunstall Way S40 ... 95 E1
Tupton Hall Sch S42 ... 131 E4
Tupton Prim Sch S42 ... 115 E1
Tupton Way S42 ... 116 B1
Turf Lea Rd SK6 ... 23 D1
Turlowfields La DE6 ... 175 E4
Turnberry Cl
Chesterfield S40 ... 114 B4
Ilkeston DE7 ... 194 B1
Turnbury Cl DE14 ... 254 A4
Turncliffe Cl SK17 ... 84 C3
Turnditch CE Prim Sch
DE56 ... 177 D1
Turner Ave NG16 ... 182 A2
Turner Cl
4 Dronfield S18 ... 56 C1
Ilkeston DE7 ... 194 B1
Turner Dr
Eastwood NG16 ... 195 D4
Staveley S43 ... 97 D4
Turner Rd NG10 ... 236 B2
Turner St DE24 ... 232 C3
Turners La DE55 ... 170 A4
Turnlee Cl SK13 ... 17 E4
Turnlee Dr SK13 ... 17 E4
Turnlee Rd SK13 ... 17 E4
Turnley Rd DE55 ... 160 B3
Turnoaks Bsns Pk S40 ... 115 D3
Turnoaks La S40 ... 115 D4
Turnpike Cl DE14 ... 143 E3
Turton Cl NG16 ... 182 A2
Tursley & Hatton Sta
DE55 ... 239 E4
Tutbury Rd
Burton u T DE13 ... 240 A1
Rolleston DE13 ... 240 A1
Tuxford Cl DE21 ... 206 A1
Tuxford Wlk NG3 ... 268 C2
Twentylands DE13 ... 240 B2
Twentywell Dr S17 ... 56 A3
Twentywell La S17 ... 56 A3
Twentywell Rd S17 ... 56 A3
Twentywell Rise S17 ... 56 A3
Twentywell View S17 ... 56 A3
Twickenham Cl S20 ... 59 F3
Twickenham Cres S20 ... 59 F3
Twickenham Dr S20 ... 59 F3
Twickenham Dr DE22 ... 218 A3
Twickenham Glade S20 ... 59 F3
Twickenham Glen S20 ... 59 F3
Twickenham Gr S20 ... 59 F3
Twin Oaks Cl DE23 ... 230 C4
Twissels Bank DE6 ... 213 D1
Twyford Cl Heanor DE75 ... 193 E4
Swadlincote DE11 ... 255 F1
West Hallam DE7 ... 207 E4
Willington DE65 ... 242 B3
Twyford Rd
Barrow u T DE73 ... 244 A3
Long Eaton NG10 ... 235 F2
Willington DE65 ... 242 A3
Twyford St DE23 ... 267 A1
Tyldesley Cl DE24 ... 231 E1
Tyndale Chase DE24 ... 231 F1
Tyndall Pl ST4 ... 269 D2
Tynedale Cl NG10 ... 236 A3
Tynefield Ct DE65 ... 230 C1
Tynefield Mews DE65 ... 229 D1
Tynsel Parkes CE Prim Sch
ST14 ... 210 A1
Tythe The DE11 ... 256 A4

Uffa Magna DE3 ... 217 E1
Ulley Cres S13 ... 44 A4
Ulley Rd S13 ... 44 A4
Ullswater Ave S20 ... 59 F3
Ullswater Cl Derby DE21 ... 205 E1
Dronfield S18 ... 56 C1
Mosborough S20 ... 59 F3
Ullswater Dr
Derby DE21 ... 220 C3
Dronfield S18 ... 56 C1
Ullswater Pk S18 ... 56 C1
Ullswater Pl S18 ... 56 C1
Ulster Terr S14 ... 269 E1
Ulverston Rd S41 ... 95 E4
Underhall DE4 ... 143 D2
Underhill Ave DE23 ... 231 E4
Underhill Cl DE23 ... 231 F3
Underhill Rd S43 ... 80 A3
Underpass The DE1 ... 267 C4
Undertown La DE6 ... 197 E3
Underwood CE Sch NG16 ... 171 F1
Underwood Terr DE1 ... 143 D4
Union Rd
Ilkeston DE7 ... 208 C4
New Mills SK22 ... 33 E4
Nottingham NG1 ... 268 B2
Swadlincote DE11 ... 256 A3

Union St Ashbourne DE6 ... 173 D1
Glossop SK13 ... 17 E4
Harthill S26 ... 61 F3
Long Eaton NG10 ... 236 C4
Mansfield NG18 ... 268 B4
Melbourne DE73 ... 252 A4
South Normanton DE55 ... 159 F3
Unity Cl DE11 ... 256 A1
Unity Wlk S43 ... 17 E4
Univ of Derby DE22 ... 204 B1
Univ of Derby (Sch of Art
& Design) DE1 ... 267 B2
Univ of Sheffield
(Research Labs) SK17 ... 85 D1
Unstone Dronfield By-Pass
S18 ... 76 B4
Unstone Hill S18 ... 76 B4
Unstone Jun Sch S18 ... 76 C4
Unstone Rd S18 ... 76 C2
Unthank La S17, S18 ... 74 B2
Upchurch Cl DE3 ... 217 E2
Upland Rise S40 ... 95 E1
Uplands Ave DE23 ... 231 E3
Uplands Gdns DE23 ... 218 C1
Uplands Rd Glossop SK13 ... 15 D3
Hackingknife SK14 ... 15 D3
Upper Albert Rd S8 ... 43 D3
Upper Bainbridge St DE23 ... 219 D2
Upper Barn Cl DE75 ... 181 F1
Upper Blindlow La SK17 ... 106 A3
Upper Boundary Rd DE22 ... 218 C2
Upper College St 10 NG1 ... 268 A2
Upper Croft S44 ... 269 D2
Upper Croft S44 ... 131 F2
Upper Croft Cl S43 ... 96 C4
Upper Dale Rd DE23 ... 218 C1
Upper Dunstead Rd NG16 ... 182 A2
Upper Eldon St SK17 ... 268 C1
Upper End Rd SK17 ... 67 E2
Upper Furlong St S14 ... 269 F1
Upper Greenhill Gdns DE1 143 E3
Upper Hall Cl DE56 ... 191 E3
Upper Hollow DE23 ... 218 A1
Upper King St S43 ... 77 F1
Upper La DE6 ... 175 F2
Upper Mantle Cl S45 ... 131 E2
Upper Marehay Rd DE5 ... 180 B3
Upper Moor St S40 ... 95 F1
Upper Nelson St DE75 ... 181 E1
Upper Newbold Cl S40 ... 95 D4
Upper Orchard St NG9 ... 223 F4
Upper Parliament St NG1 ... 268 B2
Upper School La S18 ... 76 A4
Upper Town La DE4 ... 126 A1
Upper Valley Rd S8 ... 43 D3
Upper Wellington St NG10 223 E1
Upper Yeld Rd DE45 ... 109 E2
Uppermoor Rd DE24 ... 232 C3
Upperthorpe Rd S21 ... 60 B3
Upperthorpe Villas S21 ... 60 B3
Uppertown La DE4 ... 142 B1
Uppertown La DE4 ... 143 D1
Upton Cl DE75 ... 181 F1
Upton Mount NG19 ... 135 F1
Upwood Cl S40 ... 95 D3
Upwoods Rd DE6 ... 211 D1
Utah Cl DE65 ... 228 C1
Uttoxeter New Rd DE22 ... 218 C3
Uttoxeter Old Rd DE22 ... 218 C3
Uttoxeter Rd Derby DE73 ... 217 F1
Hatton DE65 ... 227 D1
Hilton DE65 ... 228 B1
Scropton DE65 ... 226 C2

Vale Cl Bolsover S44 ... 99 D1
Dronfield S18 ... 57 D1
Vale Dr NG20 ... 119 F1
Vale House Dr SK13 ... 10 A3
Vale Mills DE22 ... 218 C4
Vale Rd Hartshorne DE11 ... 257 D2
Mansfield Woodhouse NG19 ... 136 A2
Swadlincote DE11 ... 256 A3
Vale St ST4 ... 269 E2
Vale The DE7 ... 207 E1
Valentine Ave NG16 ... 171 F4
Valerian Cl SK17 ... 85 E4
Valerie Rd DE72 ... 246 A4
Vallance St NG19 ... 136 A2
Valley Cl S45 ... 132 A4
Valley Dr S21 ... 60 B4
Valley Gdns SK14 ... 15 F2
Valley Rd Bolsover S44 ... 118 A4
Broadbottom SK14 ... 15 F4
Chesterfield S41 ... 115 D4
Clay Cross S45 ... 131 D2
Cromford DE4 ... 155 D4
Derby, Cherrytree Hill DE21 220 A3
Derby, Littleover DE23 ... 218 B1
Glossop SK13 ... 16 C1
Hayfield SK22 ... 25 E2
Ilkeston DE7 ... 208 C3
Kilamarsh S21 ... 60 B4
Kimberley NG16 ... 195 E4
Mastin Moor S43 ... 79 F2
Overseal DE12 ... 262 A2
Sheffield S8 ... 43 D3
Shirebrook NG20 ... 119 F3
Valley Rise Common Side S18 75 E2
Swadlincote DE11 ... 256 A2
Valley View Belper DE56 ... 179 D1
Ilkeston DE7 ... 208 C3
Valley View Rd DE55 ... 148 B3
Vancouver Ave DE21 ... 220 B2
Vancouver Dr DE15 ... 248 B2

Vanguard Rd NG10 ... 236 B3
Vanguard Trad Est S40 ... 115 D4
Varley St DE24 ... 232 B3
Vaughan Rd NG20 ... 119 F3
Vaughan Rd S023 ... 45 F3
Vaughan Way ST17 ... 269 D3
Vauxhall Ave DE22 ... 218 A4
Ventura Cres DE55 ... 159 D1
Verbena Dr DE23 ... 231 E2
Vere Cl DE65 ... 242 A3
Vermont Dr DE21 ... 220 B3
Verney St NG19 ... 134 C4
Verney Way NG19 ... 134 C4
Vernon Cl NG20 ... 120 A2
Vernon Dr Bakewell DE45 ... 109 D4
Derby DE21 ... 220 C2
Vernon Gn DE45 ... 109 D4
Vernon Rd Chesterfield S40 ... 95 F3
Stoke-on-T ST4 ... 269 E2
Vernon Rise S42 ... 115 F1
Vernon St Derby DE1 ... 218 C3
Ilkeston DE7 ... 194 C2
Nottingham NG1 ... 268 A2
Shirebrook NG20 ... 120 A2
Veronica Dr NG16 ... 195 E4
Vestry Rd DE21 ... 205 F2
Vetchfield Cl DE24 ... 231 F1
Via Gellia Rd DE4 ... 154 B4
Vicar La Chesterfield S40 ... 266 B3
Tibshelf DE55 ... 148 A3
Vicarage Ave Derby DE23 ... 218 C1
Ilkeston DE7 ... 194 B2
Vicarage Cl Belper DE56 ... 179 D2
Burton u T DE15 ... 248 A2
Heath S44 ... 117 D1
Holmesfield S18 ... 75 D4
Nottingham NG3 ... 268 B2
Shirebrook NG20 ... 119 F2
Smalley DE7 ... 192 C3
Swanwick DE55 ... 169 F4
Vicarage Ct S18 ... 217 E1
Vicarage Dr Derby DE21 ... 220 A4
Stramshall ST14 ... 210 A2
Vicarage Gdns Heanor DE75 181 F1
Swadlincote DE11 ... 256 B2
Vicarage La
Ashford in t W DE45 ... 108 C4
Dore S17 ... 55 E4
Duffield DE56 ... 190 C2
Hayfield SK22 ... 25 E1
Ironville NG16 ... 170 C1
Little Eaton DE21 ... 205 E4
Rowsley DE4 ... 110 C1
Vicarage Mews DE55 ... 170 C3
Vicarage Rd Belper DE56 ... 190 C4
Derby, Chellaston DE73 ... 232 C1
Derby, Mickleover DE73 ... 217 E1
Stoke-on-T ST4 ... 269 D2
Swadlincote DE11 ... 256 B2
Woodville DE11 ... 256 C1
Vicarage St DE7 ... 194 B2
Vicarage Way ST17 ... 269 D3
Vicarage Wlk DE7 ... 268 B3
Vicarwood Ave Derby DE22 204 C1
Holbrook DE56 ... 191 E4
Victor Ave DE24 ... 218 C4
Victor Cres NG10 ... 223 E2
Victor Rd S17 ... 55 F4
Victoria Ave
Borrowash DE72 ... 221 D1
2 Buxton SK17 ... 85 E4
Draycott DE72 ... 235 D4
Hadfield SK13 ... 10 A3
Heanor DE75 ... 181 E1
Netherthorpe S43 ... 79 D2
Nottingham NG2 ... 268 C1
Victoria Cl DE11 ... 217 F2
Victoria Cotts DE55 ... 159 E2
Victoria Cres NG10 ... 170 C2
Victoria Cl Ilkeston DE7 ... 194 C1
Mansfield NG18 ... 268 B3
Matlock DE4 ... 143 E3
Victoria Ctr NG1 ... 268 B3
Victoria Rd S8 ... 147 F1
Victoria Rd S41 ... 96 C3
Victoria Hall Gdns DE4 ... 143 E3
Victoria Park Rd
Buxton SK17 ... 85 E4
Calow S43 ... 96 C3
Victoria Rd Bamford S33 ... 40 A2
Draycott DE72 ... 235 D4
Pinxton NG16 ... 160 B2
Ripley DE5 ... 169 E1
Sandiacre NG10 ... 223 D3
Selston NG16 ... 171 F3
Stafford ST16 ... 269 D4
Victoria Sq DE63 ... 173 E1
Victoria St Alfreton DE55 ... 159 D2
Brimington S43 ... 118 A4
Castle Donington DE74 ... 247 D3
Chesterfield S41 ... 266 B4
Clay Cross S45 ... 131 E2
Creswell S80 ... 81 F1
Derby DE1 ... 267 B3
Dronfield S18 ... 56 C1
Glossop SK13 ... 17 E4
Ilkeston DE7 ... 194 C2
Ironville NG16 ... 182 B2
Langley Mill NG16 ... 182 B3
Long Eaton NG10 ... 236 A3
Melbourne DE73 ... 252 A4
New Mills SK22 ... 33 D3

Victoria St continued
Nottingham NG1 .... 268 B1
Ripley DE5 .... 169 F1
Shirebrook NG20 .... 119 F2
Somercotes DE55 .... 170 B4
South Normanton DE55 .... 160 A3
Stafford ST16 .... 269 E4
Stapleford NG9 .... 223 E4
Victoria St N S41 .... 76 C1
Victoria St W S40 .... 95 E1
Victoria Terr DE55 .... 148 A4
Victory Ave S42 .... 115 E1
Victory Cl DE55 .... 169 F1
Victory Cl NG10 .... 236 B3
Victory Dr NG19 .... 136 C1
Victory Rd DE24 .... 232 A3
View Rd S2 .... 43 D4
Viewdales Cl DE6 .... 175 F1
Vikinge Bsns Ctr DE11 ..... 256 C2
Vikinglea Cl S2 .... 44 A4
Vikinglea Dr S2 .... 44 A4
Vikinglea Rd S2 .... 44 A4
Villa St Draycott DE72 ...... 235 D4
Stoke-on-T ST4 .... 269 E4
Village Com Sch DE23 ...... 231 F4
Village Ct DE6 .... 190 C2
Village St DE23 .... 231 F4
Village The Dale DE7 .... 207 F1
West Hallam DE7 .... 207 F4
Villas Rd Bolsover S44 .... 98 C2
Toadmoor DE56 .... 167 F2
Villas The Stoke-on-T ST4 ... 269 E1
Whaley Thorns NG20 .... 101 D2
Villiers Cl S2 .... 43 F3
Villiers Dr S2 .... 43 F3
Vincent Ave Derby DE21 .... 220 C2
Ilkeston DE7 .... 208 C4
Vincent Cl DE56 .... 192 A4
Vincent Cres S40 .... 95 D1
Vincent St DE23 .... 218 C1
Vine Cl DE23 .... 231 D4
Vine Cres NG10 .... 223 D3
Vine Farm Cl DE7 .... 208 B3
Vine Row ST4 .... 269 E1
Vinebank St ST4 .... 269 E1
Viola Cl DE21 .... 206 B2
Violet La DE15 .... 254 C4
Violet Lane Sch DE15 .... 254 C4
Violet St DE23 .... 218 C1
Violet Way DE15 .... 255 D4
Virginsalley La DE6 .... 184 B1
Vista The NG9 .... 223 F3
Vivian St Bolsover S44 .... 98 C3
Derby DE1 .... 219 D4
Vulcan St DE23 .... 219 D1
Vyse Dr NG10 .... 236 B3

Wade Ave Derby DE23 ...... 218 B1
Ilkeston DE7 .... 209 D4
Wade Dr DE2 .... 217 F1
Wade St DE23 .... 218 B1
Wadebridge Gr DE24 .... 233 E3
Wadham St ST4 .... 269 E2
Wadhurst Gdns NG3 .... 268 B2
Wadsworth Ave S12 .... 44 B3
Wadsworth Cl S12 .... 44 B3
Wadsworth Dr S12 .... 44 B3
Wadsworth Rd Sheffield S12 ... 44 B3
Stapleford NG9 .... 223 F4
Wagstaff La NG16 .... 171 E3
Wain Ave S42 .... 132 A4
Wain Dr S14 .... 269 D1
Wain Way S42 .... 132 A4
Waingroves Prim Sch
DE5 .... 181 D4
Waingroves Rd
Codnor DE5 .... 181 D3
Ripley DE5 .... 181 D4
Wainwood Rise ST4 .... 269 D1
Wainwright Ave S13 .... 44 B4
Wainwright La S13 .... 44 B4
Wakams Cres DE72 .... 233 D2
Wakefield Ave DE13 .... 239 D3
Wakefield Croft DE7 .... 194 B2
Wakelyn Cl DE72 .... 234 C1
Walbrook Rd DE23 .... 218 C1
Walcote Cl DE56 .... 179 E3
Walden Rd S2 .... 43 D4
Waldene Dr DE24 .... 233 D3
Waldley La DE6 .... 211 E4
Waldorf Ave DE24 .... 233 D4
Waldorf Cl DE24 .... 233 D4
Walford Rd Kidsmarsh S21 ... 60 B3
Rollestone DE13 .... 240 B2
Walgrove Ave S40 .... 95 F1
Walgrove Rd S40 .... 95 E1
Walk Cl DE72 .... 235 D4
Walk Mill Rd SK22 .... 25 C1
Walk The DE56 .... 192 A4
Walkden Rd NG18 .... 268 B4
Walker Ave DE5 .... 169 F1
Walker Gr NG9 .... 223 F3
Walker La DE1 .... 267 A4
Walker St Hadfield SK13 ...... 10 A2
Nottingham NG2 .... 268 C1
Walkers Ave NG16 .... 182 C3
Walkers La S21 .... 60 B3
Wall Ditch DE6 .... 149 D1
Wall Rd DE14 .... 254 A4
Wall St Buxton SK17 .... 85 E4
Ripley DE5 .... 169 E1
Wallace St DE22 .... 218 B3
Wallfields Cl DE65 .... 230 B1
Wallis Cl DE72 .... 235 D4
Wallis Rd NG18 .... 268 C4

Walls La S80 .... 81 D4
Walnut Ave Derby DE24 ... 233 D4
Shireoaks S81 .... 63 F4
Walnut Cl
Aston-on-T DE72 .... 246 A4
Barrow u T DE73 .... 244 A3
Burnaston DE65 .... 229 F3
Derby DE73 .... 245 D4
Ilkeston DE7 .... 209 D4
Repton DE65 .... 243 D1
Swadlincote DE11 .... 256 A3
Walnut Dr S21 .... 60 B3
Walnut Rd DE56 .... 179 D2
Walnut St DE24 .... 232 C2
Walpole St DE21 .... 219 E3
Walseker La S26 .... 61 E4
Walsham Ct DE21 .... 205 E1
Walter Evans CE Prim Sch
DE22 .... 204 C1
Walter St Derby DE1 .... 218 C4
Draycott DE72 .... 234 C4
Nottingham NG7 .... 268 A2
Walters Cres NG16 .... 171 E3
Waltham Ave DE24 .... 231 F2
Walthamstow Dr DE22 ..... 218 A3
Waltheof Rd S2 .... 44 A4
Walton Ave DE24 .... 232 C2
Nottingham NG2, NG3 ...... 268 C2
Walton Back La
Chesterfield S40 .... 114 A4
Holymoorside S42 .... 113 F4
Walton Cl Chesterfield S40 .. 114 A4
Dronfield S18 .... 56 B1
Swadlincote DE11 .... 256 A2
Walton Cres
Ashbourne DE6 .... 173 E1
Chesterfield S40 .... 95 F1
Fenton ST4 .... 269 F1
Walton Dr Chesterfield S40 .. 95 F1
Stoke-on-T ST4 .... 269 F1
Walton Dr Chesterfield S40 .. 231 F4
Walton Drive Ct S40 .... 95 F1
Walton Fields Rd S40 .... 95 E1
Walton Hill DE74 .... 247 D2
Walton Hospl S40 .... 114 C4
Walton Rd Chesterfield S40 .. 95 E1
Derby DE21 .... 219 F3
Walton-on-T DE15 .... 254 B3
Walton St NG10 .... 223 E1
Walton Way S42 .... 114 C2
Walton Wlk S40 .... 95 F1
Walton-on-Trent CE
Prim Sch DE12 .... 259 E4
Wansbeck Cl NG7 .... 268 A2
Wansfell Cl DE3 .... 217 F1
Wapentake La DE56 .... 165 E1
Warburton Cl S2 .... 43 E4
Warburton Gdns S2 .... 43 E4
Warburton Rd S2 .... 43 E4
Ward Dr DE55 .... 170 B4
Ward La Barlborough S43 ..... 80 A4
Disley SK12 .... 32 C2
Ward Pl Mansfield NG18 ... 268 A3
Sheffield S8 .... 43 D4
Ward St Derby DE22 .... 218 C2
Tupton S42 .... 131 E4
Ward's La Breaston DE72 ... 235 E4
King's Newton DE73 .... 245 D1
Melbourne DE73 .... 244 C2
Ward's Yd S40 .... 266 B2
Wardgate Way S40 .... 95 D3
Wardlow Ave NG3 .... 220 A4
Wardlow Cl S40 .... 114 C4
Wardlow Mews S41 .... 9 E1
Wardlow Rd Ilkeston DE7 ... 194 C2
Sheffield S12 .... 44 B3
Warehouse La S33 .... 38 B2
Warhurst Fold 🖪 SK13 .... 10 A3
Warmbrook DE4 .... 165 F4
Warmbrook Jun Sch SK23 .. 47 E3
Warmbrook Rd DE4 .... 47 E3
Warminster Cl S8 .... 43 D2
Warminster Cres S8 .... 43 D2
Warminster Dr S8 .... 43 D2
Warminster Gdns S8 .... 43 D2
Warminster Pl S8 .... 43 D1
Warminster Rd S8 .... 43 D2
Warmwells La DE5 .... 180 B3
Warner St Chesterfield S41 .. 266 C1
Derby, Mickleover DE3 ..... 217 F2
Derby, St Luke's DE22 ..... 218 C2
Warney Rd DE4 .... 127 E1
Warren Ave NG9 .... 223 E4
Warren Ave Extension
NG9 .... 223 E4
Warren Cl Burton u T DE13 ... 240 C1
Pilsley S45 .... 132 B1
Warren Cres S21 .... 58 C1
Warren Ct NG9 .... 223 E4
Warren Dr DE12 .... 261 E3
Warren La Branston DE14 ... 253 F4
Castle Donington DE74 ..... 236 A1
Warren Lea SK6 .... 15 D1
Warren Rise S18 .... 57 E2
Warren St DE24 .... 232 C4
Warren Wlk S21 .... 58 C1
Warrendale Ct DE73 .... 233 D1
Warser Gate NG1 .... 268 B1
Warsop Vale Jun Mix &
Inf Sch NG20 .... 120 B2
Warwick Ave DE23 .... 218 B1
Warwick Cl Branston DE14 .. 253 F4
Glossop SK13 .... 17 F4
Swadlincote DE11 .... 256 C3
Warwick Dr DE7 .... 194 B2

Warwick Gdns DE56 .... 179 E3
Warwick Rd
Long Eaton NG10 .... 237 D4
Somercotes DE55 .... 159 E1
Warwick St
Chesterfield S41 .... 115 D4
Derby DE21 .... 219 E1
Wasdale Ave S19 .... 59 F3
Wash Gn DE56, DE4 .... 166 A4
Wash House La S40 .... 95 E1
Washbrook La DE6 .... 161 F2
Washford Rd DE65 .... 228 C1
Washhouse Bottom SK17 ... 69 F4
Washington Ave DE21 ...... 220 A3
Washington Cl DE73 .... 252 A4
Washington Dr
Mansfield NG18 .... 268 A3
Stapleford NG9 .... 209 F1
Wasnidge Cl NG3 .... 268 B2
Watburn Rd SK22 .... 24 B1
Water La Bakewell DE45 .... 109 E3
Bamford S33 .... 40 A2
Bolsover S44 .... 117 F4
Cromford DE4 .... 155 D3
Eyam S32 .... 71 F3
Hollingworth SK14 .... 9 E3
Mansfield NG19 .... 135 D2
Middleton (Nr Wirksworth)
DE4 .... 154 B3
South Normanton DE55 ... 160 A3
Stony Houghton NG19 ..... 118 C1
Tideswell SK17 .... 68 C3
Wirksworth DE4 .... 165 F4
Water Meadow La S40 .... 95 D4
Water Meadows The DE73 ... 244 B3
Water Orton Cl NG9 .... 223 F2
Water St Bakewell DE45 .... 109 E3
Buxton SK17 .... 85 D4
Glossop SK13 .... 10 C1
Stafford ST16 .... 269 E4
Stoke-on-T ST4 .... 269 F2
Watercress La S45 .... 131 E1
Waterfoot Cotts SK14 .... 9 D2
Waterfoot La SK23 .... 45 E3
Waterford Dr DE21 .... 220 A2
Watergo La DE7 .... 230 C4
Watering La DE56 .... 191 E3
Wateringbury Gr S43 .... 78 C1
Waterloo Cl DE55 .... 160 B4
Waterloo Cres NG7 .... 268 A2
Waterloo Ct DE55 .... 159 D2
Waterloo La NG9 .... 209 F3
Waterloo Pl DE11 .... 256 A2
Waterloo Prom NG7 .... 268 A2
Waterloo Rd
Matlock Bath DE4 .... 143 D1
Nottingham NG7 .... 268 A2
Waterloo St
Bramley-Vale S44 .... 117 F1
Clay Cross S45 .... 131 E2
Watermeade S2 .... 59 D1
Watermeadow Cl NG19 ..... 136 B3
Watermeadow Rd DE24 .... 233 D3
Watermeadows The NG10 .. 236 A4
Waterpark Rd DE6 .... 224 A4
Waters Edge S6 .... 23 D4
Waterside Baslow DE45 ...... 91 F3
Burton u T DE15 .... 254 C4
Hadfield SK13 .... 10 A3
Ironville NG16 .... 170 C2
Marple SK6 .... 23 D3
Waterside Cl Derby DE22 .. 205 D1
Sandiacre NG10 .... 223 D2
Waterside Jun Sch DE15 ... 254 C4
Waterside Rd
Burton u T DE15 .... 254 B4
Disley SK12 .... 32 C4
New Mills SK22 .... 33 D4
Stoke-on-T DE15 .... 254 B4
Waterthorpe Cl S20 .... 59 F4
Waterthorpe Cres S20 .... 59 D1
Waterthorpe Gdns S20 ...... 59 F4
Waterthorpe Glade S20 ...... 59 F4
Waterthorpe Glen 🖪 S20 ... 59 F4
Waterthorpe Rise 🗷 S20 ... 59 F4
Waterway The NG10 .... 223 E2
Watery La Ashbourne DE6 .. 184 C4
Bretby DE15 .... 249 E2
Clifton DE6 .... 184 C4
Ellastone DE6 .... 183 D2
Scropton DE65 .... 226 C1
Swadlincote DE11 .... 255 E3
Thurvaston DE6 .... 215 E3
Watford Bridge Ind Est
SK22 .... 24 B1
Watford Bridge Rd SK22 .... 24 B1
Watford La SK22 .... 24 B1
Watford Rd Buxton SK17 .... 84 C4
New Mills SK22 .... 24 B1
Watford St ST4 .... 269 F2
Watham La SK14 .... 9 F2
Watkin St Fenton ST4 .... 269 F1
Nottingham NG3 .... 268 B2
Watkinson St DE75 .... 181 E1
Watnall Cres NG19 .... 268 A4
Watson Ave Heanor DE75 .. 181 F1
Heanor DE75 .... 268 C4
Watson La S42 .... 114 B2
Watson Rd DE7 .... 194 B1
Watson St Derby DE1 .... 218 C3
Derby DE1 .... 218 C4
Stoke-on-T S45 .... 269 F2
Watten Cl DE24 .... 231 F1
Watts Gn DE45 .... 108 C4
Waveney Cl DE22 .... 205 D3
Waverley House Sch NG7 .. 268 A2

Waverley St Derby DE24 ... 232 B4
Long Eaton NG10 .... 236 C4
Nottingham NG7 .... 268 A2
Tibshelf DE55 .... 148 A4
Wayfaring Rd DE21 .... 206 A1
Wayford Ave S41 .... 266 C1
Wayside S43 .... 96 B4
Wayside Cl S42 .... 132 A4
Wayside Ct S43 .... 96 B4
Wayzgoose Dr DE21 .... 219 E3
Weaddow La DE45 .... 124 C1
Weakland Cl S12 .... 44 C2
Weakland Cres S12 .... 44 C2
Weakland Dr S12 .... 44 C2
Weakland Way S12 .... 44 C2
Weather Hill La HD7 .... 3 F4
Weathern Field DE21 .... 261 E3
Weaver Cl Ashbourne DE6 . 185 E4
Crich DE4 .... 156 C1
Weaver Rd ST14 .... 210 A1
Weavers Cl Belper DE56 .... 179 E3
Borrowash DE72 .... 221 E1
Weavers Gn DE3 .... 217 E1
Weavers The ST14 .... 196 B3
Weaving Ave S33 .... 38 B1
Webster Ave NG16 .... 182 C1
Webster Croft S41 .... 77 D1
Webster Cl S40 .... 95 F3
Webster St DE1 .... 267 A2
Wedgewood Cl DE15 .... 248 A1
Wednesborough SK14 .... 9 E3
Weekday Cross NG1 .... 268 B1
Weighbridge Rd NG18 ...... 268 A3
Weighman Dr NG16 .... 195 D4
Weir Bank DE15 .... 254 C3
Weir Park Ave NG3 .... 268 B2
Weirside DE4 .... 168 A4
Welbeck Ave Buxton SK17 ... 85 E1
Ilkeston DE7 .... 208 B3
Welbeck Cl
Nottingham NG3 .... 268 B2
Staveley S43 .... 97 E3
Welbeck Ct S43 .... 80 C2
Welbeck Dr S42 .... 114 C2
Welbeck Gdns NG9 .... 223 F2
Welbeck Gr DE22 .... 204 B2
Welbeck Rd Bolsover S44 ... 99 D1
Long Eaton NG10 .... 223 E2
Mansfield Woodhouse NG19 136 B2
Welbeck St Creswell S80 ..... 81 F1
Mansfield NG18 .... 268 B4
Whitwell S80 .... 82 A3
Welbury Gdns S20 .... 59 F3
Welby St ST4 .... 269 F1
Welch Ave NG9 .... 223 F4
Welch St S14 .... 269 E2
Welfare Ave S40 .... 95 E2
Welfare Cl NG20 .... 119 F2
Welfitt Gr NG20 .... 101 D1
Well Banks DE6 .... 165 D1
Well Cl DE6 .... 175 F2
Well Gate SK13 .... 10 C1
Well La Belper DE56 .... 190 C4
Blackfordby DE11 .... 257 D1
Holymoorside S42 .... 112 C4
Repton DE65 .... 242 B1
Shirland DE55 .... 146 B2
Well Rd S8 .... 43 D3
Well Row SK14 .... 16 A4
Well Spring Cl 🖪 S43 .... 96 C4
Well St Brassington DE4 .... 152 C1
Derby DE1 .... 267 B5
Elton DE4 .... 140 C4
New Mills SK22 .... 33 D4
Ripley DE5 .... 169 E1
Welland Cl Burton u T DE15 . 248 A1
Derby DE3 .... 217 E2
Welland Rd DE65 .... 228 B1
Wellcarr Rd S8 .... 43 D1
Wellcroft Cl NG18 .... 268 A3
Welldon St DE5 .... 181 D2
Weller St ST4 .... 269 D2
Wellesley Ave DE23 .... 231 E4
Wellfield DE6 .... 143 E3
Wellfield Cl S12 .... 44 C1
Wellfield St DE45 .... 143 E3
Wellgate DE45 .... 109 D1
Wellhead Rd S8 .... 43 D3
Wellington Cir 🖪 NG1 ...... 268 A1
Wellington Cl DE14 .... 143 E4
Wellington Cres DE7 .... 267 D2
Wellington Pl NG16 .... 182 C1
Wellington Rd DE14 .... 253 F4
Wellington Sq NG7 .... 268 A2
Wellington St
Chesterfield S41 .... 77 E2
Derby DE1 .... 267 D2
Eastwood NG16 .... 182 C2
Heanor DE75 .... 181 E2
Long Eaton NG10 .... 236 C4
Matlock DE4 .... 143 E3
Ripley DE5 .... 169 F1
Stapleford NG9 .... 223 E3
Stoke-on-T ST4 .... 269 D1
Wellington Villas NG7 .... 268 A2
Wells Cl NG19 .... 136 B2
Wells Ct DE23 .... 230 C4
Wells Rd DE3 .... 217 F1
Wells St S44 .... 118 B4
Wellspring Cl
Barlborough S43 .... 80 A3
Wingerworth S42 .... 115 D2
Wellspring Dale NG9 .... 223 F3
Wellwood Rd DE11 .... 256 A3
Welney Cl DE3 .... 230 B4
Welshpool Pl S40 .... 95 E2
Welshpool Rd DE21 .... 205 E1

Welwyn Ave
Derby, Allestree DE24 ...... 204 B1
Derby DE24 .... 232 C1
Mansfield Woodhouse NG19 136 A1
Welwyn Cl Chesterfield S40 .. 95 E1
Sheffield S12 .... 44 A1
Welwyn Rd S12 .... 44 A1
Wembley Gdns DE22 .... 218 A4
Wendover Cl DE3 .... 217 E1
Wenham La NG17 .... 148 C1
Wenlock Cl Chesterfield S40 . 95 E1
Derby DE3 .... 217 F1
Eastwood NG16 .... 195 E1
Wenlock Cres S40 .... 95 E1
Wenlock Dr S42 .... 115 E4
Wensley Dr DE21 .... 220 C1
Wensley Rd
North Wingfield S42 .... 131 F4
Winster DE4 .... 141 E2
Wensley Way S43 .... 97 E2
Wensleydale Cl NG19 .... 136 C3
Wensleydale Rd NG10 .... 236 A4
Wensleydale Wlk DE24 ...... 233 E4
Wentworth Ave S40 .... 114 C2
Wentworth Cl Derby DE3 ... 217 F1
Mansfield NG19 .... 136 C2
Wentworth Croft DE75 ...... 182 A4
Wentworth Ct NG16 .... 195 F4
Wentworth Dr DE13 .... 240 B3
Wentworth Rd S8 .... 56 C4
Wentworth St DE7 .... 195 D2
Werburgh Cl DE21 .... 220 B3
Werburgh St DE22 .... 218 C2
Werneth Low Ctry Pk SK14 . 15 D4
Werneth Low Rd SK14 .... 15 D2
Werneth Rd SK13 .... 17 D4
Wesley La DE72 .... 221 E2
Wesley Pl NG9 .... 223 F4
Wesley Rd Ambergate DE56 . 167 F2
Derby DE24 .... 233 D3
Stonebroom DE55 .... 146 C3
Wesley St Glossop SK13 ..... 10 C1
Hadfield SK13 .... 10 A1
Ilkeston DE7 .... 194 C2
Nottingham NG2 .... 182 B2
Wesleyan Chapel Wlk
NG9 .... 223 F4
Wessex Gdns S17 .... 55 E3
Wessington Dr S43 .... 97 E4
Wessington La DE55 .... 158 A3
Wessington Mews
Derby DE22 .... 204 C3
Gamesley SK13 .... 9 F1
Wessington Prim Sch
DE55 .... 157 F4
West Ave
Derby, Chellaston DE73 .... 232 C2
Derby, Little Chester DE1 .. 267 A4
Draycott DE72 .... 234 C4
Hilton DE65 .... 228 B3
Ripley DE5 .... 169 F1
Sandiacre NG10 .... 223 D3
Stapleford NG9 .... 223 F4
Stoke-on-T ST4 .... 269 D2
West Bank Matlock Bath DE4 143 D1
Stoke-on-T ST4 .... 269 D2
Toadmoor DE56 .... 168 A1
Winster DE4 .... 141 E2
West Bank Ave Crich DE4 .. 156 C1
Derby DE22 .... 218 C4
Mansfield NG18, NG19 .... 268 B4
West Bank Cl DE22 .... 218 C4
West Bank Lea NG19 .... 136 A3
West Bank Link NG19 .... 136 A3
West Bank Wynd NG18 ...... 268 B4
West Bars S40 .... 266 A3
West Cl Derby DE22 .... 204 C1
Stafford ST16 .... 269 F4
West Cres
Long Duckmanton S44 .... 98 A4
Matlock DE4 .... 143 D3
West Croft Ave DE23 .... 231 E3
West Croft Cl DE55 .... 125 D3
West Dr Derby DE3 .... 217 E1
Doveridge DE6 .... 211 D1
Tintwistle SK13 .... 9 F4
West Edge Cl S45 .... 182 A4
West End Alfreton DE55 .... 159 D2
Barlborough S43 .... 80 A4
Brassington DE4 .... 152 C1
Broadbottom SK14 .... 15 F4
Elton DE4 .... 140 C3
Pinxton NG16 .... 160 B2
Wirksworth DE4 .... 165 F4
West End Cl DE55 .... 159 D2
West End Cres DE7 .... 208 B4
West End Dr Ilkeston DE7 .. 208 B4
Shardlow DE72 .... 234 C1
West End View S21 .... 59 E1
West Gate Holme HD7 .... 3 F4
Long Eaton NG10 .... 236 B4
Mansfield NG18 .... 268 A4
West Gr DE24 .... 232 B3
West Hill Codnor DE5 .... 181 D4
Mansfield NG18 .... 268 B4
West Hill Ave NG18 .... 268 B4
West Hill Dr NG18 .... 268 B4
West Hill Pk NG19 .... 136 A2
West Hill Way NG18 .... 268 B4
West Lawn DE65 .... 230 B1
West Lea S40 .... 95 D3
West Lea Cotts S44 .... 80 A2
West Lees Rd S33 .... 40 A2
West Nottingham Coll of
F Ed NG18 .... 268 B4
West Par ST4 .... 269 F1

West Park Com Sch DE21 .. 220 B3
West Park Rd DE22 .... 218 C4
West Rd Buxton SK17 ...... 85 D3
  Derby DE21 .... 220 B3
West Row DE22 .... 205 D1
West Service Rd DE21 .... 220 A2
West St Bramley-Vale S44 . 117 E1
  Burton u T DE15 .... 248 A2
  Chesterfield S40 ...... 266 A4
  Clay Cross S45 .... 131 D2
  Clowne S43 .... 81 D3
  Creswell S80 .... 81 E1
  Dronfield S18 .... 56 C1
  Eckington S21 .... 59 E1
  Heanor DE75 .... 181 E1
  Langley Mill NG16 ..... 182 A2
  Nottingham NG1 .... 268 C1
  Somercotes DE55 .... 170 B3
  South Normanton DE55 .. 159 F3
  Stonebroom DE55 .... 146 C2
  Swadlincote DE11 ...... 256 A2
  Tintwistle SK13 .... 9 F4
  Warsop Vale NG20 ...... 120 B2
  Whaley Thorns NG20 .... 101 D2
West Terr 8 DE7 .... 194 C1
West View Barlborough S43 . 80 A3
  Bolsover S44 .... 118 A4
  Mayfield DE6 .... 184 B3
  Rocester ST14 .... 197 D2
  Staveley S43 .... 78 B1
West View Ave DE23 ...... 231 D4
West View CI S17 .... 55 F3
West View Dr S17 .... 55 F3
West View Rd S41 .... 95 F3
West Way DE55 .... 159 E1
West Way S17 .... 269 D3
Westacre Dr DE11 .... 255 F1
Westbank CI S18 .... 57 D2
Westbourne Gdns DE56 .... 179 E3
Westbury St DE22 .... 218 C2
Westby La Ashworth NG16 . 195 E2
  Kimberley NG16 .... 195 F2
Westcroft Cres S20 ...... 59 F4
Westcroft Dr S20 .... 59 F4
Westcroft Gdns S20 ...... 59 F4
Westcroft Glen S20 ...... 59 F4
Westcroft Gr S20 .... 59 F4
Westcross Ave NG9 .... 223 F4
Westdale CI NG10 .... 236 A3
Westdale Rd
  Mansfield NG19 .... 136 A1
  Westwood NG16 .... 171 E2
Westdene Ave DE23 .... 232 B3
Westerlands NG9 .... 223 F3
Western Ave DE55 .... 169 E4
Western Dr DE73 .... 193 F4
Western La SK23 .... 46 A4
Western Rd
  Derby, Mickleover DE3 . 217 F1
  Derby, Rose Hill DE23 . 219 D2
Western Terr NG7 .... 268 A1
Westfield Ave
  Chesterfield S40 ..... 95 D1
  Ilkeston DE7 .... 181 F1
Westfield Bank S43 ..... 80 A4
Westfield Campus S20 ... 59 E4
Westfield CI Chesterfield S40 . 95 D1
  Ilkeston DE7 .... 208 B3
  Mansfield NG19 .... 268 A4
Westfield Cres S20 ..... 59 E4
Westfield Ctr S20 ...... 59 E4
Westfield Dr Blackwell DE55 . 147 F1
  Ilkeston DE7 .... 194 B1
  Mansfield NG19 .... 268 A4
Westfield Gdns S40 ..... 95 D1
Westfield Inf Sch S40 .. 95 D1
Westfield La Barlborough S43 . 79 F4
  Mansfield NG19 .... 268 A4
  Middle Handley S21 ... 77 F4
Westfield Northway S20 . 59 F4
Westfield Rd Dronfield S18 . 76 B4
  Killamarsh S21 .... 60 B3
  Swadlincote DE11 ..... 256 A3
Westfield Southway S20 . 59 F4
Westgate St NG3 .... 268 C2
Westgreen Ave DE24 ..... 232 B3
Westhall Rd DE3 .... 217 E2
Westhead Ave ST16 ..... 115 F2
esthill La S42 .... 115 F2
Westhorpe Ave NG2 ..... 268 C2
Westhorpe Dr NG10 ..... 236 B4
Westhouses Prim Sch
  DE55 .... 147 E1
Westland Dr NG16 ...... 160 B2
Westland Gdns S20 ..... 59 E4
estland Gr 8 S20 ...... 59 E4
estland Dr S20 .... 59 E4
estland St S20 .... 59 E4
estleigh NG19 .... 136 B3
Westleigh Ave DE22 .... 218 B3
Westley Ct S40 .... 95 F3
estley Cres DE21 ...... 191 E1
estminster Ave NG10 .. 223 E3
estminster St DE24 ... 232 C4
estmoor Rd S43 .... 96 C2
estmorland CI DE21 ... 219 E3

Westmorland Way NG16 ... 171 D2
Weston Bank DE6 .... 211 F4
Weston CI S40 .... 95 D3
Weston Gr S40 .... 235 F2
Weston Park Ave DE24 ... 232 C2
Weston Park Gdns DE24 .. 232 B2
Weston Rd Aston-on-T DE72 . 246 A4
  Stafford ST16, ST18 ... 269 F4
  Weston-on-T DE72 ...... 245 F3
Weston Rise DE73 .... 245 D4
Weston Spot CI DE5 ..... 180 B4
Weston St Heanor DE75 .. 194 A4
  Swadlincote DE11 ...... 256 A2
Weston-on-Trent
  Parochial Prim Sch
  DE72 .... 245 F2
Westthorpe Rd S21 ...... 60 B3
Westwick CI ST14 .... 210 A1
Westwell PI S20 .... 59 E3
Westwick Cres S8 .... 56 C4
Westwick La S47 .... 94 B1
Westwick Rd S8 .... 56 C4
Westwick St DE7 .... 209 D3
Westwood Ave S43 .... 97 E4
Westwood CI S43 .... 97 E3
Westwood Dr Derby DE24 . 232 B3
  Staveley S43 .... 97 E3
Westwood La S43 .... 96 C2
Westwood Pk DE11 .... 255 F3
Westwood Rd Calow S44 .. 97 D2
  Nottingham NG2 .... 268 C1
Wetherby CI NG16 .... 195 F4
Wetherby Rd DE24 .... 232 C3
Wetheral Rd DE15 .... 248 B1
Wetlands La S44 .... 96 C2
Weyacres DE72 .... 221 E1
Weybridge CI DE7 .... 207 E4
Whaley Bridge Prim Sch
  SK23 .... 45 F4
Whaley Comm S44 .... 100 B2
Whaley La S43 .... 45 E4
Whaley Rd NG20 .... 100 C1
Whaley Thorns Heritage
  Ctr NG20 .... 101 D2
Whaley Thorns Prim Sch
  NG20 .... 101 D2
Whalley Ave ST14 .... 269 D1
Wharf Bank DE6 .... 266 B4
  Staveley S43 .... 78 C2
Wharf PI ST4 .... 269 F2
Wharf Rd Nottingham NG7 . 268 A1
  Pinxton NG16 .... 160 B1
Wharncliffe S43 .... 45 F4
Wharf The DE21 .... 235 D1
Wharfdale Rd NG10 ...... 236 A3
Wharmby Ave NG19 .... 135 E2
Wharncliffe CI SK13 .... 9 F2
Wharncliffe Rd DE7 ..... 208 C4
Whatstandwell Sta DE4 .. 156 B1
Wheal La Sheldon SK17 .. 107 E4
  Taddington SK17 ...... 107 E4
Wheatbridge Rd S40 ..... 266 A3
Wheatcroft SK13 .... 9 F2
Wheatcroft CI
  Clay Cross S45 .... 131 E1
  Wingerworth S42 ...... 115 D2
Wheatfield Cres NG19 ... 136 C3
Wheatland CI DE24 ...... 231 E1
Wheatlands DE11 .... 256 A3
Wheatlands La DE45 ..... 91 E3
Wheatlands Rd
  Burton u T DE15 ...... 254 C4
  Wingerworth S42 ...... 114 C2
Wheatley Ave
  Somercotes DE55 ...... 159 E1
  Stoke-on-T ST4 .... 269 D1
Wheatley CI NG19 .... 136 C1
Wheatley Gdns S43 ...... 127 E1
Wheatley La DE15 .... 248 B2
Wheatley Rd DE4 .... 127 E2
Wheatsheaf CI DE21 ..... 206 B1
Wheatsheaf La DE4 ...... 156 C1
Wheatsheaf Rd SK23 ..... 45 F3
Wheeldon Ave
  Belper DE56 .... 179 D2
  Derby DE22 .... 218 C4
Wheeldon Cres S43 ...... 96 B4
Wheeldon Way DE6 .... 175 F2
Wheeler Gate NG1 .... 268 B1
Whenby CI DE21 .... 217 E1
Whernside S43 .... 219 E4
Wheston Bank SK17 ...... 69 D3
Whetmorhurst Rd SK6 .... 23 F2
Whieldon Cres ST4 ...... 269 F1
Whieldon Rd ST4 .... 269 F1
Whilton Ct DE56 .... 179 E2
Whilton Cres DE7 .... 207 E4
Whinacre CI S8 .... 57 D3
Whinacre PI S8 .... 57 D3
Whinacre Wlk S8 .... 57 D3
Whinbush Ave DE4 .... 232 C3
Whinney Bank NG19 ...... 136 B2
Whinney Hill NG19 ...... 136 B2
Whiston St DE23 .... 219 D1
Whitaker Gdns DE23 ..... 218 C1
Whitaker Rd DE23 .... 218 C1
Whitaker St DE23 .... 219 D1
Whitby Ave DE21 .... 205 E1

Whitcombe PI DE5 .... 169 E1
White Edge CI S40 ...... 95 E3
White Edge Dr DE45 ..... 91 F3
White Gate Rd HD7 ...... 3 E4
White Gates DE5 .... 181 D4
White Hart St NG18 ..... 268 B4
White Hart Yd DE56 ..... 191 F4
White Knowle CI SK17 ... 85 E3
White Knowle Rd SK17 ... 85 E3
White La Highlane S12 .. 44 B1
  Shottle DE56 .... 177 E2
White Leas S40 .... 95 D2
White Leas Ave S42 ..... 132 A4
White Lion Sq DE7 ...... 208 C4
White Lion St ST17 ..... 269 E3
White Lodge La DE45 .... 91 F3
Whitecarr La
  Ashover DE55 .... 145 D2
  Brackenfield DE55 .... 145 D3
Whitecotes CI S40 ...... 114 C4
Whitecotes La S40 ...... 114 C4
Whitecotes Prim Sch S40 . 114 C4
Whitecross Ave S17 ..... 69 E2
Whitecross Gdns DE1 .... 218 C4
Whitecross St S17 ...... 69 E3
Whitecross St DE1 ...... 218 C3
Whitefield La Ashover S45 . 129 D3
  Chelmorton SK17 ...... 106 B4
Whitehall Terr SK23 .... 34 B1
Whitehead CI DE7 .... 194 B1
Whitehead Dr NG16 ...... 182 B4
Whitehead St S44 .... 78 C1
Whitehough Head La SK23 . 34 C4
Whitehouse CI DE24 ..... 232 B2
Whitehouse Rise DE56 ... 178 C3
Whitehouses S41 .... 266 C1
Whitehurst St DE24 ..... 232 B4
Whitelea La DE4 .... 45 E2
Whiteleas Rd SK23 ...... 34 C4
Whiteley Rd DE5 .... 180 C4
Whitely La Dore S17 .... 55 D4
  Ible DE4 .... 153 F4
Whitely CI NG9 .... 223 F4
Whitemoor Hall DE56 .... 179 E3
Whitemoor La DE56 ...... 179 E3
Whites CI DE55 .... 159 E1
Whites Croft View S43 .. 80 A3
Whiteway DE22 .... 204 C1
Whitewell Gdns DE24 .... 233 E3
Whitewells La DE56 ..... 178 B4
Whitewells Rd DE56 ..... 167 F1
Whitfield CE Prim Sch
  SK13 .... 17 D4
Whitfield Cross SK13 ... 17 E4
Whitfield La DE45 ...... 124 C1
Whitfield Pk SK13 ...... 17 E4
Whiting Ave NG9 .... 223 F1
Whiting St S8 .... 43 D3
White Bank Rd SK22 ..... 24 A1
Whitley Way DE6 .... 184 C3
Whitmore Ave S42 .... 115 F1
Whitmore Rd DE21 ...... 219 F3
Whitstable CI DE21 .... 231 E4
Whittaker La DE21 ..... 191 E1
Whittaker Mews S41 .... 76 C1
Whiting Valley Rd S41 . 77 D1
Whittington Hall Hospl
  S41 .... 77 E2
Whittington Hill S41 .. 77 D1
Whittington La S18 .... 76 C3
Whittington Rd
  Chesterfield S43 .... 77 F2
  ... S43 .... 77 F2
Whittington St DE24 .. 232 B3
Whittington Way S41 .. 77 D1
Whittlebury Dr DE23 .. 230 C4
Whitton PI S41 .... 98 A3
Whitwell Ave S80 ..... 63 D2
Whitwell Rd DE21 ..... 127 C2
Whitworth Rd
  Chesterfield S41 ... 96 A3
  Darley Dale DE4 .... 127 D2
  ... DE4 .... 208 C3
  Northwood DE4 ..... 127 D2
Whitwell Prim Sch S80 . 82 A3
Whysall St DE7 .... 181 F1
Whyteleafe Gr DE21 ... 206 A1
Wickens PI S43 .... 79 D2
Wickersley CI DE22 ... 204 B1
Wickets The DE5 ...... 254 C4
Wickfield CI S12 ..... 44 C3
Wickfield Dr S12 ..... 44 C2
Wickfield Gr S12 ..... 44 C2
Wickfield PI S12 ..... 44 C3
Wickfield Rd S12 ..... 44 C2
Wicksteed CI DE56 .... 179 E3
Widdop CI S13 .... 44 B4
Widdop Croft S13 ..... 44 B4
Widdybank CI DE47 .... 220 C2
Wideshaft DE11 .... 256 B2
Widmerpool St NG16 ... 160 B1

Wigley CI NG3 .... 268 C2
Wigley Prim Sch S42 .. 93 F2
Wigley Rd S43 .... 97 E3
Wigmore CI DE3 .... 217 E2
Wilberforce Rd NG16 .. 135 E1
Wilbury Dr S12 .... 44 A3
Wilcox Ave NG19 ...... 136 A3
Wild Hill NG17 .... 148 C4
Wild La DE4 .... 157 D2
Wild St DE22 .... 218 B3
Wildaygreen La S18 ... 75 D1
Wilderbrook La DE56 .. 178 A4
Wilders Lea Ct DE56 .. 179 D1
Wildhay La DE6 .... 183 E4
Wildman St NG7 .... 268 A2
Wildpark La DE6 ...... 202 B3
Wildsmith St DE24 .... 233 D4
Wilford Rd NG2 .... 268 B1
Wilford St NG2 .... 268 B1
Wilfred PI ST14 ...... 269 D2
Wilfred St DE23 ...... 219 D1
Wilhallow La NG16 .... 171 F1
Wilkin Hill S17 ...... 75 F1
Wilkins Dr DE24 ...... 232 C4
Wilkinson CI
  Chesterfield S40 ... 115 D3
  Pleasley NG19 ...... 135 D3
Wilkinson Dr S43 .... 97 D4
Will Shore's La DE4 . 142 B3
Willcock Rd DE14 .... 254 A4
Willerby Rd DE14 .... 143 E1
Willersley Ct S41 ... 95 E4
Willersley Rd DE4 ... 155 E4
Willesden Ave DE22 .. 218 A4
Willetts Rd DE21 .... 220 A4
William Allitt Sch DE11 . 255 F4
William Ave NG16 .... 182 C1
William Booth Inf Sch
  NG2 .... 268 C1
William CI S20 ...... 59 E3
William Cres S20 .... 59 E3
William Gilbert Endowed
  Prim Sch DE56 ..... 190 C2
William Howitt Jun Com
  Sch DE75 .... 181 E1
William Levick Prim Sch
  S18 .... 56 B1
William Lilley Inf Sch
  NG9 .... 223 E3
William Nadins Way DE11 . 255 F2
William Newton CI DE65 . 241 D3
William Rd NG2 ...... 223 E4
William Rhodes Prim Sch
  S40 .... 266 A1
William Shrewsbury Prim
  Sch DE13 .... 240 C1
William St Belper DE56 . 178 C2
  Chesterfield S41 .. 96 A3
  Derby DE1 .... 218 C1
  Eckington S21 ..... 59 E2
  Long Eaton NG10 ... 223 E1
William St N S41 ... 76 C1
Williamson Ave SK17 . 66 B1
Williamson Cres S23 . 45 E4
Williamson Rd SK23 . 45 E4
Williamson St NG10 . 268 A4
Williamthorpe CI S42 . 132 A4
Williamthorpe Ind Pk
  S42 .... 116 B1
Willington Rd Etwall DE65 . 229 E2
  Findern DE65 ..... 242 B4
  Repton DE65 ...... 242 A2
Willington Sta DE65 . 242 A3
Willn St DE23 ...... 218 C1
Willoughby Ave NG10 . 223 E2
Willoughby CI DE72 . 235 F4
Willoughby St NG9 .. 195 D1
Willow Ave
  Long Eaton NG10 .. 223 E1
  Ripley DE5 .... 180 B4
  Shirebrook NG20 .. 119 E3
  Stapleford NG9 ... 223 E3
Willow Brook CI DE65 . 228 B1
Willow CI Alfreton DE55 . 159 D3
  Aston-on-T DE72 .. 246 A4
  Creswell S80 ..... 81 F1
  Derby DE72 .... 245 F4
  Pilsley S45 ...... 132 B1
  South Normanton DE55 . 160 A3
Willow Croft DE24 .. 233 E2
Willow Ct S45 ...... 97 D2
Willow Dr
  Chapel-en-le-F SK23 . 47 D3
  Mastin Moor S43 .. 79 D2
  Swadlincote DE11 . 255 F4
Willow Farm Ct DE65 . 230 B1
Willow Garth Rd S41 . 95 E4
Willow Meadow Rd DE6 . 185 E4
Willow PI DE15 ..... 254 C4
Willow Rd
  Castle Donington DE74 . 247 D3
  Killamarsh S21 ... 60 B3
Willow Rise NG10 .. 223 D3
Willow Row DE1 .... 267 A4
Willow St S21 ..... 146 B1
Willow Terr S43 ... 80 C1
Willow Way DE4 .... 127 C2
Willowbath La DE4 . 165 F4
Willowbrook Grange DE21 . 233 D1
Willowcroft Rd DE21 . 220 C2
Willowdale Ave ST4 . 269 F1
Willowfields DE65 . 228 B1

Willowherb CI DE24 . 231 F1
Willowpit La DE65 . 228 C3
Willows Ave DE55 .. 159 D3
Willows The
  Hulland Ward DE6 . 175 F2
  Pleasley NG19 ... 135 D3
Willowsend CI DE65 . 230 B1
Willriding La DE6 . 183 E4
Wilson Ave DE23 ... 231 E4
Wilson Rd DE23 .... 231 E4
Wilsons Wlk SK13 .. 10 A3
Wilmington Ave DE24 . 233 D3
Wilmore Rd DE24 ... 232 A3
Wilmorton Tertiary Coll
  DE24 .... 219 F1
Wilmorton Tertiary Coll
  ... DE7 .... 219 F1
Wilmot Dr DE7 ..... 192 C3
Wilmot Rd Belper DE56 . 179 D2
  Swadlincote DE11 . 256 A2
Wilmot St Derby DE1 . 267 B2
  Heanor DE7 ...... 181 F1
  Ilkeston DE7 .... 194 C1
  Long Eaton NG10 . 236 A3
  Matlock DE4 ..... 143 D3
Wilmslow Dr DE21 .. 206 A1
Wilne Ave NG10 .... 236 A2
Wilne CI NG10 ..... 235 F2
Wilne La Breaston DE72 . 235 E2
  Shardlow DE72 ... 235 D1
Wilne Rd Draycott DE72 . 235 D3
  Long Eaton NG10 . 235 F2
Wilshaw CI SK23 ... 47 E3
Wilson Ave Blackwell DE55 . 147 F1
  Clowne S43 ...... 80 C3
  Denby S18 .... 181 D2
Wilson CI Burnaston DE3 . 230 B4
  Clay Cross S45 .. 131 E1
Wilson Dr DE55 .... 170 B4
Wilson La S44 ..... 117 D3
Wilson PI S8 ...... 43 D4
Wilson Rd Derby DE21 . 219 F4
  Dronfield S18 ... 57 E2
  Eastwood NG16 ... 182 C1
Wilson Rise DE73 .. 252 C3
Wilson St Alfreton DE55 . 159 D2
  Derby DE1 .... 267 B2
  Dronfield S18 ... 76 A4
  Pinxton NG16 .... 160 B2
  Radmanthwaite NG19 . 135 E1
Wilson's Terr SK13 . 17 D4
Wilsthorpe Rd
  Breaston DE72 ... 235 F4
  Derby DE21 ...... 220 A4
  Long Eaton NG10 . 223 D1
Wilsthorpe Sch NG10 . 223 D1
Wilton CI DE24 .... 231 E1
Wilton PI DE7 ..... 194 C1
Wilton St DE7 ..... 194 C1
Wiltra Ave NG16 ... 171 D2
Wiltshire Rd DE21 . 219 F4
Wimbledon Rd DE22 . 218 A4
Wimborne Cres S41 . 95 F4
Wimbourne CI DE73 . 233 D1
Wimpole Gdns DE22 . 218 A3
Wimsey Way DE55 ... 159 D1
Wincanton CI DE24 . 219 E1
Winchcombe Dr DE15 . 248 A1
Winchcombe Way DE21 . 206 A1
Winchester Cres DE7 . 209 D4
Winchester Dr
  Burton u T DE14 . 254 B4
  Linton DE12 ..... 261 E3
  Mansfield Woodhouse NG19 . 136 B2
  Swadlincote DE11 . 256 B3
Winchester Rd S41 . 95 F4
Windermere Ave
  Dronfield S18 ... 56 C1
  Ilkeston DE7 .... 208 B3
Windermere Cres DE22 . 204 C2
Windermere Dr DE21 . 220 C3
Windermere Gdns NG10 . 223 D2
Windermere Rd
  Chesterfield S41 . 95 E4
  Clay Cross S45 .. 131 D2
  Long Eaton NG10 . 223 D1
  Matlock DE4 ..... 170 B3
Windley Cres DE22 . 204 C1
Windley Dr DE7 .... 194 B2
Windley La
  Idridgehay DE56 . 176 C3
  Turnditch DE56 .. 177 D1
  Windley DE56 .... 189 F4
Windley Sch NG7 .. 268 A3
Windmill Ave DE55 . 192 A4
Windmill CI
  Castle Donington DE74 . 247 D1
  Elvaston DE24 ... 233 E2
  Ockbrook DE7 .... 221 E3
Windmill Dr ST14 . 224 C2
Windmill Greenway S20 . 59 F3
Windmill La DE72 . 221 E2
Windmill Hill La DE22 . 218 C3
Windmill La
  Alderwasley DE56 . 166 C3
  Ashbourne DE6 ... 173 E2
  Belper DE56 ..... 179 D2
  Denby S18 .... 71 E3
  Mansfield NG18 .. 268 C4
  Nottingham NG2 .. 184 C1
  Unstone S18 ..... 77 D3
Windmill Rd DE65 . 229 D2

Windmill Rise
Belper DE56 .... 179 D3
Somercotes DE55 .... 170 B4
South Normanton DE55 ..... 159 F3
Windmill St DE11 .... 256 A1
Windmill View DE56 .... 179 F4
Windrush Cl DE22 .... 205 D3
Windses Est S32 .... 53 E1
Windsmoor Rd NG16 ...... 182 B4
Windsmoor St ST4 .... 269 E1
Windsor Ave Derby DE73 ... 231 D4
Melbourne DE73 .... 252 A4
Windsor Cl
Ashbourne DE6 .... 173 E2
Borrowash DE72 .... 221 E1
⬛ Chesterfield S40 .... 95 E1
Heanor DE75 .... 181 F2
Swadlincote DE11 .... 256 A3
Swanwick DE55 .... 170 A4
Trowell NG9 .... 209 D3
Windsor Cres
Ilkeston DE7 .... 208 C2
Stapleford NG9 .... 223 F4
Windsor Ct Derby DE3 ...... 217 E1
Sandiacre NG10 .... 223 D2
West Hallam DE7 .... 207 E4
Windsor Dr Derby DE21 .... 221 D3
Dronfield S18 .... 56 B1
Wingerworth S42 .... 114 C2
Windsor Gdns NG18 .... 268 C3
Windsor Park Rd SK17 ...... 85 E4
Windsor Rd Buxton SK17 ... 85 E4
Linton DE12 .... 261 E3
Mansfield NG18 .... 268 C3
Uttoxeter ST14 .... 210 A1
Windsor St NG9 .... 223 F4
Windsor Wlk S41 .... 115 E4
Windy Fields Rd S42 ...... 113 E4
Windy House La S2 .... 44 A4
Windy La DE21 .... 191 E1
Windyridge SK17 .... 121 D3
Winfield Gr SK6 .... 15 D1
Wingerwork Ave S8 .... 56 B4
Wingerworth Cotts S42 ... 115 F2
Wingerworth Park Rd
DE21 .... 220 C3
Wingerworth St S42 .... 115 F2
Wingfield Cl S18 .... 56 B1
Wingfield Cres S12 .... 44 B3
Wingfield Dr Derby DE21 ... 205 F1
Ilkeston DE7 .... 194 B2
Wingfield Gr SK13 .... 17 F4
Wingfield Rd
Alfreton DE55 .... 158 C2
Tupton S42 .... 131 E4
Winhill Rd S32 .... 24 B1
Winkburn Rd NG18, NG19 .. 268 A4
Winn La DE6 .... 174 C4
Winnat Pl S43 .... 97 E4
Winnats S33 .... 37 F1
Winnats Cl Chesterfield S40 .. 95 E3
Glossop SK13 .... 17 F4
Winney Hill S26 .... 61 F3
Winney La S26 .... 61 F2
Winnington Rd SK6 .... 23 D4
Winshill Inf Sch DE15 ..... 248 A3
Winslow Ave SK14 .... 9 D1
Winslow Grn DE21 .... 220 B3
Winster CE Prim Sch DE4 . 141 E3
Winster Cl Belper DE56 .... 179 D3
Clay Cross S45 .... 131 D3
Winster Gn DE11 .... 255 F3
Winster Gr SK17 .... 85 F4
Winster La DE4 .... 140 C3
Winster Market Ho DE4 ... 141 E3
Winster Mews SK13 .... 9 F1
Winster Rd Derby DE21 .... 205 F1
Staveley S43 .... 97 E4
Winster St SK17 .... 85 F4
Winster Way NG10 .... 235 F3
Winston Cl NG9 .... 223 F4
Winter Closes NG16 .... 171 F1
Winterbourne Dr NG9 ..... 209 F1
Wintercroft La DE6 .... 161 F1
Wintergreen Dr DE23 ...... 230 C3
Winton Sq S14 .... 269 E2
Wintonfield St ST4 .... 269 F2
Wire La DE55 .... 148 A2
Wirksmoor Rd SK22 .... 33 D4
Wirksworth CE Inf Sch
DE4 .... 165 F4
Wirksworth Hall Gdns
DE4 .... 165 F4
Wirksworth Ind Est DE4 ... 154 C2
Wirksworth Jun Sch DE4 .. 154 C1
Wirksworth Jun Sch DE4 .. 155 D1
Wirksworth Rd
Duffield DE56 .... 190 B2
Idridgehay DE56 .... 176 C3
Ilkeston DE7 .... 208 B2
Kirk Ireton DE6 .... 165 E2
Shottle DE56 .... 177 E2
Windley DE56 .... 177 E2
Wisbech Cl S40 .... 114 C4
Wisgreaves Rd DE24 .... 232 C4
Wishing Stone Way DE4 ... 143 F3

Witham Cl S41 .... 96 B3
Witham Cl S40 .... 95 E2
Witham Dr DE23 .... 231 E3
Witney Cl DE24 .... 232 B4
Witney St S8 .... 43 D4
Wittering Cl NG10 .... 236 C3
Woburn Cl
Blackwell DE55 .... 147 F1
Swanwick DE55 .... 169 F4
Woburn Croft NG10 .... 223 D2
Woburn La NG19 .... 135 E2
Woburn Pl Derby DE22 .... 218 A3
Radmanthwaite NG19 .... 135 E2
Woburn Rd NG19 .... 135 E2
Wolds Rise DE4 .... 143 E4
Wolfa St DE22 .... 218 C2
Wolfcote Cl S45 .... 131 E1
Wolfe Cl S40 .... 95 E1
Wolfe St S14 .... 269 E1
Wolfscote Dale DE11 ...... 255 F1
Wollaton Ave S17 .... 56 A3
Wollaton Dr ⬛ S17 .... 56 A3
Wollaton Rd Derby DE21 ... 219 F4
Sheffield S17 .... 56 A3
Wollaton Rd S DE21 .... 205 F1
Wollaton St NG1 .... 268 A2
Wollen Cl S80 .... 81 F1
Wolseley Rd Sheffield S2 ... 43 D4
Stafford ST16 .... 269 F4
Wolverhampton Rd ST17 .. 269 E3
Wolverley Grange DE24 ... 233 E3
Wood Ave Creswell S80 .... 81 E1
Sandiacre NG10 .... 223 D3
Wood Cl S42 .... 114 B2
Wood Croft DE23 .... 231 E4
Wood End Rd DE75 .... 181 F1
Wood Gdns SK22 .... 25 E2
Wood La Belper DE56 ...... 190 C4
Creswell S80 .... 100 B4
Hanbury DE13 .... 238 A2
Hayfield SK22 .... 25 E2
Horsley Woodhouse DE7 .... 192 B3
Idle DE4 .... 153 F3
Idridgehay DE56 .... 176 C4
Kniveton DE6 .... 163 D1
Market Warsop NG20 .... 120 C4
Pentrich DE5 .... 169 D2
Pleasley NG20 .... 119 F1
Scarcliffe S44 .... 118 C3
Shirebrook NG20 .... 119 F1
Smalley DE7 .... 192 B3
Swadlincote DE11 .... 256 A4
Wood Nook Cl NG16 .... 171 F3
Wood Rd
Derby, Chaddesden DE21 .. 220 A4
Derby, Oakwood DE21 ...... 205 F1
Derby, Spondon DE21 .... 221 D3
Wood St Alfreton DE55 .... 159 E3
Codnor DE5 .... 181 D4
Derby DE1 .... 267 C4
Eastwood NG16 .... 182 C2
Glossop SK13 .... 17 E4
Hollingworth SK14 .... 9 E3
Holmewood S42 .... 116 C1
Ilkeston DE7 .... 194 C1
Mansfield NG18 .... 268 B4
New Mills SK22 .... 33 D4
Nottingham NG2 .... 268 A2
Ripley DE5 .... 169 E1
Somercotes DE55 .... 170 B4
Swadlincote DE11 .... 256 A1
Wood St N DE55 .... 159 E3
Woodale Cl DE23 .... 230 C3
Woodall La S26 .... 61 E3
Woodall Rd S21 .... 60 C3
Woodall Service Area
S21 .... 61 D3
Woodbeck Ct DE21 .... 206 A1
Woodberry Ave ST4 .... 269 D1
Woodberry Cl S14 .... 269 D1
Woodborough Rd
Mansfield NG19 .... 135 F1
Nottingham NG3 .... 268 B2
Woodbourne Rd SK22 .... 33 D3
Woodbridge Cl DE21 ...... 232 C1
Woodbridge Jun Sch
DE55 .... 159 D2
Woodbridge Rise S40 ..... 114 A4
Woodbrook Cl S43 .... 45 F4
Woodbrook St DE23 .... 45 F4
Woodall La S26 .... 61 E3
Woodchester Dr DE24 ..... 233 E3
Woodcock Gr SK13 .... 10 C1
Woodcock Rd SK13 .... 11 D1
Woodcote Way DE23 .... 231 D4
Woodfall La DE56 .... 189 F2
Woodfield Cl SK13 .... 9 F3
Woodfield Dr Ripley DE5 ... 180 B4
Swadlincote DE11 .... 256 B3
Woodfield Rd NG16 .... 160 B2
Woodford Rd DE22 .... 218 A4
Woodford Way S43 .... 78 A2
Woodgate Dr DE73 .... 233 D1
Woodhall Dr DE23 .... 230 C4
Woodhead La S45 .... 130 B1
Woodhead Rd Glossop SK13 . 10 B3
Holme HD7 .... 2 C3

Woodhead Rd continued
Sheffield S2 .... 43 D4
Tintwistle SK13 .... 10 A4
Woodhouse Ct NG19 ...... 136 B1
Woodhouse La
Barlborough S43 .... 79 F3
Bolsover S44 .... 98 C2
Mastin Moor S43 .... 79 E3
Rowsley DE4 .... 126 C4
Scropton DE65 .... 226 C4
South Normanton DE55 .... 159 F3
Winster DE4 .... 141 E3
Woodhouse Rd
Kilburn DE56 .... 192 A4
Mansfield NG18 .... 268 B4
Woodhouse St
Nottingham NG3 .... 268 C2
Stoke-on-T ST4 .... 269 E1
Swadlincote DE11 .... 256 B2
Woodhouse West Fst &
Mid Sch S13 .... 44 C3
Woodhurst Cl DE21 .... 219 E4
Woodland Ave
Borrowash DE72 .... 221 E1
Ilkeston DE7 .... 194 B2
Sutton in A NG17 .... 148 C2
Woodland Dr
Scropton DE65 .... 226 B2
Sheffield S12 .... 44 A1
Woodland Gr Clowne S43 .. 81 D2
Mansfield Woodhouse
NG19 .... 136 B2
Woodland Pl S17 .... 55 F3
Woodland Rd Derby DE22 . 218 C4
Sheffield S8 .... 43 D2
Swadlincote DE15 .... 255 D2
Woodland View Dore S17 .. 56 A4
Sheffield S12 .... 44 A1
Whaley Thorns NG20 .... 101 D2
Woodland Views ST14 .... 224 C1
Woodland Way
Clay Cross S42 .... 131 D3
Eastwood NG16 .... 182 C1
Woodland Wlk S40 .... 94 C3
Woodlands Brimington S43 . 96 B4
Wirksworth DE4 .... 165 F4
Woodlands Ave
Breaston DE72 .... 235 F4
Derby DE24 .... 232 C2
Woodlands Brow DE6 ...... 173 E2
Woodlands Cl
Little Eaton DE21 .... 205 D4
Melbourne DE73 .... 252 A4
Tintwistle SK13 .... 9 F3
Woodlands Com Sch
DE22 .... 204 B2
Woodlands Cres DE12 ..... 262 A2
Woodlands Gr S42 .... 131 D3
Woodlands La Derby DE73 . 245 D4
Quarndon DE22 .... 204 B3
Woodlands Rd
Chapel-en-le-F SK23 .... 47 D2
Derby DE22 .... 204 C3
Disley SK12 .... 32 A3
New Mills SK22 .... 33 D4
Overseal DE12 .... 262 A2
Woodlands The
Mansfield NG19 .... 136 A1
Melbourne DE73 .... 252 A4
Whaley Thorns NG20 .... 101 D2
Woodlands Way DE73 ...... 252 A4
Woodlands Yd DE73 .... 245 D4
Woodlea Gr DE21 .... 205 E4
Woodleigh Cl S40 .... 94 C3
Woodmans Croft DE65 .... 227 E1
Woodminton Dr DE73 ...... 232 C2
Woodnook Cl S40 .... 95 D2
Woodnook La S40 .... 94 C3
Woodnook Way S40 .... 94 C2
Woodpecker Hill DE7 ...... 208 A1
Woodrising Cl DE21 .... 206 A2
Woodroffe Wlk DE23 ...... 231 F4
Woodrove Ave S13 .... 44 A4
Woodrove Cl S13 .... 44 A4
Woods La Burton u T DE15 . 248 A1
Derby DE22 .... 267 A1
Woodseats Rd SK13 .... 16 A3
Woodshop La DE73 .... 244 B3
Woodside Buxton SK17 ...... 85 E4
Eastwood NG16 .... 182 C2
Horsley DE7 .... 192 B2
Woodside Ave
Holmesfield S18 .... 75 D4
Killamarsh S21 .... 60 C4
Woodside Cl
Bakewell DE45 .... 109 E3
Chesterfield S40 .... 95 D2
Woodside Cres
Ilkeston DE7 .... 194 B3
Long Eaton NG10 .... 236 A4
Woodside Dr
Bakewell DE45 .... 109 E3
Derby DE22 .... 205 D2
Woodside Pl S45 .... 131 D2
Woodside Rd
Sandiacre NG10 .... 223 D3
Shirebrook NG20 .... 119 F3
Shireoaks S81 .... 63 F4
Woodside St SK22 .... 33 D3

Woodside View S18 .... 75 D4
Woodsorrel Dr DE21 .... 206 A2
Woodstock Cl DE22 .... 204 B2
Woodstock Dr S41 .... 115 E4
Woodstock Rd NG9 .... 223 F2
Woodstock Rise S41 .... 115 E4
Woodthorpe Ave
Clay Cross S45 .... 131 D2
Derby, Allenton DE24 ...... 232 C2
Derby, Chaddesden DE21 .. 219 F3
Woodthorpe CE Prim Sch
S43 .... 79 E1
Woodthorpe Cl
Bolsover S44 .... 98 C4
Sheffield S2 .... 44 A4
Woodthorpe Cres S13 ...... 44 B4
Woodthorpe Rd
Bolsover S44 .... 98 C4
Sheffield S13 .... 44 B4
Woodthorpe S43 .... 79 E1
Woodthorpe Sec Sch
S13 .... 44 B4
Woodvale Cl S40 .... 114 A4
Woodview Cl S42 .... 114 C1
Woodview Rd DE11 .... 255 F3
Woodville CE Jun Sch
DE11 .... 256 C1
Woodville Inf Sch DE11 ... 256 C1
Woodville Rd
Hartshorne DE11 .... 257 D3
Overseal DE12 .... 262 A2
Woodward's Pl DE11 ...... 256 B2
Woodward's Rd DE11 ...... 256 C2
Woodyard La DE65 .... 221 E1
Woolaton La SK17 .... 138 B1
Wooley Cl S42 .... 131 D4
Wooliscroft Way DE7 ...... 194 B1
Woolley Bridge Rd SK13 .... 9 F3
Woolley Cl SK14 .... 9 E2
Wooley La
Hollingworth SK14 .... 9 E3
Hollingworth, Woolley SK14 . 9 E2
Woolley Mill La SK13 .... 9 F4
Woolley Rd DE4 .... 143 D3
Woolley Yd DE4 .... 141 E3
Woolpack La NG1 .... 268 B1
Woolrych St DE23 .... 218 C1
Woolsthorpe Cres DE7 .... 208 B2
Woosnam Cl DE14 .... 254 A3
Worcester Ave NG19 .... 136 B3
Worcester Cres DE21 ...... 219 F4
Worcester Gr SK13 .... 17 F4
Worcester Mews NG19 .... 136 B3
Worcester Rd DE15 .... 254 C3
Wordsworth Ave
Derby DE24 .... 231 F3
Mansfield Woodhouse
NG19 .... 136 A2
Wordsworth Dr DE24 ...... 232 A3
Wordsworth Pl S18 .... 76 B4
Wordsworth Rd
Awsworth NG16 .... 195 E3
Chesterfield S41 .... 95 F4
Works La S44 .... 97 D2
Works Rd S43 .... 78 A1

Worksop Rd
Mastin Moor S43 .... 79 E2
Nottingham NG3 .... 268 C2
Thorpe Salvin S80 .... 62 C4
Whitwell S80 .... 81 F3
Worrall Ave NG10 .... 223 F1
Worthington La DE73 ...... 252 C1
Wortley Ave NG9 .... 209 E2
Wortley Cl DE7 .... 209 D4
Wortley Ct S33 .... 51 D4
Wragley Way DE24 .... 231 E1
Wray Cl NG3 .... 268 C2
Wreakes La S18 .... 56 C1
Wren Cl DE11 .... 256 C2
Wren Nest Rd SK13 .... 10 A1
Wren Nest Terr SK13 .... 10 B1
Wren Park Cl
Belper DE56 .... 178 B3
Chesterfield S40 .... 114 C4
Findern DE65 .... 230 B1
Ridgeway S12 .... 58 C4
Wren Park Prim Sch
DE3 .... 218 A1
Wrenpark Rd S42 .... 114 B2
Wretham Cl DE3 .... 230 B4
Wright Ave DE5 .... 169 F1
Wright St DE1 .... 181 D4
Wroxham Cl DE24 .... 232 B2
Wulfric Cl S2 .... 43 F4
Wulfric Pl S2 .... 43 F4
Wulfric Rd Eckington S21 .. 59 E2
Sheffield, Deep Pit S2 .... 43 F4
Sheffield, Manor Estate S2 .. 44 A4
Wyaston Cl DE22 .... 204 C1
Wyaston Rd
Ashbourne DE6 .... 185 E3
Osmaston DE6 .... 185 E3
Wybersley Rd
High Lane SK6 .... 32 A4
Marple SK6 .... 23 D1
Wychwood Dr NG9 .... 209 E1
Wycliffe Rd DE55 .... 159 D2
Wye Bank DE45 .... 109 F3

Wye Bank Gr DE45 .... 109 F3
Wye Dale DE11 .... 255 F1
Wye Gr SK17 .... 85 E3
Wye Head Cl SK17 .... 84 C3
Wye St Buxton SK17 .... 85 E3
Derby DE24 .... 233 D4
Wye Terr DE4 .... 126 C1
Wyedale Cl Bakewell DE45 . 109 F3
Buxton SK17 .... 85 E3
Wyedale Cres DE45 .... 109 F3
Wyedale Ct ⬛ S41 .... 95 F4
Wyedale Dr DE45 .... 109 F3
Wyedale View DE45 .... 109 F3
Wyelands Cl SK17 .... 84 C3
Wyming Brook Dr S10 .... 42 B3
Wynd The S21 .... 79 C2
Wyndale Dr DE7 .... 208 B4
Wyndham Cres DE15 ...... 248 B1
Wyndham St DE24 .... 233 D4
Wynton Ave DE24 .... 233 E3
Wyntor Ave DE4 .... 141 E3
Wynward Cl DE7 .... 194 C3
Wysall Cl NG19 .... 135 D1
Wystan Ct DE65 .... 242 B2
Wyston Brook DE65 .... 228 B3
Wythburn Rd S41 .... 95 F4
Wyver La DE56 .... 178 C4
Wyvern Ave NG10 .... 236 B4
Wyvern Cl Eastwood NG16 . 195 F3
Matlock DE4 .... 143 D3
Wyvern Gdns S17 .... 55 F3
Wyvern Way DE21 .... 220 B2

Yardley Cl DE55 .... 169 D4
Yardley Way DE56 .... 179 D3
Yarncliff Cl S40 .... 95 D5
Yarrow Cl DE24 .... 231 D1
Yates Ave DE72 .... 246 A3
Yates Rd SK22 .... 33 D4
Yeardsley Ave SK23 .... 33 F3
Yeardsley Grange SK23 .... 33 F3
Yeardsley La SK23 .... 33 F3
Yeld Cl DE45 .... 109 F4
Yeld Rd DE45 .... 109 F4
Yeld The DE45 .... 109 F4
Yeldersley Cl S40 .... 95 D3
Yeldersley La
Brailsford DE6 .... 187 E1
Osmaston DE6 .... 186 C1
Yelt La DE6 .... 224 B2
Yeoman Park Sch NG19 ... 136 B2
Yeoman St DE4 .... 154 A2
Yeovil Cl DE24 .... 233 E3
Yerley Hill DE6 .... 172 A4
Yew Tree Ave DE72 .... 235 D2
Yew Tree Cl
Chesterfield S40 .... 114 A4
Clay Cross S42 .... 131 D3
Killamarsh S21 .... 60 C3
Shirebrook NG20 .... 119 E3
Sutton in A NG17 .... 148 C1
Yew Tree Gdns DE12 ...... 260 C4
Yew Tree Hill DE4 .... 156 A2
Yew Tree La Bradley DE6 .. 186 A3
Elvaston DE72 .... 234 A3
Yew Tree Rd Hatton DE65 . 227 D1
Rosliston DE12 .... 260 B3
Swadlincote DE12 .... 255 E1
Yewdale Gr DE21 .... 206 A1
Yews Cl DE73 .... 233 D4
Yewtree Cl DE15 .... 233 A4
Yewtree Cres DE15 .... 254 C4
Yokecliffe Ave DE4 .... 165 E3
Yokecliffe Cres DE4 .... 165 E3
Yokecliffe Dr DE4 .... 165 E3
Yokecliffe Hill DE4 .... 165 E3
York Ave Sandiacre NG10 .. 223 D3
Westwood NG16 .... 171 E3
York Cl DE11 .... 256 C2
York Cres S44 .... 117 D1
York Pl North Wingfield S42 . 132 A3
Shireoaks S81 .... 63 F4
York Rd Derby DE21 .... 219 F3
Long Eaton NG10 .... 223 D1
Shirebrook NG20 .... 119 E3
Swadlincote DE11 .... 256 C1
York St Chesterfield S41 ... 115 D4
Derby DE1 .... 218 B3
Glossop SK13 .... 10 C1
Mansfield NG18 .... 268 B4
Nottingham NG3 .... 268 B2
York Terr Glossop SK13 ...... 17 F4
Pinxton NG16 .... 160 B2
Stoke St NG19 .... 136 A4
Yorkshire Way SK13 .... 17 F4
Youlgrave All Saints CE
Prim Sch DE45 .... 125 E3
Youlgreave Cl DE21 .... 205 F1
Youlgreave Dr S12 .... 44 B3
Youlgreave Dr S12 .... 44 B3
Young St DE23 .... 218 B1
Younger St ST4 .... 269 E4
Yoxall Ave ST4 .... 269 D1
Ypres Rd DE22 .... 204 C1

Zetland Cres DE24 231

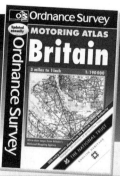

Ordnance Survey

MOTORING ATLAS

Updated annually

Britain

The best-selling *OS Motoring Atlas Britain* uses unrivalled and up-to-date mapping from the Ordnance Survey digital database. The exceptionally clear mapping is at a large scale of 3 miles to 1 inch (Orkney/Shetland Islands at 5 miles to 1 inch).

A special feature of the atlas is its wealth of tourist and leisure information. It contains comprehensive directories, including descriptions and location details, of the properties of the National Trust in England and Wales, the National Trust for Scotland, English Heritage and Historic Scotland. There is also a useful diary of British Tourist Authority Events listing more than 300 days out around Britain during the year.

Available from all good bookshops or direct from the publisher:
Tel: 01933 443863

The atlas includes:

◆ 112 pages of fully updated mapping
◆ 45 city and town plans
◆ 8 extra-detailed city approach maps
◆ route-planning maps
◆ restricted motorway junctions
◆ local radio information
◆ distances chart
◆ county boundaries map
◆ multi-language legend

Ordnance Survey

STREET ATLASES
ORDER FORM

Ordnance Survey
Northwich Winsford Middlewich
Every named street at extra-large scale

STREET ATLAS
PHILIP'S

Ordnance Survey
STREET ATLAS
Lancashire
COMPLETE COUNTY-WIDE COVERAGE

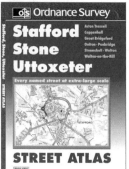

Ordnance Survey
Stafford Stone Uttoxeter
Acton Trussell, Coppenhall, Great Bridgeford, Oulton · Penkridge, Stramshall · Walton, Walton-on-the-Hill
Every named street at extra-large scale

STREET ATLAS
PHILIP'S

PHILIP'S

The Street Atlases are available from all good bookshops or by mail order direct from t publisher. Orders can be made in the following ways. **By phone** Ring our special Credit Card Hotline on **01933 443863** during office hours (9am to 5pm) or leave a messag on the answering machine, quoting your full credit card number plus expiry date and your full name and address. **By post or fax** Fill out the order form below (you may photocopy it) and post it to: **Philip's Direct, 27 Sanders Road, Wellingborough, Northants NN8 4NL** or fax it to: **01933 443849**. Before placing an order by post by fax or on the answering machine, please telephone to check availability and prices.

COLOUR LOCAL ATLASES

PAPERBACK	Quantity @ £3.50 each	£ Total
CANNOCK, LICHFIELD, RUGELEY	☐ 0 540 07625 2 ➤	
DERBY AND BELPER	☐ 0 540 07608 2 ➤	
NORTHWICH, WINSFORD, MIDDLEWICH	☐ 0 540 07589 2 ➤	
PEAK DISTRICT TOWNS	☐ 0 540 07609 0 ➤	
STAFFORD, STONE, UTTOXETER	☐ 0 540 07626 0 ➤	
WARRINGTON, WIDNES, RUNCORN	☐ 0 540 07588 4 ➤	

COLOUR REGIONAL ATLASES

	HARDBACK	SPIRAL	POCKET	
	Quantity @ £10.99 each	Quantity @ £8.99 each	Quantity @ £4.99 each	£ Total
MERSEYSIDE	☐ 0 540 06480 7	☐ 0 540 06481 5	☐ 0 540 06482 3 ➤	
	Quantity @ £12.99 each	Quantity @ £8.99 each	Quantity @ £5.99 each	£ Total
BERKSHIRE	☐ 0 540 06170 0	☐ 0 540 06172 7	☐ 0 540 06173 5 ➤	
	Quantity @ £12.99 each	Quantity @ £9.99 each	Quantity @ £4.99 each	£ Total
DURHAM	☐ 0 540 06365 7	☐ 0 540 06366 5	☐ 0 540 06367 3 ➤	
	Quantity @ £12.99 each	Quantity @ £9.99 each	Quantity @ £5.50 each	£ Total
GREATER MANCHESTER	☐ 0 540 06485 8	☐ 0 540 06486 6	☐ 0 540 06487 4 ➤	
TYNE AND WEAR	☐ 0 540 06370 3	☐ 0 540 06371 1	☐ 0 540 06372 X ➤	
	Quantity @ £12.99 each	Quantity @ £9.99 each	Quantity @ £5.99 each	£ Total
BIRMINGHAM & WEST MIDLANDS	☐ 0 540 07603 1	☐ 0 540 07604 X	☐ 0 540 07605 8 ➤	
BUCKINGHAMSHIRE	☐ 0 540 07466 7	☐ 0 540 07467 5	☐ 0 540 07468 3 ➤	
CHESHIRE	☐ 0 540 07507 8	☐ 0 540 07508 6	☐ 0 540 07509 4 ➤	
DERBYSHIRE	☐ 0 540 07531 0	☐ 0 540 07532 9	☐ 0 540 07533 7 ➤	
EDINBURGH & East Central Scotland	☐ 0 540 07653 8	☐ 0 540 07654 6	☐ 0 540 07656 2 ➤	
NORTH ESSEX	☐ 0 540 07289 3	☐ 0 540 07290 7	☐ 0 540 07292 3 ➤	
SOUTH ESSEX	☐ 0 540 07294 X	☐ 0 540 07295 8	☐ 0 540 07297 4 ➤	
GLASGOW & West Central Scotland	☐ 0 540 07648 1	☐ 0 540 07649 X	☐ 0 540 07651 1 ➤	
NORTH HAMPSHIRE	☐ 0 540 07471 3	☐ 0 540 07472 1	☐ 0 540 07473 X ➤	

Ordnance Survey

STREET ATLASES ORDER FORM

COLOUR REGIONAL ATLASES

	HARDBACK	SPIRAL	POCKET		£ Total
	Quantity @ £12.99 each	Quantity @ £9.99 each	Quantity @ £5.99 each		
SOUTH HAMPSHIRE	☐ 0 540 07476 4	☐ 0 540 07477 2	☐ 0 540 07478 0	➤	☐
HERTFORDSHIRE	☐ 0 540 06174 3	☐ 0 540 06175 1	☐ 0 540 06176 X	➤	☐
EAST KENT	☐ 0 540 07483 7	☐ 0 540 07276 1	☐ 0 540 07287 7	➤	☐
WEST KENT	☐ 0 540 07366 0	☐ 0 540 07367 9	☐ 0 540 07369 5	➤	☐
NORTHAMPTONSHIRE	☐ 0 540 07745 3	☐ 0 540 07746 1	☐ 0 540 07748 8	➤	☐
OXFORDSHIRE	☐ 0 540 07512 4	☐ 0 540 07513 2	☐ 0 540 07514 0	➤	☐
SURREY	☐ 0 540 06435 1	☐ 0 540 06436 X	☐ 0 540 06438 6	➤	☐
EAST SUSSEX	☐ 0 540 07306 7	☐ 0 540 07307 5	☐ 0 540 07312 1	➤	☐
WEST SUSSEX	☐ 0 540 07319 9	☐ 0 540 07323 7	☐ 0 540 07327 X	➤	☐
WARWICKSHIRE	☐ 0 540 07560 4	☐ 0 540 07561 2	☐ 0 540 07562 0	➤	☐
SOUTH YORKSHIRE	—	☐ 0 540 07667 8	☐ 0 540 07669 4	➤	☐
WEST YORKSHIRE	☐ 0 540 07671 6	☐ 0 540 07672 4	☐ 0 540 07674 0	➤	☐
	Quantity @ £14.99 each	Quantity @ £9.99 each	Quantity @ £5.99 each		£ Total
LANCASHIRE	☐ 0 540 06440 8	☐ 0 540 06441 6	☐ 0 540 06443 2	➤	☐
NOTTINGHAMSHIRE	☐ 0 540 07541 8	☐ 0 540 07542 6	☐ 0 540 07543 4	➤	☐
STAFFORDSHIRE	☐ 0 540 07549 3	☐ 0 540 07550 7	☐ 0 540 07551 5	➤	☐

BLACK AND WHITE REGIONAL ATLASES

	HARDBACK	SOFTBACK	POCKET		£ Total
	Quantity @ £11.99 each	Quantity @ £8.99 each	Quantity @ £3.99 each		
BRISTOL AND AVON	☐ 0 540 06140 9	☐ 0 540 06141 7	☐ 0 540 06142 5	➤	☐
	Quantity @ £12.99 each	Quantity @ £9.99 each	Quantity @ £4.99 each		£ Total
CARDIFF, SWANSEA & GLAMORGAN	☐ 0 540 06186 7	☐ 0 540 06187 5	☐ 0 540 06207 3	➤	☐

Name..

Address..

....

....

....................................Postcode.................

◆ Add £2 postage and packing per order

◆ All available titles will normally be dispatched within 5 working days of receipt of order but please allow up to 28 days for delivery

☐ Please tick this box if you do not wish your name to be used by other carefully selected organisations that may wish to send you information about other products and services

Registered Office: 2-4 Heron Quays, London E14 4JP
Registered in England number: 3597451

Total price of order £ ☐

(including postage and packing at £2 per order)

I enclose a cheque/postal order, for £ ☐

made payable to *Octopus Publishing Group Ltd*,

or please debit my ☐ Mastercard ☐ American Express

☐ Visa account by £ ☐

Account no

☐☐☐☐ ☐☐☐☐ ☐☐☐☐ ☐☐☐☐

Expiry date ☐☐ ☐☐

Signature..

Post to: Philip's Direct, 27 Sanders Road, Wellingborough, Northants NN8 4NL

Ordnance Survey

STREET ATLAS
South Essex
BEST BUY AUTO EXPRESS
Unique comprehensive coverage
SOUTHEND-ON-SEA
Plus Chingford, Dagenham, Ilford, Romford
PHILIP'S

Ordnance Survey

STREET ATLAS
West Yorkshire
NEW EDITION
COMPLETE COUNTY-WIDE COVERAGE
NEW BRADFORD HALIFAX, LEEDS WAKEFIELD AT EXTRA-LARGE SCALE
PHILIP'S

Ordnance Survey

STREET ATLAS
Glasgow
and West Central Scotland
Comprehensive coverage from Stirling to Ayr and Greenock to Lanark
PAISLEY
GLASGOW CITY CENTRE AT EXTRA-LARGE SCALE
PHILIP'S

PHILIP'S